Mutually Beneficial

Mutually Beneficial

The Guardian and Life Insurance in America

Robert E. Wright and George David Smith

New York University Press

NEW YORK AND LONDON

NEW YORK UNIVERSITY PRESS
New York and London
www.nyupress.org

Library of Congress Cataloging-in-Publication Data
Wright, Robert E. (Robert Eric), 1969–
Mutually beneficial : the Guardian and life insurance in America / Robert
E. Wright and George David Smith.
p. cm.
Includes bibliographical references and index.
ISBN 0–8147–9397–5 (cloth : alk. paper)
1. Guardian Life Insurance Company—History.
2. Insurance, Life—United States—History.
3. Insurance companies—United States—History.
I. Smith, George David.   II. Title
HG 8963.G942W75   2004
368.32'0065'73—dc22   2004001240

New York University Press books are printed on acid-free paper,
and their binding materials are chosen for strength and durability.

Manufactured in the United States of America

10 9 8 7 6 5 4 3 2 1

For our fathers,
Robert Gene Wright
and
Frank Hoxie Smith

Contents

Illustrations

Unless otherwise noted, all illustrations are reprinted by permission from the archives of the Guardian Life Insurance Company of America.

Illustrations appear as a group following page 120.

Figures

Sources: Guardian's data is based on Annual Reports, various dates, and Annual Statements, various dates, GLIC archives. Industry data is adapted from *Life Insurance Fact Book,* various years. The authors designed and drew the models depicted in figures 1-1, 1-2, 8-6, 12-2, 14-1, and A-1.

Tables

Sources: Sources used to construct the tables are supplied immediately below each table.

Preface

As Guardian Life Insurance Company President James A McLain observed in the mid-twentieth century, "Life insurance has inspired a whale of a lot of uninspired writing." That sad fact remains true, especially for the history of life insurance, which has gone largely undeveloped save for the myriad of vanity publications that companies have generated to celebrate corporate anniversaries and the like. This particular publication will not inspire people put off by academic research, but it will, hopefully, help to redress the paucity of serious literature on the industry. Though one company is the focus of this volume, its history is meant to illustrate the larger progress of life insurance in the American economy. Though celebratory in the sense that any work on a long-lived company necessarily affirms its success over time, this history is also a critical examination of the evolving economic structure and fortunes of life insurance since its modern development in the mid-nineteenth century.

The main title of this book, *Mutually Beneficial,* stems from an expression common among eighteenth- and nineteenth-century American businesspersons, who believed that they should be free to do business with each other if, and only if, the exchanges were profitable to all parties. The founders of Guardian Life Insurance Company of America, which styled itself the Germania Life Insurance Company from its establishment in 1860 until shortly after America's entry into World War I, were deeply imbued with that nineteenth-century conception of economic liberty and mutuality of interest. They were democratic revolutionaries who had been thwarted in the uprisings that rocked Europe in 1848, and conceived of their company as an exercise of their inalienable right to pursue life, liberty, and property as a community of interest. It was no accident that the new home that they adopted, and that in turn adopted them, was the emerging commercial metropolis of Manhattan.[1]

The title also refers to a form of corporate organization and governance that, until relatively recently, was popular among life insurers. In the latter part of the twentieth century, most life insurers converted into stock corporations, but Guardian's top leaders continued to believe that the life insurance business was more effective when organized *mutually*. Dan Lyons, one of the company's most important chief executives, imbued Guardian's sales personnel during the 1960s with the simple credo "Don't do any deals . . . unless they are good for the policyholder, the agent, *and* the company. It has got to be good for each of the three parties to the deal." That creed has held fast through a succession of chief executives into the twenty-first century.[2]

Mutual life insurance is based on the premise that policyholders are in effect "owners" of the enterprise. Throughout the history of American life insurance, many stock companies have thrived, but because a portion of their profits must enrich their stockholders, such companies cannot consistently offer policyholders the lowest-cost, highest-quality life insurance possible. On the other hand, the managers of mutual companies may not have sufficient incentives to create large profits for their policyholders. Hence the relative merits of mutual and stock ownership are not easily discerned. Guardian has had to work hard to make mutuality work.[3]

The book's subtitle, *Guardian and Life Insurance in America,* is more than a word play on the company's current name. It signals that this book is not so much the history of a corporation as it is the history of an idea, or rather an ideal. Life insurance is at base a financial instrument, but it is also a social and political statement, one particularly American in flavor. Americans historically purchased far more life insurance per capita than any other nation. In so doing, they effectively turned away from more socialist forms of welfare. Every insured American was a capitalist, an owner of a type of financial capital known as the life insurance policy, a contract that rationally distributes the risk of premature death over a large pool of policyholders, and that does much more.[4]

This work was undertaken at the behest of The Guardian Life Insurance Company through an intermediary, The Winthrop Group, Inc., an association of economic, business, and technology historians. Guardian made all its documents and personnel available to us in exchange for a promise from Winthrop that Guardian could review text for factual errors. The authors sought out the comments and criticisms of Guardian executives and employees with the understanding that there would be no censorship of any kind. The New York University Press reviewed and accepted the text on its scholarly merits.

With that in mind, it is worth recalling the words of the insurance historian R. Carlyle Buley, who once remarked that "one of the advantages of writing on historical subjects of some past period is that the characters involved cannot argue back with the historian. Living characters can and do."[5] Guardian executives and employees indeed helped us to correct some errors of fact, and occasionally debated with us on points of interpretation. In short, the questions asked and the views expressed herein are ours alone.

The labor, a joint intellectual effort, was divided between the authors as follows. The concept for the book, the questions and the themes, were developed jointly in a series of meetings in the spring of 2002. Robert Wright bore the primary onus of the research, and wrote the initial chapter drafts. The drafts were then passed back and forth, in several critical iterations, as the authors met frequently to discuss and revise their ideas.

Our objective for the book was to provide a solid narrative history of Guardian, while also addressing particular facets of the life insurance business in depth. Hence, the book is divided between chronological and topical sections. Following a conceptual introduction, part I of this volume (chapters 1, 2, 3, and 4) provides a chronological overview of the company's evolution. Established as a mixed company in New York in 1860, Guardian soon began to sell policies in a number of states. Shortly thereafter, it spread into Canada and several European nations, especially Germany. Guardian was always a medium-sized insurer, but its importance to the industry was larger than its market share, particularly after its exculpation in the Armstrong Investigation in 1905. During World War I, the company changed its name and refocused on the U.S. market. Soon after its mutualization in 1924, Guardian faced, and met, the investment challenges posed by the Depression and World War II. After the war, the company flowered, growing in both size and breadth. In the 1950s, for example, it expanded into accident and health and began developing group lines of business. By the late 1960s, it recognized and prepared to meet the challenges posed by inflation that would threaten it, and the entire industry, in the 1970s and 1980s. While other life insurers went bankrupt or had their reputations severely tarnished in the 1990s, Guardian continued to thrive and enjoy an enviable reputation.[6]

Parts II and III, chapters 5 through 13 inclusive, analyze each phase of the life insurance process illustrated in figure 1-2. Chapters 5 and 6 focus on product creation and development, from the basic whole life policy to annuities to Guardian's other major contracts, including term life, disability, health, and a variety of employee-benefit and group insurances. Chapter 7 details the evolution of Guardian's advertising and marketing campaigns. It shows, for instance, how Guardian's advertising evolved as life insurance itself changed from a means to protect the economic well-being of widows and orphans to a mechanism for accumulating an estate free of taxes. In chapter 8, we describe how the methods by which Guardian sold or distributed its products to individuals and businesses changed over time. Since World War II, Guardian has built up a large career field force composed of field representatives paid a salary and bonus and managed by entrepreneurial, commissioned general agents. Starting in the 1960s, the company also greatly expanded the brokerage channel.

Chapter 9 argues that Guardian managed to attract and retain quality employees because it offered them a good work environment, extensive training and educational opportunities, and a superior job evaluation program that underlay an entrepreneurial, meritocratic human resources culture. In chapter 10, we explore regionalization and automation as largely successful attempts to increase administrative efficiency. Adoption of computers and advanced telecommunications technologies allowed the company to move many of its back office operations to regional offices where the cost of doing business was lower, customers were closer, and good employees cheaper and more plentiful than in expensive, crowded Manhattan.

Expense management, including descriptions of Guardian's struggles against unjust taxes and inefficient regulations, is also the central focus of chapter 11. We concentrate on Guardian's relationship with the New York insurance department for several reasons. First, Guardian is a New York–domiciled company. In other words, New York granted the company its corporate charters and New York regulators are primarily responsible for overseeing its activities. Second, New York insurance superintendents are, and have long been, the most important of all insurance regulators, regardless of a company's state of domicile. Part of the reason for that is that the insurance regulators of other states often look to New York for guidance. More importantly, any life insurer that wishes to do business in New York—and most do because of the Empire State's large population and wealth—must follow New York's rules and regulations.[7]

In part III, chapters 12 and 13, we explain the causes of Guardian's highly successful investment history. Guardian's investment philosophies, liquidity management techniques, and asset allocation decisions have helped it to exceed the industry's average net rate of return almost every year for *at least the last seven decades.* That is truly an amazing record and a crucial aspect of Guardian's long-term success.

Part IV, chapter 14, attempts to tie together the earlier parts of the book by examining the recent history of the company from the top down. It overviews Guardian's corporate culture and governance, including executive succession and compensation, in an effort to understand how Guardian manages change without losing its traditional emphasis on the policyholder. The final chapter also chronicles Guardian's recent past, current path, and likely future obstacles. Finally, it assesses the importance of the company's deep-rooted ethical corporate culture and its firm commitment to mutuality.

More broadly, throughout the entire book, the emphasis is on net costs. We are most interested in how Guardian responded to changes in the economy, the competition, and the regulatory, tax, and technological environments as it endeavored to provide policyholders with quality but low-cost life, disability, and health insurance. Costs are a function of expenses, investment returns, and mortality experience, the three legs of the proverbial life insurance "stool." Part II concerns itself with mortality and expense management. Part III is about investment returns. Part IV shows how top management juggled those three major variables. Part I overviews the evolving nature of the stool and management's strategic responses to those changes.

The source materials for this work were abundant. Guardian has excellent archival resources, even by the standards of most businesses its age. It is important to note that while the authors relied extensively on Guardian's corporate archives, we took great pains to verify and expand on the written record through interviews of key personnel, active and retired. The claims of company employees were tempered by thorough reading of the public record, including regulatory documents, court records, industry publications, and news and scholarly articles. The relevant secondary source literature has been exhausted, at least to the point of our knowledge of it. The primary source documents that we utilized, both manuscript and typescript, have been silently corrected for misspellings and obvious typographical mistakes. Editorial insertions in quotations appear in square brackets; unless otherwise noted, all emphases in quotations appear in the original. Finally, readers should note that we relied on contemporary translations of German-language documents.

We incurred many debts before bringing this book to fruition. First and foremost, we want to thank the many Guardian managers and retirees who granted interviews: John Angle, Ashby Bladen, Joseph Caruso, Armand de Palo, Miervaldis "Wally" Dobelis, Robert Evraets, Art Ferrara, Leo Futia, Frank Jones, Ed Kane, Eric Larson, Gary Lenderink, Dennis Manning, Howard Most, Jim Pirtle, Bob Ryan, Joseph Sargent, Tom Sorell, and Don Sullivan. We must also thank those who provided us with valuable information, especially Cliff Kitchen, Steve Scarpati, and Charlotte Stacey. We are most indebted to Sargent, Caruso, Dobelis, Kane, and Faith Drennan for reading, and rereading, the entire manuscript and offering suggestions that saved us from much embarrassment. Thanks are also due to Guardian employees who helped the authors to arrange those interviews, to access the company's archives, and to obtain industry documents: Joanne Chippi, Arlene Duffy, Faith Drennan, Susanne Perez, Helen Plakas, Karen Olvany, Liz Snyder, and Ann Treanor.

Industry experts outside of the Guardian were also helpful. Ed Graves, Virginia Webb, and Marge Fletcher of the American College provided important guidance and assistance. Economic historian Richard E. Sylla read the entire manuscript and provided valuable advice, comments, and insights. We also thank Anita Rapone for her book, *Guardian Life Insurance Company, 1860–1920: A History of a German-American Enterprise* (New York: New York University Press, 1987), which proved invaluable in the preparation of the present study, though we cite it only when necessary to point readers to the primary source material upon which both of our books are based. Readers interested in the personalities of Guardian's founders or additional details about the company's first six decades, especially its close relationship with the German-American community, should read her fine work. Finally, a special word of thanks is due to the great television character SpongeBob Squarepants, who lives in a pineapple under the sea, for keeping our children amused at least part of the time while we wrote—that is, when we weren't watching ourselves.

Robert E. Wright
George David Smith
New York 2003

Abbreviations

CSO   Commissioners Standard Ordinary (mortality table)

ERISA   Employee Retirement Income Security Act

GA   general agent (a commissioned, independent sales manager)

GAAP   Generally Accepted Accounting Practices

GAMCORP Guardian Asset Management Corporation

GDP   Gross Domestic Product

GIAC   Guardian Insurance and Annuity Company

GIS   Guardian Investor Services, LLC

GISC   Guardian Investor Services Corporation, now GIS, LLC

GLIC   Guardian Life Insurance Company of America
(the parent company)

GLICOA Associates   Guardian Life Insurance Company of
America's broker-dealer, later GISC, now GIS, LLC

LEAP   Lifetime Economic Acceleration Process

LOMA   Life Office Management Association

MONY   Mutual of New York

NAIC   National Association of Insurance Commissioners

NASD   National Association of Securities Dealers

NRO   Northeast Regional Office, GLIC, Bethlehem, Pa.

NYLIC   New York Life Insurance Company

SEC   Securities and Exchange Commission

TNEC   Temporary National Economic Committee

UL   Universal Life

YRT   Yearly Renewable Term (aka Annual Renewable Term)

Introduction

In Arthur Miller's *Death of a Salesman,* Willy Loman is contemplating suicide. Distraught by a deep sense of personal failure as a husband and father, Loman thinks he might at least provide his family with a $20,000 life insurance death benefit. He worries about a suicide exclusion in his policy, yet he rationalizes, "Didn't I work like a coolie to meet every premium on the nose?" Perhaps mercifully, the audience is not made privy to the details of his policy (the play would have closed at intermission), but we can plausibly imagine that if Loman were a New Yorker aged about sixty years in 1950, it is almost certain that his policy would have been paid off, even if he had left a suicide note. For, you see, while Miller may have been a great playwright, he knew little about life insurance. By the early part of the twentieth century, all life policies issued in New York contained a suicide clause requiring the insurer to pay the policy's face value if the insured committed suicide two or more years after policy issuance.[1]

Moreover, were it not for the sake of the drama, Miller's hapless protagonist need not consider ending his own life. Loman, who has been having trouble finding and retaining a job due to psychological problems that impair his driving and work skills, may very well be eligible for a disability benefit. Most policies (then as now) waive premiums if the insured becomes disabled. Others waive premiums and provide monthly cash payments. Even better, Loman's policy probably has substantial cash value that he could use to purchase an annuity on his life and that of his betrayed but worthy spouse, Linda. The income provided by the annuity would be modest, but the couple's mortgage would be paid off. If Loman were foresighted enough, he could even take out a policy loan to help set up his sons in business. His premium payments, like his mortgage payments, are a significant form of savings that could be tapped by less desperate means. In short, Loman's claim that he is "worth more dead than alive" is not true, at least from a financial standpoint. This is because the life insurance contract provides more than a death benefit, more than a

1

mechanism for spreading the financial risk of premature death over a pool of policyholders. It truly is a policy for the whole of life.[2]

Life

Since time immemorial, people have fretted about risk, especially when potential losses are expected to be large. Members of highly organized societies have always sought insurance or other risk-sharing mechanisms to protect themselves against a wide range of calamities, including shipwrecks, fires, weather, business losses, and, more recently, automobile accidents, liability suits, and even changes in interest rates and stock prices. Of all forms of insurance, life insurance is the most essential form of protection. Life insurance helps families—the fundamental units of social organization—reduce the risk associated with the loss of income should a wage earner die prematurely, that is, before expected retirement.[3]

What precisely is involved in the risk associated with death? After all, unlike fire, drought, or loss of goods, death is certain. The problem is that in social terms, one's death is not "final." Quite aside from spiritual considerations, those who have produced offspring live on genetically and emotionally in their children, and their children's children, for whom the loss of a loved one is often accompanied by the loss of a significant source of economic support. Even the death of an individual without spouse or child can have profound economic impact on extended family, friends, business partners, and creditors.

Nor is the timing of one's death predictable in any meaningful sense. If it were, it would be easier for a responsible wage earner to plan for survivors' fortunes—to decide how much to save and how much to spend. It is death's uncertainty that gives life insurance its value.

The case for the value of live insurance is amply supported by the work of social scientists. Evolutionary anthropologists have long argued that humans (like many species of animals) tend to behave not as individuals but rather as principals in organizations composed of extended family members (and sometimes even unrelated individuals whose contribution to the group is unquestioned). To use a business analogy, people generally attempt to strengthen their "family firms" through their life's labors, and hope to leave their kin a legacy—a kind of bequest of equity after they are gone. Recently, many economists, too, have come to view bequest motives as strong components of economic behavior, accounting for up to 80 percent of aggregate capital accumulation.[4]

If a family "head" or other particularly productive family member fails to provide adequate protection for the rest, potential beneficiaries may demand a purchase of insurance, in the same way that children routinely spur the purchase of diapers, clothing, and other commodities that parents transfer to their offspring. In business contexts, beneficiaries often demand the purchase of protection. "Key person" and credit life insurance, for example, is purchased at the behest of the beneficiaries, employers, and creditors, respectively. (Slave insurance, though written by life companies, was really a form of property and casualty insurance because it indemnified the policyholder against a fraction of the current market value of the slave, not the present discounted value of the slave's expected future income. Otherwise, it would have been too tempting for slaveholders to murder or overwork their slaves.)[5]

Given the strong motivations to bequest property (a stock) and to reduce income risk (a flow), one might conclude that life insurance would be among the easiest contracts to sell. After all, we are all going to die, almost all of us have loved ones who will survive us, and we all are accustomed to reducing risk by purchasing insurance. Ironically, however, life insurance is one of the most difficult products to sell. It has always been, as many have said, "a sold good, not a bought good." Psychologists and sociologists have confirmed what insurers themselves have long known: that people resist life insurance purchases because they do not like to think about their own passing or the passing of loved ones. There may very well be a good deal of truth to that argument, but it is only a partial explanation, at best. It implies that people allow their irrational fears to get the better of them. There are at least two other, more rational explanations for most individuals' resistance to purchasing life insurance. For one thing, people have to incur costs now to hedge against some event in the future, a universal problem of weighing the relative costs of paying now or later. For another, individuals do not resist life insurance, per se, as much as life insurance *companies,* the firms that underwrite the policies.[6]

Why is this so? When people buy insurance, they must have reasonable faith that the insurer will pay their claims promptly and without hassle. In the case of life insurance policies, the problem of trust is especially acute. After all, the insured will not be around to pursue his or her claim personally. Beneficiaries are left to fend for themselves, and often lack the information necessary to present an iron-clad case for their claims. Potential policyholders know but little about the companies attempting to win their business. Which companies are most reliable? Which have good track records in honoring their claims? Which are most likely to be around years from now to pay their claims? The gap in information between the potential policyholder and the insurer is extremely large, as is the cost of acquiring information to bridge that gap. Potential customers know that some insurance companies have gone bankrupt, but few realize that state guaranty associations protect their interests as fully as FDIC insurance protects bank depositors. Prospects also know that some of the largest and most well-known insurers have overpriced policies or engaged in other predatory practices like "churning" and misrepresenting life insurance as a retirement annuity benefit. And rapidly rising health care costs have not helped matters. It is little wonder that life insurance salespersons must search diligently for prospects and often face stiff initial resistance to their overtures. It all boils down to a problem of trust.[7]

Trust

As insurance executive William C. Johnson pointed out in 1907, "there is no higher form of trusteeship than that which a life insurance company undertakes." Indeed, buying life insurance is not like buying other financial liabilities, such as bank deposits. Trust in one's bank need not run nearly as deep as trust in one's life insurer. First, it is much more difficult to price life insurance policies than bank accounts. Second, depositors can quickly access their funds if need be, and, should a dispute arise, depositors can press their claims personally. Life policyholders, on the other hand, must be absolutely certain that their life insurer will remain solvent for long periods of time.[8]

The solvency of life insurance companies is important for broader social reasons, as well. This is because, in order to thrive as businesses, much less to meet their obligations to make good on their policies, life insurers must invest premiums paid by policyholders in remunerative assets. Thus, like banks, life insurers are essentially financial intermediaries. They gather numerous small premiums from policyholders into huge pools of investments. They link savers (policyholders) to borrowers (entrepreneurs, governments, and households) by channeling funds into productive sectors of the economy. Life insurance companies invest their premiums in various debt instruments, including mortgages, government and corporate bonds, loans to policyholders, and cash instruments like bank accounts and commercial paper. They also, to a lesser degree, purchase equity stakes in corporations and real estate. As a class of investors, life insurers usually are relatively conservative, more likely to invest in high-rated bonds than equities, and in more established sectors of the economy than in new or distressed ventures, striving to earn relatively low but safe and steady returns.[9]

The existence of life insurance has thus augmented economic growth by increasing society's total savings. Indeed, life insurance has long been thought to induce thrift in ordinary citizens so that they can pay their premiums. Those increased savings, in turn, reduced the cost of borrowing for entrepreneurs, governments, and homeowners by increasing the supply of investment funds, thereby establishing a complex web of mutually beneficial relationships among insurers, policyholders, direct beneficiaries, and what we call "social beneficiaries." As increased financial intermediation has been a major cause of economic progress, life insurance companies have made significant contributions to the general weal.[10]

Yet that simple fact has not been widely appreciated. Historically, the life insurance industry has not enjoyed a very good reputation, despite its economic importance and despite the large number of very good companies that populate it. Part of the problem is simply guilt by association. As a category of business, finance has been held in low public esteem in the United States ever since the early days of the republic. Americans have always mistrusted financiers and their institutions. Robert Morris, who largely financed the last phase of the American Revolution on his personal reputation, and Alexander Hamilton, who established the nation's credit, were vilified by people who mistrusted financial power. Famous and largely ethical private investors such as John Jacob Astor, Jay Cooke, and J. P. Morgan may be heroes to economic historians, but in their own time, they were regarded by many as nothing more than greedy financial alchemists. Banks have provided vitally needed services to ordinary citizens, but are remembered as often as not for their denials of credit to the economically weak and their foreclosures on the victims of financial distress. Insurance companies appeared on the economic landscape in the early days of the industrial revolution as large, "moneyed" behemoths, and thus, they too were fitting objects of fear. Given the abiding populist strain of American culture, the unethical or illegal actions of a single company can still taint the entire industry for an extended period.[11]

In the 1820s, for example, several scandals involving the issuance of notelike bearer bonds and stock manipulation schemes by insurance companies rocked Wall Street. The failure of several life insurance firms in the 1850s, ascribed to outrageously high policy dividends (return of premiums paid) and the acceptance of promissory notes in lieu of cash for premiums, again weakened public confidence. After the Civil War, numerous joint-stock life companies fell into the hands of unscrupulous managers who enriched themselves while running their firms into bankruptcy.[12]

Consider, as but one example of many, the case of American Life of Philadelphia, which in the late nineteenth century designing financiers destroyed by surreptitiously purchasing a controlling interest and then equally stealthily possessing themselves of American's assets. In the last decades of the nineteenth century, the largest life insurance firms developed cozy securities purchasing relationships with much-maligned investment bankers, including J. P. Morgan; Kuhn, Loeb, and Company; and Kidder, Peabody, and Company. Scandals, schemes, and investigations, including the Armstrong Investigation in 1905, the Temporary National Economic Committee (TNEC) inquiries in the late 1930s, and the Celler probe of 1942–43, repeatedly shook the public's faith in life insurance firms, even when the insurers were not culpable. In our own time, the "churning" of policies by some major insurers has added needless costs while providing little benefit to their holders. Such scandals and probes scarred the industry precisely because trust is the most important attribute of the service.[13]

"The sale of a life insurance policy by an agent to a prospective buyer hinges more than anything else on one essential point," wrote an industry analyst in 1927, "and that point is confidence." In practical terms, the life insurance agents most of us encounter at some points in our lives have to establish personal bonds of trust, and then do even more. They must also convince potential clients that the companies underwriting the policies they sell are inherently reliable. In doing so, agents will point to a firm's size, longevity, and reputation for keeping promises. The firms themselves will support their agents with images of solidity, like the Rock of Gibraltar; familial warmth, like the Pelican, or friendly familiarity, like Snoopy, the dog from the Peanuts cartoon.[14]

The insurance agent, of course, is not merely the insurance company's salesperson; she is the critical link between the policyholder and the larger economy. "We have it as the boast of life insurance companies and the confession of policyholders," noted industry chronicler Paul Geren in the 1940s, "that much of the savings accumulated in life insurance would never have been made were it not for the importunity of life insurance agents." That agents have been quite adept at selling life insurance is evidenced by the fact that even during the Great Depression, some 83 percent of families with an annual income below $2,500 had more debt than savings, and yet most owned some life insurance. In 1976, at least one family member in some 83 percent of U.S. households had life insurance protection; in over half of all families, all family members were insured, the same levels as in 1960. In 1998, there were some 358 million life insurance policies in force in the United States, more than one per capita. The average amount of life insurance in force per household in that year was $141,000. All this "reflects the disposition of the typical American," opined Geren, "to guard his life insurance . . . and to add to it even at the sacrifice of other assets or the increase of liabilities."[15]

Trust, and the corresponding growth of life insurance over time, has been buttressed to some degree by government regulation aimed at both protecting policyholders against misrepresentations, price gouging, and the like and also ensuring that insurance companies do not abuse their considerable financial power on the investment side. Of course regulation is a burden to companies, and in that respect the life insurance industry's contribution to social beneficiaries has redounded to its benefit. Despite the generally poor reputation of insurance, the life sector has avoided major regulatory scrutiny at the federal level. At the state level, however, regulatory control of the life insurance industry has been much stiffer. State regulators impose restrictions on policy provisions, premiums, agent commissions, and insurance company investment strategies and accounting practices. In turn, insurers, and to a lesser extent agents, interact with regulators, both directly through negotiations and indirectly through "loophole mining" and product innovation. When they act in the public interest instead of their own interest, regulators attempt to balance the competitive needs of insurers with the rights of policyholders and the interests of society at large.[16]

Figure 1-1 illustrates the *general structure* of the institution of life insurance. On the left is the life insurer, divided into its presale, postsale, and back-office components. Projecting from the company are its owners—stockholders, policyholders, or a combination of both. Also projecting from the company is its policy, proffered through the firm's own salespeople, its agents, or independent brokers. If the company is partly or wholly a mutual, the policyholder essentially becomes a member of the firm, hence the physical connection of the owner projection to the direct

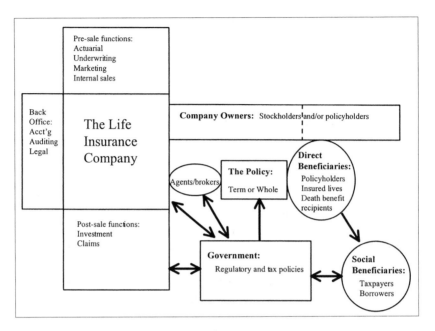

FIGURE INTRO-1 *Life Insurance Structure*

beneficiary circle. The dotted line in the owner projection severs the connection for stock firms.

Likewise, the dotted line in the direct beneficiary circle serves to separate the policyholder from the insured and from death claim beneficiaries. The policyholder and the insured are often the same person, but they need not be, as long as the policyholder has a significant economic interest in the life of the insured. Similarly, the policyholder and the recipient of the death benefit do not have to be related. Literally *anyone* can be a death claim beneficiary.

Because death claim recipients need less assistance from society, literally *everyone* is an indirect or social beneficiary of life insurance, hence the heavy dark arrow leading to the social beneficiary circle. As noted above, society also benefits from investments made by life insurers.

The final major player in the structure, the government, regulates the life company's investments, sales, and policy provisions. It also influences the demand for life policies through its tax policies and its provision of involuntary insurance substitutes such as Social Security.[17]

Figure 1-2, in contrast, illustrates the life insurance *process*—the creation, sale, servicing, and payment of major products sold by life insurance companies. The squares list the major functions of life insurance; the circles list the major departments that perform those functions. The left part of the figure reminds readers that the key to the entire life insurance process, i.e., to the efficient creation and provision of those functions, is management.

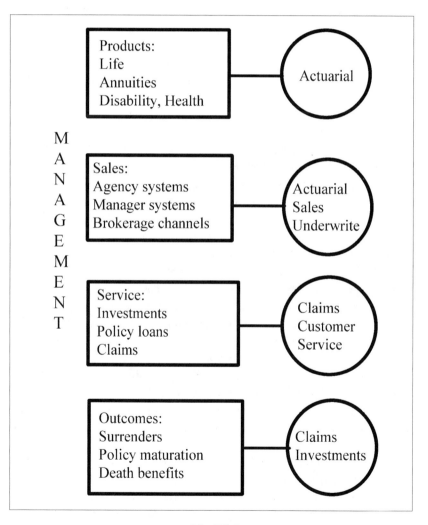

FIGURE INTRO-2 *The Life Insurance Process*

Mutuality

"Mutualization," Guardian general agent Charles Rudd noted in 1918, "carries confidence with the buying public." For much of the twentieth century, almost all of the most important life insurers were constituted as mutual companies, that is, as business cooperatives beholden to policyholders and not to shareholders. In the past, stock corporations often converted into mutuals. In recent times, most of the largest mutual life insurers have "demutualized," converting into stock corporations. Because the relationship between trust and mutuality in ownership is no small matter, it is important to consider why insurance companies would choose to reorganize themselves as stock, rather than mutual, companies, or viceversa.[18]

Stockholders own the vast majority of large U.S. corporations. The profits, if any, of such companies accrue to the stockholders, to whom managers owe a special, fiduciary responsibility. Though stockholders have nominally held the power to hire and fire the managers, in practice, managers, even if they owned little or no stock, ran firms for long periods with little stockholder interference. Increasingly, however, managers have also become significant stockholders in their firms, on the notion that the interests of the principals (the owners) and the agents (the managers) will thereby be brought into closer alignment.[19]

At their best, stock companies are very effective producers of a broad range of goods and services, from automobiles to soap to tax advice. Stockholders push management to keep the firm's stock price high. Managers, in turn, strive to maintain profitability in order to retain their jobs, earn bonuses, and cash in on stock options. In many lines of business, such constant attention to the bottom line keeps firms lean, mean, efficient, and willing to exit temporarily unprofitable businesses without compunction. When firms are unwilling or unable to run efficiently, outsiders—other companies, corporate raiders, or buyout funds—stand ready to purchase their stock, take control of their management, and drive them back to profitability.[20]

Stock companies are not, however, the optimal organizational form for all business sectors. Law firms, for instance, are forbidden by law to organize as joint-stock companies. There are several reasons for this, the most pertinent here being that attorneys need to make decisions that are in the best interests of their clients, not in the best interests of stockholders. The attorney-client relationship is an intimate, often long-term one, and so clients could not trust their attorneys if they had to fear that stockholder interests were paramount. Imagine, for instance, a scenario where the stockholders in a law firm wanted a one-dollar-per-share dividend declared but where the firm had only enough profits to pay ninety cents per share. The attorneys in the firm might decide to prematurely settle a case rather than wait for trial in order to meet stockholder demands for a one-dollar dividend. The attorneys, in other words, might induce a client to take a paltry settlement now instead of a larger one later, solely to satiate stockholders. Similar reasoning applies to life insurance firms, a long horizon business requiring a high degree of trust. The relatively short-term perspective of most stockholders and the long-term perspective of policyholders do not mix well.[21]

As early as the colonial period, Americans understood that all insurance is essentially mutual in principle. The first life insurance companies chartered in the United States organized as joint stock firms, probably to distance themselves from earlier, inefficient and rum-soaked "friendly society" insurance schemes. Those early stock companies, however, sold few policies. While most survived by transforming into asset management firms, or "trust companies," not until mutual firms arrived on the scene around 1840 did the U.S. life business thrive. From the 1840s until very recently, while most life insurers have been stock companies, mutual firms have held most life insurance industry assets. In other words, a relatively few, giant mutual firms came to dominate the life insurance business. That outcome was not accidental.[22]

Mutual companies commanded confidence, even though they, like stock companies, were far from perfect. Policyholders were even less able than large corporate stockholders to exercise their rights with respect to managers, which reality, under some conditions, has allowed mutual company managers to become inefficient, self-interested, or predatory. Indeed, several studies suggest that mutual financial firms performed best in staid, well-understood lines of business requiring relatively little management effort. Mutual companies also lacked the opportunity to raise funds in the equity markets and sometimes faced disadvantageous tax treatment.[23]

Offsetting those disadvantages is the fact that mutual policyholders cannot easily or cheaply "vote with their feet" by exiting the firm through policy surrenders or loans. They cannot sell their policies outright, and to insure again at a higher age, if indeed they are insurable at all, would mean higher premiums. But disgruntled policyholders can easily avoid buying additional insurance, a major source of revenue for many insurers. Moreover, they can cheaply tell their friends and family to avoid contact with the underperforming company. As MONY historian Shepard Clough put it, "Events had proved that an unsuccessful management would eventually have the policyholders down on its head and have the public doing business with competitors." Mutual managers thus have a powerful incentive to keep their principal source of funds satisfied. In addition, mutual policyholders have been less likely to falsify claims than policyholders in stock companies. Competition for customers from the many joint stock firms in the life insurance market, moreover, has often stimulated the better mutual managers to become more productive. Finally, the identity of customers and owners in a mutual company simplifies the matter of allegiance. As MONY actuary Joseph MacLean put it, "the cost in a mutual company depends largely on the efficiency of management," the emphasis being on *efficiency*. To serve the policyholder well, the mutual must be prudently managed and governed.[24]

Guardian

To be successful in competitive markets in the early twenty-first century, mutual life insurance companies must be particularly *well run*. They must discover ways to induce management to work vigorously for the benefit of policyholders. First and foremost, therefore, mutual companies need good governance structures and quality leadership. The thesis of this book is that Guardian Life Insurance Company of America, one of the few remaining mutual life insurers, learned how to structure its business and corporate culture so as effectively to "maximize" policyholder value.[25]

Guardian began its existence in the nineteenth century as a hybrid or mixed company owned partly by stockholders and partly by policyholders. Technically, it became a wholly mutual company on 1 January 1946, though it was almost entirely mutualized in 1925. Moreover, since the formation of the company in 1860, management has always run it like a mutual, i.e., strictly in the interests of policyholders. As early as 1862, for example, the Board noted "that in a Life Ins. Co. the interest of the Stock holders is quite insignificant compared with that of the policy holders." Again in 1869 it told regulators that the company was "essentially on the mutual plan."[26] This early orientation of the business resonated over the decades. Guardian became, and then persisted as, a wholly mutual company into the twenty-first century, even after other large insurers abandoned the principle.

The principle is important, since this book will show that as a mutual company, Guardian has managed consistently to provide policyholders with quality, low *net cost* insurance protection. (Net cost of insurance is simply premiums paid minus dividends [retroactive premium adjustments] credited. Premiums are *estimates* of the cost of insurance based on conservative expectations of the insurer's future mortality experience, expenses [commissions, taxes, administration costs], and investment returns. Through dividends, mutual life companies [and stock companies that offer participating policies] return premiums to policyholders based on their *actual or ex post* mortality, expense, and investment experience. If management is efficient, it will keep mortality and expense costs relatively low and investment returns relatively high, and thus maximize the policyholder's return by minimizing the net cost of insurance.)[27]

Guardian has also been "profitable" as measured by return on net wealth, that is, net income as a percentage of average net worth.[28] One reason for this kind of success may be that as a mutual Guardian was better able than a stock company might have been to focus on the long term. Another important reason is that Guardian generally emphasized efficiency over scale, both in the nineteenth century when size was all-important in the life industry and again in the mid-twentieth century when the prevailing obsession in American big business was asset growth. Thus even though there were times when scale constraints became important to the company's strategy, Guardian's strict adherence to the interests of its policyholders kept its growth rates relatively modest.

This was important when one considers that beyond a certain size, bigger was not necessarily better when it came to life insurance. Scale economies in insurance are not unimportant; big life insurance companies are generally more efficient than small ones, to be sure, but, as Guardian has long understood, *really big* life insurance companies are no more efficient than *merely big* ones. Moreover, economies of scope, that is, efficiencies derived from sheer variety of product offerings, are not always present. Recognizing that after a certain point, growth for the sake of growth would not further the interests of existing policyholders, Guardian has never sought to be among the largest or most diversified of life insurers, just among the more efficient and effective.[29]

Finally, the history of Guardian is interesting, not just in its own right but also as an exemplar of the larger industry. Though never among the gigantic life insurers, the company has been an important intellectual leader in the sector for over a century. It has repeatedly helped to shape industry opinion, practice, and even regulation, always in the name, and interests, of its policyholders. NYLIC chronicler Lawrence Abbott once claimed that "the annals of financial institutions are generally supposed to be dry and statistical." Though the pages that follow contain numerous data tables, statistical charts, and discussions of technical issues, the story of insurance is as important and compelling as that of any enterprise.[30]

Part I

Historical Overview

What relevance can events that occurred over a century and a half ago possibly have today? Some Germans got together and formed a life insurance company. So what? Those men have long since died, as have their children, and even their children's children. And, perhaps more importantly, the world they inhabited also appears to have died. The United States is a vastly different place today than it was in 1860. A nineteenth-century denizen of Manhattan transported to the present would get mugged before he figured out where he was or why seemingly everyone was jabbering into little music boxes festooned with glowing, numbered buttons.

But then again, a part of the founders and their world *does* live on. The founders themselves, however, would not recognize it, at least on the surface. The company they founded on the eve of the Civil War has grown many times over, changed its address, radically expanded its product offerings, and even changed its name. The founders, though, might very well recognize the company's spirit. Moreover, if they wished, they could trace the company through successive stages of development, day by day, week by week, quarter by quarter, year by year, decade by decade right to the present, in one unbroken chain of life, death, constancy, and renewal.

We humans do not spring fully formed from the head of Jove, and neither do our institutions. History, therefore, is a vital part of any business organization. It is especially important, however, to life insurance companies due to the long-term nature of their contracts. Consider, for instance, the case of a policy issued by Guardian in 1899. The insured died in 1929. The widow elected to receive interest on the proceeds for her lifetime and the lifetimes of either of her two children. Some sixty-five years after the policy had been issued, Guardian was still sending checks to the last surviving child though not a single person who had been with the company in 1899 was still active. Or consider the case of J. F. Brunjes, who signed up with Guardian in 1868. In 1923, Guardian paid his policy to him as an endowment because he had reached his ninety-sixth birthday. Again, the Guardianites who helped to underwrite the initial policy were long gone. The company, however, lived on and fulfilled its solemn obligations. As James P. Sullivan, chief actuary of Chicago's Sullivan Organization, put it, "The operators are, after all, only the changing veneer of the whole institution which we all hope will go on to permanently successful service for the people whose common interest has built it." Life companies, in other words, are sort of supra-individuals. In that respect, this book is more of a biography than a history.[1]

As Guardian's second president, Cornelius Doremus, once noted, "length of life, whether of an individual or a corporation, establishes character." Guardian's character today is very strong because of the efforts of its current personnel but also because of circumstances that it faced and decisions that it made last week, last month, last quarter, last year, last decade, and, yes, even last century. And because the company did not arise sui generis, but rather emerged from the peculiar circumstances of the nation, the insurance industry, and its founders, some consideration must also be given to the period before the company's formation, back to the origins of life insurance itself. Before readers can fully appreciate the historical origins of Guardian, they must first understand the contextual milieu in which it arose.[2]

Most scholars of the subject contend, with very little direct evidence, that the industry was a product of urban industrial democracy. In other words, the usual story is that life insurance arose because demand for it increased due to changes in where people lived, how they earned their livelihood, and the nature of their political system. We wish to stress here that increases in the supply of life insurance due to technological advances in legal matters, actuarial methods, and company organization were just as important. Moreover, though demand for insurance indeed increased over the course of the nineteenth century, it did so because of the use of commissioned sales agents, not because of broad socioeconomic changes. (A more formal summary of our argument, which is essentially Druckerian, appears in the appendix.)[3]

Upon first hearing, the view that urbanization, industrialization, and democratization caused the growth of life insurance sounds quite plausible. Life insurance grew along with industrialization, having gained some importance in England in the mid-eighteenth century, about the same time as steam engines and mechanized factories appeared, labor became specialized, and large numbers of workers moved from the farm into towns and cities to seek employment in the then "new economy." Successful early industrializers, Holland, Britain, and the United States, were the first to develop modern life annuities and legal reserve life insurance. Great Britain, the United States, and Canada remain the leaders in life insurance and have long been the world's foremost urban industrial democracies.[4]

Industrial democracy was certainly compatible with modern life insurance, but demand for protection had always existed. Indeed, the roots of life insurance extend far back in history, well before the advent of urbanization, industrialization, or democratization. Several ancient societies, including Babylonia, Egypt, and Rome, experimented with various forms of life and burial insurance and life annuities. In fifteenth-century Barcelona, slaveholders insured the unborn offspring of their pregnant slaves and creditors insured the lives of their debtors. Individuals who insured the lives of others for short terms were active in Britain and elsewhere in the seventeenth century. Colonial America was home to several life insurance societies, established for the benefit of the family of clergy, well before republicanism evolved into democracy, agriculture gave way to industry, or cities and suburbs began to dominate the landscape.[5]

Essentially, it was the universal fear of death's adverse income effects combined with the ability to hedge against it that produced life insurance. It is difficult to believe, as many scholars have argued, that self-sufficient farmers, who comprised most of the populations of preindustrial societies, had little need for the protection of life insurance. If anything, given the greater dangers they faced, they had in fact *more* need for insurance. Almost all humans, especially farmers, need life insurance and always have. Consider in the abstract the case of two men, each with a spouse, two small children, and the same disposable wealth and income. The first, a farmer, invests his savings in land, farm improvements, and livestock. The second, an employee, invests in bonds. If the farmer dies, his assets remain unworked, generate no income, and lose value. If the employee dies, his bonds continue to pay interest. Ceteris paribus, the farmer, essentially a small business owner, needs life insurance at least as badly as the employee.[6]

As one of Guardian's house organs noted in 1961, "it is a funny thing about life insurance. It has to be paid for whether or not it is bought." In other words, humans always carry some form of life insurance; it is just that a good many of them, too many of them, are self- or clan-insured.

People traditionally relied, in other words, on what they owned (or what their clan owned) at any given moment to provide for their spouses and children should they perish. The real question is, then, not when did people start to need life insurance but rather what unleashed modern legal reserve life insurance? Or, to put it another way, what enabled organized businesses to provide contracts for this natural need for protection cheaply enough to induce people to purchase them?[7]

Part of the answer lies in the financial revolution that transformed England in the 1690s and America a century later. Good financial systems were necessary to industrial progress, and nations that possessed them had developed a number of interrelated monetary and financial institutions, including a relatively reliable and cheap contract enforcement system; a stable unit of account; a reliable money supply, usually regulated by a central bank; securities markets, exchanges, and broker-dealers; and a variety of private intermediaries, including banks and property and casualty insurance companies. Legal reserve life insurance also grew up in this environment—a part of the institutional package—selling annuities and death payment policies to increasingly affluent urbanites, middle- and working-class alike, and then using the proceeds to finance investment in other parts of the industrial/financial system. (Farmers bought life insurance, too, but only as they emerged from mere self-sufficiency, and only after the financial revolution sufficiently monetized the economy to allow them to turn some of their physical assets into the cash necessary to pay premiums.) In eighteenth-century England, the investment side of the equation bore fruit early. Once the conditions were ripe for the emergence of insurance companies, they quickly became backers of that country's farm enclosure movement, which generated an increase in agricultural productivity that then freed up people to work in the factories of the industrial revolution.[8]

Successful completion of a financial revolution, however, was necessary but not sufficient for the proliferation of modern life insurance. Life insurance was the laggard of the Dutch and Anglo-American financial revolutions. Britain did not get its first major life company, the Amicable Society for a Perpetual Assurance Office, until 1705, nearly fifteen years after its financial revolution began in earnest, and that company functioned more like an assessment society than a legal reserve insurer. The Insurance Company of North America, chartered by Pennsylvania in 1794, had the legal power to write policies upon the life or lives of any person or persons, but it wrote a few term policies related to its main business, marine insurance, and did nothing to develop a life business. Early life insurers were few and far between. They possessed little actuarial expertise and relied on rudimentary underwriting practices. But they had to earn profits for eager stockholders. Given this particular combination of know-how and profit seeking, most policies were inflexible and overpriced. Few were sold. The United States did not get its first dedicated life company, the Pennsylvania Company for Insurance on Lives and Granting Annuities, until more than twenty years after its financial revolution entered high gear under Alexander Hamilton's guidance in the early Federal period. The Pennsylvania Company and the trickle of life insurers that followed it wrote very little life insurance, relying instead on their asset accumulation business to stay afloat. What they gained was some investment experience that would serve their more successful corporate followers in the years to come.[9]

In more precise terms, life insurance lagged behind other financial services sectors for four reasons: the highly interdisciplinary nature of the gathering and coordinating of relevant knowledge; the information problems associated with pricing policies; the fact that life insurance is a "sold" rather than "bought" product; and the strong sentiments against it from some religious as well as secular quarters that believed insurance to be "criminogenic," i.e., an inducement to criminal activities such as murder and immoral activities such as speculation. To sell life insurance demanded technical and organizational capabilities for the cultivation of customers and efficient methods for writing and honoring contracts. The knowledge problems were the toughest nuts to crack.[10]

Life insurance is indeed an interdisciplinary line of business that requires a great breadth of expertise. To excel, life insurers must have state-of-the-art competence in economics, finance and financial mathematics, history, law, medicine, psychology, and statistics, in addition to general business skills like accounting and writing. In the eighteenth century, legal knowledge was common enough, but some now-indispensable branches of knowledge, like the medical sciences or economics, were so little developed that the relevant expertise simply did not yet exist. Other important fields were understood by only a handful of leading researchers. Medical knowledge was rudimentary and accumulated at a stately pace, and economics was a series of real-time observations and interpretations that were more art than science.[11]

Statistics, however, could be applied with some precision. The mathematical principles underlying modern life insurance had been developed by the latter part of the seventeenth century, but they were not widely understood for more than two hundred years. America's first actuaries found a big market for their skills. Many served as consultants to multiple companies. (Indeed, as late as 1889 only eighty to one hundred actuaries lived in the United States, just about one per company.) Skills were thus pooled, and many large companies, such as Mutual of New York (MONY, est. 1843), hired consultant actuaries into the late nineteenth century just to calculate dividends.[12] One Sheppard Homans served as a consulting actuary for more than thirty different insurers before he founded his own firm, the Provident Life Insurance Company, in 1875. Guardian was blessed with several good actuaries, including the scholarly mathematician Dr. August Zillmer, early on.[13]

It is likely that eighteenth-century insurers did not envision the relatively complex nature of the mathematical issues that they faced. Help came from scholars. Practical mathematicians of the Enlightenment like the astronomer Edmond Halley (1656–1742) and, later on, Richard Price (1723–91) *derived* the present value formula and the annuity formula for their scientific readers because they felt that the formulas were not familiar enough to be taken as given. Once life insurers got the correct formulas down pat, sometime after the 1725 publication of *Annuities upon Lives* by the brilliant mathematician Abraham de Moivre (1667–1754), they faced the gargantuan task of assembling the most *relevant* actuarial data possible. The applied mathematics proved useful enough, considering that Britons and Americans, men and women, annuitants and insureds, urbanites and rural residents, rentiers and commoners faced significantly different mortality risks at different ages. Insurers had to plug the data into the correct formula and calculate the correct answer to, as Halley put it, "a not ordinary number of Arithmetical operations." And they had to do all that with quill pens under candlelight, not computers under halogen lamps.[14]

The computation tasks were as arduous as they were off the mark. The first "mortality tables," Richard Price's Northampton Table (1783) and Joshua Milne's Carlisle Table (1815), were really only population tables, so their use for insurance purposes was problematic. For instance, Price's so overstated mortality that when the British government used it to price life annuities, it lost millions of pounds sterling. Even in the nineteenth century, construction of a good mortality table was a difficult process, so much so that most early U.S. insurers used the first decent U.S. mortality study, Sheppard Homans's American Experience Table, for nearly a century.[15]

Possession of a good mortality table did not mean that the insurer would use it properly. The Equitable Assurance on Lives and Survivorships in England in 1762 adopted a formal set of actuarial techniques designed by mathematician James Dodson. Led by Dodson, that company made some attempt to calculate policy reserves and level premiums, but, again, it would be a century more before such practices were widely disseminated. Not until the mid-nineteenth century did the concepts of the level premium and policy reserves, perfected by Elizur Wright, take hold.[16]

Wright was *the* leading technical light in American life insurance. With the proliferation of his level premium concept, insurance premiums remained constant over the entire contract instead of increasing each year as with yearly renewable term policies. Under a level premium plan, early premium payments exceed what is needed to cover mortality. The overplus, which in early policy years is substantial, the insurer invests on behalf of the policyholder. Those invested funds the insurer applies to later premiums so that they do not have to increase as the insured ages (and hence becomes more likely to die in a given year). Wright's concept of reserves, special insurer liabilities, helps insurers to calculate the value of funds they need to set aside to ensure that they will have sufficient funds to pay all death claims in a timely manner.

The information problems facing both the insurer and the policyholder were considerable. The former had to wonder if the latter had the economic and moral wherewithal to tell the truth on the application, to continue to pay the contracted premiums, and not to commit suicide (if he was also the insured) or homicide (if he was not the insured). The policyholder, on the other hand, could not easily discern whether his or her premiums were being rationally invested or if they were being used to pay for a company director's scullery maid, mistress, and coach-and-four. And until market interest rates and mortality rates became less volatile in the latter half of the nineteenth century, neither party knew what interest or mortality assumptions were optimal.[17]

In short, life insurance, a business that must combine strong emotion and pure mathematics to be successful, was, and largely remains, a much more intricate and difficult business than banking, securities dealing, or even property and casualty insurance. Its steep learning curve, requiring both left and right brain functions, best explains its historical timing. Institutional developments, such as the passage of wives' insurance legislation, which in the 1840s allowed widows to receive premiums unencumbered by the claims of their husbands' creditors, and the rise of mutual companies and participating business in the 1830s and 1840s, were also factors in the spread of affordable life insurance.

In short, demand for life insurance protection always existed but technical knowledge and its dissemination had to improve before protection could be supplied to significant numbers of people at a mutually beneficial price. Increased technical expertise and the consequent decline in insurance costs were the most important factors in the growth of life insurance in the mid-nineteenth century. New sales techniques, the so-called American agency system, induced further sales. The cold fact is that for psychological reasons people rarely purchase life insurance unless strongly, repeatedly, and artfully urged to do so. As late as the Great Depression, Guardian's *own* employees carried only a small amount of insurance. To rectify the situation, company executives induced department heads to become internal agents and encourage the purchase of more insurance by employees.[18]

As figure I-1 shows (note the log scale), significant new entry in the decades between 1840 and 1870, which included the establishment of Guardian in 1860, stimulated further growth in the industry. Moreover, increased competition led to significant policy reforms, such as the introduction of surrender provisions, the refinement of actuarial tables, includ-

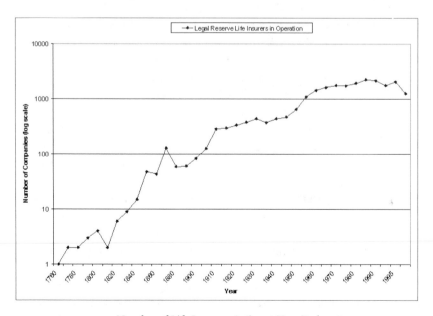

FIGURE I-1 *Number of Life Insurers Active at Year End, 1760–2000*

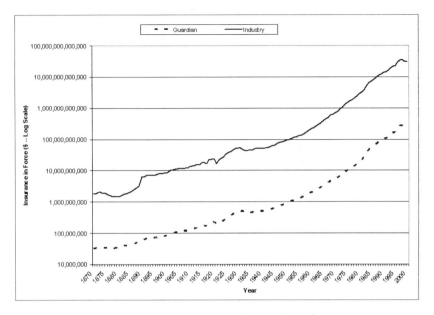

FIGURE I-2 *Life Insurance in Force, Guardian vs. the Industry, 1870–2000*

ing Sheppard Homans's American Experience Mortality Table, and the as-
cendancy of level premium whole life over term insurance. By the Civil
War, the technical aspects of legal reserve life insurance, the benefits of the
mutual form of company organization, and the need for commissioned
sales agents were finally widely enough understood that life insurance
could be sold at affordable prices to large numbers of people.[19]

After the Civil War, life insurance costs improved and religious prejudices against life insurance largely faded into memory. In the late nineteenth century, except during economic downturns, total life insurance in
force grew rapidly. (See figure I-2. Note the log scale.) The economic and
social importance of the industry was established. But the rapid growth of
life insurance led to the institutional amassment of large pools of assets,
subject to managerial abuse. By the dawn of the twentieth century, the industry was under attack.

The first part of this book, which includes chapters 1, 2, 3, and 4,
sketches the history of Guardian, the life insurance industry, and, to some
extent, the economic and political history of the United States of America.
As one early life insurance historian put it, "every great corporation is the

TABLE I-1
Timeline of Major Leaders and Events

Name	Title(s)	Years	Historical Events	Company Events
Hugo Wesendonck	President	1860–97	Civil War; Reconstruction; Second Industrial Revolution	Begins operation; establishes branch offices overseas, including Berlin
Cornelius Doremus	President	1898–1914	Spanish American War	Builds new home office in Union Square
Hubert Cillis	President	1915–20	World War I	Changes name from Germania to Guardian
Carl Heye	President (Board Chairman)	1921–39 (1939–44)	Roaring Twenties; Market crash; Great Depression; New Deal	Mutualizes; introduces Graph Estate sales plan
James A McLain	President (Board Chairman)	1940–56 (1957–63)	World War II; Korean War	Moves into health and accident insurance
John L. Cameron	President (Board Chairman)	1957–63 (1964–68)	Coldest part of the Cold War; Kennedy assassination	Moves into group insurance
Daniel J. Lyons	President (Board Chairman)	1964–68 (1969–70)	Vietnam War escalates; "Great Society"	Exceeds $4 billion in force and $100 million premium income
George T. Conklin	President (Board Chairman)	1969–76 (1977–80)	Watergate; oil crises; stagflation	Exceeds $1 billion in assets and obtains stellar investment returns
Leo R. Futia	President (Board Chairman and CEO)	1977–80 (1980–85)	Continued economic woes	Exceeds $1 billion in premium income; direct recognition program improves dividends
John C. Angle	President (Board Chairman and CEO)	1980–84 (1985–89)	Economy worsens but then improves during Reagan administration	Regionalizes by moving back-office operations to remote locations in Pennsylvania, elsewhere
Arthur V. Ferrara	President and CEO (Board Chairman and CEO)	1990–92 (1993–96)	Gulf War; start of long bull market on Wall Street	Easily weathers life insurance industry bankruptcy, consolidation, and demutualization waves
Joseph D. Sargent	President (President and CEO) [Board Chairman and CEO]	1993–96 (1996–2001) [2002]	Asset bubble breaks; terrorism hits home	Launches large advertising and branding campaign; relocates home office to Hanover Square
Dennis J. Manning	President and COO (President and CEO)	2002 (2003–)	Global political unrest and soft economy	Implements FOCUS plan to prune expenses

Source: Office of the Corporate Secretary.

product of two forces—the one internal, the other external—the management, and the times in which it has its existence." So the three narratives intertwine in ways numerous and deep. Macroeconomic and regulatory forces set general parameters in which the industry and Guardian had to function. In turn, life insurers influenced the economy and the regulatory framework in sundry fundamental ways. Similarly, the life industry's beliefs, traditions, mores, and, most importantly, competitive practices had a major impact on Guardian's development. Guardian, in turn, has at times profoundly influenced the life insurance industry.[20]

Life insurers, and Guardian is no exception here, face three major tradeoffs: expending vs. saving, risk vs. return, and tradition vs. innovation. How well Guardian has handled those three tradeoffs has largely determined how well it has done *relative to other life insurance companies.* The overall performance of Guardian and the industry, on the other hand, has largely been a function of the health of the economy and the quality of regulation. So while Guardian takes center stage in part I, it cannot be the only actor to which we refer. (Readers whose expertise lies elsewhere than history should refer to the timeline in table I-1.) Throughout the four chapters in part I, emphasis is placed on Guardian's strategic management of its net costs. Details about products, distribution, and expense management, asset management, and management and governance can be found in parts II, III, and IV, respectively.

Germania
Origins and Progress to World War I

Multimillionaire moguls under legislative investigation. Rampant accusations of managerial self-dealing, corruption, and fraud. Creative accounting. Growing public distrust of an entire industry. Heads of top corporate leaders rolling. Sound familiar? Except those accusations are not from today's headlines but rather from the Armstrong Investigation, a New York State legislative probe that changed the face of the life insurance industry in the latter half of 1905.

The life insurance industry grew rapidly in the second half of the nineteenth century. Ironically, however, economic success hurt the industry by giving rise to new anti–life-insurance sentiments based on America's deep-seated fear of a "moneyed aristocracy" led by greedy financiers. The Armstrong Investigation showed that big insurers were indeed engaged in sundry nefarious activities, few of which were in the interests of policyholders. That probe also showed, however, that some life insurance companies, including Guardian, were true blue.

Guardian was a rare breed, a type of company that Americans in 1905 were eager to see proliferate more widely. Little has changed to this day. Guardian remains a rare breed that many Americans, jaded by a seemingly endless stream of corporate-governance and insider-trading scandals, would like to see reproduced more widely. Guardian's story is not a sensationalistic one rife with intrigue and wrongdoing. As a model for both moral *and* profitable corporate success, however, it is an interesting and crucially important one.

The most important traits that characterize Guardian today—commitment to policyholders, long-term financial strength, and ethical corporate culture—were ingrained into the company from its earliest days. After a rocky start, the company set out on a path of solid growth that soon earned it a sterling reputation among stockholders and policyholders alike. It also led American companies into overseas markets. Neither recession nor regulatory repression could injure the company, which waxed stronger with each passing decade until tested first by a Great War, then by a Great Depression, and finally by a Great Inflation.

Germania Rises

On 28 March 1860, just months before the election of Abraham Lincoln to the presidency would split the nation asunder, a group of twenty-one men composed largely of prosperous German immigrants, assembled at Delmonico's Restaurant in lower Manhattan to discuss the formation of a company, which they intended to charter under the State of New York's 1853 Life and Health Insurance Companies General Incorporation Act. Many of the petitioners had been on the losing side of the Revolution of 1848, unsuccessful champions of political liberalism in their native lands. By that time seeking their fortunes in the land of opportunity, they hoped to supply other German-Americans, then about one million strong, with life insurance, now a well-established business in the United States, but still a high-growth business with plenty of untapped markets.[1]

The leader of the group, Hugo Wesendonck, had been born in 1817, in Elberfeld, a vital textile center situated on the Rhine. Trained in the law, Wesendonck was attracted to liberal legal and political movements that were spreading throughout the German states in the 1840s. His work on civil rights and his involvement in drafting a pan-German constitution in 1848 as a participant in the Frankfurt National Assembly earned him the wrath of authorities. With an indictment for treason hanging over his head, he fled Germany and sought asylum in the United States. After arriving in New York in 1849, he received help from his brother, Otto, a textile importer, who had preceded him. Hugo then followed in Otto's footsteps by opening an importing business in Philadelphia. As he rose to affluence, he busied himself once again with German-American cultural and social movements, which rekindled his interest in politics. He joined antislavery organizations and became a local leader in the new Republican Party. He befriended Carl Schurz, the political activist, journalist, and later Civil War hero, the most famous German-American of his generation. In 1859, Wesendonck moved to New York and teamed up with like-minded Germans to organize an insurance venture.

Wesendonck steered Germania as its commanding, paternal leader until 1897, nearly working himself to death (he died just three years later at age eighty-three). He was a man of some charisma, and attracted a number of prominent German-Americans to his business, including August Belmont, the Rothschilds' representative in the United States, and Joseph Seligman, an influential Wall Street financier, who sat on Germania's board. The portrait of Wesendonck that hangs outside Guardian's boardroom conveys a kind of benign severity. Anita Rapone described him in this way: "His full white beard and deep, resonant voice, complemented by impeccable dress, lent him an air of indisputable gravity and authority." As one of his employees remembered him, Wesendonck was "a courtly gentleman of culture and nobility." He ruled his business with a benign, yet iron, hand.

It was not at all unusual for immigrants or other affinity groups in the nineteenth century to form mutual aid or "friendly" societies, many of which offered, among other services, some limited forms of life insurance such as burial insurance. What was unusual was that these Germans, most of whom were prominent businessmen, lawyers, or bankers, wanted to form a company on a scientific, legal reserve basis and to offer legally binding contracts with life contingencies—insurance and annuities. In the terms of their native tongue, they sought *Gesellschaft* (society), not *Gemeinschaft* (community).[2]

Founding a life insurance company was a profit-seeking venture, but it was a venture imbued with idealism. Germania's founders wanted to do well by doing good, not simply make a mint off their German brethren. They had wanted to form a fully mutual company, a company owned only by its policyholders, but were constrained by law to issue shares in their venture. In New York, life insurance companies had to raise at least $100,000 worth of equity capital before commencing operations. Wesendonck felt that since the firm had to be a mixed (joint stock and mutual) company anyway, the founders might as well signal their support by raising $200,000 in equity capital. It turned out to be good advice. "It is doubtful whether it would have survived the early struggles of its infancy" had it started on a slimmer base of equity, wrote Cornelius Doremus, Wesendonck's successor, in 1901.[3]

The company, through the agency of five stock commissioners, held an initial public offering of stock, and sold four thousand shares at a par value of $50 each to 127 different subscribers, who took an average of about 31.5 shares each. The largest subscription, for 478 shares, was taken by Otto Wesendonck, Hugo's brother. Three of the subscribers were women, one of whom, Mary Berly, took the smallest subscription, two shares. The median subscription was for twenty shares. Most of the subscribers were men with German-sounding surnames like Holthausen and Schumacher. A few, however, had Irish- or Anglo-sounding surnames like Sullivan, Davidson, and Morgan.[4]

The subscribers fully paid for their subscriptions by early June. The company used $100,000 of their payments to purchase U.S. 5 percent coupon bonds of 1858 for deposit with the office of the New York superintendent of insurance, which on 10 July 1860 allowed the company to begin business. On 16 July, after filing the superintendent's certificate with the county clerk, Germania Life Insurance Company of New York opened shop, and sold its first policy the following day to a Brooklyn cigar merchant, Selig Kling. The company wrote other policies quickly enough, and rejected some of the applicants, four of them, in September, the same month in which it insured its first female life. By the end of 1860, the company, which had invested over $1,200 in advertising, had sold 152 whole life policies, ten term policies, and seven endowment policies, giving it a total of $500,979.02 in force. The youngest policyholder was only sixteen years old, the oldest fifty-eight. Most of the company's policyholders were in their thirties and early forties. The company paid its first death benefit, $500, and its first surrender benefit, in 1861.[5]

The general business revival that followed the Panic of 1857 explains the timing of the company's formation. As Germania was fully formed before Lincoln's election, it was not one of the several insurers established, in the words of historian R. Carlyle Buley, to take advantage of "the inevitable artificial war prosperity." Indeed, Germania began to struggle a little in the spring of 1861 because it found its business seriously checked by the war. "The various Agencies have almost entirely ceased to do business," President Hugo Wesendonck informed the board in June, "and in this city, only by extensive and persevering canvassing, may Risks be obtained." Indeed, most of the company's first policies were written on the lives of friends and family in the greater New York City area. In order to break loose from its doldrums and increase its business, Germania began a rapid expansion of its agency force.[6] (See table 1-1.)

Expansion continued after the war; by 1868 Germania had some 279 agents. The company could not expand quickly enough; non-German

TABLE 1-1
Number of Germania Agents, 1860–65

Year	New York Agents (#)	Agents Elsewhere (#)	Total Agents (#)
1860	4	10	14
1861	10	53	63
1862	10	55	65
1863	20	108	128
1864	19	116	135
1865	21	117	138

Source: Annual Statements, various years.

companies like the Mutual Benefit, Union Mutual, and Metropolitan Life also tried to cater to, in the words of historian Mildred Stone, the "floods of intelligent, thrifty German immigrants" streaming into the country.[7]

The agency development program bore fruit perhaps beyond expectations, and by spring 1862, the Special Committee reported that "an increasing proportion of the business . . . has been acquired outside of the City," with new policyholders in Boston, Chicago, Cincinnati, Detroit, Hartford, Indianapolis, Milwaukee, Newark, and Philadelphia. By the autumn of 1862, Germania had added policyholders in Bloomington, Buffalo, Cleveland, Davenport, Fond du Lac, New Haven, Reading, San Francisco, Springfield, and West Bend, in (Union-controlled) Mississippi. By March 1863, it had policyholders in cities too numerous to list.[8]

From the start, however, Germania's avowed emphasis on the "safety of the assured" served as a brake on sales. Many life insurers in the mid-nineteenth century issued their own promissory notes or "scrip" in lieu of cash dividends. Most of those same companies also accepted "premium notes," the promissory notes of policyholders, for payment of premiums. Many observers rightly derided such excessive use of credit as a dangerous means of drumming up business and inflating dividends. After all, it was much easier to afford a policy or a dividend scale if one had only to sign for it! Germania realized the dangers of the system and hence was one of a handful of companies that were from the start "cash only." Premiums and cash dividends were both paid completely in honest-to-goodness money—bank notes, bank deposits, or coins—and not in IOUs or scrip.[9]

As often is the case, what was good for the policyholder in the long run was not what was good for the company's sales in the short run. By the end of the 1860s, some important companies like NYLIC moved to an all-cash system. Eventually, the entire industry was cash only. In the meantime, however, Germania found it necessary to supplement its agency force with so-called traveling agents. In 1861, for instance, Wesendonck traveled to Philadelphia to drum up business. The traveling agents helped inexperienced local agents to drum up leads and close deals—in cash.[10]

Wesendonck himself emerged as the early Germania's biggest producer. Unable to afford a press agent, he wrote to his numerous friends and induced them to make "known as widely as possible that Hugo Wesendonck, one of the great 'Forty-eighters,' and an intimate friend of Carl Schurz . . . would be in town on a certain day and would make a very interesting address on the Revolution of 1848" in some informal location. Wesendonck proceeded to spellbind his audience with stories about the revolution, then skillfully and subtlely switched to the subject of life insurance. After the stirring orations, large numbers of his listeners placed their signatures on the dotted line. In 1862 his travels in the West were so successful that the staff and board could scarcely believe the unexpectedly large business that he signed. Upon his return from one two-month-long sales sojourn, Wesendonck told the board that it appeared to him "advisable to push the Western business by all reasonable means." "A steady business may be expected in future from the West," he correctly surmised.[11]

Even by the standards of the day, the rate of growth of Germania's insurance in force was phenomenal, registering in the triple digits in each of its first four years and in the double digits in the next six.[12] By the end of 1870, the company had over $32 million in force, approximately 1.8 percent of the legal reserve insurance in force nationally. (See figure 1-1.)

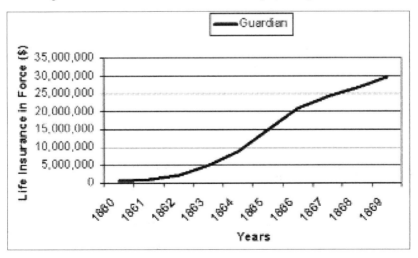

FIGURE 1-1 *Guardian's Life Insurance in Force, 1860–69*

Wesendonck and the other early agents did a good job selecting risks, too, as Germania's losses by death were far lower than predicted by the life tables adopted by the company. Mortality rates thereafter deteriorated somewhat, and were higher than the industry average, but remained well within safe limits. (See table 1-2.) The acceptable rates were in part attributable to the fact that Germania did not accept war risks during the Civil War, returning the value of the policy upon the enlistment of an insured life.[13]

From early on, Germania's directors were much concerned about agency and other expenses. As early as June 1861, Wesendonck assured the Board that expenses did "not exceed those of any other company doing business in this City," some indication that he was alert to what his competitors were doing.[14] (See table 1-3.)

Germania's management expressed relief when it was able to report that the company's expense ratio (defined as cash expenses/cash receipts x 100) had dropped from 37.83 percent in 1863 to 29.71 percent in 1864. It expected "that with the increase of business, [the expense ratio] will

TABLE 1-2
Germania's Mortality Rates, 1862–69

Year	Mortality Payments/Insurance in Force (%)
1862	.684
1863	.867
1864	.876
1865	1.072
1866	1.277
1867	1.065
1868	1.115
1869	1.113

Source: "Special Committee" Minutes, various years.

TABLE 1-3
Germania's Expenditures, 1862

Expenditure	Amount ($)
Salaries	456.60
Advertising	50.00
Law Expenses	20.00
Office Expenses	68.78
General Agencies	147.26
Commissions	158.81
Examination fees	117.00
Total	1,018.45

Source: President's Report, 31 May 1862, Box 42, GLIC archives.

show further steady decrease in future years." The expense ratio indeed did decrease, to 22.21 percent in 1868, well below the industry average of 27.78 and median of 27.42. In 1869, the expense ratio dropped further, to 18.77 percent, even though the company had suffered the necessarily heavy expenses of the organization of a branch office in Berlin. That was a good start to what would be half a century of successful overseas business.[15]

Competing in a Cyclical Economy

As Germania matured, its rate of growth as measured by insurance in force necessarily slowed. Triple-digit growth rates were relatively easy to attain starting from a base of zero. By the early 1870s, Germania could not maintain double-digit growth rates. After the Panic of 1873 led to a depression, the worst in the nation's history to that point, growing at all became a struggle. In four out of five years between 1874 and 1878, the company's total insurance in force actually shrank, but it managed to survive where most others did not. Of the 129 life insurers in operation in 1870, only fifty-five remained in 1882. In fact, relative to the rest of the industry, Germania weathered the depression quite well. As shown in figure 1-2, Germania's share of all life insurance in force increased during the depression years, even when the dollar value of its insurance in force was shrinking (dark bar below zero, light bar above zero). In other words, during the recession Germania did not sink as fast as the industry. That pattern would repeat itself numerous times, most notably in 1894, and 1907, and 1917. It helped that Germania sold into a well-to-do market niche. Many of its policyholders were small businessmen, a group unlikely to become unemployed during economic downturns. Furthermore, Germania was always a highly respected insurer with a good reputation and excellent credit ratings. During economic downturns, therefore, policyholders and prospects did not have to tremble in fear of Germania's demise. In other words, tough times brought a sort of "flight to quality" that redounded to the well-managed Germania's benefit.[16]

The life companies that failed in the 1870s did so either because they invested badly or suffered relatively high expenses and mortality. Many had been reckless in writing policies and speculating with or otherwise squandering their shareholders' and policyholders' money. Germania survived because it wrote business on "good" lives, did not allow commissions to

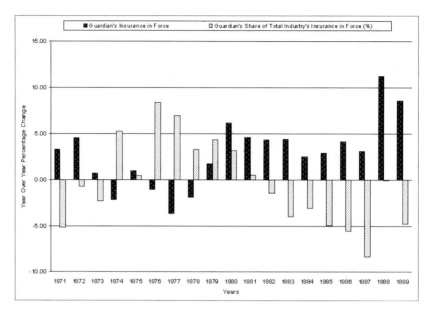

FIGURE 1-2 *Guardian's Share of All Life Insurance in Force in the U.S., 1871–89*

get out of hand, did not waste resources on a showy home office or excessive advertising, and enjoyed a relatively diverse and remunerative investment portfolio. Germania's mortality experience, in the troubled 1870s, remained relatively stable, its expense ratio continued to trend downward, and, by at least one measure, its persistency rate over the period 1859–81 far exceeded the industry average.[17] (See tables 1-4, 1-5, and 1-6.)

Over its first half-century of business, Germania's management kept expenses down by paying constant attention to the relative costs and benefits of all expenditures, especially those related to agents. It kept mortality in line by requiring medical examiners to focus on answering all of the questions in its examination forms, completely and accurately. It achieved superior investment results by investing heavily in mortgages and keeping its cash balances low. Moreover, the growth rate of Germania's insurance in force was positive throughout the 1880s. Except for 1888, however, its growth lagged behind that of the rest of the industry. (See figure 1-2.) Germania therefore found it absolutely necessary to follow the ways of the industry leaders and to appoint managers for large districts and high commissions. The reorganization worked, as by 1893 the company's business

TABLE 1-4
Germania's Mortality Rates, 1870–78

Year	Mortality Payments/Insurance in Force (%)
1870	1.347
1871	1.186
1872	1.350
1873	1.659
1874	1.553
1875	1.484
1876	1.315
1877	1.670
1878	1.625

Source: "Special Committee" Minutes, various years.

TABLE 1-5
Germania's Expense Ratio, 1870–74

Year	Expense Ratio (%)	Explanation for Change
1870	16.85	Decreased from 18.77% in 1869 because the European business was no longer draining resources.
1871	18.49	Increased due to the purchase of agents' renewal commissions.
1872	15.91	None given.
1873	14.96	None given.
1874	14.56	None given.

Source: "Special Committee" Minutes, various years.

TABLE 1-6
Comparative Persistency Ratios of Selected Insurance Companies, 1859–81

Company	In force 1858 (in millions $)	Sales, 1859–1881 (in millions $)	Cols. 2 plus 3 (in millions $)	In force 1881 (in millions $)	Col. 5/4 (%)
Mutual Life of New York	32.58	707.96	750.54	315.9	42.7
Mutual Benefit	19.11	308.49	327.60	127.41	38.9
Germania	**0**	**95.65**	**95.65**	**36.37**	**38.0**
National Life (Vt.)	1.54	23.76	2530	9.52	37.6
New York Life	13.58	445.23	458.81	151.76	33.1
New England Mutual	10.41	172.57	182.98	57.80	31.6
Equitable	0	638.22	638.22	200.68	31.4
Northwestern	0	250.11	250.11	74.50	29.8
Massachusetts Mutual	2.50	102.65	105.15	30.14	28.7
Industry Average	141.50	6,663.85	6,805.35	1,676.93	24.6

Source: Williamson and Smalley, *Northwestern Mutual Life,* 85. Courtesy Northwestern University Press.

had increased and, according to some officers, "bid fair to further increase."[18]

By that time, growth was straining the company's administrative capabilities. In 1893, Max A. Wesendonck, Hugo Wesendonck's son, became a salaried special director charged with assisting "generally in the management of the Company's business, and especially to superintend the Company's exterior service," a grueling task that William Cohn, the company's general inspector, could no longer perform. The position soon came to be known as second vice president. By 1895, when business was again falling off, Germania offered to assist those sales managers who made efforts to better organize their territories to procure more new business from places other than the seats of their agencies. Germania then treaded water in its U.S. markets until a series of industry scandals and their public investigation provided an unexpected boost to its reputation.[19]

It makes sense then that in the 1870s and 1880s the stock market's response to Germania was quite favorable, especially after insiders like Otto Wesendonck gobbled up shares during the company's early struggles for existence, before the market had acquired implicit confidence in the institution. Germania's stock, however, was much more like a preferred than a true common stock in that its dividends were capped at 7 percent per annum for "interest" and 5 percent per annum for "surplus" and were senior to policyholder dividends. Stockholders had no other claim on the company's surplus and could be outvoted by policyholders in corporate elections. Policyholders ruled, at least in spirit. The managers really controlled the business, and all its policyholders and shareholders were ultimately left to rely on the competence and integrity of management.[20]

After 1868, the maximum 12 percent dividends ($6 per share) were dutifully made every year. In 1876, the market priced Germania's shares at between 140 and 160 percent of par, i.e., between $70 and $80 per share. The following year, the company's shares touched $100 before falling back to the $75 range in 1878. After trending back to $100 in 1879, the company's stock price dropped in 1880 to around $70 per share. It treaded water for several years before dipping to $60 per share in 1885. Thereafter, it trended higher. By January 1886, the company's shares traded at between 125 and 132 percent of par ($62.50 to $66). By September 1887, sellers of Germania shares again sought as much as $80 per share.[21]

Germania's stock was rarely quoted in the financial press after 1887. Life insurance stocks generally were not of great interest to speculative Wall

Street brokers, and in any case, the company's stock was "closely held," hence infrequently traded. Between 1860 and 1918, there were on average fewer than nine exchanges of Germania shares per year, and of course many of those were bequests. The average annual stock turnover rate (average annual shares traded/number of shares outstanding or 276.61/4,000) was very low, just under 7 percent. The stock did trade on occasion, and President Cornelius Doremus mentioned in a 1901 meeting that the company's shares were fetching $100, or twice the par value. In 1913 an undetermined number of shares again traded at $100 each. In 1915, eight shares traded at $93.50 and thirty at $100. In 1916, fifty shares went for $97.50 and eight for $90. In 1918–19, three trades were made, one for twenty shares at $72.50 per share, one for ten shares at $70, and one for two shares at $68. (The price differences on the last three trades mentioned were probably a function of the date of the trade and/or the ownership of the next dividend, which amounted to $4.25 per share in January and $1.75 in July. Par value was $50, so $6 per year was a 12 percent dividend, 7 of "interest" and 5 of "surplus" as described above.) But again, the volume of trades in Germania's stock was so low that when speculative interests tried to take over the company in 1901, they were unable to purchase enough shares to dislodge the insiders. As the expansion of its business slowed in the United States, Germania's overseas business began to take up much of the slack. It was right after the Civil War that Germania had begun to look for opportunities in foreign markets.[22]

The Quest for Multinational Business

Life insurance firms had some natural advantages in seeking geographic breadth. They were more amenable to expansion than, say, banks, where customers made constant demands to obtain loans, make deposits, and withdraw cash. Savings bank depositors and a few infrequent commercial bank customers sometimes resided a considerable distance from their banks, but rarely lived more than a day away. Except for financiers and international wholesalers, no one maintained a permanent demand account in a distant land. Moreover, stringent legal restrictions against branching meant that banks could not readily expand their geographical reach.[23]

Life insurance was a different story. Whole life policyholders generally remitted premiums once a year, and insurers needed to contact them only occasionally, to inform them of dividends, the company's progress, and the like. Additions in coverage, changes of address, and other routine correspondence, while important, were not urgent. Most importantly, life insurers, unlike commercial banks, found it necessary, and legally possible, to establish networks of sales agents who personally assisted policyholders in a variety of matters. The geographical constraints on life companies were, therefore, minimal, a fact that some were quick to realize. English life companies, for instance, had penetrated the U.S. market as early as 1807, when London's Pelican Life Insurance Company established an agency in Philadelphia. Similarly, Robert Steward Buchanan had served as the New York agent of the Albion Life Insurance Company of London in the 1850s.[24]

As for Germania, most of its founders were worldly men, not native to America, for whom expansion north, south, and into Europe seemed as natural as their simultaneous effort to extend the company's reach across the United States. There was a compelling economic rationale, too. Geographical expansion brought not only more policies but also a more diversified base of premium revenue, which could help the company weather the depressions that periodically stalled economic progress.

All things considered, the company's first international foray was disappointing. Germania entered Canada in 1867 but withdrew the following year after the Canadians imposed a federal licensing law and demanded a hefty security deposit. Not until 1887 did Germania, NYLIC, and a few other U.S. insurers return to Canada. Germania also attempted to go south, appointing general agents in Cuba, Costa Rica, and Chile in 1867. But little business followed from those sources.[25]

Europe was different. In 1868, Germania took a decisive step into the international arena by sending Prussian-born Hermann Rose to Berlin to establish a branch office. Rose used his commanding personality, his wide knowledge of affairs, and his energy to make the branch a great success. The business of the branch eventually extended from Prussia into all the different parts of the German Empire and beyond its boundaries into Western, Eastern, and Southern Europe. Only Britain and Scandinavia eluded its reach. Rose headed up a special European board of directors that enjoyed entire charge of the company's European affairs subject only to such regulations as the company's New York board might require.[26]

Germania's business outside the United States was disproportionately large for an American insurer. Germania was fourth in the international field by the 1880s, following NYLIC, MONY, and Equitable, three of the

TABLE 1-7
Foreign Business as a Percentage of Germania's Total, 1868–1925

Year	Foreign Business/Total (%)
1868	1.54
1870	5.99
1875	18.22
1880	28.03
1885	34.60
1890	42.86
1895	47.31
1900	47.60
1905	43.34
1910	45.57
1915	39.39
1920	21.21
1925	1.20

Source: "Foreign Business Guardian (Germania)," Office of the Secretary, Scott, Box 64, GLIC archives. A few numbers differ very slightly from those reported in Rapone, *Guardian*, 97.

country's five giant insurance companies. By 1885, a third of Germania's total business came from outside of the United States. By 1895, foreign revenues accounted for 47 percent of its business.[27] The growth of the relative importance of Germania's foreign business continued until 1900. (See table 1-7.)

U.S. insurers could do well overseas because they realized sooner than their foreign competitors that life insurance was a sold product, not a bought one. American sales methods, especially the commission agency system, were aggressive in comparison to European practices. U.S. insurers also introduced what were policy innovations in Europe, such as cash surrender values and policy loans, along with generally increased policyholder service standards. They easily outflanked competitors until the locals adopted the innovations, and then turned the tables by using their superior domestic political connections to gain market advantages. For example, NYLIC and MONY faced considerable political resistance in Germany, especially as their success mounted in the last decade of the nineteenth century. But Germania, run by Germans and German-Americans, enjoyed relatively good access to Germany's market. Cultural and language barriers were not nearly as large for Germania as for other expansion-minded U.S. insurers. Germania's top brass communicated effortlessly in both German and English, and the company also enjoyed lower regulatory, transactional, and cultural costs due to the effectiveness of its relatively autonomous Berlin board. The Equitable entered Germany in 1877, but it could not match Germania's ability to cope with local regulations, so it retreated in 1893. NYLIC entered in 1882, and got booted in 1895. (It returned seven years later.) Mutual Life also entered in 1883, but lost its authority to do business in Germany in 1895.[28]

The Armstrong Investigation

Big business was never popular in the United States, especially when times were bad. In the relatively unregulated economy of the nineteenth century, big business corporations seemed like rampaging behemoths, sweeping away small businesses, exploiting workers, and establishing monopoly power in critical sectors of the then "new economy." Multimillionaire moguls emerged, making unheard of sums of money. Even worse, they conducted their affairs in secrecy. Scandals abounded, as bondholders and stockholders were fleeced in fraudulent undertakings. Managerial self-dealing and corruption seemed commonplace, as did "creative accounting." Financial institutions were especially untrustworthy, if only because it was difficult for people to understand what they were up to. Insurance companies with their vast pools of money, often ill invested, loomed large as corporate villains.[29]

Though costs had greatly improved over time, Americans generally believed that life insurance policies were artificially expensive. It was easy to blame managerial excesses, high sales commissions, and other expenses. *Collier's,* for instance, expressed its outrage over commissions that represented between 17 and 42.5 cents of each dollar paid in premiums. "The cashier of the savings bank," the author of the article noted, "does not . . . take out $42.50 and ram it down his own pocket before putting $57.50 in the vault."[30]

By the early twentieth century, news stories abounded about life insurers who lobbied extensively by utilizing their family, personal, and business connections and who made outright bribes to politicians from their ever-deepening coffers. To some extent, life insurance executives were their own worst enemies. They regularly excoriated each other's companies in the industry and popular presses, hoping thereby to gain some competitive advantage. They damaged the entire industry's reputation by widely publicizing accusations of wrongdoing (that were too often true). Understandably, the public deeply resented and feared the political power that the big life insurance companies represented, and industry executives exacerbated the situation by pointing out that they enjoyed bigger revenues than the federal government, and owned assets worth more than entire nations.[31]

After decades of lurid stories, the public became convinced that the largest life insurance company managers had gone too far in serving their own interests rather than the interests of their policyholders. America was becoming more democratic in its polity, but its largest public corporations remained the lucrative fiefdoms of autocratic managers. Policyholders and shareholders were unorganized, and managers enjoyed considerable refuge from any public accountability. Everything was left to the individual integrity of managers in a corporate economy that had few institutional checks and balances. Under such conditions, life insurance managers, sitting as they did on enormous pools of cash premiums, were in a position to aggrandize themselves. Managerial opportunism abounded on a scale from outright corruption to the simple desire to expand one's corporate empire, whether such expansion was economically justified or not.

In the late nineteenth century, many life companies strove mightily to get bigger—larger reserves, more assets, more insurance in force—at any cost. Increased size meant higher executive salaries. Richard A. McCurdy of Mutual Life of New York and his son earned five times more than the president of the United States. They made more than the governors of all U.S. states and territories *combined*. Size also meant more influence with investment bankers, opportunities to participate in high-profile syndications, more social prestige, and more bragging rights within the industry.[32]

Conflicts of interest abounded in the relationships between insurers and other financial institutions seeking to tap their cash. One of the most egregious examples of the commingling of interests (egregious, at least, by modern standards) was the case of George W. Perkins, the first vice president and effective CEO of NYLIC, the largest insurance company in the United States at the turn of the twentieth century. Perkins was a skillful dealmaker and had used his position at New York Life to operate as an investment banker. In November 1900, he was invited to take a desk in J. P. Morgan's firm, and he did, operating as both Morgan partner and New York Life executive. By all accounts, Perkins was an honest and humane manager, fiercely opposed to corruption, good to his workers, careful with his policyholders' money, and transparent with his accounts. But the conflict of interest, albeit legal at the time, was enormous. The nation's largest insurer had become a captive slush fund of the world's greatest investment banker. Policyholders were left to the mercy of Morgan's and Perkins's personal integrity.[33]

The scale of a business has too often in the course of economic history become a sham substitute for efficiency, and for early-twentieth-century policyholders, size provided little more than a false sense of security. The social efficacy of life insurance provided cover for managers who argued that the sheer growth of insurance in force was a good thing. Some executives even resorted to religious terminology to describe their "missionary" efforts. Given those attitudes, too many companies concentrated on landing new business rather than on improving the cost or quality of their services to existing policyholders, who were left to complain that their premiums were subsidizing the increasingly lavish compensation of life insurance executives and their ill-advised battles to acquire the next batch of business.[34]

Conditions for public outrage to ripen into political action may fester for a long time, until some event or revelation brings them to a head. In this case, the ball started rolling when a market speculator, Thomas Lawson, penned an exposé of shady investment practices in insurance companies. This set the table for the efforts of professional "muckraking" journalists, who leapt upon the brazen extravagance of one company, the Equitable Life Insurance Company, where an in-house struggle for power was underway.[35]

Prior to the exposure, directors of Equitable had become concerned about the investment of funds in competing banks. The industrialist Henry Clay Frick led an internal team of investigators to look into the matter and discovered a number of apparently fraudulent accounting procedures and bad investments. The company's board rejected the findings, touching off a highly publicized struggle for power. Frick and the railroad financier Edward H. Harriman resigned from their seats on the board, which alerted a state insurance commissioner to investigate. A public scandal erupted.

It was easy for the press to personify the problem in the form of Equitable's flamboyant young vice president James Hazen Hyde. Hyde, among his extravagances, was found to have charged to the company's tab $200,000 (roughly $4 million in 2002 dollars) for private parties. When other managers sought to mutualize the Equitable and oust Hyde, their effort touched off a lengthy and highly publicized struggle for corporate control involving arch financiers J. P. Morgan and E. H. Harriman. The tawdry events leading to the struggle for control of the company was the spark that set long-smoldering public opinion aflame. But exorbitant expenses, unnecessarily high costs and lapse rates, and general disregard for the safety of the assured were the fuel that made the subsequent explosion so large and so brilliant.[36]

Insurance executives had been fighting a long siege from regulators and tax collectors, and had managed, through intensive lobbying—and perhaps some well-placed payoffs—to keep key members of the state legislature pretty much on the side of minimal regulation. Now the industry's reputation was shot, and in 1905, the New York legislature unleashed a wide-scale inquiry into the entire spectrum of industry management and financial practices.

The investigative body, known as the Armstrong Committee after its chairman, state Senator William H. Armstrong, hauled the most important industry executives before it. They had no choice, though many went into the proceedings hoping that little would come of them. They were quite wrong. Armstrong would humble, even humiliate, most of them, setting the stage for modern insurance regulation.

The life force behind the Armstrong Investigation was the committee's ambitious chief counsel, Charles Evans Hughes (1862–1948), a man destined to become governor of New York and ultimately chief justice of the U.S. Supreme Court. Hughes's performance was as masterful as it was zealous. To maintain public interest, he artfully spaced sensational disclosures over the entire investigation period, from 6 September to 30 December 1905. His probing questioning of top life executives revealed rampant nepotism, almost complete directorial control of proxy votes, executives more interested in high finance than safe insurance, outrageously costly marketing methods that hurt existing policyholders, unrealistic sales illustrations, declining dividend scales, attempts to buy control of politicians, dubious accounting techniques, and outright fraud. NYLIC, for instance, made fictitious sales of junk bonds at par so that it could list the dubious assets at unrealistically high prices on its annual statements.[37]

Hughes's considerable wrath embraced all the big players in the industry. He hammered away, tarnishing reputations, personal and institutional. When it was over, the committee's 450-page report provided a framework for a spate of new insurance laws in Albany, and what came out of the legislative mill was a host of reforms that profoundly altered the financial practices, and health, of the industry. Tontine policies were abolished and investment options considerably narrowed. Companies were required to issue annual dividends to shareholders and policyholders alike. Company surpluses, i.e., profits not returned to policyholders or stockholders, were limited to 10 percent of liabilities. Agency rebates were outlawed. Lobbying efforts were curbed. Commission rates and the volume of new business that could be sold in a year were also capped.[38]

The most important *structural* reform was to require divestiture of the equities of industrial corporations, financial institutions, and trusts. This made it harder for financial intermediaries and their friends in the executive suites of insurance companies to use policyholder premiums as slush funds for investment schemes. The idea, overall, was to lower the risks on the asset side of the balance sheet, risks that had all too often resulted not only in personal corruption but also in institutional failure.[39]

Many states, twenty-nine of the forty-two that met in 1907 to be exact, enacted legislation similar to that of New York's. The tide of new regulation crested by 1908 and began to recede somewhat by the end of 1909, but the most important legislation remained substantively in place for decades. Many top life executives had to pay fines and repay their insider loans. A good number of them, especially at the largest insurers, lost their jobs.[40]

Out of this gale of exposure and reform emerged Germania, unscathed, even triumphant. The Armstrong Investigation had inadvertently served the company by providing an independent forum in which it could demonstrate its financial solidity and frugal management. Despite their proximity to the Big Five, all of which were headquartered in Manhattan or northern New Jersey, Germania's managers had convincingly demonstrated that their business practices had been honest and aboveboard. They had never involved themselves in underwriting syndicates and had donated a grand total of less than $1,000 to lobbyists. That Hughes's probe turned out to be "a valuable advertisement" for the company is seen in the *Insurance Monitor,* which noted,

> President Cornelius Doremus . . . had the good fortune to be called. We say good fortune, because his testimony put his company in a most favorable light before the public—so favorable that even the yellowest [most sensationalistic] of the daily papers had only words of commendation for it.

Germania's actuary John Fuhrer had also testified, and in doing so was able to publicize the fact that when New York regulators had examined the company's books a few years earlier, they had concluded that the management of the Company has been devoted more to the attainment of a strong financial position than to the acquisition of any great amount of new business, and its condition today shows the result of wise, intelligent and conservative administration.[41]

Also disclosed in the proceedings were the salaries of Germania's officers, which were substantially lower than those of other New York insurers. In 1901, the presidents of the biggest three companies each earned twice as much as the salary of Germania's president, vice president, *and* stock dividends added together. In 1905, President Cornelius Doremus (a "grand old gentleman," according to an industry journal) made just $15,000 per year (roughly $280,000 in early-twenty-first-century dollars). Corporate Vice President Hubert Cillis earned just $12,500, and Second Vice President Max A. Wesendonck, $10,000. Those salaries were, if anything, embarrassingly *low*; the public revelation of them may have been the factor that spurred Germania in 1907 to grant modest increases to the president, both vice presidents, the secretary, and the head actuary.[42]

Germania's clean bill of health was earned on the backs of its founding generation. Hugo Wesendonck was noted for his frugal and effective management, as was his financial right hand, Frederick Schwendler, who had guided the company's investments to 1890. Their legacy of competence and integrity spilled over well into the next generation. Wesendonck's successor, Cornelius Doremus, had to confront numerous challenges during his tenure. He fought off a takeover attempt, engaged in a losing power struggle for managerial control of Germania's Berlin office, brooked dissent within the company's board (opposition led by the venerable Carl Schurz!), and managed the company's response to the Armstrong probe. But incompetence and misbehavior among his managers were not among his problems.

Following Doremus's testimony in the Armstrong Investigation, other life companies clamored for a chance to show the committee that they too were clean businesses that served their policyholders well. Since such stories did not create headlines, Hughes quickly learned to avoid calling executives of the better-managed insurers to the stand. He also shunned the smaller companies, and so most of the honorable insurers did not get a hearing. Of those insurers explicitly exculpated by the hearings, only Mutual Benefit Life, Manhattan Life, and New England Life came close to approaching Germania in size and importance. It was a rare breed, a type of insurance company that Americans in 1905 were eager to see proliferate more widely.[43]

Armstrong's Aftermath

In the aftermath of the Armstrong shakeup, general agents like Charles Ives led a movement to professionalize life insurance salesmanship. Ives, who is best known for musical compositions like his Pulitzer Prize–winning *Third Symphony*, was a principal in Ives and Myrick, a general agency of the Mutual Life that was located at Nassau and Liberty Streets, right around the corner from Guardian's old downtown home office. Ives, a Yale graduate, began his insurance career in the actuarial department of Mutual Life in 1898. The following year, unsuited to the work, he joined the Raymond Agency, Mutual's most important New York agency, as a clerk. There he met future partner and lifetime friend Julian Myrick, who at a later stage in his career came to be known as "Mr. Life Insurance."

The Raymond Agency was one of the Armstrong Investigation's many victims. Ives and Myrick made the best of the uncertain post-Investigation environment in 1907 by opening their own general agency for the Washington Life Insurance Company, a small insurer not implicated in any fraudulent activities. The agency thrived despite the Washington's woes. Within a year the Washington reinsured with a Pittsburgh-based insurer not authorized to write business in New York. Ives and Myrick therefore rejoined the Mutual Life, this time as managerial agents with fixed salaries and commission overrides. The agency excelled. First it became the Mutual's most productive agency, then the top agency in New York City, and finally, by 1929, the largest agency (without an exclusive territory) in the entire country. Honesty, professionalism, and extensive use of well-trained brokers were the keys to the agency's success.

The bashful Ives never solicited business himself, instead concentrating his efforts on writing effective ad copy and, more importantly, writing training materials that both inspired the agency's direct solicitors and brokers and helped them to eschew emotional, self-serving salesmanship in favor of dispassionate, scientific financial counseling. The courses that Ives authored used the case analysis approach made famous by the Harvard Business School; they helped to transform his trainees from mere peddlers of policies into professional estate planners. Thanks in part to Ives's artistic yet profound articles, including the famous pamphlet "The Amount to Carry," and Myrick's extraordinary social skills, the agency, like Guardian, did well by doing good, by concentrating on helping people rather than on raking in commissions. The rewards of good service, they realized, would come naturally. Indeed, Ives personally cleared $56,000 in 1922 alone, a heady sum for the day. The most direct evidence of Ives's influence on Guardian is the name of his agency's monthly bulletin, *The Estate-O-Graph*, which may have inspired the moniker of Guardian's famous Graph Estate sales program. Guardian began drifting toward estate analysis during Ives's heyday. Moreover, given the agency's reputation and proximity to Guardian, it is likely that Guardian's early sales training programs may also have been inspired by this prolific composer of music and business literature. Of course, Guardian may also have influenced the thinking of Ives and other industry reformers.[44]

A new crop of insurance executives also came to power in the wake of the Armstrong probe, stressing industry-wide cooperation and soundness over size and competition. To foster cooperation, the life industry formed a number of professional associations, including the Association of Life Insurance Presidents and the American Life Convention. Germania was a founding member of the former and one of the first large eastern companies to join the latter, in 1922. Its officers regularly attended the conventions and learned much from them. In the new environment, life insurers also reduced their use of negative advertising.[45]

The Armstrong report had strongly advocated the mutual form of organization over the stockholder corporation. As insurers reconsidered their reputations and their finances, the mutual form became more popular, as Prudential, Equitable, and MetLife fully mutualized, while MONY and other longer-established mutuals strove for more sustainable, moderate growth in lieu of rapid gains at all costs. This and other reforms were largely self-imposed. Self-regulation became more commonly accepted as a hedge against more government intervention. This was a wise course. The federal government stayed away, leaving insurance, as distinct from banking or securities regulation, almost entirely to the states and the industry, itself.

S. S. McClure, editor of *McClure's* magazine, concluded that the New York investigations had a "tonic effect" on insurers. The beneficial upshot was that security and economy became the watchwords of the entire industry, not just a few conscientious companies. Over the longer haul, major insurers followed the lead of smaller companies like Germania, as they began to recruit men more interested in the eleemosynary aspect of the industry than its potential to accumulate great wealth and power. The selection tactic worked. By the mid-1920s, Hughes and the insurance industry had made amends. Hughes told a meeting of life insurance presidents,

> I am not here to review the past save as I am permitted to congratulate you upon the unparalleled growth and the soundness of the life insurance enterprise under your management, upon the broadly diffused benefits which you are conferring upon the nation. . . . I believe that there is no safer or better-managed business in our country than yours.

By the mid-twentieth century, insurance executives were regarded as the most community oriented and best educated, albeit lowest paid, business leaders in the nation. They took satisfaction from their jobs, even if, as the sociologist C. Wright Mills observed, they were no longer members of America's "power elite." They realized what Guardianites had long understood, namely, that good profits and high principles go hand in hand.[46]

The higher ethics and service orientation of life companies greatly aided the industry as a whole. Despite the emergence of competitors, including savings bank life insurance, the old-line legal reserve insurers thrived. Life insurance in force surged and insurers avoided the worst of the Depression by largely avoiding risky, volatile assets like junk bonds and common stocks. Somewhat more favorable tax treatment came in the 1930s and 1940s. Perhaps most importantly, the industry easily thwarted New Dealers' attempt to federalize life insurance regulation in the late 1930s and early 1940s. The life industry thrived in good times and survived in trying times because it had turned into a group of gentle guardians.[47]

Germania, soon to become Guardian, excelled in the new environment, which was much more to its liking than the old. Its U.S. business grew relatively rapidly after 1905, and what had been a downward slide in its share of total insurance in force was largely reversed until the end of the Great War. (See figure 1-3.) Moreover, its mortality experience, which was about 73 percent of expectations in 1904, remained favorable.[48]

In 1910, the company used its semicentennial anniversary as a reason to build a new home office, to overhaul its policies, and to reorganize its ad-

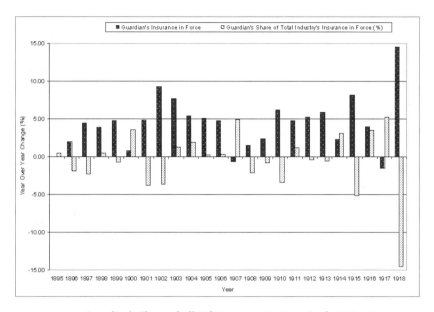

FIGURE 1-3 *Guardian's Share of All Life Insurance in Force in the U.S., 1895–1918*

ministration. Guardian's home office had been at 20 Nassau Street since 1884. Prior to that purchase, the company had shuffled in and out of three different leased buildings along Broadway. The new twenty-story home office, which was located on the corner of Seventeenth Street and Park Avenue South, the northeast corner of Union Square, was not finished in time for the golden anniversary, but Guardian moved in the following year. The landmark building, extensively renovated and enlarged by an annex occupied in early 1962, served as Guardian's home for most of the twentieth century.[49]

The new policies introduced during the semicentennial celebration in 1910 embodied all competitive features, including lower premiums, higher guaranteed values, incontestability after one year, automatic nonforfeiture, reinstatement, and other attractive provisions. The future president, Carl Heye, then a young manager, convinced Cornelius Doremus to establish an agency department in the home office headed by T. Louis Hansen, who would figure prominently in executive discussions in the years to come. Regular executive meetings became the norm, and new office procedures were designed to keep everything at a high level of efficiency. The company did so well in the following years that, in 1914, when its share of the industry's life insurance in force increased 3.10 percent, it granted an unusual bonus to its top six officers. That bonus was but small compensation for the travails the company's management would face in the coming few years.[50]

2

Retreat

The German Problem and Its Painful Resolution

The last survivor of Germania's founding directors, Hermann Rose, died at age eighty-five on 11 September 1910. He had been the company's leader in the highly successful Berlin office, from which he extended its business throughout much of Western Europe, and his passing marked the apogee of Germania's highly successful forays into international markets. Under the supervision of Rose, and then his son Heinrich, the volume of the Berlin office's new business came to exceed that of the home office for a number of years. And now, on the elder Rose's passing, Germania, standing astride the Atlantic, was poised to become one of the world's foremost international financial institutions. World events interceded, however, and by 1917, Germania's international business, like that of all of the multinational insurance companies, became just another casualty of the Great War and other regional conflicts.[1]

The first cracks in Germania's international business appeared during the Mexican Revolution. Germania had entered Mexico in 1902, and its business grew modestly there—most of the insurance it had written in Mexico consisted of German immigrants who married Mexican women—until it was forced to pull out of the troubled nation in 1916. By then, ongoing revolutionary conflict had resulted in a series of changes in governments that so destabilized the Mexican economy that it was no longer feasible to do business there. That blow, however, was not as major a one as America's entry into World War I. The Great War jolted the company to its foundations, forcing it to change its name and to begin the difficult process of unwinding its European operations.[2]

The main problem was Germany and all it implied. Even though, by World War I, the largest part of the company's U.S. business by far was derived from Americans not of German descent, Germania remained for the time being a "German" company, as the surnames of many of its New

York and Berlin directors on 1 January 1915 attest: Ahlemann, Becker, Bernuth, Borsig, Caesar, Cillis, D'Oench, Doremus, Goepel, Kloenne, Kuttroff, Pagenstecher, Roelker, Rose, Schieren, Schnakenberg, Watjen, Wesendonck, and Wesendonk. Once the English and American propaganda machines went into high gear, images of the "Hun" raping and pillaging the innocents of Europe and torpedoing commercial vessels on the high seas unleashed enormous social and political prejudice against Americans of German descent. Anti-German hysteria reached a fever pitch, as films like *The Prussian Cur* and *The Kaiser, the Beast of Berlin* became popular, as pretzels were banned from bars and Bach from symphonic programs, as sauerkraut became "victory cabbage" and German toast became French toast, and as German-Americans were imprisoned and deported by the government and physically assaulted by their neighbors.[3]

As bad as the outbreak of war in Europe was for all German-Americans, it was particularly awkward for those doing business with the fatherland. Well before the United States was drawn into the conflict, the onset of the fighting in Europe disrupted communications between the home and Berlin offices and between the Berlin office and agencies located outside the Central Powers. When the company did receive dispatches from Berlin, it was only after much delay, via the U.S. secretary of state. By 1917, communication with the Berlin office was at a virtual standstill, and Germania's board scrambled to keep the European business afloat by tying the Western and Southern European agencies directly to the home office in New York, bypassing Berlin altogether, as the cessation of all communications with the company's European branch forced Germania to concentrate solely on its American business.[4]

In 1914, Germania was contending with the issue of war exclusions on two possible fronts—a war brewing between the United States and Mexico and war in Europe. During America's Civil War, Germania was careful to avoid insuring war risks, but that had changed in the Spanish-American War of 1898, when the company waived its policies' war clause and granted free permits to engage in military service. Policies issued in the United States after 1 January 1907 contained no restriction of any kind on military service. In May 1914 it decided, after thoroughly investigating the competitive situation, to consider insuring professional military personnel upon their completion of a supplemental application form that asked for their consent to a single extra cash premium equal to 4 percent of the face amount of the policy. Policies issued to servicemen, however, had to be relatively expensive whole life policies, not cheap term, could not contain a disability clause, and were limited to $2,000 face value or less. Overall, wartime difficulties in Europe were mitigated by strong U.S. policy sales. In 1915, when the industry did well generally, Germania's domestic sales grew rapidly, and were even stronger in 1916 (see figure 1-3), in amounts equal to the best year the entire company had ever had.[5]

In fact, Germania did fairly well at home *and* abroad during the Europe-only phase of the war. The mortality experience on its European business was quite good because the company had not assumed war risks in Europe. It kept its European investments to the bare minimum required by law. Germania innovated at home. In 1915, it instituted the National Economic Mobilization of Life Insurance Policyholders program, which was part educational campaign and part innovation thought pregnant with possibilities, and introduced a Health Reclamation Service aimed at lengthening policyholders' lives. The program, especially Germania's food garden bulletins, was a rousing success as measured by the hundreds of letters received from policyholders and nonpolicyholders, and numerous letters of commendation from federal and state officials.[6]

At the end of 1914, Cornelius Doremus retired, giving way to Hubert Cillis, just the company's third chief executive in fifty-five years of business. Cillis had joined Germania as an actuary in 1869, when he was but twenty-one years old, and had risen to prominence as a founder of the Actuarial Society of America. Doremus had apparently long given up a struggle to impose more centralized home office control of the prosperous Berlin operations and their headstrong managers. Cillis would have to spend much of his presidency, which lasted until the end of 1920, worrying about how to pick up the pieces of the European business, as it was left in shambles by Germany's defeat in World War I.

Loyalty at a Premium

After the United States declared war on the Central Powers—Germany, Austro-Hungary, and Turkey—in April 1917, Germania's management went out of its way to prove its loyalty to the United States, directing its agents to sell U.S. war bonds without profit or commission of any kind to the company. Germania was the first life insurance company to subscribe on its own account to the first war loan. It stopped its traditional practice of translating its annual statements into German and publicized its employees and agents who enlisted in the armed services. To top it off,

Germania took pains to promote the government's competing life insurance program for soldiers and sailors.[7]

None of those efforts sufficed to insulate the company from the virulent anti-German emotions sweeping the nation. Since the outbreak of the war, Germania had come under attack more or less continuously, and all the negative publicity induced company sales managers to broach the question of changing the company's name. T. Louis Hansen, Germania's superintendent of agencies, managed to quiet such agitation to some extent, but the issue reappeared with renewed force in September 1917 at the first annual convention of Germania Life fieldmen. At that New Orleans meeting, members of the company's sales force bluntly explained to Hansen that "the name of the Company and the precarious situation of the European Branch" had become a major "handicap" that had rendered "it impossible . . . to secure new Agents."[8]

Hansen reported the agents' sentiments to the Finance Committee upon his return to New York. Confronted with those agency and publicity pressures, the company felt compelled to study the name change in great detail. After an intensive internal study, Germania's management decided that if it were to change the company's name, it should do so before German forces inflicted casualties on American troops. The anonymous author of the study, elaborating on the comments made by general agent Frederic Doremus at the New Orleans convention, stated the matter bluntly:

> When the American forces have suffered losses in Europe, however, when transports have been sunk, when the first ships arrive with the caskets of fallen soldiers; when the transports return to the United States with mutilated and maimed men, blind soldiers . . . and paralyzed and other wrecks of humanity carried on stretchers, a change of name at that time would be commented upon—not as an act of patriotism, but of compulsion, and would probably be too late to have much beneficial effect.

Company studies also showed that other insurers with the word "German" in their names, like the German American Fire Insurance Company of Baltimore, the Buffalo German, the Germania Fire Insurance Company, and the German Mutual Life Insurance Company had already changed monikers or were in the process of doing so.[9]

Some directors and agents, however, still opposed the name change. Their arguments, which rested mainly on emotional sentiment and vague claims about the unimportance of names, were easily rebutted. The name "Germania," the proponents of change agreed, had been important early in the company's history when some three-quarters of the company's policyholders were either German or of German descent. And the name was important in Europe. But with the future of the European branch in serious doubt, and the percentage of ethnically German policyholders in America not much greater than the proportion of the German population in the United States, the company had no choice but to change its name. T. Louis Hansen sealed the matter when he gave a speech filled with anecdotes that showed that "Germania" offered no competitive advantage, even with Germans. In the most telling example, a German sea captain who put in at Baltimore early in the war eschewed a Germania agent and bought a policy from Northwestern Mutual![10]

The next question was what the company's new name would be. An ad agency repeatedly urged it to adopt the name "Liberty." The company rejected those overtures because a company with that name had recently gone bankrupt. Moreover, Germania had other ideas. On 22 November, Cillis wrote New York regulator Jesse Phillips to ask permission to use the name Union Life Insurance Company. The proposed name presumably tied in with the location of the company's home office in Union Square, its Civil War vintage, and its strong affection for the United States. But then it learned that a company named "Union" had failed in 1909.[11]

In December 1917, Germania's directors instead settled on the name Guardian Life Insurance Company of America. One director, Albrecht Pagenstecher, dissented. "Guardian" had a nice ring to it, implying safety and security, and carried the added benefit of saving money on altering the home office sign—same initials and same number of letters, with only two of them changed. The name change caused some minor inconveniences, like the need to have some of its bonds reregistered and seemingly endless paperwork, especially in Wisconsin, where a company with the name Guardian Life Insurance Company of Wisconsin was already in existence.[12]

The name change certainly made news. "The Directors [of Germania] decided upon this course of action," the *New York Times* reported, "in order to remove any doubts caused by the company's old name as to its nationality." The name, which many thought implied that the company originated in Germany and did business in the United States as a branch of a German institution, was hurting the interests of its agents and policyholders and therefore had to be abandoned. The decision, Hubert Cillis later noted, "was not taken with a light heart" but "had become imperative under prevailing conditions." At the same time, the directors announced that they would confine the writing of new business to the United States.[13]

Exiting Europe was, under the circumstances, a regrettable decision but a sound business move; Guardian had a lot to lose if it stayed. Its directors believed that under the prevailing conditions new business transactions in Europe would undoubtedly prove as unprofitable as they had in Spain. In the short term, the company could do little about the depreciation of its European securities. Only because its domestic business was prospering did Germania's securities portfolio hold up during the war— quite well, in fact, when compared to its peers. (See tables 2-1 and 2-2.) The larger danger was that the taint of association during wartime would undermine the company's domestic business as well.[14]

Guardian Life Insurance Company was now poised to focus its business on U.S. markets only. It had ample room to grow domestically; it was doing business in only thirty-six states. But withdrawal from foreign markets would not be easy.

Extortion, Political and Otherwise

The name change officially took effect on 1 March 1918, but Guardian continued to come under attack, especially from the many hack papers that did little other than sell advertising and steal stories from such legitimate business news sources as the *Journal of Commerce.* In one particularly egregious case, J. Frazer Kempson, editor of *The Insurance Times,* maliciously contended that Guardian discriminated in favor of its European policyholders and against its American policyholders. Kempson did even worse by writing to New York's superintendent of insurance arguing that Guardian was "hopelessly insolvent," and accusing the superintendent of "not doing his job." As the superintendent tried to explain to Kempson, "You are in error when you state that the Guardian . . . is hopelessly insolvent." If Guardian's European assets became valueless, so too would its European liabilities. Kempson shot back that Guardian's percentage of European securities to capital and surplus was 900 percent, while those of the Mutual (44 percent), Equitable (59 percent), and NYLIC (60 percent), the other major U.S. companies with interests in Central Europe, were much lower. The superintendent dismissed the ratio in question as irrelevant.[15]

It was difficult to fathom what drove Kempson in his apparent vendetta against Guardian until he revealed it in the form of a letter dated

TABLE 2-1
The Decline in Value of Germania's European Securities, 1914–18

Year	Cost (Purchase Price) of European Securities ($)	Market Value ($ on 31 Dec.)	Cost over Market ($)
1914	7,481,222.00	6,540,697.00	940,525.00
1915	8,203,225.00	6,629,971.00	1,573,254.00
1916	8,710,745.01	6,738,504.54	1,972,240.47
1917	9,353,521.57	7,043,472.83	2,310,048.74
1918	10,159,389.71	7,768,851.64	2,390,538.07

Source: "Correspondence with Department of State," Office of the President, Heye, Box 48, GLIC archives.

TABLE 2-2
Amortized Value to the Market Value of the Assets of Top Life Insurance Companies, 31 December 1917

Name of Company	Market Value of Securities ($)	Amortized Value of Securities ($)	Excess of Amortized over Market Value ($)	Rate of Excess (Col. 4/ Col. 2—%)
National Life (Vt.)	23,350,991	23,625,291	274,300	1.17
Germania	**12,222,087**	**12,418,576**	**196,489**	**1.61**
Connecticut General	4,195,039	4,348,683	153,644	3.66
Columbian National	7,538,507	7,836,040	297,533	3.95
Penn Mutual	64,040,976	66,699,525	2,658,549	4.15
Fidelity Mutual	8,680,599	9,081,530	400,931	4.62
Metropolitan	307,924,344	322,297,104	14,372,760	4.67
Travelers	34,466,892	36,106,083	1,639,191	4.76
Phoenix Mutual	9,047,161	9,510,684	463,523	5.12
Prudential	256,094,054	269,956,474	13,862,420	5.41
Berkshire	11,597,317	12,234,276	636,959	5.49
Provident Life & Trust	51,564,258	54,525,481	2,961,223	5.74
New England Mutual	46,758,259	49,456,930	2,698,671	5.77
John Hancock	51,772,540	54,865,374	3,092,834	5.97
Mutual Benefit	56,392,892	59,811,896	3,419,004	6.06
Mutual	379,849,703	403,190,925	23,341,222	6.14
State Mutual of Massachusetts	23,261,416	24,771,559	1,510,143	6.49
Home	17,387,244	18,600,574	1,213,330	6.98
Massachusetts Mutual	39,036,514	41,795,253	2,758,739	7.07
Aetna	40,453,056	43,348,921	2,895,865	7.16
Connecticut Mutual	23,751,661	25,855,864	2,104,203	8.86
Equitable	302,059,778	329,290,902	27,231,124	9.02
Northwestern Mutual	99,785,203	109,708,766	9,923,563	9.94
New York	499,877,911	550,191,467	50,313,556	10.07
Average				**5.83**
Median				**5.76**

Source: "Securities Held by Life Insurance Companies on December 31, 1917 as per New York Insurance Report," Office of the President, Heye, Box 48, GLIC archives.

27 April 1918, in which he warned Guardian's president, Hubert Cillis, that unnamed sources were supplying him (Kempson) with information. Cryptically he wrote that those individuals would receive "a great deal more money" if they continued to work "for the other side." Kempson went on to say that the mysterious informers "would rather be on our side than on the other side" because "respectability is on our side." "That being the case," Kempson explained, "I think that a rather substantial retainer should be forthcoming." Kempson was certainly audacious, if not outright reckless. He scrawled at the bottom of the page in his own script the following: "I fully believe that if the correspondence between these parties and superintendent were published that it would eternally D[amn] the Guardian Life Ins."[16]

In his response of 30 April, Cillis virtually dared Kempson to publish the correspondence while feigning ignorance of what Kempson had meant by "retainer." "If you have reference to a retainer in a legal sense," Cillis advised, "such question would have to be submitted by us both to the Company's counsel and to the Superintendent of Insurance . . . and you will appreciate that no hurried action can be taken in this matter." At the same time, he dashed off photostatic copies of Kempson's letter to the superintendent and to the alien property custodian with a note stating that the "letter we are sure requires no comment."[17]

That very day, Guardian Vice President Carl Heye received one F. J. Andrews, agent for a mysterious Mr. Stinson. The subject of the meeting was Andrews's contention that various parties wanted to oust the superintendent of insurance in the elections to be held that November, and they needed funds to help them, to the tune of $10,000. Guardian officials knew that the two incidents were related, and so when the pair met again on 2 May, Heye presented Andrews with Kempson's blackmail letter, while a hidden Guardian stenographer recorded their conversation from an adjacent room. "Remember one thing," Heye said. "If you go ahead [with publication], you must all [Andrews, Kempson, Stinson] take the consequences." The matter was dropped.[18]

To combat other, continuing attacks from the tabloid journals, the company made a show of its loyalty by subscribing heavily to the government's war loans. Even after the war had ended, Guardian hastened to respond to an extraordinary request from Treasury Secretary William McAdoo and New York Federal Reserve Governor Benjamin Strong, pledging a $1 million subscription to the fourth liberty loan, an amount twice its subscription to the third loan. This occurred at a particularly bad time. A spike in mortality rates due to the great influenza epidemic of 1918, along with skyrocketing interest rates in Europe, severely strained the company's cash holdings, so much so that it had been forced, in November, to ask the Manhattan Bank to discount $250,000 of its time deposits.[19]

To make matters worse, the alien property custodian, headed by the infamous "red" basher A. Mitchell Palmer, forced the company to go another mile in its attempts to appease the authorities and burnish its image. Though all but one of its directors and all of its officers were U.S. citizens, its board still sounded very German. Its six Berlin-based board members were technically "alien enemies" and hence, like all of the company's other German owners, no longer lawful stockholders. Palmer wanted more than to control shares; he was pushing for the right to appoint nine new board members. Guardian thought that foreign holdings of the company's stock, which probably was not much in excess of 35 percent, entitled Palmer to appoint only eight. The company's lawyers, Dulon and Roe, however, thought that Palmer had no say in the matter whatsoever because the alien property custodian was at best a minority stockholder and it was never intended that minority stockholders should control the action of the majority in the selection of directors or otherwise.[20]

Nevertheless, under the circumstances the company thought it wise to conform entirely with Palmer's wish. Accordingly, on 22 August 1918 the alien property custodian replaced nine "German" directors, the six Berlin directors and three others, with men with Anglo-American names like Austin, Edwards, MacDonald, and Moore by assigning them each ten shares, formerly the property of Karl von Wesendonck, and voting them on the board. The men served as representatives of the alien property custodian until 19 June 1919. On 8 May 1919 Hubert Cillis, in trust for Germania directors, officers, employees, and fieldmen, purchased the 1,548 shares of stock under the control of the alien property custodian for $68.50 per share, dividend off. At that price, they heavily oversubscribed for the sale, a fact that the company did not disclose to the Alien Property Custodian. George C. Austin stayed on as a regular director but the other new directors left, though the company invited several of them to stay on. "Anglo" names became increasingly common in the company's higher echelons, Germans became scarcer in the company's ranks, and by 1928, Guardian could not even find a competent German stenographer to help prepare correspondence required to liquidate its European business. Some tension between the German old guard and the newbies persisted into the 1930s, but it never bubbled to the surface.[21]

The Lingering Dissolution of the European Business

As bad as the shenanigans surrounding the German issue were, the company had a multitude of problems to worry about in this period. The worldwide "Spanish influenza" epidemic of 1918 greatly increased general mortality, mostly among those in the prime of life. As the ravages of the scourge continued, some life insurance companies suffered five or more times their normal rates of mortality. Health officials predicted a renewed outbreak of the plague in a more virulent form. To add to the problems, losses on real estate mounted, expenses piled up, and investment earnings plummeted, largely due to the company's liberal subscription to the government's various liberty loans. Expecting to take a bath on its European securities, Guardian decided to cut its dividends by 50 percent. The decision was unpopular with policyholders but necessary.[22]

In January 1919, a minor disaster struck; influenza took the life of a $100,000 policyholder. Luckily, Guardian had reinsured half of the risk. But even with the reduced dividend scale, the unexpected $50,000 payment still sent the company scrapping for liquidity, which it secured through the sale of liberty bonds and the discounting of a time deposit about to mature. Agency manager T. Louis Hansen reported that the company's fieldmen had taken the dividend reduction in stride. They undoubtedly realized, as New York regulators did, that Guardian had staggered through the epidemic much better than many life companies, some of which, like Kansas City Life, almost went under. To boost morale and business, Guardian launched a sales campaign in February 1919, called "President's Golden Jubilee Month," to honor Hubert Cillis's fiftieth anniversary with the company. The campaign met with strong demand for life products, thanks to the high death rates, and helped to ease the financial squeeze. The episode convinced Guardian management, once and for all, that the company's name change was not enough. It would have to make good on its promise to exit foreign territories.[23]

The immediate postwar European situation was not as disastrous as feared. In February 1919, the home office had gathered enough information to conclude that

> the business had been allowed to continue normally, without interference on the part of the German or Austrian Government authorities, and that the net losses by death during the first three quarters of the year had been

but 60% of those for the previous year. . . . [Moreover] the European Agency apparently had had no difficulty to further finance itself without any assistance from the Home Office.[24]

The war, however, greatly diminished the importance of the Berlin branch, as table 2-3 shows.

Despite this unexpectedly good news, the company stuck with its decision to exit foreign territories. Guardian's home office had been concerned by the laxity of management in the Berlin office even before the outbreak of war. (Hermann Rose's successors failed to live up to his standards.) Mortality rates for the European branch had been abnormally high since 1910. Resources to send someone competent for the mission to reorganize the Berlin office were scarce. "No one capable of this work," the company's leadership believed, "could possibly be spared." Certainly the European business looked no better after the conflict, with the economies of Central Europe in tatters. As early as October 1917, company officials had met, secretly and confidentially, with three of Wall Street's top European experts: a leading partner of one of the great international banking houses, a vice president of the National City Bank, who was considered an international expert among financiers, and the head of the foreign exchange department of the Equitable Trust. They had painted a gruesome picture of postwar Europe's financial scene, one rife with partial repudiations of national debts and significant volumes of lost trade. Austro-Hungary and Germany were the worst cases. The Equitable Trust executive predicted, with great prescience, that those countries could only retire their debts by issuing reams of fiat paper money. Hyperinflation indeed ensued.[25]

For a variety of regulatory, political, and economic reasons, the exit from Europe was a slow one. The first barrier was the New York State Department of Insurance, which forbade Guardian from reinsuring its

TABLE 2-3
Relative Decline of the Importance of the Berlin Branch during World War I

Year	Home ($)	Europe ($)	Total ($)
1914	12,778,614	5,493,789	18,272,403
1915	13,842,379	1,352,896	15,195,275
1916	19,682,971	1,378,149	21,061,120
1917	22,969,053	2,102,915	25,071,968
1918	22,785,670	1,872,257	24,657,927

Source: "Germania Life Stock Subscription," 8 May 1919, Office of the President, Heye, Box 48, GLIC archives.

European business with any firm not admitted to do business in New York. The superintendent insisted that any deal made in the course of winding down the business in Europe not adversely affect U.S. policyholders. There could be no large remittances to Europe, nor any contingent liabilities. Foreign governments, too, made exit as difficult as they had often made entry. U.S. life insurers operating in Germany repeatedly tried, in vain, to induce the host government to pass a law that would allow a syndicate of German companies to assume foreign insurers' German policies and all the liability attached to them.[26]

One reason Guardian's directors hesitated to liquidate the European business quickly was that they felt obligations toward the company's agents and employees there, especially those in Germany. The company remitted considerable sums to the Berlin office to help the staff to cope with the economic dislocations that rocked Germany after the draconian peace imposed by the Allied Powers. In March 1920, for instance, Guardian's home office wired 250,000 Reichsmarks for the relief of lower-salaried German employees. In 1921, after the mark's value had virtually vanished, the parent company shipped U.S. currency and even food to the Berlin office.[27]

The economics of liquidation proved nettlesome. With the breakup of the Austro-Hungarian Empire, it was not clear how to handle policies denominated in a defunct unit of account in a polity that no longer existed. Europe's postwar economic dislocations so adversely affected financial markets that the value of Guardian's foreign securities vanished into the ether. Liquidation would force the company to recognize those losses. As Guardian did not want to hurt any of its policyholders, it proceeded slowly, searching for solutions that would minimize the damage. In the face of what seemed to the company to be insurmountable difficulties, patience was deemed the best policy.[28]

Meanwhile, Guardian pushed business development in the United States as far as possible in order to reduce the proportion of its business in Europe to the lowest possible figure. In the long run, it succeeded. The impact that liquidating the foreign business had on the company would decrease with each passing year.[29] (See table 2-4.)

Of the European business in force, about two-thirds was in Germany, one-fifth in the former Austro-Hungarian Empire, and the remainder in Belgium, France, Holland, Switzerland, and Spain. When approached by Swiss companies in 1921 about reinsuring its policies in Switzerland, Guardian replied that it was not interested in the proposition. Its strategy

TABLE 2-4
European Business as a Percentage of Domestic Business,
1900–1921

Year	Percentage
1900	92
1910	84
1913	76
1914	72
1915	65
1916	56
1917	49
1918	44
1919	35
1920	27
1921 (estimated)	24

Source: Finance Committee Minutes, 9 November 1921, Box 15; Memorandum, 7 November 1921, Office of the President, Heye, Box 46, GLIC archives.

was to dispose of the business in the inverse order of its desirability, i.e., business in the former Austro-Hungarian Empire first, then Germany, Belgium, Spain, Holland, and, finally, Switzerland. Guardian pressed to find a buyer for its policies in newly formed Austria, Czechoslovakia, and elsewhere in Central Europe and the Balkans, but it held back to await the results of negotiations pending between NYLIC and Czechoslovakian representatives.[30]

Given the anticipated cost of liquidating the European business and the destruction of the Reichsmark, Guardian eliminated dividends on German and Austro-Hungarian policies in 1922. In the summer of that year, members of the board urged the company's new president, Carl Heye, who had gone to Germany, to bring about a speedy liquidation. Heye, who was negotiating with the Phoenix Life Insurance Company of Vienna to assume the company's business in Europe, stalled. Baseler Lebens Versicherungs Gesellschaft signaled that it wanted to treat with him over Guardian's Swiss, German, Dutch, and Belgian business. After some time, Heye felt compelled to reject Baseler's offer, because it wanted, in addition to Guardian's European assets, a share of Guardian's surplus. He believed that Guardian could make a better deal, and eventually, it did.[31]

In June 1923, Phoenix reappeared, offering to take Guardian's German and Eastern European policies on a liabilities-for-assets basis. Guardian dispatched T. Louis Hansen to Berlin to make a deal, but a nasty little surprise awaited him upon his arrival in the German capital. German law would not allow a life insurance company to transfer its liabilities without the consent of its policyholders. Thus Guardian was left with the option of reinsuring policies, which left it with some liability. (If the acquiring company failed, in other words, Guardian would have to reassume the risks.) Hansen therefore could approach only solid companies unlikely to go bankrupt, and good German insurers were nearly impossible to find. Most had massive problems of their own—foreign liabilities that they could no longer afford and tremendous expense burdens that were mounting almost in geometric progression due to hyperinflation. German companies without foreign liabilities were mostly small and those who sought Guardian's business would probably fail.[32]

For a number of technical legal reasons, Hansen also rejected the idea that Guardian buy out its European policyholders directly. He was at wit's end until Dr. W. W. Berliner of the Phoenix Life called on him to reconsider Phoenix's interest. The main sticking point was that Vienna-based Phoenix was also a foreign company and it was not clear if it had regulatory approval to transact business in Germany apart from its existing southern Germany concession.[33]

Hansen got around all these problems the old-fashioned way. He courted a key German regulator, who consented to the deal so long as Phoenix would refrain from writing new business in Germany unless it paid handsomely for a regular Reich's concession. Hansen then obtained Munich Re's guarantee for the deal and submitted the proposed contract to German regulators. It seemed that he had the whole messy business under control when again, much to his surprise, German insurance regulators scotched the deal by insisting on contract language that neither Guardian's board nor the New York Insurance Department could ever approve. Hansen was furious. He threatened to take the next steamer home and reminded the German regulators that the New York Insurance Department had already ruled that the assets deposited to cover the company's German liabilities would have to suffice. For the deal to fall through, he argued, would not be "in the interest of the German policyholder."[34]

What had been motivating German insurance regulators to obstruct was their belief that American companies would be more likely to pay off policies in gold if prevented from transferring or reinsuring their assets. Hansen explained that no American company was going to pay off policies in gold and that nothing could force them to do so. Still, German regulators pressed for a reason as to why Guardian wanted to leave Germany at all. Hansen explained to them that the company's main "reason for desiring to dispose of the business [was] that it involved work out of all proportion to its value." Finally, the regulators agreed to modify the disputed language, and the deal went through in late 1923.[35]

Issues regarding the German policies continued to crop up, but for the most part Guardian had freed itself from day-to-day concern with the German business. The reinsurance agreement enabled Guardian all but completely to close its Berlin office. German regulators, who had been uneasy with the prospect of a large layoff, were satisfied with Hansen's promise that Guardian would treat its former employees well.[36]

Severance was accordingly expensive. The Berlin employees were no fools. They had anticipated that under the watchful eye of insurance regulators they would collect a generous severance from Guardian, even as they drew salaries from a new employer. In 1924, Guardian indeed made good on a severance offer, remitting a "final" payment, totaling $26,735, to thirty-nine European directors, officers, employees, and apprentices. It paid a further $500, in total, to an unspecified number of general agents. Later that year, though, it remitted another $6,500, most of it to Emil Natonek, the company's general agent in the former Austro-Hungarian Empire. Smaller sums continued to trickle out to widows and other familial supplicants for years thereafter.[37]

For Phoenix, the acquisition of Guardian's business was a loss leader. "No profit can possibly accrue to that Company from the transfer of the German business," Hansen noted, certain that "the officials of that Company [had] signed in the hope that the Swiss, Dutch, Belgian and Spanish business would follow." Events would not work out that way. But the deal was done, and in September 1923, Guardian sold its tiny Romanian business to Steaua Romaniei of Bucharest under the guarantees of both Munich Re and Phoenix. Elbe Life bought up Guardian's Czech policies around the same time. Then in 1924, Guardian informed Phoenix and Munich Re that it was interested in selling the rest of its Western European assets, but that it would have to wait for the regulatory backlog regarding the Central European policies to clear before it could take decisive action. New York's regulators moved at a snail's pace, checking every fact and noting every typo. Not until 1925 had regulators formally approved all the transactions.[38]

Yet again, legal barriers surfaced, this time in Switzerland and Spain, while Phoenix complained that it did not want to be bound to match Guardian's dividends on its U.S. policies. Furthermore, Phoenix wanted to pay Guardian only 25 percent of the benefits of the transferred business, or $3,000 yearly for ten years, or an immediate lump sum payment of that stream at 5 percent for immediate transfer of all its Western European business.[39]

All that slowed negotiations. Worried about the drag the small European business was having on the company's corporate resources, Carl Heye returned to Berlin once again in 1927 to negotiate with Phoenix the reinsurance of the company's remaining business in Europe, which consisted mainly of policies written in Spain, the Low Countries, and Switzerland, along with a few policies in France and Germany contracted in foreign or defunct currencies. He struck a deal contingent upon its acceptance by the New York superintendent of insurance and Phoenix's admission to do business in Switzerland. By the terms of the deal, Phoenix was to effectively assume all of Guardian's liabilities and responsibilities arising out of all of its remaining European business, as if the same had originally been written by the Phoenix. As a further safeguard, Munich Re would guarantee Phoenix's liabilities arising out of the agreement. The extraction would cost Guardian $220,864 in cash but the company would retain title to its European real estate and other European assets, including an office building in Berlin's financial district near Deutsche Bank and a property in northern Berlin that it had foreclosed upon in 1914. Hansen thought the properties were worth a total of some $250,000, at least when stable conditions returned. The company also owned a good office building in Vienna. All told, Guardian expected to break about even but rid itself of the risks and costs.[40]

This deal, too, was never consummated, because of a revalorization problem. The German government tried to force Guardian, NYLIC, and other American companies to contribute to a "revalorization fund" pursuant to a German law that sought to undo some of the inequities Germany's hyperinflation had inflicted on creditors, including policyholders. (The companies had paid off mortgages on real estate and paid dividends in depreciated Reichsmarks.) Unfortunately for Guardian, Phoenix declined absolutely to make a contribution to the revalorization fund, and under German law, Guardian would be solely liable for the German government's claims.[41]

German authorities demanded $670,000 from Guardian, which, with support from the New York insurance superintendent, managed to negotiate a settlement for less than half that amount.[42] That was the price of avoiding expected nuisance lawsuits. The German authorities had gone along because they realized that any suits against the company would eventually have to be enforced in U.S. courts, a risk. After the 1930 revalorization settlement, Guardian's general director in Berlin, Rudolf Goose, congratulated Guardian on what he termed "this success."[43]

By then Guardian's remaining business in Europe was small and rapidly decreasing. It was still too much, requiring disproportionate attention at a time when the home office could ill afford to bestow it. The remnants of the European business generated an extra profit of about $58,000 through the sale and redemption of securities in 1931 and 1932, but the opportunity cost of the long liquidation period became apparent during the depths of the Great Depression. The Finance Committee spent too much of its time worrying about European interest rates, securities prices, and economic conditions at a time when the domestic business was on the ropes.[44]

Following the settlement of the revalorization issue, Guardian continued to make overtures to Phoenix in hopes that the small business remaining in Belgium, the Netherlands, Spain, and Switzerland could be advantageously disposed of during the current year. Talks dragged on until late 1936, when Phoenix went into receivership following revelations that it had fraudulently paid out big sums to Austrian politicians and media moguls. A consortium of German insurers then formed the Isar Life Insurance Company to assume Phoenix's insurance liabilities in Germany, while the Austrian insurer Ovag picked up the pieces of Phoenix's business in its home country. Just as that mess began to clear, the outbreak of war once again disrupted commerce and communications between the Old and New Worlds. Guardian tried to reassure its remaining European policyholders that it would make good on any proper claim under the policy in case of war, either through the now tiny Berlin office or directly from New York. But the vicious efficiency of the German blitzkrieg effectively rendered the promise worthless, and so Guardian and its policyholders had little choice but to wait out the conflagration.[45]

After the war, Guardian's European bank deposits fell into the hands of the emerging communist government of East Germany, whose currency was devalued by 95 percent. The company had lost all control of its real estate in Berlin, and only eventually received some small reparation for its lost European assets from some confiscated German and Japanese assets. It was only in the late 1940s that the company was once again able to try to shed its remaining European liabilities. In 1947, Guardian paid off its Spanish policies, some thirty-nine of them totaling less than $50,000 including paid-up dividend additions. It thereby unburdened itself of expenses that had been running at $6,000 per year, savings that would offset the payoff in five years. A year later, Guardian resolved to liquidate all its remaining small residue of European policies in force. The remaining Swiss policies were liquidated in 1949–50, the Dutch in 1951, and then finally the Belgian and French policies were paid off. A policy worth $1.40, where the policyholder could not be located, was eventually canceled. The dollar value of the policies was trivial compared with the time and expense needed to liquidate policies on a grueling case-by-case basis. In the end, the $27,516 difference between the cost of liquidation and the policy reserves was a wise expenditure. By the end of 1952, Guardian was finally out of Europe, its international business consisting only of a residue of policies in Mexico.[46]

Otherwise, all that remained were some Eastern European claims that trickled in from time to time. Those claims were simply denied on the grounds that it was unlawful for the company to make payments to people living behind the Iron Curtain. Guardian had suffered confiscation of its assets in the region by communist regimes, though in 1967, compensation payments to the company from European governments resumed. All business in that region was finally wrapped up in 1972.[47]

By the mid-1950s, Guardian ceased writing new business in Canada, where stringent regulation posed barriers to group insurance. In 1970, the board of directors authorized a plan for providing insurance to U.S. citizens residing abroad, foreign nationals employed by United States companies either in the United States or abroad, and foreign nationals employed by foreign companies who spend a substantial amount of time in the United States. The board stressed that the resolution did not authorize the officers to open agency offices in foreign countries. By the twenty-first century, even as other life insurers sought new market opportunities outside the United States, Guardian continued to steer clear of foreign entanglements.

The decision to remain focused on the domestic market was made easier by the fact that Guardian for much of the twentieth century found its home market a profitable one. As we shall see, however, those profits did not come easily as the company, industry, and economy faced repeated shocks, including a depression, a second world war, and increased levels of inflation, taxation, and regulation.[48]

3

Boom and Bust

Guardian's domestic business in force grew rapidly in the 1910s and early 1920s because of the successful reorganization of the agency force in 1910 and the unusually large demand for life insurance that took place after World War I. Problems with its overseas operations aside, Guardian emerged from war and pestilence to enjoy its share of prosperity during the "Roaring Twenties." Big business was triumphant. The world of finance had grown respectable, or at least less mysterious, as more and more ordinary people invested their own funds in the bond and stock markets. Once-feared giant industrial corporations—railroads, electric power companies, and producers of chemicals, metals, and machinery— had lived up to their promise as great wealth-creating machines, and the wealth trickled down to ordinary working families who now enjoyed sub-stantial "disposable" income. Working families aspired to increase their income and social status, and more and more people could afford appli-ances powered by electricity, such as motor-driven fans, radios, and toast-ers. They could own their own Model-T Fords and Chevrolets, and install telephones in their homes. Not surprisingly, the demand for life insur-ance also grew.[1]

The "New Era" of the 1920s brought a rising tide of prosperity that came crashing down in the stock market crash of October 1929. As the Great Depression of the 1930s dragged on, big business lost its luster. More and more industries became subject to regulation, much as insur-ance had some thirty years earlier. New sales of whole life policies fell off sharply and remained sluggish until the outbreak of World War II in 1939. Wartime expenditures propelled the economy out of its doldrums but did not significantly lift household consumption, which would resume with force only after the guns fell silent in 1945. Over the momentous two and a half decades from 1920 to 1945, Guardian became a different kind of company. It not only withdrew from its foreign markets, as we have seen;

it also standardized its distribution arrangements and reorganized itself into a full mutual company, which it has remained ever since.

Mutualization and Its Impacts

Carl Heye had observed, in 1916, that there was a general belief among his company's leaders that mutualization would be a good thing. Apparently that belief had been held for some time. Following their decision to change the company's name, in July 1918, Guardian's officers concluded that the psychological moment had come to rid the company of its shareholders and fully mutualize. The fieldmen welcomed the prospect. Charles Rudd, a Guardian sales manager in Evansville, Indiana, for one, in a letter to Heye, said, "There is no doubt in my mind, that the quicker we can mutualize, the better it is going to be. You have no idea how contemptible and dirty the competition is on the firing line." He urged the home office to use the pending auction of its stock by the alien property custodian as a springboard for full mutualization.[2]

Guardian's officers were unable to implement the plan, however. There simply was no time to obtain regulatory approval. As World War I drew to a close, the influenza epidemic wreaked havoc with mortality rates, and then, after the war, the recession of 1921 further squeezed the company's finances, forestalling any hope of financial restructuring until the mid-1920s.[3]

We could not fully appreciate, in retrospect, just how bad things were had not Albert Conway, an official of the New York Insurance Department, conveniently recorded a history of the company's woes. As summed up by that critical observer, Guardian's combined war and influenza losses were especially heavy by industry standards because of the large percentage of the company's business that was outstanding in Germany. The company's mortality ratio more than doubled in the plague year of 1918, as the ratio of surplus and contingency reserves to net policy liabilities fell to the dangerously low ratio of .0263. One of the company's responses to the looming possibility of insolvency was to cut its dividends in half for the following year. But what really saved Guardian from that prospect was the large surplus it had accumulated before the outbreak of war and influenza. The collapse of securities markets in the 1921 recession sharply reduced the value of assets for all life insurance companies, as much as 6 percent of total industry assets. Guardian's investment portfolio, noted Conway, consisted largely of mortgages, "which happened to be very fortunate under the then existing circumstances. It was therefore able to weather this second storm."[4]

One effect of the 1919 dividend reduction was to cut into sales, which prompted Guardian to raise dividends for the three following years. The pressures to do so were manifest from field reports. When 1920 dividends increased to 70 percent of the 1918 level, sales managers complained that the rise was too modest. The net cost of Guardian's policies had increased enough to make it difficult to procure new business. Agents scrambled to convince their prospects that "the personal factor, liberal policy features, our service program, et cetera" were worth the higher cost of Guardian policies. For some individuals, perhaps just one out of ten, this was a losing argument. But it was the large cases that were vulnerable, and the loss of large cases destroyed morale and created dissatisfaction. The cost increases dampened the recruiting of sales agents and adversely impacted persistency rates. The lower-cost Massachusetts Mutual, for instance, had second-year persistency of 92 percent compared to about 75 percent for Guardian.[5]

The weakened market brought these problems in the field into sharp focus. Corporate sales managers, who recruited and oversaw commissioned general sales agents, began to worry about the nonstandard nature of the agreements they made with those agents, who, in turn, could be very arbitrary in the ways they compensated the local agents they recruited to serve as their field force. A 1920 corporate memo on the subject explained that under the present system, "or lack of system," there was no uniformity in agency contracts. Commissions for successful policy renewals were capricious. "Intelligent men will not knowingly enter into such [individualized] contracts," a corporate memorandum concluded. Disgruntled agents, who felt they might have been treated inequitably, would, and did, encourage policyholders to lapse. A larger danger was that entire agencies, built up with the company's funds, might move to competitors who offered better, more certain deals.[6]

That the agency contracts were problematic can be seen from the case of a Tulsa general agent, one Mr. Doyle, who died in 1922, leaving his accounts in such disarray that a corporate sales manager, future Guardian president James McLain, had to trek out to Oklahoma to straighten them out. McLain, to his horror, discovered that Doyle had not been paying renewal commissions to his agents for several years. He also discovered that in some cases Doyle had been accepting promissory notes in lieu of cash payments for premiums. McLain urged his superiors "to instruct the Tulsa Agency to make the changes in keeping the agency records" similar to those "that have been installed at a number" of other Guardian agencies. In response to those pressures, the company adopted an agency development program that purported to save it $100,000 over two years. More uniformity in contracting procedures and commissions made agency building easier, attracted a better type of man, and reduced the company's lapse rate.[7]

The process of shoring up the sales force was inevitably intertwined with the problem of corporate organization. When Guardian's board in 1921 finally moved to buy out shareholders and fully mutualize the company, the decision was taken with the field agency problem very much in mind. Though Guardian had always been a mutual in spirit, agent Charles Rudd had pointed out, the public did not appreciate that fact. And the general trend toward mutualization of insurance companies after the scandals of the early twentieth century—Equitable, Home Life, Metropolitan Life, Provident Life and Trust, and Prudential had all moved from stock to mutual forms of organization—had left Guardian looking retrograde. The progress of the industry, combined with the lingering belief that Guardian was a "foreign" company, had eroded "the reputation that Guardian had earned during the Armstrong Investigation," Carl Heye acknowledged. Guardian desperately needed a gambit to attract new salesmen to the company, and full mutualization would be of great value in that important endeavor.[8]

As usual, nothing came easily. The New York superintendent of insurance postponed the company's conversion because it considered the time inopportune. Samuel Untermyer, a prominent trial lawyer and influential crusader for financial reforms, had been busy casting aspersions on the mutualization of life insurance companies. (It was believed in some quarters that stockholder governance, as weak as it had proven to be, was stronger than mutuality, and would, hence, provide better discipline of management.) Another problem was with the terms under which Guardian executives had personally acquired company stock that had been confiscated from German shareholders. A syndicate Hubert Cillis had formed to acquire the stock from the alien property custodian had paid 137.5 percent of the stock's par value. Two years later, the officers proposed to sell the shares to policyholders for twice that amount. The superintendent warned, "It might do the Company considerable harm if it became known that such stock was now being sold by the Company's Officers and their friends at nearly double the price paid two years ago."[9]

Guardian's head sales executive, T. Louis Hansen, was taken aback by the superintendent's intervention. "After all," he wrote to Heye, "it is not a question as to what we paid for the stock sold by the Alien Property Custodian so much as the fact that the Company is under a perpetual obligation to pay 12% on its stock." As for the profits pocketed by the company's directors on the stock transaction, "Surely [the superintendent] does not expect those who participated in the syndicate to give up an 8.6% investment which is perpetual without compensation, even on the part of the Company's officers." The book value of Guardian's stock, after all, was a lofty $1,000. In any case, he argued, criticism of the transaction "would not last one month while the advantages of mutualization would continue so long as the Company transacts business." Besides, it was generally conceded that the only way to mutualize was to buy out stockholders at a fair price, and the current market price of the company's stock could well be deemed fair, owing to decreases in interest rates and improving prospects for business.[10] Such defenses were unavailing.[11]

Seeking an alternative means to their goal, Cillis, Heye, and Hansen agreed personally to acquire any Guardian shares that came on the market. To avoid any criticism, they donated any proceeds from the resale of shares to the company, some $7,500 in all, to the Guardian Welfare Trust, which had been set up to benefit needy home office employees.[12]

In 1924, a new superintendent took office. He understood some of the disadvantages of the mutual form—he noted that directors could use their field force to control policyholder proxies and thereby perpetuate themselves in office—but he was friendlier to Guardian's efforts to get on with it. Guardian had pleaded that its principal shareholders were "well along in years, and that the matter would be likely to be considerably complicated and delayed through their death." That prediction turned out to be all too true.[13]

When the company finally got the regulatory go-ahead in November 1924, it worked fast to obtain stockholder and policyholder acceptance of the plan. Guardian deposited $600,000 in the Bank of the Manhattan Company to provide for the purchase of the company's four thousand shares at $150 each, or 300 percent of par, with the promise that the usual interest and surplus dividends of $4.25 per share would also be paid. Since the going market price for the shares was about $95, it was no great surprise that the voting shareholders were unanimously in favor of the plan. The policyholders were nearly so.[14]

The benefit to policyholders was clear. Guardian would no longer have to pay stock dividends, and since the company had repurchased the outstanding shares from a contingency reserve, mutualization left its statutory surplus unaffected. Most important, full mutuality would restore Guardian's ability to compete more effectively. President Heye wrote an individualized letter to each policyholder who voted against the plan to assuage any fears that the move would somehow cost them money. At least it would not cost them involuntarily. Mutualization became a useful occasion for Guardian's agents to contact their existing clients and sell them more insurance. The change in organization seemed to have very positive effects in the market. Company sales for the first half of 1925 were 30 percent greater than those of the same period a year earlier.[15]

Still, one small thread remained loose in the whole business, and it would prove somewhat nettlesome. Legal complications connected with the liquidation of the estate of a deceased stockholder left ten shares of stock unredeemed. Its conversion hung in limbo for many years, so Guardian technically remained a mixed company and continued to pay dividends and to create stockholder documents. Guardian at long last became a fully, bona fide mutual company in January 1946. At first, the rating agency Moody's and some policyholders had been a little confused with the situation, but the economic effect of the twenty-year delay was minimal, since Guardian was essentially paying dividends to itself on all but the ten stray shares.[16]

Happy Days in the New Era

Following a steep drop in business in the depression of 1921, Guardian increased its dividends. This fortunate offset to the economic crisis had been possible because of decreased agency costs and strong investment earnings. But the board also decided to mark to market the value of its European business on its 1921 annual statement, a change that posed a shock for the company's balance sheet. The German mark was then worth just a penny; its traditional rate had been closer to twenty-four cents. "While the material decrease in the assets at first glance may seem disturbing," Carl Heye told the company's managers, "it should be borne in mind that an exceptional financial strength of the Company is thus revealed more clearly than ever before."[17]

Heye, Hansen, and the other executive officers discussed how best to report the write-down in the annual report and to the insurance press, in particular the insurance rating agency Best's. After much bickering over language—Hansen, the salesman, wanted to accentuate the positive; Heye, the buttoned-down executive, wanted to avoid "self-glorification"—it was decided to refer to the new surplus fund created to account for the write-down as a "Special Reserve for Contingencies." This was probably better than the original name for it: "European Exchange Fluctuation Fund."[18]

The following year Guardian made a slight change in its calculation of dividends to lower the net cost of its insurance policies, bringing them into closer alignment with competing companies. The change increased dividends from 5 percent to 30 percent, the benefit accruing principally to life policies of recent issue at the younger ages. Again, the more liberal dividends were made feasible by the company's improving financial condition, which brought its surplus, which generally ran high, closer to maximum statutory levels. Indeed, by 1924, Guardian's investment portfolio was in great shape. Only one mortgage was in default and in that case the equity in excess of the mortgage was at least 80 percent. Very few of the company's securities were in default and the amortized value of its securities was less than 0.5 percent greater than its market value.[19] And its European assets, battered as they were, still had market value entirely sufficient to cover any liabilities that might arise. Guardian increased dividends again in 1925, which placed it in the highest class of low-cost insurers. Thus, just a few years after the Great War had threatened to wreck its business, the cost of Guardian's core whole life product was by some measures lower than that of all other companies, except Union Central and Sun Life of Canada.[20]

Guardian's superior market position became crystal clear in November 1925 when one of its Rochester, New York, agents, Ernie Houghton, set a world's record for the most business submitted in one month by a life insurance agent: $876,300, spread over 690 policies. Houghton also broke the record for the most applications submitted in one day: 117. That topped the measly 101 applications submitted, interestingly enough, by Guardian's Shreveport agent E. A. Gillespie the previous 31 August! Guardian was most proud of the fact that none of Houghton's business had been "forced"; most applications were accompanied by checks for the entire first premium. Houghton hit his mark because he shrewdly publicized his bid for the world's record. Of course, all conceded that he could not have broken the record had he not been an outstanding underwriter selling a highly competitive product.[21]

Guardian's products were so competitive in the mid-1920s because its investment earnings were relatively good, being well above the industry average. Moreover, its mortality experience was good. Like many insurers, Guardian had launched a Health Services program, aimed at educating people to basic facts about self-care and hygiene. It was effective. And the company reinsured effectively by reinsuring anything, in the words of Guardian actuary Irving Rosenthal, "which looked a bit off-color." The cost of reinsurance was low and the company's expenses were low. In addition, because of more carefully written general agent contracts, low home office salaries, and modest increases in staff, Guardian did so well that by 1926 it was about to exceed its statutory limit for writing new business. Then, in 1927, the company's sales force set a new record for paid in business. The rate of return on invested assets increased—from a low of 4.47 percent in 1920 to 5.82 percent—and mortality registered at a mere 48 percent of expectations. The following year, Guardian cut its premiums on term policies and significantly slashed its surrender charges, and the company finished the decade with an enviable reputation for its efficient agency organization and its financial acumen.[22]

The one sour note was the passing in 1927 of T. Louis Hansen, whose unexpected death was caused by the onset of an infection. Hansen, who had joined the company as an actuarial clerk in 1896, had moved over to the newly formed agency department in 1910, and over the next seventeen years oversaw the growth of the distribution side of the business. His restructuring efforts in that area had yielded enormous efficiencies, and he had been one of the company's key voices in policymaking. That he was to be succeeded by James McLain turned out to be an unexpected stroke of good fortune.[23]

The Relentless Debacle

The morning of 29 October 1929 had dawned bright and clear. When Guardian's employees arrived at their desks and began the day's work, as usual, they had no inkling of the portentous events the day would bring forth. By midmorning, Union Square was teeming with people talking and gesticulating as if discussing something of importance. Newsboys rent the autumn air with the ominous shouting of headlines that Guardian employees, toiling at their desks, could not decipher. Then word arrived by wire that the stock market had broken and that a panic was on in Wall Street. A flood of telephone calls, telegrams, and face-to-face visits then swamped the policy loan department as frenzied policyholders sought immediate loans to cover margins to prevent their being wiped out. A wild-eyed, harried crowd besieged the office for the rest of the day. The policy loan department had to borrow clerks from other departments to keep up with the demand. And it only got worse; within a few months, the department doubled in size.[24]

The panic was the beginning of a protracted market decline that would last three years, but then it was *just* a market crash. Generally the year wound up as another solid chapter in Guardian's performance, as did 1930, the first full year of the Depression. Mortality rates increased a bit due to a rash of suicides and accidents tied to the adverse economic situation. But people were also queuing to buy larger amounts of term insurance to offset the blow to their estates wrought by the market downturn. The onset of the Depression meant lower prices, which helped the company keep its operating expenses in line, even while aggregate salaries increased because the rapid expansion of the company's business required the engaging of twenty-one more employees than anticipated. Investment returns increased as risk premiums on bonds increased, and since the company held no stocks of any kind, the stock market plunge affected Guardian only indirectly, in an increase in the volume of policy loans.[25]

Carl Heye waxed optimistic as the economy drifted into depression. There was no reason to assume that the slump would be uncharacteristically long. The business cycle could be great in amplitude, but historically downturns had generally been as mercifully brief as they had been sharp. In 1930, Heye addressed his employees, looking forward, he said, to "the splendid future which lies in store for our Beloved Company." The splendid part of the future was farther off than he thought.

The Great Depression presented a multitude of severe challenges to the insurance industry. Guardian survived the period, doing well at times, for a complex set of reasons that changed from year to year. No one factor—changes in sales volume, mortality rates, investment income, expense ratios, cash management, regulatory policy—determined the outcome. The dynamic mix of factors was what mattered. A bad year in one arena might be offset by success in another. The trick was to do enough things well to stay afloat.

For example, when sales slumped sharply in 1931, mortality rates saved the day. They were just 47 percent of the expected toll, the best in a decade, and directly opposite the industry trend. Guardian managed also to maintain a relatively high yield on its investment portfolio, 5.71 percent. Low strain from new business, lower costs, improved mortality, and good investment income all combined to help Guardian achieve a $4.1 million gain in its surplus, a record high. The gain was based on the National Association of Insurance Commissioners (NAIC) valuation of bonds, not their current market rates, but even if marked to market, Guardian's balance sheet was in good shape.[26]

The Depression seriously caught up with Guardian late in 1931, when the Finance Committee resolved, in October, to decide upon dividends quarterly, instead of annually as it traditionally had. The announcement of this new policy caused enough of a stir that the committee backed off a bit, promising, in effect, not to alter the dividend unless an unexpected contingency should arise. The contingency surfaced in the third quarter of 1932, when Guardian bent to the inevitable and decreased its dividend by 15 percent.[27]

Guardian's underwriting was certainly not to blame; the company's mortality results remained extraordinarily low at the rate of 49.75 percent of expectations, some ten points lower than the average for comparable life companies. (Over the period 1924 to 1931, Guardian's mortality experience was significantly better than the average mortality of thirty-one leading companies.) Guardian's mortality experience would remain extremely favorable until the first half of 1934, and then it worsened somewhat. In the meantime, blame for the dividend reduction was placed on a host of other ills: increases in taxation, postal rates, and cash calls and decreases in interest rates on investments suitable for life insurance companies, in sales of new business, and in confidence about the future. Defaults in Guardian's mortgage portfolio also increased. There had been almost no significant mortgage defaults from 1918 through 1927. Defaults rose a bit in the later 1920s, then surged to over $3 million by the end of 1931, and continued to occur as the Depression ground on. Securities yields fell, too.[28]

Carl Heye positioned the lowering of the dividend as "a proper and conservative step under the prevailing conditions." Newspapers that covered the rate cut noted that the company remained strong and that it technically could have maintained dividends if it thought that economic conditions would soon improve.[29]

Hard times often make for good discipline, and opportunistic spending. Guardian responded to the Depression by inaugurating a series of operating reforms. To improve mortality rates Guardian installed new equipment for the medical department, including an X-ray machine, electrocardiograph, and fluoroscope. Cost-reducing reforms included the creation of a statistical department, the rewriting of cards in the premium record department, and personnel reductions that offset salary increases for the most efficient employees. Guardian's executives slashed their own salaries by 10 percent, along with those of their employees, except for low-paid clerical help. Salaries remained lower until business picked up in the latter part of the 1930s.[30] (See table 3-1.)

As for policies in force, the major setback came in 1933 when sales of ordinary insurance slumped and policy surrenders increased. For Guardian, it was the worst year of the Depression, made worse for the Guardian by the termination, in late 1932, of its most productive general agent, the John C. McNamara Organization, in a dispute over expenses. McNamara's agency, which boasted forty-four full-time and hundreds of part-time agents, had directly accounted for about a third of the company's new business since 1925, and indirectly for more, since McNamara had willingly shared his considerable sales and training expertise with other Guardian agencies.[31]

TABLE 3-1

Guardian's Employees, Total Payroll, and Average Payroll, 1926–37

Year	Total Officers and Employees (#)	Total Payroll ($)	Average Payroll ($)
1926	235	460,045	1,957.64
1927	249	477,506	1,917.69
1928	248	497,929	2,007.78
1929	278	530,458	1,908.12
1930	308	604,069	1,961.26
1931	306	610,925	1,996.49
1932	305	602,122	1,974.17
1933	—	575,268	—
1934	—	570,101	—
1935	—	579,919	—
1936	—	595,919	—
1937	—	625,838	—

Source: Minutes of the Board of Directors, 26 April 1933, 19 December 1934, 18 December 1935, 16 December 1936, 15 December 1937, Box 5, GLIC archives.

By then, according to some accounts, Guardian was on the brink of failure. Some observers had been predicting the collapse of a large number of life insurers because they did not appreciate the gravity of the "banking" features—policy loans and cash surrender values—built into modern life contracts. Guardian, which kept very low levels of cash, appeared very much at risk. Accounts of Guardian's troubles, however, appear to have been grossly overblown. The internal record certainly does not support them. (See table 3-2.) What they show is that Guardian emerged relatively unscathed from the 1933 banking crisis, during which time a large number of financial institutions either failed or were simply padlocked by the federal Treasury Department. In general, the insurance industry enjoyed a high survival rate, experiencing nothing like the rash of bankruptcies and failures it had endured in the 1870s.[32]

After the Democrats took the White House under Franklin D. Roosevelt, Carl Heye rankled at the ensuing New Deal social welfare programs. He extolled life insurance as the ultimate tool for obtaining economic and social welfare "without involving political expediency and class strife, which only too often have proved to be the incentive for ill-advised social measures."[33]

Those qualms notwithstanding, it helped that government regulatory policy was on the company's side. Guardian received succor in three ways. First, many jurisdictions in the United States called a moratorium on policy loans and other voluntary cash benefits. Though life insurers still had to pay death and other core benefits promptly, the sources of the most serious strains on their cash flows were held in abeyance. The moratorium worked because many Americans supported it as a necessary though unpalatable measure. Second, state regulators gave life companies some leeway in the valuation of their assets, which enabled companies to dress up their balance sheets. Third, the federal government instituted a wide range of reforms—from deposit insurance to securities regulation—that began to restore some faith among investors in the financial sector.[34]

TABLE 3-2
Guardian's Bank Deposits and Cash on Hand, March 1933

Date	Balance in Banks ($)	Cash on Hand ($)	Total ($)
3 March 1933	390,100.97	3,360.74	393,461.71
9 March 1933	381,878.23	4,588.65	386,466.88
28 March 1933	805,010.21	3,309.65	808,319.86

Source: Finance Committee Minutes, 29 March 1933, Box 16, GLIC archives.

The second half of 1933 brought substantial improvement in new sales and a marked decrease in policy loan applications, so much so that Guardian's Finance Committee toyed with the idea of restoring dividends. "Owing to the difficulty . . . of determining with any degree of assurance what the outcome of the recent revolutionary changes in the general and financial situation of the Country would be," however, the committee "concluded that the conservative action on the dividend question was indicated, which would result in a further strengthening of the Company's financial condition." Moreover, Guardian's net rate of return was sagging due to lower interest rates and higher cash holdings. Thus, as an alternative to increasing dividends, the company bolstered two of its "special" reserves: those against depreciation of the home office and other real estate holdings, and a reserve against other contingencies.[35]

The decision proved wise when, in January 1934, new paid-for business ran 33 percent ahead of the previous year's figures. Sales remained at those levels throughout the year, as policy terminations decreased by 24 percent. It was another reasonably favorable year for mortality, at least by industry standards. On the other hand, double indemnity claims, due largely to increased automobile accidents, rose 9 percent.[36]

Publicly, Carl Heye, like other financiers, waxed optimistic about the state of the economy, the industry, and the company. "It is true that the outlook for business generally is still somewhat obscure," he told leading sales agents at the Leaders Club convention at the Waldorf-Astoria in July 1935, "but after all, a remarkable improvement has taken place since 1932, when the lowest point in the depression was reached. . . . The forces making for recovery continue strong." Privately, the general pessimism of the Depression era had become indelibly etched in the behavior of Guardian's executives. They could not but forecast a grim future for their company's long-term earnings. Guardian's new investments, like the investments of many of its peers, went mainly into ultra-safe, hence ultra–low-yield, securities—not a bad idea, since by the end of 1934, the market value of Guardian's securities actually *exceeded* the more liberal convention values by some $300,000. Along with other leading life insurers, Guardian slashed to 4 percent the interest rate assumption in its dividend scale, and then did so again, to 3.75 percent in 1935. It went to a 3.5 percent basis in 1938. The lower assumptions meant moderately lower dividends to policyholders but much greater safety.[37]

What Guardian did not dare to do in this period was to risk its reputation with policyholders for fair and prompt treatment of claims. If anything, the company went out of its way to demonstrate its magnanimity toward beneficiaries. When Edward Nelson of Chicago died in early 1934, he owned a $10,000 Guardian policy. But he also owed a $1,500 policy loan and a $12,500 mortgage. Guardian could have applied the $8,500 net due on the policy to the mortgage but thought it "unfair to the widow to insist upon the Company's right." Instead, the company disbursed $3,500 in cash to the grieving spouse, and kept the remaining $5,000 on deposit as security for the balance of the mortgage.[38]

There was the usual mix of positive and negative factors—but generally positive—in 1936, when Guardian achieved some gratifying progress after pushing the sale of higher-premium forms of policies. Assets grew, income exceeded disbursements by a wide margin, and new paid-for business, bolstered by a national advertising campaign, jumped 13.3 percent. Total life insurance in force increased and surplus and reserves remained strong, though investment returns continued to sag due to lower interest rates and continued emphasis on government and high-grade corporate debt. Tax increases adversely affected operating expenses, though, and mortality rates spiked. Luckily, those losses were offset, as agents began more reliably to repay their advances and as income from real estate improved. Another strong year followed, setting records for premium and total income. Mortality improved markedly. Among the problems was the discovery of shortages in the company's agencies, which prompted an increase in agency fidelity bond coverage by $100,000. A bigger worry was that, according to a study by Northwestern Mutual, Guardian's net cost ranking had deteriorated to twenty-first place among insurers.[39]

After a period of slow recovery, just when the struggles of the 1930s seemed over, the economy turned sharply downward in 1937–38. The causes lay in the political system. Monetary mismanagement by the federal government and political affairs in Europe were roiling the markets and dampening investment. Business cratered in the renewed despondency of depression, and Guardian, cautious as ever due to the prevailing worldwide economic conditions, established a special investment fluctuation reserve of $1 million. The company cut its dividend scale again in 1939, losing further ground in the cost category.[40]

Guardian's high net costs eventually began to cut into sales. (See table 3-3.) To stem the decline, Guardian's sales department introduced the Graph Estate, a sales presentation designed to garner new or extended

TABLE 3-3

*Insurance Industry Twenty-Year Net Cost of
Policies Continued and Surrendered, 1939*

Company	20-year net cost, policy continued ($)	20-year net cost, policy surrendered ($)
Prudential	361.69	50.69
Penn Mutual	364.06	56.48
Northwestern	367.56	39.98
Metropolitan	370.15	37.31
Provident Mutual	371.79	61.79
New York Life	373.83	46.83
New England Mutual	387.58	60.00
Mutual Benefit	388.10	60.52
Equitable of Iowa	389.44	78.44
Massachusetts Mutual	392.45	64.67
National Life (Vt.)	393.88	66.30
Equitable of New York	396.12	69.12
State Mutual	398.79	71.21
Connecticut General	404.03	93.03
Mutual Life of New York	404.08	76.50
Connecticut Mutual	405.04	77.40
Union Central	407.72	97.72
Banker's Life	408.05	97.30
John Hancock	410.11	99.11
Guardian	**410.16**	**82.58**
Phoenix Mutual	410.38	78.93
Aetna	414.73	83.73
Pacific Mutual	435.36	132.36

Source: Williamson and Smalley, *Northwestern Mutual Life*, 253. Courtesy Northwestern University Press.

business from existing policyholders. Agents were trained, in this new program, to focus more on their clients' estate planning needs. The Graph Estate, so called because it laid out each client's estate in an easy-to-understand graphical format, was designed to have a positive influence on income settlements, whereby Guardian paid beneficiaries interest on benefits in lieu of the full face value of the policy. Income settlements left assets under Guardian's control and helped to smooth out cash flows. The company advertised that the settlements under the plan aided beneficiaries by helping them to budget more carefully. "People spend more wisely when they receive money in small, periodic payments," the company claimed, "than when they get it in big lump sums." The market success of the Graph Estate helped Guardian plow slowly ahead for the balance of the Depression. The company registered modest improvement in most categories, though new sales continued to slack off.[41]

"Shaking Off the Blues" with James A McLain

Slumping sales may have spelled the end of Carl Heye's presidency. At age sixty-three, he was replaced in the job with an agency man, James A McLain, effective in January 1940. Another salesman, agency manager Frederic Doremus (son of the former company president Cornelius Doremus) was appointed to the board. Though Heye, in a letter to Berlin director Wilhelm Remppis, insisted that his resignation was "entirely voluntary," it was certainly a good time to shift the orientation of top management from financial management more to the sales side of the business. Change was certainly afoot, so clearly the aging and conservative Heye was no longer the best person for the top spot. Whether nudged aside, "kicked upstairs," or not, Heye continued to serve as chairman of the board through 1944.[42]

McLain, just forty-one years old, hailed from Urbana, Ohio. Like another Midwesterner, Harry S Truman, McLain possessed a middle initial but no middle name. More important, he represented a symbolic, as well as substantive, change in the company's top management. He was the first native-born, non-German ethnic president of Guardian, and the first to come from the nation's heartland. After a stint with the Provident Mutual of Minneapolis, McLain, a "very progressive" individual, had joined Guardian in 1920 as an agency assistant. The son of a life insurance agent, he graduated from Urbana University, the Case School of Applied Science, and the Carnegie Institute's school of life insurance salesmanship. He hit the floor running, touring the nation with T. Louis Hansen before setting foot in the home office. His talent and enthusiasm brought quick promotion to assistant superintendent of agencies in 1924 and inspector of agencies in 1925. He replaced Hansen as superintendent of agencies in 1928, and two years later, became a vice president. After Guardian made him president, he would serve in the post for seventeen years. He remained as chairman until the end of 1963, when he retired into a consultancy role at age sixty-five.[43]

McLain was animated, if not boisterous, a hard drinker, and tough as nails, according to those who knew him. When he died in 1977, the board could state without exaggeration that his "dynamic leadership, innovative ideas and boundless energy . . . were key factors in shaping the company."[44]

Most of all, McLain was the quintessential salesman, a hale-fellow-well-met person who made friends throughout the industry. Industry insiders joked that his middle initial stood for "affable." He served in a number of industry posts, including president of the American Life Convention. At various times, he was a member of the board of directors of the Institute of Life Insurance and the chairman of a committee appointed by the Life Insurance Association of America to examine certain life insurance regulations, a director of the Central Mercantile Association of New York, and president of the New York Chamber of Commerce. McLain's personality and many professional connections helped Guardian to attract quality directors, much as Hugo Wesendonck had done in the late nineteenth century. According to Edward Kane, for many years Guardian's general counsel, McLain was such a magnetic motivational speaker that one could roll him into bed at four in the morning, get him in an eight o'clock meeting, and he would have the agents going, "Yeah, Jim! Yeah, Guardian!" But McLain was not all show; there were some serious brains behind his slick style, as evidenced by his publications and plans.[45]

The new president, it was hoped, could spark the sales force, and he did. Sales increased somewhat in 1940 and literally surged, some 13 percent, in 1941 on the back of the continued success of the Graph Estate program and McLain's efforts to improve agent training.[46]

Additional help came from improvement in the mortality rate in 1941: 43.83 percent of expectations, the lowest recorded rate during the entire history of the company to that time. The rate of return on investments, however, continued downward, slightly below the industry average. "There seems no likelihood of any important change in the [investment] situation at an early date," McLain advised the policyholders.[47]

The industry's net rate of return would not trend upward again until the early 1950s. World War II was very good for the U.S. economy. Enormous federal expenditures, financed by unprecedented deficit spending, was just what it took for the country to go back to work—for companies to produce, for laborers to toil. The government was the most important consumer, and consume it did. The Great Depression was over. It took the war to "fix" the economy, but since the war years were financed with paper currency and pegged yields on government securities, the sagging investment fortunes of Guardian could not improve much until interest rates rebounded. Low investment earnings due to massive purchases of low-yielding government bonds necessitated further dividend reductions. Patriotism had its price. In 1943 all policies went to a 3.3 percent basis, applied to the mean reserve instead of the initial reserve as before, which led to a further 20 percent reduction in dividends. The cumulative effect of dividend reductions between 1932 and 1943 had been to reduce dividends by about 50 percent.[48]

The December 1941 bombing of Pearl Harbor had many effects on the company, some positive. The most immediate was to force the home office to extinguish the light from its enormous sign, high atop Union Square, lest it become a beacon to enemy aircraft and submarines. The threat of attack, if only sabotage, seemed imminent, so Guardian began microfilming its most important records and even snapped shots of its bonds, just in case the originals burned in their safe deposit storage. The home office installed a new siren, which the local authorities refused to allow it to test. Fortunately, it was never needed.[49]

Six months into the conflict, McLain formed Guardian's War Cabinet, a committee of eight employees charged with coordinating and accelerating the company's war-related activities. The War Cabinet had authority to draft for service any member of the staff at any time. Among other activities, the cabinet established a Guardian "community chest" for disbursing donations of the four staples of life—blood, books, cash, and clothing—and created a special newsletter, *The Bond*, for Guardianites serving in the armed forces. It coordinated everything from fire drills to recycling campaigns, and urged employees to save at least 10 percent of their salaries by purchasing war bonds.[50]

A new War Service Bureau served as a "watchdog within the company for policyholders-in-Service." It helped its armed-service insureds to make or delay premium payments under such government programs as the Soldiers and Sailors Relief Act. The bureau also aimed to help discharged veterans to update their insurance coverage and to obtain suitable employment. It was not all patriotism. Common business sense prevailed soon after America's entry into the war, when Guardian thumbed a war exclusion clause into its new contracts. There were still plenty of Guardian policyholders in combat, and by early 1942, the first killed-in-action claims were received and paid.[51]

Even though some Guardian policyholders faced bonsai attacks, kamikaze raids, Normandy's deadly hedges, and Tiger tanks, the company's wartime mortality experience was extremely favorable, reaching all-time lows in 1941 and 1942. Not until 1944 did the mortality rate exceed 50 percent of expectations. The reason for the low mortality had less to do with the war exclusion clause than with some of the leading causes of death in Americans. Save for Pearl Harbor, the war barely touched American soil. The denizens of Castle America did not have to face the horrors of the Blitz or invasion by land. Battle casualties were but a small fraction of the yearly death toll. (During all of World War II, about four hundred thousand Americans died in service. In the same period, an annual average of some 390,000 Americans died of heart ailments alone.) Antibiotics and improving medical treatment reduced many conventional forms of mortality, and even the war itself reduced some causes of death. Gasoline rationing, for instance, sent the traffic death rate plummeting. As soon as the war ended, Guardian removed war and aviation restrictions on new policies.[52]

Another by-product of the war was a spike in the company's labor productivity. During the war, total assets and insurance in force reached record levels as Guardian continued on its moderate growth path. Guardian, like most other large employers, had extended liberal benefits to employees who joined the armed services even before U.S. entry into the war, and it continued those benefits with an employment reinstatement guarantee. For that reason, and because the government imposed salary controls, Guardian did not replace employees who left for military service (or for other reasons), instead attempting to squeeze more output out of remaining workers through a work-week extension of 2.5 hours (7 percent) and more diligent work. Thus the increase in sales occurred as the home office staff shrank by a quarter and its field staff shrank some 40 percent by the autumn of 1943. The reduced field force sold increasing amounts of more persistent new business, as the Graph Estate plan met with appreciative acceptance by new and old policyholders. Guardian salesmen produced an average of $127,000 of new business in 1944, compared to only $99,000 per agent in twenty comparable companies. It is well to remember that Guardian served a higher-than-average market niche, but quality training and sheer sweat accounted for much of the company's increased efficiency.[53]

Guardian responded to its net cost pressures by appealing to the patriotism of policyholders. The 1941 annual report was devoted to a fourfold explanation of how Guardian contributed to the war effort.

• Directly—through the purchase of securities issued by the United States, thereby supplying the sinews of war.

- Indirectly—through the financing of various corporate and individual enterprises. . . .
- Directly—through furnishing both trained and untrained man-power for active military . . . service.
- Directly—through the use of its trained sales organizations . . . to help in the widest possible distribution of Defense Bonds.

The company also pointed out that its officers and staff were personally investing in Treasury bonds, and that the company was establishing a payroll deduction plan to facilitate employee purchase of government bonds.[54]

It was favorable mortality and flat expenses that canceled out the company's decreased investment earnings in the last years of the war, allowing the board to maintain the dividend scale adopted in 1943. Some expense reductions were achieved through reduced agency allowances and reorganization of the home office. No savings was considered too small. In early 1944, Guardian took advantage of reader interest in advertising media by distributing its annual report as advertisements in newspapers and magazines rather than printing the report separately as a pamphlet. The tactic may help explain the surge of business that followed, a 26.5 percent first-quarter increase in sales. Ultimately, said Irving Rosenthal, the company's chief actuary, "our biggest selling point was the fact that we hadn't gone broke."[55]

The Outbreak of Peace

Many business leaders feared that the end of war, with all the buildup of "excess capacity," would plunge the nation back into depression, but the outbreak of peace unleashed enormous pent-up consumer demand. There was a brief downturn, a postwar adjustment, but another American economic "boom" was about to begin, this one characterized by a great growth in population, massive migration to the suburbs, and high rates of household consumption.

At Guardian, skepticism was the order of the day. Irving Rosenthal and other executives fretted that the company was headed for deep trouble. Its annual earnings were $4 per $1,000 of insurance in force less than Northwestern Mutual, $3 less than Connecticut Mutual, and $2.50 less than Massachusetts Mutual. Rosenthal felt that "something fairly drastic had to be done to keep us alive and moving in the new competitive atmosphere which was about to be born."[56] Lots of life insurers—perhaps too many—had come through the Depression intact. Only the strongest would survive.

Guardian's business, already sprouting nicely, bloomed in 1946. Its new life sales soared 47 percent above previous year levels. Income and surplus levels also showed double-digit increases. The company's lapse rate in 1946 was 1.3 percent, a strong improvement over 1939, when lapses ran at 4.22 percent. But nothing was to be taken for granted.[57]

Jim McLain responded to Rosenthal's challenge by launching a six-pronged plan of attack that was little short of a complete restructuring. First, he moved to shore up the board of directors by recruiting commercial banker James A. Jackson and Brooklyn Dodgers owner Branch Rickey in December 1945. Rickey, who owned life insurance policies valued at hundreds of thousands of dollars, had known McLain since their boyhood days in Ohio.[58]

Second, McLain authorized a new category of sales agent, the field representative, who would be a company employee remunerated with a salary and merit bonus rather than a subcontractor paid on straight commission, as had been the custom. Moreover, in 1948, McLain bolstered the company's sales training programs, creating the office of director of field training and staffing it with a certified life underwriter named Paul E. Van Horn.[59]

Third, the company put the brakes on reinsurance, which had grown increasingly expensive after 1938. Guardian's board had long since discussed the fact that much of the standard business that it reinsured might profitably be retained by the company, but postponed action until sufficient mortality studies could be concluded. The war delayed action on this matter, but in 1947, the company listened to the world's leading expert on retention limits, none other than its own Irving Rosenthal, and increased its retention limit for policies for ages twenty-six to fifty inclusive.[60]

The fourth reform was cultural in nature, an attempt to shore up office morale and efficiency by relaxing what Rosenthal termed the company's traditional "Prussian office discipline." The Teutonic reference may have reflected some prejudice on Rosenthal's part, but it is true that during the long German-dominated period of the company's history, from Hugo Wesendonck to Carl Heye, office discipline was tight, not atypical of the times, but certainly formal by postwar standards. A scan of Rules for the

Guidance of Home Office Clerks from various years reveals such stipulations as the following:

1. The office hours are from 9 A.M. to 4 P.M. (Saturdays 9 to 1)[61] with thirty minutes for luncheon, except on Saturdays.
2. Each clerk must be at his desk at 9 A.M. sharp.[62]
3. It is desired that some kind of coat be always worn in the office.
4. Smoking is not permitted [hard medicine for mid-twentieth-century employees].
5. Communications between male and female clerks must be confined to matters pertaining to the company's business.
6. Clerks must not leave their desks during business hours, except on business of the company.
7. Clerks must see that their desks present a neat appearance.
8. Each clerk is to confine his attention strictly to his own work.
9. Each clerk is employed on trial and is not entitled to any notice of dismissal until he has been in the employ of the company for at least one year. Thereafter a month's notice will be given unless dismissal is due to misconduct or a violation of these rules.[63]

Another rule, promulgated by Doremus in 1907, was that anyone caught "playing the races" would be dismissed "instanter." (Employees could play cards at lunch as long as no wagering was involved.) Though such rules seemed reasonable for the workplace, the tone was severe and the day-to-day reality very authoritarian. Managers pronounced, employees responded, and that was the end of it. As small group underwriting manager Helen Sulyma later recalled, "in the old days, you just did as you were told."[64]

Guardian's postwar office environment would change radically. Higher salaries and formal job evaluation schemes were the order of the day. More traditional forms of patronage gave way to meritocracy. Managers learned to listen better. In 1946 Guardian had in place an employee-run advisory board charged with studying problems affecting employee welfare and efficiency. The new body, which consisted of a diverse group of seven members elected by fellow employees, met monthly to generate constructive suggestions for improvement of relations with the members of home office staff and with policyholders. Having kept employee salaries as low as possible for most of the century, Guardian right after the war increased the salaries of home office employees, other than officers, by 8.33 percent in order to maintain wage parity with other New York City life insurers. In accordance with strong employee sentiment, Guardian began to pay clerical salaries biweekly instead of semimonthly, and in 1947, in recognition of exceptional efforts, the board of directors granted the clerical staff an additional 8 percent bonus.[65]

All these moves probably reflected increasing competition for good clerical help, and Guardian thereafter kept pace with employee salary trends becoming evident in the New York area. Corporate officers were not overlooked. Company executives, whose salaries remained flat during the war, were granted a 20 percent pay increase on average. McLain was the big winner; his salary increased from $35,000 to $50,000—about $500,000 in end-of-century terms.[66]

As compensation levels were raised, the company shelved its "antiquarian manual procedures," rules that were simply "inefficient and high cost," according to Rosenthal. The home office building was modernized in 1948 at a cost of $98,000,[67] as new time-saving office equipment was installed.

Finally, Guardian appointed a new manager to oversee its investment fortunes, a young finance genius named George Conklin. Conklin predicted that if given the authority he could lead Guardian back to the top of its industry in investment returns. He got it, and he did, in just a few years.[68]

4

Good Times, Hard Times
in the Postwar Era

As the second half of the twentieth century dawned, Guardian's chief actuary, Irving Rosenthal, was pleased with his company's state of affairs. Guardian, he wrote, had finally overcome its struggle to achieve more "economies in operation . . . without lessening the quality of service." Rosenthal may have been sanguine, but his CEO, Jim McLain, was decidedly impatient. New policy sales were not increasing rapidly enough to suit him. While the company was putting on a good face to its existing policyholders, he was reading the riot act to his sales managers. "What's wrong?" he demanded to know in a June 1949 meeting of Guardian's Field Advisory Board.[1]

The sales managers had an answer: the home office, they complained, was not doing *its* job. Get tougher with underperforming managers, for one thing, they said; we need more support.

One thing was certain. Guardian had to grow. Only that way could it spread expenses over more policies in force while continuing to look for ways to extract more productivity out of its workforce and administrative systems. A new growth plan was already taking shape that embodied three initiatives: to increase the number of Guardian sales representatives, to arm those sales people with more products, and to improve the relative net cost of the company's products.[2]

Guardian's growth was not to be achieved by altering its time-honored strategy of selling into middle- to higher-income market segments. Instead, the company could try to increase sales in its existing territories with the development of new products at lower premiums, and by embellishing its existing policies. It would do both. But the big opportunities for growth, in McLain's mind, at least, loomed in newer, distant territories. Guardian must first and foremost expand its geographic reach and find familiar-looking customers in more places. McLain's objective was nothing less than to expand, if possible, to all the states of the United States, state by state.[3]

The chief constraint was on the supply side. How could Guardian attract desirable agency men? It would not be easy to find raw talent and nurture it from afar. So rather than establish its own sales offices, the company's agency director, George Mendes, set about enlisting already established independent brokers, a strategy that would prove generally to be successful. By the end of 1949, the push was on to blanket the continental United States with Guardian agents.[4]

The Golden '50s

Geographic expansion was an echo from Guardian's past. It reversed a trend that dated back to before World War I, when the company began its exit from Europe and then contracted its U.S. operations, to become a northeast regional player. In 1917, Guardian had agencies in thirty-six states; in 1931, just thirty-one. Later, Guardian had ceded even more territory.[5]

As Guardian extended its agency coverage westward and southward, it rode a billowing tide in postwar industry fortunes. Higher family incomes coupled with an increase in single-earner middle-class families pushed the demand for life insurance sharply upward. The demand for group insurance grew, too. Pressed by organized labor demands in World War II (when wages and prices had been controlled by the federal government), companies large and small had begun tacking on health and life insurance benefits to worker's compensation. What workers got, managers wanted even more of, and so as the economy boomed in the 1950s, corporate America assumed more and more burdens for social welfare in the form of nonwage benefits. Group insurance was part of the package.

As sales increased in its traditional lines of business, Guardian plowed proceeds back into both new product and new agency development. When the books closed on 1955, marking what purported to be the best year in Guardian's ninety-five-year history, the company made a big investment in agency expansion, pushing into five midsized cities in Virginia, in Texas, and on the West Coast. The following year, it opened ten new offices, bringing the total number of its agencies to eighty, up from sixty-four five years earlier.[6]

Guardian's march into new territories was met by competition from not only other major insurers but also smaller ones, some of which could pose unexpected problems. What could Guardian do, for example, about the nuisance presented by the Guardian Life Insurance Company of South Carolina, just a small, local concern, but one that was poaching on the larger company's reputation? Guardian offered to pay its namesake $20,000 to change its name, and so it did, to the People's Guardian Life Insurance Company! Soon thereafter, the People's Guardian reinsured its business and padlocked its door. The experience was enough to remind Guardian's lawyers to register some six iterations of the company's name, along with three advertising slogans, with the U.S. patent office.[7]

Constrained by its higher-end market strategy, Guardian's annual growth rates, while robust, were lower than the industry average. The company's insurance in force increased from a 6-to-7–percent range in the early 1950s to an 8-to-9–percent range at the end of the decade. During the same period, however, the company's overall share of insurance in force dropped from 0.99 percent to 0.90 percent. This was of no great concern so long as the company could increase both earnings and productivity. The point was to achieve scale, not share, in a growing market.

As much as Guardian rode the rising tide, much of its good fortune in the 1950s was company specific: lower-than-expected mortality, above-market returns on its investments, and an improved expense ratio. To some extent, efficiency gains were mandatory, as new technologies and techniques spread throughout the industry, speeding up data processing and reducing collection costs. The simplest measure of productivity was the volume of insurance it wrote, in constant dollars, per employee, and in the early postwar years, Guardian's productivity by this measure trended upward. Some of this improvement was the result of increasing sales of group insurance, as that new business line grew rapidly relative to ordinary whole life. Dollar for dollar, group insurance was cheaper to write and maintain than individual whole life.[8]

Productivity increases would help Guardian to grow larger still. Efficiency gains came, too, from the ripening of a merit-based compensation system that had begun in the 1940s. Instead of granting a general increase in clerical salaries, as financial institutions had generally done in the past, salary ranges in each employment classification were broadened, giving managers more discretion to reward superior performance.[9]

All this was good news. Guardian's one-hundredth anniversary arrived in 1960 on the heels of the postwar era's first serious recession, when despite some softening of the general business economy, the year ended with new highs in nearly all phases of its operations. An extensive promotional campaign featured the company's history in national advertisements, a short book, and publicity junkets. Guardian also exploited the anniversary to introduce such new products as five- and ten-year term policies convertible to permanent insurance without medical examination. The field force was reportedly delighted by the boost in business they attributed to new products and technical streamlining. When the books closed on its centennial year, the company boasted to its policyholders of its "97 agency offices and district agencies, a dynamic program appealing both to the brokerage market and our full-time sales organization, a strong financial position and an up-to-date investment policy, and a home office organization alert to the challenges ahead." After one hundred years, there was no better time to be in the business.[10]

"No More Rabbits"

When John F. Kennedy took the oath of office in January 1961, optimism ruled: renewed prosperity; space exploration; restored faith in the American way of life; Camelot. For its part, the life insurance business was at the top of its game. Public opinion about the industry was as favorable as it would ever be. The whiff of scandals of bygone years had abated; Armstrong and TNEC were ancient history. Insurance agents were no longer nuisances to be avoided so much as useful service providers, even trusted advisors, for matters of family and employee security. More than 110 million Americans, some 60 percent of the population, owned some life protection. Every family that could afford insurance had some, though of course not as much as the industry thought they should. People were living longer, healthier, wealthier lives, and the future looked bright, as far as the actuarial eye could see.[11]

Of course, nothing good lasts forever. For life insurers, the reversal in fortune began slowly, almost imperceptibly, in the early 1960s, and it accelerated in the following decade. From the end of World War II until about the mid-1960s, the biggest threats to Guardian's business had been intra-industry ones. By the late 1960s, the greater threats to its business loomed from the larger environment in the forms of competition, inflation, and disintermediation.

Years of industry growth had attracted new life insurance ventures, while existing companies continued to expand. (See figure 4-1.) In 1966, Shale Goodman, a Guardian general agent, complained, "There apparently is no such thing as writing a case anymore without the waters becoming muddy with competition." Competition, the bane of all profit seekers, grew ever more intense as new business began to level off. Excess capacity in the industry meant once again, as it had decades earlier, that only the strong would survive a shake-out.[12]

By 1960, the competitive advantages that Guardian had created for itself had already begun to disappear as other insurers slashed term premiums and introduced a quantity discount system similar to its own. Many officers believed that Guardian could gain new competitive advantages by investing heavily in the research necessary to continue to move forward in newer fields. But cutting premiums was the immediate fix. Term premiums were reduced and disability and whole life policy contracts were liberalized to meet competition. However, as Irving Rosenthal put it, "there were no more rabbits left to pull out of the hat." To stay competitive, Guardian was going to have to award bigger dividends. And that would mean increasing earnings, improving mortality, and lowering expenses yet again. Back to the grind.[13]

Another danger of fierce competition was that agents throughout the industry, in their struggle to survive, might cut corners. Cases of fraudulent agency practices grew in number and gravity, once again tarnishing the industry's reputation. Regulatory agencies, in the meantime, tried to lessen the bureaucratic burdens of oversight on companies, which in some cases opened the door for even more shenanigans. Due to its large investment in its lifetime field force, Guardian was largely free of agency graft. The company could not so easily insulate itself, however, from other major sources of turbulence.[14]

A more fundamental challenge to the industry was lurking just beneath the surface of the financial market's awareness. It became manifest by the 1970s: an accelerating trend toward "disintermediation." Householders were shifting savings into mutual funds, pension plans, and direct-investment vehicles that reduced the role of banks, insurance companies, and other traditional financial intermediaries.

And to make matters worse, after years of progress keeping them in check, rising expenses became a problem once again as the rate of infla-

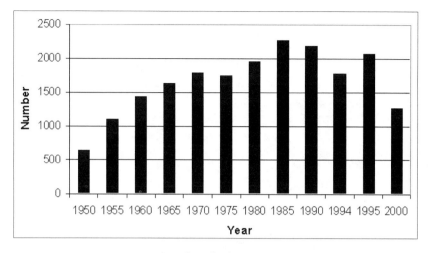

FIGURE 4-1 *Number of Life Insurers, 1950–2000*

tion quickened. The rampant inflation of the 1970s would batter the entire industry, driving up administrative expenses while savaging the real
returns on fixed-income investments.[15]

How did Guardian fare in this changing environment? The company
was not in a "survival situation," Rosenthal wrote in a confidential mem-
oir—its surplus was a healthy 7 percent of liabilities—but it was not terribly competitive, either. Between 1954 and 1963, Guardian had managed to
increase dividend scales seven times, four across the board, and three for
certain classes of policies that made extraordinary contributions to the
company's earnings. But the increases were modest compared to those of
its major competitors. If the problem was how to match the dividends of
its rivals, where would the money come from? Guardian's investment
earnings were already superior to most other life insurers', so little more
could be done on that front, except to work hard to keep them above the
industry average. The company's expense ratio and mortality experience,
on the other hand, were far from enviable and hence ripe for improvement. The task, however, was easier outlined than accomplished.[16]

In 1961, the company implemented the suggestions of a consulting
study by Robert Walker and Associates to try to streamline its administration and update compensation practices. All this was undertaken simultaneously with the implementation of a computerized data processing
system and the construction of a home office annex. A program was

launched in 1963 to spruce up the performance of managers on the firing line—to help the company's first-line supervisors do their jobs more effectively and to help new ones become effective as quickly as possible. Those reforms had only modest effect. In 1963, while Guardian was once again able to proclaim its best year "ever," to its policyholders, an internal report noted that it was only Guardian's "superior investment yields" that were keeping the company competitive. Mortality experience was slipping, and little headway had been made on expenses. Moreover, the company was suffering from some noncompetitive product lines. Guardian was so out of line on annuities, for example, that many field agents thought it better for Guardian simply to withdraw from that business rather than carry them in the rate book at uncompetitive rates.[17]

Two years later, Guardian seemed poised to turn itself around yet again. The group and individual health divisions became profitable even though the introduction of Medicare put something of a damper on both lines, and computerization finally began to pay off. The company also breathed new life into its old workhorse, the Graph Estate, with the introduction of a new electronic Graph Estate that produced strong results wherever the field force could be induced to use it. It was further refined in 1967, to bring it to a more advanced level of estate planning.[18]

Guardian in the mid-1960s increasingly specialized in the small businesses market, especially in group sales. Concentrating on the small business market was still a good long-term strategy. Small business owners generally, then as now, did not purchase enough life insurance to cover their estate tax liabilities. All they needed was to be made "aware," for someone to sit down and talk with them about retirement plans.[19]

By now geographic expansion had given way to extending markets within existing territories. To bolster its sales to small businesses, Guardian launched in 1966 a number of new small business products, including the Guardian Executive Fifty, a novel, easy-to-understand package that offered small firms $50,000 of life insurance, $50,000 of major medical, and $1,000 per month of salary protection for their owners and top executives. The product was launched with aggressive advertising designed to display the tremendous diversity of the company's policies:

> A manufacturer of ballpoint pens has protected himself against the loss of his company's key men—and at the same time set up a tidy cash reserve.

> Two brothers who own a knitting mill have guaranteed each other cash to continue the business if tragedy strikes either of them—and guaranteed the deceased partner's widow a fair price for her share of the business.
>
> The professional employees of a large photography studio enjoy the protection of group life and health insurance and the benefits of a pension plan.

These were followed by an ad in which a dour judge brandishing a gavel looks down upon the viewer, while the question is posed, "How'd you like to have *him* telling you how to run your business?" In the fine print, viewers learned how Guardian could help to protect small businesses from going bankrupt after the death of a partner. "Anyone Can Insure Your Life," the punch line went, but "We Insure Your Life's Work."[20]

Restless Agents

In the small business arena, Guardian was a champion. Yet the company's managers knew that problems were mounting, and that Guardian's overall competitive position was weakening. Expenses and turmoil in process innovation continued to dog the company. What Guardian most sorely needed was improved net costs. In 1967, savings from a program to improve salary management proved negligible, and agency morale sank as home office service deteriorated in a wave of seemingly intractable computer glitches. Some fifty-two critical job vacancies remained open for a long time in 1967, simply because the personnel department found it difficult to fill them with suitable employees.[21]

Faced with growing complaints from the field, Guardian's management promised the old panacea: higher dividends and policy revisions. But unusually high mortality and concerns about the future course of inflation and interest rates prevented it from increasing dividends. (None of that prevented Guardian from announcing "the finest year in its history," which it was able to do by highlighting absolute rather than percentage increases in key categories.) Some relief did come in 1968, when the company raised dividends on the back of strong investment earnings. Mortality, expenses, and taxes remained relatively high, however, almost dashing hopes for a second dividend increase in 1969.[22]

Increased sales agent training and calls to the field for higher-quality business met with an angry response. Guardian's sales managers excoriated the company's officers at a meeting in May 1969, telling them that they had better improve the competitiveness of the individual life products, provide better service to both policyholders and sales agents, and in general respond to the field force with more flexibility. Computer system failures continued to cause headaches for agents trying to service their customers, and headaches spelled lost commissions. Moreover, a sudden and heavy increase in policy loan requests, policy surrenders, and automatic premium loans made life in the field all the more difficult. Irving Rosenthal explained that the home office computer staff would need "another year to iron out all the bugs that now exist in the system," a prediction that proved roughly correct but must have seemed incredible at the time.[23]

Perhaps the biggest irritant to the sales agents was their feeling that they were not trusted to write good business. The gist of their complaint was that Guardian's management, in its desire to impose more quality controls, was disrespectful of their entrepreneurial status. They did not like being treated like employees, with lectures and training on how to sell policies and to whom.[24]

The ferocity of the field's attack on management in 1969 is interesting in several respects. Clearly, the agents were disgruntled, but they did not up and leave. They must have had some faith in Guardian's long-term prospects. The company's investment performance was superior, its lead actuaries among the best in the business, and its officers seasoned professionals, willing to listen and able to respond. If that is what they thought, then they were right. In the short term, President George Conklin launched a special project designed to more precisely identify and improve policyholder service trouble spots. He worked to reduce the number of "people complaints" caused mostly by entry-level employees who were not yet fully "Guardianized." Guardian also concentrated on improving its mortality and expense ratios, and on improving morale in the field and in the home office. The best program for improving morale was to reduce the number of computer problems, which finally happened with the completion of the changeover to the IBM 360 and Guardian's proprietary software, Life Computer System.[25]

The field agents did not always know best; it was also possible for good ideas to emanate from the home office. In 1971, Guardian announced a low premium, low dividend strategy that infuriated members of the field force. Their remuneration, after all, was a percentage of premiums, and they could not imagine that the volume of business stimulated by lower premiums could increase sales enough to compensate them for their lower unit commissions. Policy sales took off, however, and field agents began to clamor for more advertising of the strategy, to emphasize the fact that Guardian's insurance policies were falling in price while everything else was going up.[26]

Decentralization

Since its inception, Guardian had been led by a succession of strong leaders who could, and largely did, run the whole show (the exception being the period when the European business was separately administered). Such centralization of authority was possible in modest-sized corporations, but by the 1960s, Guardian's growth placed too many demands on its president. George Conklin, ever alert to new management concepts, relied on consultants and introduced formal strategic planning meetings, management by objective, and the like, in order to bring more brainpower to the top management table. But the problem remained—too much information overwhelmed the chief executive's office. Market and operating problems were not getting solved in timely fashion. One solution was to share the labor. For much of the 1960s and '70s a "great triumvirate," composed of Dan Lyons, George Conklin, and Irving Rosenthal, ran the company. According to Art Ferrara, the triumvirate gave Guardian a dimension that no other company had. In combination, the triumvirate possessed "genius, guts, and understanding." Of the three, only Rosenthal failed to win the title of CEO, but his imprint on the company was almost as great as that of the company's other prominent leaders.[27]

In 1973, Conklin and Rosenthal implemented a radical reorganization of Guardian's administrative structure. The new organization divided Guardian into business-specific "profit centers," including individual life, health, and group. Instead of having all tactical and operating issues come to the top management for resolution, each profit center had its own general manager. This kind of decentralized organizational structure was nothing new in American business—it extended back to the prewar era in such great companies as General Motors, Dupont, and Procter and Gamble—but had not spread widely throughout the corporate economy until more and more large companies embraced decentralization in the late 1960s.[28]

The idea behind the more decentralized structure was to unleash entrepreneurial activity at lower levels in the company and speed up the resolution of day-to-day problems. Profit center managers were granted considerable autonomy within their scope of operations, while being held accountable for their results, as corporate management now became responsible for monitoring managerial performance instead of creating product-specific strategies and tactics. One beneficial result was to open up high-level career opportunities for ambitious managers who otherwise might never have the opportunity to apply their latent talents for general management. As to compensation, successful profit center managers were remunerated handsomely; there would be no cap on the bonus.[29]

Thus Guardian became almost a federation of companies, all with a common goal but each with a different means of achieving it. The new profit-center structure better enabled the company to expand and diversify its business base without sacrificing control. Guardian's profit-center managers could evaluate new business opportunities related to their product lines. The company would then assess the prospects for investing in new ventures in accordance with the concept of "risk capital," a measure of resources that could be safely invested in new ventures. Rosenthal and Conklin adapted the concept, first developed by Swedish actuaries who specialized in the mathematical theory of risk, defining it for Guardian as surplus that could afford a level of "unfavorable loss" without cutting into dividends. Thus new-venture risks were hedged in that the potential investment losses related to them could be justified as expendable from a policyholder standpoint. On the other hand, a successful new venture could at a minimum cover some of the company's fixed costs. Better, it could help subsidize the traditional individual whole life segment of the company.[30]

With some key problems brought to heel and with a new organization in place, Guardian began to hit on all cylinders again. The year 1972 had been a good one financially, due to high investment earnings and strong profitability in its individual life and group businesses. The next year was even better. The improvements came in the nick of time, for the environment was about to grow worse. The so-called Arab oil shock struck, driving wholesale and consumer prices soaring. Thereafter, for the rest for the decade, accelerating inflation racked the economy, and the insurance industry was especially hard hit.[31]

Inflation and Its Discontents

Inflation was a long-standing fear of the insurance industry. Guardian had sounded frequent alarms about it in its annual reports over the years. In 1947, when the nation's aggregate price level spiked by nearly 15 percent, the company identified inflation as the country's chief domestic problem. In 1958, despite the slowing economy, the annual report identified inflation as "one of the most serious problems our country faces." In 1969, George Conklin wrote that inflation was once again "the life insurance industry's most important problem," and five years later, when inflation soared into the double digits, he cited inflation as "the number one problem in the United States and throughout the free world." He had not seen anything yet. In 1979, as inflation again surged to double-digit levels, Guardian's annual report called inflation "the single greatest danger to our nation's economic health and stable social environment."[32]

In a socially perverse respect, inflation might at first blush seem good for life insurers. As the prices of all goods and services increase, the "real" value of an old policy, which is to say the purchasing power of the face value of the policy, declines. Policyholders, ergo, must purchase more insurance to provide their loved ones with the same level of material comfort. Guardian's management had observed this fact in 1946, noting that "life insurance holdings that might have been considered adequate just a few years ago [before the surge in wartime price levels] fall about 50 per cent short of meeting minimum requirements today." Just as fathers had to increase their sons' allowances for college, that year's annual report explained, companies had to increase their business life insurance, and veterans had to purchase additional policies to supplement their now inadequate government coverage.[33]

The reality has always proven to be different. In inflationary environments, expectations of higher prices might encourage advance buying in a number of markets, as happened dramatically in the high-inflation years of 1978–81. (The effect, of course, was to drive prices even higher.) One can easily envision how this might happen with the purchase of a car or refrigerator, for example. But with insurance the opposite generally occurs; inflation expectations severely dampen insurance sales. The reason for this is simple: when people buy $x of protection, they want to know what goods and services that amount will purchase. Any uncertainty in their minds about the real or inflation-adjusted value of the policy will raise doubts that sales agents will find difficult if not impossible to overcome. More concretely, consider the case of a $25,000 policy purchased with a single premium of $10,000 in a year when one dollar would purchase a savory McDonalds hamburger and Coke. In essence, the policyholder has paid ten thousand lunches today to provide beneficiaries with twenty-five thousand lunches in the future. But suppose that after purchasing the contract, erosion of the value of the dollar forces the price of the McLunch to $3. Now, the policyholder has paid ten thousand today to acquire 8,333.34 (25,000/3) lunches in the future. That is not a very good deal. Admittedly, this example is a bit simplified. Most people pay life insurance premiums annually, not in a lump sum, price increases do not occur all at once, and taxes and dividends are left out of the picture. Add in as much complexity as you like, though, the principle remains the same—inflation can reduce or even eliminate the real returns of ordinary whole life insurance policies.[34]

The litany of problems inflation poses for insurers is lengthy. A summary will suffice. First, inflation kills insurance sales and reduces persistency. Because insurance policies are long term and nominally denominated, even low levels of inflation eat into the purchasing power of a policy's face value, reducing its attractiveness. That induces people to surrender policies, take out policy loans, and slam the door in the face of insurance salespeople. Similarly, inflation can wreak havoc with health insurance lines. Health premiums, unlike life premiums, can be adjusted fairly quickly, but rapid increases in the price of health benefits sometimes outstrip premiums, leading to losses.[35]

Second, inflation increases administration expenses, as everything from paper clips to labor rises in price. Budgets become uncertain and employee efficiency declines. Recruitment, especially of top people, grows more difficult. And, of course, higher expenses means higher net cost to policyholders.[36]

And all that is only one side of the picture. On the asset side of the balance sheet, insurers invest largely in conservative, fixed-income instruments, exactly the kinds of investments that get hammered by inflation. As inflation causes nominal interest rates to increase, the value of existing fixed-income securities, like the bonds and mortgages that compose the bulk of life insurers' assets, declines. (Guardian, like many life companies, had a negative market value for brief periods when nominal interest rates rose quickly.) High rates of inflation and high nominal interest rates also lead to increased delinquencies and defaults. Moreover, high nominal interest rates increase demand for policy loans. Whenever market rates exceed the fixed contractual interest on policy loans, policyholders respond rationally, draining life companies of cash just when they could make investments at propitious rates. Worse yet, policy loans often result in surrenders. Of course, higher nominal interest rates do not always mean higher real interest rates. If inflation increases faster than nominal interest rates, it leaves *lenders* at the end of a loan period with less purchasing power than they started with. Life insurance companies therefore lose purchasing power on many of the loans that they make during inflationary periods.[37]

In short, life insurance and high inflation simply do not mix. As Irving Rosenthal said, "In an inflationary period you have to run faster and faster just to stand still."[38]

Life companies, therefore, have always attempted to hold the line against inflation. In the late nineteenth century, they were solid "gold bugs," lobbying for the conservative monetary policies of William McKinley over the "silverites" like William Jennings Bryan, who wanted to expand the money supply. Guardian was especially sensitive to this debate, which dominated the politics of the era. (The company, recall, had begun its life on the eve of the inflationary Civil War, and later, as it wound down its European business, it suffered more from inflation than most U.S. life insurance companies.) Its employees dutifully lined up for the McKinley Sound Money Parades held in New York in 1896 and 1900. In the 1896 parade, Guardian furnished two full companies of eighteen abreast, fully decked out in brand new brown fedora hats furnished by the company, with huge chrysanthemums (signifying gold standard) on their lapels, and toting solid silk flags on five-foot hickory poles.[39]

In 1933, at the depths of the worst *deflation* in the nation's history, Guardian sponsored a conference where one of the guest speakers evoked the specter of runaway inflation! The prevailing worry was that debtors would pressure the government to depreciate the dollar. As soon as the war buildup began to pull the economy out of its doldrums, insurance companies again began to fret about price increases. In the 1940s, life insurers jumped on the wishful notion that increased sales of life insurance might serve as a brake on inflation (it did not), and tried to combat inflation during the war through professional associations, including the Institute of Life Insurance and the Life Insurance Association of America.

For its part, Guardian warned policyholders of the dangers of inflation, hoping that the price level would follow the same cyclical periods of inflation and deflation that it had in the past. Three years later, Guardian joined 161 other life companies in a far-flung anti-inflation campaign that lasted through the balance of the war. The advertising campaign, which appeared in about three hundred newspapers and periodicals, reached some thirty-five million families.[40]

After World War II, Guardian claimed that its second most important goal, behind financing war and recovery with the purchase of government bonds, was to push with renewed vigor against the peril of inflation. The 1948 annual report complained bitterly of the prevailing inflationary spiral, and George Conklin cheered loudly as Federal Reserve chairman Marriner Eccles took a politically suicidal stand against the central bank's inflationary policy of propping up the market prices of Treasury bonds. In 1950, Guardian devoted an entire section of its annual policyholder report to "The Fight against Inflation." "Not all the dangers we face today," Jim McLain noted just months after the start of the Korean War, "are external." "An even greater potential threat to our national security than armed aggression," he argued, "is that of impairment of our economic health through further inflation." It "bleeds . . . our country's strength." McLain urged policyholders to back six anti-inflationary policy suggestions made by the Institute of Life Insurance, proposals that included higher taxes, higher savings, and lower consumption. It would take "willing, patriotic sacrifice" to swallow those pills.[41]

In March 1951, Guardian's management was elated by the end of the Federal Reserve's pegging of Treasury prices. "For the first time," the company's annual report observed, "a real step forward was taken in the fight against inflation." Budget deficits were now the main worry, because, as George Conklin explained it, growing "deficit financing by the government poses a very serious threat of still further inflationary pressures." Guardian suggested that government slash its deficits by eliminating all nonessential spending, a tactic that it employed itself to great effect. McLain urged policyholders to contact their representatives in Congress and urge them to observe "all possible economy in governmental spending," to cut taxes, and to cease deficit financing. The company's near-obsession with inflation continued unabated over the years. Any inflation was too much. In 1952, McLain warned against the dangers of "creeping inflation": sustained low increases in the aggregate price level that eat away "the value of our money slowly, almost unnoticed."[42]

The problem with "creeping inflation" is that it edged people away from whole life policies toward term insurance. Fearful that rising price levels would erode the real value of their whole life policies, Americans were increasingly buying term at what seemed like bargain prices so that they could invest the savings in mutual funds, common stocks, commodities, real estate, and other forms of wealth expected to provide protection for the owner against inflationary forces.[43]

Five years later, inflation, which conventional macroeconomic doctrine favored as a means to buoy employment, was still creeping away. But Guardian was not so enamored of this social policy. The company made an $8,000 contribution to the Institute of Life Insurance's anti-inflation cooperative advertising program. In 1958, Conklin told life insurance executives that inflation could be stopped if only the government would balance its budget, pull back the reins on the welfare state, tighten up monetary policy, alter tax laws to encourage saving, and induce labor unions to stop pushing for wage increases in excess of productivity gains. That was quite an agenda, and not a winning argument in the political arena. Still, the company insisted that "inflation is neither desirable nor inevitable" and urged its policyholders to support a balanced federal budget. The following year, Guardian pledged its complete cooperation in all steps to prevent continued inflation. In 1963, following a federal tax cut, Conklin raised his voice publicly in favor of more income tax breaks to spur productivity gains. And so on, and so forth, to no avail.[44]

The entire life insurance industry fought the good fight against inflation, but in the end, there was little it could do about U.S. monetary policy or the long descent from gold standard to "fiat" currency. Over the course of the twentieth century, the United States slowly slid off the gold standard. The creation of the Federal Reserve System in 1913 was the first step in the process. By exchanging its liabilities (notes or deposits) for loans, bonds, or other assets, the Federal Reserve could increase the money supply. At first, that power was not a major problem because the banking system still had to convert its liabilities into gold, a crucial and time-tested constraint that served to limit expansion of the money supply. During the Depression, the federal government devalued the dollar and ended its retail convertibility into gold. After World War II, under the Bretton Woods system of fixed exchange rates, the U.S. government maintained huge stockpiles of gold, in Fort Knox and elsewhere, that it pledged to exchange for dollars held by overseas central banks. The system functioned well enough as long as foreign governments were content to hold Federal Reserve notes instead of bullion.[45]

But by the late 1960s, inflation was putting enormous pressure on the fixed-exchange-rate system. (To many financial experts, inflation seemed to dwarf even the Red Menace of communism.) As U.S. inflation increased during the Vietnam War and the massive funding of the Great Society programs, foreign governments began to redeem dollars for gold en masse. The U.S. government ran out of gold, or nearly so, during the Nixon administration, which, in 1973, abandoned convertibility completely. The new dollar was no longer backed by any physical commodity, so all it took to increase the supply was to print notes or, more simply, to credit reserve accounts. The era of the currency "float" and discretionary monetary policy had arrived. And so had the rapid depreciation of the dollar and record levels of inflation.[46]

Though the abandonment of the gold standard disrupted financial markets, Guardian and most other life insurers handled those disruptions with but minor difficulty. The persistent, unprecedented inflation rates of the 1970s, however, would prove more difficult to negotiate. Rapid increases in the aggregate price level raised the net cost of insurance while lowering its net benefit to a degree that became all too obvious to policyholders.[47]

"The fires of inflation," Rosenthal noted, "fried a lot of fat out of all the old line insurance companies." In one respect that was not so bad. If prices rose, companies were forced to find ways to cut expenses, which was good, if there were expenses to cut. It was not so good where expenses rose for critical services. Between 1973 and 1975, for example, Guardian's home office fuel and electricity costs soared from $234,000 to $639,000. Employees were not generally expendable, and as prices rose, their demands for higher wages rose apace.[48]

After 1973, the life industry responded to the devastation of inflation in four major ways. First, it kept a close eye on the Federal Reserve System and the executive branch of the federal government. Few had faith in the U.S. central bank, and for good reason. Historically it had been unable to combat inflation without inducing recession, which was only marginally better than inflation, as far as Guardian was concerned. In early 1977, the company's management feared that the Carter administration would not be able to keep inflation in check. "There is not sufficient awareness in the Administration," Conklin argued shortly after President Carter's inauguration, "of the dangers of renewed inflation." As usual, Conklin proved prescient. By autumn of that year, widespread unease prevailed in the financial market and in the business community generally because of the Carter administration's failure to grapple effectively with rising prices. (By one measure, inflation hit 6.62 percent in 1977, up from 5.75 percent in 1976.) By the spring of 1978 inflation was worsening still, to 7.59 percent, and at the end of that year, Conklin hoped that the Federal Reserve would control money growth, even if it risked a recession. After Paul Volcker became chairman of the Federal Reserve, in 1979, the central bank's board of governors did exactly that.[49]

Federal monetary policy was pretty much outside the industry's control. How could life insurance companies help themselves? In the inflationary 1970s, John Angle recalled, life insurers became more sophisticated about trying to match their fixed income investment maturities with their liabilities and about running stress tests to better judge the condition of their balance sheets. Guardian addressed the problem by investing increasingly in corporate common stocks, a strategy considered risky by most of its peers. Unlike bonds and other forms of loans, which decrease in price as inflation, and hence nominal interest rates, increases, common stocks could appreciate during inflationary periods as the nominal prices of physical assets like factories, real estate, and inventories rose. Guardian also continued and intensified its efforts to achieve increased productivity, implementing programs designed to cut operating expenses in all its business lines. Increasing use of computer technology and the use of microphotography to reduce storage costs also helped.[50]

The pace of new product introductions increased throughout the industry, as did the experimentation with new strategies. Insurers also probed for profitable chinks in the armors of regulation and taxation. Those companies that responded conservatively to the adversity of the late 1970s tended to get left behind. Guardian's Rosenthal believed that inflation forced insurers, "on pain of a lingering death, to think and act like" young companies, "to press harder and harder for new production, and to avoid like the plague the natural tendency to coast comfortably on the pool of old business."[51]

Perhaps most important, Guardian pushed ahead a long string of dividend hikes in order to stay up front in what Rosenthal called "the inflationary rat-race." Rising dividends did wonders for agency morale, not to mention the relief it provided to policyholders. The company's field agents took advantage of the company's strong dividend showing to argue that the era's unusual combination of inflation and recession—"stagflation"—showed the value of buying life insurance with the company. By the mid-1970s Irving Rosenthal, who was not prone to optimistic exaggeration, proclaimed, "Happy Days are here again." Mortality was down, and Guardian continually bumped up against New York's surplus limitation law, which prohibited the company's surplus from exceeding 10 percent of liabilities.[52]

Fret as it did about inflation on into the end of the decade, Guardian was coping with it reasonably well. The company had turned adversity into good fortune. Its new management structure was functioning smoothly, and by 1977, the cost of permanent Guardian policies was among the lowest in the industry. Guardian's general agents, not usually prone to express their gratitude, complimented the company on its net cost position. Between 1967 and 1978, Guardian increased the dividend scale on its individual life policies for eleven consecutive years, a record it believed unmatched by any other company.[53]

Still the toll on the industry was great. As figure I-2 demonstrates, the industry's assets and insurance in force continued to grow in absolute terms. As table 4-1 shows, however, the life industry's *relative* importance as a financial intermediary shrank dramatically after 1959, and would continue to do so to the end of the century. In other words, over the last four decades of the twentieth century, individuals invested an increasing percentage of their savings in assets other than life insurance policies. The disintermediation of financial services was the other great challenge of the era.

TABLE 4-1
Life Insurance Industry's Share of the Financial Intermediation Market, 1945–99

Year	Total Assets of Financial Intermediaries (billions $)	Life Insurance Industry's Share (%)
1945	103.70	43.2
1959	310.90	36.6
1970	1,313.07	15.3
1980	4,034.78	11.5
1990	10,811.20	12.5
1999	25,999.15	11.8

Sources: Brimmer, *Life Insurance Companies*, 39; Federal Reserve Flow of Funds Accounts, various years, http://www.federalreserve.gov/releases/Z1/current/data.htm, accessed 18 May 2002. Courtesy Michigan State University Press.

Disintermediation

"Traditional guaranteed cash value life insurance," Leo Futia reassured Guardianites in 1981, "has endured for 150 years, through good times and bad, inflation and deflation, prosperity and depression, war and peace." Futia's remarks came at a time when it appeared to many industry observers that whole life insurance was a dying product. He was actually worried about the trend. Whole life was out; term insurance was in.[54]

This was but one aspect of the way the trend toward disintermediation was impacting insurers. Since the mid-1950s, beneficiaries, fearing inflation and seeking higher returns elsewhere, had become increasingly loath to leave death benefits in the hands of Guardian, more often electing single sum payments over income plans. The insurance industry saw the writing on the wall—an emerging trend away from permanent insurance (see figure 4-2)—but could do little about it. By 1970, financial services firms were aggressively soliciting policyholders in an attempt to convince them to raid the cash values in their policies, buy cheaper term policies, and reinvest the difference. Why not buy term and invest the rest?[55]

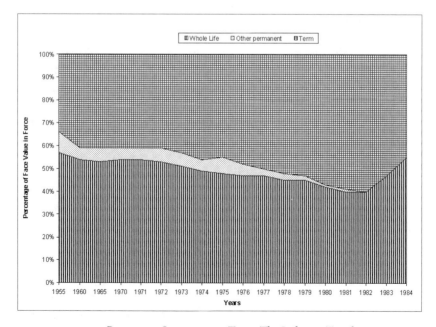

FIGURE 4-2 *Permanent Insurance vs. Term: The Industry Trend, 1955–84*

The shift to term was influenced, too, by inflationary pressures. The average inflation-adjusted net cost of whole life *quintupled* between 1965 and 1980 by some measures, while the cost of term—more closely linked to the secular decline in mortality rates than the secular increase in prices—actually decreased. (The net cost increases were highest for stock companies' nonparticipating policies and lowest for mutuals, but dividends, on average, did not keep pace with inflation.) As a consequence, term became much easier to sell than whole life. Term was a highly competitive, low-margin business, sold as it was by savings banks as well as other insurance companies. But Guardian agents had to put food on the table, so they increasingly pressed management to promote term conversion, hoping, sometimes beyond hope, that they could make a living by selling cheap term policies that policyholders would later convert into higher-commission whole life contracts.[56]

Guardian's management knew all too well that life companies had become increasingly less competitive for the savings dollar and hence clearly recognized the threat of disintermediation. Guardian developed new products, such as group universal and individual variable life insurance policies, largely in response to the twin threats of competition and inflation. Such products developed slowly, however, in part because a cloud of unresolved taxation questions loomed over them, but largely because Guardian's management believed that such fancy new products were rarely in the best interests of policyholders. As for the threat of disintermediation, the best response seemed to move the company into the sale of equity products. In 1968, the company's top brass, including Conklin, Futia, and Rosenthal, personally formed a broker-dealer subsidiary, GLICOA Associates, to facilitate the sale of its new mutual funds—the Compass Income Fund and the Compass Growth Fund—through its sales agents. Guardian, the first major New York insurance company to offer its field force a mutual fund product, also sought to enable policyholders to participate in the growth of the American economy. Instead of leaving dividends to accumulate with the company's general account, policyholders could transfer them to the higher-yielding mutual funds. "Life insurance and mutual funds are complementary products," the company noted, stressing, however, that they were "designed to meet different financial needs."[57]

In 1970, Guardian established a new mutual fund, the Guardian Park Avenue Fund, run by yet another wholly owned subsidiary, Guardian Advisors, Inc. Guardian Advisors joined the brokerage affiliates of three other life insurers two years later to contest the SEC's attempt to block stock exchange membership for brokerage subsidiaries of big institutional investors. Guardian Advisors and the three other brokerages were members of the Philadelphia-Baltimore-Washington Stock Exchange (PBW Inc.), the SEC's chief opponent in the institutional membership controversy. The brokerages fought to cross-examine witnesses in an apparent attempt to prove that the SEC's proposed policy was designed to preserve the minimum brokerage rate structure on the New York Stock Exchange. In early 1973, the SEC imposed requirements that made continued membership of Guardian Advisors on the PBW exchange unfavorable. Guardian Advisors and two other insurers instituted suit. When PBW rules changes rendered Guardian Advisors redundant, Guardian merged it with GLICOA in January 1974.[58] The merged entity continued to lose money in 1974 because of the regulatory troubles and lower mutual fund sales brought on by a particularly difficult year for the stock markets and for the sale of equity products. Though by early 1974 it was gaining some ground in direct sales to the public, the Park Avenue Fund's primary function was to serve as the underlying security for variable annuities issued by Guardian Insurance and Annuity Company, Inc. (GIAC), yet another new subsidiary created solely to market Guardian's variable annuities and variable insurance products. By 1972, GIAC was licensed to sell variable annuities in twenty-two states.[59]

By mid-1975, GLICOA was on much firmer ground because the stock market turned around and an increasing number of Guardian agents, 435 by midyear, became registered to sell the company's mutual funds. GLICOA made further gains in 1976 and 1977 though Guardian and its affiliates did not always find it advantageous to use GLICOA facilities for their security transactions and the market value of the company's seat on the PBW exchange decreased. GLICOA's nominal profits disappeared in 1978, when Guardian began to charge it for field expense overhead, i.e., for recognition of the benefits GLICOA derived from being able to use the agency force of Guardian Life to market its own products and services. The loss was a minor one, however. GLICOA came back strong in 1979 but faltered somewhat in 1980. GLICOA became Guardian Investor Services Corporation (GISC) in 1982. GIAC also began to do fairly well in 1976, increasing sales 383 percent. It experienced an influx of premature redemptions in 1977 and 1978, which it checked to some extent by introducing a withdrawal penalty provision.[60]

By 1977, GIAC's sales were skyrocketing, finally putting it in the black. In the high interest rate environment of the late 1970s, Guardian's fixed annuities foundered, but GIAC's variable annuity products held up well. New sales in 1978, however, suffered a sharp decline because GIAC strove to improve profit margins. The unprecedented increase in interest rates in 1979 knocked GIAC for a loop because investors dropped annuities for other savings and investment media, particularly in the period following the Federal Reserve's dramatic actions in October. GIAC made its name in 1981, when it teamed up with Value Line Securities to offer a new no-load, single-premium, deferred-variable annuity aptly called "Value Guard." The product was very successful, straining GIAC's surplus to the point that Guardian had to infuse it with $10 million of new capital.[61]

Guardian considered entering into other financial services, but such gambits did not prove viable. One possibility—an idea that had been bruited about as far back as 1945—was to enter the savings and loan business. The idea that policyholders could make "straight savings, etc. deposited through agency offices" turned out to be too costly, and so the plan was dropped. Another unfruitful effort was the Annex Realty Company, a subsidiary that Guardian formed in 1969 to allow it to invest in real estate developments on an equity basis, so that it could profit from inflation-induced real estate price appreciation. By 1974, Annex was turning a profit, but had no new ventures underway because high construction costs and static rents dampened returns to the same level that Guardian could make elsewhere, with less risk. Annex lumbered on until 1980, when it was folded back into the parent company.[62]

Such false starts did not incur serious losses; they were just ventures that failed to prove out. Nothing ventured, nothing gained. Generally, Guardian remained focused on its core enterprise. Diversification, which was all the rage in mature industries of the time, turned out not to be Guardian's strategy. Pulling back from temptation, the company took a page from Peter Drucker's counter-trend advice in *Managing in Turbulent Times,* and pretty much "stuck to its knitting." The company poured its capital into the areas that it knew best—individual life, group insurance, and equity products. In 1979, Futia said with confidence that "Guardian faces these troubled financial times in a significantly better position than our competition."[63]

Four years later, Guardian passed the largest dividend increase in its history, an astronomical 359 percent advance over the 1964 dividend scale. The large increase was linked to the introduction of LifeGuard, a new series of policies that offered very favorable dividends on policies against which no loans were taken. The Dividend Update Program offered existing policyholders, in Guardian's usual style, the same benefit. Sales of new business skyrocketed. By 1984, Guardian's dividend rate on nonloaned policies was once again probably unmatched in the industry. Guardian's 1984 annual report identified the elements of the company's success: "cost-competitive quality product innovation, outstanding investment performance, carefully managed expenses, and aggressive management."[64]

Portents

Guardian had to be strong if it were to survive: the period from the mid-1980s to the mid-1990s would be a difficult time for life insurers. The difficulties stemmed from a variety of factors that, acting in unison, created the "perfect storm." Group and health lines simultaneously experienced a cyclical market downturn while declining interest rates pressured investment spreads. An increasing percentage of new sales of relatively low-priced variable and universal life policies reduced margins, just as policyholders increasingly replaced their ordinary insurance policies with those lower-priced products. Finally, competition in the industry grew fiercer with the rapid entry of new companies and the expansion of old ones, financed through the sale of Guaranteed Investment Contracts (GICs), which were backed by the assets of insurance companies.[65]

In combination, those pressures could be deadly. Beginning in April 1991, several score of life insurers—including such venerable names as Executive Life, Fidelity Mutual Life, Monarch Life, Mutual Benefit Life, and Old Colony Life—gave up the ghost. Of course, throughout history, hundreds of life insurers have failed. What distinguished this wave of failures was the size and age of the insolvent companies. Most had invested too heavily in either junk bonds or commercial real estate, the markets for which collapsed in 1990. Home Life, long Guardian's "sister"—historically most comparable—company, also exited, though by folding into mutual insurer Phoenix Life, it did so more gracefully than most.[66]

The top managers of the great insurance firms, worried that their core markets offered little hope for increasing growth and profits, had begun to diversify their businesses into a broad array of financial services and real estate. Diversification strategies unfolded in one major insurance company after another, as companies like MetLife, MONY, Prudential, and the Equitable took on the aspect of financial conglomerates.[67]

The conglomeration of life insurers had proceeded apace during the 1980s in concert with a like trend in the broader financial services industry. (This trend ran counter, ironically, to the mass *de*conglomeration of companies in the nonfinancial sectors of the corporate economy.) Conglomeration was enabled somewhat by the progressive loosening of regulations that had discouraged common ownership and control of assets in the "buy" and "sell" sides of financial services.

In the meantime, the relatively stable legal environment in which insurers had operated since early in the century was being transformed, as changes on the regulatory front gathered force. Since the 1970s insurers had been urging state officials to clean up outdated rules. At the outset, the most important problem with regulation was the 10 percent maximum statutory surplus law that had been in force since the Armstrong movement. The original intent of that law was to compel insurers to return profits to policyholders, but by the 1970s insurers had come to view it as *anti-safety*. The law, having been tolerated for decades, now came under fierce attack. It seemed like a legitimate argument at a time when a critical mass of leading economists was challenging time-honored premises of regulation and government's competence to determine how managers should allocate resources in the private sector. It was also a time when politicians in both major political parties were more prone to respond to calls for limiting the scope of government power over business.[68]

Guardian, recall, had always sought to be as highly capitalized as possible to protect its policyholders from loss. As its statutory surplus approached the legal maximum in 1974, the company appealed to Albany for relief. "When the present restriction was adopted," John Angle argued, "individual life was essentially the only business of the life insurance companies." Since World War II, however, group life and health and individual health had grown rapidly. Approximately 50 percent of Guardian's premium income, for instance, stemmed from group premiums and individual health premiums. "Our surplus limits," the company reasoned, "should reflect the risks entailed by these forms of insurance."[69]

In 1981, New York's Heimann Commission, which had been organized to consider updating insurance regulations, went further, recommending that strict Armstrong-era limitations on life insurers' investments and organizational structures be replaced by a Prudent Man standard. Actions regarding retention of earnings and their investment should be judged by what prudent business executives would be expected to do under prevailing circumstances, not by rigid rules. This was, in effect, a clarion call for deregulation. Life companies were subsequently allowed to invest, through creation or acquisition of subsidiaries, in any lawful business *except banking.* What had begun as an argument to preserve the safety of policyholder interests had evolved into a green light for managers to redeploy policyholder cash outside the traditional confines of the insurance business.

As diversification gained steam, insurance executives began to view their policyholders in a new light. How could executives justify to their policyholders their more aggressive deployment of corporate cash flows into the acquisition and management of noninsurance assets? Regulators were not inclined to give managers a wide berth in the disposition of the surplus, but executives could always lobby politicians to change the rules. In 1988, the New York legislature did exactly that; it enacted a law allowing mutual insurers to demutualize, that is, to convert into stockholder owned corporations. Thus life insurance managers, who had formerly desired more freedom to return cash to their policyholders, wound up with permission to abandon the principle of policyholder governance altogether. One after another, life insurance companies demutualized, and became beholden, at least nominally, to their new shareholders. Insurance in the more diversified financial corporations became just another division of a large holding company, and an unglamorous one at that. The corporate-level monitoring of insurance sales and services practices grew weaker, just as the pressures on middle managers and agents to "make their numbers" grew stronger.[70]

A new epidemic of scandals broke out in the early 1990s, the evidence of which aroused the public and the government in a way reminiscent of the Armstrong era. Staid industry giants like Prudential and Metropolitan were tarred by allegations of misconduct ranging from unethical behavior to outright fraud. As the stories, and proofs, of malfeasance piled up in the prime-time network news, newspapers, and industry press, public and political attitudes toward life insurers grew testier than they had been since the Armstrong era.

Guardian was never implicated in the scandals. Yet it was in this cauldron of industry woes and regulatory change that Guardian confronted its most important policy decisions in three-quarters of a century. Indeed, Guardian would buck the industry trends. It would remain focused on its core business, developing new services only in close relation to it. It would remain a mutual company, one of only four large life insurers to do so. Guardian would even move its home office downtown, to the old financial district of New York, just at a time when other great Wall Street firms were moving out.

We'll pick up this story in chapter 14, following more detailed accounts of Guardian's operational history.

Part II

Product, Distribution, and Expense Management

Operation "Sure Buck" was two and a half years in the works when Guardian participated in a "sting" of a group of seventeen physicians in Mexico and their American co-conspirators in California, including two bankers, a billing service owner, and medical equipment suppliers, who had hatched a clever cross-border scheme to defraud U.S. health insurers of what could amount to millions of dollars. One of the physicians had detailed his operation to a group of American confidants who, so he thought, were insurance brokers and who invited him to a meeting in Manhattan to pitch a key component of his plan—an HMO for Mexican citizens residing in the United States—to three top executives of Guardian Life Insurance Company of America. The insurance brokers were in fact FBI agents from San Diego, and the men in Guardian's boardroom were not executives, but rather members of the company's Special Investigation Unit (SIU). After the faux executives reviewed the physician's business plan, they induced the doctor to bring a group of his cronies to a credentialing session in Texas. They were all arrested and tried. By that time the conspirators had already netted some $800,000 through the submission of claims for services never provided and inflated fees.[1]

Guardian's SIU had been organized to investigate potentially fraudulent claims, which were always an unfortunate fact of life for insurers. Such intricate and potentially large cases as the one described above were handled by the SIU in the late twentieth century. More mundane fraud cases, like lying about age or smoking habits, were handled as a matter of routine by the claims department.

Claims investigations, large and small, like all administrative activities, of course require investment. The only thing that justifies the investment for a company like Guardian is the return on the investment to the policyholder. In a suspicious claims case the question arises, will it cost more to pay the claim immediately or to challenge it and perhaps incur significant investigation and legal fees? As with all life insurance companies, Guardian has had to make difficult claims decisions involving gun wounds, falls from tall buildings and bridges, and so forth. If the death took place before the incontestable period or suicide clause expired, the company could fight the claim. If the death were an accident and not a suicide, it would have to pay twice the policy's face value if a double indemnity rider was in effect. Of course, most such claims were relatively small in the scheme of things, but cumulatively, if allowed to go undetected (or worse, if they were simply tolerated as a cost of doing business), they would constitute a large tax on policyholders. One could go overboard: if the company were to contest every claim, it would lose lots of money in investigation and court costs and lost business. Still, it mattered to pay attention, to devote resources to the scrutiny of odd or suspicious cases.[2]

Claims investigations are but one aspect of the simple tension that permeates the administration of the life insurance business: the tradeoff between spending and saving. This tradeoff is the focus of part II of this study. In chapters 5 and 6, we examine Guardian's major life insurance products, including various forms of individual life, health, and disability policies; annuities; pensions; and group life, disability, and health lines. We will see that actuaries, in each case, designed and priced life contracts in a process that was neither easy nor inexpensive.[3]

Once created, products had to be advertised and sold, the topics of chapters 7 and 8, respectively. Again, the process was neither easy nor inexpensive. Life insurers could expend relatively little on distribution—advertising and sales commissions—but would in turn sell relatively few policies. They could also spend exorbitant sums and do a huge but ultimately unprofitable business. Insurers strove to find the most efficient tradeoff between expending resources and saving them. That goal was never precisely attained, in part because the optimal tradeoff was always a moving target and hence in constant need of management attention.

Chapters 9, 10, and 11 examine the other major areas of expense management, including policyholder service, tax engineering, regulation adaptation, technology adoption, and human resource development. In each case, considerable investment of time and money was required. In each case, the costs had to be justified in terms of the long-term welfare of the company's policyholders.

Hugo Wesendonck,
founder of Germania Life
Insurance Company,
President 1860–97.

Carl T. Heye, President
1921–39. (Courtesy Henry
Hoelzer)

James A McLain, President 1940–56. (Courtesy William F. Draper)

John L. Cameron, President 1957–63. (Courtesy Frank C. Bensing)

Daniel J. Lyons, President 1964–68. (Courtesy Frank C. Bensing)

George T. Conklin Jr., President 1969–76. (Courtesy Paul W. Wood)

Leo R. Futia, President 1977–80. (Courtesy John Cullen Murphy)

John C. Angle, President 1980–84. (Courtesy Everett Raymond Kinster)

Arthur V. Ferrara, President 1985–92. (Courtesy Ned Bittinger)

Joseph D. Sargent, President 1993–2001. (Courtesy Dan Nelken)

Dennis J. Manning, President 2002–Present. (Courtesy Dan Nelken)

7 Hanover Square, built in 1983, became the home office to Guardian employees in April 1998 and currently houses over thirteen hundred employees. (Courtesy Todd Weinstein)

The Premium Loan and Payment Office located on the mezzanine level of the former home office building, 50 Union Square, New York, New York.

The Premium Loan and Payment Office converted to the company cafeteria, circa 1940.

Architectural detail in the entranceway of the Premium Loan and Payment Office/company cafeteria.

The Bethlehem, Pennsylvania, regional office, the first of the company's regional home offices, was built in 1983 and currently houses over sixteen hundred employees. This office services Guardian's group, individual life, Berkshire individual disability and equity businesses. The company also has regional offices in Appleton, Wisconsin; Pittsfield, Massachusetts; and Spokane, Washington.

Life Insurance Policy Form, circa 1930.

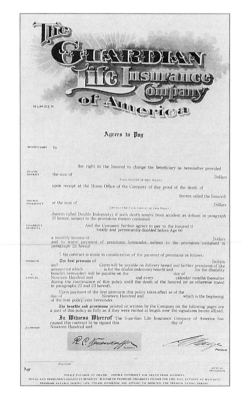

5

Product Development
The Actuarial Problem and Individual Insurance

Shortly after the Civil War, Missouri was in a state of anarchy. One Mr. F. Brandt was murdered by a marauding band of ex-Confederate soldiers and mercenaries known as Quantrill's Guerillas, who forged a path of terror and plunder in the region until they were brought to heel in 1868. The killers gave no thought to the fact that Brandt had loved ones who depended on him for their sustenance; but Brandt, at least, had made provision for them, a whole life policy with Germania. His family received succor by the speedy arrival of a bank draft from New York. With that they were able to survive and put their lives back into some semblance of order.[1]

Fast forward to Christmas 1952, when a young husband and father, aged thirty, was struck down by a drunk driver less than two years after purchasing a Guardian policy. The policy had a family income rider, an accidental death benefit, and a face value of $6,000. For the price of two annual premiums totaling $480, the man's widow and two young sons received over a period of eighteen years almost $42,500. The foresight of the deceased was enshrined in that year's annual report. "In what other way could he have invested his premium . . . to provide an income that will help" his beneficiaries to live "in comfort and decency?"[2]

Such anecdotes put a human face on the tribulations that families have always faced in their struggle to survive in an uncertain world, and have always been an important part of the message insurers must deliver to the young and healthy, who see death as a remote, or deferrable, question. *Tragedy strikes even those in the prime of life.* And what if Brandt or the young father had not been killed but rather disabled, to live on unable to work? Or, in an equally cruel twist of fate, what if they had escaped early death and disability, only to face the prospect of an impoverished old age? Or what if they were in business with a partner who died, forcing dissolution of their business assets at unpropitious prices? Or what if they lived and grew wealthy, only to leave their heirs with a messy and expensive tangle of taxes and other estate charges?[3]

Life insurance is not just for the dead. All the foregoing possibilities, and more, could actually be insured against in some fashion. Since its beginnings in 1860, Guardian has been part of an industry that fashioned a creative array of products that provided for many of life's adverse contingencies. This chapter and the next trace the development of Guardian's major insurance products—whole life, term, variable life, annuities, pensions, disability, dental, and health—in both group and individual forms, and the related equity products and reinsurance treaties that help augment those products and hedge the costs of providing them. It all begins with the actuary, who makes the provision of insurance economically feasible.

Engineers of Liability

The economics of a life insurance policy is simple to grasp and hard to manage. The irreducible fact is that the cost, hence price, of a policy is the critical variable that makes it an affordable good. That cost is a function of the insurer's mortality experience, administrative expenses, and investment earnings. A life's contingency makes pricing the policy—or averaging the price of all policies—extremely tricky. It is a dynamic problem, one that changes over time depending on a host of environmental and personal factors. Solving the problem is the job of the insurance actuary, who assesses the risks and costs of the life insurance policy.

Ascertaining the likelihood of death is both art and science. The science part is mortality tables, statistical compilations of the probability of death of persons of certain characteristics at different ages. Given a large and random sample, the tables, which have been refined over time, are quite good at predicting *the number* of people who will die in a given year. They say nothing, however, about *who* will perish. Moreover, policyholders do not randomly assign themselves to insurers. Each life insurance company tends to specialize in one part of the total insurance market, seeking out policyholders that fit their particular *niche.* The mortality characteristics of a market niche will inevitably differ, sometimes greatly, from those of the overall population. Thus each insurer not only has to know what the industry knows but also must develop firm-specific knowledge about mortality.

The art of mortality assessment comes from trying to ascertain precisely who is likely to die soon and who is likely to live long. Home office underwriters are charged with making those individual determinations. Some applicants they must reject altogether. Some can be insured, but only at a higher age or higher risk class so that they pay higher premiums. In making such decisions, underwriters receive help from actuaries, who adjust the general mortality tables to reflect the experience of their respective companies. Actuaries also analyze the risks imposed by policyholders with certain characteristics or behaviors, such as occupation, place of residence, personal vices, even hobbies. If a group of policyholders poses an added risk, actuaries must decide if they are, *as a class,* insurable at all, insurable only with certain types of policies or below certain dollar levels, or insurable with payment of an extra premium. To see how this works, consider what happened in 1940, when Guardian's actuaries made four adjustments to accommodate changes in aviation technology and world events that impacted U.S. demographics.[4]

1. They eliminated the extra premium for air transportation because of the airline industry's "record of progress."
2. They included, however, an exclusion for piloting due to an increased "tendency among many young men . . . to evince more and more interest in flying instructions and actual flying." (This was one of the added risks of Guardian's upper-income market niche.)
3. They limited the amount and plan of insurance available to those in military training.
4. They initiated a policy of postponing decisions on the applications of European refugees "until such time as they have become well enough established in this country to indicate the absence of any abnormal hazard in insuring them."

Once the probability of death is ascertained, and an interest rate assumed, premiums can be calculated. Consider, for example, the premium for a one-year term policy for a forty-year-old female using the 1980 CSO table. According to that table, 2.42 out of every one thousand females will die in the fortieth year. If one hundred thousand females each bought $1,000 worth of insurance, the insurer would have to earn $242,000

(240.2 deaths out of one hundred thousand insured lives x $1,000 insurance each) to pay the claims likely to arise. Those funds will come from premiums, but also from investment of the cash. As a final step, some allowance for sales and administration expenses must be made.

The time value of money is also involved: a dollar today is more valuable to a prospective insured than a dollar in the future. But unlike a bond or loan with a maturity, or payoff, that will occur at a certain future date, the maturity of the life insurance policy is uncertain. The insured could die next week or in a hundred years. Actuaries must determine the premium not just by considering the likelihood of death but also by factoring in a projection of interest rates and the likelihood of inflation.

Though the pricing problem gets much stickier as the contract lengthens beyond a year, the principles remain the same. Since the mid-nineteenth century, life companies have priced most of their multiyear contracts on the level premium principle developed by Elizur Wright. Under that principle, the insured pays the same nominal amount each year over the term of the policy, essentially overpaying in the early years to subsidize premiums due in the later years. Were it not for the level premium concept, most older people would find life insurance prohibitively expensive. The level premium principle, however, puts a great obligation on life insurers, particularly their actuaries, to maintain the proper level of reserve liabilities to meet claims.

To ensure that the company can meet its obligations, actuaries try to peer into the future and estimate the crucial cost factors of mortality, investment, expenses, and lapse rates. Actuaries make "conservative" projections, i.e., assumptions that overstate the premium by being pessimistic about the number of death claims the company will face, the expense of administration, and future interest rates. In other words, they skew the premium in favor of the company. Policyholders understand this, of course, which is why some life insurers provide participating policies, which return excess premiums to policyholders, after the fact.

Except for a period prior to 1913, when Guardian issued a few policies at nonparticipating rates, all of the company's policies have been issued on a participating basis. Guardian and other insurers with participating policies collect more than they need in premiums, do the best job they can on mortality, investment, and expenses, and then, on the basis of their actual experience, return part of the premium to policyholders. Of course, actuaries are also intimately involved in the rational calculation of those repayments or "dividends."[5]

Calculating dividends is a tricky business best left to professional actuaries. A simplified example from 1910, however, may help to clarify the basic principles:

Ordinary Life—Age 35—$1,000	
Premium charged	$27.67
Net premium, American 3 1/2%	19.91
Loading	7.76
Mean reserve (first year)	15.84
7/8% of same (4 3/8% earned minus 3 1/2%)	.15
42% of loading (7.76)	3.26
Deduct expense charge of $.50 per 1,000	.50
Loading element refunded	2.76
Add interest as above	.15
Total (dividend)	2.91

For policies that have been longer in force the same process applies, thus:

Year	Loading Refund	+ Interest Element	= Dividend
2	$2.76	.24	3.00
3	2.76	.35	3.11

That is a rather simple calculation. Since 1910, actuarial science has become far more sophisticated, involving highly complicated mathematics. That is why it is not uncommon to find actuaries who began their careers in mathematics, engineering, physics, or even, literally, such "rocket sciences" as astronomy, ballistics, and meteorology.[6]

Actuaries are the engineers of the liability side of the life insurer's balance sheet and are so adept at mathematics that they often help out with investment decisions on the asset side too. They are the cerebral cortex of any good insurance operation, the computers before computers, the interface between what the market says it wants and the reality of what its providers can afford. But actuaries are also hard-nosed businesspeople. They understand competitive issues as well as arcane actuarial rites. At their best, they can explain to the sales representative the disadvantages of competing products and the advantages of their own policy forms.[7]

Since World War II, Guardian has been home to many leading actuaries, at least five of whom—John L. Cameron, Daniel J. Lyons, Irving Rosenthal, John C. Angle, and Armand de Palo—became famous in their chosen profession. The Brooklyn-born Cameron was a graduate of Williams College and a fellow of the Society of Actuaries. After stints at Travelers and the actuarial consultant firm of George B. Buck, he joined Guardian as assistant actuary in 1930. He was later promoted to associate actuary and then, in January 1941, to second vice president. A "bright, bright actuary . . . loaded with integrity," he was elected to the board of directors and given a full vice presidency in 1943. Known to Guardianites as "Honest John," he succeeded McLain as Guardian's president in 1957. He served in that capacity until the end of 1963. The following day, 1 January 1964, Cameron, who is perhaps best remembered for his cautious approach to the business, succeeded McLain as chairman of the board, a position he relinquished to fellow actuary Daniel Lyons at the end of 1968.[8]

Dan Lyons was a very bright, Catholic boy from Randolph, a suburb of Boston, the son of a salesman and a schoolteacher. He went to Harvard and later trained as an actuary, which appealed to his love for mathematics. He worked for the Travelers and Columbian National for a few years but his employment fell casualty to the Great Depression, and he found himself out of work in 1934. He found refuge in the New Jersey Insurance Department, where he served as an assistant chief actuary and wrote a few papers that came to the attention of James McLain, who hired him in 1943. Lyons quickly advanced to second vice president in 1948, reporting to vice president John Cameron, and was responsible for coordinating all new business activities, including sales, underwriting, and actuarial planning.[9]

Lyons was busy developing the individual health business when McLain tapped him to serve as agency vice president. Lyons possessed an entrepreneurial streak a mile wide and the brains to back it up, and his superiors knew it. They appointed him administrative vice president at the end of 1953, and he became a director of the company in 1957. He finally made it to the presidency in January 1964. In 1969, he resigned the presidency but remained chairman of the board until the end of 1970, and then beyond that remained active on Guardian's board until he turned ninety, still sharp as a tack. His value was his steadiness. He liked to remind his colleagues, "When things look real bad, they're not really as bad as they look, and when they look real good, they're not really as good as they look." Lyons was to the insurance side of the business what George Conklin was to its investment side, the man who laid down the tracks that subsequent leaders followed closely.[10]

Lyons's right-hand man was another actuary, Irving Rosenthal, a native of the Lower East Side. Rosenthal graduated from City College magna cum laude and joined Guardian in 1930, at the age of twenty-two. He was the elder of two sons of a Jewish immigrant from Russia who became professional actuaries, passing his examinations at age twenty-five, the youngest age allowed into the Society of Actuaries. Possessed of a keen analytical mind and an even keener sense of humor, he is remembered as the most popular guy in the company during his time there. He had a mischievous sense of humor. He once pompously informed Guardian's sales managers that an important policy change could not possibly be implemented because the forms had already gone to the printer. In one meeting of the group profit center, Rosenthal opined that it was "idiotic . . . to try to predict the future but who has a better right to be idiotic than an actuary, particularly one approaching the age of senility?" On another occasion, he told a sales representative that he would gladly write a special policy for him, longhand, and suffer the $1,000 fine and year in jail that such an action would entail, just so he could write a little business for a change! None of that should belie the more serious side of his personality; he was a well-published and well-respected scholar in his field.[11]

When he had something serious to discuss, the beloved Rosenthal liked to take a colleague for a stroll in Union Square, which stretched out beyond the southwest corner of Guardian's home office building. Even then he found it difficult not to crack a joke. He promoted Edward Kane to become Guardian's general counsel on one such walk, wisecracking all the way. As they made the rounds through the park, Rosenthal observed that Jewish lawyers were the toughest. Since Guardian did not have a Jewish lawyer, though, it had to settle for the next toughest kind, an Irish lawyer. His offbeat, often sarcastic sense of humor worked well for him.[12]

Rosenthal was Guardian's perennial master of ceremonies, as his career advanced from 1941, when he was vice president and chief actuary, to his promotion to senior vice president in 1963. In recognition of his quasi-co-CEO role during the latter stages of his career, the board minutes recorded that "his extraordinary value to The Guardian is not fully reflected in any chart of organization, for it lay in the down-to-earth wisdom and soundness of his judgments when complex and critical decisions were required." After his retirement, Rosenthal, like most former Guardian top executives, stayed on as a consulting director until July 1977.[13]

Rosenthal's successor as chief actuary was John Angle. After growing up and attending public school in Lincoln, Nebraska, Angle went off to the University of Michigan in 1941. America's entry into the Second World War at the end of his first semester interrupted his studies. He joined the army, which put him in the program for weather officers. He obtained training at the University of Chicago and served out the war stateside as a second lieutenant in the Air Weather Service. When he returned to Lincoln after the war, with a new bride, he did not have the foggiest notion what he was going to do because the government had trained large numbers of meteorologists, few of whom could hope to find employment in the field. A family friend stepped in and landed Angle a job with the fourteen-year-old Union National Life of Lincoln. Angle started in the investment department but the company, which was subsequently absorbed by American General Life, quickly discovered that he knew more mathematics than the company's part-time actuary. Angle took up his new duties with enthusiasm, becoming only the second Nebraskan ever to become a fellow with the Society of Actuaries by examination.[14]

After the Korean War, Angle joined the Woodmen Accident and Life Company of Lincoln, Nebraska, as its chief actuary. In that position he had accounting, underwriting, and data processing all reporting to him. When Woodmen in the early 1960s installed one of the first computers to be used in Nebraska, Angle gained cutting-edge experience overseeing the adaptation of generic IBM mainframe insurance software to his company's particular needs.

Woodmen made Angle a director, but could not offer him a chance to become the company's CEO. It was largely a family business and would remain that way at the top, so Angle responded to the blandishments of a headhunter, who put him in touch with Guardian in 1973. At first, Angle had rejected the opportunity, but his wife urged him to reconsider. As a graduate of Smith College, Catherine Angle had friends in the Northeast, and the couple's children were already out of high school. Angle contacted the headhunter, found Guardian "a terribly exciting place to be," landed the job, and moved to Greenwich Village. He started in his new post, as senior vice president and chief actuary of Guardian, in July 1973.[15]

Guardian had sought Angle out because of his compatible experience, and because of an unusual talent gap among its internal candidates for the work that Angle would take on. The Woodmen, like Guardian, wrote participating whole life policies, group insurance, and individual disability insurance. Moreover, Guardian had a strong health insurance program, a line of much interest to Angle. The company placed Angle in charge of group insurance, individual insurance, equities, and the individual life actuarial department. Data processing, also lacking strong leadership, was soon added to his portfolio. Thereafter, Angle's ascent was swift and steep. He became executive vice president in 1977, and within three years succeeded Leo Futia as Guardian's president. He got the job because both Futia and Arthur Ferrara, the most likely successor, were agency men at a time when the board felt that a change in emphasis was due. (The major industry problems of the time were more related to products and pricing than to distribution.) Angle succeeded Futia as board chairman and CEO in 1985; he retired from both posts at the end of 1989 but in good Guardian style remained active on the board.[16]

Angle was noted for his dry wit, which often revealed itself in the course of business. When he complained, for instance, about a Texas insurance department's demand that insurance executives submit detailed biographical information, he said, "Texas seems to be suspicious that the mob is taking over the life insurance business and will reveal itself in a well-designed questionnaire." But he was also a serious student of life insurance. He contributed a chapter on risk selection and substandard risks to a technical life and health insurance handbook that went through several editions in the 1960s and 1970s. In that chapter, Angle and his coauthor John McCuistion compared health insurance underwriters to "university admission officials, the educational testing services, bank loan committees, licensing and professional examination boards of every sort, and personnel officers"—all occupations that "examine and classify applicants by closely following a set of 'admission' standards." They held that health insurance underwriting was "more of an art than its life insurance counterpart" because of the relatively subjective nature of "health," the relative plethora of "rating factors," and the large degree of adverse selection. Only 80 percent of individual health applicants, they noted, were accepted as "standard risks," compared to 91 percent of individual life insurance applicants.[17]

Finally, Armand M. de Palo, who came to Guardian on 5 January 1976, picked up where Angle left off. Like many of Guardian's top honchos, de Palo, a native of New York City, is well studied, well published, and well respected in his field. Unlike many actuaries, he has not formed a narrow specialization, preferring to stay abreast of all the major actuarial areas, including agent compensation, actuarial reserves, life product pricing, and life dividends. Indeed, he is the sole author of the Society of Actuaries' "Advanced Policyowner Dividend Study Note." A skilled public speaker, de Palo is a leading spokesperson for the more conservative segment (business, not politics) of the actuarial profession and indeed the entire industry.[18]

In many ways, de Palo is a classic Guardian success story. He joined the company very early in his career and was quickly rewarded for his brains and commitment to the policyholder. On 1 January 1986, just ten years after joining the company, he became a vice president and life actuary. Exactly four years later he moved up to chief actuary. In that role, he has made a number of important contributions to Guardian's business, including its management accounting system and its innovative executive compensation program. Perhaps more importantly, he has been Guardian's conscience, its soul, and one of its most powerful officers. Only the company's CEO can overrule his decisions; they have rarely done so because de Palo always has logic, evidence, and the policyholders' best interests on his side. Only in gray areas, where real judgment calls have to be made, are his recommendations occasionally set aside.[19]

Whatever the state of the art and science, the key task for Guardian's actuaries has always been to help Guardian walk the thin line between innovating with new products and serving its existing policyholders. Innovation is key to meeting the challenges from rivals in a dynamic industry. Servicing its policyholders is key to its reputation. Both are essential to sustaining Guardian's ability to compete.[20]

As home office employees, actuaries work closely with field sales agents to develop the products most in demand in the marketplace. Guardian's actuaries and its field force have had an unusually peaceful and productive relationship. Underlying the histories of all of the policies described in this chapter is the cumulative brainpower and sweat of Guardian's chief actuaries and the people who have reported to them.[21]

Whole Life Insurance and Variations on the Theme

Guardian's flagship product has always been the individual whole life policy. It was the mainstay of the entire life insurance industry from the 1850s until the 1970s, and is deceptively simple. The policyholder pays to the insurer an unchanging nominal premium each and every year until the death of the insured, at which time the insurer pays to the beneficiary the face value of the contract. That basic framework, however, is simply the chassis for a great variety of policies. For instance, the policyholder could opt to pay premiums for a certain period, e.g., ten, fifteen, or twenty years, instead of for the entire life of the insured. In either case, premiums cease and the policy matures when the insured dies. Obviously, premiums are larger if limited in number. In the extreme, the insured can pay a single, very large premium.[22]

In another variation, known as an endowment policy, the insurer pays the face value of the policy upon the death of the insured or a fixed date, whichever happens first. (Technically, all whole life policies are endowment policies because they can be surrendered for their full face value when the insured hits a very advanced age—formerly ninety-six but now generally one hundred—where mortality tables end. In general parlance, an endowment policy is one that pays off at an age less than the terminal age assumed in standard mortality tables.)[23]

In the 1870s, Guardian's endowment policies were highly competitive because their premiums were lower than nearly all of its competitors' premiums. A healthy thirty-five-year-old man could receive $1,000 in ten years, for example, by paying Guardian $101.04 annually. While it may at first glance look like a bad deal to pay $1,010.40 to receive $1,000, it was not, as the insurer stood ready to pay the $1,000 if the insured died, and it would pay dividends too. Moreover, Massachusetts Mutual charged more, $106.30 per annum for a similar policy, and Union Mutual of Maine, $110.50![24]

In 1886, Guardian introduced two new endowment policies. The first it called a "pure endowment" that did not pay out until after a fixed number of years had passed. If the policyholder died before the expiration, premiums would cease but no death benefit would be paid until the fixed maturity date. The second new endowment policy it called a "duplex endowment." Under that policy, a death benefit was paid if the insured died. If he or she lived until the date fixed in the policy, the amount insured would become payable in any event after the end of yet another period stipulated in the contract.[25]

A life income endowment policy is an endowment policy that automatically turns into a life annuity at some prespecified age, often sixty to sixty-five. According to one Guardian agent, the policy worked much like the old Cherrelyn horse car that supplied transit between Cherrelyn and Englewood, Colorado, in the pre-automobile era. A horse pulled the passenger trolley up rails to the top of the hill separating the two towns. The teamster then placed the horse on the rear platform and allowed it to rest while gravity finished the job. In this analogy the policyholder is like the horse. If he worked hard during his prime to pull his income endowment policy to the proper height, he could retire and coast for the rest of his days on the power of compound interest.[26]

Whole life policies have varied in other ways as well. Between 1870 and 1906, insurers greatly liberalized policies by allowing for surrender values, premium payment grace periods, provisions for reinstatement, policy loan provisions, and incontestability. Late-nineteenth-century policies also grew less restrictive about travel, residence, and occupation.[27]

Guardian was rarely a leader in policy liberalization, but it was never one of the reactionary forces that sought to retain the status quo, which of course favored the insurer rather than the policyholder. Guardian implemented liberalizations only after it was certain that a new provision was unlikely to endanger the company's financial position.

A good case in point is the evolution of the incontestable clause. During the difficult 1870s, troubled life insurers found it convenient to contest policies for any number of trite and trivial reasons simply to avoid, or at least delay, full payment. Prospective policyholders naturally winced at such practices. As one nineteenth-century critic of life insurance put it, "no man desires to leave a lawsuit as an inheritance to his widow and children." It was only a matter of time, therefore, before life companies began to promise, contractually, not to contest policies. In 1879, the mighty Equitable copied the concept of incontestability from Manhattan Life, which had incorporated, but without much fanfare, an incontestability clause into its policies as early as 1861, just seven years after three British insurers first adopted the practice. To protect themselves from premeditated fraud, insurers usually made incontestability clauses effective only after the policies had been in force one or more years.[28]

Incontestability was not only just, but also much needed. Sales agents could not very well sell insurance as "peace of mind" if the policyholder/insured had to fret about the insurer's intentions. Yet, the clause met much resistance from certain life insurers. In 1882, for instance, John Taylor of Connecticut Mutual questioned the motives of companies that used the incontestable clause. Taylor thought the clause unnecessary because "contesting the payment of claims, either for technical or meritorious reasons, does not pay." The market forced companies to pay up because "the notoriety, disfavor, loss of new business, and added payments in damages, interest, counsel fees, and legal expenses" that came with contesting claims was simply too great to bear. Inclusion of the clause, therefore, was merely a ruse to "get new business at all costs." Prospects, however, liked the clause, probably because it freed them from the large search costs that Taylor's market-driven solution would have imposed on them.[29]

Guardian took the middle ground. In 1883, after careful study of the issue, the company began to issue policies with a three-year incontestable clause. Five years later, the board allowed the issuance of policies incontestable from the start instead of after three years but only when necessary and when demanded. In 1892, it made all policies, new and existing, incontestable after one year for misrepresentations in the policy. It also loosened limitation of coverage on account of travel, residence, occupation, and suicide. It maintained the one-year incontestability period and liberal suicide clause until 1931, when it increased the period for both to two years. Guardian was responding to a long-observed pattern: many dubious claims were made right after the one-year anniversary. That observation, along with an increasing incidence of suicide during the Depression, drove the changes.[30]

From the policyholders' standpoint there was the danger that after paying premiums for many years, they might fall on hard times and be forced to forfeit their policies. Companies and regulators came to realize that each whole life policy had an equity value or "cash value," its legal reserve minus a surrender charge. To help sell whole life policies, insurers offered the insured access to the cash value of their policies through two major mechanisms, policy loans and surrender values.[31]

It is precisely because of their surrender benefits that whole life policies could be viewed as savings instruments. Consider, for example, Guardian Policy No. 63135, a ten-payment whole life policy issued to a male, age twenty-seven, on 4 October 1873. The annual premium was $88.70 for $2,000 worth of coverage. After forty-five years, the policy netted the policyholder over $1,250, plus almost half a century of protection on his life. The accounting was as follows:

Ten payments of $88.70 each	$887.00
Less dividend returns	849.49
Cash surrender value after 45 years	1,288.70
Net profit	$1,251.19[32]

Surrender values could be paid in three forms: (1) cash; (2) paid-up reduced insurance (i.e., the cash value is used to purchase a small policy that will be paid upon the insured's death); (3) paid-up term insurance (i.e., the cash value is used to purchase a term policy that will pay the face value if the insured dies before the term expires). By 1877, Guardian allowed surrender values in cash or paid-up insurance, at the option of the policyholder.[33]

Whole life policies were also savings tools in that as the need for protection diminished, their cash value could be tapped via policy loans to fund purchases of other income-generating investments while maintaining the policy in force. Insurers did not recognize this benefit right away, but when some companies allowed them around 1885, sales increased. Still, the practice of making policy loans was limited before 1892, when New York regulators explicitly condoned their use. Guardian made loans on its policies in the nineteenth century but not until 1902 did it include an explicit policy loan provision in its contracts. After Armstrong, many legislatures mandated the inclusion of policy loan provisions in whole life policies.[34]

Policy loans helped policyholders in innumerable ways. In just one example, a Guardian policyholder related to his agent in 1965 that a policy loan had given him the cash necessary to buy a new home while holding onto his first house in anticipation of a firmer market. Because the policyholder did not have to make a sacrifice through a quick sale, the loan saved him $1,000 on the sale, much more than the interest charge on the loan.[35]

Policy loans were not an unalloyed blessing. They were risky to insurers. Traditionally life insurers contractually fixed the interest rate on policy loans at 5 to 6 percent per year. Because of that rigidity, policy loans at times seriously dogged the industry. The volume of policy loans outstanding spiked either in deep recessions when people were desperate for cash or when market interest rates were extremely high. In either case, the loans hurt life companies by converting them into quasibanks that could be run upon for liquid funds. In fact, insurers had even fewer protections against runs than banks because, unlike banks, insurers could not turn policy loan applicants away nor raise the interest rates charged.

Insurers worried most about the ill effects of fixed-interest policy loans on their business in a highly inflationary environment. In 1980, when inflation soared to its worst levels in modern U.S. history, many life companies joined efforts to seek, at state and federal levels, legal changes that would make permanent life insurance more viable in an inflationary environment. One such proposed change would have permitted insurance companies to issue policies with variable policy-loan interest rates. Guardian strongly backed the initiative; its CEO Leo Futia wrote all company field personnel with a request that they support it. His letter contained a summary of the Model Policy Loan Interest Rate Bill and bulleted points that essentially argued that traditional fixed policy loan rates hurt nonborrowing policyholders, Guardian's investment returns, and ultimately, the entire institution of guaranteed cash value life insurance. The proposed bill linked policy loan rates, with a two-month lag, to Moody's corporate bond index, but gave individual companies some discretion in the precise rate offered to policyholders at any given time. The NAIC adopted the model bill in December 1980, and the state legislatures followed.[36]

Adoption of the bill was slow, however, and so Guardian solved the policy loan issue more quickly on its own. In 1983, the company created separate, much more favorable dividend scales for policies that were not encumbered with loans. Guardian simply assigned lower dividends to policy borrowers. The justice of this—which Guardian called "direct recognition"—was almost perfect. After all, policyholders who borrowed at 5 or 6 percent when market interest rates were 10, 15, or 20 percent were already reaping a large "dividend," the rate spread between their loans and the going market rate for money. Direct recognition spelled much higher dividends for nonborrowers. Consider what happened in the case of a male aged sixty, a nonsmoker in good health, with policy paid up by age sixty-five. The policy, which had a face value of $100,000, yielded a dividend of $5,812 under direct recognition compared with just $2,121 under the old scale. The program, with a boost from a clause in the 1986 Tax Reform Act that eliminated the tax-deductibility status of interest paid on policy loans, was a success. Ever since, policy loans have been less dangerous to insurers while remaining important as benefits for policyholders.[37]

Surrender benefits—cash values, policy loans, dividends, and other forms of "living benefits" paid to the policyholder instead of the beneficiary—are extremely important parts of whole life insurance. In 1915, Henry Reis, president of Old State National Bank, could state without exaggeration that "modern life insurance is largely a thing of life. No longer is it only a protection for a man's family after he has been called away. It is with him all his life—an every-ready resource—always a reliable ally in fighting life's battles." Since Reis wrote, the living benefits of life insurance grew ever more important until by 1945 the benefits paid to the living exceeded those paid to the beneficiaries of the deceased. One might be surprised to hear that insurers have since paid out more in living benefits than in death benefits.[38] (See table 5-1.)

Over the course of the twentieth century there were other major individual life policy innovations, including the proliferation of credit, sub-

TABLE 5-1
Benefits Paid by the Life Insurance Industry, 1945–70

Year	Total of All Living Benefits ($000,000 Omitted)	Death Benefits ($000,000 Omitted)
1945	1,388	1,280
1947	1,633	1,339
1949	1,988	1,490
1951	2,275	1,709
1953	1,525	1,990
1955	3,142	2,241
1957	3,950	2,711
1959	4,421	3,110
1961	5,230	3,581
1963	5,819	4,209
1965	6,586	4,831
1967	7,628	5,665
1969	8,768	6,758
1970	9,431	7,017

Source: *Life Insurance Fact Book,* 1967, 37; and 1971, 43.

standard, preferred, juvenile, and wife policies, the advent of the double-indemnity clause, and the rejuvenation of term policies. Guardian was almost invariably in the middle of the pack, never assuming the initial risk of innovation but always willing to follow if policyholders were benefited.[39]

For instance, Guardian made a serious foray into the field of credit insurance only after it could copy the Equitable's mortgage redemption plan, which it thought worthy of emulation because it was based upon extended experience. After experimenting with that policy for six years, Guardian introduced in 1946 a mortgage insurance policy, on the level premium plan, in units of $5,000 that decreased progressively to $1,000 over fifteen, twenty, or twenty-five years. The idea was to match the standard loan amortization schedule so that if the insured died, the policy would pay off the mortgage. At first, Guardian offered mortgage insurance policies only to insureds aged twenty to forty-five years. Due to considerable demand for this type of coverage at ages above forty-five, however, Guardian in 1947 decided to accept risks up to fifty years of age, but only on mortgages of fifteen years or less. In 1955, Guardian introduced a similar product to accommodate the growing popularity of thirty-year mortgages.[40]

Artifacts: Industrial Insurance and Tontines

The affordability of whole life policies has always been an issue. In the nineteenth century, millions of urban and rural poor in Europe and the United States could not afford to pay the premiums on whole life policies or even term policies, especially at higher ages. Many life companies responded by developing a special form of whole life policy known as "industrial insurance," which had low face values and modified provisions that enabled companies to offer them at lower prices. Premiums for industrial policies were in fact extremely small, and were personally collected every week (or sometimes month) by a salesman, or "debit man." The personal collection service kept policyholders' remittance costs down and surrender rates lower than they might otherwise have been. Moreover, the visits allowed the agent to collect significant amounts of information about the policyholder/insured and the situation of his family and neighbors. Through repeated visits, a good debit man became a respected financial consultant for a large number of the working poor.[41]

Industrial policies were, however, generally nonparticipating and usually did not allow for policy loans or third-party assignments. Policy loans on such small policies would have been prohibitively expensive and also would have mitigated the forced savings intent of industrial policies. Insurers believed that most industrial policyholders were unlikely to understand the meaning of collateral or assignment, so they forbade assignments to protect policyholders from designing lenders.[42]

Eyeing the tremendous growth of Prudential and other industrial insurers, Guardian decided to enter this new, burgeoning field. It wrote industrial insurance for only eight years, from 1880 until 1887, before leaving the field. Most of the policies were on the lives of German immigrants and their offspring and a sprinkling of Irish stock along the Atlantic seaboard from Massachusetts to Virginia. The decision to enter the industrial field, short-lived as Guardian's experience in it proved to be, was not a bad move. Millions of poor Americans needed the type of coverage provided by industrial insurance. Most new German immigrants were poor, manual laborers. Group and social insurance were still decades off. Assessment societies and fraternal schemes were generally unsound and some were outright flimflams. The problem was that Guardian was ill equipped to serve this market.[43]

Industrial insurance required scale economies that Guardian did not possess, and in the final analysis did not want to possess. The most promising fields for expansion of industrial insurance were in the rural South, particularly among populations of poor white and black share-croppers with which Guardian had little contact or experience. In other words, Guardian's entry into the industrial field was somewhat incongruous with the company's ordinary whole life niche, which was relatively up-market, even if not necessarily carriage trade.[44]

The best thing that can be said about Guardian's foray into industrial insurance was that it quickly saw the writing on the wall and withdrew before it lost its shirt. During the Armstrong Investigation, Guardian explained that it had done no better than to break even on its foray into industrial insurance. Guardian may have gained some new business that could be converted into its more traditional policies, but mainly it faced the prospect of serving already-in-force, unprofitable industrial policies for several decades to come. In 1910, Guardian forgave premium payments on all its industrial insurance after the insured reached seventy-five years of age. In 1921, it considered lowering that age to seventy but instead sought, unsuccessfully as it turned out, to interest MetLife in buying its remaining industrial policies. In 1925, almost fifty years after it stopped writing industrial policies, Guardian decided to make systematic efforts to convert into regular insurance the small, industrial policies initially written on minors. At the very least, it sought to induce industrial policyholders to pay commuted premiums annually instead of weekly, a mode of collection that was extremely costly for a company that had long since terminated its debit men. In 1940, only 146 industrial policies with a total face value of $15,784 were still in force, so Guardian decided to waive all further premium payments after 1 January 1941. The nickels and dimes were simply too expensive to collect and process.[45]

In the historical sweep, Guardian's aborted entry into industrial insurance was of little lasting importance. Industrial insurance all but evaporated by the late 1960s, a victim of Social Security and the proliferation of modern group insurance. (About $12 billion remains in force today, barely a proverbial spit in the bucket.) As figure 5-1 makes clear, group life swallowed industrial whole and even took a nice chunk out of the market share of ordinary insurance.[46]

Guardian's move into the other major innovation in nineteenth-century whole life insurance, tontine or "deferred dividend" policies, turned out much more favorably for the company. Pure tontines were invest-

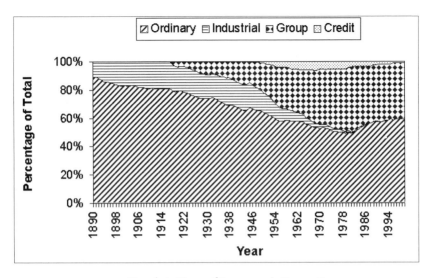

FIGURE 5-1 *Trends in Types of Insurance in Force, 1890–2000*

ment pools where all of the profits accrued to the last living investor in a given pool. Guardian's tontine policies were not so severe. Under its policies, policyholders did not receive dividends annually as was the case with ordinary whole life. Rather, they received dividends every five, ten, or twenty years. Deferring the dividends allowed remaining policyholders to appropriate the accumulated dividends of those who had died or lapsed. Like other forms of whole life, the face value of the policy was paid when the insured died, but the accumulated dividends were not. So unlike a pure tontine, all policyholders received basic coverage, but those who lapsed or died during the deferment period did not reap dividends.

In the latter part of 1873, Guardian began to issue modified tontine policies. By 1875, it expressly preferred to issue whole life policies with the tontine clause. By 1877, it offered a tontine or expected endowment plan, in which benefits were payable upon the insured's death or when one-half of the insured pool died. In 1889, the company began to issue tontine policies with removal of travel, residence, and occupation restrictions after three years.[47]

In the British farce *The Wrong Box*, the relatives of one of two remaining survivors of a true tontine attempt to do away with the other survivor, with predictably benign comedic results. And tontines were always somewhat tainted in real life. After the Armstrong Investigation, tontines became viewed as monstrosities, not because they inspired murder, but because deferred dividends appeared to be a mechanism for "gambling" or *increasing risk*. That made it diametrically opposed to the principle of insurance as a means of spreading, i.e., reducing, risk. In 1906, W. G. Langworthy Taylor stated the case against tontines thusly: "Life insurance is not at all a gambling business . . . but the endowment feature [in tontines] . . . is a gambling on one's own survival and on the inheritance of the property of those who die before."[48]

Until recently, most observers have jumped on the bandwagon of tontine condemnation. Those observers forget that the tontine principle had a long history. Tontines were popular in France and elsewhere as early as the seventeenth century. Tontine schemes were also popular in colonial and early national America. In 1805, several hundred members of the Chesapeake elite bought shares in the Washington Tontine, an early real estate investment trust that paid one big dividend at the end of twenty years to survivors instead of the semiannual dividends paid by most corporations. Other examples abound.[49]

Moreover, tontine life policies received the blessings of New York regulators and noted actuaries like Sheppard Homans. Of the major insurance policymakers of the era, only Elizur Wright expressed reservations about them. Critics rely on the lore that only three companies, Mutual Benefit Life, Connecticut Mutual, and Provident Life and Trust, never offered any type of tontine policy and excuse others only on the grounds that competitive pressures forced them to offer the pernicious contracts.[50]

Modern scholarship, however, argues against such a moralistic view. One can argue convincingly that tontine policies were actuarially sound and an attractive investment. Many nineteenth-century Americans agreed; by 1905 some two-thirds of all life insurance in force was of the tontine or deferred dividend variety. Few contemporaries had problems with tontine policies. Though the policies often failed to live up to illustrations, largely because insurers did not appreciate how fiercely policyholders would cling to them, tontines could pay large returns. Moreover, many policyholders refused to consider the purchase of nontontine policies and clearly demonstrated that they understood the basic nature of the tontine concept. William C. Johnson also clearly distinguished between tontine contracts, which were widely used in unregulated Britain without abuse, and the misuse their large surpluses engendered.[51]

In the final analysis, the problem with tontines was not the policies themselves; they were simply contracts, freely entered, that returned more to the insured the longer he lived and hung onto his policy. The problem was with the huge undivided surpluses that deferred dividend policies created. Many companies found the surpluses irresistible and used them to embark on a variety of risky schemes. Guardian's sale of tontine policies, therefore, should not be viewed as a stain on its history but rather as a tribute to its upright management. It faced the same temptations all insurers did, but there is no record that it ever gave in to them.[52]

Accommodating Exceptional Risks

Although Connecticut General Life and a few other insurers experimented with the writing of insurance on substandard risks as early as 1865, insurance for those deemed to be a greater than normal risk did not become widespread until the twentieth century. As late as 1903, for instance, Guardian instructed its agents to immediately reject persons "who have taken the 'Kelley' Cure, or who are of abnormal size, either small or large, deaf and dumb, blind or badly crippled." "Aside from the extra hazard involved in such risks," the company reasoned, "their acceptance tends to lower the standing of the Company in the eyes of the public." Furthermore, it instructed agents to steer any borderline applicants into high-premium endowment policies rather than whole life, or to assign them a higher age (and hence higher premium).[53]

By 1922, however, Guardian had changed its cold-hearted, though economically justifiable, position and began to underwrite substandard risks in a systematic way. By 1937, Guardian had five risk classes, a standard one that applied to about 90 percent of policyholders and four classes of riskier lives, of 125, 150, 175, and 200 percent of standard, that had to pony up "extra premiums" because they had a somewhat questionable medical history, worked in hazardous occupations, were young and underweight, or were old and overweight. By 1943, the company occasionally wrote policies on very high-risk lives, i.e., greater than 200 percent of standard, but reinsured the overplus. Until 1952, Guardian completely reinsured substandard risks rated over 400 percent of standard mortality. In 1954, Guardian cut its substandard premium charges in light of its experience and competitive pressures from other companies actively engaged in this field of underwriting.[54]

By the late 1960s, many life insurers, for an extra premium, regularly insured applicants with histories of heart attacks, cancer, diabetes, and other serious illnesses. Guardian agents began to complain that home office underwriting on substandard applications was too "strict." The underwriters shot back "that the *good* companies" had underwriting rules "not much different" from those of Guardian.[55]

Guardian also began to write policies for superior or "preferred" risks. After dabbling with the idea in 1939, and again in 1945 and 1946, Guardian introduced a preferred risk policy in 1948 that proved increasingly popular with purchasers of new insurance in the late 1940s and early 1950s. A quantity discount, or "policy fee" system further spurred sales of preferred risk policies.[56]

By 1953, the company issued three preferred risk policies. The contracts, which were only offered in amounts of $10,000 or more, and on lives first class in every respect, were unusually attractive because of their low net cost. The low cost came from slightly reduced commissions, better mortality, and expense savings due to their relatively large size. Preferred policies were often purchased by companies to protect their investment in key personnel. If the important person lived and stayed with the firm, the company could use the cash value of "key-man" insurance to provide retirement benefits. If the key person died, the company would be indemnified for his lost abilities and firm-specific human capital.[57]

Another formerly exceptional category was women. Guardian had long insured married, self-supporting businesswomen but rarely pushed for such business. In 1957 the company, "hen-pecked but hard-headed," reduced premiums on policies on the lives of women issued for $10,000 or more. This marked Guardian's entrance into the so-called wife insurance market. "We've thought women a good risk for some time now," an unnamed Guardian official told the *New York Times*, "but until recently, they did not own enough insurance to make it worth our while to reduce the prices." "It costs much the same to issue a policy for $1,000 as it does for $100,000," the official confided. Before World War II, most policies on women were for small sums designed to cover final expenses. After the war, average policy sizes for women grew with their increased economic importance. By 1955 some 10.5 million families counted on the earnings of both husband and wife for family support, up from four million working couples in 1940.[58]

In the postwar era, Guardian became as eager as any insurer to provide for June Cleaver as well as Rosie the Riveter or Rosalind the Real Estate Agent. The death of a wife and mother, the company now said, "leaves her husband and family not only bereft of her company but also of a Federal income and state income deduction and a possible Social Security allowance." So, the company offered a policy designed to allow a widower to purchase "at least a few of his wife's services." In the New York area in the 1950s, a professional cook cost $55 a week and a nurse about the same. Cleaners demanded $1.25 an hour on average, over $24,000 for a decade's worth of work. "And she's not deductible either," noted one young insurance broker. Starting in 1966, Guardian introduced a new term rider that provided inexpensive extra protection on wives' lives.[59]

Such policies were designed to indemnify family members for the lost income of a loved one. Except for industrial policies on the lives of working children, most of Guardian's juvenile policies were designed more as savings vehicles. In 1896, for instance, Guardian offered a novel child endowment policy in amounts ranging from $1,000 to $20,000. Under the terms of the contract, the life of the policyholder or donor was insured as well as the life of the child. If the policyholder died after making the first premium, the policy at once became paid up and the company would pay the face value upon maturity. If the child died before the endowment matured, the company returned all but the first premium to the donor. If both the donor and child lived, the child received the face value of the policy and the donor, the dividends. Premiums were low because the company earned a small profit (the first premium plus any earned interest on other premiums paid) if the child died and did not have to pay the death benefit on the adult until the end of the endowment period. This innovative juvenile policy was probably the product of actuary B. R. Nueske, who came to the United States from the Berlin branch in 1893.[60]

Guardian, however, did not write ordinary whole life policies on children below the age of fifteen years unless the father also carried insurance upon his life. In 1923, the company loosened that restriction somewhat, allowing its underwriters to sign a child if the father was uninsurable due to a medical impairment. If the father was uninsurable on account of moral hazard, however, the boy likewise became ineligible. The fear was that a morally suspect father might murder, endanger, or fake the death of the child.[61]

In 1945, Guardian announced a new series of juvenile policies, including endowments to the sixteen to twenty-one age group. The following year, it developed a Juvenile Insurance policy that returned premiums with interest at 3 percent if the child died before age ten and the full face value of the policy thereafter. In 1955 Guardian liberalized its juvenile line yet further, providing a full benefit after age one month and 25 percent before that. It also waived premiums on juvenile policies until the insured's twenty-fifth birthday if the policyholder (probably a parent or grandparent) died or became disabled. If the child became totally and permanently disabled after age twenty-five, he or she would also receive a premium waiver.[62]

In keeping with its name, Guardian also offered a variety of family-oriented policies. One such policy was designed to provide income for family members for ten to twenty years before payment of a lump sum. Policyholders gave the Family Guardian policy, the brainchild of Irving Rosenthal first issued on 1 March 1940, a hearty reception. The new policy's main target was relatively young family men seeking maximum protection at a low premium rate. For $65.52 a year, a thirty-year-old man received $5,000 of coverage to age fifty, by which age presumably his youngest children were nearing adulthood. Thereafter, he had the option to pay just $45.70 a year for $2,000 worth of coverage or to continue coverage at the $5,000 level upon payment of an additional premium. The policy offered regular cash and loan values, as well as the usual dividend options. Guardian updated the policies in 1950 by liberalizing conversion privileges and raising premiums slightly. In 1958, Guardian's Family Protector policy offered a $5,000 life paid-up-at-sixty-five policy for the breadwinner, a $1,250 term policy on the wife (adjusted by her age differential), and $1,000 of term to age twenty-two on the lives of each of his children. Accidental death benefits on both parents and disability waiver of premium were integral parts of the policy.[63]

Guardian had added accidental death benefits to many of its policies beginning 1 January 1917. The benefit, called double indemnity, paid double the face of the policy if the insured died due to an accident of any kind, like traveling on a common carrier such as a licensed streetcar or passenger train or other traumatic accident not linked to suicide or military service. At first the benefit was limited to those under sixty-five years of age, but later it was extended for life. Again, Guardian was neither the leader of the pack nor a straggler. After 1918, most whole life insurance written in the United States contained a double indemnity clause.[64]

Term Insurance and Annuities

Double indemnity also became a popular benefit of term policies. Term policies, unlike the whole life policies described above, generally do not have cash values, loan provisions, or surrender benefits. If the insured dies during the term of the policy, the death benefit is paid. If the insured lives, the insurer makes no payment. Term policies provide protection and temporary peace of mind, but little else.

Purists argue that there are weighty arguments against term insurance. They viewed its rapid strides with alarm. For starters, because premiums are almost solely a function of life expectancy, term is very costly at high ages. For instance, at one Massachusetts-domiciled insurer, a seventy-year-old male currently pays around $14,500 for a one-year term policy with a face value of $500,000. For the same amount of coverage at the same company, a thirty-five-year-old pays only $400. Moreover, policyholders generally misunderstand the nature of the coverage. Few realize that they are essentially renting protection, that the cost of rental will increase as they age, and that if their health slips they may not be eligible to continue renting at any price. Fewer still realize that although term premiums are much lower than whole life premiums for identical coverage, the mortality charge that they incur is usually *higher* on term policies. That is because, ceteris paribus, mortality rates are higher on term policies. Basically, people who believe that they are likely to die young or soon buy "cheap" term insurance while those who believe they will have average or better mortality buy whole life.[65]

Guardian has generally taken the middle position in the term controversy. It has never been a term enthusiast, but it has long offered it. At the most basic level, term coverage is better than no coverage at all. And term can become a stepping stone to whole life. The young breadwinner who does not yet have the resources to purchase a whole life policy, for instance, could be encouraged to buy term until his income increases. Then a conversion to permanent protection would be possible as well as desirable.

Guardian offered a type of convertible term policy, Accommodation Life Insurance, as early as 1875. The policyholder paid term rates for the first ten years, when, if still living, he or she could walk away from the valueless contract or convert it to a whole life or endowment policy at a rate that the company claimed was lower "than the established rates of this or any other company." Guardian could afford the low rates because before the twelfth year the policies were nonparticipating and had no surrender value. The policies were designed to help those whose means were limited to obtain cheap life insurance for a decade and to provide them with reduced rates and a conversion option without a new medical examination should they live and obtain greater means.[66]

Life insurers, including Guardian, have also long offered a type of contract, called a life annuity, that is, in many respects, the mirror image of life insurance. In consideration of the payment of one or more premiums, insurers pay annuity policyholders, known as annuitants, a sum of money annually until the annuitant dies. (Life insurance pays *when* the insured dies; annuities pay *until* the annuitant dies.) People purchase annuities to provide themselves a stream of income that they cannot outlive. Insurers generally do not physically examine applicants for life annuities because there is no incentive for a sickly person to apply for such a contract and because insurance companies do not feel that they can reject applicants for being too healthy.[67]

Guardian issued all the usual forms of annuity contracts but, like many insurers, did relatively little business with them until the Depression, when its Special Income annuities became popular. Under those deferred contracts, the annuitant received death benefits if he or she died before the life income payments began. The contracts also had paid up and loan values. Sales of annuities boomed after the Second World War because of the growing recognition of old age dependency. Due to increased longevity, mandatory retirement ages, and expectations of enjoying "the golden years," growing numbers of people stopped working years and even decades before they died. Annuities were never a major part of Guardian's business, however. In the mid-1960s, Guardian's rates on single premium annuities were among the lowest 10 percent of American companies. That, however, was not low enough to be competitive in the extremely price-sensitive annuity market. It also quickly shuttered its short-lived group annuity business.[68]

Disability Insurance

Death was not the only tragedy that could befall individuals. Physical illness and disability also had negative effects on family earnings. In the short run they could require large out-of-pocket expenses. By World War

I, life insurers were entering this nascent market, offering life policy riders and even full-blown health and disability policies.[69]

Fidelity Mutual Life Insurance Company of Philadelphia had issued a disability clause in its life policies in 1896, and may have been the first company ever to do so. Proliferation of such coverage was slow, however, until the 1920s, by which time most companies offered at least some kind of disability protection. Once again, Guardian was neither leader nor straggler. Its board had first authorized a disability clause rider on life policies in 1911, but one of a conservative variety that only forgave premiums should a policyholder become disabled. An extra premium was charged for the rider, and the benefit ended when the insured reached age sixty.[70]

In late December 1915, Guardian amended its charter to allow it to "make insurance upon the lives or the health of persons . . . and also to make insurance against injury, disablement . . . resulting from traveling . . . and . . . from sickness." This decision opened the door for a much more dangerous disability protection product that offered the insured an income should he become disabled. The company began to offer policies that paid an annuity of 10 percent of the policy's face value to any insured who became totally and permanently disabled. In 1919, Guardian increased its coverage by promising a monthly income of 1 percent of the policy's face value to disabled policyholders.[71]

Guardian's executives did not foresee the immense moral hazard problem that such policies would create, namely, that it was too easy for insureds to feign disability and defraud insurers. Fraud raised costs well above expectations. When times were hard, it got worse. Consider the Depression-era case of Julius Rosenbaum, who filed a claim for tuberculosis. When a medical examination turned up no evidence of that disease, he continued to claim disability, this time on the basis of having either an indeterminable throat condition *or* neurosis. More concretely, consider in table 5-2 the sums that Guardian spent corroborating disability claims versus death claims in the early 1930s. Corroboration costs included inspection, investigation, legal, and medical costs. Disability experience was particularly bad during the Great Depression, but it was never very good up to that time.[72]

Years before, in 1922, Guardian's managers, especially those conversant with Bismarck's ill-fated social disability scheme, correctly discerned that competitive forces had driven them to be far too liberal with disability benefits. It increased disability premium rates by between 20

TABLE 5-2
Guardian's Claims Investigation Expenditures, 1932–34

Year	Death ($)	Disability ($)
1932	5,613.85	38,156.44
1933	8,917.50	20,830.68
1934	3,036.70	12,004.73

Source: Memorandum, 14 February 1934, Claim Department Records, Box 77, GLIC archives.

and 25 percent effective in 1926. Rates were still not high enough given the relative ease with which policyholders could force long-standing claims against the company. For instance, in January 1925 an Indiana policyholder named Wilbur E. Barry, a minor, claimed a severe case of *ichthyosis hystex,* an untreatable disease that left both of his legs and his lower torso covered with a scaly condition that made his skin look like a piece of dried-up wood or alligator skin. According to his doctor and attorney, the condition made it "almost impossible for the insured to walk" and hence left Mr. Barry unemployable. Guardian resisted, arguing that Barry had been afflicted with the scaly disease since birth. The company disputed the claim on the grounds that "public policy inhibits bounty on fraud," and went to court. The judgment compelled the company to make monthly payments to Barry. In 1941 Guardian's Claim and Surrender Department again insisted on proof of Barry's disability. Proof arrived and Guardian continued to make the monthly payments, chafing over just one more instance of what it considered to be nothing more than fraud triumphant.[73]

All insurers suffered similar problems, and many exited the field. After exhaustive study, Guardian took the path less traveled and simply strengthened its underwriting, updating its disability provisions in 1932 and again in 1938, and reducing the monthly payment to 0.75 percent of the policy's face value. But claims arising from policies issued before 1932 continued to plague the company for years, despite a reduction in dividends on those policies.[74]

In 1938, Guardian sent a home office employee to personally visit each and every doubtful disability claimant whose policy predated 1932. The visits were designed to help the company to decide whether to continue paying the claims without doubt or to terminate payments. In cases still under doubt, the inspectors had authority to purchase the disability clause for up to three years' worth of benefits. They purchased a number of clauses, and in some cases entire policies. After regulators clamped down on this practice during World War II, Guardian discontinued it, even though it had worked up an actuarially sound basis for purchasing the contracts. What made justifiable business sense did not always win acclaim in the public arena.[75]

To try to reduce disability claims in the future, Guardian began to give agents basic instructions to help them screen out potential frauds. "Consideration of the often intangible, but nevertheless quite real, moral hazard constitutes one of the most important phases of Disability underwriting," the 1938 agent's manual explained. To estimate this intangible, agents were advised to give consideration to each applicant's character, reputation, insurance claim record, earnings, occupation, employment history, and credit rating. "An insurance company must appraise the moral hazard," in other words, "somewhat after the methods used by a bank or commercial house." "Lack of control in personal habits, drinking, gambling and speculating, and disregard of the rights and opinions of others," the manual urged, "strongly militate against the granting of Disability Benefits." The manual also noted that immigrants and females had much higher rates of disability and hence had to be screened with even more care. And of course legitimate occupational hazards had to be considered as well.[76]

Due in part to this training, the company's disability experience, like those of other companies that stuck it out and implemented underwriting and policy reforms, eventually became satisfactory. By 1940, Guardian was again pushing its individual disability clause, which it included in an increased proportion of eligible policies. In 1941, the company announced an extra dividend on policies with waiver-of-premium disability protection written since 1 January 1932 and with monthly-income disability protection written since 1 September 1934. It did so because the experience on the newer policies was greatly improved relative to the heavy losses on older business. The additional dividend, the company believed, was "a unique action by a life insurance company issuing disability coverage."[77]

After World War II, Guardian was one of the few companies that continued to offer protection against the hazard of permanent and total disability in the form of a monthly income. It increased coverage to 1 percent, or $10 per month for every $1,000 of insurance. When new entrants finally appeared in 1950, Guardian responded by broadening and improving its disability coverage. A new policy rider that provided disability benefits on term life policies was "an unprecedented innovation," according to Irving Rosenthal, one that placed Guardian "way out in front in term competition."[78]

In 1952, Guardian began to offer disability policies that could be purchased separately from any life policy. No longer was disability a mere adjunct to life insurance, so it could more easily evolve to meet changing market conditions and customer needs. The two most important characteristics of stand-alone disability products are renewability and definition of disability. At first, Guardian wrote "any occ" (any occupation) policies that paid only if the policyholder due to disability could no longer work at any occupation. Now, Guardian only offers much more liberal "his occ" (his occupation) policies that pay if a disabled policyholder cannot return to his or her precise occupation. A surgeon who suffered nerve damage in his hands but who could still work as a general practitioner, for example, would not receive benefits under the earlier "any occ" policies, but would under the newer "his occ" policies.

Similarly, early on Guardian wrote commercial policies, where it could increase individual policyholder premiums annually; guaranteed renewable policies, where it could only increase premiums for entire classes of policyholders; and noncancelable policies, where premiums could never increase. Today, it specializes only in the last-mentioned type, known in the business as "noncan" policies. In summary, Guardian's niche in the disability market today is in "noncan his occ" policies, not surprisingly the Cadillac of the market. But changes leading to that specialization did not come all at once, nor were they the only innovations the company undertook.

In 1958, Guardian rolled out three new disability products, the Reliance Total Disability policy, Income Guardian Disability policy, and, at the highest end, Income Defender Disability policy. For competitive reasons, those policies had 15 percent lower premiums than similar Guardian products. Since dividends were also lower, however, the net cost of the new policies was the same as the company's existing products.[79]

By 1965, Guardian's long-term disability rates were well above those offered by casualty companies. Guardian actuaries, however, believed that the casualty companies' rates were inadequate. The 1970s brought economic difficulties and with them, increased disability claims as the un- or underemployed found their disability coverage a useful supplement to government unemployment insurance. Guardian actuaries, much to the chagrin of agents, therefore remained conservative about pricing disability products, including long-term group disability. By the mid-1970s, intense competition and new Social Security disability provisions had cut deeply into the sale of disability income products. By the late 1970s, the company warned that a great deal of "over-insurance" had been written. It refused to exit, but became extremely cautious, with John Angle publicly wondering whether disability insurance had become "a demolition derby in which the winning car will drive off stuck in second gear on wobbly wheels and with its fenders dragging on the track."[80]

In 1987, Guardian learned another lesson about disability insurance. Policies became incontestable two years and a day after they went "in force," but neither statutes nor policy provisions adequately defined exactly when a policy became "in force," the effective date or the date of issuance. Because the courts hold that contract ambiguities must be resolved against the drafter of the contract, Guardian was forced to pay a fraudulent disability claim made more than two years after the date of issuance (4 December 1981) but before two years as measured from the effective date (25 February 1982).[81]

Disability insurance has always been a cyclical business. Guardian's experience with disability, though generally better and less volatile than that of the many companies that repeatedly entered and exited the business, was checkered. The profitability of the line experienced its ups and downs. In the 1990s, for instance, Guardian sold large amounts of disability insurance, much of it as a supplement or backup to Social Security disability benefits, but not all of it was for a profit. With its 2001 acquisition of Berkshire Life, Guardian wedded itself to the disability market for the foreseeable future. Berkshire had a good policyholder base, but all the risks of the business remained. And the acquisition made Guardian the second largest issuer of noncancelable disability insurance in the nation. Thus the question is begged: why did Guardian move so aggressively, deeper into the business? Quite simply, Guardian found that over the long haul it can sell disability policies for a profit and that it has an ample surplus to cover any losses incurred during cyclical downturns. That ability to focus on the long term, of course, is one of the great advantages of its mutual form.

As John Angle noted, disability insurance and certainly medical expense insurance are somewhat akin to casualty coverage. After all, if your automobile crashes, your property and casualty insurer picks up the cost of fixing it, after the deductible. If your body crashes, your life insurer pays the cost of fixing it, again after a deductible. Your car goes to a "body shop," you go to the hospital. So how did life insurers get into a line that looks like property and casualty? The answer lies in the intertwined relationship between death, disability, and health in people's lives. Clearly, dying puts a damper on one's earnings. But so too does crippling, long-term disability, and at younger ages the risk of disability is many times higher than the risk of death. Moreover, a disabled person continues to consume resources, so disability coverage is absolutely critical to every family's financial safety. So, too, Guardian realized soon after World War II, is health and accident insurance, which pinches the pocket two ways. When ill, one's income is reduced for a period of days, weeks, or months. Worse yet, the cost of health care can easily run into many thousands of dollars. As Guardian's advertisements put it, "your health is your wealth." To help people hedge health risks, Guardian, led by Gerald Parker, began in 1952 to offer health and accident insurance policies in addition to life and disability insurance.[82]

Health and Accident Insurance

Guardian's experience in the health field also dates back to the World War I era, when it was one of few companies that priced rudimentary health services into their life policies. Its participation in the field was small, however. It did insure the health of its own employees on an individual basis as a benefit. For many years, it reserved two beds at Lenox Hill Hospital for its employees. By 1941 that was no longer an adequate system, so it paid for individual hospitalization benefits for home office employees through the Associated Hospital Service of New York. In 1944, it extended the fully paid benefit to include full family coverage. It was expensive. When the AHSNY jacked up rates some 20 percent in 1949, Guardian began to explore lower-cost alternatives. In 1952, the company decided to enter the health and accident field, after receiving some technical aid from Monarch Life.[83]

Guardian thought of health and accident insurance as a natural extension of its traditional life and disability businesses. "These new forms," it explained to policyholders, "will equip us to offer an even more complete plan of protection against life's hazards." The first policies were designed to provide protection against the financial losses that usually follow an accident or a serious illness by providing monthly income during a period of disability and cash payments to help pay the cost of medical treatment and hospital and nursing expenses.[84]

Stories about accidents made for good publicity. For instance, in 1953 a twenty-five-year-old stenographer suffered a compound fracture of one of her legs in a skiing accident. Hospital and surgical bills came to more than $600. Luckily, she had been one of the first people to take out a Guardian health and accident policy. Guardian promptly paid her bills. "I am so thankful that I insured with The Guardian," she wrote. "An accident is bad enough without the necessity of paying for it over the next year or two." Two years later, a little girl got a piece of glass stuck in her eye while playing. Her doctors managed to save her vision, and Guardian footed the $1,000 bill.[85]

Thanks to such stories, increasing health care costs, and structural changes in the health care industry, health insurance grew rapidly between 1950 and 1955. Again, Guardian appeared in the middle of the pack, neither leading the charge nor lingering in the rear. On the urging of actuary Dan Lyons, it started off with only five policy forms until the company learned the business. And there was much to learn, including new, more stringent underwriting rules, and more accurate claim tables that would have to be developed.[86]

In 1954 Guardian, led by Gerald Parker, introduced a major medical policy, NC 11, that enjoyed considerable success in the individual market though its growth was somewhat limited by the company's refusal to sell the new policy to families with annual incomes over $25,000. Guardian, like several other insurers, believed that higher-income individuals demanded more expensive care, partly because they tended to reside in big cities, where medical costs were high. Moreover, high barriers to entry slowed progress. Michigan, for instance, required a $300,000 deposit before it would allow Guardian to write health contracts.[87]

Health insurance was rife with actuarial problems and moral hazard. The development of Guardian's 1954 individual major medical policy highlights some of the daunting difficulties that its actuaries faced. They started with a large but somewhat problematic study published by Prudential. The first difficulty was that most, but not all, of the lives in the study were male. Second, the study did not consider several important factors, including higher utilization of medical facilities due to the presence of insurance, individual selection by the insurer and elimination of preexisting illnesses, income understatement by claimants, and expense padding by claimants and doctors. The report also made no allowance for future price inflation. Guardian decided to ignore that shortcoming because it believed that if and when such inflation occurred, premiums could be appropriately increased without incurring policyholders' wrath.[88]

But the other shortcomings of the study could not be easily overcome. The Prudential analysis did not account sufficiently for the moral hazards of medical insurance. Guardian's actuaries decided to add 50 percent to the Prudential table to account for the fact that people will seek out more treatment if insured. As John Angle noted in a 1973 article, in health insurance "one sees situations where the applicant at his option can seek medical treatment for an existing impairment or chronic condition so as to make frequent or prolonged disability quite likely." The actuaries also added 33.33 percent for the underestimation of income (people would tend to lowball their income expectations), and 25 percent for expense padding by medical providers. After subtracting 10 percent for anticipated deselection of the worst cases, the actuaries had made what they thought were conservative estimates.[89]

But such issues turned out to be only the tip of the iceberg. Health costs seemed always to increase faster than inflation. "The demand for medical services tends to increase more rapidly than the supply," Irving Rosenthal noted in 1961, "so the purveyors of such services are increasingly in a stronger economic position. The medical profession is certainly taking advantage of this strong position so that the cost of medical services is increasing more rapidly than the general price level." Members of the public, therefore, have had to shell out an increasing percentage of their income for health insurance and they have not been happy about it. Moreover, health costs at times rise so rapidly that insurers lose significant sums before they can increase premiums. More difficult still, health care costs vary considerably from region to region. Over time, the average length of hospital stays decreased, but per diem fees soared, often enough to compensate for the shorter stay. Worst of all, the statistical relationship between age and health costs and income and health costs was not static; it changed over time.[90]

It turned out, too, that new business production in the individual health line could be increased with relatively little effort and expense. And it was a business amenable to constant refashioning. To stay competitive, therefore, Guardian's actuaries had to stay extremely busy. Their correspondence, which included any number of exciting theoretical games related to health insurance, is enough to make the layperson's head spin.

As health insurers began to accept, of course for an extra premium, a broader range of health impairments, Guardian began to offer health insurance for people with physical impairments or a history of illness— "impaired risks"—in 1956. It seemed like a good move, as gains in accident and health surged upward in the first three-quarters of 1957. In 1958, Guardian updated its individual major medical policy line and began to write group major medical business modeled on its successful individual policies. But the market turned, and individual major medical lost money in the late 1950s, inducing Guardian to withdraw two major medical forms and to increase premiums.[91]

Individual health insurance in force grew steadily in the late 1950s and early 1960s, with premium revenues increasing from almost nothing in 1952 to over $12 million a year a decade later. Guardian continued, however, to place more emphasis on the writing of life insurance. By the early 1960s, the company believed that major medical health insurance would never contribute to surplus. It needed to continue to offer such policies, however, to keep up the morale and cross-selling opportunities of the field force. "The moral of this story," Rosenthal argued, "is that by watching experience carefully and by changing policy forms and rate levels as frequently as we dare we can just about keep on an even keel financially in our Major Medical lines." Guardian, like other companies, hoped that the health line would help to save new field representatives from failure by providing them with policies that were easier to sell than ordinary life policies.[92]

Ergo, the company continued to innovate and adapt in this challenging field. One major innovation in Guardian's major medical policy was a renewable provision, introduced in 1959. The company offered a Guaranteed Issue Option that essentially "insured insurability" by allowing policyholders to buy additional health insurance at specific ages up to age forty, regardless of changes in health or occupation. Though of course popular with prospects, that feature was somewhat risky as it was guaranteed renewable. Moreover, though by the terms of the contract Guardian could increase premiums, regulators often dragged their feet signing the necessary approval forms.

In 1960, Guardian introduced a new Senior Citizens Hospital and Medical Expense reimbursement policy, the first of its kind to offer guaranteed coverage, renewable for life, to people in the sixty to eighty age bracket. Two years later, it joined with six other New York companies to establish the New York 65 Health Insurance program, which covered New York State residents age sixty-five or over for basic hospital and surgical benefits and major medical expenses. The proliferation of policies and broadening of coverage was almost irresistible.[93]

Guardian's individual health lines broke even in the fourth quarter of 1962 and again began to show a profit in the first quarter of 1963. Guardian revamped its major medical program on 1 April 1964 and rolled out a new line of individual health policies on 1 February 1965. The new individual health policies, which included a new occupational classification system, were designed to improve the company's competitive position and to increase the proportion of health insurance business accounted for by the loss of income types of coverages as contrasted to hospital and medical expense coverages. This new loss-of-time program took hold very well.[94]

When Medicare was enacted in 1965, the company revamped its medical expense policies. It took advantage of the partial socialization of health care by offering a lower-priced policy that was renewable until Medicare benefits kicked in. It also created a policy designed to supplement the benefits of Medicare where no coverage or only a limited coverage was afforded by the new law. "Among the most important of these," Lyons informed the board, "are hospital confinement after the exhaustion of Medicare benefits, private duty nursing care and provision for some of the medical expenses in excess of those provided for by Medicare." The death knell for Guardian's senior citizen products was not Medicare, however, but the reluctance of regulators to grant premium increases. Delays of a year or two, combined with the rapidly rising cost of health care, forced Guardian to play constant catch-up in a game with the rules stacked against it.[95]

The continuous upward trend in medical costs and frequent government forays into the area made health insurance a highly dynamic field. Premiums were based not on current medical costs but rather on expected future medical costs. Guardian's projections were not always accurate. The company's health care business took a beating in the first half of 1966, for example, because its actuaries had not fully anticipated a sudden acceleration of the upward secular trend in medical care costs. Volatility in the individual health market plagued Guardian into the late 1970s. The area was restored to profitability under the direction of Joseph D. Sargent, who moved it from the red to the black during his six-year stint as its head (1979–85), partly by moving Guardian out of the individual major medical field in 1980.[96]

Fundamental changes in health care subsequently stymied the individual health field. The importance of individual health slowly shrank to insignificant portions of the company's overall business, despite forays into HMOs like Physicians' Health Services and Foundation Health Systems. Today, Guardian does not sell individual health insurance.[97]

Equity and Variable Products

Inflation, in the words of Irving Rosenthal, knocked "the hell out of all" the company's traditional products, especially those with large saving components. As John Gray, Guardian's somewhat eccentric group actuary, noted, life insurers had become "less and less competitive for the savings dollar" since World War II. Though in absolute terms, savings in debt instruments through life insurers had increased, life insurers' percentage of total savings was shrinking rapidly. The public realized that "the record over the last 10, 20, 50, 100 years (and longer) shows that equity investments have proved superior to debt investments." If Guardian and other insurers wanted to compete for the savings dollar, Gray contended, they would have to establish "separate accounts," an accounting device that would allow insurers to offer equity-based products similar to those offered by banks and mutual funds. Compared to mutual funds, especially, permanent life insurance seemed, in inflationary periods, a relatively poor investment.[98]

Insurance diehards continued to urge investors to purchase huge amounts of permanent life insurance and fixed annuities before considering mutual fund investment. They noted that people die at unpropitious times, including market downturns. They argued that life products provided an adequate income in the long run, as opposed to a higher income that might run dry during retirement. And they pointed out that term insurance had a higher rate of expense than whole life or endowment policies. For the "buy term" strategy to work, therefore, investors had to earn a return materially higher than that of the insurer. Those were logical but often losing arguments.[99]

It was safer for a number of insurers to take the middle ground. Investment in life insurance and mutual funds could be "blended," tailor-made for individual investment strategies. Benjamin Woodson stated the case most clearly when he wrote that life insurance was "the ideal investment for *some* of the investment dollars of *all* persons, for *most* of the investment dollars of *most* persons, and for *all* the investment dollars of *some* persons." The "blenders," as they were sometimes called, argued that mutual funds hedged against inflation and life products hedged against deflation. So investors should have equal amounts of each. The blender strategy made particularly good sense in the early 1960s when inflation was still relatively low and investors believed that they were equally likely to face inflation as deflation in the years ahead.[100]

By the late 1960s, however, inflation began to look like a more permanent part of the economic landscape. Companies like Prudential had already introduced variable life products linked at least in part to the performance of equity funds. Guardian, however, hewed to the blenders' credo. It would use investor interest in equity products to spur demand for the company's traditional life products. Such an approach fit perfectly with Guardian's durable Graph Estate sales program.[101]

Guardian made two forays into the equity field. First, under the stewardship of George Conklin, William Brown, and, later, Jack Smith, the company began to invest increasingly heavily in equities for the company's general account. (This development is covered fully in part III.) Second, Guardian established separate accounts to back its mutual fund offerings. To sell those funds, in 1968, several of Guardian's officers formed a legally independent broker-dealership, GLICOA Associates, as a closely held stock company. The following year, after regulators approved the move, Guardian bought the firm. GLICOA had to register with the SEC and forty states under their so-called Blue Sky laws. It joined NASD and set about training Guardian agents in the ways of equity products.[102]

Guardian urged its new equity products offspring to move quickly, and its managers complied. William C. Brown took the helm and produced quick results. In April 1969, Guardian became the first major New York life company to offer its field force mutual fund products, the Compass Income Fund and the Compass Growth Fund. Sales of those funds were limited in the early going, due to poor performance, low commissions, and the need for each agent to obtain NASD certification. Not a propitious start. Sales lagged behind expectations into the early 1970s but then improved markedly, prompting Guardian to roll out its flagship Guardian Park Avenue Fund. That fund outperformed the S&P 500 eleven out of thirteen years between 1974 and 1986, inclusive. It ranked among the top-rated funds from its inception until at least the mid-1980s, sporting annually compounded returns in excess of 20 percent. In 1981, Guardian began offering a cash management account linked to a money market mutual fund. The Guardian Cash Management Trust, a no-load money market fund with check-writing and Visa card service, allowed customers to participate in the high yields then available in the money market while providing prompt liquidity. The product was one of several offered by Guardian Investor Services Corporation (GISC), a subsidiary formed out of GLICOA Associates. (GISC also sold Real Estate Limited Partnership programs, which allowed individuals to invest in real estate in a tax-advantaged investment vehicle.) "We did it to grab clients," explained Joseph Caruso, the corporate secretary. The idea was to position sales representatives to cross-sell Guardian's Park Avenue Funds. The strategy was successful, and by the early twenty-first century, Guardian was offering an array of equity products through its equity profit center.[103]

Guardian was a more reluctant player in the new arena of variable life insurance products backed by equity investments. The company took the position that people should purchase guaranteed life insurance of the traditional type first. Upon that solid, permanent chassis, the reasoning went, the rest of one's estate, the "at risk" part of an individual's wealth, could be built.[104]

In thinking about variable life insurance, Irving Rosenthal favored the adoption of a British-like system. In Britain and Canada, life insurers offered a guaranteed death benefit but cash values at the insurer's discretion. That allowed them to invest relatively heavily in equities on their general account. When the stock market was high, they could afford more generous nonforfeiture benefits and paid up additions. When the markets were low, they continued to pay the guaranteed death benefits but cut back on cash surrender values. "The guaranteed cash value," Rosenthal argued, "is both the glory and the bugbear of American life insurance." Other managers felt that variable products, though better than no protection at all, were simply too volatile, too much at risk, to serve the essential protection function. That belief colored all of Guardian's actions in the variable arena.[105]

The basic problem with nonguaranteed variable products was that, tied as they were to the vicissitudes of the equities markets, they placed investment risks squarely on the shoulders of the insured. A variable life policy might be worth, say, $100,000 one year, $120,000 the next, but only

$90,000 the year after that. To purists, variables offer another way to speculate in the stock market, not protection. The attraction of variable products was, according to Joseph Caruso, "the sizzle as much as the steak." Guardian therefore pretty much stayed clear of the variable bandwagon. As late as 1972 the company stated that it had no immediate plans to develop a variable life policy, though its executives realized that "some degree of price inflation is likely to be with us indefinitely and, therefore, a variable life insurance product cannot help but be attractive to a large proportion of prospective life insurance purchasers." After Guardian decided to create a variable life contract, its plans got bogged down in regulatory tangles and the company's firm belief that in most instances whole life better suits the needs of its prospects and policyholders. Guardian still sells mostly standard whole life; variable products represented only about 20 percent of its new business in 2001, compared to about 80 percent or more of new business at some other companies.[106]

Variable annuities were treated somewhat differently. Guardian had been aware, since 1966, that variable annuities would at some point in the not-so-distant future be an important part of the industry's operations. The company had less of a problem with variable annuities because they could be used to bolster investment in fixed income annuities as a hedge against high inflation. It decided to hold off on their development, however, until the government clarified the laws and rulings governing variable annuity products. By August 1968, Guardian thought the legal ground clear enough to establish a separate account to handle its new variable annuity policies, which it hoped would prove helpful in retirement planning.[107]

By February 1969, the company had a Group Variable Annuity policy prepared for sale. The development of individual variable annuity policies, however, faced higher regulatory barriers and turned out to be a much longer process. SEC oversight of the variable products was in the offing and had to be provided for. In late 1969, therefore, Guardian decided it was best to write individual variable annuities through a subsidiary, though the tactic would take some time to implement. Indeed, the SEC delayed introduction of Guardian's variable annuities until 1971. Conklin promised skeptical agents that he would be the first to buy one of the annuities. It was worth the wait. For a time, in the early 1980s, Guardian's variable annuities were the best in the business, particularly after the company teamed up with Value Line in 1981 to offer a product called Value Guard.[108]

Competition caught up when Guardian failed to develop newer equity products quickly enough. In 1997, the company, stung by the loss of investment guru Chuck Albers to Oppenheimer, felt the need to introduce some new blood. So the company's CEO, Joseph Sargent, and chief investment officer, Frank Jones, recruited Bruce Long, the president of New England Variable Life Insurance Company. Long came to the company as a senior vice president, with a mandate to fortify the equity profit center. He put in a new, more flexible operating system, developed new products, and improved the company's "Dalbar" policyholder service ranking from 41 (out of 48) in January 2000 to 12 (still out of 48) in December of that year. Those were not transient gains; in 2002, the center won two Dalbar awards, one for mutual fund servicing and one for servicing variable annuities. Improvements like those allowed Long to land a sales agreement with broker-dealer A. G. Edwards, a relationship that expanded Guardian's equity product distribution system to over twenty thousand registered representatives. But Long was not done yet, adding the mammoth UBS Paine Webber to Guardian's distribution chain in 2003.[109]

Finally, it should be noted that Guardian has completely eschewed nonvariable, "universal life" policies. Credit for developing universal life (UL) is generally given to George R. Dinney of Canadian insurer Great-West Life, who developed this kind of policy in 1971. Universal life is a flexible-premium, adjustable death benefit policy. Its hallmark is flexibility. Subject to certain restrictions, UL policyholders can pay whatever premium they wish, whenever they wish. Subject to underwriting requirements, they can adjust their death benefits upward or downward whenever they like, as they see fit. Some companies went further, fashioning hybrids known as "variable UL" policies tied both to the stock market and to the policyholder's decisions regarding premium payments.[110]

Because of regulatory restrictions and tax liabilities, the first universal life policies did not appear in the United States until 1979. By 1987, however, 375 companies sold universal life products. No life product has gained acceptance so readily in the industry. Indeed, by 1985, universal life accounted for over a third of all individual life premiums paid. But, as usual, Guardian did not jump on the bandwagon before considering the implications for the policyholder. Simply put, it found UL sorely lacking. The problem here was that UL policies were *too flexible.* Premiums were too easily skipped and face values too easily reduced. Commissions fluctuate too much for the liking of career agents. Moreover, due to the uncertainties of the cash flows, insurers who sell UL policies cannot invest as long-term and hence, ceteris paribus, they reap lower investment returns. Finally, Guardian's strategy for selling insurance, now as it had been in the past, was to emphasize the safety of insurance over the potential windfalls from investment. It was a conscious strategic choice that kept Guardian from becoming swept up in industry trends that may not have the policyholder's best interests at heart. That same strong commitment to the policyholder also pervades Guardian's other major products, individual and group policies designed as employee benefits, the subject of the next chapter.

6

Product Development

Group, Benefits, and Reinsurance

This chapter describes products, both individual and group, designed to serve as employee benefits. Sometimes, as in the case of pension trusts and franchise insurance, Guardian's individual life field force marketed individual policies through employers to multiple individuals. Group insurance, however, was generally a more efficient way of delivering employee benefits. Group is an umbrella term for a variety of products offered to entire groups of people rather than individuals. Group policy types include life, disability, health, and dental insurance. Group is a huge business in the U.S. economy today, yet it is relatively modern. At Guardian, group insurance is now a distinct part of the company's business, with an economic structure that is fundamentally different from that of its individual life and health business.[1]

A fundamental difference is the relative efficiency of group insurance. Expenses on group policies are considerably lower than on individual policies. Sales efforts may be more intensive, but their yield is higher. It might take, say, ten thousand person hours to sell one thousand policies to individuals, but only one hundred hours to close a group deal with a company with one thousand employees. After the sale, it would take untold hours to service those one thousand individual policies. But in a group sale, the insurer issues only a single master policy to the company, which does most of the rest of the business of selling, administering, and collecting premiums from its employees.[2]

Group underwriting is also a different animal than its individual-line cousin. Life insurers generally underwrite the "group" rather than the individuals composing it. They more or less assume that anyone able to work (or be a member of the group) is a decent enough individual risk. What the insurer needs to ascertain is the average quality of lives that select into particular groups. While certain groups might not be wanted at all, the group underwriting game, for larger groups anyway, is really more about determining the appropriate premium than accepting or rejecting risks.[3]

Guardian's niche in the group market is relatively small groups with as few as one or two members. That niche has, for the most part, been extremely profitable. Because of those two facts, Guardian's individual life agents have repeatedly sought a piece of the pie, sometimes through direct sales of individual employee benefit policies like pension trusts, sometimes through indirect attempts to capture some of the Group Department's profits. That is somewhat ironic given Guardian's tenuous initial exploration of the group marketplace.

Fits and Starts in Group

Modern group life insurance, characterized by its low-cost, standardized product for pools of customers, was in part a response to the demands of the burgeoning labor movement of the late nineteenth century. One possibility for insuring masses of uninsured workers was to socialize insurance. Wisconsin, the leading Progressive state of that era, actually implemented a program in which the state offered its citizens level-premium, whole-life insurance at cost. Since commissions for distributors were low, the state did not write much business, but the program was a worrisome harbinger of things that might come, as far as insurance executives were concerned. Some companies responded to the threat of social insurance by developing products that could be made low cost enough to cover large numbers of people who might not otherwise afford their standard products.[4]

The logic of group insurance was not apparent right away. Life companies at first tried to sell wholesale life insurance to workers by sending agents to their places of employment. It was an efficient way to sell, if employers were willing to provide access. It seemed a natural tack for industrial policy insurers, but Guardian, too, entered into this arena when it insured all of the employees of a large manufacturer in 1890. Yet, while all the employees of this and similar workplaces were covered, insurers issued the policies to individual workers; employers played little if any role in the transaction, probably regarding it simply as a goodwill gesture toward their employees. It was not until 1911, when Equitable managed to insure 125 employees of the Pantasote Leather Company in one stroke, that industry leaders began thinking more seriously about the possibilities of group insurance. The following year, Equitable persuaded Montgomery Ward, as an employer, to purchase the first true group policy, blanket coverage to its workers as an employment benefit.[5]

Fraternal societies and companies with large stakes in industrial insurance cried foul, claiming that such group policies were unsound if only because they did not require medical examination. But in fact group policies were quite sound. They were almost always term coverage, written for modest amounts. Many companies, including industrial companies, sold nonmedical insurance in individual lines as well. Because the face value of such policies was low, it simply made sense to skip the examination, as the calculated costs of meeting claims were generally spread across large enough numbers of lives to offset the increased risk of individual mortality in the group.[6]

Group life grew slowly at first, simply because most employers did not want to foot the bill. By the same token, employees could not be easily persuaded of the benefit of paying for insurance out of their own pockets. As principles of "scientific management" and "industrial relations" began to take hold in the second decade of the century, employers began to recognize the value of providing some measure of worker compensation, in the form of retirement and other benefits, as a spur to productivity. In many cases, employers agreed to split the bills for group insurance, which generated more demand for it. When payroll deduction schemes became more popular in World War I (as unions made great gains in the industrial sector), insurance premiums were increasingly deducted from wages. Pay stubs provided employees with constant reminders that they were receiving quality protection at dirt-cheap rates. It was then that group insurance began to make serious inroads into the market for industrial insurance. Company sponsors had begun to realize that group insurance was a much more efficient way to protect large numbers of the working poor, while remaining flexible enough to also help insure managers and even executives.[7]

Guardian began writing group life policies during World War I. Its first group insurance sale was made to another life company, the venerable Pennsylvania Company for Insurance on Lives and Granting of Annuities, in 1916. The policy was for $220,000 of participating renewable term insurance (roughly $3 million in 2001, a large amount for the time). Guardian maintained that client, which it later shared with Aetna and Equitable, until sometime after World War II, during which time the coverage on over five hundred employees grew to over $1 million, which turned out to be a very profitable piece of business.[8]

Guardian's policy in the early years, however, was not to entertain any application for group insurance, so the company regularly turned away agent requests to approach prospects in that market. The company's officers did not want to undertake the anticipated expense of creating a dedicated group insurance department. Continuing pressure from field salesmen changed their minds in 1924, when they agreed to consider group policies that came to the company without competition. The company would also step up its efforts in more traditional wholesale insurance.[9]

Because Guardian was not prepared to go out and meet competition in this market, group and wholesale business merely trickled in at first, until John C. McNamara, Guardian's most productive field agent, prevailed on the company to become more aggressive. In 1925, the company introduced a Salary Allotment Plan, whereby Guardian issued individual whole life policies without medical examination to the employees of any company that agreed to make monthly payroll deductions to cover premiums. Guardian continued writing such quasi group business until after World War II.[10]

In fact, by the end of the 1930s, Guardian had in force only two true group policies, its share of the Pennsylvania Company's business and its own employees'. From 1910 through 1936, Guardian offered to employees and officers who had been at the company for ten or more years a death benefit equal to a percentage of the final salary of two times the number of years employed, up to 100 percent if employed for fifty or more years. In 1937, the company substituted term insurance for all of its U.S. employees equal to the high end of their salary group range. For instance, the family of any employee who earned between a then-substantial $1,501 and $2,000 per year would receive a payment of $2,000 if the employee died while still employed by Guardian. In 1940, the company provided group coverage to all its sales agents to the tune of $1,000 each.[11]

As World War II ended, of Guardian's peer companies, only Home Life was selling group insurance. But Guardian once again was coming under pressure from its sales representatives, who sensed that the labor market was going to be quite different from that of the Depression. Government freezes on wages during the war had whetted employee demand for "fringe benefits," which aggressive unions were able to extract from large-industry employers that were in no position to take a strike during the

FIGURE 6-1 *Guardian's Share of the Group Market, 1960–2000*

conflict. In 1947, Guardian's chief actuary, Irving Rosenthal, completed an exhaustive study of group insurance that suggested that the company should shy away from the group field. The company, especially Dan Lyons, continued to monitor group developments. It finally decided to enter the group market in a serious way in 1955, once the company had put its individual life segment back on firm ground and the market for group had increased to such levels that it was impossible to ignore. By then, the nation's major corporations had assumed the role of welfare providers, at least as they now routinely wrote retirement benefits and group insurance coverage into their employment contracts. The demand for wholesale insurance, in the meantime, had virtually vanished. It had higher rates than group and did not enjoy the more favorable tax treatment that the government provided for group insurance, so politically popular it had become among unions and employers alike.[12] (On the growth of group, see figure 6-1.)

Group Forges Ahead

Guardian's decision to enter group rested squarely on Rosenthal's acceptance of an actuarial analyses performed by Robert Wilcox, the firm of Milliman and Robertson, and Robert C. McQueen, consultants the company had hired to study the matter. Group's growth would continue to accelerate, McQueen had reported, because of the increasingly onerous nature of income taxation. "Group insurance is a means of partially relieving highly paid personnel from their responsibility to purchase substantial amounts of personal insurance." "Because of today's high tax rates," he explained, citing *Business Week,* "it is much more expedient for a company to provide a liberal Group insurance plan for its staff than raise salaries sufficiently so that the individuals themselves may buy personal insurance." Even better, New York had lifted restrictions that historically limited the face value of group policies to less than $20,000. Now, group could serve as more than a glorified industrial policy, and develop into a full-fledged employee benefit. It could serve as more than the traditionally modest coverage for low-paid workers; white-collar managers could enjoy substantial coverage under group. Moreover, Guardian realized that it could sell group disability and health policies as well, essentially offering an entire employee benefits package. The company decided to jump in, and never looked back.[13]

Group insurance turned out to be a good fit for Guardian, which had long specialized in the upper-income part of the market, and which was particularly adept at servicing small business owners. Moreover, Guardian already had a firm foothold in another area of the employee benefits business, pension trusts.[14]

Pension Trusts and Group Pensions

As with life and health insurance, Guardian had gained pension experience with its own officers and home office employees, to whom it first offered modern pension coverage on 1 January 1942, after four years of study. Before the war, Guardian made ad hoc decisions regarding retirement benefits by placing employees on the so-called retired list. Under the new plan, employees were entitled to at least their contributions plus

2 percent per annum interest and were vested upon attaining age twenty-five and completing one year of service with the company.[15]

As late as 1940, Guardian was turning away outside pension business because such deals required it to issue annuities and special life income endowment policies with which it had little expertise. But just two years later, Guardian reversed course and entered the pension field. It did so in response to requests from two organizations, the Telephone Company Workers Union and the Egyptian Lacquer Company. At first Guardian's managers worried that existing competition might be too well established, and that the cost of setting up an organization for the profitable handling of such business was too high, but they at least decided to investigate the possibilities. They learned that recent tax code changes had made the pension business more attractive, and so they dedicated one home office employee to help agents to write pension trusts. It was enough. Pension trust business began to flow in the following year, and Guardian struggled to find personnel to help administer the load. The company then launched an agent training course on pension trusts to bring its sales force up to speed.[16]

Thus the market beckoned and the company responded. In 1943, Guardian introduced a Pension Trust series of policies designed to provide companies with a means of paying pension income to retirees. In 1946, it expanded its pension line with policies that placed particular attention on the practical problems facing medium-sized firms employing between twenty-five and 250 persons. By 1947, it had begun servicing firms with as few as ten employees and by 1952, with as few as five. Small firms would also become important in Guardian's other employee benefit lines.[17] Technically speaking, pension trusts were not group policies at all but legal trusts established to carry out the terms of a pension plan for a group of individuals, usually employees of a common employer. Essentially, they were individual life insurance policies, sold by field agencies, but specifically designed to fund employee pension programs.

What became an intriguing interplay between regulation, taxation, and policy innovation enlivened the pension field as it developed in the 1950s. Insurers had to scramble, not merely against each other but also against banks and trust companies that exploited certain tax advantages to spirit a good deal of the pension business away from life companies. Tax changes eventually crippled the pension trust business and in 1974 the passage of the Employee Retirement Income Security Act (ERISA) changed the landscape altogether. ERISA, which was designed to protect the retirement savings of American workers, spawned the now-familiar 401(k) and like plans. Guardian's board hastened to form an unincorporated subsidiary to provide pension consulting services. The new entity was to render sales assistance and pension plan management services, including consultation, actuarial work, installments, government reporting, and data processing to interested parties, whether they owned Guardian policies or not. Regulatory approval to enter this business came in 1975.[18]

But by the end of the decade, the pension trust business had lost its luster. A sea change had occurred in the market for pensions. As Rosenthal noted, "low employee turnover, stable prices, stability of the employer, and predictable political action were all taken for granted" when Guardian had first entered the pension business in the 1940s. Now, high inflation, increases in Social Security benefits, rapid employee turnover, and corporate mergers were turning the pension field into something more akin to a minefield. Facing such challenges, pension trusts slowly disappeared, leaving Guardian without a pension product for approximately a decade and a half.[19]

In 1995, Guardian decided to fill that void by creating a new group pension profit center. Guardian hoped to make the line profitable by selling true group pension products, primarily 401(k) plans, instead of multiple individual policies to its small business niche. The company struggled to make this business work, but was unable to achieve sufficient scale to become profitable. It stopped writing new group pension business in 2002.[20]

Group Insurance and the "Baby" Market

The same social forces that made group life insurance and pensions more attractive in the 1950s were also at work in the health field. It was 1955 when Guardian first stuck its toe in the group health insurance waters. That year it wrote a group health policy for its own home office and field employees. Two years later, Guardian began writing commercial disability, accidental dismemberment, and medical policies for other companies.[21]

Early on, group health and accident insurance lost money for the company. Publicly, Guardian blamed acquisition expenses. More likely was that the company had bitten off more than it could chew, having chased such large potential clients in the nation's center industries, such as General Motors, General Electric, and General Dynamics. Guardian could not compete in that jumbo arena with the big boys in group insurance, the likes of MetLife, Prudential, Mutual Benefit Life, and Connecticut General.[22]

Because its new Group Department, which began operations in March 1957, was small, Guardian lost only $122,000 in the first nine months of 1957, even after accounting for development and operating expenses for both the home office department and the field office. The situation improved when the department's leading light, Arthur Ferrara, shifted gears and reoriented the company's group insurance strategy to go after the smaller "baby group" market. Most group insurers had ignored the smaller companies under the assumption that writing small business would not be profitable. It turned out to be a good, traditionally apt niche market for Guardian. Once the decision was made, Guardian moved rapidly to secure its share of this, as it turned out, growing market throughout the country, and the company soon became among the largest underwriters in the small group market. McLain immediately saw that Guardian was poised to make a big splash in the market. Legend has it that he added an additional floor to the planned home office annex to house the Group Department at a time when it consisted of a couple of salesmen and a secretary![23]

In 1957, the "baby" market was defined as companies employing ten to twenty-four people. Guardian did try to crack slightly larger companies—it encouraged its sales representative to try to write business for companies with seventy-five to one hundred employees. But the competition was boring down into that somewhat larger market from above, and so by 1964, four out of five Guardian group policies were written on cases under fifty lives. As long as the company concentrated on baby groups, it could make money, particularly after it learned how to select the cream of the crop. Good margins, less competition. That was the place to be.[24]

Indeed, the most interesting aspects of Guardian's group experience revolved around its efforts to write increasingly smaller groups. Its first major foray was something of a step backward to the age of wholesale insurance, but it filled a need. In 1961, it began to offer so-called franchise insurance, discounted individual disability insurance, to organizations with five to twenty-four employees. The policy was designed for groups that did not legally qualify for a true group policy or that desired greater benefits than those provided in typical group policies.[25]

Conscious of the shortcomings of franchise insurance, Guardian in 1962 slashed franchise premiums and simultaneously began to work on a policy, unveiled in 1964, that offered both life and health coverage to groups of four to nine lives. The ad copy was brief and catchy: "Two's a couple, Three's a Crowd and Four is a Guardian group." The gambit worked: the Group Department broke about even in 1964 and went "in the black" in both 1965 and 1966. The department kept its costs low by remaining perpetually "understaffed" by traditional standards. And the staff was in turn hampered by what its managers felt were unfair regulatory restrictions, "imposed . . . on us that our competitors do not have."[26]

Guardian took another major step in 1967, when it joined forces with the Rhode Island Hospital Trust Company to create the Multiple Employer Trust (MET) program. MET—no one said what MetLife thought about it—allowed employers with from two to nine employees to purchase group insurance. Unlike most group policies, employees had to show evidence of insurability and were subject to medical examination if they opted for additional coverage. By 1969, 3,203 companies were participating in the trust. Like most of Guardian's early group endeavors, the policies were actually a bundle of insurances, including life insurance with an accidental death benefit, loss of time insurance, hospital, surgical, and pregnancy benefits, and supplemental major medical.[27]

New York regulators took notice. Two employees, they thought, did violence to the concept of "group," and so the MET program could not be approved. Guardian general counsel Ed Kane fought back. The company's arguments went as follows. First, MET pooled employers that were of the same type and hence of similar risk. Second, the company did not abandon individual underwriting procedures. Finally, and most importantly, Guardian asserted that New York had no jurisdiction in the matter; Rhode Island had no group insurance laws. For good measure, Guardian contested the jurisdiction New York regulators had over contracts entered into by small businesses even in New York. After protracted litigation, the regulators finally approved the practice, in 1972.[28]

Thus Guardian had set out looking for bars of gold but learned instead that it could forge bars from many little nuggets. By the mid-1960s, Guardian was one of the princes of group insurance, a king in its small-market niche. In October 1966, Provident Mutual managers visited Guardian to learn the secrets of Guardian's success. Guardian had become an industry benchmark. And the market was huge and relatively untouched for decades. As late as 1979, over half of all small businesses had no group insurance at all.[29]

The Elements of Success

How *did* Guardian do it? Irving Rosenthal's analysis of the group experience is revealing. Rosenthal noted that there was "no doubt that luck has also played a part, bad luck on their part and good luck on ours." But companies, like people, make their own luck. Rosenthal chalked up Guardian's superiority to its sales strategy, underwriting, dividends, expenses, and managerial incentives.

To use the inquisitive Provident Mutual as a counterexample, that company did not write major medical policies or any groups below ten lives, the presumed minimum for making good money. Provident, a close proxy for Guardian's competition in the small market, routinely wrote policies limited to accident and health insurance, instead of the entire package or bundle of insurances, a concession that Guardian rarely made to prospective clients. Provident's limits, moreover, were less liberal than Guardian's. For its part, Guardian was "tougher . . . in checking back for previous experience, . . . enforcing actively at work provisions, and in insisting on life coverage cutbacks at retirement." And it kept its dividends low. Perhaps most important, Provident's sales representatives were simply not as good, or motivated, as Guardian's: they received lower pay and displayed higher turnover.[30]

Guardian was better able to increase rates when it needed to precisely because its sales force was motivated enough to "*sell*" the rate increases, along with the insurance. As Rosenthal put it, Guardian's group sales force was not "bothered as much by price competition because it believes in its product and knows how to take full advantage of its quality features." They were good at making the case that Guardian's group health policies provided "richer benefits" to counter prospective customers' price resistance. (To this day, the company's group health policies, which are PPOs, provide much richer benefits than HMOs and even most alternative PPOs.) It was a case of loyal salespeople selling product differentiation, pure and simple.[31]

For many years the Guardian group sales force enjoyed relatively high compensation and considerable autonomy while having a strong rapport with the home office. But things deteriorate when unattended to, and by

1977, Guardian's group representatives were complaining, more vociferously than usual, that the company's group policies had become too expensive to sell. Group executives were in a bind. They were convinced that the competition was underpricing their offerings, but that would not comfort the sales force. Two years passed before the industry generally faced up to the pricing problem, but tensions between the home office and the field lingered.[32]

When dealing with the field force, group officers confronted many of the same problems that faced their colleagues on the individual insurance side. They periodically had to rein in aggressive salespeople, reminding them to sell the company's products to prospects, and not to sell prospects' policies to the company. On one documented occasion, a sales representative asked the Group Committee to alter the psychiatric language in its major medical policy so that he could quote on a large prospect that would be sensitive to the provision as it was. When the committee quickly declined the business, it could not have helped but alienate the agent.[33]

Other pressures were brought to bear on the group managers by the individual lines agency force. When Guardian sold group it sold *term* insurance. Agents, on the other hand, champed at the bit to offer *ordinary* life policies to groups on the belief that the demand would burgeon. A 1969 internal study showed that such policies were likely to be unprofitable—not likely to be a winning argument for the sales force. In the end, the Internal Revenue Service came to the rescue when it imposed tax rules that effectively impaired the value of ordinary group insurance, in 1971.[34]

Small-group policies had a specific category of risk about which managers had to remain alert. They were subject to the risk that a workplace catastrophe would cause a major spike in claims. Guardian suffered just such a spike in early 1969, when a flash fire in a small building in midtown Manhattan resulted in life claims of $150,000. It had to cope with a much bigger spike, obviously, when the World Trade Center was destroyed by terrorists in September 2001, until then among the least likely of events to be envisioned by group actuaries. Still, such risks were statistically small compared to the benefits of writing group lines.[35]

Quickening Pace of Competition

The Group Department turned its first profit in 1965, and by 1970 it was making a substantial contribution to the company's progress and profits, freeing up resources for Guardian to invest in other areas that might not have been possible otherwise. But again, time and competition did not stand still. Group insurance early on involved much "blocking and tackling"—doing the little things to keep agents and brokers happy and customers buying. Through the 1970s, every now and again, a new entrant would stir things up with a rate cut or new product wrinkle. But in general, the market quickly returned to equilibrium, often with Guardian emerging with increased market share.[36] (See figure 6-1.)

In the 1980s, competition in group insurance quickened and became more fluid, and by 1990, the pace of change seemed out of control. To remain a player in the market, a company had to stay on the cusp of innovation. Regulations changed, and as old-line mutual companies converted to stock corporations, they proved more willing to make abrupt changes in pricing policy, if only to shore up short-term earnings. In some cases, larger insurers began to see group insurance as a loss leader for other insurance and investment products.[37]

Rapidly changing markets called for rapidly evolving strategies. In the 1970s, the average Guardian group consisted of six to seven lives. By 1990, the fastest-growing segment of the company's group business remained groups of fewer than ten lives. After that, though, Guardian felt confident in moving "up market"—like Toyota from the Corolla to the Lexus—so that by the end of the century, its average group approached fifty lives. (When competitors invade your markets, invade theirs, provided that you are strong enough.) Similarly, as traditional products like indemnity health insurance disappeared, Guardian worked hard to find new markets, such as group dental, to take up the slack.[38]

Changing regulations also affected aspects of the group market. Group health, for example, fell casualty to increasingly burdensome government regulations. In 1993, for instance, New York State compelled insurers to accept all applicants and to charge all policyholders the same rate. Whether lawmakers anticipated the response or not, insurers simply exited the Empire State. The situation was especially difficult for Guardian, which lost some fifty thousand small group customers covering some 250,000 individuals. Moreover, Clinton administration proposals to socialize health insurance, combined with the rapid emergence of health maintenance organizations (HMOs), created much uncertainty and hence hindered long-term planning efforts.[39]

Despite setbacks in group health, Guardian remained a major force in the group marketplace as it widened its small-market niche. In 2001, the company's 220 group salespeople grossed about $750 million annually, spread over a wide array of products. So few could sell so much because they did not sell directly, but rather seeded the field for the company's basket of group wares, preparing independent agents and brokers to place larger blocks of business with the company.[40]

The foregoing does not do justice to the many corners of the group insurance field Guardian ventured into or rejected along the way. In 1957, the company took a share of the Federal Employee's Group Life program. Four years later, it toyed with, but abandoned, the idea of bidding on major medical coverage for all employees of New York City, but quoted on occupational accidental death insurance for the city's cab drivers, one of many small specialty coverage gambits. In 1973, the St. Louis Cardinals wanted to insure its first baseman, Joe Torre, for up to $150,000 a year for three years, back in the days when that amount reflected a healthy salary for a prime player. Guardian studied Ball Players Keyman Disability Insurance intensively. Rosenthal may have gotten a kick out of poring over the disabled lists of major league baseballs players. Or maybe not. His notes include mention of such early 1970s stars as *Ernest Banks* of the Chicago Cubs, Pittsburgh's *William Mazeroski,* the Giants' *William L. McCovey,* Kansas City's *Louis V. Piniella,* and Oakland's *Reginald M. Jackson.* One wonders if Rosenthal would have referred to Babe Ruth as George Herman or Sudden Sam McDowell as Samuel.[41]

In the final analysis, the group profit center's most important contribution to the company may not have appeared on any balance sheet or P&L statement. In a 1969 speech, Rosenthal celebrated the advent of group insurance and paid homage to what he saw as its remarkable impact on the corporation. In a nice rhetorical device, he juxtaposed group, the "New Guardian," with the more traditional "Ordinary division" or "Old Guardian." The New Guardian, he noted, was younger. At its head was Iowan John Gray, a self-confident, even brash executive, strongly perfumed with the smell of success. Gray, a highly controversial and extremely competitive ex-Met man who joined Guardian in 1963, was onto something. Part of his secret, perhaps, was that renewable term group policies were very forgiving. If mistakes were made, they could be fixed the following year. "If the old Guardian makes a mistake," Rosenthal said, "it takes 10 years to discover it and 20 years more to live down its effects." The New Guardian, moreover, was better adapted to the inflationary world that dogged traditional life insurance. The Old Guardian benefited from the new ideas and the sheer vigor of the group managers and sales force, whose "tremendous volume of new business" had surpassed expectations. Despite its traditional conservatism, the Old Guardian's executives had given the youngsters a great deal of leeway to conduct their business as they saw fit, to open and close offices, to experiment with products and pricing. As the Old and New Guardians closed their "communication gap," they recognized themselves as part of a continuum in the company's history. "Both Guardians believe in developing unique products which appeal particularly to small businesses—our best clients," Rosenthal concluded. If he were alive today, he would no longer need to make the distinction.[42]

Insurance for Insurers

The essential residual of an insurance company's business is *reinsurance.* It is the means, in part, by which conservative insurance underwriters compensate for the enthusiasm of their sales forces. Life insurers inevitably write policies that fall outside their tolerances for risk. Policies may be too large, too burdened with outlying or uncertain characteristics. To reduce their exposure to large or uncertain risks, life insurers regularly reinsure policies that exceed their so-called retention limits, the maximum policy size for a particular class that they wish to take on. Reinsurance, in short, is insurance for insurers.[43]

Consider the example of one thousand male insureds, each forty years of age. According to the 1980 CSO table, 3.02 of those men will die before reaching their next birthday. The insurer knows that simple "fact" with a great deal of precision. What it does not know is who among the insureds will perish, those with $1,000 policies or those with $1 million policies? As one can imagine, the difference is quite important. To the extent that small and large policyholders are of the same "class," i.e., have the same mortality rate, there is no way for insurers to predict which outcome will occur. What reinsurance does is to reduce that uncertainty, by providing a means by which insurers can share large risks.

Reinsurance also reduces the strain of new business on the insurer's surplus. When a company writes a new policy, it must immediately establish an actuarially sound reserve to pay it should the insured die. Given that new business often costs more to acquire than is received in first-year premiums, new business "strains" surplus because insurers must allocate part of surplus to cover the policy reserve. By reinsuring the risk—sloughing the risk off onto another company—the original writer of the policy avoids the need to reduce surplus to cover it. Through reinsurance, companies with ample surplus, like Guardian, can essentially lend part of their surplus to smaller, less well-capitalized insurers.

Reinsurance also enables insurers to arbitrage premium spreads between companies. That is, the original writer is able to extract a larger premium from the policyholder than it has to pay to reinsure the risk. The spread or difference between the two premiums is gross profit. For instance, a company might write a $100,000 policy with a $2,000 premium on a risky life. It might be able to reinsure $90,000 of that risk with a company with less stringent underwriting requirements for risky lives for only a $1,000 premium, and then pocket the difference.

Guardian has been both seller and buyer in the market for reinsurance. On the one hand, it has acted as a direct-writing or "ceding company," i.e., a company that originally wrote a policy and wished to divest itself of some of the risk. On the other, it has sometimes acted as a reinsurer or "assuming company," i.e., the company taking on the risk. Historically, ever since its first major reinsurance treaty was signed with NYLIC in 1875, Guardian has acted mostly as a ceding company. Though it reinsured policies for the temporarily troubled NYLIC in the 1870s, it did not regularly act as an assuming company before the 1980s.[44] Since the early 1950s, Guardian has also been an active participant in various reinsurance risk pools.

For Guardian, ceding certain types of business was conventional practice until 1922, the year when Guardian's management began to consider that reinsurance was quite profitable to the assuming company. In 1924, it reported on a study of the advantages of taking on the excess business of other companies, and then experimented with so-called facultative reciprocating agreements, whereby it traded policies with a reciprocating company. The practice ran into resistance from Guardian underwriters, who balked at the incoming business in such deals. Because the contracts were "facultative," as distinct from automatic, Guardian reserved the

right to reject such business, and did so often enough to make the recip-
rocal nature of its agreements a moot point.[45]

Before that development, Guardian had ceded most of its reinsurance
business to MetLife, at least until 1923 when it formed what would prove
to be a long-lasting relationship with the Lincoln National Life Insurance
Company of Fort Wayne, Indiana. In the years leading up to World War
II, Guardian did most of its reinsurance with Lincoln in accordance with
a hybrid yearly renewable term/coinsurance contract. (In general, reinsurance contracts are either coinsurance contracts, where the reinsurer
assumes a proportionate share [say 50 percent] of any liability arising
under the original policy in exchange for a proportionate share [say 45
percent] of the policy's premiums, *or* yearly renewable term [YRT] contracts, where the reinsurer assumes the policy's net amount at risk in exchange for the payment of a term premium by the ceding company. The
Guardian-Lincoln contract was literally a hybrid between the two arche-
types.) The unusual contract raised regulatory eyebrows, but was perfectly legal.[46]

In the years leading up to World War II, Guardian also signed YRT
contracts with MetLife and three smaller companies and entered into
coinsurance contracts with MetLife and ten other companies. Those reinsurance treaties, Irving Rosenthal later showed, were profitable because
the company's underwriters proved particularly adept at identifying the
good lives for the company to keep while reinsuring those who died. Its
mortality rate on ceded business was 150 percent of expectations, against
50 percent of expectations on the business it kept. Almost all of those
losses were on high policy value borderline risks, a class for which reinsuring companies were notoriously optimistic. In other words, as Irving
Rosenthal implied in his review of the experience, reinsurers got just
what they asked for, even if they did not know it.[47]

After years of getting the short end of it, Lincoln and MetLife, which
had taken on the lion's share of Guardian's reinsurance business, began to
sour. Said Rosenthal, "It took all of Mr. McLain's formidable persuasive
powers to convince Mr. McAndless, the boss of the Lincoln National, to
continue as our sole reinsurer." Lyons suggested that only McAndless's
friendship with McLain—they were drinking buddies perhaps—kept the
contract in force. Higher rates were the answer. In the mid-1950s, when
Guardian was still reinsuring mostly with Lincoln and MetLife on automatic as well as facultative agreements, it began to enter into modified

coinsurance contracts, that is, contracts in which the reinsurer lends the policy reserve back to the original company, with MetLife and four other companies. The amounts were small at first but soon grew. For the next twenty-five years, Guardian preferred ceding by means of automatic treaties on a modified coinsurance form.[48]

After World War II, Guardian sought to lay off new categories of catastrophic risks, as the risk of war-related catastrophes, including nuclear strikes, increased. Commercial reinsurers like Lloyds shied away from such astronomical risks, so in 1952, Guardian agreed to subscribe to the Joint Committee on War Problems' pooling arrangement "for the equitable distribution among life insurance companies of serious, but presently undeterminable losses on account of catastrophic war deaths within the Home area." In more commercially related risks of potentially outsized proportions, Guardian became active in "pool reinsurance," where it joined with other carriers to insure such exotic special risks as jumbo jet hulls, space vehicles, satellites, and the like.[49]

As for standard reinsurance, Guardian had been tapering off its historical habit of ceding business since the beginning of World War II. This trend was reflected in increases in retention limits, which were raised from $75,000 in 1930 to $150,000 in 1952 (more than a mere offset to inflation), and then, more dramatically, to $250,000 in 1956. To hedge some of the added risk that it was taking on, Guardian entered into various "catastrophic loss" contracts. The contracts did not cover individual policies but rather the possibility of a single, tragic event causing a spike in claims. In 1960, for instance, Lloyds of London covered Guardian's "excess losses," any losses greater than $525,000 arising from any one accident or catastrophe, up to $3 million. Lloyd's later upped Guardian's coverage to $10 million and its deductible to $750,000. At the time, Guardian was channeling most of its regular reinsurance business, what little of it there was, to North American Reinsurance, Lincoln National, Security Benefit of Kansas, and Cologne Re.[50]

By the mid-1960s, Guardian was using reinsurance as sparingly as possible, retaining every risk that it possibly could. This position held until April 1979, after which the company began to cede a much larger volume of life insurance. The motivation for this reversal of policy was to take advantage of price concessions on bulk sales and to reduce exposure to the perceived growing risks of certain classes of individual life insurance. By the end of 1980, Guardian was ceding all risks in excess of $1 million and 90 percent of the risk on nonpension trust policies that were valued on standard actuarial tables. In addition, the company ceded business facultatively in those underwriting situations in which it preferred not to keep its full retention limit. Later that year, Guardian decided to reinsure 40 percent of the risk under all pension series policies and 40 percent of the risk on all policies valued on the 1958 CSO table of mortality. By purchasing this additional reinsurance, Guardian stabilized the levels of its mortality experience and decreased the surplus strain of writing new business. By using the modified coinsurance form of reinsurance, the reinsurers took on part of Guardian's mortality, investment, and expense risks. The large volume of ceded business, moreover, gave Guardian significant negotiating power.[51]

As Guardian ceded record levels of its own business, it also became a major reinsurer or assumer of other companies' risks. John Angle was the champion of reinsurance, and in the years immediately preceding his ascension to the presidency, he made the case for it in numerous papers and memoranda. He understood that the market for reinsurance was purely caveat emptor, but also that it had grown to be quite efficient. From the detailed historical analysis that pervades his writings on the subject, one gets the sense that he was frustrated by the company's modest presence in this market. Guardian had slipped into reinsurance in the mid-1960s, when it joined the American Accident Reinsurance Group (AARG) and the Extended Reinsurance Group (ERG). By the early 1970s, after giving much thought to the peculiar problems of pricing insurance pools, Guardian covered catastrophic losses with AARG and by joining a consortium of ninety-three life insurers known as Special Pooled Risk Administrators, Inc. By 1979, the company had earned a modest cumulative profit of $1.3 million from various reinsurance pools, but that was a pittance compared to what could be had. And the timing was right. There was a fortuitous opportunity for a surplus-heavy company like Guardian to move boldly into the reinsurance business on the basis of the prevailing inflationary environment.[52]

"More companies appear to need financing assistance today than 10 years ago," Angle wrote, "because . . . inflation, and improved mortality experience, have rendered existing valuation standards too conservative and often require insurers to set up deficiency reserves." In some cases, he noted, "deficiency reserves exceed 100 percent of the first year's premium in magnitude." Any company that did not have sufficient surplus to finance the sales volume that would be required to keep pace with inflation would be ripe for reinsurance. As Angle noted, Guardian could lend some of its surplus to needy companies "by means of the device of reinsurance."[53]

There was also a sound strategic reason for entering the business related to the industry intelligence one could gain only from a reinsurer's perspective. Reinsurance gives the reinsurer an opportunity to gain information of considerable value. Reinsurers rapidly learn the forms of insurance that are selling so well that the issuing companies need reinsurance assistance, and the pricing returns to both ceding and reinsuring companies. Reinsurers, finally, know the identity of companies that are pressed so hard that they need to obtain reinsurance. Some of those could become candidates for acquisition.[54]

When he became president, Angle committed the company to reinsurance, and by 1985 he reported that the assumption business, with help from Thomas Kabele, was growing "rapidly and profitably." But by the late 1990s the company found that it had gone too far, that it had taken on esoteric risks that it wished it had not. After the events of 11 September 2001, Guardian retreated from the assumption market, selling some of its reinsurance subsidiaries. By early 2003, it was essentially back where it started.[55]

The same does not hold true for Guardian's advertising history. For much of its existence, as will become apparent in the next chapter, the company remained reluctant to make a major investment in advertising. In the mid-1990s, however, it decided to capitalize on its good name and reputation by greatly increasing advertising expenditures for the Guardian brand name. By 2003, the company showed no signs of deviating from its new, more intensive advertising strategy.

7

Spreading the Word

If one were to think about insurance advertising, one might envision a couple discussing the vicissitudes of life that may require buying protection for the family. Or one might dimly recall hearing an electronic voiceover, warning of unexpected bad news. *What if, heaven forbid, you are not always around to care for your family?* Or, one might remember a print advertisement extolling the benefits of building a secure financial future through insurance. But all in all, while people may recognize the names of particular insurers, they will be unclear as to how they heard of them. Particular advertising campaigns are not easy to associate with particular companies. Prudential's Rock of Gibraltar and MetLife's Snoopy (that warm and fuzzy icon of shrewd innocence, romping in a field that makes people otherwise uncomfortable) are rare exceptions.

Of course, the objective of life insurance is at root an unpleasant subject. Advertising insurance may motivate, but fear also induces inaction. Because it has always been difficult to determine the cost-effectiveness of advertising generally, and of insurance advertising in particular, life companies have not made the levels of financial and creative investments in ad campaigns that, say, consumer goods companies—for whom advertising is like life's blood—have done. Guardian, certainly, has not been famous for its ads, but that is not to say that its advertising campaigns have been unimportant. Insurance advertising has always served as a necessary and useful vehicle for raising awareness about insurance, per se. It has, on occasions, boosted new products into the marketplace. And it has supported sales agents in their sales pitches to their prospects.[1]

In the nineteenth century, life insurance companies seized upon train wrecks or other newsworthy disasters to advertise their products. It was not uncommon for readers to come across planted news items about widows and orphans who had either been helped by insurance or ruined by the lack of it. Such tactics did not sign much new business directly, but gave sales agents the ammunition they needed to get prospective customers' attention and to explain the risk and reward considerations of insurance.[2]

As one might expect, from the beginnings of the industry, insurance advertising stressed the protection of loved ones. Consider the late-nineteenth-century Northwestern Mutual ad portraying a mother, two children, and the empty chair of the deceased father. It was surely intended to melt the heart of Ebenezer Scrooge. The good news was that the bereaved family was amply provided for materially, and the light streaming in from the window suggested that it was also provided for emotionally or spiritually. This theme suffused all the literature that was distributed to the public, right down to the early-twentieth-century letterhead of Guardian general agent Charles Rudd, which proclaimed, "Wives may object to life insurance. Widows never do."[3]

It was in more recent times that industry and corporate advertising began to focus less on family catastrophes and more on such positive themes as the savings and tax benefits of insurance. Insurance as a means to personal financial well-being! A 1968 Guardian advertisement that ran in several magazines illustrates the point nicely. Above an eerily familiar icon—a white-bearded man, bedecked in stars and stripes, hand outstretched, palm up, with greedy eyes aglow—was the caption, "If you think you're leaving everything to your wife and kids there's something you should know about your Uncle Sam."

But questions were begged, then as now, as to the efficacy of advertising. Did such powerful images add to the bottom line? Did such ads actually induce people to buy insurance? If so, did they attract potential customers to the advertiser, as opposed to any insurer? And if so, did it cause enough new prospects to actually sign up to justify the expense of the ad? Or was advertising effective only in molding general public perception about a company and its products? Was it enough to expect that good life insurance advertising might accomplish two simple things: (1) convince the audience of a need for insurance; (2) persuade those who feel a need to contact the advertiser or his agent, not the closest or cheapest source of supply? The latter was certainly harder to achieve than the former. And all of it was hard to quantify.[4]

Regardless of the need to be filled, neither objective of the advertising process was easy, but both were necessary lest the advertiser merely throw its money away or simply stimulate sales for more conveniently located competitors. Of course, advertising, if it worked, redounded to the benefit of the industry as a whole. A free-rider problem? Not really. Many companies, including Guardian, historically contributed to various industrywide cooperative advertising programs designed to drive up the aggregate demand for life insurance.[5]

Early Promotional Strategies

Such industry advertising aside, Guardian has always invested in advertising and promotion aimed at selling its own products, developing its own brand, and providing guidance to its sales force. As early as 1861, Guardian had developed a prospectus that contained a set of responses to all the major objections to life insurance. They went something as follows. If a prospect worried that life insurance was contrary to morals or religion, the sales agent could point to the ethical value of insurance. Morality and faith demanded lawful provision for the consequences of unexpected death. To those who argued that their surviving wives and children could work for their livings, the salesman could point out the fact that female and child labor were unremunerative. To those who claimed that they had already accumulated enough assets to cover the needs of their loved ones, a salesman could observe that a collapse of the financial markets (a frequent occurrence in the nineteenth century) could easily wipe out any fortune. *Why not buy insurance and be doubly sure?* To those who said that they were too poor, the salesman could show that just six cents a day would insure a thirty-year-old man for a robust $1,000—more than a year's wages for, say, a typical practicing lawyer or clergyman. To those who showed indifference to their mortality—a common affliction of youth—salesmen were loaded up with stories of healthy young men who had been cut down in the prime of life. And savings was an added feature. One could argue the added benefit of life insurance as a way to save for retirement, in addition to its protection.[6]

The prospectus, and the salesman's pitch, went to prepared, or potentially prepared, buyers. To attract prospects required broadcasting. One of Guardian's first means of advertising was to print copies of its corporate charter and bylaws, which it did in 1860, 1867, 1891, 1899, and several more times throughout the twentieth century. Dry reading, to be sure, but the documents at least introduced the company, its history, and its governance procedures to potential policyholders.[7]

Most of Guardian's early advertising was flat-out boring, aimed at informing while projecting the solemn solidity of the enterprise. That was considered good. Often, the company's advertising consisted of a balance sheet, the names of directors, and other strictly factual or statistical information. In 1870 Guardian boasted that it had met the rigorous requirements of the laws of Germany, Austria, and Switzerland, no doubt of passing interest to Central European immigrants. In 1909, the company actually published a pamphlet listing *every single death claim* that it had paid since 1860. The pious might have found more excitement in *The Book of Numbers*. The pamphlet provided the name and residence of the insured, the amount paid, premiums received, the year of issue, the year of death, and even the policy number. There was no attempt to highlight the more compelling cases, such as that of Claude Rebard, who met his demise having paid $161.66 in policy premiums. Did he die happy? The payoff to this family was a tidy $3,000.[8]

What Guardian liked to stress in its more aggressive advertising was that its policies were "simple and liberal," that its management was "prudent, economical and successful," and that its financial condition was "unequaled." Agents, closer to the customer, were a bit more creative and certainly more reader friendly. Agents spent their own funds to promote their local business, and often wrote their own copy. In their advertising they tended to reach for the heartstrings. In one 1900 advertisement of a Guardian agent in Colorado, a small boy playing with a toy boat inquires,

> "Papa, if you are called away on a long journey, you would leave mama and me some money to use until your return, wouldn't you? How about that journey you will some day be compelled to take, and from which you will never return? Don't you think you ought to make some provision for us then?"[9]

For advertising claims to be effective—that is, in the long-run improvement of the business—they had to be independently corroborated. Guardian repeatedly *requested* the New York superintendent of insurance to audit its books and examine its operations. In 1878, the superintendent demurred; he had no budget to undertake such a project. Guardian responded by hiring outside auditors to undertake the chore. Guardian passed the audit, and the superintendent stamped the company with his imprimatur, certifying that the company operated under "the most skillful management." (By the end of the century, Guardian had to undergo direct examination by regulators whether it wanted to or not.)[10]

Guardian's annual report to policyholders served double duty as an advertising pamphlet. That the company put out a report at all made it somewhat unusual, placing it in the relatively small class of conservative insurers who believed in cultivating existing policyholders as much as planting the seeds for new ones. It was good business. Its 1871 policyholder report claimed that Guardian was "possessed, over and above its Capital Stock, for every One Hundred Dollars it owes, of an amount of One Hundred and Thirteen Dollars and Fifty-eight cents." "It is evident therefrom to all, and beyond cavil," the broadside claimed, the "absolute security" and the "large Dividend paying capacity" of Guardian. In 1877 the annual report enumerated, in English and German, the names of the company's directors and officers, the company's balance sheet and basic cash flow, and the quality of its investments, policies, dividends, and premiums relative to leading competitors. The twenty-one-page pamphlet also listed the company's premiums on three major policies—whole, accommodation, a form of convertible term, and endowment.[11]

Publicity in the Pre–World War I Era

Guardian's most interesting promotional activities in the late nineteenth and early twentieth centuries were not technically advertising at all, but rather fell under the more general rubric of publicity. Insurers were not always as decorous as they liked to represent themselves as being. Many companies attacked their rivals in newspapers whose editors gleefully accepted side payments to run vituperative stories aimed at undermining corporate reputations. Because of its own good reputation, Guardian generally avoided the worst of such attacks, except of course during World War I.

Industry publications were also important vehicles for publicity, and it was useful to exploit them. (The company's agents read them. Prospective agents read them, too.) In 1904, for instance, the company was concerned to take bragging rights away from New York Life, noting that it, Guardian, had pioneered American insurance in Germany. The following appeared in the *Insurance Monitor*.

The Germania Life Insurance Company of this city has issued a circular to its agents calling attention to the fact that it was the first American company to enter Germany—in 1868—and has uninterruptedly done business in the German Empire ever since. This circular was called out by a newspaper dispatch announcing the fact that the New York Life Insurance Company was the first to comply with the requirements of the new insurance law of Germany. The Germania announces that it has now in force in the Empire M. 140,000,000.[12]

Guardian often demanded credit when it thought credit was due, and released the equivalent of the modern public relations dispatch whenever it wanted to get its achievements into the press.

Yet, for the most part, Guardian's attempts at publicity were as dull as its advertising. Consider the following 1907 blurb in the *Insurance Monitor*.

The Germania Life Insurance Company had a premium income of nearly five million last year, and returned over three millions to its policyholders. A liberal part of the difference was employed in so strengthening its reserve that all its policies, both old and new, have now been put on a 3 1/2 per cent basis. The total assets now stand at about thirty-seven and a half millions, insuring over one hundred and fourteen millions of risks. During the past forty-six years this company has returned to its policyholders nearly two dollars for every dollar of assets which its holds, and has paid out and now holds by six and a half millions more funds than it has ever collected from them, besides paying the expenses of management.[13]

The best publicity Guardian ever received was not its own doing. The clean bill of health given to the company by the Armstrong committee investigators helped Guardian differentiate itself from its more tainted rivals and from the mass of new stock companies that sprang up in the West and South. All the company needed to do was to point out that it was a New York–domiciled company and everyone knew that it was closely regulated. It was possible to go overboard. So proud of its executives' testimony before the New York State lawmakers was Guardian that it published the verbatim transcripts, certainly valuable to historians.[14]

Other than media coverage, Guardian and its more prosperous agents dispensed a considerable variety of promotional materials, including address books, desk calendars, mini calendars, memo books, and miniature almanacs that, alongside lists of facts like the population of U.S. cities and the time needed to digest certain foods, conveniently contained tables of premiums on various Guardian policies. Guardian also used postcards featuring the home office on the front and witty little sayings on the back, some in mock-biblical prose. One card read, "The prudent man foreseeth the evil and insureth well, but the simple pass on and leave their families to suffer the consequences of their selfishness or lack of foresight." Said another, "If a man cannot spare one-tenth of his income for life insurance how does he think that his widow can manage to spare the whole ten-tenths?" Even if one made allowance for the deceased's gambling and drinking expenditures, the point was no doubt well taken.[15]

Guardian rarely missed an opportunity to proselytize. In 1912, an illustration of the new home office in Union Square—itself an advertisement to all who beheld its monumental solidity in one of New York's more cheerful neighborhoods—graced its receipts. In the 1930s, the back of the company's receipts solicited requests for a free booklet that explained "how to keep well, how to keep a policy in force, how to save and spend wisely, how to name the beneficiary properly, how to protect the beneficiary against loss." The receipts were emblazoned with the policyholders' service department credo: "Of use to the Policyholder while living."[16]

The Advertising Age

Probably more effective were the pamphlets that reprinted letters from grateful policyholders and beneficiaries that appeared after World War I. In 1926, Guardian supervisors were asked to send a copy of letters expressing appreciation or thanks for unusual service to a company officer for possible use as advertising. The pamphlets that were produced from such comments, though by their nature anecdotal, were quite forceful in stressing the importance of insurance and the quality of Guardian's service. Consider, for instance, the missive of Mrs. W. J. Morrison of Etna Mills, Virginia:

> Am in receipt of my draft. Feel so very grateful to you. Your courtesy and promptness will be a fine ad in this vicinity. I was so much opposed to my husband having his life insured, but he did so in spite of opposition. Now I have found it to be of the greatest comfort and consolation.

Or the letter of Miss Florence Candler of Denver, Colorado: "I certainly appreciate very much the infinite amount of time and effort you have spent in locating us and paying a policy, the existence of which was not even known to us."[17]

As the twentieth century progressed, Guardian agents became ever more adept at placing useful stories in their local newspapers. Guardian's advertising also loosened up, became more creative, and focused more clearly on Guardian's competitive advantages. In 1913, Guardian pitched its nine great virtues in a little sheet called "A Few Reasons Why to Apply for Insurance to The Germania Life Insurance Company."

1. Its Great Financial Strength
2. The Conservatism in its Investments
3. Its well defined Policy of steady growth
4. Its Record of Dividends to Policyholders
5. The Results achieved for its Policyholders
6. Its Care for the Interest of Its Policyholders
7. Its fairness in dealing with its Policyholders
8. Its unequaled record in Foreign Countries
9. The Attractiveness of its Policies.[18]

It was in the consumer revolution during the "Roaring Twenties" that Guardian, right in step with corporate America, entered the modern advertising age. Guardian's advertisements became more succinct, more punchy—denser in content yet lighter in words. Writing ad copy had become an art. The foregoing "reasons" were whittled down, in 1927, to just five words: Age, Control, Strength, Policies, and Service.[19] More impact; easy to remember.

The yearly reports to policyholders continued to serve as a primary means of advertising to the fold. Along with the company's balance sheet, an illustration of its recent growth, and a letter from the president was a solicitation for additional information. The president's letter might outline Guardian's current sales theme, or it might attempt, in a bad year, to put a positive spin on the future. In the company's 1919 statement, President Hubert Cillis explained that mortality rates, which had soared the year before due to the historic influenza epidemic, had dropped to 66 percent of expectations. He then noted that "Life Insurance is practically the only commodity which has not risen in cost during the last few years, notwithstanding the fearful ravages" of the epidemic. That was, in fact, untrue. Premiums had not risen, but Guardian and other insurers had slashed dividends. The really good news of the year, ironically, was that the epidemic had impressed upon millions of Americans the urgency of insurance protection.[20]

In 1923, the leading themes of the annual report were Guardian's decision to diversify its mortgage portfolio in the different localities where it wrote business, and its program for further increasing the efficiency of its agency organization. In 1927, the company extolled its rapid growth and high investment returns as sure signals of its value to policyholders. In the 1929 statement, President Carl Heye stressed that the stock market crash had not adversely affected Guardian. Instead, he claimed, the lesson of the preceding October's stock market crash was that the "economic value of life insurance as an asset always worth 100-cents-on-the dollar was realized to a greater degree than ever before." He then wrote about Guardian's "ready response . . . to the urgent demand for loans on policies to tide over financial emergencies."[21]

Obviously, the annual reports served several purposes. First, they kept policyholders informed about the company's current fortunes in an effort to reduce surrender and lapse rates. Second, they reminded policyholders of their need for life insurance and suggested the possibility of acquiring more protection, with Guardian. Third, the statements were effective little sales brochures that were easily passed from policyholder or agent to a prospect. Beginning in 1939, the annual report almost always included a list of Guardian agency offices, with addresses, and often contained at least a paragraph or two devoted to Guardian's product line.[22]

Financial planning became more of a concern in Guardian's advertising and promotional campaigns, reflecting the increasing affluence of its target market in the 1920s (and the increasing anxiety of the same in the Great Depression). In the late 1920s, Guardian unveiled "Jack Horner," "an everyday he-human," a professional blessed with a wife, a child, a car, a high golf handicap, and a mortgage. The pipe-smoking, bow-tied Jack faced a major problem. "His earnings stretched just about far enough to cover the demands of living . . . with . . . just a bit left for saving." Jack's great fear was that he would never be able to create an estate. But now that a friend had introduced him to a Guardian agent who set him straight, Jack could "eat his pie and have it too."[23]

The Depression did not force Guardian to retreat from advertising; quite the opposite. Up to that point, the company's advertising had been targeted and localized. In 1934, Guardian became only the seventh life insurance company to advertise nationally on a large scale. The field force was the main impetus behind the new coast-to-coast campaign. The board agreed to finance the campaign because it had become convinced that national advertising would enhance the prestige and standing of Guardian in the eyes of policyholders, field agents, competitors, and the public, and that it would leverage celebration of the company's seventy-fifth anniversary. The campaign would help morale by increasing the company's name and product recognition by touting its background of safety and service. Guardian retained the New York advertising firm, Hanff-Metzger, which placed some two dozen different ads in such major periodicals as the *New York Times Magazine, Saturday Evening Post, Collier's,* and *Time* on a budget of $30,000. What was considered the most effective of the ads appeared in the June 1935 issue of *Parents' Magazine,* which featured a young housewife with a baby in one arm and a toddler on her hip, saying "bravely and in all sincerity" that "we'd get along . . . *somehow.*" "But," ominously, "the landlord asks for his rent . . . and gas and electric companies send their bills on the first of the month, whether men live or die." The campaign came in under budget, and was judged to have been a success.[24]

The board then authorized an advertising expenditure of $35,000 for 1936, $40,000 for 1937, and $42,500 for 1938. It only expended a little over $24,000 of that sum in 1938, as the economy faltered, and the budget was lowered to $34,000 for 1939. That year's campaign included a great variety of half-page ads in *Fortune* magazine, each touting a different product or service. One ad featured a little girl playing with blocks to promote the Guardian Family Income Plan. Another depicted an elderly couple in support of the company's guaranteed retirement income policies. In yet another a father explained to his son the virtues of (what else?) the Father-and-Son Plan. A businessman introduced the public to the Graph Estate. To help bring in new agents, a mother exclaimed, "I want Billy to be a life insurance man just like his dad." Guardian continued to advertise in *Fortune* over the next decade. The ads were thought to have great prestige value, the tear sheets helped sales agents, and more of the magazine's three hundred thousand readers were interested in Guardian insurance than the three million readers of low-brow popular magazines. Good "demographics."[25]

In 1940, Guardian issued a very detailed annual report that included extracts from the reports of the various officers charged with the conduct of the major divisions in the company. This unprecedented detail on the company's operations was an industry innovation, and met with the broad approval of policyholders. When the United States joined World War II, Guardian seized upon the patriotic utility of life insurance: it increased morale, staved off inflation, and generally strengthened national defense, so the story went. "It is in the light of these and other *obvious facts* [emphasis added], and with no thought of selfish Company interest," Guardian claimed, "that we urge you in your best interests and the nation's, to maintain existing protection as far as possible."[26]

Guardian dramatically increased advertising during World War II. It put out large annual reports in 1942, 1943, and 1944 to back its national advertising campaign, the so-called War Year Report to Guardian Policyholders that appeared in *Business Week, Fortune,* and other major business periodicals. It used the ad campaign to make more prospects aware of its Graph Estate method of tailoring life insurance to the individual's needs and means and to push a slogan, "Guardian of American Families since 1860," first unveiled during the company's seventy-fifty anniversary advertising campaign. Guardian dropped the slogan after the war but continued to legally protect it and a number of other slogans and symbols.[27]

In 1946, Guardian launched a major advertising campaign, alternating two-hundred-line and one-hundred-line advertisements weekly in nine major markets to push its juvenile insurance-education endowment policies. Generally, however, Guardian cut back on advertising in the postwar period, largely limiting itself to *Fortune* and the insurance press. As table 7-1 shows, its advertising expenses in the first half-dozen years after the war were quite low by historical standards.[28]

TABLE 7-1
Guardian's Advertising Expenditures, 1947–54

Year	Amount Expended ($)
1947	19,994.56
1948	16,597.74
1949	12,903.65
1950	10,388.17
1951	29,729.66
1952	60,014.08
1953	38,430.48
1954	45,415.13

Source: Name Cases, Legal Department, Box 219, GLIC archives.

Annual Reports

Guardian continued to leverage the advertising potential of its annual report, which each year stressed a different theme. In 1948, on advice from outside consultants, it introduced policyholders to top management and their responsibilities, then a novel idea. By then, annual reports were taking on a distinctively modern air as advertising media.[29]

The 1949 annual report featured a policyholder known as Mr. X. His story began in 1933, when he was a bachelor purchasing a $5,000 ordinary life policy payable to his mother. Mr. X elected to have his dividends automatically deposited with Guardian at interest. In 1935, Mr. X got a new job in a different city. Guardian's "Stencil division" noted the change of address on the company's records. The new job must not have panned out because in 1937 Mr. X did not have the cash to pay his annual premium. A helpful cashier at his agency office explained that he need not surrender the policy for cash. Instead, he could take a small paid-up policy or take out a policy loan. Mr. X chose the latter, paid off his premium with the proceeds, and had some cash left over besides to help him cover other necessary expenses. Mr. X met his next annual premium but only after receiving a grace extension of 120 days. In 1940, after marrying into some money and obtaining some more from a matured endowment policy, Mr. X repaid his policy loan, made his wife the beneficiary, and began to meet with his agent at regular intervals to review his insurance needs.[30]

The following year's edition stressed the importance to the economy of Guardian's investments. It contained black-and-white photographs of Guardian's investments at work—in corporations like Granite City Steel Company, Pacific Telephone, Marden Clothing Company, and Fruehauf Trailer Company, in municipal governments like Pittsburgh, in single-family homes in Louisiana, Michigan, Minnesota, and Ohio, and in a modern shopping center in Texas. Six years later, the annual report contained four stories of how Guardian policies muted the effects of prolonged illness and early death. The anecdotes were real cases. And though the size of the annual report was scaled back, beginning the following year, Guardian continued to tug at policyholders' emotions with one or two true stories of how the company helped to provide dignity and hope for the families of those who died before their time. The section, called "Your Guardian in Action," tried some cross-selling, encouraging health policyholders to buy life insurance and life policyholders to pick up some health coverage.[31]

In was not until the 1980s that Guardian's annual reports blossomed into large, colorful, glossy affairs lavished with photographs of executives, the home office, the regional offices, and Guardian's successes. A twenty-year dividend history was a new feature that graphically illustrated Guardian's stunning success. The reports, by this time, were really magazines of more than thirty pages in length, and were distributed to all policyholders, employees, and other parties interested in the company.[32]

Advertising in the Postwar Era

To compensate for its lower expenditures on national advertising, Guardian in the postwar era increasingly sought out publicity of the best kind: unpaid. Many of the company's officers were prolific writers who published articles in various specialized trade presses seemingly at every opportunity. In 1952, for instance, Guardian attorney Daniel J. Reidy, after reading of the woes suffered by a law firm after one of the principals died, published an article urging law firms to purchase life insurance as a means to lower estate taxes and to ward off unwanted liquidation of assets. James McLain wrote an extensive article on life insurance for *The Encyclopedia Americana,* contributed to important journals like the *Commercial and Financial Chronicle,* and made frequent speeches. On one such occasion in 1949 he spoke at the opening of *For Some Must Watch,* a documentary film about the life insurance needs of a typical U.S. town, Oneida, New York, which starred Guardian agent Jack Sutton.[33]

The company also began to explore new methods for spreading the word. In 1940, it sponsored a "Guardian Life Day" at the World's Fair in New York in conjunction with its eightieth anniversary convention. In the 1950s, it conducted direct mail programs and sales promotion campaigns that included leaflets, folders, pamphlets, an agent's magazine, a brokerage bulletin, birthday cards, and policy wallets. In 1963, it sponsored one-quarter of play in each of the Notre Dame football games broadcast over the radio in the New York metropolitan area. Recruiting of sales personnel was the first advertising theme of that campaign. Reaction to the first broadcast was good, eliciting seven or eight serious job inquiries.[34]

Guardian also compiled lists of its more famous policyholders. The lists contained the names of many top corporate executives, including several duPonts; government administrators, such as Shreveport City Commissioner John McWilliams Ford; politicians, most notably President Franklin D. Roosevelt[35] and congresswoman Florence Bolton; medical, dental, legal, and finance professionals; artists and cartoonists; entertainers like Benny Goodman; media moguls Joseph Pulitzer and Frank E. Gannett; and infamous types, like the spy Richard Weber. In the last instance, Guardian's tips led to a conviction and sentence of twenty-five years.[36]

Guardian returned to national advertising in 1955, when it conducted a drive for sales growth, implementing a major campaign that included a local radio component in selected cities. The company sought additional business, it explained to policyholders, in order to spread costs among a larger group and thus reduce the expense per policy. It felt that more people should know about Guardian's tradition as a sound, progressive, friendly company. Though the campaign would lead to few direct sales, it created a more favorable climate for the sales activity of its representatives by increasing the company's name recognition. One of the ads featured a Marcus Welby–looking doctor making a 3:00 A.M. house call to save a feverish baby. Ads run in *Newsweek* and elsewhere in 1958 stressed particular Guardian policies, like Income Guardian, Family Guardian, Preferred Risk 60, Junior Guardian, Life Income Endowments, or, more generally, the nondeath benefits of life insurance such as saving for education, retirement, emergencies, or business opportunities.[37]

Because by this time it was clear that practically everyone believed in life insurance as basic family protection, the full-page ads featured dads frolicking with the kids on the front lawn, retired gentlemen golfing and fishing, young men graduating from college, businessmen enjoying record earnings, and everyone always smiling, even the housewife telling a well-meaning relative that the family did not need a loan simply because the husband was laid low by an accident. Such ads made clear that life insurance was about life, not death. Morbid stories about families ruined by explosions, horrific traffic accidents, and the like were relegated to pamphlets doled out by agents at the optimal moment in the sales pitch.[38]

In 1959, in preparation for its centennial, Guardian ran five history-related spots: "Couriers of Civilization," "17 New States and 99 Years Later," "The Guardian and the Pony Express Ventured on Exciting Careers in 1860," "When Men Scorned Women's Rights The Guardian Insured Women," and "This Was Wall Street." In the late 1950s, Guardian greatly reduced the scope of its annual reports, reducing them from pamphlets with dozens of pages to simple foldouts. Partly to compensate for this, the company commissioned a brief history, *Guardian of a Century,* to commemorate the company's centennial anniversary. It gave a copy gratis to each policyholder who requested one. Historical stories and anecdotes related to the centennial also generated much publicity and added attention. For example, the company induced New York Mayor Robert F. Wagner to declare the week of 16 July 1960 "Guardian of America Week." It also received major press for its presentation of "Guardian of America" awards to four U.S. service academies.[39]

The company also commemorated the occasion by launching a new national advertising campaign. In this round, Guardian focused its efforts on major news magazines like *U.S. News and World Report, Newsweek,* and *Time.* The most striking ad featured a photograph of a young father tying a life preserver around his daughter at the beach. The caption, "Guardian Guarantees Protection for Her—Good Property for You," dramatized the theme and objective of the campaign. Though the message was far from new, the effect was positive. Again, the ads were upbeat, the people, even the seriously ill mother, all smiles. Again the emphasis was more on the life benefits and investment value of life insurance than on the death benefit.[40]

The increasing emphasis on the investment aspects of life insurance products was a response to the threat that increases in Social Security benefits and group sales posed to traditional whole life policies. The new drumbeat accordingly went on, in 1963, when Guardian ran one of its more clever series of advertisements, the "Joe Scott" column in *New Yorker* magazine. The ads looked like short articles and had provocative titles like "Which Is the Stronger Sex?" "Positive Dreaming," and "A Good Way to Spoil Your Grandchildren." Then, in the following year, Guardian unveiled a new slogan, "Your Guardian for Life," employing a unique and distinctive letter "G." One of the ads, which featured a teenage girl sobbing because her widowed mother could not afford to send her to her prom, broke the au courant "happy, happy, smile, smile" mold, and in the process became a raging success. People actually sent contributions to the company to pay for the girl's prom dress! (Even more earnest: the offers to escort the pretty young model to the prom.)[41]

Creative efforts aside, Guardian's investment in advertising still lagged behind that of the rest of the industry. In 1965, for instance, Guardian spent $3.03 per $1,000 of premium income on advertising, compared to the industry median of $3.52. Guardian then opened a new ad campaign, in 1966, that targeted small business owners, long a key constituency for the company. This one explained how Guardian agents helped small concerns with such problems as the death of partners or "key men" and how to attract and retain top professional talent by offering good benefits packages. The campaign featured mention of a different local representative in each national ad, followed up by local promotion on radio and in newspapers. In addition, the new campaign stressed just "Guardian" instead of "Guardian of America."[42]

By contrast, Guardian's new equity products received virtually no advertising support. Equity products were subservient to policyholder welfare as a matter of policy and strategy, and even after Guardian introduced a range of products for its field force to sell, its training materials and advertisements continued to emphasize that the goal was to meet each client's individual needs, not to sell certain hot investment products. For instance, if an endowment had just matured or a death claim were to be paid, Guardian agents might opportunistically offer their customers or families a mutual fund through GLICOA. But the company's sales force and ads continued to stress the importance of obtaining guaranteed whole life protection before making riskier investments. *If you pay the premiums, you get the guaranteed rewards without any fret or worry. Stock market buckling? Don't lose sleep over it! Your insurance is still there, protecting your family's future like . . . a guardian! That's the ticket.*[43]

In the 1970s, as equity products became more important to its business, Guardian still refrained from advertising them on the grounds that other companies had suffered tremendous losses in the promotion of their equity products. Its agents, however, urged the Equity Department to provide more creative marketing ideas. They wanted more support. In any case, Guardian's equity products got so much free publicity in the normal course of market scrutiny that sales boomed without the expenditure of large sums on advertising.[44]

Life insurance products unfortunately did not generate as much free publicity. So in the mid-1970s, Guardian took out ads in the *Wall Street Journal* that bragged, and rightly so, about its impressive dividend record. Similarly, a 1983 ad campaign claimed, "The Weight of Evidence Is in Our Favor." The advertising budget was still relatively small, however, in the range of $350,000 in the early 1980s, or a mere .0007 advertising-dollar-to-premium-income ratio. Guardian still regarded advertising as a useful tool on which the fewest possible resources should be expended.[45]

In the last quarter of the twentieth century, Guardian's management found it appealing to stress the *age* of the company as a proxy for strength and desirability. Old was good in the insurance industry, if not in automobiles, steel, or electronics. Yet it was important not to suggest that the company was a dinosaur in what many people thought of as a staid and unglamorous industry. In 1985, Guardian unveiled a new "diamond G" logo, suggesting progressive entrepreneurialism, even while retaining the more classic logotype in the spelling of its name, suggesting a tradition of financial robustness. How much the symbols may have mattered to the public, even subliminally, is unclear, but inside the company the mix of modernity and tradition took on increased importance, especially in the early 1990s, when several large insurers ran into financial distress. "We must continue to tell the story of our financial strength [tradition] and the quality of our products and distribution system [sleek and up-to-date]," Art Ferrara noted in 1991, especially if the company were to maintain its triple-A credit ratings.[46]

Targeted competitive marketing pieces have also been effective. For three decades Guardian sales agents had made effective use of a brochure called "Guardian Plusses," which rested on a long tradition of Guardian talking points. The company also developed a new document called "How to Choose a Life Insurance Company: Executive Presentation Client's Guide," which it updated annually. "How to Choose" was a kind of hybrid annual statement and guide to competition, its purpose being to help prospects understand why they needed life insurance and then why they should purchase it from Guardian. Still in use, it is thirty pages of text and tables designed to reduce prospects' search costs by offering them a fairly objective overview and analysis of the company's recent history and competitive position. It is not an exciting document but it was not designed to be, precisely in the spirit of Guardian's promotional materials some 140 years earlier.[47]

In 1996, Guardian embarked on a major advertising program designed to unleash an asset that it has long held largely in reserve, its strong brand name. The company greatly increased advertising expenditures, revamped its logo yet again, and ventured into new advertising media, including television and the Internet. It also developed a new theme, that Guardian is the company that makes dreams happen, the company that enriches all the people that it touches. But the old themes remain alive and well. In the early twenty-first century, Guardian's sales representatives and ads, alike, continue to stress the company's mutuality and trustworthiness, the high grades that it receives from independent ratings agencies like Moody's, the relatively strict regulatory oversight it is subject to as a New York company, its successful investment strategy, its strong capitalization ratio, its high persistency rates, and its long-term ability to pay significant dividends. Those are the hallmarks of a mature company, but not a stale one.

Guardian also reiterates what it had been telling its customers for more than sixty years: that its agents are more than just insurance salesmen; they are trusted financial advisors. *Guardian's Financial Security Analysis* booklet at the dawn of the third millennium is basically a modern, beefy version of its old Graph Estate workhorse. The next chapter will describe more closely the role of Guardian's sales management and field force in the company's success.[48]

8

Selling Insurance

Leo Futia was a meticulously organized man of predictable routine in search of unpredictable results. One cold morning in Buffalo, he brushed off the lake-effect snow that had fallen on his head and shoulders during the five-minute walk from his automobile to work. It was December 1962, and Futia, a Guardian field representative, riffled through his extensive card file system to line up telephone calls for the day. How many, he thought, would lead to face-to-face interviews? The list done, he dashed letters off to a few warm prospects and then completed some committee work for the Life Underwriters Association. He then gave some thought to the interviews he had already scheduled for later in the day. Using Guardian's convenient tool, the Graph Estate, he could quickly match each prospect's known needs up with the appropriate life insurance products. He knew he had yet to brush the snow off his car and check his tire chains for the treacherous trip down icy Elmwood Avenue, but he had a few minutes to spare. So he returned to the card file and pulled the numbers of a few existing policyholders that he had not talked with recently. *Tom and Norma Prowd may have a child on the way; they will need much higher coverage if they do. Ann Dilimon is a single mother; she should increase her coverage as soon as she can afford to do so. Michael O'Leary just became a partner in his law firm; ka-ching!* It was not a simple matter of money, though. Futia liked financial success, but he also liked people. It was one important reason why he was in the insurance business.[1]

Futia had learned that the key to success in selling insurance rested upon three things: his personal rapport with prospects and policyholders; the reputation and policies of his employer, Guardian; and, not least, his ability to move people efficiently from a cold call to a closing. He knew from experience that every ten telephone calls yielded about three initial interviews, and three initial interviews led to one sale. He worked that simple formula into a business that had earned him a steady membership in Guardian's million-dollar sales club since 1950.[2]

The Insurance Salesperson's Burden

Selling insurance was far from easy. As much as he liked meeting people, Leo Futia knew that people did not always want to meet him. "Rejection is a big part of selling life insurance," he said. It took a salesperson's cast-iron stomach to deflect the inevitable rebuffs and move on. Woody Allen said it even better. In *Take the Money and Run,* an unruly chain-gang inmate is sentenced to twenty-four hours in the "hole"—not solitary confinement, but a torturous session with a blue-suited insurance peddler, all smiles, briefcase in hand. Leo Futia did not have the luxury of a captive audience. His burden was to overcome the natural inertia, if not sheer aversion, of his potential customers.[3]

Generally speaking, people will not, if left to their own devices, purchase life insurance. Before insurance became part of a standard benefits package, the U.S. government found it difficult to persuade *soldiers* to sign up for and retain highly subsidized (really cheap!) term policies. Most people who have ever tried to sell life insurance have failed to make a living at it. It takes a particular kind of personality, sales skills, and discipline. Steering prospects to policies they do not need simply to reap high commissions never works over the long term. Successful career agents forgo the temptation to push the high commission policy and instead offer the contract that makes the most sense for the prospect. Honest salesmanship leads to long-lasting friendships, add-on sales, referrals, and the satisfaction that comes from doing the right thing.[4]

Insurance salespeople must articulate clearly to their prospects the two major features of insurance: protection and savings. Different prospects have different needs for both. The key is to find the right product for their particular circumstances. Generally speaking, the relative importance of protection and savings has changed over time. As late as the early 1960s, protection was still the most important reason cited in consumer surveys, but savings was a close second. Today, with the proliferation of the two-income family, protection has generally taken a back seat to tax-deferred savings and estate planning. Successful agents change the emphases of their sales pitches, in other words, to account for individual prospects and for secular trends. They become, in short, trusted financial advisors.[5]

Whether or not a sale is made, and whether or not that policy stays sold until it becomes profitable to the company depends on the agent's skill and determination. The quality of the average agent, in turn, largely depends upon the company's selection processes and training programs. "When you realize that insurance is a product . . . that needs to be sold and is not a product that is bought," Joseph Caruso notes, "a distribution system becomes very important."[6]

General Agencies vs. Branch Offices

There are two archetypal ways to organize life insurance distribution. Sales management can be established either around commissioned general agents or around salaried managers. Each has its advantages and drawbacks. Over its long history, Guardian experimented with both of those pure forms, as well as with hybrids. All of Guardian's systems were based on the creation of a geographical area or territory where either the "general agent" or the "sales manager" reigned supreme. In either case the leader of the territory was recruited and oversaw the work of sales agents, or "fieldmen," as they were historically known, their contracts, and their responsibilities.[7]

In its infancy, Guardian established new agencies wherever it could, and then evaluated and kept those that did the most efficient business, as measured by agency expenses as a percentage of premiums received. "Time only will show," said the report of the Special Committee in 1863, "which of the Agencies should be continued, and which should be discontinued." Guardian's general agents enjoyed geographical territories that they defended quite vigorously. Sometimes the boundaries of a state and an agency were coterminous. In more densely populated regions, however, a state could be sliced and diced into numerous general agencies. In the sparsely populated West, a single agency would span several states.[8]

As table 8-1 shows, by 1873 Guardian had made deep inroads into several states but had barely scraped the surface of others. In 1896, California was Guardian's top U.S. producer, followed by Colorado. New York was a distant third, just ahead of North Dakota. Missouri, Wisconsin, Texas, and Pennsylvania were other important states. After Armstrong, New York's importance rebounded and California and New York battled each other for prominence through at least the 1950s. The spread of Guardian's business was partly a function of economic demography. Early on, it did best in areas, like Pennsylvania, where there were lots of Germans. Throughout its history, due to its relatively affluent and well-educated market niche, it has done better in wealthier areas. But part of its success in some states, North Dakota and Colorado in particular, was due largely to the efforts of skilled general agents. For example, Frederic S. Doremus, son of future Guardian president Cornelius Doremus, spearheaded the company's growth in its far-flung western territory.[9]

TABLE 8-1
Guardian's Net Premium Income by State, 1873

State	Net Premium Income ($)	Share of Total (%)
Alabama	10,914.07	0.80
California	170,945.59	12.53
Canada	2,681.17	0.20
Colorado	4,368.95	0.32
Connecticut	9,412.24	0.69
Cuba	7,680.65	0.56
Delaware	103.53	0.01
Florida	0.00	0.00
Georgia	30,435.00	2.23
Illinois	68,644.71	5.03
Indiana	39,066.59	2.86
Iowa	8,439.26	0.62
Kansas	4,966.04	0.36
Kentucky	52,289.99	3.83
Louisiana	59,754.76	4.38
Maryland	32,701.94	2.40
Massachusetts	18,080.78	1.33
Michigan	16,772.70	1.23
Minnesota	16,069.20	1.18
Mississippi	8,633.23	0.63
Missouri	44,724.61	3.28
Nebraska	2,927.88	0.21
New Jersey	17,145.81	1.26
New York	461,724.76	33.80
Ohio	69,739.99	5.11
Pennsylvania	107,935.64	7.91
Rhode Island	673.59	0.05
South Carolina	4,228.60	0.31
Tennessee	9,074.33	0.67
Texas	26,296.09	1.93
Virginia	6,479.54	0.48
West Virginia	12,583.52	0.92
Wisconsin	29,900.64	2.19
Wyoming	8,410.60	0.62
Total	1,363,806.00	100.00

Source: Annual Statement, 1873, Box 1, GLIC archives.

In the nineteenth century, Guardian provided each general agent with a liberal outing of canvassing matter, a sign, and books of blank forms. General agents were not allowed to represent any other life insurance company or death benefit provider. If visited by one of the company's special, traveling agents, the local agent was supposed to assist him and also allow him to audit his books. If the general agent could not produce the numbers to stay in business, Guardian terminated his contract and either hired a new general agent or allowed the territory to lie fallow until a propitious opportunity for reentry presented itself.[10]

Distribution strategy evolved with the times. For example, by 1870, Guardian had established general agencies in eight cities in Massachusetts, including Boston, Worcester, and Springfield, but every one of them soon failed. For many years thereafter, the company was not represented in Massachusetts, at least not until the 1920s, when one Guardian general agent prospected the Bay State anew for wealthy and healthy customers. Competition in that populous state, however, was intense; the region was home to many first-class life insurers. Guardian reentered, appointing Joseph E. Lockwood as local manager and then supporting him with a new relationship it had struck with the Old Colony Trust Company of Boston. Whatever foothold the company gained in New England was then stymied by the Great Depression, but instead of eliminating nonproductive agencies, which was the traditional response, Guardian tried to make its existing agencies there more productive by encouraging its agents to increase average policy size and decrease first-year lapse rates. The territory was deemed too rich to abandon. Fortunately World War II came in time to redeem the company's position in New England, and in 1945, Guardian moved aggressively to further develop the territory, even entering little Rhode Island for the first time in the twentieth century.[11]

In the wider scope of things Guardian's mode of distribution also changed. Before the 1920s, the company had relied entirely on commissioned general agents, whom it nonetheless called sales "managers," a confusing misnomer. Each was in fact an independent contractor, operating a commercial fiefdom over which Guardian had little control short of the threat of terminating the relationship. Many companies, such as New York Life, had long since abandoned general agencies in favor of setting up branch office systems with salaried managers. The control was greater, but so was the ongoing financial and organizational burden of supporting and nurturing the careers of salaried managers.[12]

Guardian had stayed with the general agency system in part because of its entrepreneurial quality. Commissioned agents were more driven to sell. But the onset of the Depression changed the company's thinking, and a hybrid system quickly developed. The records show that while some Guardian sales "managers" were simply traditional general agents who operated on a straight commission basis, others were salaried employees who also received commission "overrides" on business written by their field force. Yet others received salaries plus commissions on their personal business only. The mix could change rapidly. In 1937, thirty-one of the company's sales managers were commission-only general agents and twenty-five were salaried managers, but by 1940, thirty-four were general agents and only twenty, salaried employees. Ideally, the company still preferred the general agency system to the branch system.[13]

Guardian's top management was wed to the idea that general agency contracts generally attracted men of greater vision, fortitude, and ambition. But since such men were difficult to find, especially when the company was trying to expand aggressively, it could not afford to forgo hiring salaried managers, as well. In fact, when James McLain presided over sales force policy, he assumed that a mix was desirable from a strategic and economic standpoint.[14]

Regardless of the type of contract, the home office had always to monitor its sales force closely. At the roots of the business, the interests of the salesman and the company were at odds. General agents needed their commissions; sales managers needed to meet their quotas. Both, in other words, had to drive to put new business on the books. The company, on the other hand, needed business that would persist, i.e., that would not lapse. Obviously, the lower the lapse rate, the better the agent sold the policy. Historically, lapse rates have varied widely from company to company, from less than 10 percent to well over 50 percent. Guardian also needed to keep mortality rates in line and in this the field force also played a large, though not exclusive, role.[15]

So the home office paid attention not only to the quantity of business emanating from particular agencies but also to its quality. In the 1910s, Guardian made frequent studies of the persistency of business. By 1939, those studies included the experience of other companies conducting similar research, and soon afterward, Guardian began analyzing each of its agencies in detail, starting with the one located in Rochester, New York, which was conspicuous for its low persistency record and the questionable financial condition of many of its policyholders. But that was nothing compared to the problems that would become apparent at the Kansas City general agency, which included the solicitation of business from applicants "sick in bed under medical attendance!"[16]

By the mid-twentieth century, Guardian had sixty-three agency offices licensed to do business in all forty-eight states and the District of Columbia; it was a truly nationwide insurance provider. But many of Guardian's agencies were too small to be viable. The company therefore concentrated on building up its smaller agencies into units of economic size, jettisoning those that could not make the grade. By the end of 1960, the company's one hundredth year in operation, Guardian had ninety-seven agency offices and district agencies. Guardian has regularly terminated general agents for a variety of causes beyond mere underperformance. In 1979, for example, it bounced a general agent in Sacramento for improper use of company funds, and the following year it sent an Albany general agent packing for noncompliance with company procedures. (For the total number of Guardian GAs and managers, see figure 8-1.)[17]

From the 1930s until the 1960s, sales managers were engaged in one of three different types of contracts: straight commission, salary plus commission, and straight salary with incentive bonus. By 1950, the contracts in each category had been rendered uniform with respect to each manager's duties and responsibilities, differing only with respect to the computation of compensation. By the 1960s, virtually all Guardian territories

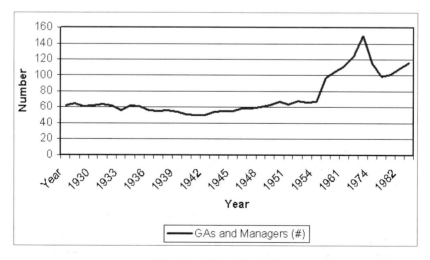

FIGURE 8-1 *Number of Guardian Sales Managers*
(GAs and Branch Managers), 1925–84

were run by managers with true or slightly modified general agent contracts where a general agent-in-training received a salary for three years
while he built up a block of business.[18]

The main reason why Guardian moved away from salaried managers—reverting to historical form—was that they did not fit the company's entrepreneurial sales culture. The company's officers would have
agreed with Irving Rosenthal when he said that the "branch-office or
salaried manager system [was] no good for a company of [Guardian's]
type and size." The managerial system simply did not provide enough incentives to offset the sustained costs of their employment.[19]

The entrepreneurial quality of the general agency system can be illustrated by the career of Dennis Manning, who spent much of his adult life
setting up and running small businesses—first his own pension consulting firm, then a moderate-sized Guardian general agency in Houston,
Texas. When he was coaxed into joining the home office in 1991, he found
the transition from agent to corporate manager so personally unsatisfy-
ing that he returned to the field, this time to run a large general agency in
White Plains, New York. The scaling up helped prepare him for his second, more rewarding, stint at corporate headquarters, until he rose to the
presidency, putting him once again in charge of a business.[20]

Traditionally, Guardian employed agency directors to attract, train,
and retain general agents. Despite the training programs, Guardian general agents have always been fiercely independent of the home office, re-
sistant to every perceived encroachment upon their domains, and persistent about their needs for support. The more successful of them had great
institutional leverage, and were not afraid to use it to demand better service and better products. Whenever the New York metropolitan area general agent John C. McNamara "cracked his whip," Irving Rosenthal noted,
"everybody in the Home Office jumped."[21]

Guardian's management was smart enough to tolerate, even cultivate,
the independent streak among its general agents, but at a known price.
The home office had to ensure that communication channels were wide
open. It had to be vigilant as to what was going on in the field that might
harm the company's business and reputation. It had to avoid the types of
conflicts that would lead to misunderstandings or hurt feelings that
would reduce efficiency, but it had to challenge agents on performance.

Guardian's Field Advisory Board was established in 1948 to help navi-
gate these difficult waters. The board consisted of seven agency managers
representing all sections of the country, and acted as a direct liaison be-

tween the company's sales organization in the field and management at the home office. It met several times a year. At its first meeting, President McLain set the tone of the board by encouraging sales agents and managers "to present candidly and 'with no holds barred' their questions, suggestions and advice on: (1) Problems of general interest to the Company and field at large—including the agency program of the Company, and (2) Problems of limited or local interest." McLain also asked questions of the general agents. He would get what he asked for.[22]

Guardian's general agents utilized the committee to influence the company's direction. For instance, in the mid-1970s, when business was tough, general agents wanted to be able to sign general agency contracts with other companies to allow them to place business that Guardian could not, or would not, write, and openly requested the right rather than trying to mask their intentions, or worse, their practice. Leo Futia initially balked, but was gradually persuaded that the agents had a point. He allowed them to write outside business on an ad hoc basis, i.e., without a general agent's contract, if, and only if, Guardian did not offer the right product for a prospective policyholder's needs. In this way, he staved off what might have been a silent wave of treacherous behavior among the sales force.[23]

Finding and Training Salespeople

Guardian's 1965 annual report observed, "a good insurance man can be as valuable as a good lawyer, a good accountant or the family doctor." Without a trusted guide, people find ways to avoid purchasing basic protection. It was a process that required personal contact. In a famous failed contrarian strategy, Sears, Roebuck tried to sell life insurance through its voluminous and highly successful catalogue. In one four-year span, Sears sold a grand total of eighteen hundred policies, a single day's worth of production for any decent-sized insurer using the commission agency system. Finding a good insurance man, however, was never easy.[24]

The basic problem is that selling life insurance has long been a skilled profession for which it takes time to build up the requisite expertise. It is rare for anyone in the business to do well quickly. Further complicating matters, even after a field agent gets pretty good at what he or she does, it takes years of solid production figures to build up the big base of renewal commissions and relatively easy add-on business that provide for a generous and stable flow of income. For those reasons, most commission-only sales agents leave the business for greener, or at least easier, pastures. Historically, agency turnover has always been a big problem for insurance underwriters.[25]

The general approach to finding, and then training, agents in the nineteenth century was a numbers game. General agents hired as many fieldmen as possible and did little to cultivate them. General agents then pitched the battered careers of the poor performers overboard, usurped their renewal commissions, and sought out replacements. The few who survived the ordeal often wrote most of the agency's business. Still, the many who had failed were a major drag on resources.[26]

In the early years of life insurance, agents were recruited on the fly and received no specialized training whatsoever. At best, they received sketchy instructions and some promotional literature. Early agents of Northwestern Mutual, for example, received only the following advice:

1. Insure yourself first.
2. Be familiar with the company's policies. Sign your friends first, then try to sign the most influential persons in the area.
3. Circulate the advertising documents sent by the Home Office.
4. "Persevering industry and unflinching determination to succeed by personal effort, will insure complete success—and nothing else will."

Not bad advice, any of it, but hardly a substitute for comprehensive training, which was essential to, though no guarantee of, success.[27]

There is evidence from the early records that Guardian tried at least to predict those prospective or recently signed agents that were most likely to fail, and sent them away before they cost the company a lot of time and money. By 1889, the company was screening applicants by having them provide satisfactory references. If approved, the new agent then had to obtain a surety bond to ensure his good behavior.[28]

The company learned over time that hiring fewer agents allowed general agents to devote more training resources to each. There was a tradeoff. Guardian had higher success *rates* with individual agents than companies that did little screening, but because it hired fewer agents to begin with, the end result was much the same, a chronic shortage of good agents. The dearth was particularly severe in rural areas, so Guardian until the late 1950s contracted with part-time agents, who sold only in areas more than ten miles from cities with populations exceeding fifty thousand according to the latest U.S. census. Hence Guardian's approach to finding and training agents was not necessarily the best industry practice, but it was at least consistent with the company's preference for slow and steady growth.[29]

That Guardian paid some attention to training issues early on is seen in a thirty-one-page pamphlet containing business instructions for general agents and their agents in 1889. The prescriptions therein were fairly rudimentary, but certainly better than, say, Northwestern Mutual's contemporary advice simply to try, try, and try again. After outlining the company's underwriting standards, the pamphlet reminded agents to fill out applications completely, in ink, and of many other administrative niceties. It then briefly described the company's policy forms and its general business policies, like minimum and maximum face values, and explained certain basic insurance laws. Most importantly, the pamphlet tried to imbue agents with Guardian's core values. For instance, it adamantly stated that changes of existing policies were always unwelcome because it was in the interests of both policyholders and the company that existing insurance be continued. The pamphlet said precious little about how to actually sell insurance, noting only that its agents should thoroughly acquaint themselves with the subject of life insurance and then personally solicit applications. By 1903, Guardian added an unremarkable reminder that agents should "always bear in mind, that in order to become successful in their calling and build up a prosperous business, they must be industrious, systematic and enthusiastic."[30]

Industrywide, most commissioned agents did work diligently—they had to—but most found that in the early years they could barely make ends meet. Persistence of character mattered. So did integrity. The pressures to abandon the field, to seek out high-risk customers, or to perpetrate fraud were intense. There had to be a better way. Yet progress in the commission agent system came slowly. Call after call for change from within the industry went unheeded, especially during good times when insurers did not wish to rock the proverbial boat. Education and training were obviously important, and made great strides, but what was also needed was a radically different approach to compensating sales agents.

Everyone in the industry knew that a pure salary scheme would fail just as miserably, if not more so, than the pure commission system. Without clear monetary incentives, no one would sell much product. Moreover, agents were expected to perform both pre- and postsale services.

Presale services include selection of the proper policy type and the amount of premium in light of the prospect's needs and ability to pay. Postsale services include keeping the policy in force until its purpose is accomplished, keeping the policy up to date, i.e., in line with the client's changing needs and abilities, answering the policyholder's questions, and occasionally even persuading policyholders to submit a valid but perhaps embarrassing claim. A pure commission system gave agents little incentive to perform any service other than selling policies. Agent incentive systems are crucial to the agents themselves, of course, but also to life insurers and policyholders, so it was important to get it right. What was needed—and it took a long time to figure this out—was a hybrid compensation structure that would allow a new agent to subsist while he learned the skills and built up a block of business that would smooth out his income, and that would at the same time give him some incentive to perform both pre- and postsales services.[31]

New York Life (NYLIC) was the first major company to confront the sales conundrum. After Armstrong, it jettisoned its general agents, replacing them with the salaried manager or branch system. It then built a compensation system—the eponymous Nylic system—that attempted to attract, reward, and retain good, long-standing agents. The Nylic system was designed to tie the interests of its agents to those of the company and in the process to dignify the profession of selling insurance. Communication between the headquarters office and the agencies improved. New York Life began to recruit agency managers into the executive ranks, which in turn improved the monitoring of the agents overall. The Nylic approach worked for New York Life, but did not prove transferable to smaller companies. Guardian searched out an alternative, and in 1920, it considered a plan to finance new agents along the lines of Phoenix Mutual's plan, which involved more up-front costs but resulted in no net loss to the company over time. But rather than make a radical change, Guardian decided at that time to spruce up its agent-training program.[32]

Guardian had already made systematic improvements to agent training during World War I. In 1916, it had introduced a monthly news magazine, aptly named *Service,* for its agents. The periodical won immediate acclaim from the insurance press. A year later, it had held the first of what would become annual national field agent meetings. The first meeting included numerous discussions of such topics as Selecting and Training Agents, Where Shall We Look for New Agency Material, How Shall the New Agent Be Started, How Can the Old Agent Be Made More Productive, Writing Big Business, Writing City Business, Writing Country Business, Selling Insurance to Women, Securing Prospects, Preparing for the Interview, The Approach, and, most importantly, Closing. Starting in 1922, Guardian provided agents with written study materials, such as "Guardian Guardianship, a Course of Study for Guardian Agents," which provided information about the company's history and business philosophy as well as specific policy information.[33]

Another major change came in the Depression, when Guardian's sales managers hired salaried agents who made from $50 to $100 per month plus a 20 percent commission on new business and renewal considerations. In this approach, Guardian was following the lead of a number of other leading life insurance companies that apparently believed prevailing economic conditions justified a salary scheme for new agents that would secure the services of quality men. A stick replaced the carrot of commissions. Salaried agents had to maintain at least $11,250 of gross insurance for each $10 of monthly salary or face termination. The break-even point for Guardian was a robust $15,000, a level that most salaried agents would not be able to achieve. The salaried agent plan did not work out to the company's satisfaction and was slowly abandoned, as salaried managers were replaced by commissioned general agents, and as salaried field agents were terminated for falling below minimum production levels.[34]

In 1940, the company's new agency vice president, Frank Weidenborner, reported that Guardian's field force had become more concerned with pension plans than any other major aspect of their compensation. Guardian's officers would not move on pensions, however, because they thought agency costs were too high to justify them. (At the time, only three life insurance companies had formal pension plans for fieldmen.) Two years later, as wages were frozen during wartime, and pension plans became widespread in the corporate world, Guardian reconsidered, and created a pension plan for its agents. Through successive tinkerings, the company established so attractive a pension system for its fieldmen that Dennis Manning, for one, claimed that he joined the company partly because of its generous agency retirement benefits.[35]

Frank Weidenborner, in the meantime, had been a staunch advocate of professional recognition for the life insurance field underwriter. He had joined the company as agency assistant in 1924 after graduating from the School of Life Insurance Selling at the Carnegie Institute of Technology. He earned an industrywide reputation for pushing Guardian forward in the selection, monitoring, and training of new agents. His approach to the problem was so successful that the company published a booklet about it in 1938, just preceding his promotion to the top job in his specialty. By the end of 1940, some thirteen hundred U.S. business leaders requested copies of the booklet, which Guardian distributed freely in the belief that it would learn as much as it had to teach on the subject. Continuous research and testing in subsequent years enabled the company to improve its salesmen selection process so that it could reduce the size of its agency 40 percent without adversely affecting sales.[36]

Then, with the blessing of Guardian's president, James McLain, himself a former agency man, Weidenborner weaved the reinvigorated selection program around Guardian's Graph Estate program. The Graph Estate placed a premium on agent training because it forced agents to custom fit an insurance program to the needs of a client and to his ability to buy and *retain* that program. In all, the program created an atmosphere of high energy for agents but low pressure for prospective policyholders that proved good for both sales and Guardian's reputation.[37]

In 1941, McLain unveiled a new sales course for neophyte agents. The course evidently worked as the average production of first-year agents appointed in 1941 soared 131 percent over that of 1940 appointees. (The new training and programming methods appeared several years before the appearance of an influential scholarly monograph on insurance sales that essentially validated the Graph Estate approach.) It was one instance when Guardian was well out in front of the industry, pioneering.[38]

However, the findings of that same publication, *Compensation of Life Insurance Agents,* also called into question commission-only compensation systems. "The need of the present is improved service, not first-year production," the authors argued, "yet the old compensation system . . . has remained for more than three decades practically unchanged." "Before qualified college graduates and successful young men looking for greater opportunities will turn to life insurance in large numbers," the authors argued, "companies must offer satisfactory training programs and well-rounded compensation systems, including first-year financing, profitable opportunities for established agents, and a plan for retirement." Like many other companies in the industry, Guardian took such advice seriously and began to consider how it could successfully update its field force compensation system without unduly increasing expenses.[39]

The failure of the salaried agent scheme during the Depression had only reinforced Guardian's traditional posture against salaries for salesmen. But compensation remained tricky in an economically harsh environment. Guardian allowed new agents to draw against commissions in order to smooth out their incomes in the waning days of the Depression era, and during World War II, when recruiting new agents became extremely difficult, general agents began to dispense cash to "encourage" people to sign on as field agents. The home office assisted by cutting the interest rate on cash advances from 5 to 4 percent. As the war dragged on, those remedial practices evolved into a guaranteed salary or "earn-learn" program. A new field salesperson now received a salary of $25 per week in exchange for a reduced first-year commission on business written during his first four to seven months in business.[40]

With the help of Dan Lyons the "earn-learn" program was elevated into a full-blown Field Representatives' Plan in 1946. Whether field sales representatives hired under the plan worked for a commissioned general agent or a salaried manager, they were now treated as Guardian employees, not agents. Under the plan, first-year field representatives received a base salary. Thereafter, salary increases were tied to certain production credits. After the third year, the incentive compensation included a persistency component based on the difference between actual and expected insurance in force. The emphasis on persistency synchronized nicely with the Graph Estate sales method and Guardian's overall philosophy. "Usually," the company observed, "first year lapses are caused by over-selling or high pressure," neither of which were in the best interests of the policyholder or the company.[41]

It was a continued tight market for sales agents that had prompted the company to adopt the Field Representative Plan. After World War II, it was difficult to attract quality applicants due to strong competition both from other insurers and other businesses. There was a generational shift also, in that young men and women were loath to sign up for commission-based jobs. What made Guardian financially able to implement the field rep plan was that its screening process had improved so much over the years that it effectively eliminated most applicants not suited for insurance sales. Sales projections were also precise enough so that the company could calibrate salary schemes for field representatives that provided a realistic minimum base while allowing for performance-based increases.[42]

Guardian advertised the Field Representative Plan as an employment plan tailored to the career targets of young men entering business. It played up the assured income but unlimited upside opportunity, the scientific selection and training, the fringe benefits, and the vital service to society provided by life insurance salesmen. Although the plan elicited a good deal of enthusiasm, good candidates did not flock to sign on because the base salary seemed too low. Nor did the sales managers do a particularly good job of selling life insurance as a career.[43]

Guardian played around the edges of the plan to make it more attractive. In 1950, the home office distributed the "Guardian Program for Successful Selling" to new representatives, and offered to more seasoned veterans new literature, courses, programs, and conferences. The training programs paid off, especially in making sales agents more adept at discerning the highest price a prospect would pay for a given insurance coverage. Properly trained fieldmen had better opportunity to discover information that enabled them to tailor policies optimally.[44]

It is important to understand that the field representative system supplemented, rather than replaced, the traditional commission-only sales agent. General agents and salaried managers recruited and trained both commissioned sales agents and field representatives, but all hires and training methodologies were subject to home office approval. That said, the relative importance of field representatives has waxed over the years. In 1961, commissioned agents produced around 40 percent of new business, field representatives about 30 percent, brokers around 25 percent, and general agents and sales managers the balance. By 1972, field representatives generated 42 percent of the company's new business and by 1975 their share had increased to 56 percent.[45]

By the early 1980s, field representatives outnumbered commissioned agents. Into the twenty-first century, Guardian's field force still consists of both agents and field representatives, but field reps now account for some 80 percent of the field force. There are two good reasons for this. First, the Field Representative Plan, which in essence smoothed out income flows, made particularly good sense for Guardian's field force, which typically sold into a relatively affluent niche where sales were relatively few, but also relatively large. Second, the Field Representative Plan is neither a training program nor an equivalency plan. Ceteris paribus, field reps who remain with Guardian earn more than commission agents and substantially more than field representatives who leave the company.[46]

The field representative contract had some problems. One issue that arose during the 1960s and 1970s was that the representatives' total remuneration did not always keep pace with inflation. Under those circumstances, many representatives begged to be switched to commission contracts. When the company relented and adjusted compensation upward, however, representatives were content.[47]

While salary programs like the Field Representative Plan reduced attrition, field force turnover remained high. It was an industrywide problem. Even with salary supports, only one in three sales trainees at major companies like Equitable, Home Life, Mutual Benefit, MONY, Mass Mutual, Northwestern, NYLIC, and Penn Mutual lasted through their first year. Those companies that paid higher starting salaries had higher success rates. A company might pay no salary and retain only one in every one hundred trainees, or it might pay $100,000 per annum and retain all the trainees, even those who could not sell water in the desert. The key was to find the optimal tradeoff between salary and production. Throw training expenses into the mix and the solution became even more complex. Despite those minor shortcomings, the Field Representative Plan continued to grow in popularity. Figure 8-2 details the growth and composition of Guardian's field force from 1930 to 2001.[48]

Of course Figure 8-2 begs the question, how did Guardian recruit all of those sales representatives? The first challenge was to attract a pool of prospects. Guardian did so by advertising for new agents in trade publications like *The Eastern Underwriter* and by interviewing the graduating

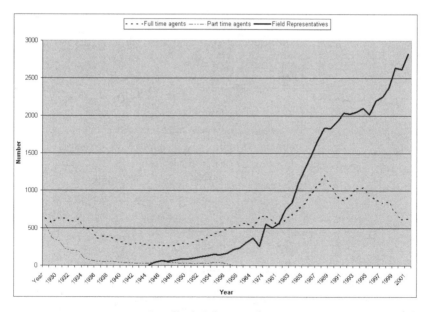

FIGURE 8-2 *Guardian's Sales Force by Type, 1930–2001*

class of the country's few insurance programs. (It was by the latter technique that it landed Leo Futia.) Sometimes a general agent might try to steal agents away from another Guardian general agent—a practice that was of course frowned upon as it was a zero-sum game for the company. Guardian's general agents were not above raiding the agency forces of other companies, an invitation to intra-industry warfare. But that was the nature of competition.[49]

Most desirable was to be able to sign up an entire functioning general agency. Historically, the biggest of such general agent acquisitions was the John C. McNamara Organization, which after 1924 represented Guardian in the boroughs of Manhattan, Richmond, and the Bronx and in the counties of Westchester, Putnam, Ulster, Orange, and Rockland in upstate New York. McNamara had a proven track record, so when he projected that he would have $100 million insurance in force within a decade, tremendous volume for the time, Guardian scrambled to sign him up. For his part, McNamara was happy to join Guardian, if only because he already sold more business than the company with which he was then connected could write![50]

At first, McNamara was a great find for Guardian as the agency was always up among the national leaders, like the giant Knight agency of the Union Central, the famous Woods agency of Equitable, or MONY's Ives and Myrick. But in 1932, Guardian and McNamara parted over a contract dispute. McNamara responded, at first, by appealing to Carl Heye's conscience in a piece of doggerel that McNamara thought carried an important message. He called it "The Stoic's Prayer" or "The Good Indian's Prayer":

> O Powers That Be, make me sufficient to my own occasions.
> Teach me to know and to observe the Rules of the Game.
> Give me to mind my own business at all times and to lose no
>   good opportunity of holding my tongue.
> Help me not to cry for the moon or over spilled milk. . . .
> Give me always a good comrade, and to view the passing show
>   with an eye constantly growing keener, a charity broaden-
>   ing and deepening day by day.
> Help me to win, if I may win; but—and this, O Powers; espe-
>   cially—if I may not win, make me a good loser.[51]

The poetic effort was sufficiently persuasive that the two sides struck an uneasy peace that evaporated in 1938, shortly after Guardian rejected

McNamara's overtures regarding a large pension trust deal. After settlement negotiations broke down, the agency sued Guardian for $467,000 for unpaid commissions and expense allowances on the basis of alleged oral modifications of its contract. Guardian appeared close to settling for $25,000 or $30,000 in 1939 but McNamara remained steadfast. It broke off negotiations and tried to "twist" at least one large Guardian policyholder. When the case finally came to trial in 1943, the judge ruled that McNamara had failed to prove any balance due it and directed judgment in favor of Guardian. McNamara appealed but again lost. The ordeal cost Guardian some $45,000 in attorney's fees, the price of six huge bound typescript volumes that detail the proceedings.[52]

Retaining Salespeople

The troubles with McNamara point to an abiding concern. How well did Guardian retain its salespeople? After the first year, quite well, in fact. In 1940, the average length of service of a full-time Guardian field agent was 9.5 years. Moreover, as demonstrated by table 8-2, most of its agents had five or more years of service with the company.[53]

Most, but not all, of those agents were men. As early as the Great War period, Guardian contracted with several female agents, a few of whom were exceptionally good. Maude McCallister, for instance, was a leading producer from 1919 until at least 1931. In the 1970s, the big female producers were Rosita Fu, who developed New York's Chinatown district, and Janice Poland of Clifton. According to Poland, women made good agents because they were more apt than their male counterparts to listen

TABLE 8-2
Tenure of Guardian's Field Force, 1940

Years of Service (#)	Share of Total Agency Force (%)
Less than 5	36
5 to 10	29
10 to 15	15
15 to 20	10
20 to 25	6
25 to 30	3
30 to 50	1
Total greater than 5	64

Source: Annual Report, 1940, Box 2, GLIC archives.

carefully to prospects' needs. There is no statistically significant basis, however, for knowing whether women were more or less easily retained than men.[54]

In 1950, the distribution of field employee experience was much the same as it had been in 1940, adjusting for the postwar growth of the field force and the addition of field clerical workers to the data.[55] (See table 8-3.)

What did Guardian do to achieve such retention? First and foremost, it tried to keep its general agents, especially the most productive ones, happy. After all, loss of a general agent entailed loss of a number of field-men as well. Guardian made major concessions to the McNamara agency, for instance, because it had accounted for over $2.35 million of new business out of a total for all agencies of about $13.3 million for the first quarter of 1925. It created a special home office account in McNamara's bank to induce it to provide the agency with a substantial line of credit. The company made further concessions to McNamara in 1926. After World War II, establishment of bank accounts for new general agents became common practice. In 1951, for example, Guardian established an account with a Houston bank to facilitate the conduct of business by an agency that it recently established in that city. Guardian also allowed GAs to specialize as they sought fit. For instance, Guardian GAs Robert Spaulder, T. Arthur Warshall, and Jerry Schnur concentrate on writing business through general brokers. In contrast, Holcombe Greene, a Guardian GA in Atlanta, concentrated on selling term policies to students, many of whom later became successful professionals who bought big whole life policies from Green's coterie of field reps. Whatever worked and was fair was alright with Guardian.[56]

Second, Guardian lavished encouragement, gifts, and conventions on its producers, especially the best ones. In the 1920s, Guardian held an annual convention for its sales agents. It dropped $15,000 to

TABLE 8-3
Tenure of Guardian's Field Force, 1950

Years of Service	Field Employees (#)	Total Share (%)
Less than 5	321	54.13
5 to 10	97	16.36
10 to 15	43	7.25
15 to 20	53	8.94
20 to 25	37	6.24
More than 25	42	7.08
Totals	593	100

Source: Annual Report, 1950, Box 3, GLIC archives.

$20,000 on each event, which was part training session and part vacation jaunt to destinations like Atlantic City, Chicago, and Montreal. When regulators complained about the cost of certificates, tie bars, money clips, mugs, rings, and plaques that the company doled out to top producers, Guardian pleaded that the costs were truly of small intrinsic value in the light of the very high qualification requirements. Regulators cracked down on the practice in 1969, so Guardian scaled back on the symbolic trinkets and gewgaws. Conventions, however, remained an important part of the compensation of successful field personnel.[57]

Third, Guardian did everything it could to see its fieldmen through business downturns. The Great Depression of course was anything but great for agents. Commendations for spirit and loyalty were nice, but what really mattered was that the company began to advance first-year premiums. By 1934, some of Guardian's general agents operated on a drawing account basis for the purpose of equalizing the manager's income, his total first year and renewal earnings, collection fees, and the like. The company went far beyond that to retain its top agents. In the fall of 1933 the company purchased the renewal interest of veteran top producer Leon Alexander so that he could extricate himself from personal financial difficulties brought about by his endorsement of a note that had gone into default.[58]

Throughout the Depression, Guardian continued to hold its annual agency conventions. It wined and dined its high-yielding agents, members of the so-called Leaders Club, at the Waldorf-Astoria and other posh Manhattan hotels. In 1935, the general agents were regaled with speeches by the top home office brass, received certificates of merit from Jim McLain, visited the military academy at West Point by boat, and supped at a seventy-fifth anniversary dinner during which New York State Superintendent of Insurance Louis H. Pink praised the life industry for attempting "to help bring the country through this trying time." In 1940, the agency men met to celebrate the appointment of one of their own, McLain, as president of Guardian. Guardian also sponsored a President's Club for its very top producers.[59]

In the final analysis, the most important factors in retaining sales reps were Guardian's selection and training programs. Selection ensured that only those with the best prospects of long-term success were chosen in the first place. Training ensured that those quality prospects could make a good go of it.

After World War II, Guardian again stressed sales training, especially for reemployed Guardian salesmen returning from the service. As in the past, that initial training was supplemented with a continuous training program synchronized with the agent's progress as a salesman. In 1946, it implemented a new screening procedure, which consisted of a series of thorough tests and several weeks of intense initial training. Applicants were selected on the basis of their showing in qualification tests, including The Guardian Personal Rating Chart, the Strong Vocational Interest Chart, the Inspection Report, and the Aptitude Index Blank. The company dropped the aptitude index for a time, but reinstated it in 1978. The screening was quite rigorous; about 40 percent of all applicants for field representative positions were declined at some point during the screening procedure.[60]

In 1958, new sales training material received a very favorable reception in the field and helped to increase sales. By the late 1960s, however, development of new career manpower became a paramount problem for the industry as a whole and especially for Guardian, whose general agents felt that they were not being given adequate help and tools to meet their training needs. The company revamped its field force programs by providing general agents with more training in recruiting and selection. It also launched a new program designed to acquire, retain, and promote elite field agents and representatives with management potential.[61]

In 1985, Guardian boasted of over one thousand career agents, up from just six hundred four years earlier. By that time, many of the company's agents were certified as chartered life underwriters and/or chartered financial consultants. Guardian continued to add quality agents and field representatives to its field force under the straightforward supposition that more minds in the field meant more sales.

That is not to say, however, that field force growth was linear. In 1995, Guardian planned to add, on net, 205 field representatives. It managed to land only a net of fifty, however, partly because individual life sales were very disappointing and partly because the public's perception of life insurance sales had soured due to numerous "churning" and "vanishing premium" scandals. The following year, when Guardian suffered a net decrease of eighty-two field personnel, it began writing financial rewards and penalties regarding sales force retention into its general agent contracts.[62]

By 1999, Guardian had turned the trend around, mostly beating recruiting goals, which boded well for future sales. During the downturn that gripped the equity markets in the first years of the new century, Guardian's sales, true to past experience, jumped. And strong sales meant more recruiting success. The company added on net 202 new reps in 2002, bringing its career agent force to 2,825.

Open communication between the home office and field was yet another aspect of successful acquisition and retention of salespeople. As far back as 1901, Cornelius Doremus held a convention at the home office where he provided the company's agents with detailed information concerning the company's transactions and financial condition. Bolstered by the company's then-outstanding condition and the president's call to sales, agents significantly increased their production over the next several years. Decades later, company president Dan Lyons made frequent trips throughout the United States to visit the field staff. The trips contributed greatly toward the high morale that usually existed among Guardian field reps. Compared to the industry average, Guardian came to have an excellent reputation for facilitating effective communication between the field and home office and for treating its field force fairly. The company continued to update its contracts, including the Field Representatives' Plan, to meet changing conditions.[63]

Ultimately, Guardian had to supply its agents with a wide enough variety of quality products, including equity products like mutual funds, to give its field force the opportunity to walk away from every encounter with a prospective customer with some sort of sale. Indeed, many of the company's product development decisions, particularly after the mid-1960s, were driven primarily by the need to keep the field force and general agents happy. Until 1988, the company also allowed its sales force to sell the equity products of other companies but since then has made them channel all such business through Guardian or one of its subsidiaries.[64]

More recently, Guardian introduced a sales strategy known as the Lifetime Economic Acceleration Process, or LEAP, sales system. Developed in 1980 by one Robert Castiglione, the basic premise of LEAP, that people should purchase as much whole life insurance as the insurers will sell to the individual, was quite radical at the time. Though LEAP was criticized in some quarters, Guardian viewed LEAP as a good way to stimulate sales that was consistent with policyholder welfare. LEAP stressed the tax-free nature of the "inside buildup" of life policies and was designed to maximize a policyholder's wealth under most tax and economic scenarios.[65]

Group Sales

In the early years, Guardian sold products directly from the home office. Of course, save for the company's first few years, the direct sale of whole life was insignificant, and if a lead came into the home office—the mortgage department was a continuing source of such leads—it was promptly turned over to the appropriate member of the field force. Group insurance, on the other hand, has largely been the bailiwick of the home office and group branch office employees, not general agents. The expansion of group insurance has been responsible for much of the company's recent growth.[66]

In 1956, Guardian named T. Robert Wilcox secretary in charge of the new Group Insurance Department. When Guardian entered the group field in 1957, it asked Connecticut General, a pioneer in the field, for some materials on its group business, which it got. But Connecticut General probably did not appreciate how Guardian repaid it, by "cherry picking" the person assigned to deliver the materials: Arthur Ferrara.[67]

Ferrara was a Bronx-born insurance veteran who joined Guardian on 27 January 1957. After taking a B.S. in business administration from Holy Cross, he had done a stint in the army right after the Korean War, and then put in a few productive years at Connecticut General. Like many insurance executives, Ferrara had fallen unintentionally into the business; he just happened to click with the Connecticut General interviewer, who was also a veteran. Though he knew nothing about insurance at first, Ferrara took full advantage of Connecticut General's group training program, which was at the time state-of-the-art.

Just three years after joining Guardian, almost to the day, Ferrara became Guardian's regional sales manager. In 1967 he became director of group sales for the eastern division and in 1972 agency vice president. In 1981 he became executive vice president and joined the board. A tenacious competitor, inside and out, he became president of Guardian on 1 January 1985 at age fifty-four. At the beginning of 1990 he also became CEO, a post he relinquished in 1996. Ferrara stayed on as a board director.[68]

Guardian opened its first group office at 150 Broadway, and from there gradually established regional offices spread around the country. The second group office was established in Atlanta, Georgia, in 1959, and soon after, offices were opened in Dallas and San Francisco. Fearful that this part of the business was growing too fast, Irving Rosenthal for a few years imposed a moratorium on the spread of group offices. As business conditions warranted, the ban was lifted, and by 1970, Guardian's group business was ensconced in some twenty major cities, including Boston, Chicago, Los Angeles, Philadelphia, St. Louis, and Washington, D.C. Some of the growth was premature, and the company shut down several unprofitable group offices, including the one in Dallas, by 1974.[69]

Still, group insurance was a high-growth business. A problem was how to staff it with qualified sales and service personnel. The traditional life insurance sales agent model was insufficient to the need. Whether physically located in the home office or in one of the regional offices, group sales representatives were fully Guardian personnel, not sales agents or even field representatives. They received salaries, bonuses, and benefits on the same basis as home office employees.

The bonuses paid to group employees were based on the *profitability* of business that they wrote, not the quantity. The group compensation system worked extremely well. If group salespeople smelled something rotten in Denmark, or any other defined group for that matter, they would route it, through brokers, to either less astute vendors or to those who were geared to price for higher risks. In 1971, Guardian produced about twice as much new premium per salesperson as the industry average. Earnings per salesperson were also at the top. Most important, there was little *voluntary* turnover. There was the occasional firing, but Guardian's group representatives were durable folks, less likely to be discouraged and less tempted to switch employers.[70]

Yet one can always find a fly in the ointment. Though they received generous—some said overly generous—overrides on group business, general agents were for many years jealous of the Group Department. And because group was highly profitable, the inevitable internal struggle ensued for its surplus. In 1971, after Guardian appointed district agents for the direct writing of group insurance, some general agents threatened to resign because they questioned the value of their franchise as a result of the new arrangement. General agents complained that the change turned the Group Department into a separate company, competing with the general agents for business from brokers. The GAs wanted to know why they should not get it all, even though generally speaking they did little to acquire the business.[71]

The outcries from the general agents did not amuse Irving Rosenthal. "Some of our general agents," he complained in 1971, "simply don't understand our company philosophy of independence of action for each of our product lines." "They don't understand that independence is perfectly compatible with co-operation, with friendship, with mutual profitability. A few of them even act like petty feudal lords demanding highly privileged treatment because the Company has bestowed a title on them." The spitting match was hardly one-sided. Group's head, the brilliant but cantankerous John Gray, countered that the overrides for general agents amounted to an evil "tax." Rosenthal rejected that position, too, and set both interests straight—group's profits belonged to the policyholders and would be distributed to the Group Department, the general agents, dividends, or wherever else Guardian's top management saw fit.[72]

And it was a good thing that Rosenthal and the rest of Guardian's management kept general agents and group out of each other's faces because for the balance of the twentieth century, group continued to grow by leaps and bounds. At the end of 1970, Guardian had 8,701 group policies in force. By 1992, that number had soared to over seventy thousand! Total group insurance in force jumped from about $1.6 billion in 1970 to over $80 billion as the twentieth century closed.[73]

Insurance Brokers

At the other extreme of the sales spectrum were brokers, who technically represented the interests of the prospects rather than any particular company. In reality, though, brokers represented themselves and the small coterie of companies with which they had brokerage contracts more than they represented the interests of their clients. That said, brokers were valuable because they moved a lot of product and moved it in a hurry. Guardian's use of insurance brokers extends back into the early twentieth century, and one of the company's most successful general agents had no field representatives at all. The Spaulder, Warshall, and Schnur Agency in New York City earned its commissions by inducing property and casualty brokers to locate and conduct initial screening of life insurance prospects.[74]

An early Guardian foray into the brokerage field was both costly and embarrassing. The company's informal relationship with All American Brokers, Inc., whose mission it was to steer Irish-American and German-American business away from "English" companies, soured Guardian on brokerage contracts for a time, but was not serious enough to perma-

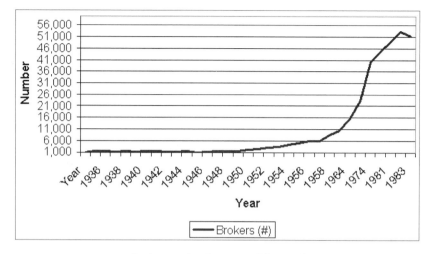

FIGURE 8-3 *Brokers under Contract with Guardian, 1935–84*

nently prevent it from attempting to cultivate the brokerage channel. By 1935, Guardian had contracts with about a thousand brokers, a figure that stayed largely constant until the early 1950s. (See figure 8-3 for details.)

Despite their growing numbers after World War II, brokers were responsible for only about a quarter to a third of Guardian's total production. The explanation for that is simple enough—Guardian did not treat brokers as well as some other companies, like Prudential and Continental Assurance, did. Brokers naturally sent more business to those companies. By 1960, Guardian changed its posture, offered better terms, and thereafter came to rely greatly on the brokerage market, especially to sell group insurance and equity products. Brokers had a far wider reach than the company's field agents alone. Moreover, they were relatively inexpensive as distribution channels.[75]

Controlling Surrender and Mortality in the Field

Brokers are cheap, but what Guardian's sales force does that brokers cannot do is help keep good policies alive and bad risks in check. In this respect, the role of the Guardian salesperson is critical to the growth and survival of the business. To be sure, insurance surrender rates were largely

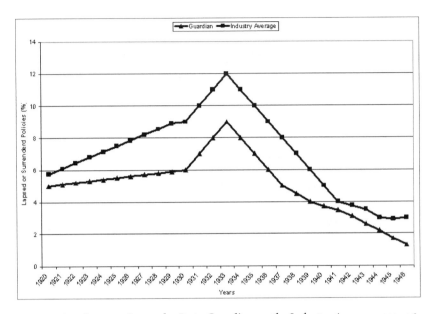

FIGURE 8-4 *Lapse or Surrender Rate: Guardian vs. the Industry Average, 1920–46*

a function of exogenous forces, in this case forces that affect the insured's disposable income. "There is a direct tie-in," Guardian told policyholders in 1947, "between what is left of the nation's income after essential living costs are paid and the way people hold on to their life insurance." Yet Guardian's surrender experience relative to other life companies was an indication of the relative skill of its agents and the relative quality of its policies and services. Surrender (and lapse) rates were in part under the control of the field force, which could always help or persuade policyholders to persist. We find in figure 8-4 that Guardian's performance was superior to that of the industry average, usually by a considerable margin, especially when industry rates were trending higher.[76]

As important as keeping policies in force was selling policies in the first place to people with good prospects for a long life. The health of any insurance company is ultimately dependent on mortality, and as James A McLain reminded industry leaders in 1935, "company mortality—to an extent frequently underappreciated—is a reflection of the character and caliber of its sales force."[77]

Of course, life insurance mortality is not merely selected at the point of sale. Since Guardian's founding, there has been a secular downward trend in mortality rates as the pace of medical advancements largely outstripped the proliferation of what one critic called the "Twentieth Century Habits . . . of wine, women and song." Increased longevity has greatly aided the overall industry. Life insurers have helped to reduce mortality in general by sponsoring important medical research and encouraging prophylactic or "preventive medicine." The secular downward trend in mortality rate helps the life insurance industry, but it helps specific life insurance companies only to the extent that they take advantage of it through enlightened and modern underwriting techniques.[78]

As figure 8-5 shows, through its long history, Guardian sometimes experienced very favorable, sometimes average, and sometimes high mortality. For much of its history, Guardian's mortality experience was average or better. As John Cameron, then associate actuary, noted in 1940, that generally favorable experience was, in large measure, due to "the careful selection used by our field representatives over a long period in the past in securing policyholders who measure up to The Guardian's standards."[79]

What were those standards? The evidence goes back to 1889, when once a suitable prospect had been found, and persuaded to purchase a

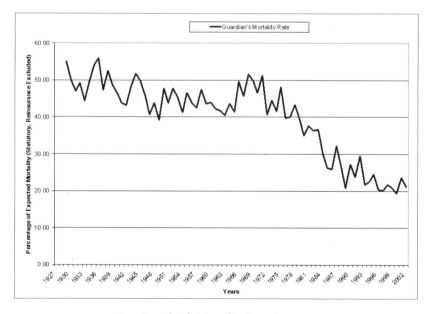

FIGURE 8-5 *Guardian's Mortality Experience, 1927–2002*

policy, Guardian sales agents had to ensure that the prospect himself, and not a proxy, was examined. The agent had to do so, however, without actually being present at the examination, which the examiner had to make in private, presumably so as not to be biased by the agent in his judgment. The agent then had to pay the examiner $3 for a routine exam, or $5 for an exam and urine test, which was required of all applicants involved in the alcohol industry and anyone applying for insurance totaling more than $5,000. If the prospect sought more than $10,000 worth of coverage, a second examination was required.[80]

In the nineteenth century, temperance was a key test. Again, in 1889, Guardian informed its agents to steer clear of "those who lead other than a temperate life" because according to statistics and the experience of all companies, heavy drinkers were the worst risks. Accordingly, the company at that time would insure "parties who are in any way engaged in, or connected with, the manufacture or sale of beer, wine or any intoxicating liquor" only for short-term endowment policies (i.e., high premium policies) taken out fairly early in life. When agents continued to forward applications for whole life policies for alcohol risks, Guardian sent out a circular that showed that mortality among those in the liquor business was substantially higher, from 50 to almost 70 percent, than the standard mortality tables. Other occupations adverse to longevity were those of stonecutter, butcher, baker, druggist, and, due to frequent proximity to contagions, physician. The ill effects of particulates were not as well understood as they would be in the late twentieth century, but any trade in which particles of dust were inhaled by workers was suspect. It was not until well into the postwar period that tobacco consumption became a red flag.[81]

By 1903, Guardian decided that as a general rule its salesmen should only approach people aged twenty-one to sixty years. Younger persons presented a special hazard because their physical constitutions, habits, and future occupations were usually unclear. Those over sixty should be solicited only if their habits, personal history, and family record were impeccable. "Persons who are ruptured," Guardian's instructions noted, would also be considered, but "only if a suitable truss is worn by them."[82]

Guardian had caught on to the fact that some savvy customers were beating the life insurers at their own game. The scheme was simple, legal, and effective. The applicant induced the agent to "rebate" his first year commission. Such rebating, essentially a form of price discrimination, was a common practice before the Armstrong Investigation. Agents gave some or all of their commissions back to the applicant in order to make bonus levels and, perhaps, secure renewal commissions in future years. But some applicants took the rebate, then "lapsed" the policy in the second year. By repeating the process year after year with different companies, the shrewd could secure very low-cost insurance. And when their health deteriorated, or age increased, to the point that they were no longer insurable, they would then maintain their last policy. The practice severely damaged companies interested in their long-term profitability rather than their new sales rankings. Guardian, when it could, refused to approve the applications of such designing persons.[83]

By 1909, the list of unacceptable or questionable occupations had grown longer and more complex. Applicants in some occupations, the company told agents, would be outright declined. Acrobats, aeronauts, professional soldiers, and racecar drivers, among others, were among that group. Applicants from certain other occupations, like baseball players, cowboys, and steamboat engineers, could only purchase on the endowment plan. Applicants in some other occupations, like electrical workers, hatters, and insane asylum attendants, had to fill out a form detailing their job functions before they would be considered for medical examination. Also in 1909, the company provided agents with a specific list of diseases and ailments that would lead to automatic declination. Among the conditions were appendicitis, cancer, epilepsy, hernia, syphilis, and excessive overweight or underweight. Those who were known to have attempted suicide would also be declined automatically.[84]

Gender was also an underwriting issue. Guardian in 1889 flatly told agents that the company did "not desire to write at all on female risks," but would grudgingly consider applications from the wives of men insured by the company. In 1895, however, the company reversed course, announcing to agents that it encouraged applications from women whose husbands were insured by Guardian or any other legal reserve life insurance company. Two years later, it went yet further and dropped the extra 0.5 percent premium on the lives of women. By 1920, Guardian told its agents that unmarried female risks engaged in gainful occupations were "generally desirable." "Married women," however, were "less desirable." Sufficient insurable interest and complete freedom from moral hazard, the possibility of the husband knocking off his "ball and chain" to collect her insurance, had to be shown, in part by the husband's insurance with Guardian or another insurer. As further safeguards, the company would not insure any female for more than

$10,000, would not grant her term insurance, and would include the disability rider only for unmarried professional women, not for factory operatives, car conductors, domestic servants, or other wage laborers likely to claim disability.[85]

There is no evidence that race per se was ever an underwriting consideration at Guardian.[86] After the company gave up on industrial insurance in the nineteenth century, it did not pay much heed to lower income groups, regardless of race. It was more than content to sign up members of the growing black middle class, right square in its target market. By the 1950s Guardian wrote policies on what it considered "a goodly number of colored people . . . where living conditions and occupations warranted." The company calculated that mortality was generally higher for African-Americans due to their socioeconomic standing, but the company felt as a matter of policy that it could not charge a higher premium based on a broad category of race. Most African-Americans who insured did so with fraternal organizations, industrial insurance giants like MetLife, or smaller companies that specialized in providing blacks (and sometimes poor rural whites) with life and disability insurance.[87]

By 1922, Guardian provided agents with a special pamphlet devoted to the selection and rating of risks. The pamphlet detailed how the company wanted to handle a variety of medical conditions, from abortion to varicose veins, and occupations. Because the company now accepted substandard risks, and offered disability and double indemnity riders, the pamphlet was more nuanced than earlier instructions. Coppersmiths in shipbuilding yards, for instance, would be insured, if healthy, at regular rates and allowed to purchase a disability rider but not a double indemnity rider, presumably because too many died of accidents on the job. The electrician next to him, if healthy, would be insured at a minimally substandard rate and likewise could obtain disability coverage but not double indemnity.[88]

In 1938, Guardian examined mortality by agency after it was noted that the agencies in the South had made an unfavorable showing. After study, the company attributed the poor performance to the small exposure of the southern agencies. In other words, the high mortality could have been a statistical anomaly. By 1938, Guardian's agent manual had grown into a small book—169 pages of tiny type—that attempted to be comprehensive as the warning on the cover, "Consult This Manual before Writing for Information," suggested.[89]

Guardian in 1924 began to cautiously write non–medical-examination insurance after initial rejection of the idea and a great deal of study. By 1938, it allowed sales agents who completed its correspondence course and who met minimum production requirements to write insurance, up to $5,000 (ages fifteen to thirty-five) or $3,000 (ages thirty-six to forty), without the insured having to take a medical examination. It simply made economic sense not to require exams on relatively young lives insured for small amounts. Over time, Guardian edged up both the maximum nonmedical policy value and the age limit.[90]

For larger policy values, however, medical examinations remained an important part of the underwriting or screening process. Not until 1949 did Guardian allow a single examination of its largest policyholders. At that time, the growing number of large cases forced it to designate certain trusted examiners as "preferred" and to allow them to provide the only exam. By the 1970s, Guardian mandated that one "regular" examiner validate applications up to $100,000. Above that level, to $250,000, a "special" or "preferred" examiner had to complete the physical. Above $250,000, Guardian again required two examinations, at least one of which had to be conducted by one of its "special" examiners. Within a few years, however, the soaring costs of health care induced Guardian, following closely on the heels of industry leaders, to use paramedical facilities for most cases. Agents at first resisted the change, arguing that paramedical staff were incompetent and that their facilities tended to be located in inconvenient places. By 1974, however, more than 20 percent of the company's exams were conducted by relatively inexpensive paramedical facilities. Guardian continued to push the use of paramedical examinations in lieu of less cost-efficient doctor's exams.[91]

The final screen before policy issuance was the home office underwriter, who reviewed medical or paramedical results and policy applications before their final acceptance by the company. The underwriter double-checked and if necessary rejected or rated applications made by persons with serious medical impairments or with personal histories that suggested the excessive use of intoxicants. He or she also rejected applicants in extremely hazardous occupations or those who applied for amounts of insurance out of line with what appeared reasonable for the applicant's financial condition. To make the underwriter's job easier, field agents were enjoined, in the words of Leo Futia, to "disclose to Home Office underwriters any adverse information known to them about any risk submitted to the company," on both group and individual cases and in all product lines.[92]

This second line of defense was necessary because some sales personnel simply did not appreciate all of the risks involved in writing certain types of business. They complained bitterly, for instance, about the apparent automatic declination of small policies at high ages. Home office underwriters patiently explained the adverse selection problem inherent in this type of application. Elderly people who had never bought but suddenly wanted insurance usually did so because they knew how they felt. They had an alarming tendency to pass away soon after the ink on the contract dried.[93]

Similarly, home office underwriters had continually to remind sales agents that total insurance in force for each policyholder should bear some reasonable relationship to the insured's financial situation. Otherwise, it becomes too tempting to cause or attempt to fake a death. With big commissions looming, agents rarely liked to consider this facet of the business. Companies therefore needed to be careful that they did not issue too much insurance.[94]

Thus agents disdained negative underwriting decisions, as necessary as they were to keeping the long-term health of the business viable—even for the agents. "It would be most important that the underwriters at the Home Office," Guardian agents argued in 1971, "have some sort of feeling of what an agent must do to earn a living, and then have the whole thing fall down in a heap by stumbling over a matter of getting the contract issued." That comment was made at a time when Guardian's underwriting was much more lax than it had been historically. The reason was the prevailing pressure to generate sales growth, or as one Guardianite put it, "Volumitis." The company simply wanted to grow rapidly. So rather than strive, as it had in the past, for the lowest mortality possible, it strove for "optimal mortality." In other words, it had made a calculation of the tradeoff between strict underwriting, profitability, and new sales growth and sought to reach the top of the curve. (See figure 8-6.)[95]

The top of the curve was a perilous place. In the late 1960s, mortality rates surged to unexpectedly high levels. That was when Dan Lyons brought Leo Futia down from Buffalo to the home office to help rectify the situation.[96]

Leo Futia hailed from Buffalo, and had graduated from Canisius College with a degree in business administration in 1940. He extended his business studies at the Wharton School until Pearl Harbor induced him

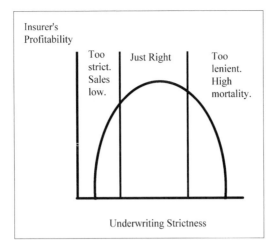

FIGURE 8-6 *Tradeoff among Sales, Profitability,*
and Underwriting Strictness

to join the Coast Guard for a four-year stint. He rejoined Guardian after the war as a full-time sales agent, and soon became one of the company's first field representatives. He thrived selling life insurance to his fellow Buffalonians, and in the mid-1960s, he took over as general agent of Guardian's Buffalo territory. After three years in that post, Futia joined the home office in New York, at Lyon's behest, as a senior vice president. From then it was all uphill, and quick. In 1971 he was promoted to executive vice president, from where he advanced to the presidency upon George Conklin's promotion to chairman and CEO in 1977. Futia became chairman and CEO in 1980, and then ceded those posts at the end of 1984 to John Angle. Futia then remained on the board of directors, as was the custom for former Guardian CEOs.[97]

The reason that Lyons had settled on Futia to change Guardian's adverse mortality situation was that the agent had proven that he not only could sell large amounts of insurance consistently but at consistently high quality. Futia's policyholders were a healthy lot, with excellent mortality rates. Lyons hoped that Futia could help the entire agency force to become better field underwriters.

Futia knew from experience that risk selection was more art than science. But if approached properly, it was not a complicated process. The three main elements of selection, as he understood it, were the prospect's health, financial situation, and moral character. If a sales prospect lived in a van down by the river or greeted you at the door with breath reeking of alcohol, do not write the business. Simple enough. In one instance, Futia was about to deliver a small endowment policy to a young woman when he noticed a blurb in the paper that stated that this new policyholder had attacked her boyfriend with a broken bottle. He mailed the policy and the clipping back to the home office with the note, "I don't think this is what we want." Obviously, not all cases were so cut and dried, so easy to identify. In borderline or suspect cases, the agent had to take the time to investigate the situation more deeply, or have the wit to grant less insurance, or the integrity to rate the prospect as substandard and charge a higher premium.

What George Conklin had realized was that Guardian's agent training program was more than sufficient to help the field force to take such precautions. Futia agreed. The mortality problem was probably not systemic. It must have been that a few rogue agents were writing high-risk policies. Futia investigated and sure enough, just a few agencies, including Guardian's largest, were the sources of most of the company's unexpectedly early death claims. Guardian terminated the worst offenders and kept a close eye on a few others, warning them to shape up or ship out.[98]

Futia's investigation yielded some good news, as well. His report showed that most of Guardian's agencies were top drawer. Still, the cautionary tale was that it took only a few incompetent or venal underwriters to wreak havoc with the company's actuarial calculations. As Irving Rosenthal put it,

> Each life insurance company may be likened to an apple orchard; each row of trees represents an agency; each tree in a row represents the issues of one calendar year of an agency. A company has bad mortality if it has too many trees producing disproportionate amounts of rotten fruit. The mortality ratio may be likened to the ratio of the number of rotten apples which prematurely fall to the ground to the much larger number of apples which remain on the trees and ripen normally and in due season.

To which John Cameron could not help but add in mock-biblical tones, "every tree which bringing not forth good fruit is hewn down and cast into the fire." Fruity metaphors abounded.[99]

Policyholder Hyman Miller was one such bad apple. Mr. Miller was a very sick and clever individual who took the company for more than

$100,000. Miller had diabetes and hypertension, but managed to hide his ailments from friends and family, even his wife, for a decade. When a medical examiner caught on, Miller bribed him not to report it, quickly lost weight or took medicine, and tested lower. When a company examiner finally caught his diabetes, Miller professed surprise. He did not stick around for the fallout. He died of coronary heart disease at age forty-eight, and while the company managed to contest two of his policies, eight more had long since become incontestable.[100]

In the Vortex

"Mortality," Leo Futia noted, "is what we are in the business to deal with." Whether one viewed that fact as a social or moral obligation, the life insurance industry certainly did better as people lived longer, because it received more premium payments and had more time to invest them. It is no wonder then that life insurance associations have always sponsored medical research, hygiene programs, and other endeavors to lengthen human life. And at the end of the day, society benefited.[101]

The problem facing an individual company, however, has always been how much it alone can spend on such broadly useful endeavors. At the end of each year, policyholders, as a selfish matter, were hardly demanding that the company's surplus be invested in improving social welfare. And for basic research or programs that aid the entire community, a free rider problem exists. Why fund a project that will benefit everyone? Let the other guy do it! One solution to the free rider problem was to jointly fund associations that, in turn, sponsor general programs of benefit to everyone. Another solution was to provide health-related services to one's policyholders only. In this conflicted arena, Guardian, like most insurers, took both approaches. One can only have faith that in the long run, corporate and social welfare will generally advance in tandem, as they are mutually interdependent.

At the same time, the particular circumstances of selling life insurance were always rife with conflict, even at the corporate level. Guardian had always to defend its business against high-risk individuals seeking insurance, no matter how deserving as human spirits. The company constantly demanded that its sales force be selective in choosing the company's new policyholders, if only to protect its older ones. The sales force, on the other hand, was populated with entrepreneurial spirits who needed to make a living and who wanted to be successful in business terms. They responded to the positive incentives to earn commissions and bonuses, to the demands of their customers for service, and to the pressures they felt to meet the company's sometimes contrary demands for safety and growth. Whether or not one ever thought of these matters systematically, the insurance salesperson's greatest challenge was to find a way to do business in a conflicting vortex of social, corporate, and individual welfare.

Of course, the quality of an insurance policy only begins with the initial sale. How satisfied a policyholder will be with a policy largely depends on how well the insurer services the policy after the sale. Some of that service burden falls upon the shoulders of the sales rep. Much of it, however, ultimately depends on the quality of the back office, the administrative personnel and systems that track policy changes, bill policyholders, pay claimants, and provide myriad other services. The quality of administration, as we shall see in chapter 9, hinges on the selection, training, and compensation of the insurer's home office employees.

9

Administration
Process and People

From the policyholder's standpoint, the administration of an insurance company is about one thing: policyholder service. Would-be policyholders want the protection best geared to their needs, at reasonable cost. Efficient policyholder service for these and a myriad of other transactions is just good business. It helps to keep down lapse rates and to bring in new customers. Existing policyholders want timely policy loans and quick responses to requests for policy changes. Policyholders' beneficiaries want prompt, hassle-free payoffs of their claims.

Guardian has staked its reputation for paying claims promptly since at least 1877, when its annual report noted that "thousands of widows and orphans will bear witness to the liberality and promptness with which the Company has fulfilled its obligations." In 1940, the company reported that the claim department made "every effort to see that every claim, whether to beneficiaries or to living policyholders, is paid on the same day when completed proofs are received." By that date, the company had established a long-standing practice. When claims were problematic, on account of technical matters, Guardian had normally settled them without resort to legal proceedings. It was more intent on pursuing suspicious claims made soon after the policies were taken out. The company won a strong majority of the cases that it actually took to court, because it contested claims only after careful investigations were made and competent evidence secured. Indeed, regulators agreed that every one of the seventy-two death and double indemnity claims that Guardian disputed between 1935 and 1937 was warranted. Strict office discipline and record keeping were crucial to good policyholder service and to protecting the company from false or erroneous claims. In the nineteenth century Guardian kept every check it drew as proof of payment. In 1894, for instance, policyholder Elie Charlier of New York had apparently forgotten that he had received his dividends. When he complained that he had not received "the usual checks," Guardian pulled out the canceled instruments with his endorsement on the back.[1]

Keeping policyholders was not an easy task. Any slip in service might elicit a complaint, and it was essential to keep complaints to a minimum. A policyholder's opinion of the company was based on the treatment received from the least friendly employee or agent, so Guardian's internal memorandums warned. We do not know precisely what prompted the following letter from a disgruntled policyholder (a crackpot?) in 1937.

> Inasmuch as we have not yet received any reply to our December communications [the policyholder wrote] we must assume that your holiday spree on monies stolen from widows and other unsuspecting clients has lasted longer than two weeks. When the entire staff at 50 Union Square recover from the headaches induced by carousing on other people's money we hope one of them will find time to honor us by answering our airmailed letters.

But Guardian took it seriously enough to handle it with care. His complaint, whatever it was, was eventually settled without fuss.[2]

Policyholders usually filed complaints about home office administration with the agents or representatives who had sold them the policies. The sales force, in turn, tended to sympathize with their clients. Agents confronted with complaints in the context of lapsed policies, refusals to purchase additional coverage, and other pocket-wrenching scenarios were likely to put pressure on the home office to upgrade its service, personnel, and procedures. This often put the home office on the defensive. "There are many things which the Company would like to do," President McLain told sales managers in 1948, but "it can do only those things which are feasible financially." Such cost-benefit arguments did not always sit well in the field.[3]

The home office had learned over time that policyholder service was not merely the sum of individual contractual relationships; it was a systematic process. R. C. Neuendorffer, who was employed by Guardian from 1908 until 1947, was the company's first expert on "scientific management." Following the expertise of Harry A. Hopf, one of the leading innovators in life insurance office management in the early twentieth century, Neuendorffer worked constantly to streamline office procedures and to engage employees in their improvement by rewarding them for good suggestions. He was the first of a series of in-house experts on office administration and expense management, all aimed ultimately at pleasing policyholders.[4]

Early Administrative Procedures

In 1926, Guardian collected into a supervisory manual various office administration rules that had been previously stated from time to time in memorandums. The amount of detail compressed into the eleven-page document is impressive. The manual instructed department heads not only to keep "all equipment . . . clean and in good repair and . . . good running order" but to inspect the equipment frequently so as to "prevent break-downs which might cause delays." Heads were also to requisition supplies well in advance so that work would not be interrupted. Each head had to see to it that the office was opened by 9:00 A.M. and that at the close of business "all lights and fans are turned off, desks clean, files and cabinets tightly closed, all work . . . completed, and all outgoing mail sent to the Mail Department." The head had full authority to extend the hours of his office whenever the work of the department justified it. In addition, he had to see that economical use was made of electric current and had to prevent the waste or excessive use of supplies of all kinds. At least once a month, on every fourth Thursday, department heads had to supervise a clean-up day designed to ensure that all equipment, files, and blanks were put away in their proper places. The head was to ensure that desk drawers were removed to see if any papers had fallen behind them. On top of all that, he or she was supposed to see that all clerks kept their wraps in the places provided. And this was just the first page of the manual![5]

The manual offered a number of useful suggestions. It called for department heads to keep a daily production record on form X-110. The form, the manual claimed, was "an indispensable aid to control." To make the most efficient use of the company's human capital, the manual also advocated that each clerk know at least two jobs, his own and a higher or at least parallel job. Finally, it suggested that supervisors warn clerks not to bury cases that were complicated or unclear, but immediately to refer such cases to the department or section head for advice. "If a clerk is absent," the manual ordered, "the department or section head will see that the papers in his basket are given attention by another clerk without delay."[6]

Does the manual suggest that Guardian was "form happy"? In addition to form X-110, the manual mentions at least three other forms, including X-107, which had to be completed in order for clerks working overtime to receive their $2.00 "supper money," and form X-83, which had to be completed to ensure return of certain types of paperwork, i.e., other forms. The danger was the mindless proliferation of paperwork; the company could drown in a sea of red tape. Pruning was necessary from time to time. A 1940 review of stationery and forms resulted in the discontinuation of 148 obsolete forms. Following the advice of the budding management guru Peter Drucker, in 1954, Guardian tried to remember to purge itself of obsolete forms every few years, as a matter of sound bureaucratic practice. One could only stem the tide for so long. Growth, greater size, and greater complexity brought more forms. By 1963, Guardian had such a plethora of forms that it placed the production of all of them under the supervision of the General Planning Department, which was charged with making all the "buy vs. make" decisions for the company—regarding its forms. Rather than go directly to outside printers, supervisors who wanted forms now had to fill out the correct form, X5. No mention of what supervisors who could not find an X5 form had to do, but presumably it entailed . . . yet another form![7]

All this was necessary because the volume of information an insurance company had to track was nothing less than mind-boggling. Never mind what information an insurance company had to cope with by the year 2000. In 1940, when Guardian was quite small by modern standards, it had over 130,000 policyholders, some twenty-six thousand of whom changed residence in that year alone. In addition, another 10,585 policyholders changed beneficiary designations, over forty thousand had policy loan accounts, nearly seven thousand reinstated lapsed policies, 5,322 changed the frequency of their premium payments, and some three thousand asked for policy changes or conversions. Similarly, the company's 1946 rate book required more than one hundred thousand separate mathematical calculations, most completed by hand or with the use of Burroughs mechanical adding machines. No computers.[8]

Like all companies, Guardian had little control over prevailing wage rates or taxes, or the price of office supplies and other equipment. It could only obtain substantial savings by using its physical and human resources wisely. Guardian first analyzed its office efficiency in a formal way in 1893, when Assistant Secretary Gustav Meidt asked each employee to delineate his respective duties. The responses were used to help the company understand its own evolving administration.[9]

Thirty years later Guardian was growing fast enough that its administrative costs seemed to be getting out of hand. The home office engaged the services of a management consultant, the Leffingwell Ream Company, for $750. William Henry Leffingwell himself promised to save the company at least $3,000 per annum in administrative expenses and noted that he would be surprised if he could not save it $15,000 per year. Guardian accepted his offer because Leffingwell had written the first textbook on "scientific" *office* management and stood in a class by himself. It is hard to say whether his efforts paid to promise, but in 1942, the company again employed "management engineers" to make a study of procedures, practices, and methods of various departments with the idea that they might be improved, made more economical, or both. On the back of the recommendations that came from that second study, Guardian reorganized its office procedures in 1944. In 1952, a special expense committee, composed of four executive officers, was charged with making continuing studies of the company's operations and suggesting methods of keeping expenses to an absolute minimum without impairing the services provided to policyholders.[10]

Make or buy decisions were constantly reviewed. In 1953, the company joined the Eastern Card Library, a nonprofit consortium that furnished insurers with Medical Information Bureau data that proved helpful during the applicant screening process. Annual expenditures for the service, $30,000, were far less than the $45,000 Guardian spent for the maintenance of its own files.[11]

Communications were costly. In 1945, Guardian conducted a study of its Western Union service to ensure that its use of telegrams was efficient. In 1957, Guardian reminded employees that they should weigh the costs and benefits of the four major communication routes available to them—first-class mail, air mail, telegram, and telephone. The tradeoffs were clarified. Mail was cheaper but slower, best used for conveying large amounts of information or materials that were not highly time sensitive. Telephone calls were best for immediate contact or where significant discussion was involved. Telegrams served best to convey short, unidirectional messages where time was of some essence.[12]

It was never easy to get compliance to initiatives to keep the bureaucracy trim and sleek. Efficiency programs came and went. In 1961,

Guardian, with the aid of consulting firm Robert Walker and Associates, implemented the Supervisors' Work Analysis Program, or SWAP. During the program, supervisors conducted minute, Tayloresque studies of the work processes of each of the jobs under their respective control, "laboriously charting every minute detail of [the] processes, determining frequency of all the variations, applying motion time values to determine a 'standard' (reasonable) time for each process, and finally comparing this standard with the actual time which his people are now taking." Resistance to the program came not from the rank and file but from the supervisors. To get them to get behind the program and sell it to the organization, Guardian executives considered tying the salary policy of the company to the SWAP program. They took such an extreme step because the pilot program showed that SWAP was a great money saver, with the time needed to complete many routine procedures being sliced in half. Moreover, according to the report, SWAP taught at least some supervisors to think more readily in terms of time and its cost.[13]

When computer conversion delays hurt policyholder service in the early 1960s, Guardian strove to reestablish rapport with its policyholders and agents. As a first step, it reviewed the recent history of its policyholder service-related decisions. It then generated several concrete suggestions, including the establishment of a systematic procedure for reviewing all complaints from policyholders, agencies, and the general public. The out-of-pocket expense of improved policyholder service, the report projected hopefully, would be amply repaid in higher persistency rates and additional sales.[14]

In the late 1960s, after a recurrent series of computer conversion glitches, the company, with the help of a consulting firm, Profit-Improvement, undertook an intensive study of its clerical operations. Under the program, Guardian redesigned administrative jobs to make them richer and more meaningful. In the first department studied, personnel savings of 25 percent were achieved. In May 1970, President Conklin reported that the program had provided the company with substantial performance benefits. Loan processing times dropped from seven days to three to four days, cash surrenders from ten to four or five, and conversions from between ten and fifteen days to six days. The program was so successful that Guardian made it a permanent part of its administrative policies.[15]

Employee Selection

No amount of bureaucratic fixing can work without good, well-trained, yet thinking employees. Guardian general counsel Ed Kane was a clerk in the claims department when an irate policyholder came in, insisting that he be paid the *face value* of his policy on demand. Kane patiently explained that Guardian would pay the $5,000 value of the policy only after the man died or turned ninety-six, whichever came first. Not to be dissuaded, the man returned the next day, brandishing a gun. Kane made a quick calculation, relented, and offered to cut a check immediately. The customer gratefully accepted the check, which, of course, was never paid. He was later arrested. Not all situations were so challenging. But creative employees were more valuable than mere bureaucrats. The problem was how to find and then retain them.[16]

Like any asset, the company's human capital had to be purchased. Unlike its financial capital, more than cash had to be tendered. Salaries were important, but so were the benefits, both the formal ones, like retirement and health insurance, and the informal ones, like glee clubs, outing days, and office atmospherics. Perhaps most important of all was the corporate culture. Many people who wanted to "do well by doing good" found Guardian an amenable place to work, if only because, historically, it placed an explicit emphasis on ethics. By the same token, character was an important hiring screen.[17]

In the early days, employment decisions were necessarily ad hoc. The company was a small, tightly knit team. Everyone knew what everyone else did, or in some cases did not do. So hiring and promotion decisions were fairly easy. Salaries were relatively low, though, and "sticky." Guardian was not unusual in either respect. Its employee salaries and promotion policies were similar to those of, say, the early MONY.[18]

Whether mutual companies should grant employee bonuses was a heated question. One side held that bonuses increased efficiency and retention. The other felt that all profits ought to accrue to policyholders. (MONY, for example, had stopped paying bonuses when it felt the sting of sharp criticism of the practice in the late 1860s.) By the 1910s, however, Guardian was routinely awarding "special compensation" to a few outstanding employees each year. From 1896 to 1932, the company granted Christmas bonuses ranging from 5 to 6.67 percent of annual salary, based on seniority, preferring such a scheme to a general salary increase. The holiday cheer was dropped in 1960 when two peer companies granted general salary increases to their employees, exacerbating pressures in the intensely competitive employment market in the New York metropolitan area.[19]

When noncash incentives could be used effectively, they were. Before World War II the company granted paid half-day vacations for departments that maintained a good record. The company hoped that under that system supervisors and other clerks would quickly punish any shirkers. Clerks with good individual attendance records also received one day off each quarter. That was in addition to the two weeks of annual vacation enjoyed by clerks in the employ of the company for more than a year.[20]

Before World War II, Guardian typically raised wages only under pressure. It hiked the salaries of its lowest-paid employees during World War I in order to mute the effects of the prevailing high cost of living. The company also increased salaries during World War II to combat increased living costs, sagging morale, and high turnover. Just ten days after the attack on Pearl Harbor, for instance, it passed an emergency salary increase of 6 percent. By then it was the company's practice to offer two broad types of salary increases: the more desirable practice of granting individual raises based roughly on merit, and the less desirable practice of granting across-the-board increases, based on the aggregate price level. For many years, the company granted raises for individual employees in January, until Carl Heye moved the increases to April, purportedly because any employees disgruntled by the size of the bonus would find it more difficult to find a new job then. Later on, the company staggered individual salary increases by granting them on the anniversary of hire.[21]

It was inflation that made across-the-board increases inevitable. In inflationary periods, Guardian generally tried to raise salaries ahead of price increases so that employees would not suffer from extended periods of decreasing real wages. It made clear, however, that it could only afford to do so if worker productivity increased.[22]

In the early 1920s, Guardian realized that its ad hoc individual increase system was suboptimal for recruiting then-coveted college graduates. In April 1923, the company sought for the actuarial department a female correspondent with college training and mathematical qualifications. At the same time, it was also decided to employ a younger actuary or actuarial student who was well along in his examinations. The company also desired two bright young men, preferably college graduates, one with planning and organizational talents, the other with legal qualifications, to serve as assistants to the secretaries. But the company did not find filling such positions easy. Guardian tried to modernize by basing salary increases, after 1926, on a report, or rating, scale that it enjoined its supervisors to fill in "carefully and fairly."[23]

The new system was an improvement but was eventually found to be inadequate. In 1937, therefore, the company invested considerable time evaluating its salary structure. The ill effects of that year's deep recession, however, made it hard to adopt any changes, which were postponed until wartime, when Guardian would lose many of its key employees, at least for a time. One issue was how to sustain the corporate culture—Guardian-specific traditions, objectives, and methods—amid an unusually large influx of new employees. Another was whether to share more information about how compensation was determined. Guardian's top managers wanted to render personnel policy more uniform across the company without threatening the contentment and loyalty of its older employees. The means was to make job classifications and salary scales more "scientific" and to simultaneously lift the curtain of mystery that had long surrounded salary principles. Guardian also geared up for an intensified program of in-house education that stressed insurance principles and the background and philosophy of Guardian practices.[24]

Meritorious Careers

At the end of World War II, Guardian had established a long tradition of careerism. Guardian had made, and would continue to make, the occasional, notable hire from outside its ranks, but the company much preferred to groom and promote from within. By the end of the twentieth century, Guardian's supervisors and managers almost always came up from the rank and file. Two major benefits arose from the policy. First, as Guardian Vice President Don Sullivan explained, "by the time we make somebody a manager, we know those people." Second, it was good for morale. To go to work for Guardian was to stake a career on it. And those who excelled could expect to be rewarded. From time to time, Guardian's personnel managers would remind employees that the company's objective was to fill jobs by promotion from within and to base all promotions on merit.[25]

This was particularly important if Guardian were to attract more college graduates. Though few undergraduates were trained in life insurance, life insurers saw successful pursuit of a baccalaureate degree, in any field, as a positive signal of the applicant's desire to rise above the clerical ranks into management. Moreover, Guardian and other life insurers were generally pleased with graduates' basic business skills and especially with their interpersonal skills. The big problem was attracting college graduates to the company. Stock and mutual companies paid virtually identical salaries. Those salaries, however, did not compare favorably to those available to college graduates hired by burgeoning "center" firms in the manufacturing sector. Moreover, most college graduates in the 1950s thought insurance a relatively uninteresting line of work and believed that within insurance companies advancement would be too slow, based more on seniority than merit.[26]

Historically, advancement and compensation was subject to the opinions—and prejudices—of individual supervisors. Managers operated under instructions to permit the transfer of any employee who qualified for an open position, and were asked simply to keep their eyes peeled for young clerks who showed ability and interest so that they might be trained for responsible positions. In 1948, Guardian began to systematize its approach to promotions and compensation in ways that differed markedly from its prewar practices. That year, the company adopted a program using a merit rating scale that allowed new employees to earn a raise after six months on the job, to seek a raise on their respective hire anniversaries, and to negotiate a raise as soon as ability to perform the new job was demonstrated. Supervisors graded employee performance in seven key areas on an eleven-point scale:

1. Punctuality and attendance
2. Initiative and creativeness
3. Co-operation
4. Ability to learn
5. Quality of work
6. Quantity of work
7. Knowledge of job.[27]

The merit program had an unplanned benefit. Supervisors quickly discovered that by providing their employees with scheduled, measurable feedback about job performance, the supervisors themselves learned more about their own organizations and how their personnel might best be used. The "basic idea of [merit] interview is not to criticize but to try and get improvement," noted a memorandum on the program. Supplemented with training opportunities to help low-rated employees to improve, the program was thought to have a powerful effect on efficiency.[28]

In 1955, the merit program was enhanced when managers moved to implement the recommendations of a study aimed at nurturing high-level talent. The study recommended that Guardian

1. plan for the replacement of officers as they retire with "relatively young, vigorous, and competent persons who have grown up with the company";
2. provide leader prospects with "work sufficiently stimulating to keep these employees contented until they are ready for managerial responsibility";
3. rotate leader prospects to keep them interested and to help them to understand all aspects of the business;
4. expect and encourage continued education;
5. make it clear that managers are "genuinely interested" in each leader prospect's progress and that they intend "to place them in positions of responsibility when the openings occur";
6. seek out family men because "such individuals find the security of home office employment more important than do unmarried young people";
7. provide formal training.[29]

The merit program evolved into a permanent feature of Guardian's compensation and promotion system, and was revisited from time to time. In 1963, for example, Guardian's home office managers convened a series of meetings to evaluate, critique, and generally explicate the techniques and philosophy underlying its performance rating system. Basic—timeless?—questions about employee performance were readdressed.

- Should an individual's salary ever be reduced? Why? Why not?
- What is the meaning of a promotion-from-within policy?
- What is meant by excessive absences and tardiness?
- How can turnover be reduced?[30]

As to wages, the company generally paid better than the national industry average after World War II. The idea was to attract and keep the best personnel available on the market. This worked in an economic sense, of course, only if the company's employees were more efficient than those of the industry at large.[31]

Thus whenever Guardian's relative efficiency showed any downward turn, it was a cause for concern and adjustment. The mid-1960s was such a time, and this fact helped prompt the reviews of work regimes, technology interfaces, and merit ratings noted above. Guardian began to make more routine studies of the company's salary scales and salary policy, and to consult with outside experts.[32]

Benefits

Benefits—or nonsalary compensation—came to the corporate world in gradual steps throughout the twentieth century. They were driven in small part by paternalistic considerations, but in large part by competition and broader social factors. The modern corporate practice of providing retirement contributions and medical insurance to employees grew largely out of the wage freeze during World War II, when organized labor unions fought successfully for such non–wage-based increases for their members. Managers followed suit. U.S. corporations have since been critical providers of "social insurance," especially since government programs to extend social insurance universally as a matter of entitlement do so at low levels. Guardian's history in this regard followed the larger trend.

Guardian's first pension plan was devised for its home office and Berlin office employees in 1908. It was a direct response to German insurance regulatory pressures to provide pensions for the Berlin employees. Germany, the world's pioneer in social insurance, had long compelled domestic corporations to participate in its comprehensive system for compulsory disability insurance and pensions. What was good for the Berliners was good for the New Yorkers. Guardian thus became the first New York insurer to offer a pension plan to its employees, but not before it was confronted by the state's superintendent of insurance, who wanted the company to wait for permissive legislation. William G. Choate, the company's counsel, actually had to make the argument that there was no legal prohibition to providing such benefits! The early benefits were surely modest, and were modestly augmented in 1926, when Hubert Cillis, T. Louis Hansen, and Carl Heye contributed $2,500 each to form the Guardian Life Welfare Trust, Inc. The trust, which by World War II had swelled to $45,000 through additional gifts and interest, benefited company employees who were in need of pecuniary assistance beyond that which the company itself could grant them. Essentially a private charity, the trust encountered no regulatory hurdles.[33]

Guardian's employee benefits package did not take substantial, modern form until 1942, when it adopted the Guardian Employees Retirement Plan. Despite the name, the plan provided employees with a range of benefits, including a service retirement annuity, a disability annuity, long-term sickness benefits, and a death benefit. To fund the benefit, employees paid 2 percent of their salaries to $3,000 and 3 percent on salaries over $3,000 and below the $12,000 cap, while the company contributed any necessary additional funds. Employees were automatically retired on the first 31 December following their seventieth birthday. In subsequent years, the company tweaked the plan to keep pace with changes in the competitive, tax, and Social Security environments.[34]

By the end of 1952, Guardian offered the following welfare benefits to its employees:

1. Lunches (home office only);
2. Noncontributory group life and disability (home office); contributory group life and disability (field reps);
3. Noncontributory hospitalization memberships in Blue Cross;
4. Reduced rates on regular Guardian life insurance and deferred annuities;
5. Welfare trust fund;
6. Retirement plans.

We shall review the history of such benefits in more detail.[35]

In 1917, Adelaide Smithers, the ladies' auxiliary to the home office employee association, complained that most of the company's "girls" had to bring their lunch from home and eat it cold. She suggested that if the company would not institute a lunch room in the building as so many other companies had done, it should at the very least install a small electric stove and an urn for keeping water hot, which would enable the girls to make tea, coffee, or cocoa. During the winter of 1938, the company did Smithers one better and began to provide free tea, coffee, milk, and soup to its employees. (Other major life insurers also provided employees with free or subsidized lunches, some of them for many years.) Citing the dearth of restaurants in the neighborhood, the company provided free lunches until 1966, when tax code changes induced the company to subsidize only half of each meal. To this day meals remain subsidized, though not as heavily.[36]

In 1937, Guardian adopted a long-term sickness allowance, or "salary continuation" plan, for employees with fewer than eleven years of service with the company. The plan allowed for full pay for up to seven months followed by half-pay for up to six months. For employees with eleven or more years' tenure, the plan called for the cases to be handled individually. At that time it also adopted a group life policy for all home office employees, except those of the home office Collection Department, who were added to the plans in 1939. In 1956, a study indicated that Guardian's benefits compared favorably with those of other life insurance companies in the New York area, except for the group life insurance feature, which was so much less favorable than that offered elsewhere that it placed the company at a disadvantage in the personnel market. Guardian immediately beefed up its coverage, and by the 1960s, the Group Department was advising the corporation on its employee benefits, essentially selling the company on additional coverage whenever it noticed that Guardian's benefits were in danger of slipping below the industry average.[37]

By 1950, Guardian had three retirement plans, one for commission agents, one for salaried field employees, and one for home office staff. Although the expense was considerable, it was necessary. An employee who enjoyed reasonable provision of financial security for himself and his family in event of death, disability, or retirement, the company explained to policyholders, was a happier employee who provided the company with more efficient work and the policyholder with better service. "It would be incongruous," President McLain noted, "if those who work to provide security for others were not to enjoy a reasonable measure of security for themselves." Unstated was the harsh reality of competition. Employees were now seeking out not simply the best wage, but the best benefit plans, too.[38]

Accordingly, Guardian continued to revamp and update its benefit plans over the balance of the twentieth century. It added dental coverage in the late 1980s and now also offers a long-term care group insurance benefit (written by another carrier). It now offers employees group life coverage of twice annual salary up to $400,000; employees can purchase whole life at a discount, with no commissions included in the premiums. Guardianites can also purchase Guardian's mutual funds with no sales loading.[39]

But true to form Guardian did not follow every benefit fad. In the 1990s, for example, when most companies jettisoned their defined benefit plans in favor of cheaper cash balance or defined contribution plans, Guardian retained its defined benefit plan. Though defined benefit plans and other top-notch benefits are expensive, Guardian believes that in the long run they pay off in the form of increased employee efficiency and loyalty.[40]

Investing in Loyalty

Employee satisfaction is reflected by the turnover rate. By the mid-twentieth century, Guardian was keeping tabs and reported that it typically experienced its highest turnover in the clerical ranks and other entry-level positions. At higher job grades, however, turnover dropped precipitously, as table 9-1 suggests. The average length of service of home office staff in 1940 was 13.5 years. One of five employees had been employed for fifteen or more years. As table 9-2 shows, much the same was true ten years later.[41]

"We're accustomed to long service records here at The Guardian" noted Charlotte Reidy in 1950 (at least for people who survived the first five years). Low turnover was considered highly desirable. It lowered switching costs, it resulted in improved intra-organizational communication, and it bolstered the efficiency of experienced employees. Guardianites were encouraged to think of themselves as "lifers" interacting with other lifers. It was in everyone's best interest, therefore, to do a good job

TABLE 9-1	
Tenure of Guardian's Home Office Employees, 1940	
Years of Service	Total Share (%)
Less than 5	40
5 to 10	16
10 to 15	24
15 to 20	8
20 to 25	4
25 to 30	3
30 to 50	5

Source: Annual Report, 1940, Box 2, GLIC archives.

TABLE 9-2		
Tenure of Guardian's Home Office Employees, 1950		
Years of Service	Home Office Employees (#)	Total Share (%)
Less than 5	150	41.67
5 to 10	91	25.27
10 to 15	21	5.83
15 to 20	27	7.50
20 to 25	39	10.83
More than 25	32	8.90
Totals	360	100

Source: Annual Report, 1950, Box 3, GLIC archives.

and to get along. And getting along was encouraged by company-sponsored events aimed at extra-hours socialization. Fifteen years of service qualified an employee for membership in the Service Club, which sponsored dances, choral societies, a bowling league, championship baseball and softball teams, and basketball, card, and golf tournaments. Long-time service was also honored with great ceremony.[42]

In fact, one can go back at least to 1916 to find evidence of Guardian's attempts to forge a community of interest among its employees. The Germania Life Home Office Association signed up practically all of the company's employees who would enjoy listening to the "victrola" that had been purchased for $111. Two rooms on the fifth floor were made available for meetings of the association. The following year the company expended $2,000 to endow the association with a gymnasium, social rooms, and showers. "Use of the space for these purposes, and the aforesaid expenditure," the Finance Committee reasoned, "seemed entirely justified in view of the fact that thereby the employees will be better satisfied with their positions and thus more attached to the Company, with their loyalty strengthened and their efficiency increased."[43]

The company also sponsored a "Guardian outing" day each year. In 1965, 634 people, including 250 employees and officers, attended the event. To help everyone in the Guardian "family" feel more at home on the road as well as in the home office, Guardian long encouraged the attendance of spouses at its agent conventions and other meetings. A large percentage of spouses in fact did attend company gatherings. Furthermore, spouses often accompanied managers on prolonged business trips, at least until regulators cracked down on the practice in the 1960s.[44]

A *Home Office Newsletter* was Guardian's means for communicating among its employees. It was a useful vehicle for lauding employees who excelled at their posts. The October 1955 issue gave a tip of the hat to the company's switchboard operators for exceeding standards in a service analysis conducted by New York Telephone. The *Newsletter* was not always all good news. That same issue noted that "the services of seven members of the staff were terminated during the past month because of unsatisfactory work and/or absenteeism." Such notices were by no means unusual. Thus the newsletter had a salutary effect on the careless. (To punish less severe transgressions, the company held back salary increases.)[45]

Such company-sponsored recreational activities, honors, and perquisites were commonplace in U.S. corporations by midcentury, as companies liked to compare themselves to employees' extended families. Loyalty went both ways in organizations that strove to nurture long-term careers. Stability in employment was a high good. (The General Electric of Bernard Swope was vastly different, in this regard, from the General Electric of Jack Welch.) People who worked together played together, even informally. In fact, during his very first week on the job, Ed Kane hit the daily double with his boss, much to the chagrin of the elevator operator, who was also the bookie. He then found a date in the dividend department, and somehow ended up in a golf tournament in a foursome with the CEO and two vice presidents. Kane won the tournament, made a killing playing cards with his superiors later that night, and then worried all weekend about getting fired for it. Fortunately Guardian did not fire people for their golf skills or shrewdness in poker. Perhaps they were signs of enterprise.[46]

The corporate family ethos came under increasing pressure in the postwar era, particularly in the 1970s when U.S. businesses generally underwent massive restructuring under inflationary and global competitive pressures and adapted to new technological systems. Private lives had changed, too, with more dual-income families living farther away from their workplaces. And company-specific careers were giving way to the notion of individual professional careers that may involve several employers in one's lifetime. Formal recreational activities and other company-sponsored events began to wither away. To help keep payrolls down, Guardian began to rely more and more on temporary workers for which a brisk market developed in the 1970s. Historically, the company had preferred giving overtime to regular employees rather than relying on "temps" for peak-load work or transitional jobs because the temps' company-specific knowledge seemed insufficient to allow them to perform as efficiently as regular employees, even on a compensation-adjusted basis. But in the 1970s the company found that temporary hiring was another kind of screening process in which it could make regular employment offers to the best. This was yet another sign of the increasing flux in the nature of employment.[47]

Signs of a breakdown in the traditional corporate "family" dated back to the mid-1960s, when Guardian began to lose too many of its mid-to-low-level personnel at the home office. In 1964, the percentage of home office employees with less than three years of experience reached fifty. The company looked for ways to solve the problem, but its rapid growth in that era made it difficult to find good people. Managers resorted to asking employees to recommend friends and relatives for the jobs, but that was not enough. The company began offering cash incentives to employees to bring friends and family on board. Still, the drain continued. High turnover brought service problems, a point brought home in 1968 when sales agents complained that policies were often mailed to the wrong addresses.[48]

As the turnover problem grew more desperate, Guardian resorted more directly to financial incentives. In 1968, it began matching employee retirement savings up to 3 percent of employee salaries. The company pledged a further contribution if the increase in surplus exceeded 5 percent of the increase in liabilities, a profit-sharing bonus of up to 10 percent of salary. (The company changed the calculation of its Employee Incentive Savings Program in 1971 to include three variables, expense control, increase in new premium income, and net earnings as related to liabilities.) In 1969, Guardian's turnover rate in the home office was just under 40 percent, a historic high for the company though lower than the average for other life insurance companies in New York.[49]

Guardian's profit-sharing program helped retain employees and even better news was that despite the turnover, employee efficiency was improving greatly in this period. The number of Guardian home office employees per million of premium income was halved from 6.7 in 1968 to 3.2 in 1976. While some of that gain was attributable to inflation, the more impressive fact is that Guardian actually cut staff devoted to the life business some 16 percent between 1968 and 1976 while the number of in force policies grew. For every one thousand policies in force in 1968, Guardian employed 0.92 persons. By the end of 1976 that number had dropped to 0.74.[50]

The field force, however, continued to fret over home office performance. Turnover in the early 1970s was running at about 30 percent, but sometimes spiked higher when salaries did not keep pace with inflation. Recessions helped by reducing employees' options, but stagflation ate away at morale. In 1974, for instance, agents complained of what they termed the "lackadaisical" attitude of many entry-level employees. "Newly-appointed general agents," they noted, "are comparing the Guardian unfavorably with their previous companies." The company responded by cross-training employees to do several jobs and authorizing more overtime. It also implemented a system of service indices to track the performance of entry-level employees more precisely. Finally, it encouraged frustrated general agents to send carbon copies of correspondence to the department manager.[51]

Guardian tried a lot of little things to improve employee morale and retention rates. For example, if an employee was transferred at the company's convenience, it was policy to buy the employee's home at a good price. Dan Lyons tried communicating more about senior management plans and policies. George Conklin hired consultants to advise the company on a job-enrichment program that might help employees find their duties more satisfying.[52]

During the deregulation wave of the 1980s and 1990s, Guardian feared that banks and other financial services companies accustomed to dealing extensively with customers would enter the life insurance business and begin to outcompete it in policyholder service. The company responded to the threat by putting everyone in the company, CEO included, through an extensive "customer service" training program. As a result of the program, Guardianites felt better prepared to treat with both internal and external clients.[53]

By the end of the century, Guardian was doing a better job of matching employees with the jobs that most suited their individual characteristics and aptitudes and then to empower them to make more decisions, thereby softening some of the traditional big-business, hierarchical approach to organization. Each employee was given a so-called certificate of empowerment that conferred considerable discretion to act within the company's broad core values. That is, in spirit at least, a throwback to practices in the much smaller company Guardian had been during World War I, when managers urged employees simply to "do what is right!" All of those changes brought increased employee satisfaction and a return to low turnover rates.[54]

Employee Training

More generally, in the late twentieth century, Guardian redoubled its efforts to provide employees with the intellectual tools they needed to do their jobs better. Company-sponsored education had become more than ever both company necessity and individual perk.

Employee training and education at Guardian in one form or another dated back to 1916, when the company provided employees with access to an extensive library of insurance literature. By the 1920s, all clerks and office boys were ushered through formal training courses, which, if they passed, guaranteed them a reasonable trial period of employment. The courses were more than merely remedial. They stressed "writing and figuring," and were quite rigorous; students had to pass an examination *and* write a paper, a workload equivalent to that of a good college course. Experienced clerks often got low grades. About one-seventh of the students failed.[55]

At the higher levels, in 1922, two decades before it became common practice among most corporations, Guardian encouraged employees to further their education, offering five scholarships for office employees who wished to take the Columbia University extension courses on life insurance. Dorothy Goldsmith was actually granted a half-time leave of absence to enable her to finish her program of academic studies. Guardian routinely granted workers time during office hours for study, lectures, and examinations unless it led to an undue accumulation of undone work. By 1930, fully half of the company's employees were said to be "studying on the outside."[56]

In 1945, Guardian introduced an orientation course for new hires, with the ugly-sounding title "Indoctrination Program," which began with a lecture on the insurance field, and the history and policies of the company, followed by

1. Open discussion and question period.
2. Showing of films such as "Search for Security."
3. Tour of the building.

Incoming employees were then armed with copies of "Life Here at the Guardian," "The How and Why of Guardian Pay Scales," "The Handbook of Life Insurance," and the company's "Civil Defense Plan."[57]

The next phase of training, two months after the employee's appointment, was the more friendly sounding "Get Acquainted Course," which provided a general explanation of life insurance principles and terminology, compared Guardian's first policy and first annual statement with its most recent policy and statement, and explained the company's field and home office organization.[58]

By 1952, Guardian extended higher education financial assistance to those who successfully completed approved courses of study with the Insurance Society of New York, Life Office Management Association, the Actuarial Society, and other accredited extension schools and colleges. Guardianites were generally good students. In 1963, the passing percentage of employees sitting for Course I actuarial examinations continued to be better than that of the industry. The percentage of employees participating in tuition assistance ranged from 10 to 15 percent in the 1960s. In 1965, the company implemented a plan designed to provide more consistency among departments. That plan liberalized tuition assistance for general education courses and provided a degree of assistance that varied according to grades attained, a policy that continued into the twenty-first century.[59]

Other forms of specialized training were offered in-house. Officers could take supervisory training courses, for example. After World War II Guardian letter dictators and takers, alike, could use the Hower Letter Improvement Service to obtain objective feedback about how their letters sounded to others or how their letters looked to persons receiving them. In 1963, 1966, and 1967, Guardian engaged Mona Sheppard, a then-noted consultant on letter writing, to conduct specialized correspondent training for the company. The goal was to improve the quality of correspondence and to decrease its turnaround time in accordance with a formula that boiled business correspondence down to the four S's: Simplicity, Shortness, Strength, and Sincerity. To this day, Guardian continues to help its employees to improve their writing and presentation skills.[60]

As a general rule, Guardian tried to find a balance between investment in new training for older employees and making aptly skilled new hires when systems problems surfaced. If management thought—as it did about the group actuarial force in 1960—that a unit was inefficient, it might opt for intensive training rather than simply hire more workers. On the other hand, if a unit appeared to be working well but still could not keep up with its workload, Guardian sought to add additional workers to relieve bottlenecks in the workflow.[61]

By the 1980s, Guardian relied on helping employees to finance additional formal education rather than training. The reason? Jobs required more independent thinking than formerly; Guardian increasingly found it best to hired seasoned people rather than newbies out of college. Such employees, Guardian believed, needed to broaden their horizons rather than train for a narrow job description.[62]

Guardian's education program was and remains very generous; the higher the grade earned, the lower the employee contribution. Overall, Guardian's investment in education and training paid off, its managers believed, because it produced more informed, more efficient, and more loyal employees. It is little wonder then that the company's house organs often pushed employees to make good use of the education benefits the company provided.

Education and training never cease at Guardian. By 1993, the company offered no fewer than forty-five management training programs. More recently, it implemented a mentoring program designed to help managers hired from outside the company to adjust quickly to Guardian's policyholder-centered corporate culture. Management quality became especially important in the 1970s when then-president George Conklin modernized the company's management structure by delegating more authority to the heads of the newly formed profit centers. The profit centers had wide latitude to run their businesses as they saw fit, so Guardian had to make certain that it had well-educated people in those posts. In the 1980s, President John Angle placed a further premium on executive education when he implemented modern strategic planning initiatives that helped to focus Guardian's top management on the future.[63]

Opening Up the Ranks

Ideally, merit-based organizations discriminate on performance but not on ascriptive criteria. Before World War I, Guardian's hiring most certainly reflected ethnic and gender affinities, but the German connection diminished over time. Guardian's German origins may explain some of its acceptance of other ethnic minorities. The company's founders were "foreigners," outsiders. The company's extensive overseas business before World War I gave its managers a more cosmopolitan outlook than was true of the vast majority of American corporations, large or small. And some of Guardian's managers themselves felt the sting of discrimination during and after World War I. It may have had a palliative effect. As a Catholic of Irish descent, for instance, Ed Kane found little place in the higher echelons of Wall Street. There were limited venues for a Jew like Irving Rosenthal. Yet they both made careers at Guardian, as did many other Catholics, Jews, and other non-WASPs.[64]

There is no evidence, in the modern era, that Guardian's selectivity in hiring had anything to do with such individual characteristics as race or religion. Guardian's record on open hiring advanced along with that of most U.S. corporations. By the 1960s, when the broader civil rights movement pressed the issue, Guardian made it explicit policy to hire promising young college graduates wholly without regard to race, creed, color, or national origin. Regulators took notice, and gave Guardian a clean bill of health in 1964, the year of the Civil Rights Act.[65]

Prior to World War II, Guardian had hired African-Americans primarily for low-level jobs. In the 1950s, female African-Americans served in clerical roles. The company's practices in hiring and promoting female employees generally reflected the inequalities of the society at large. In the 1920s, for example, Guardian did not look with favor upon the retention of women after marriage. Single women contemplating matrimony, however, were invited to ask permission to hold their jobs after marriage, because the company was willing to entertain exceptions to the general rule.[66]

Guardian eventually hired large numbers of single females to do clerical work. Women who achieved influence at high levels did so as executive secretaries, controlling access and dispensing trusted advice to their bosses. Guardian's first female employee, Kate Hargreaves, Cornelius Doremus's secretary, was regarded by one employee as "quite a man!" She may have been imposing, but there were limits. She was eventually ousted from the firm for "bossing" some of the company's officers around.[67]

In 1913, only two of Guardian's one hundred or so home office employees were women. Like textile manufacturers and telephone companies before them, life insurers during the manpower shortage caused by World War I discovered the price efficiency of female labor. There was no looking back. By 1953, female Guardianites outnumbered their male counterparts two to one. At that time, women supervised other women. Dorothy Rush, Ruth Napfle, Ann Hanus, Louise Pitone, and Dorothy Morehouse each headed up a section of "girls" in the clerical staff. The home office mailroom, which employed mostly young boys, was managed by one Gertrude Helwig, who, according to the then–group administrator, was a "holy terror," which earned her some respect. Women often survived by acting tough, but it did not move them up the ranks.[68]

There were the rare exceptions, like Dorothy "Dottie" Goldsmith, who ran the personnel department for over four decades beginning in 1920. She was a well-regarded corporate gatekeeper, and was personally responsible for what her contemporary male managers described as important hires. Sophie Bulow headed up the Issue Department. Goldsmith and Bulow held masters degrees from Columbia University. Similarly, Lillian Nitka, a graduate of Drake's Business School who joined Guardian in 1949, was supervisor of the Agency Department in 1960.[69]

It was in the 1960s when women began to make it into the managerial ranks more frequently. Pearl Goldman had headed up the Pension

Department since 1967, and was joined at that lofty level by Helena Sulyma, who took charge of the group underwriting department. The late-
twentieth-century technological revolution sped the careers of women
along, as many came to Guardian armed with expertise in computer operations and programming, which earned them relatively high pay when
such skills were scarce in relation to the burgeoning demand for them. But
not until 2000 did Eileen McDonnell become Guardian's first profit center
officer and first female senior vice president, for individual markets.[70]

The big push towards equality in hiring and promotions had come in
1971, when Guardian and seven other major insurance companies and the
New York State Commission of Human Rights agreed to increase the
number of minority and female workers in higher-paying categories. The
agreement, which had been brewing since Martin Luther King's 1966 boycott of MetLife, called for at least doubling the number of members of
minority groups and women in technical, sales, professional, and executive jobs within two years. The companies also promised in general terms
to "work toward bringing the number of women and members of minority groups . . . to their statewide population percentages."[71]

That was a significant commitment because female and minority employees accounted for only 2 percent of higher-level life insurance jobs at
the time. The accord was reached in response to accusations that the life
industry was "lily white" and predominantly male in the higher-salaried
jobs. Guardian had already implemented a similar policy in May 1970,
when the board approved employment during the next twelve months of
four "hard core disadvantaged persons" with the understanding that
Guardian pay for their training and salaries with no reimbursement from
the government. Results of those and like endeavors of course took
decades to come to full fruition, especially in companies like Guardian
where turnover in the higher ranks was extremely low. Yet by 1993
Guardian could point to the fact that women held 43 percent of its management positions and minorities about 9 percent, up from 10 percent
and 3 percent, respectively, in 1980.[72]

Whatever their color, creed, or gender, employees are limited by the
tools of the trade at their disposal at any given time. Newer office technologies are usually more productive than older technologies. But they
are also usually more expensive, both in terms of acquisition cost and
training time. In the next chapter, we detail Guardian's constant struggle
to put the most *cost-effective* office tools in the hands of its employees and
agents.

10

Managing Administrative Expenses
Regionalization and Automation

As in all other businesses, controlling expenses was a constant problem for the Guardian Life Insurance Company. How, as the annual report of 1950 had put it, could the company "keep all controllable expenses as low as possible *without impairment of essential services* to our policyholders and beneficiaries"? Not to spend on important things was inefficient in the long run. At what point between waste and parsimony did optimal efficiency lie?[1]

The insurer's time-honored "expense ratio"—expressed as cash expenses/cash receipts x 100—allows for comparisons over time and across firms, but does not in itself resolve the question of what levels of expenses are efficient for particular firms under particular circumstances. Still, as a crude measure of efficiency, it is important. Though historical industry data are hard to find, we have continuous data for the period spanning 1916 through 1925 that shows that Guardian's expense ratio was squarely in the middle of the distribution of sampled companies. (See table 10-1.)

Guardian has generally been content to strive for the middle ground. Economies of scale among the larger insurers (Guardian was never among the largest companies) no doubt may have enabled them to spread certain administrative expenses over larger numbers of policies, but there were other considerations, too. Just as companies with very high expense ratios were likely to be spendthrift, companies with very low ones could run the risk of short-shrifting service.

Figure 10-1 illustrates Guardian's expenses as a percentage of total disbursements in a later period, from 1946 to 1966, when the company managed to keep its expenses below 20 percent the entire period, but did not break the 10-percent barrier.

Figure 10-2 shows the company's expense breakdown in 1948.[2]

The foregoing figures are merely illustrative. The sum of Guardian's operating expenses embraced field force expenses, investment expenses, executive compensation and board fees, employee compensation, real estate, and equipment. It included expenses on policyholder service, technology, regional offices, home office employee salaries (below the officer

TABLE 10-1
Expense Ratio of Selected Companies, 1916–25

Company Name	Ten-year Average of Expense Ratios
Mutual	3.80
Equitable	3.82
Northwestern Mutual	3.83
Mutual Benefit	3.84
New York Life	3.85
Penn Mutual	3.90
Massachusetts Mutual	3.99
New England Mutual	4.06
Union Central	4.12
Bankers (Iowa)	4.20
Provident Mutual	4.27
Connecticut Mutual	4.31
State Mutual	4.35
Missouri State	4.37
National	4.43
Kansas City	4.55
Phoenix Mutual	4.56
Columbian National	4.56
Guardian	**4.57**
Lincoln National	4.58
Equitable (Iowa)	4.60
Fidelity Mutual	4.62
Reliance	4.69
Home	4.70
Northwestern National	4.73
Acacia	4.75
National Life and Accident (Vt.)	4.75
Illinois	4.75
Berkshire	4.75
Jefferson Standard	4.77
International	4.77
State Life	4.77
Central Life Assurance	4.84
Atlantic	4.88
Franklin	4.90
Great Southern	4.90
National of the U.S.	4.91
Mean	**4.46**
Median	**4.57**

Source: Palyi, "Life Insurance and the Financial Frontier, Continued," 208.
Courtesy University of Chicago Press.

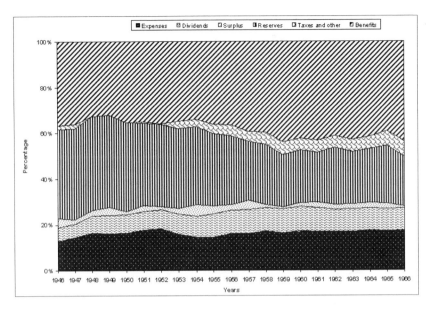

FIGURE 10-1 *Guardian's Disbursements, 1946–66*

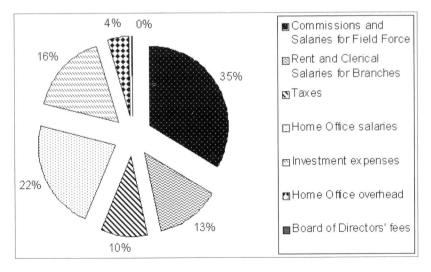

FIGURE 10-2 *Guardian's Expense Breakdown, 1948*

level), and taxes—both direct, or explicit, and indirect, or implicit, such as expenses imposed by regulation. This chapter deals with attempts to reduce costs and increase the efficiency of service by means of moving office functions out of the Manhattan home office and by means of automation.

Regionalization

Manhattan has long been an extremely expensive place to do business. After finding its migration upstate blocked, Guardian decided to lower its expenses by moving its back-office operations to regional centers throughout the country. In addition to being cheaper than Manhattan, the regional offices also proved more convenient to agents and policyholders, most of whom now have an office in their time zone with which to communicate.

"Regionalization," broadly defined, began as early as 1933, when Guardian leased space in the Empire State Building. During the 1920s, the home office building had slowly filled up with people and records. The company gained some time by utilizing the building's basement and sub-basement for storage and by accelerating obsolete record destruction, both part of the company's so-called Five Year Space Program. Storage pressures mounted, however. Between 1924 and 1926, for instance, the volume of incoming mail, most of which had to be retained for a period of years or decades, increased 50 percent.[3]

The search for additional space continued after business accelerated in the post–World War II period. Though it had had an ongoing schedule for destruction of old records in place since at least 1926, the lag between new business acquisition and records destruction was necessarily a long one. As the decades rolled by, the papers piled up and up. During World War II, Guardian began to use microfilming equipment, at first purchased to safeguard important documents, as a means of reducing storage needs. It also periodically rearranged its storage space and purged it of old furniture and other detritus.[4]

But even that was not enough. By 1951, Guardian began to store various accounting records in the National Bank of Canaan, Connecticut. It later transferred those microfilms and hard copies of vital records to a vault in Iron Mountain, in Hudson, New York, as its document security and defense program again gelled with its need for more storage space.

But the space problem simply would not go away. By 1953, in fact, the company, now four hundred strong spread over fourteen floors, was having difficulty storing its employees. Home office elevators were so crowded at lunchtime that the company had to adopt and enforce a staggered lunch schedule. The home office building had six additional floors, but Guardian could not use them until the leases of its tenants expired.[5]

So it was at that time that Guardian considered moving its home office out of Manhattan, to White Plains, New York. The issues were many: the high cost of the city, the nearly hysterical fear of nuclear attack, engendered by the news that the Soviets had acquired the technology to make a hydrogen bomb, and the deterioration of the once-fashionable neighborhood around Union Square. When they heard about management's plan to move, Guardian's employees objected, and got some help from New York's superintendent of insurance, who blocked the move because it believed that it would disrupt policyholder service. Guardian sued, but lost in court, as the judge ruled simply that the company's New York headquarters "were not inadequate for the convenient transaction of its business."[6]

Guardian hired Fantus Factory Locating Service to study the matter further. The consultants advised a move to New Rochelle, if only because White Plains, the seat of Westchester County, had become overcrowded. Guardian made plans to build a "dramatic" new home office there, this time with more employee approval. By 1956, regulatory approval for the move seemed likely, but what the company had not anticipated was the opposition of New Rochelle residents to zoning changes that would have allowed for the necessary commercial construction. Nasty court battles ensued, prompting Guardian in 1957 to again thoroughly review the subject of the future location of the home office. It dropped the New Rochelle project along with all thoughts of leaving the city in the near future. Manhattan was expensive, but at least the company was welcome there. Guardian decided to invest in modernizing and expanding its Union Square office building. In 1962, renovations to the original twenty-story tower were completed along with the construction of a new three-story "annex" that displaced several small apartment buildings.[7]

Guardian perforce became a strong supporter of the general upgrading of its Union Square or Park Avenue South neighborhood in the 1960s, even making contributions to the Park Avenue South improvement project in 1961. In 1967, the company supported community groups to fight a zoning variance obtained by its neighbor, Max's Kansas City restaurant, which operated a "cabaret" at night that many regarded as a nuisance. In the mid-1970s, Guardian became a key mover in efforts to clean up the neighborhood, and in 1980, it donated money to the Fourteenth Street–Union Square Local Development Corporation, which promised to implement a sanitation program on the streets and sidewalks around Union Square, which had long since become one of the more "colorful" places in the city—so colorful, in fact, that company newsletters gave advice on how to avoid getting mugged. Security was a big issue. On the night of Friday, 22 May 1981, the cashier's department was burglarized. The thieves made off with about $600 in cash and thousands of dollars of securities.[8]

Guardian's rapid growth and development continued to strain its aging home office and Manhattan continued to be an expensive place to do business and an inviting target for criminals and terrorists. The success of small, regional companies, like Lincoln National of Fort Wayne, Indiana, suggested that life insurers could thrive by tapping the efficient but relatively cheap labor force available in many rural or deindustrializing areas. In 1970, Guardian engaged Fantus again, this time to explore the idea of establishing satellite operations outside of the metropolitan area. As technology improved and communication expenses decreased, the creation of regional offices became increasingly feasible.[9]

Rather than attempt to move upstate again, Guardian took the "back door" approach and established regional offices throughout the country: Spokane, Washington; Appleton, Wisconsin; Norwell, Massachusetts; Bethlehem, Pennsylvania; and, most recently, Pittsfield, Massachusetts. It was able to do so because it leased a satellite channel that greatly facilitated communication. Regulators who had twice nixed Guardian's attempts to move upstate could not keep the company from moving back-office operations to lower-rent districts and moving policyholder service representatives closer to policyholders.[10]

Regionalization proved successful. Most of Guardian's back-office clerical work, including collecting premiums, paying claims, and issuing policies, can now be done in locales where high-quality workers can be hired at 55 to 85 percent of what they would cost in New York. The largest regional office, the Northeast Regional Office (NRO), established in 1986, was situated just ninety minutes from both Manhattan and Philadelphia near Bethlehem, Pennsylvania. A core group, including Robert Ryan and Don Sullivan, was dispatched from New York to manage the NRO, though 91 percent of the employees came from the Lehigh Valley region.[11]

The company created several regional offices rather than just one be-cause it wanted to get employees into every major time zone. Since the company did not want to assume the burdens that come with dominating local labor markets, it decided to stop the growth of its Bethlehem facili-ties after it became the Lehigh Valley's second largest employer with about twenty-two hundred employees. A new Berkshire office was tar-geted for expansion in 2001.[12]

Sales and claims were also regionalized to a degree. As early as 1964, Guardian had concluded that agents and brokers preferred to do business with companies that offered local claims service. "Complaints . . . in those areas where we provide local claims service," one executive explained, "is practically non-existent by comparison to the complaints we receive on claims processed through the Home Office." By the end of the century, Guardian maintained four regional sales and claims offices for group in-surance. Those offices, which were small, enabled the company to keep its extensive agency and brokerage bases fully informed about the company's product innovations and to serve as a liaison between the home office and general agents.[13]

By then, the company had also made considerable progress in "out-sourcing" many of its operations that had been traditionally managed in-house. For instance, after a home office employee forged a few checks, Guardian hired regional banks to collect the checks and wire the proceeds to New York. "So if you live in the mid-West," John Angle explains, "you send your premiums to a post office box in Milwaukee and the bank there opens that box eight times a day, deposits the check and then that night, transfers that money to our account in New York so the following morn-ing, our investment department knew what cash had come in." Eventu-ally, such "lock box" banks would even update Guardian's computer files.[14]

Regional offices did not, ultimately, solve the problem of growing strains on the capacity of its home office. In 1979, desperate for space, Guardian rented offices along Park Avenue South, between Union Square and Grand Central Terminal. But Guardian, in time, found it too ineffi-cient to run people all around New York City, so once again, in the mid-1990s, its managers pondered leaving the city, this time for the former Pepsico Building in Somers, New York. The mayor's office, loath to lose jobs, offered Guardian $7.8 million in tax concessions to stay put in the Big Apple. Guardian agreed to the deal and in 1999 it sold its landmark headquarters in Union Square to Starwood Hotels, leased (with an option to buy) a larger home office facility in Hanover Square, consolidated its core legal and management functions there, and continued to move its back-office and peripheral units to regional offices spread throughout the nation.[15]

Guardian took regionalization to its logical conclusion in the 1990s by implementing a "telework" or telecommuting program. It began experimenting with work-at-home employment when its western regional office in Spokane, Washington, ran out of space for its more than six hundred employees in the early 1990s. By 1998, fifty claims and policyholder service representatives worked full-time from their homes. Allowing certain employees to telecommute reduces the company's overhead while simultaneously increasing employee productivity, job satisfaction, and retention rates. "I'd hesitate to change jobs even for more pay," telecommuting claims analyst Denise Loehlein said. "I attribute the success of our telework program," Director of Regional Administration Kathleen Greco explained in 1998, "to the fact that we did our homework." Teleworkers reported to the office a few days a week, but only to attend meetings and pick up paperwork. Most communication with supervisors and customers took place by telephone or computer. Teleworkers took fewer sick days, more readily worked overtime during peak periods, and performed more work per hour. Telecommuting was so successful that some office employees were encouraged to spend parts of their days at home, processing claims without the usual office interruptions.[16]

Automating Work Processes

What made regionalization feasible was the modern—second—revolution in telecommunications, and Guardian's ability to tap into it. Guardian had done business in Europe in the nineteenth century largely on the basis of its ability to move information rapidly via telegraph, but the Berlin branch had been an autonomous, self-sufficient operation, and, as its experiences during the First World War showed, in some ways almost another company. The regional offices of the late twentieth century, by contrast, did clerical and other support work for the corporation as a whole; they would not last long without direction from the home office. As noted above, one major piece of technology, a telecommunications satellite, was decisive. Guardian was one of the first life insurers to lease a satellite channel and its home office was the first building in the Union Square area to have a satellite dish on its roof.[17]

According to John Angle, the modern Guardian was an efficient user of technology. His assessment was largely correct, and was based on a longer history than he may have realized. Guardian hired its first stenographer and typist around 1900. Before that time, all letters were written by hand and all copies by press copy. The systems, though manual, worked extremely well. In 1901, New York regulators noted that the company's "books, accounts and records are so intelligently devised and so well kept that the making of a thorough examination is greatly facilitated thereby." Also around 1900, Guardian purchased mechanical adding machines. (Prior to that time, Guardian employees had laboriously added figures by hand and had colleagues double-check their work.) Still, the calculation of the annual statement alone consumed weeks. In 1929 the company installed two bookkeeping accounting machines, which sped things up a bit. That same year, Guardian employees discovered a number of short-cuts for finding the error if an account did not balance.[18]

Though primitive by today's standards, the company's limited technology did not interfere with its top priority, the prompt payment of death claims. As the volume of business became increasingly burdensome after Armstrong, however, the company, like other large insurers, adapted, making numerous organizational and technological improvements that reduced unnecessary duplication.[19]

Some duplication, of course, was necessary. During World War I, Guardian obtained a photostat machine, an early mechanical copier. A few years later, a Beck duplicator caused quite a stir when it joined the heavily used photostat. In 1929, Guardian replaced its photostat machine with a Super-Rectigraph that made the photographic process entirely automatic and continuous. In 1938 it added a mimeograph machine to its duplication arsenal. In 1942 it began leasing Recordak film equipment in order to microfilm policy loan cards and other records. In 1946, it surveyed life insurance companies about their use of photocopying. By the 1950s, Guardian duplicated memos by having its internal print shop typeset and print them. In the early 1960s, a manager reported that the company's experience with Xerox copiers had been favorable.[20]

In 1916, to save time and labor, Guardian started to lithograph the signatures of the president and secretary on all insurance contracts. A little over a decade later, it began to use the Todd check-signing machine, at first renting it until it was certain that it wanted to adopt it permanently.

It later added two additional check-signing machines. By 1939, all three were in poor condition. After study, Guardian decided to replace them with a more modern and efficient National Check Writing and Signing Machine. A second such machine was added by 1950. Such technological advances, then as now, did not go unnoticed in the underworld. In 1949, one Mearle Markley, an enterprising felon, used the Utah state prison print shop to create artful Guardian and Sears Roebuck checks. Fortunately, he was unable to pass any of the checks, largely because the signatures were fictitious.[21]

In 1922, Guardian considered replacing its worn-out postage stamping and sealing machine, a so-called Mailometer Machine, with a Pitney-Bowes postage meter machine. After an officer queried other companies about the proposed Pitney-Bowes machine, however, Guardian thought it more profitable to simply purchase a new Mailometer. That year it also purchased a movie projector that it rented out to sales managers for showing life insurance films. Also in the 1920s, Guardian utilized a colored printed card system and a date-time stamp machine to track policy dividends.[22]

In the days before everyone had a phone, much less e-mail, Guardian ran a fifteen-minute messenger service, and a pneumatic tube and a dumbwaiter comprised its document delivery system. Both were designed to keep clerks on task at their desks rather than roaming from office to office. As late as the 1960s, Guardian tried to keep visits to other departments at a minimum. It went so far as to ascertain that 2,305 personal visits to the mail and printing departments were made in the first two months of 1964, a figure thought to indicate serious interference with the operation of those departments.[23]

Guardian had an interdepartmental telephone system in place by 1924. By 1926, the system was already feeling the strain of the company's rapid growth. It also had outside lines, which it upgraded in 1925. In 1961, it finally automated some of its telephone functions in order to reduce the mounting workload of its busy operators. By 1964, the company had about four hundred phones for eight hundred employees. It added eight trunk lines, just for agents, in 1969 and ten more only two years after that. In 1977, the board agreed to spend $350,000 for a new home office telephone system, the Dimension 2000 PBX system. The system ended up costing $435,000, but it was much more efficient than the older technologies, including the Simplex machine that Guardian employees had used for sending and receiving telegrams ever since 1930.[24]

By 1940, the sheer weight of all of Guardian's automation machines began to take a toll on the floors of the home office building. Engineers ordered that there be no material adding of further equipment until the tolerance of the floor construction could be ascertained. One of the company's heaviest machines was a large mechanical printing press or "addresseograph," a dinosaur that printed premium notices and many other forms. In one continuous operation, the machine, which most insurers adopted, unrolled blank paper, printed on both sides, cut the paper to the proper size, and even filled in names and addresses. Compared to today's PC, laser printer, and mail merge program, the machine, which filled half a room, was a noisy monstrosity. It got the job done faster, and about $1,000 a year cheaper, than by hand, however, and that was all that mattered. The company added a second addresseograph in 1944 and updated the machines the following year.[25]

After World War II, Guardian used a series of large, specialized office machines like the addresseographs for simplifying routine tasks like calculating dividends, keeping track of policyholders' addresses, and preparing standard acknowledgments. Guardian had accumulated so much mechanical office equipment that it found it necessary to organize a Machine Service Department. None of those technologies, however, was cutting edge. Guardian's strategy here was to take advantage of tested methods of mechanizing accounting and other office work in order to scratch out some savings, not to break new ground in office technology.[26]

More often than not, Guardian followed rather than led in the introduction of new technology, and was somewhat a reluctant spender on labor-saving devices. Consider that in 1946 Guardian put off for a year an experiment with electromatic typewriters, though in 1949, it installed an auto-typist that utilized a punched roll to handle, like a player piano, about two-thirds of the mechanical production of various types of standard contracts. In 1966 the company was *still* debating whether or not to introduce electric typewriters—common as they were by then—as standard equipment in agency offices. As recently as the late 1970s, even the home office apparently did not have enough typewriters (or perhaps typists) to go around. Agents repeatedly complained about the company's practice of printing up form letters with blank spaces that clerks shoddily filled up in their own hand instead of typing out. "Can't typewriters be used for policyholder correspondence?" they repeatedly queried. Often, the clerks simply had to wait to receive "hand me downs" from higher ups.[27]

The same was true for dictation machines. By the eve of the Depression, Guardian used a so-called ediphone, a primitive dictation device, which allegedly was a great time saver. By World War II, Guardian owned a battery of dictating machines. (The contraptions, called dictaphones, used a wax cylinder.) To keep costs down, however, Guardian did not buy as many machines as were needed during peak periods, forcing employees who wanted to use them to dictate after hours.[28]

Computers

High-speed computing, along with the development of word-processing and spreadsheet software, has become such an integral part of business life that it is easy to forget how modern it is. The introduction of computers into life insurance, which is an enormous generator and consumer of quantitative data, dates back to the early twentieth century. In 1921, Guardian, about a decade after adoption by the largest insurers, introduced extensive systems of Hollerith cards for tracking premiums, payments, and other important information. Use of the cards also made computation of company-specific actuarial statistics, including mortality rates, and investment statistics much easier. In 1922, Guardian introduced the ditto system, a multiplying card-writing device that helped to render the company's cards more uniform. The machine released two clerks for other duties. By 1938, the noisy Hollerith machine was in constant demand, so the company rented an extra one for special projects. In the ultimate irony, Guardian even used Hollerith cards to track the efficiency of its use of the Hollerith technology. By the 1930s, McBee key sort card technology appeared as well.[29]

In 1946, Guardian streamlined its clerical operations further by moving to stub-accounting and microfilming. Apparently Guardian *was* at the cutting edge of this technology because the following year "office engineers" A. B. Dick and Company published a case history of Guardian's procedures for reproducing various policy record cards, and made up an exhibit, which it displayed at the industrywide Life Office Management Association (LOMA) meetings. Guardian's officers regularly attended LOMA meetings and came away with cutting-edge ideas, some of which, like the Dvorak keyboard, did not pan out, others of which, like the possible insurance applications of electronic devices (computers) would turn out to be crucial. As early 1947, several years before the Census Bureau began using UNIVAC I, Guardian's Burgh Johnson advised the company's officers that "in the near future" life insurance companies would install "a central computing machine" that would have "numerous subsidiary installations throughout the organization." By early 1948, the company had conducted a study that suggested that it could install just such a central computing machine for about $40,000, plus up to 150 service outlets at $75 each.[30]

Clearly, something needed to be done to keep up with the increased volume of its business. In 1944, Guardian mistakenly sent a policy loan check to Jessie B. Smith of Minneapolis, for far more than the face value of her policy, instead of to the policyholder who made the request, Jesse B. Smith of Indianapolis. Predictably, Mrs. Smith tried to cash the check and Mr. Smith wondered what the holdup on his loan was. The matter was quickly rectified but it was just one clear example that the card method of tracking policyholders was getting awkward and inefficient. But electronic computers, which held some promise in this area, were still unproven and extremely expensive. So before resorting to the computer, Guardian tried other things, such as pumping the soothing strains of Muzak into the mail and application departments, lunch room, addresseograph and tabulating room, and supply department, in the hope that it would improve employee effectiveness. "The general comment both in the office and by visitors" regarding the Muzak was reportedly "favorable." There is no accounting for taste.[31]

By the early 1950s, Guardian had jettisoned its Hollerith and McBee card systems in favor of eighty-column edge-punched IBM cards. Before that time, the clerical staff, which included young folks like neophyte Ed Kane and what seemed to him at the time like "a million old ladies," shook swordlike spindles filled with cards. Those that fell out they updated that day. IBM card sorters, collators, and tabulators with sophisticated wired control boards replaced the relatively inefficient human laborers, but did not necessarily leave them jobless. McBee sort card operators, for example, were eventually retrained as key-punch data-entry clerks.[32]

By the early 1950s, trade journals were abuzz with predictions about the efficiency of electronic computers. Life insurance executives were beginning to grasp the broad outlines of the coming information revolution. They knew first that "the information that we compress today on punch cards will be further compressed by storing the necessary figures and words on magnetic tapes which can be scanned at the speed of many thousands of words a minute." They also foresaw that "since a computer's output, in its raw state, is in the form of electronic pulses, there are also possibilities for relaying these pulses simultaneously to remote points before reducing them to words" and figures. Exciting but as yet expensive and unproven stuff. So Guardian continued to monitor the cost-benefit tradeoff of the emerging industry.[33]

In 1955 Guardian made its move, embarking on a program to acquire modern electronic data processing equipment that operated at what were for the time "incredible speeds." Accordingly, the company appointed Robert W. Deisler, who had joined the company early in 1932, as coordinator of electronic methods and procedures. But Deisler and Vice President Burgh Johnson felt that they needed expert *in-house* advice. So Guardian went into the market in search of someone who could help the company to develop a state-of-the-art IBM mainframe statistical system. By 1961 Guardian had found its man, Gordon F. Gilchrest.[34]

Gilchrest was a rare breed in those days. He had years of experience in electronic programming, and could translate his expertise well enough so that the company's president could rely on him for making important electronic operations decisions. In 1960, impressed by the almost unbelievable speed of the IBM technology, Guardian outright purchased the IBM 650 drum memory mainframe that it had been renting since 1956. In 1964, it purchased another, refurbished IBM 650 to back it up. Although the original machine had been in service only seven calendar years, it had aged more like fifteen years because it had been almost continuously in service on a three-shift basis. The 650, which ran on punch cards, represented a major shift to both mass-produced mainframes and electronic processing—faster and more reliable than the truck-sized UNIVAC or even the older, more compact IBM systems, so long favored in the industry. The second 650 also helped to facilitate the testing of advanced system concepts and logic.[35]

By the end of 1960, Guardian, with the help of programmers like William Portela, Susan Underdahl, Ann Hanus, and Miervaldis Dobelis, had shifted to the electronic processing of premium billing, commission accounting, and individual policy transactions. About that time, Dobelis covered a wall with a huge flowchart that helped the programmers and analysts to see how all the individual programming parts that they were working on would interact to form an integrated system, which Guardian would eventually call its Life Computer System (LCS).[36]

The changeover to the computerized system increased expenses and caused some delays and errors, but the difficulties were only temporary. "The increased complexity of our business," President Cameron explained, "requires that we face these problems now even though visible results may not be evident in the immediate future." And some areas were showing great promise. The conversion of old records from the so-called hernia books to computer punch cards, for instance, ran some months ahead of schedule.[37]

Not everyone was happy with Guardian's adoption of the IBM 650. Actuary Irving Rosenthal, so progressive in many ways, was something of a high-technophobe. He complained that IBM's "super-salesmen" were selling "baloney." He was impatient with the bugs in the system, and harped about the disruptions in services to policyholders and agents and unanticipated expenses. He claimed that the computer system was so inflexible that upon presentation of any new type of policy, like a joint life policy, the computer would "spit, cough, hiccup, throw a tantrum, lay down on the floor and scream." Never mind that computerization was rapidly improving service in areas of furnishing status information, prompt handling of premium collections, and various other procedures associated with policy service.[38]

In 1962, IBM's supersalesmen struck again, selling the company an IBM 1401. It added a second, which replaced seven old manual accounting machines, the following year. (The 1401s were not major technological advancements and were used mostly for printing.) In 1963 the company brought in consultant Joseph K. Blum and Co. to assist in the planning of the physical facilities for the advanced computer system. The company originally envisioned the purchase of an IBM 1410-1302 system but scrapped that idea on the advice of Price Waterhouse, which argued that the new IBM 360 Model 40 was the way to go. Approval for the 360 came in April 1966.[39]

The IBM Systems/360 had come on the market in 1964 and represented a major revolution in the already transforming technology of computing. It was designed in part to reconcile differences between systems that were optimal for scientific computing and those that were optimal for data processing. The system included several computers, an operating system, and peripherals, such as disks, tapes, card input and output equipment, and printer, all based on a common architecture, so that any part of the system could be expanded, upgraded, or augmented incrementally. The system's compatibility drove costs, particularly software costs, down sharply. Guardian's management had come to recognize that the 360 had compatibility features that would make corporatewide systems management much easier. Most important, in their minds, was that the 360/40 could be upgraded without changing programming codes. [40]

By late 1966 Guardian was testing its advanced 360 computer system. All seemed well after approximately 15 percent of the company's policies had been transferred to the new system. Hardware failures, software problems, and programming bugs, however, slowed conversion. Development of the homegrown, full-blown Life Computer System (LCS) created further delays. The LCS was very advanced for its day, using a transaction-oriented input notation for routine loan, dividend, and other policy maintenance. GAIN (Guardian Automatic Input Notation) and RAIN (Reentry Automatic Input Notation) saved time by enabling clerks to issue simplified commands. For more complex work, Guardian created a "substitution change" routine. The "Purify" program tested posttransaction results against prescribed rules to ensure that records were error free. Finally, Guardian programmers developed a letterwriter (Policyholder Document or PhD for short) to notify policyholders of transactions automatically. With updates, LCS is now in its fourth decade. But its original development was not as easy as anticipated.

Perhaps most vexing of all, punch cards had to be converted to complex variable-length disk records. Portela and his programmers, and actuaries Roberto Pope and Ronald Telesnick, worked on new coding while policyholder service managers like Edward Kerswig, John Fagan, William Magnussen, Manuel Tutunjian, Phyllis Auliano, and Ed Cohen and their crews worked around the clock to repair internally inconsistent records that could not pass through the exacting conversion process. [41]

To lure programmers to put in a half-day each Saturday, the testing supervisor threw Saturday afternoon picnics, complete with kites, sandwiches, Shakespeare-in-the-park, and jugs of Chianti on "Hippie Hill" in Central Park. Anthony Peloso recalled that at the time he felt as if he literally lived in the home office. [42]

The hard work, wine, and free drama paid off; the pace of conversion quickened substantially late in 1969, and was largely finished by May 1970. Completion of the conversion was important because the operation of two separate and distinct systems had burdened the operating departments and created substantial service problems. By then, as table 10-2 shows, Guardian's IBM 360/40 system was clearly a positive net present value project at a 5 percent rate of discount.[43]

There were casualties, though. The process of introducing new computer technologies had been fraught with bugs that had constantly to be ironed out. Computer glitches evoked a constant stream of complaints from the field and policyholders. And Gilchrest, who had managed Guardian through the mainframe revolution, nursing the company through several computer systems planning projects, resigned in 1969 after apparently overstepping his bounds by demanding a big self-promotion. The loss proved not so severe, though, as the crew he left behind continued to do their work, refining the company's computer systems into higher degrees of efficiency.[44]

In the meantime, Guardian had purchased another $100,000 worth of additional computer core storage capacity in 1970, and had installed new Mark IV software, which helped to improve performance. In May 1971, President George Conklin, who had personally monitored the progress of the program on a daily basis, reported dramatic improvement in the company's service to policyholders and the field. Complaints from those quarters had been sharply reduced, and morale was noticeably improved.[45]

Two important points must be made here. First, the company's computer difficulties were the rule in the industry, not the exception. Second, the Life Computer System was a cutting-edge project, closely watched by the rest of the industry. Guardian's systems developers innovated in a number of important technical areas, including disk storage. And the

TABLE 10-2

Guardian's IBM 360/40 System, a Positive Net Present Value Project

Year	Estimated Incremental Cost ($)	Present Value at 5% ($)	Estimated Incremental Benefit ($)	Present Value at 5% ($)
1964	200,000	200,000	10,000	10,000
1965	280,000	266,667	**20,000**	19,048
1966	320,000	290,249	**200,000**	181,406
1967	330,000	285,066	**300,000**	259,151
1968	200,000	164,541	500,000	411,351
1969	200,000	156,705	500,000	391,763
1970	200,000	149,243	500,000	373,108
Totals	1,730,000	1,512,471	2,030,000	1,645,827

Note: Figures in boldface are the authors' estimates based on various sources, various dates, Box 43, GLIC archives.

Source: Figures are from President's Report, 28 October 1964, Box 43, GLIC archives.

pace of change was almost maddening. "If you dropped a pencil and bent down to retrieve it," joked Dobelis, "you'd be technologically outdated by the time you straightened up."[46]

Out of sheer necessity Guardian continued to upgrade its hardware and software on a regular basis. Its transition in 1976 from its two IBM 360s to the new IBM 370/158 went smoothly, though it had to shell out an extra $60,000 for a new control device and $478,000 for a used 370 and additional core storage in 1978 and 1979. In 1981, it went ahead with plans to purchase a new IBM 3033N computer and to modify the home office computer room environment to accommodate it. Again, Guardian soon found itself paying out hundreds of thousands of dollars for additional electronic storage capacity for the new system.[47]

Guardian's mainframes, though sometimes more expensive than bargained for, paid for themselves. By 1974, Haskins and Sell and Arthur Anderson reported that Guardian's data processing division was among the best in the industry. By the end of the 1970s, Guardian had what it thought to be a sizeable and excellent computer staff in place. And they were much needed. By 1986, the company's numerous electronic data processing systems generated so much heat that it proved profitable to channel it into the home office's climate control system![48]

Despite its eventual successes with its mainframes, the company remained true to its cautious tradition, erring on the conservative side in its technology expenditures. In 1973, Guardian rejected Telex terminals as too expensive for the benefits that they provided. When PCs first appeared, not every employee needed a PC on his or her desk to perform his or her function efficiently, so not every employee had a PC. As John Angle explained in 1981, Guardian did not believe that "the computer, by itself, increased productivity. A computer when combined with the right knowledge and applied on a large enough scale can bring dramatic increases in productivity." The key was expense efficiency. The company routinely made projections to help it to judge whether it should embark on a project or not. If it could not decide, it retained consultants to help with the analysis. Only as computer expenses, especially storage and software expenses, began to decrease, did it become increasingly desirable to put first a terminal, then a PC, on just about everyone's desk.[49]

The advent of the computer age initially did more to transform back-office operations. In 1978, for instance, the Group Claims Department converted to a computer system that involved the use of computer terminals by each claim analyst. The new system, which required an outlay of some $355,000 for 116 terminals, significantly improved the analyst's work routine. ClaimFacts, a new claims system installed in 1992, increased efficiency of this most important back-office function a further 25 percent by 1994.[50]

Computerization initially had less impact on the day-to-day work of the company's professionals. Credit analyst James Pirtle, for example, remembers assembling spreadsheets himself, by hand, in the 1960s and 1970s. He thought that the manual process gave him deeper insights into the company that he was studying, noting that fancy new computerized spreadsheets had not helped the ultimate efficiency of the purchasers of WorldCom and Enron securities.[51]

General agents had a difficult time convincing Guardian's top brass that they needed computer terminals to enable them to communicate with the home office more cheaply, quickly, and efficiently to service policyholders and to prepare for sales interviews. They broached the subject as early as April 1972 but met rebuff time and again. By the end of 1979, they were fed up. They claimed that telephone charges were getting outrageous, that home office clerks did not answer their letters, and that the U.S. postal service was dog slow. Then came the kicker: "Most agencies of companies comparable in quality to The Guardian has [*sic*] some form of terminal system," said an agent in the field. Arthur Ferrara, who feared that agents used computers as an excuse to stare at CRTs all day rather than go out and work, shot back that any such system had to be cost justified. It was, and the company installed a system in early 1981. In 1985, it upgraded its electronic marketing system to "GEMS II," which provided instantaneous information on existing policies, proposals for prospective clients, and a wide variety of automated office functions.[52]

Not all of the company's new technology was computerized, and sometimes creativity was the key to increased efficiency. After the cost of photocopying came down around 1970, for example, some smart Guardianite ascertained that it was cheaper to photocopy checks in its favor and deposit them immediately than to wait several days for the clerks to enter the checks into the accounting system. But most technological innovations of the late twentieth century were linked to the computer, especially to the personal computer. Still, Guardian resisted PCs for a long time. Personal computers were not judged by Guardian to be sufficiently cost effective until around 1995 or so, when the Microsoft operating system became a little more stable, and when programs fell in price while increasing in flexibility, and networking came into vogue.[53]

Likewise, Guardian was slow to adopt such related technologies as e-mail, which the company did not use extensively until 1997. Far from technophobia, the slow adoption of such technologies was simply a function of Guardian's financial caution. It adopted e-mail when it became cheaper than paper memorandums and other older means of communication. "It's just that we're very careful with how we spend the policyholder's dollar," noted Joseph Caruso, the corporate secretary. E-mail systems, like many other technologies, were thought to appear cheaper than they actually were. Many computer systems had both high fixed costs and high maintenance costs, running as high as 20 percent of the acquisition cost per year.[54]

On the other hand, Guardian was one of the first life insurers to realize the power of the Internet in fueling business transactions. Its website, http://www.glic.com, which won Golden Webby awards in 2000 and 2001, became operational in January 2000. It became an important marketing tool by 2001, when Internet statistics tracker eMarketer ranked it as the third most active insurance web portal out of the ninety insurance websites that it ranked.

Also during the 1990s, Guardian invested heavily in PC technology, particularly in its group administration and variable annuity administration systems, both of which were highly transaction oriented. Likewise, it updated its agency computer system, first to "Vision," then to "Guardian Online." The new systems used new networking technologies, direct dial-up, and the Internet. By the end of the century, Guardian also extensively used PCs for conducting actuarial and financial analyses.

Guardian successfully avoided the so-called Y2K threat, and the $42 million it spent to thwart it had side benefits in improving the company's systems functionality. New computer technology was also an integral part of Guardian's 2001 changeover to a strategic sourcing methodology that was designed to save the company tens of millions of dollars annually.[55]

Other areas of expense management are more difficult because they fall largely outside of the control of the individual insurer. Though, as we will learn in chapter 11, Guardian was far from a passive actor, taxes and regulations were not amenable to close company management. Guardian almost continually struggled against the more unjust or inefficient aspects of IRS and New York State Insurance Department policies, but by and large it had to bend to their dictates. Occasional victories in important contests, however, made it all worthwhile.

11

Burdens of Corporate Citizenship
Regulation and Taxes

Regulation begins at home, and like all life insurance companies, Guardian has had to devote considerable resources to *self-policing*, in order to limit third-party, policyholder, and agency fraud. An example of the first of these was recounted in the introduction to this section—the case in which Guardian cooperated with the FBI to uncover a cross-border health insurance billing scam. Policyholder fraud, in the form of falsified medical records and false claims, has been subject to perennial vigilance as a matter of routine. Most important for the firm's reputation and, hence, ongoing ability to sell policies is the problem of agency fraud against policyholders.

As far back as World War I, Guardian attempted to steer its agents away from the common practice of "twisting" rivals' policyholders into canceling their existing policies in exchange for what might not be a better deal. To steer agents away from such practices, it cut their commissions. When a few rogue agents persisted in "twisting," Guardian cut them loose. It also taught its field force effective methods for countering the twisting efforts of other companies. In general, between 1920 and 1961, when Guardian established two complaint files, one for complaints against agents made by policyholders, the other for home office problems with agents, recorded examples of agency malpractice were few and far between.[1]

From the 1960s forward, inflation and disintermediation combined to put considerable pressure on agency forces, as it became more difficult to make a decent living selling into the rising demand for low-commission term policies. Some desperate agents cut corners, and the publicly disclosed incidence of insurance fraud increased throughout the industry. Guardian monitored its agency forces closely, ousting agents, even general agents, whose personal problems affected their business judgment.

Guardian defended its practice of aggressively terminating agency contracts whenever suspicions merited it—though it could adversely affect new production, in the longer run, it conserved policyholder wealth.[2]

Guardian included in its annual reports warnings to policyholders against allowing agents to exchange old policies for new, while warning agents against what it referred to as "over enthusiastic" selling. A spate of circular letters was aimed at keeping agents on the straight and narrow path. The company routinely enjoined its agents not to engage even in such lawful, though ethically dubious, practices as writing too much minimum deposit business, i.e., arrangements by which policyholders systematically fund premium payments from policy loans,[3] and from "piggy-backing" new policies onto older ones.[4] In the 1990s, when agency fraud seemed rampant in certain sectors of the industry, Guardian was occasionally sued for overrepresenting the potential benefits of so-called vanishing premium policies—policies sold with the oral promise that dividends would offset future premium payments. But in general, Guardian remained above the fray. Its agents were financially dedicated to the company and so were sensitive to corporate ethical admonitions. When in the mid-1990s, a new conventional wisdom spread among life insurers that agents should not act merely as salespeople but rather as long-term developers and educators of their clients, Guardian could rest on the same principle that extended back to the introduction of the Graph Estate at the tail end of the Depression. Of course, the public does not trust insurers to behave well entirely on their own. Ethics alone do not suffice. And the public demands that insurers pay their share of taxes.[5]

Formal Regulation

In the life insurance business, government agencies conduct a number of oversight functions, including scrutinizing the information that insurers provide their policyholders, placing limitations on insurers' assets and liabilities, and restricting their relationships with other financial institutions. Much of the regulatory story is embedded elsewhere in this study. Here we discuss the general problem of regulatory and tax pressures as they have impacted Guardian's management.

In the United States, state governments regulate insurers. The spate of New Deal banking and securities legislation, enacted during the economic crisis of the 1930s, put most financial services under federal regulation of one kind or another, but left insurance relatively untouched. Thus legal tradition that supported state regulation was left intact. Until 1945, the status quo was grounded in an 1869 U.S. Supreme Court ruling, *Paul v. Virginia,* which had held that insurance was not "commerce" and hence not subject to the commerce clause of the U.S. Constitution. That decision was reversed by *United States v. South-Eastern Underwriters Association,* in 1944, which caused near-panic among insurers, but Congress was too preoccupied with war to take any action. One year later, the Mc-Carran-Ferguson Act left regulation of insurance to the several states, though it did not bar the possibility of future federal regulation. Political pressures on the insurance industry have ever worked their way through the legislative halls and regulatory agencies of the several states. The result is something of a patchwork of rules governing both policies and investment of policyholders' funds.[6]

New York State, following the Armstrong Commission reforms, has often served as a bellwether of standards. It is a fairly rigorous regime. Historically, New York has taken three approaches to regulation: mandatory, inducing, and enabling. Mandatory regulations force companies to take particular actions, e.g., invest in the securities of the state, or to avoid taking certain actions, e.g., giving policies misleading names. Inducing regulations, in contrast, provide insurers with incentives, such as tax breaks, to act in preferred ways. Enabling regulations are the most liberal of all because they allow insurers to engage in new and potentially profitable activities, like the issuance of variable policies. After World War II, inducing and enabling regulations increasingly supplanted the more traditional and, from the insurance industry's point of view, heavier-handed mandatory regulations with respect to the sale and servicing of life policies.[7]

On the investment side, New York's insurance statutes have tended to be *positive* laws, which explicitly list the types of securities insurance companies may invest in, thereby excluding all others. The alternative is *negative* legislation, which explicitly forbids investment in certain types of securities but allows investment in all others. Positive laws are, of course, more restrictive; as new securities instruments are developed, insurers have to get explicit permission to invest in them.[8]

Regulation has proven necessary. No one at the Guardian Insurance Company would seriously argue otherwise. But it is inevitably flawed if only because, as one student of the subject puts it, "most legislators, even those on the insurance committees, have little or no understanding of the insurance industry." Insurance company managers are prone to agree. Fortunately, the people who write the laws do not enforce them. That is the job of insurance commissioners and their staffs of professional regulators, who, in theory anyway, *know* the industry. Their job is not an easy one; insurance commissioners must wear many hats. "Sometimes the insurance commissioner is an official clerk, sometimes he is a judge, sometimes he is a law-giver," explained Columbia law professor Edwin Patterson in his seminal study of the insurance commissioner, "and sometimes he is both prosecuting attorney and hangman. He is partly executive, partly judicial, and partly legislative; and yet he is not confined within any of these categories." It is not a stretch to say that the insurance commissioner is also a politician.[9]

Insurance regulators wield great power. Patterson characterized their "visitorial and inquisitorial powers" as "drastic." "No other official . . . has an equal power of making his own search-warrants." Insurance commissioners have a broad array of weapons at their disposal; they can sue in court, use very informal methods of persuasion, or do just about anything in between. Generally, the executive branch of government has not been able to keep commissioners in check, but legislative and judicial procedures have been known to curb any excesses. Guardian, therefore, has generally treated insurance commissioners, especially New York commissioners, with deference.[10]

Public confidence in life insurance does not hinge much on regulation. According to one recent survey, about 75 percent of Americans have no idea how, *or even if,* life insurers are regulated. Nonetheless, there are good reasons why life insurers, good ones anyway, value at least some degree of regulation. The failure of one life insurance company negatively impacts the sales of other life companies, even the most solid ones. So, to the extent that regulation prevents the failure of insurers, it is a good thing. Second, regulators can provide objective confirmation of a good company's conduct and performance. There is no evidence that life insurers have moved from stronger to weaker regulatory states in order to lighten the burdens of oversight. Though Guardian was domiciled in New York, the nation's most stringent insurance regulator, it never gave serious thought to moving to another state.[11]

Rule-Bound Everywhere

Before World War I, Guardian was regulated in Europe as well as in the United States. Every country had its own rules. In Britain, where modern insurance was born, a so-called sunshine approach was generally preferred to more heavy-handed rules. In that country, insurers had to publicize widely their reserve equations, mortality and interest rate assumptions, and other key management information. Prospects and policyholders were then left to decide which company, if indeed any, deserved their patronage. Guardian, however, was closely tied to Germany, where the rules were more stringent. Generally, the relations between the company and the German government were smooth, though the Reich mandated the kind of investments Guardian could make and on various occasions intervened to compel the company to alter certain clauses in its policies and even provide employee pensions. In the United States, Guardian had likewise to adapt to varying regulatory rules in each state where it set up shop. And there was a lot to complain about.[12]

In the United States, state insurance regulations tended to be more directive than those of Great Britain, and as they varied from one jurisdiction to the next, the rules could be confusing and idiosyncratic. For Guardian, the rules of many states in which it did business seemed irrelevant, but they were nonetheless time consuming. When the company sought to reenter Massachusetts in 1926, for example, the board of directors had formally to resolve not to insure "in a single hazard a sum . . . larger than one tenth of its net assets," which then stood in the neighborhood of $60 million. (Guardian was shy of $60,000 policies much less $6 million ones! Not until 1930 did it up its retention limit to $75,000.) The board minutes are replete with legalistic resolutions prompted by the queries of insurance commissioners, many of which, the company frequently argued, were based on erroneous facts, limited understanding of the law, or non sequitur.[13]

Regulators could be fickle. Guardian was one of the last institutional mortgage lenders to insist that the titles of premises mortgaged to it be examined by company counsel, who had to furnish an abstract of title with searches annexed and certificates of searches for taxes, assessments, and all other liens. The practice put Guardian at a competitive disadvantage with mortgage lenders that required only policies of title insurance, which were comparatively inexpensive. So in 1905, the company sought and received regulatory approval to join other financial institutions in accepting title insurance in lieu of the much more costly traditional process. Then in 1908, New York's new superintendent of insurance insisted that insurers return to the older, more expensive method. Guardian relented and changed its bylaws to reflect the new requirements of the insurance department.[14]

Regulators could be petty. When Mississippi floods caused widespread distress in May 1927, for instance, Guardian voted a $1,000 donation to the Red Cross as a matter of goodwill and good business. (There was always a danger of the outbreak of epidemic illness in the flooded area.) The donation had to be approved by the superintendent of insurance, who asked Guardian to reconsider on the grounds that other life insurance companies had not asked to make donations.[15]

Regulatory audits could be nettlesome. Examiners delved into nooks and crannies of the company's accounting procedures, seemingly searching for anything to criticize. Invariably, they turned up a few things, some of which defied reason. A fairly straightforward example of this occurred in 1921, when regulators criticized Guardian because it included the expense of collection in its general loading factor (then 21.5 percent) instead of reporting it as a separate item. During the Depression, one examiner explained to Guardian that property taken under foreclosure ought not to be sold for an amount in excess of the actual cost value. In a rare outburst against authority, company officials complained that the examiner must have been "severely handicapped by an utter lack of understanding of the effect of the unprecedented worldwide business depression."[16]

And regulators were expensive. In addition to their salaries and overhead, they traveled. Their expenses were absorbed by the public and by the industry. Perceived expense account abuses got to the point where Guardian once threatened to sue in the 1990s. Especially vexing was the late-twentieth-century proliferation of so-called *market conduct* examinations, which, unlike general solvency probes, are not systematically grouped by standard National Association of Insurance Commissioners zone. So while Guardian faces only one periodic solvency inspection conducted by a group of regulators from different states, it now also faces a multitude of largely redundant examinations of its marketing procedures.[17]

Guardian has also often noted that regulators are simply too slow. Cornelius Doremus, for instance, noted the problem of regulatory lag in the nineteenth century: the pace of business simply outstripped the ability of regulators to respond appropriately. It was no different in 1964, when a Guardian executive felt it necessary to create a memorandum devoted to furnishing a history of Guardian's filing difficulties with New York regulators. The memorandum could not have been appealing to the regulators who read it. It showed them as bumbling bureaucrats, confused, slow, and unable to come to good decisions. Over the years, many in industry and academe have observed similar phenomena.[18]

Despite the obvious shortcomings of its regulators, it would have been unwise for Guardian to be too brusque with them, if only because every three years—New York's regulatory audits were triennial—the company came away with a clean bill of health. Not atypical was the regulatory report of 1947:

> [Guardian] is in a strong financial condition; . . . all investments are legal and the assets valued conservatively; . . . the affairs of the company are ably managed and . . . the business is being conducted in the interest of the policyholders.

Who at Guardian would want to argue with that? The company also earned accolades for outrunning the regulations on occasion, making more conservative financial and actuarial assumptions, allowing policyholders more liberal voting rights, and being more generous to policyholders than required by contract or law.[19]

There were occasions, on the other hand, when regulators had to bring the company into line with the law and prudent standard practice. During the Depression Guardian's officers began to advance considerable sums to sales managers for extended periods without board authorization. The company's officers contended that such loans were well secured by renewal commissions, but the law did not recognize renewals as adequate collateral. The company was told to write off uncollected agents' advances over two years. Similarly, in the late 1970s regulators compelled Guardian to change the names of some of its policies to make them more readily identifiable.[20]

Guardian sometimes tried to dance around regulations that did not suit it. In 1909, for instance, it realized a profit of $831,000 from the sale of its home office building at 20 Nassau. According to the law, which capped surplus at 10 percent of liabilities, all the profit from the transaction would have to be distributed to policyholders. That, however, would have constrained the company's cash flow at a time when it was building its new home office building in Union Square. To get around the problem, Guardian lowered the assumed rate of interest for its reserves, thereby increasing the required policy reserves—a simple accounting maneuver that allowed the company to keep the cash received from the sale of 20 Nassau by calling it "reserves" instead of "surplus."[21]

In 1974, Guardian asked regulators to allow it to hold a higher level of surplus, which was still capped at 10 percent of insurance liabilities. The company felt that this cap, a holdover from the days when it wrote mainly ordinary life insurance, made no sense in the age of group life, health, and disability. Guardian made ultraconservative calculations of its group accident and health claim reserves and liabilities in order to maneuver around the law until regulation finally caught up with reality. The issue came to a head when one of Guardian's investment officers, Henry Spencer, realized a windfall profit on a municipal bond deal. The state Insurance Department finally allowed Guardian to create a formal, realized capital gains fund, a special surplus over the 10 percent cap, set aside to cover against fluctuations in the market prices of equities. (A statute legalizing the change was actually called the "Guardian Amendment.") Despite the new law, Guardian continued to run up against the cap on surplus.[22]

Similarly, when Guardian decided to put the brakes on policy loans at the height of the 1970s inflationary spiral, it hit upon a simple solution— pay higher dividends to those who did not take out policy loans. Sales boomed.[23]

But none of this is to say that regulators ever gave Guardian a free pass. One major disappointment for the company occurred when the state blocked Guardian's entry into the property and casualty field. Life insurance and casualty insurance are both insurance in that they both entail a sharing of risks. In most other ways, however, the two businesses differ fundamentally. Nevertheless, Guardian and four other New York life companies flirted with expansion into the fire and casualty insurance business in 1960. Although none of the life companies had definite plans for such an expansion, they broached the subject to a state legislative committee. During the meeting, the companies emphasized the growing competition from fire and casualty companies that had established life insurance affiliates. Guardian was interested in the change because, as John Cameron noted, it received a good deal of business from general insurance brokers who might begin to funnel their business to the life affiliates of the fire and casualty companies that they represented. Despite the anticompetitive possibilities of excluding life insurers from the fire and casualty market, the New York State Insurance Department urged the legislature to reject the life companies' overtures.[24]

Guardian renewed its overtures to enter the fire and casualty field again in the early 1970s. Despite Guardian's significant experience and human capital, the government again denied it and other life insurers entry into casualty lines. This may have been a longer-term blessing. While other life insurance companies eventually diversified into property and casualty lines, Guardian found it to be a strategic and financial virtue to have stuck more closely to its core business.[25]

Watching the Watchers

Following the Armstrong Investigation, Guardian banded with other life insurers to lobby for industry interests in the public arena. It was a charter member of the Association of Life Insurance Presidents, an organization formed in the wake of the Armstrong difficulties to oppose the enactment of more restrictive legislation. Later, the company joined the American Life Convention. Guardian was also a charter member of a state association, Life Insurance Companies of New York State. More temporary alliances served, from time to time, to accomplish specific tasks, such as in 1978, when Guardian joined in a class action suit that sought to have California's usury law declared unconstitutional.[26]

Guardian also relied on its own resources to mount support for its positions on public policy. In 1978, its Alert program was designed to inform members of the field force about national issues affecting insurance. Guardian hoped to mobilize its sales agents to put pressure on their local elected representatives. The company made use of the Alert program to support passage of the Disability Amendments Act of 1979, which was intended to reduce Social Security disability benefits. The issue at hand was set forth in a memo dated 6 July 1979 from President Leo Futia, which beseeched all Guardian personnel to "call, wire or write your representatives immediately to urge their support" of the bill. If the bill did not pass, Futia warned, "pity the poor taxpayers in the future. Some day, the retirement age will have to be increased, or the taxes will rise enormously."[27]

Of Guardian's top officers, Dan Lyons was perhaps the most influential, and most assertive, with public policymakers. In the 1960s, Lyons frequently projected himself into the forefront of the life insurance industry's struggle to better serve the public and to provide a strong and unified voice in its relations with regulatory authorities. It was he who presented the industry's case on various matters before New York and other state legislatures. It was Guardian's posture historically to try to be on good terms with the state insurance commissioner, and Lyons continued that tradition. Some of the goodwill he fostered with the New York State regulators, however, deteriorated somewhat during George Conklin's tenure, but relations were repaired subsequently by Angle.[28]

Bound to New York

State regulation of the life insurance industry makes jurisdictional arbitrage possible. Companies can withdraw from states with unreasonable or expensive regulations. Theoretically, they can even move their home offices to another state. On at least one occasion, Guardian contemplated moving to a different state but it abandoned the idea as too expensive. In the 1970s, New York's regulators were causing enough troubles to induce some Guardian officers, including Chief Investment Officer Ashby Bladen, to urge the company to redomicile in Connecticut. The expense of relocation was deemed too high, however, and the company would still have to face New York regulators as a "foreign" company. There would have been some savings in expenses down the road, but not enough to make the change worthwhile. (The alternative, as seen in chapter 10, was regionalization.) So for all intents and purposes, for better or worse, Guardian remained wed to the Empire State.[29]

Guardian did cease operations in other states whenever regulatory barriers became too high. Withdrawal, or the threat of it, was effective in getting changes in the law. Guardian, like numerous other insurers, withdrew from Wisconsin in 1907 because its laws simply mandated more policy details than the company was willing to tolerate. It reentered the state in 1916, after the repeal of the problematic regulations, only to exit again, in 1918, and then apply for reentry in 1920. Guardian's response to Texas's 1907 Robertson Law, which *required* that life companies invest 75 percent of their reserves on Texas business in *taxable* Texas securities and deposit them with that state, was also swift and sure. Guardian and twenty-one other major insurers withdrew from the state, calling the law an act of "confiscation" that could "lead only to insolvency." There, however, the state was unyielding. As late as 1925, Guardian refused to make loans in Texas, though many considered it a very attractive mortgage field, partly to continue its protest of the Robertson Law and partly because it feared adverse tax consequences. The company did not write new business in the Lone Star State until 1947, and Texas did not repeal the law until 1963.[30]

More recently, instead of completely withdrawing all lines from a state, Guardian and other insurers withdraw only the specific products that hit regulatory barriers. For example, in 1976 Guardian decided to stop writing new medical expense policies in New York because the state mandated that all health insurance policies provide maternity benefits. Guardian and other health insurers thought the measure unconstitutional, unreasonable, and unprofitable because they viewed pregnancies as consciously planned decisions, not random illnesses. In 1993, the company threatened to withdraw its group policies from New York due to the passage of community rating legislation that adversely affected small group medical insurance. The new law forced the company to charge the same premium throughout the state, even if the group was located in the much more expensive downstate region. Guardian ultimately stayed in the market, but increased its premiums.[31]

Bones of Contention

The Texas Robertson Law had no intrinsic merit, but even less obnoxious investment restrictions were onerous to Guardian, because what it wanted most, on the asset side of its balance sheet, was flexibility. Regulators could not know better than the company's professionals how its cash should be deployed, went the argument. There were times when regulatory decisions seemed capricious or politically motivated. In 1925, for instance, the New York superintendent of insurance forced Guardian to sell its holdings of Kansas City Terminal Railway Company bonds simply because he did not like the bonds. In 1933, Guardian *loosened* conditions on one of its Madison Avenue mortgages after New York Superintendent George Van Schaick strongly urged the company to do so.[32]

Bond valuations were a particularly sensitive area of contention between the company and its regulators. The general rule was that if a bond's issuer was in receivership, life companies had to value the bonds in statutory reports at their market values as of 31 December, while other bonds they could list at amortized value, which could be significantly higher than market value. But evidently there was a gray area that Guardian and other companies tried to leverage. When Guardian discovered that MetLife had been allowed to list Toledo, St. Louis, and Western Railroad Company 3.5 percent coupon bonds at amortized value, even though the company had been in a receiver's hands for a number of years, it pressed the Insurance Department to allow it to continue to list its Brooklyn Rapid Transit system bonds at amortized value on the grounds that, though the system was in receivership, it continued to service its bonds promptly.[33]

The expenses devoted to coping with regulation remained major irritants to life insurers. The annual statements that they had to prepare for regulators did little to help managers figure out exactly what was happening to their businesses and resulted in what were almost comical duplications of effort. Traditionally, life companies kept accounts designed to help them to complete the Convention Blank, a mandatory annual statement designed to help regulators assess each company's ability to pay claims, i.e., its forward-looking solvency. The statutory statements (STAT) cast little light, however, on the company's value as a going concern. Pressure for life companies to keep two sets of books, one for regulators and one for company stakeholders, began in earnest in the 1960s at stock companies. Guardian executives with strong mathematical backgrounds, like Lyons, Conklin, Rosenthal, and Angle, realized that the company had to develop better management information. (John Angle joked that he often had the feeling that Guardian had accounting systems for everyone but the people running the company!) To help it better judge the company's progress, Guardian adopted GAAP accounting methods. Now the company had two sets of books, the stodgy regulatory ones and the real GAAP ones. The tax authorities required yet a third. But even those were insufficient to ascertain precisely what was adding value to the company. In the 1990s, chief actuary Armand de Palo developed a fourth set of books, Economic Value Added (EVA), that measure the present value of the future stream of profits.[34]

Examinations were also costly, time-consuming affairs. Examiners sent Guardian a draft report, which the company could respond to before its revision and publication. An exchange of ideas occurred. If Guardian was frustrated with the conclusions, it could have called a hearing. Otherwise, it reached compromises on language. It was always an open, though generally unspoken, question that the process was worth the expense.[35]

Even in the era of deregulation, the 1980s and 1990s, state regulators still were a major factor in the quotidian life of Guardian managers. As Guardian moved into mutual funds and variable products, federal regulation, in the form of SEC oversight, also loomed. Guardian successfully alleviated the impact of SEC oversight by setting up a special subsidiary solely for the purpose of issuing variable contracts. The subsidiary had to answer to the SEC, but Guardian itself did not.[36]

In other ways, it has not been so easy to contain the burden. The Economic Retirement Income Security Act (ERISA), passed in 1974, is a case in point. Guardian supported the act's primary objective of making pensions more secure. But the multitude of reports required by the act soon placed an inequitable burden on small employers, a market important to the company. Moreover, ERISA necessitated an extraordinary increase in staff for Guardian's pension division just to help policyholders to comply with the provisions of the new law.[37]

Ever so slowly, it began to dawn on state legislators that regulation may have gone too far and yet done too little. The rise of the "gadfly press" in the 1970s, most notably Joseph Belth's critical and informative *Insurance Forum,* was ample proof of that. The principle of "sunshine" became more attractive as an alternative to restrictive regulation. As early as the Armstrong Investigation, some Americans pointed to the British experience as an example to follow. Regulations in the United States, though still far from as free as in Britain, finally began to loosen in the last two decades of the twentieth century. Taxes, however, were a different story.[38]

Taxation

Though people do not always think of it this way, taxes are a form of regulation. They shift incentives. They constrain. In the life insurance industry, since the mid-nineteenth century, taxes on companies have proliferated in both degree and kind. Early on, the main tax on the business was on real estate. Soon, however, insurance companies began paying state premium taxes, state filing fees, and, eventually, federal income taxes. The newer state taxes on life companies were usually justified as necessary to cover the costs of regulating the industry. Such "special" taxation seemed reasonable enough, but in time, industry taxes generated far more revenue than the states spent on regulatory supervision. A 1940 study, for example, revealed that 6 percent of the taxes paid by life insurers to the state of New York were applied to policyholders' purposes, while the balance went into the state's general coffer.[39]

The federal government began taxing life companies in earnest during World War I. The new federal taxes were particularly disturbing to the industry because they were based on the insurers' total income. In 1921, Washington shifted to a lower and less controversial tax scheme whereby it agreed to tax insurers only on their investment income not needed for policy reserves.[40]

Life insurers have long tried to limit taxes aimed solely at raising revenue. Their argument against them is simply that taxes levied on their business are both unjust and impediments to savings. In 1935, Guardian president Carl Heye lamented that it was "regrettable that life insurance, which plays such an important part in the life of the nation, constituting an essential factor in the protection of the economic welfare of its citizens, should become increasingly subject to what has been fitly called—a tax on thrift." The tax-on-thrift argument did little to slow the pace of new taxes. Insurance companies, with their immense troves of cash, had long been sitting ducks for state governments.[41]

In 1895, for example, life insurers paid more state taxes than banks, railroads, and other corporations combined. The taxation also tended to be very uneven. "The taxation of Life Insurance," industry chronicler John McCall argued in 1898, "cannot be said to be founded on any recognized principles of equity or of political economy when in one-half of the Union it is taxed nine times as heavily as it is in the other half." Too much and unjust. Insurers tried to reduce their tax burdens by arguing that they were not really running "for profit" businesses, an argument that became hard to sustain after the revelations of the Armstrong Investigation. The industry then tried a different tack: it was the policyholder who ultimately paid the taxes and so for the policyholder at least, insurance entailed no profit. That was not a winning argument, either. Taxes were as inevitable as the death of those policyholders. The industry's efforts, through most of the twentieth century, were aimed mainly at trying to reform tax codes, rather than abolish them.[42]

Guardian's own contests with taxation date back to the Civil War. In 1864, when a tax assessor miscalculated the company's capital at only half its $200,000, the company did nothing to correct him. Four years later, Guardian considered testing the constitutionality of a Pennsylvania tax law. (It does not appear that the company followed through.) Like its industry peers, Guardian fought taxes to minimize its expenses and, not incidentally, lower the cost of protection for policyholders.[43]

But there were ideological reasons as well. Guardian's managers believed in markets and voluntarism. They believed that government tended to bloat ever larger because, as Yale professor Thomas Adams noted, "the public has no means of accurately ascertaining whether a particular activity of government is productive or unproductive, efficient or inefficient." This attitude carried forward into the mid-twentieth century when insurers tended to oppose entitlement programs like Social Security as detrimental to the American way of life. In fact, insurers lobbied against the extension of such measures at every turn. In 1949, James McLain beseeched Guardian policyholders to rise up and oppose H.R. 6000, a federal bill that proposed extensions in Social Security entitlements. In addition to posing a threat to Guardian's disability, insurance, and annuities businesses, such measures, McLain argued, undermined "native American characteristics of initiative and responsibility." "Can the government, on the known record of past performance," he rhetorically asked, "do the job as well and as economically as the individual citizen can for himself?"[44]

The main point, though, was to cut expenses. An insurer had two major weapons in its struggle to keep its tax bill in check: the courts and tax avoidance strategies. In the early 1920s, Guardian demonstrated the efficacy of both. In 1920, the company won a $15,000 settlement against the federal government for premium taxes paid in 1909, 1910, and 1911. In 1922, Guardian faced a large liability for federal income taxes if it reported the value of its European securities holdings on the basis of the prewar, gold standard exchange rates. Partly to avoid those taxes, the company reported its European securities holdings on the basis of the much lower market exchange rates. In 1924, Guardian again disputed its federal tax bill. The negotiations went on for so long, several years, and involved so much money, somewhat in excess of $5,000, that the tax collector insisted that the company post security in the form of an escrow account or a surety bond. So angry was Carl Heye that he actually balked at the annual $60 price of the surety bond![45]

Tax Resistance in the Depression Era

The Great Depression intensified insurance industry tax struggles at all levels, federal, state, and local. In 1933, Guardian pledged $500 per annum to the Citizens' Budget Commission, a political action committee devoted to reducing expenses and to maintaining the credit of the City of New York. Though the organization claimed to have saved Guardian policyholders over $13,000 in city taxes, the company ended its contributions a year later. Since the larger insurers were making donations to the commission, it is possible that Guardian's managers calculated that they could ride along free. It is also possible that Guardian may have sympathized to some extent with New York's fiscal plight, as it turned aside policyholders' pleas for the company to boycott the city's securities.[46]

Guardian's main difficulties with its federal taxes in the period related to the relatively high costs, among insurers, of researching investments. Guardian spent much effort detailing its claims for investment expenses. All of the officers of the company who had anything to do with investments were required to submit statements regarding

1. Personal time worked in connection with investments.
2. Clerical and other time and expenses known by them to be incurred.
3. Materials or rental expenses known by them to be incurred.

Guardian also retained outside accountants to defend it against federal audits, which produced considerable savings for the company in the early 1930s. Tax experts were also retained to help the company lower its considerable real estate tax charges in New York and Chicago.[47]

In 1937, Guardian mounted a challenge to a New York law that authorized a premium tax on New York companies collected from policyholders in states where premiums were not taxable. At first, Guardian simply refused payment of the taxes and sued. The New York State Court of Appeals upheld the law in principle, though it disallowed the taxing of policy premiums from residents of states, like Massachusetts, that imposed reserve taxes in lieu of premium taxes.[48]

Guardian made annual appeals to alleviate real estate taxes levied against its properties in Hudson County, New Jersey. In 1939, the tax situation in Hudson County, which included Jersey City, reached an acute stage when three state tax officials routinely blocked Guardian's appeals without hearing. New Jersey Governor Walter E. Edge dismissed the three officials when he learned that the delays were due not to the amount of work pending before the county's tax board but rather to a deliberate decision to refuse to hear the appeals upon their merits. "This is inefficiency and neglect of duty in the highest degree," he announced, to Guardian's glee. The Hudson County Tax Board subsequently lowered Guardian's tax valuation, but Jersey City appealed the lowered assessments to the state Tax Board, which, as it happened, was also under fraud investigation. Guardian once again sued. Jersey City mayor Frank Hague was called to testify for almost five hours while his wife lay hospitalized in Boston. Apparently that did not win him much sympathy. An out-of-court settlement generally favorable to Guardian was the result. The prolonged tax battles, though costly in themselves, saved Guardian, net of attorney's fees, about $100,000. Guardian also successfully fought a New York City tax on annuities in force between 1934 and 1942, when the New York Court of Appeals ruled that the city could not tax annuity payments because state law explicitly exempted them from premium taxes.[49]

The level of taxation was one issue. The expense involved in preparing tax statements and keeping track of tax changes was another. As early as 1940, Guardian complained of the very substantial growth in the workload of its tax division. "The text of one tax bill alone," it informed policyholders, "covered 489 printed pages." "Each statute," it further explained, "must be studied to insure proper compliance—each court decision, each regulation, each ruling must be diligently followed to insure the protection of policyholders' interests." Moreover, "tax statutes are not infrequently broad and general and may therefore require interpretation as to their application to a particular situation." "In not a few instances," the company lamented, "the maintenance of necessary records . . . and the preparation of tax returns cost the Company, and consequently the policyholders, much more than the actual tax paid." The Depression, in this respect, was quite depressing. In 1940, the company filed almost eight times the number of tax returns than it had filed in 1930.[50]

Postwar Tax Fortunes

In 1952, Guardian's managers ranked taxes just behind inflation as the biggest threat to the health of the company and the industry. But fighting taxes was no easy business. Guardian had to weigh the costs against the benefits of suits, appeals, and other forms of lobbying. For example, Guardian and other life insurers protested vigorously against discriminatory premium taxes on out-of-state insurers. But after the United States Supreme Court rebuffed Metropolitan Life's suit on the issue, Guardian dropped its protests and began to pay the premium taxes without further protest.[51]

In 1958, Congress made a drastic change in the basis of life insurance taxation. Guardian and other insurers denounced the change as "pseudo-scientific." The new federal tax law, as Guardian saw it, had "created a . . . monstrosity which cannot be justified on the bases of any canon of sound taxation." Worse yet, the law's complexity of detail was so great that experts could not agree on what the appropriate tax rate was for any given transaction. The complicated tax changes presented an income tax picture so muddled that Guardian could not forecast its tax liability. It guessed, and allocated $2,154,000 for 1958 federal taxes, compared with the $1,208,000 it paid in 1957. One industry expert predicted that "it may take some time for both the Treasury and the life insurance business to find out exactly what the law and the regulations mean." In the meantime, the company's actuaries could do little but scratch their heads over the company's federal tax burden.[52]

Guardian appealed in vain to its policyholders to complain about the situation to members of Congress. When the efforts fell flat, Guardian dispatched Dan Lyons to Washington, to work with the so-called Temporary Committee on the Taxation of Mutual Life Insurance Companies. Lyons spent weeks in Washington, testifying before both the Ways and Means Committee and the Finance Committee of the Congress of the United States.[53]

Thanks to the efforts of the Temporary Committee, a new federal tax law that finally passed in 1959, based on the revived principle of a total income assessment, was an improvement, though far from optimal. For one thing, many of its features remained open to multiple interpretations, some with troubling and broad implications. Many questions remained to be resolved, but Guardian paid its taxes on the basis of its own interpretation of the new law. To be safe, it created a contingency reserve, in case the government pressed for a larger payment.[54]

During the next decade, a major area of contention was the treatment of income from municipal tax-exempt securities, which Guardian maintained should not be added to its gross income. The IRS disagreed. It audited Guardian's federal taxes for the years 1958 through 1960, inclusive. The municipal bond tax exemption issue made its way to the United States Supreme Court, where Guardian lost. So in July 1965, it had to fork over $848,000 in back taxes and interest. More ominous was the fact that the IRS found a number of other items to contest. Guardian threatened more litigation and replenished its federal tax contingency reserve to gird itself for another battle. An audit revealed a deficiency of about $1.5 million, but Guardian again appealed, and continued to tussle with the IRS about its current tax filings. In 1972, the board approved a compromise settlement with the IRS for the years 1958 to 1964. Not until the end of 1974 did Guardian settle its taxes through 1969, at which point the IRS began an audit of the company's 1970 and 1971 returns. Such audits could take years to clear, and by the 1970s Guardian's tax returns were the size of college history textbooks.[55]

Throughout the 1970s and 1980s, Guardian shifted its tax strategies more toward avoidance and away from confrontation. As early as 1971, John Gray had observed "that form and method rather than substance may be determining factors for the IRS." Guardian accordingly decided to play the tax game by the IRS's own rules, as literally as possible. There were plenty of legal loopholes to be exploited. But the managerial costs remained high. "Federal Income Tax decisions," complained John Angle in 1988, "dog every decision we make."[56]

Taxes certainly affected investment decisions. In 1973, Guardian increased its net after-tax return by implementing a program of rationally taken capital losses to offset capital gains on high-quality secondary direct placements purchased at an attractive discount. The company also learned to key its investment strategy to avoid paying the capital gains tax as long as possible. It developed a computer program that told it when it was advantageous to buy, or sell, tax-exempt bonds. And before a new business was acquired or launched, the impact on taxes had carefully to be weighed.[57]

Confrontation was not abandoned altogether. In 1979, Guardian joined the industry in efforts to wage a new campaign against the "excessive" federal income tax of life insurance companies. And in 1985, the company helped to thwart legislation that would have taxed the inside buildup of life insurance. Then in 1991, Guardian entered into the early stages of another tax controversy, this one involving the taxation of nonqualified annuity policies.[58]

A big problem for mutual insurers arose from the Reagan tax reform act of 1984. That legislation attempted to simplify the taxation of life insurance and to make the taxation of mutual and stock companies more equal. Mutuals like Guardian had enjoyed what stock companies regarded as a tax advantage because mutual dividends were considered to be wholly returns of premiums, hence untaxable. The 1984 reforms recognized a portion of mutual dividends as an equity return, similar to a dividend on stock, and taxed it as such. Industry experts warned that any tax that gave companies an incentive to reduce surplus was hazardous to the health of mutuals.[59]

Other tax changes have also stung Guardian and the industry. As discussed in chapter 6, adverse tax laws effectively killed Guardian's pension trust business in the 1970s. Later, the elimination of the tax deduction on policy loans hurt demand for life insurance by lowering its expected benefit to policyholders. Another damaging change was the taxation of the inside buildup of certain modified endowment contracts with high savings components. To this day, public policymakers continue to struggle to find efficient, equitable methods of taxing life insurers.

One unanticipated benefit of the complexity of the tax codes was the investment Guardian had to make in the development of legal and research staffs. The problems of taxation gave those functions a high value within the company. As we will see in part III, Guardian's robust legal and research capabilities were invaluable to the asset side of Guardian's balance sheet. Asset management, in turn, was often the key variable in the company's success.

Investments

Five enormous computer monitors blazing with innumerable specialized trading software programs, a big television blaring the financial channel CNBC, and a switchboard of direct telephone links to brokers surround Eric Larson, Guardian's lead equity trader. Larson toils away in this electronic jungle, exchanging a slew of highly colorful Instant Messenger squibs with an unseen coterie of brokers and traders. It is a relatively slow day in the market, and Larson enjoys the leisure, doing his job, which is to dispose of a few million shares of half a dozen different stocks at propitious prices. Then suddenly, the telephone lights up like the Christmas tree in Rockefeller Center. Larson's eyes dash from screen to screen as his right index finger hovers over the massive telephone console. A few seconds later, his finger leaps for one of the buttons, he speaks a few words into his headset, bangs in a few numbers on his keyboard, and hits the enter key. He has just "made" Guardian policyholders and mutual fund holders $70,000.[1]

Larson heads a team of several Guardian equity traders, whose job is to execute buy or sell orders generated by the company's portfolio managers. The traders do not determine what stocks to buy or sell, but they decide precisely when to execute a trade and, within limits, at what price. Larson made out on the trade described above because in the fleeting moments he had to think about it, his trading instincts, honed over the years in the dog-eat-dog world of the trading floor, told him to hold off just a bit on the sale of a certain technology stock. Sure enough, the stock briefly rose in price and Larson pounced, pulling in $70,000 more than he would have made just seconds earlier.

Almost at the same time, Larson passes up an opportunity to sell a certain bank stock at $35.50 per share. He rues that decision as the price heads "south." As the morning wears on and the stock's price continues to slide, Larson wonders aloud if he should dump it and take his losses, i.e., the difference between the current price of $35.12 and the earlier $35.50 opportunity. Or, perhaps he should hold out and wait for the market to turn. With eight hundred thousand shares to unload, the decision is worth more than $300,000. He calmly analyzes the bank's stock chart and the futures market, trying to gaze ahead, fifteen minutes into the future. There is support at the $35 level, he notes, pointing to monitor 3, and the futures market is above fair value. He holds tight, hoping for a bounce off $35.

As dramatic as such a scene may seem, its outcome is essentially insignificant. With some $20 billion of assets on the company's general account alone, a 100 percent loss on the bank stock will not even come close to endangering the institution. Moreover, Larson's "losses" are only paper losses, or opportunity costs; Guardian purchased the bank shares months earlier at an average price far below the current market price. If the stock breaks through the $35 level to the downside, and plummets below $33, Larson will contact the portfolio manager, who will then decide whether to sell the stock, hold onto it, or perhaps even acquire more.

On the other hand, every dime counts. As long as Larson and his team bring in more money than they cost, Guardian policyholders are the richer for it. The "big bucks," though, are made or lost well before the orders reach the trading desk. Where the company's fortune is made is in the decisions of its investment officers, credit analysts, and portfolio managers, the people who decide which assets to buy and which to sell. Those men and women, it turns out, are very, very good at what they do, as were their predecessors, and their predecessors' predecessors, extending back in an unbroken line to the company's founding.

As figure III-1 shows, Guardian's pretax net rate of return has historically tracked that of the rest of the life insurance industry. Clearly, life insurance company returns are closely tied to the travails of the macroeconomy, a point that Guardian has long understood. The graph starts at the beginning of the Depression, with returns heading downward as default rates increased and interest rates dropped. Returns continued downward through World War II into the early 1950s, after the Federal Reserve "pegged" Treasuries at low yields (high prices), which flooded the economy with "easy" money. Mild inflation, generally strong economic growth, rising interest rates, and low default rates explain the strong upward trend in returns during the 1950s and 1960s. The sharp increase in returns to record levels in the 1970s and 1980s was due to the extremely

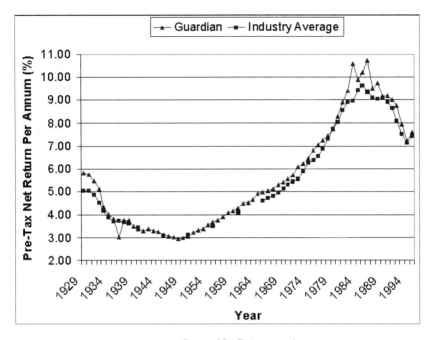

FIGURE III-1 *Pretax Net Return on Assets:*
Guardian vs. the Industry Average, 1929–95

high nominal interest rates that accompanied the great inflation of that era. Lower inflation brought lower interest rates in the 1990s, but a strong economy kept defaults low and returns at solid levels.[2]

The important point here is that since at least 1924, and probably much earlier than that, Guardian's pretax net rate of return has *almost always* exceeded the life insurance industry's average, and often quite handily. Figure III-2 illustrates Guardian's investment success relative to its industry. It is noteworthy that it did substantially better than the industry average during the Great Depression for reasons that are explored in chapter 12. During the low interest rate period in the 1940s, its performance became more or less average because the entire industry shifted heavily into government bonds. Guardian and most other life insurers became essentially government mutual funds, so there was little basis for competition. After the war, life insurers again began to compete on the basis of asset allocation decisions and credit risk analysis, and again Guardian excelled.[3]

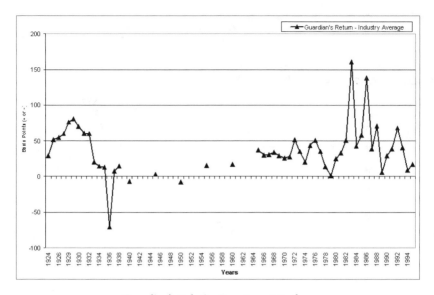

FIGURE III-2 *Guardian's Relative Investment Performance, 1924–95*

Chapters 12 and 13 explore in considerable detail the reasons underlying Guardian's long-lasting success in the investment area. Several major themes run throughout. First, Guardian kept its cash balances lower than the industry average. By staying more fully invested in income-generating assets than its peers, the company could generate higher returns. Second, Guardian could stay nearly fully invested because its economic and cash flow forecasting was among the best in the business. Simply put, it had better than average insight into future interest rates, securities prices, policy loans, and surrenders. Third, Guardian has excelled in credit analysis. In other words, it screens good risks from bad better than most life companies. Moreover, it continues to monitor borrowers closely after the loan has been made. Both techniques keep its default rates low and allow it to identify underpriced securities. Fourth, unlike many life companies, Guardian has been unafraid to take advantage of arbitrage opportunities and market glitches. Fifth, Guardian's portfolio diversification has been broad, both geographically and sectorally. That has allowed it to weather economic downturns in relatively good form. Finally, Guardian's asset allocation has been bound by reason, not tradition or the decisions of peers. The company has almost always allowed itself to become somewhat "overweight," compared to the industry average, in the asset class displaying the best tradeoff among risk, return, and liquidity then available.

Guardian thrived in those six areas because it attracted and retained a staff led by some of the best minds in the business. The company's first three presidents, with help from investment specialists like Frederick Schwendler and Casimir Tag, dominated the investment process until about 1950, when investment officer George Conklin began to assert himself. It was Conklin, his hires, protégés, and intellectual heirs, who have determined the company's investment strategies to this day.[4]

12

Investing the Premiums
Asset Management to the Mid-Twentieth Century

From the Civil War to the mid-twentieth century, insurance companies constituted the largest category of institutional investors in U.S. capital markets. Compared to banks, whose investment functions are generally better understood by ordinary citizens, life insurance companies really stand out as long-term investors. Life insurers have supplied great amounts of what banks generally could not: the very essence of financial capital, *long-term debt.* Just why that is so was summed up by Guardian's long-time chief investment officer, George Conklin. Writing in 1973, he explained the relationship between life insurers' revenues and investments this way:

> Historically, life insurance and annuity contracts have been popular savings media in the United States, and the inflow of funds from policyholders has grown at a relatively stable rate. The return flow of savings to beneficiaries and annuitants is also reasonably stable and predictable.... This reasonably predictable flow of funds, plus the long-term nature of life insurance contracts, had led life insurance companies to emphasize the long-term outlook in their investment decisions.[1]

Investment is the key component of a life insurance company's ability to survive. It is true that investment earnings compose only a fraction of life insurers' total revenues. As figure 12-1 shows, Guardian is no exception; historically its investments have accounted for only about a quarter of its annual revenues, a figure typical of the industry. Although 25 percent, give or take, may seem like an unimportant source of revenue, investments have always been, in fact, the key component of modern, legal reserve life insurance. Careful asset management separates the legal reserve insurer from mere wealth redistribution plans like Social Security,

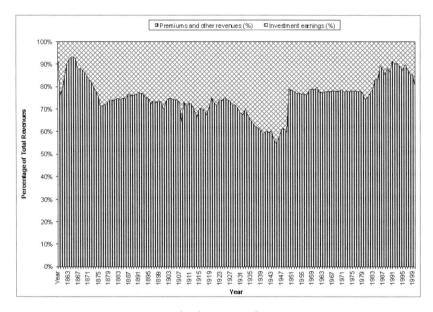

FIGURE 12-1 *Guardian's Sources of Income, 1860–2000*

fraternal and other assessment societies, or, for that matter, Ponzi schemes.[2]

Because life policies offer *guaranteed* nominal payouts, insurers have had to earn at least the minimum return assumed in their actuarial calculations or else be forced to renege on their guarantees. They have therefore tended to make return assumptions that, in the short run at least, were highly conservative. More often than not, they exceeded their conservative assumptions, refunded most of the excess to participating policyholders as dividends, and kept some, by law less than 10 percent, as surplus or reserves against negative contingencies. Lower-than-expected returns would lead to lower dividends or higher premiums, either of which could negatively affect new sales. Investment losses could also hurt new sales and induce a rash of surrenders and policy loans. Large investment losses could threaten the company's very existence. It is little wonder, then, why Guardian's board of directors considered the Finance Committee the most important of its committees.[3]

The Finance Committee is almost as old as the company itself; the company's first bylaws, passed in 1860 soon after the company organized, established the committee. For decades the committee closely monitored the company's investments, which were considered so central to the company's success that, until the early 1950s, the president chaired the committee and played the role of chief investment officer. He had help, of course, particularly from the members of the committee, which was much more deeply involved in the investment operations of the company than is true, or could be true, today. Eventually, the company also employed investment specialists to screen loan applications, perform due diligence, monitor approved loans, and execute the committee's orders.

The Finance Committee's goal was simple, but not easily obtained. It sought to earn the highest net returns possible, *consistent with the safety of the company.* The qualifying clause is key. As company executives well understood, a tradeoff between risk and return, like that illustrated notionally in Figure 12-2, permeates financial markets. The higher an investment's expected return, the higher the chance that the investment will fall short of expectations. The job of the Finance Committee was to find just the right point on the tradeoff line that would allow the company to meet its obligations and compete with other life insurance companies without endangering the company's existence. If the company's investment strategy were too conservative (point TC), the net cost of its policies would increase. Existing policyholders would begin to flee and new sales would become harder to consummate. On the other hand, if the company's strategy were too radical (point TR), its solvency would be put too much at risk. The Finance Committee needed to find the sweet spot (point SS) where the return was adequate and the risk reasonable. Moreover, the company's investment portfolio had to meet regulatory standards, provide adequate liquidity, tax, and inflation protection, and reflect the long-term horizon of the company's liabilities.[4]

As a class, life companies have historically been relatively efficient investors. They have enjoyed economies of scale that result in cost savings, they have employed people who specialized in discerning good investments from bad, and they have had enough assets under management to build highly diversified, hence lower-risk, portfolios. Guardian was fairly typical in all those respects. In broad terms, Guardian bought assets to hold over long periods. It gradually expanded its investments from local to regional to more geographically distant assets, usually by following the expansion of its policy-writing business. Like most life insurers, it eschewed market timing strategies, preferring the steady gains and low

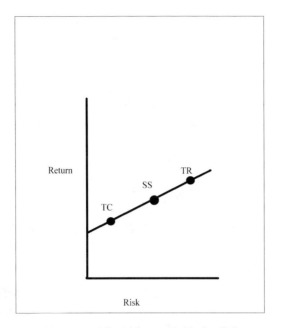

FIGURE 12-2 *The Risk-Return Tradeoff Line*

costs associated with a "buy and hold" philosophy to speculative plays. When during the Armstrong Investigation Charles Evans Hughes asked point-blank, "Have you found it necessary to watch the ticker to see where you could make a profit on a turn in securities?" Cornelius Doremus immediately shot back, "We never do." Yet unlike many life insurers, Guardian was often quick to seize arbitrage opportunities when they arose. It also had superior credit risk analysis. Guardian's investment specialists long reminded themselves and new employees of parables like the following:[5]

> *Teacher*: Johnny, if your father borrowed from you $100 and should agree to pay you at the rate of $10 per week, how much would he owe you at the end of 7 weeks?
> *Johnny*: One hundred dollars.
> *Teacher*: I am afraid you do not know your arithmetic.
> *Johnny*: Well, I may not know my arithmetic, but I know my father.[6]

Studies of investment returns indicate that something like 90 percent of an institutional investor's realized return is solely a function of its asset allocation decision. In this respect, too, Guardian was both somewhat typical and somewhat atypical of the industry. Like other life insurers, Guardian historically invested in about a half-dozen major asset classes: cash, including gold, paper currency, bank deposits, and various types of short-term loans; real estate, including its home office and investment properties; mortgages, largely limited to urban properties in Guardian's case; bonds, including government and corporate obligations; stocks, mostly preferred shares at first but later substantial quantities of common shares; and policy loans. However, Guardian's specific asset allocations, the percentage of total assets that it invested in securities, mortgages, real estate, and cash, often diverged significantly from the industry average. What most differentiated the company from its industry peers was its relative aversion to cash and its preference for holding urban mortgages.[7]

Figure 12-3 shows how the relative importance of asset classes in Guardian's investment portfolio changed significantly over time. From its inception in 1860, the company invested mostly in government bonds—treasuries and municipals—and in mortgages on city property. Later, it

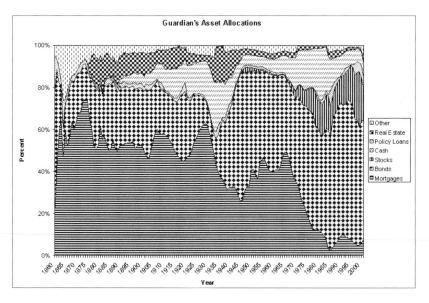

FIGURE 12-3 *Guardian's Asset Allocations, 1860–2000*

added to its portfolio corporate securities, especially railroad bonds, policy loans, and, through mortgage foreclosure and outright purchase, real estate. Policy loans trended steadily higher after their introduction in 1882, exceeding 10 percent of total assets in 1911. Real estate jumped to over 10 percent of assets during the recessions of the 1870s and 1890s but trended lower in the years immediately preceding the Armstrong Investigation, and stabilized to just under 10 percent until the end of World War I. The mix of assets would continue to evolve, and the changes reflect important differences between the company's approach to investment compared to industry norms. This chapter traces, from the company's inception to about 1950, the history of each major asset class available to Guardian.[8]

Cash

Except to evade regulatory restrictions on their investments, or to gird themselves for a rush of large claims, surrenders, or policy loan requests, life insurance companies tried to minimize their cash holdings. For Guardian, the minimum was far less than the industry average. The policy, from the company's earliest days, was to remain as fully invested as possible.[9]

The reason for that is simple enough. Returns on currency and demand deposits are zero, while returns on time deposits and financial instruments with short maturities are usually lower than returns on longer instruments of the same risk class. As Cornelius Doremus explained, holding just half a million more dollars in the bank "would cost us $15,000 per annum—the difference in interest between 2% and 5%." Moreover, life insurers, compared to other kinds of businesses, including banks, have fairly predictable cash inflows from premiums and investment earnings that almost always exceed their somewhat less predictable cash outflows for death benefits, surrenders, and policy loans. Life insurers rarely face the severe liquidity pinches that plague depository institutions.[10]

Still, life insurers are constantly receiving and making payments, so at some point they must command cash transaction media—physical currency and checking accounts. While they conceivably could have mimicked the strategy of some savings banks and met their transaction needs with credit lines at commercial banks, most life companies preferred not to have to pay interest for such a service and hence managed their own liquidity positions. Guardian sought short-term loans from banks to make payments only as a last resort because, as Cornelius Doremus put it, "it is . . . not a particularly pleasant condition for a Life Insurance Company, which should be a lender, to be a borrower of money."[11]

Until it began to pay its employees with checks in late 1928, Guardian kept on hand thousands of dollars of physical currency—coins and banknotes—in order to meet its payroll. It kept the currency, and its securities, in safe deposit boxes at nearby trust companies and further safeguarded itself with Outside Messenger Robbery and Interior Office Robbery Insurance. It doubled its insurance coverage in September 1920 in the aftermath of the worst terrorist attack against the financial district before the deadly strike against the World Trade Center on 11 September 2001. A covered wagon filled with explosives and metal shrapnel tore into the noontime crowd at Wall and Broad, killing thirty-nine and injuring hundreds more. In a bloody, smoked-filled scene eerily similar to that which would take place eighty-one years later, almost to the day, some seventeen hundred of New York's finest, seventy-five Red Cross nurses, Mayor John Hylan, and the Twenty-Second Infantry rushed to the scene. The following day, New Yorkers gathered near the rubble to sing "America the Beautiful." Given the political turmoil of the period (the era of the Red Scare, Palmer's raids, and the trial of the anarchists Sacco and Vanzetti), the edginess of Guardian's executives was justified.[12]

In 1929, the adoption of a simple technological innovation resulted in a major alteration of Guardian's cash management. The Todd check signing machine eliminated the time that had to be taken by the executive officers for the signing of checks for payments of a routine nature. The officers distrusted the technology, at first, but they managed to implement an elaborate variety of security measures[13] so that within a year, the machine had proved such a time saver that it became desirable to extend the practice to cover also policy loan and agents' commission checks. In 1932, managers were authorized to use the machine to sign a wider variety of checks up to $1,000 in value. Thereafter, Guardian kept most of its cash for transactions in the form of bank checking deposits and abandoned its safe deposit box cash system. In 1940, it updated to the most modern type of check writing and signing equipment then available. The use of checks was so ubiquitous that on 31 December 1952 Guardian had only $1,257.54 of physical currency on hand, far less than the company kept in the 1910s, when it was much smaller and the dollar went a lot further.[14]

Guardian maintained time deposits with a large number of banks, many of which were made to help Guardian's agents secure additional business. The practice began in earnest in early 1915 when Elmer F. Dekle, the company's district manager in Valdosta, Georgia, suggested "that in consideration of the making of such deposits he would be able to secure a considerable volume of new insurance." In the late nineteenth century, fieldmen at other companies had claimed that investments could be used to induce sales. Guardian, however, at first rejected the proposal on general principles. The company reconsidered when it realized that acting on the proposition would be in keeping with the present practice of all leading life insurance companies to make local investments in different states to forestall the criticism raised by a number of states against the draining of their funds by life insurance companies. The Finance Committee condoned the Valdosta deposit on three conditions: that a New York surety bond company insure it, that the return be competitive, and that the maturity be a year or less.[15]

When David A. Leon, the company's manager at Jacksonville, Florida, learned of the Valdosta deposit, he wrote the home office asserting that a deposit of $100,000 in his community could generate $400,000 of new business. The Finance Committee assented to an initial insured deposit of $50,000, with the remaining $50,000 to be deposited once $200,000 of new business came in. Such arrangements attempted to take advantage of marketing relationships between banks and life insurers that savings bank insurance in Massachusetts and elsewhere had shown to exist.[16]

Guardian also made time deposits in order to induce local banks to grant loans to its agents. In 1915, for example, the company made an insured time deposit at 5 percent annual interest in the Greensboro (North Carolina) National Bank in consideration of which deposit the bank promised to furnish proper discount facilities for the handling of notes to the company's newly appointed and promising manager, A. W. Fetter. Such agent-requested time deposits must have worked as hoped, because they became commonplace. Guardian even rushed funds to make deposits if a general agent thought that it would help him to place some insurance quickly.[17]

Over the long haul, the trend was away from gold and bank notes to other forms of "cash," which expanded to include relatively more lucrative varieties of short-term obligations such as call loans (overnight loans collateralized by financial securities), banker's acceptances, Treasury bills, repurchase agreements, and commercial paper. The important thing was that cash in any form was to be minimized in favor of being as fully invested as possible in longer-term, higher-yielding instruments and properties.

Hence Guardian kept its cash balances unusually low, generally below 4 percent, and often below 2 percent. As a percentage of its assets, the company's cash balances were almost always well below the industry average, as figure 12-4 demonstrates.

The company's policy of staying fully invested was not without risk. In August 1913, for example, the company scurried off to two banks for loans totaling $450,000 as it watched its cash position deteriorate in the face of higher demands for policy loans and increased levels of mortgage defaults. It periodically faced similar minicrises precisely because it kept fully invested. Cash crunches occurred because the company sometimes had difficulty judging demand for policy loans and because its mortgage interest payments all fell due at once, semiannually, on the first of February and August each year.[18]

At other times, Guardian faced the opposite problem of holding what it considered *too much cash.* In March 1912, for example, Guardian thought its cash holdings, then at just 1 percent of assets, too "plethoric," so it increased its time deposits and made several large mortgage loans. To help ensure investment outlets for its incoming funds, Guardian sometimes entered into "loan commitments," essentially forward contracts, or promises to make loans at specified times in the future at rates fixed today. One of the functions of the cashier's department in this period was to project future cash flows to help the Finance Committee plan its investment strategy. (Loan commitments would become a much more important investment technique later in the century.)[19]

That Guardian's cash management was so unusual is manifested by a September 1921 circular issued by the New York superintendent of insurance. In it, he chastised the state's life insurers for their high bank balances. "Good business judgment would seem to make it advisable for each company to limit the amount of its bank deposits to the necessary margin of safety and invest the balance," he noted, essentially validating, from a regulatory standpoint, Guardian's long-standing policy of remaining fully invested.[20]

In the 1920s, as it had since the end of the Civil War, Guardian continued to keep its cash balances extremely low, in the vicinity of 1 percent of total assets, except during years of high mortality or economic instability, when it allowed cash to approach 4 percent of its portfolio. The only

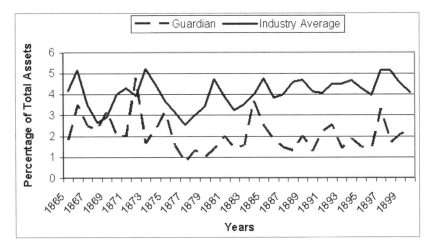

FIGURE 12-4 *Cash Position: Guardian vs. the Industry, 1865–1900*

major change in this area was that in early 1920 Guardian added New York call loans to its repertoire of short-term instruments, which also included bank deposits and Treasury bills.[21] In early 1929 it added bankers' acceptances, which the regulators had begun to allow three years earlier, because it found it increasingly difficult to secure the proper collateral for call loans. Unlike most other call loan market lenders, Guardian could not collateralize its loans with common stocks, the most widely used form of collateral in the call market. Beginning with passage of the Wales Act in 1928, Guardian could own, and hence receive for collateral, preferred shares, a type of equity-bond hybrid that paid a minimum fixed coupon like a bond but that also had upside price potential like a common share. Between 16 February 1920 and 3 January 1930 Guardian made 126 call loans at rates ranging from 4 to 10 percent per annum, nice returns given that none of the loans ever defaulted.[22]

The switch from call loans to bankers' acceptances, which were less subject to market risk, was fortuitous and not prescient. The stock market crash of October 1929 surprised most savvy investors, and Guardian was no exception. As late as 18 September 1929, just six weeks before Black Tuesday, Guardian was anticipating an attractive and sustainable market for municipal, railroad, and public utility bonds and preferred stocks.[23]

When panic enveloped the financial markets, requests for policy loans surged, forcing Guardian, fully invested as always, to scramble to sell

Treasuries. The company continued to operate on a very thin margin of cash until the national banking crisis of 1933. To allow it to do so in the face of continued abnormal demands on the company's funds for policy loans, cash surrender values, and other policy claims, the Finance Committee permitted Guardian's investment officers to borrow short-term from banks.[24]

By the autumn of 1931, Guardian had secured lines of credit totaling over $2.5 million with three leading New York banks. After obtaining the credit lines, company president Carl Heye characterized the company's present cash position as "very satisfactory." As it turned out, the company did not have to resort to the credit lines, largely because it improved its ability to forecast its liquidity needs and adjusted its holdings of short-term cash instruments, like Treasury bills, accordingly. Scholarly studies suggest that life insurance companies on average do not do a good job of forecasting cash flows, but apparently Guardian did well enough.[25]

Guardian found ways to avoid borrowing even during the Depression's darkest days. In the first quarter of 1933, as much of the nation's banking system was collapsing, it sold bonds *on a discount basis* to its banks, instead of into the market, because the bid-ask spreads in the bond pits were particularly large owing to the disturbed conditions. The banks happily discounted the bonds provided Guardian promised to buy them back if they defaulted. Guardian also received a large payment from Metropolitan Life on account of policy loans taken out on policies partly reinsured through that company. Well before the company's resources—and resourcefulness—gave way, the state imposed a moratorium on policy loans and surrender payments. The regulators had little choice, as the banking system's almost complete collapse had made it difficult for anyone to make payments. Before the moratorium took effect in March, Guardian arranged to make payments to its agents and policyholders via American Express Company money orders.[26]

Except for some two score small and a couple of large companies, the life insurance industry as a whole weathered the storm. Regulators began relaxing the moratorium restrictions by early April after the federal government had restored some confidence in the banking sector with the creation of the Federal Deposit Insurance Corporation (FDIC). Guardian probably welcomed deposit insurance. The company had tried to keep its funds in safe banks. (It rejected the overtures of the International Germanic Trust Company of New York in 1928, for example, because it was "but of recent organization.") It also had many of its deposits privately insured. Still, the huge number of bank failures during the Depression made it inevitable that Guardian would lose some of its deposits. (A 1947 study concluded that it eventually recovered about $48,500 of the $77,000 it had on deposit in failed banks.)[27]

By then Guardian had shed most of its international commitments, but what remained further complicated the company's liquidity management. When the Canadian dollar depreciated 10 percent in 1931, Guardian began to deposit its "Canadian pay" receipts in Canadian banks rather than exchange them for U.S. dollars as it traditionally had. The company refused to try to profit from exchange rate fluctuations because it did not want regulators to crack down on it for engaging in "exchange speculation."[28]

For the rest of the Depression, Guardian held more cash than it was accustomed to, reaching a high of slightly over 4 percent of total assets at the end of 1935. This reflected less a fear of another liquidity crisis than a desire to show a strong cash position in its annual statement at a time when default rates were elevated and there were few solid long-term investment opportunities. Regulators in 1935 applauded its adroit liquidity management.[29]

Real Estate

The most basic form of assets, of course, was real estate, and real estate investment began at home. Guardian invested heavily in its home office building, which in big cities were typically elaborate, stately structures that signified for all to behold the financial well-being and solidity of the insurer, and not incidentally embodying elaborate aesthetics and creature comforts for company officials. Such investments could also generate rental income. When the company decided to provide for two hospital and rest rooms in its home office in 1914, for instance, it did so on the grounds that the facilities would frequently aid its own employees in addition to providing a good talking point for the purpose of securing and holding tenants. In addition to its home office, Guardian purchased office buildings for some of its agencies. It also bought buildings as investment properties, hoping to earn good returns by leasing out offices or apartments until the buildings could be sold at an advance. It generally made out quite well in its real estate investments, so much so that according to Carl Heye its real estate returns helped it to establish "in the early part of its career . . . [its] enviable reputation of possessing unusual financial strength."[30]

Prevailing racial attitudes of the time complicated the company's view toward real estate. Beginning in earnest in the 1910s, large numbers of African-Americans migrated to northern cities in search of jobs and freedom from prejudice. The former commodity was in greater supply than the latter. Few whites took kindly to the new denizens, forcing Guardian's Finance Committee to fear the influx of "negroes" into New York neighborhoods where it owned property or had mortgages. An influx of "coloreds" would hurt property values. In 1917, for instance, white tenants fled the company's sixteen directly held properties and five mortgaged properties in the block on West 137th Street between Seventh and Eighth Avenues, present-day Harlem, after several houses in the block had been sold to African-Americans. The Finance Committee quickly approved a plan whereby architect John P. Leo took charge of the company's properties "with a view to counteracting the present demoralized condition in the neighborhood and restoring values in the block." Over twenty years later, the company still sold property when African-Americans encroached.[31]

Managing real property was a task that absorbed much time and effort, often disproportionate to the money involved. In April 1917, for example, the tenants of the Gayety Theatre in Hoboken, New Jersey, sought a rent allowance, claiming that the theater building required alterations to the extent of some $6,000. Before approving the request, the Finance Committee, already absorbed by the war claims issue, had to review detailed plans and specifications describing what the alterations would involve, for this one property alone.[32]

Guardian's real estate holdings were never much more than 15 percent of its total assets, and those high levels were due to mortgage foreclosures and not design. Real estate declined as a proportion of its investment portfolio in the 1920s, but increased precipitously in the early years of the Great Depression. By 1936 mortgage foreclosures, and hence real estate, had soared to historical levels. Finally, in 1938, Guardian began to sell a greater value of real estate than it acquired. Importantly, Guardian, unlike some major life insurers, did not suffer losses on the sale of its real estate portfolio in any year except 1934, when it posted a paltry $2,000 loss. Over the period 1929 to 1938, inclusive, the company gained on net a total of $648,000 from real estate sales. And conditions improved further thereafter.[33]

In 1939, a slight increase in activity in the real estate market in certain sections could be detected. By 1941, President McLain could report that "continued progress in the sale of real estate was made during the year." Sales of Guardian's and the life industry's real estate holdings accelerated after America's entry into the war. By the end of the conflict, only about 5 percent of Guardian's assets were tied up in real estate. Thereafter real estate's importance in the company's portfolio continued to trend sharply downward, falling to just a trace of the company's total assets by the end of the twentieth century. Real estate would have dropped even more quickly had not "purchase and lease" agreements become popular after the Second World War. Under such arrangements, Guardian purchased real property and immediately leased it, often right back to the seller, for extended periods. Guardian was one of the major innovators in this so-called net lease field. Purchase and lease arrangements afforded the lender more security than mortgages, long-term loans collateralized by real estate, long a mainstay of Guardian and the industry.[34]

Mortgages

From the beginning, Guardian was one of the industry's mortgage mavens. As figures 12-5 and 12-3, respectively, show, it was far more invested in mortgages than the industry average, and into the mid-twentieth

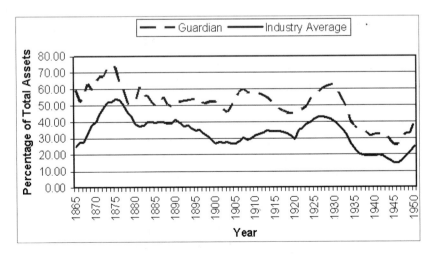

FIGURE 12-5 *Mortgage Investments: Guardian vs. the Industry, 1865–1950*

century, mortgages rivaled bonds as the largest block of the company's assets. Guardian invested heavily in mortgages because it realized that as a rule they netted a higher rate of income than equally safe bond investments. The tradeoff was that they were less readily convertible into cash or serviceable as collateral than bonds.[35]

Before World War I, most of Guardian's mortgage loans were made on real estate in the New York City metropolitan area, largely in Manhattan. The managers' and board members' intimate knowledge of conditions in the city helped the company to make intelligent investment decisions. Guardian elected Casimir Tag to its board, for instance, specifically to place him on the Finance Committee where his wide knowledge of financial matters and familiarity with real estate transactions and loans would prove of great value. Tag served in this capacity for more than two decades.[36]

The company's investment specialists knew the current conditions of the city's many neighborhoods, personally knew many of the best builders, and even considered the geology of Manhattan Island when making lending decisions. Moreover, its officers could personally run credit checks and inspect properties. By 1910, Doremus tooled around town in a company car for such purposes. In October 1913, the company sent employees out to inspect commercial properties on which it had mortgages in search of vacancies. They discovered an overall vacancy rate of 6.2 percent that was reduced to just 3.6 percent with the removal of a single troubled property from the data. Thanks to the investigation, the investment department knew that it had to monitor the mortgage on the troubled property closely. Moreover, it annually made an official search of every mortgaged property to ensure that there were no unpaid taxes, often the first sign of default. Except during recessions, defaults on mortgages were extremely rare and losses even more so. From 1 January 1900 to 31 December 1932, Guardian suffered a net capital loss on mortgages of only $217,090, or 0.18 percent of total mortgage investment.[37]

Guardian made mortgage loans on residential homes as well as much larger commercial projects, including the construction and/or sale of apartment and office buildings. Construction loans were particularly lucrative but safe because the company controlled the entire construction, had its own engineers verify the quality of the material used for the building, and could, if desired, terminate its liability when the construction was finished. If the loans were continued postconstruction, they were much preferable to loans on existing structures. Indeed, the value of modern buildings stood up much better during the Depression than that of older structures regardless of location.[38]

Many of its mortgages financed the general operations of small- and medium-sized businesses that pledged their physical plants for repayment of Guardian's long-term advances. The large loan strategy had its benefits but also its costs. All else being equal, one $1 million mortgage was cheaper to originate and service than a hundred $10,000 mortgages. If the large mortgage defaulted, however, the trauma to the company's cash flow and assets could be significant. When the James Livingston Construction Company defaulted on a $713,000 mortgage in August 1913, for instance, Guardian experienced liquidity problems so severe that it had to obtain bank loans.[39]

To help the company improve the geographical diversity of its mortgage investments, its executives, when traveling, solicited investment ideas. In 1890, for example, on his way from Cincinnati to St. Louis, Hubert Cillis paused in Louisville, Kentucky, to discuss investment in the notes of the Fourth Avenue Highland Park Company, a real estate development company. Similarly, when T. Louis Hansen was in St. Louis on agency business in 1922 he inquired into the local mortgage market and found ample opportunities at 6 percent on high-grade apartment buildings and business properties.[40]

World War I brought problems in the mortgage market. Real estate prices deteriorated sharply during the war, increasing the mortgage default rate by reducing borrower equity. By law and philosophy, life insurers were not supposed to make a mortgage loan for greater than 50 percent of a property's assessed value. As property values fell, more and more mortgages did not meet that strict criteria, forcing borrowers to reduce their indebtedness, sell the property, or default and suffer foreclosure.[41]

Foreclosure was hardly a boon to lenders. In a depressed real estate market, lenders who came into property through a borrower's misfortune either had to sell the property at a loss, i.e., for less than the mortgage principal, or attempt to rent it until property values rose. And the burdens of real estate management, as we have seen, were not well suited to a life insurance company.

In 1916, when the company took over numerous properties in default, it decided to sell, and suffer the losses, because it had sold certain bonds at a material profit that could offset the real estate loss. In 1918, however, Guardian took a different approach, ordering that properties backing mortgage loans past due or about to mature be appraised by an expert. On the basis of the appraisals and past practice, Guardian should have called in over $4 million worth of insufficiently collateralized mortgages, most of which probably would have been foreclosed. In keeping with the opinion expressed by the Mayor's Committee on Taxation and the Investigation of Mortgage Loans, however, the company resolved not to disturb any mortgages so long as interest and taxes were paid and the property was kept in good condition. The strategy worked because property prices soon rebounded.[42]

In July 1919, tight money conditions and the high default rates suffered during the war induced Guardian to raise its standard mortgage rate from 5 to 5.5 percent per annum. Rates on specific loans, however, could range between about 4 and 7 percent, depending on the credit and equity stake of the borrower, the size of the loan, and current competitive conditions.[43]

In the mortgage business, Guardian remained city bound. Many life insurance companies moved heavily into farm mortgages during and after the war, and Guardian's Finance Committee, after a thorough discussion of the subject in 1917, made preparations to follow suit. Company officers conducted extensive research on the subject, contacting other life insurance companies, at least four farm mortgage correspondents, mapmaker Rand McNally, the director of the census, the U.S. Department of Commerce, the U.S. Department of Agriculture, the departments of agriculture of eight states, and agriculture professor G. F. Warren. The officers' report, which followed closely the argument of Robert Lynn Cox's 1915 article, extolled the high-yield and low-risk characteristics of farm mortgages.[44]

But for reasons that are, in retrospect, fortunate, it did not follow through. In early 1920, after another thorough discussion of the subject the Finance Committee decided not to take up this mode of investment. That summer, it turned away a farm mortgage application forwarded by one of its top agents, Charles Rudd of Indiana, on the grounds that the company had not as yet entered the farm mortgage field. When the question cropped up again the following year, the Finance Committee took another look. After studying a favorable survey of the farm mortgage investments of life insurance companies, Guardian was still reluctant to bite. Just why is not clear. Perhaps the market had become too competitive, with lower rates and lower standards increasingly evident. In any event, farm mortgage lenders, especially ones that did not specialize in the field, would take a terrible beating in the prolonged agricultural depression of the late 1920s and 1930s.[45]

Guardian also shied away from mortgage-backed securities. In 1921, the U.S. Mortgage and Trust Company offered it a $100,000 block of mortgages on property located in different cities priced to yield 6.5 percent per year, but Guardian's investment managers sensed trouble and so the Finance Committee rejected the overture. It became implicit policy to stay out of that market, and it probably was a wise one. Despite repeated attempts to create workable mortgage-backed securities in the late nineteenth and early twentieth centuries, efficient mortgage-backed securities would not emerge until 1970.[46]

After World War I, Guardian continued to invest in residential, building, and business mortgages, but it also sought to diversify the geographical spread of its mortgage portfolio, because 58 percent of its U.S. assets were invested in the vicinity of the City of New York. This was too narrow a base for an expanding insurance business, and so the company adopted the policy of a wider distribution of its investments with a view toward adopting a proper relation between them and the liabilities on the insurance in force in the states where the company wrote business. Robert McDowell, head of the bond and mortgage department, spearheaded the initiative.[47]

The new policy shifted lending from the New York region to other cities, and it was by no means easy. To decrease lending in the New York area, the company had to turn away numerous quality local borrowers. Moreover, investing outside of the New York area required developing new sources of information. Guardian's executives tried to acquire information on distant properties personally whenever possible. For example, in 1921 Vice President T. Louis Hansen and McDowell inspected Cleveland properties on their way to a convention in Chicago. It was a good thing that they did, too, because they learned that the applicant's property was not in good repair.[48]

On occasion, Guardian made mortgage loans in order to secure additional life sales. That is not to say that it lent to bolster sales as a matter of policy, but a good word from an agent on an acceptable application clearly did not hurt the applicant's chances. In 1915, for example, Guardian lent a considerable sum to St. Edward's German Catholic Church of Little Rock, Arkansas, because the company's successful manager there intimated that the loan would help him to close a considerable volume of new business and also because the company had enjoyed satisfactory experiences with loans on church property in the past. Similarly, in 1919, the company lent $20,000 to the Young Men's Hebrew Association of Evansville, Indiana, because of the encouragement and endorsement of Charles Rudd, Guardian's fifth most productive agent. Two years later, Guardian loaned Leon Williams of Fort Smith, Arkansas, $30,000, because Williams, who already owned a $30,000 Guardian policy, pledged to purchase $20,000 more.[49]

Guardian occasionally premised acceptance of a mortgage on the purchase of life insurance. Such cases seem to have been examples of credit insurance rather than tie-in concessions, however. Applicants with good credit records who already owned Guardian life policies definitely received great respect, particularly if they first obtained loan approvals from rival life companies. As late as the 1970s, Guardian would look at investment proposals from policyholders as a "courtesy," though by that time it made clear that investment decisions would not be affected by the possibility of an insurance sale.[50]

Of course, Guardian had far more money to invest in mortgages than it could possibly hope to originate and monitor through its own executives and sales agents. So, beginning in earnest in 1922, Guardian established a system of loan correspondents roughly analogous to its agency network. Generally, the correspondents sold accepted mortgages to Guardian above par, e.g., $10,200 for a $10,000 mortgage. The overplus served as an origination fee. The correspondents then monitored the property and collected the payments, deducting half a percent for their troubles. During the 1920s, the company added loan correspondents in a number of states, including Alabama, Florida, Georgia, Illinois, Missouri, and Oklahoma. Competition among lenders was stiff; the volume of mortgages made by savings banks and life insurance companies jumped from $9.6 billion in 1920 to $27.1 billion a decade later.[51]

In the Great Depression, mortgages became much less important as a share of Guardian's assets, dropping from 62 percent of total assets in 1930 to just 32 percent a decade later. The four main causes of that shift are clear. First, Guardian foreclosed on a good number of mortgages. Foreclosures reduced the value of outstanding mortgages and augmented the value of real estate, which jumped from about 3 percent of Guardian's total assets in 1930 to almost 17 percent in 1936. Second, Guardian greatly reduced its new mortgage lending and was strict with renewals. Third, the company took advantage of low real estate prices and cheap labor to improve its own neighborhood. In March 1931, for instance, it began construction of a six-story apartment house at 107-09 East Seventeenth Street, caddy-corner to Tammany Hall, and adjacent to several of its other apartment buildings and its home office. The move was a strategic one, designed to accommodate expansion of the home office in view of the company's rapidly growing business.[52]

The fourth reason that Guardian reduced its new mortgage lending in the 1930s was that its loan correspondent system broke down. The deterioration became apparent in 1930, when the company discovered that the Mortgage Bond and Trust Company of Atlanta, Georgia, was in serious financial straits. Guardian fired the correspondent after it refused to post a surety bond. Its replacement, which did not guarantee its mortgages and which served competing life companies, was hardly ideal. About the same time, Guardian learned that the company had experienced quite a bit of trouble with its mortgages in Chicago, primarily due to the fact that, under the mismanagement of the city, taxes had been allowed to become in arrears and accumulated for a number of years. Guardian again fired its correspondent, which had not handled the company's mortgages in Chicago satisfactorily, and replaced it with Nelson, Hunt, and Company, which pledged to service Guardian's existing mortgages *without any charge*.[53]

Alas, there was no free lunch to be had in the Windy City. Nelson, Hunt, and Company had offered to service the company's mortgages because it had anticipated that with a return to more normal conditions Guardian would make additional mortgage loans in Chicago. But as Guardian was in no mood to make new mortgage loans, the correspondent desired a monthly allowance. Guardian consented to $1,000 per month, and soon had to make similar arrangements with its mortgage correspondents elsewhere. Such problems were typical of companies with mortgage correspondents.[54]

Like all life insurance companies, Guardian faced a rash of mortgage defaults in the first half of the 1930s. Owning real estate in a depressed market was, to say the least, unprofitable. Rental prices and tenancy rates were low, taxes, attorneys' fees, and maintenance costs were high, and fire insurance was not free. Guardian successfully reduced its fire insurance costs by self-insuring up to $10,000 the properties it acquired via foreclosure. The experience was so favorable that the company in 1945 upped its self-insurance against fire to $15,000. It sought ways to reduce its tax burden at every turn, but taxes still had to be paid. And it could do little about rental or tenancy rates. If it tried to economize on maintenance costs, it was certain to pay for it in the form of lower occupancy rates.[55]

Adding to the company's mortgage woes during the Depression era, borrowers often took advantage of the abnormal economic conditions by negotiating reductions in interest payments. Unlike some life insurers, Guardian rejected most such overtures on the grounds that if such a policy of interest reduction became generally known there would be an avalanche of such requests. The Finance Committee reasoned that armed with such knowledge, property owners would be inclined to default on the payment of interest or taxes, with a view to forcing the company to make interest reductions. Only if a concession would prevent the company's acquisition of the property were reduction requests countenanced.[56]

Guardian took a bath on the few score construction loans that it made in the early 1930s, so it largely avoided lending on new mortgages from 1932 until early 1935. After that, it rejected applications on unimproved and specialized properties in favor of mortgages on moderately priced modern homes, modern medium-priced apartment buildings, and business buildings. Mortgages on private homes became even more attractive after the new Federal Housing Administration began to provide guarantees, and as business properties had become relatively less attractive.[57]

In late 1936, Guardian reviewed its recent mortgage experience and developed a comprehensive set of criteria for investing in residential mortgages. All mortgages were to be completely amortized over ten to twenty years, with minimum down payments ranging from 10 percent to 20 percent, depending on the size of the loan and the age of the property. The older the building, the more attention would have to be paid to the home's heating plant, plumbing, kitchen, bathrooms, and location. In all cases, the company decided to pay particular attention to the borrower's characteristics. "He should be young, preferably, with a reasonably assured economic future, and he should be thrifty as evidenced by life insurance, bank deposits, etc.," the Finance Committee argued. Loan applications from older people, widows, and single women, either unmarried or divorced, however, called for particular care and conservative action. The increased emphasis on the borrower's credit, rather than on the security of the property alone, soon became standard in the industry.[58]

That Guardian fared relatively well in its mortgage holdings through the Depression was due largely to two historical decisions. In the 1920s it had rejected farm mortgages, which had much higher than average default rates in the Depression, and it had to some extent diversified away from the large, urban Northeast, where defaults were also higher than average. It also had a little government aid. To help life companies hold mortgages instead of foreclosing, New York regulators relaxed minimum mortgage equity rules, allowing the continuation of mortgages where depressed market prices brought the property's assessed value below that required by law. More aid had come with the passage of the Home Owners Loan Act of 1933, which had spurred Guardian to go even further than heretofore to have foreclosure proceedings delayed so as to give the owners an opportunity if possible to refinance. Guardian's stated policy was that foreclosure was not resorted to until it appeared that every effort by the owner and the company to remove the defaults would be unavailing.[59]

In early 1937, Guardian began to rebuild its tattered mortgage correspondent network, granting major producer George W. Warnecke Company exclusive rights to originate mortgages for Guardian in Westchester County. Unfortunately, Warnecke broke his promise to offer loans to Guardian first, forcing the company to turn to another, less effective correspondent. Due to the difficulty of securing acceptable new mortgage loans, Guardian did not close as many new mortgage loans in 1937 as it desired. To attract more loans, it began to pay part of the closing costs in Westchester County, Long Island, and New Jersey. Later, it loosened its requirements on weaker FHA loans in order to accommodate builders, selling off the weaker mortgages to brokers. Beginning in 1939, the company expanded its network of mortgage correspondents to include cities such as Buffalo, New York; Cincinnati, Ohio; Denver, Colorado; Houston, Texas; Philadelphia, Pennsylvania; St. Louis, Missouri; Seattle, Washington; Syracuse, New York; and Toledo, Ohio.[60]

Problems with correspondents did not go away, however. In 1940, Guardian had to replace a Jacksonville, Florida, agent when it learned that, contrary to policy, it was servicing properties through subagents. Life insurance companies faced the classic "make or buy" decision. Other life companies solved their agency problems by replacing their correspondents with employee-run branches. Guardian felt its correspondent system, with all its problems, was more cost effective. By 1945, the company had correspondents in twenty-eight cities nationwide. Two years later, the number had grown to forty-four.[61]

In 1939, the nation was recovering from its second major downturn of the Great Depression, and though war raged in Europe and Asia, it seemed remote. Major economic variables were looking up. Housing starts, for instance, were stronger than they had been since the 1920s.

Guardian shared in the general optimism, at least cautiously. It loosened its mortgage restrictions, agreeing to large "blanket" construction loans in New Jersey and Southeastern Pennsylvania, subject to *unusually* careful checkups on builders' credit, construction, closings by the company's counsel, and other safeguards. Housing starts remained strong until late 1941 when the Japanese bombed Pearl Harbor. Thereafter, the war effort diverted resources away from home construction and into war industries. Guardian responded by shifting its investment emphasis into government bonds and mortgages in defense areas, mainly for residential purposes. [62]

The business property market remained dicey, in Guardian's view. The company's reluctance to reenter the business mortgage market stemmed from too many bad experiences with that class of loans. One of the more bizarre but long-remembered experiences in that regard involved the Pickwick Theatre in Greenwich, Connecticut. Guardian lent the owner of the stage performance facility $350,000 in 1929. The owner then leased the property to a company that wanted to convert the theater for motion pictures. The business flopped because the tenants were unable to obtain first-run pictures to be run concurrently with competing theaters in nearby Stamford and Port Chester. The tenants managed to interest the federal government in prosecuting a suit against Hollywood film companies, who were both film producers and distributors, in what would converge with a landmark antitrust action. In 1939, the tenants induced the theater's owner and Guardian to make large rent concessions by threatening bankruptcy and offering to pay much larger rents from their anticipated legal winnings. The tenants indeed won on the merits of the case but could prove no damages, the film producers arguing that Greenwich was not a lucrative movie town. The tenants appealed, but then settled out of court for $165,000, net of attorney's fees. The mortgage and arrears amounted to $211,000. Guardian approved the settlement, foreclosed, and cut its losses. [63]

Guardian did make exceptions to its mortgage preferences on occasion. In 1941, it approved an application of Sands Hotel Incorporated, parent company of the pioneering Las Vegas casino. The company's high operating profit and heavy amortization schedule made it a very attractive investment. (It is not known if the Finance Committee appreciated the pedigree of the Sands's true owners, the elite of organized crime.) Still, the company remained wary enough to reject the University of Miami's request for a mortgage on new construction. The buildings it sought to erect were deemed too specialized in purpose, not readily saleable should default occur.[64]

During World War II, commercial mortgage loans were one of the few areas where decent investment earnings could be had. Sizable commercial loans, however, had to be screened carefully. In 1943, the Finance Committee tentatively approved a $400,000 mortgage loan, to be shared with the Society for Savings of Cleveland, on J. R. Sharp's oil fields in east and west Texas. The deal fell through, however, when a representative of the Investment Department visiting Dallas discovered negative information about the borrower. Safe new investments proved hard to find anywhere, and Guardian wound up settling for returns so low that it was forced to cut dividends by 1943.[65]

The mortgage field rebounded after the war, but other forms of investment proved even relatively more attractive as the years rolled on. Today, mortgages represent less than 10 percent of Guardian's investments.

Bonds

From 1868 to the Roaring Twenties, Guardian invested between a quarter and a third of its assets in bonds, debt obligations of governments and corporations. The company invested in Treasuries, some municipals, and the obligations of corporations, especially railroads and utilities. To a much lesser degree did the company invest in corporate equities, which in the pre–World War II era were regarded as a highly speculative class of securities and were sometimes illegal for life insurers to own.

In the first half-century or so of its business, Guardian learned of new corporate bond issues the way most everyone did, through printed circulars. Such circulars typically listed the size of the issue, the coupon rate and place of payment, and the names of the underwriters. They also usually presented a brief overview of the issuer's history, its proposed uses of the funds, and basic financial information like dividends, surplus, gross earnings, net earnings, and return on equity. Government issues were also advertised via printed circulars. In 1870, for example, George Sistare sent Guardian a printed circular urging it to purchase "New York City 7s."[66]

For smaller issues investment bankers sometimes sent handwritten circulars, probably to persuade the recipient that he had received private information. In 1888, for instance, William T. Meredith wrote Hugo Wesendonck a letter urging Guardian to purchase the bonds of the North

Hudson County Railway of New Jersey. "J. H. Bonn, the President, is an old citizen of Hoboken, wealthy and highly respected," Meredith confided, adding that Bonn "is a large stockholder and his sole business is the management of the Road."[67]

Of course Guardian could not completely trust the issuer or its bankers, so it sought additional information about bond investment opportunities through credit agencies like R. G. Dun and Company, Moody's, and an informal network of brokers and bankers. This network was crucial, because, as distinct from its mortgage and real estate investments, Guardian's bond investment opportunities were necessarily nationwide, even international. Thus when the company studied the value of the real estate security backing the Pacific Railroad Company's real estate 8 percent bonds, it relied on the judgment of St. Louis bankers Matthews and Whitaker through its investment banker-broker, Vermilye and Company (predecessor to the modern Warburg Dillon Read). The bankers deemed the bonds "absolutely good" because the real estate backing it was seen as indispensable to the railroad. Similarly, Spencer Trask and Company of New York endorsed an issue of 5 percent gold bonds of the Chicago, St. Louis, and Paducah Railway Company. "We have personal knowledge of all the facts in reference to this Company and the new Road," the bankers informed Guardian, "and unhesitatingly recommend the Bonds as an investment of exceptional merit and security."[68]

Far more intricate scrutiny was required of equity investments, which never constituted much of the company's investment portfolio during the time period in question. Guardian owned very few common, or even preferred, stocks. The industry as a whole was averse to equities because their prices were too volatile. Moreover, equity holders were the last in line to collect should a company fail. Regulation played a role, too. Before the passage of the so-called Armstrong laws in 1906 and 1907, Prussian regulators forbade Guardian to own equities. After Armstrong, insurance companies doing business in New York were no longer permitted to invest in or loan upon any shares of stock of any business corporation. Life companies were likewise forbidden to invest in corporate bonds if the bonds were largely secured by collateral consisting of shares of stock. The Armstrong laws also forbade a number of other practices, including underwriting new securities issues. The legislation allowed insurers twenty years to dispose of equities that they already owned, but the stipulations had little effect on the staid investment practices of Guardian, which had generally eschewed equity investment and call loans since its founding.[69]

Hence bonds were the order of the day, and the company's investment specialists kept a keen eye out for opportunities in the secondary as well as the primary bond markets. In July 1913, for instance, Guardian sold $120,000 of low-yield railroad bonds due in 1915 to finance the purchase of $135,000 of Chicago, Rock Island, and Pacific Railway Company Equipment Trust gold bonds due in 1922. With those two transactions, the company essentially exchanged short-term bonds yielding less than 4.5 percent for a security of undoubted merit netting over 5.5 percent for nine years. It executed equally successful maneuvers on several other occasions.[70]

The firm's international scope greatly complicated its investment portfolio. Most foreign nations required Guardian to deposit bonds to serve as a reserve in support of the company's contractual liabilities. It was not uncommon for a government to insist that its own bonds make up a significant portion of such deposits, which moved Guardian into questionable holdings that it would never tolerate at home. For instance, Mexico, in the midst of its revolution, demanded that the company purchase several different issues of its bonds, most of which later defaulted. In 1918, the company tried to withdraw its deposits from a Mexican bank that managed to get itself placed on the Enemy Trading List. The transaction, however, turned into an ordeal that generated scores of letters and dragged on for months. Similarly, before America's entry into the First World War, Germany enticed Guardian to invest in German war loans.[71]

As a matter of course, Guardian's home office had to make remittances to its foreign branches. Those remittances, which were sometimes heavy, exposed the firm to exchange rate risk. Moreover, when unexpected, the remittances interfered with the firm's investment strategies. In 1913, for example, the home office, as usual thin on cash, obtained a bank loan and sold bonds in order to finance an emergency remittance of 1 million marks to the Berlin office. It replaced those bonds, at a higher price, in February 1914. Likewise, the home office sometimes received remittances from overseas branches. When unexpected, such remittances could not easily find productive investment outlets, and exchange risk was also a problem. In 1914, Guardian's Mexican agent inflicted a blow to the company by purchasing exchange on New York at the prohibitive exchange rates then prevailing.[72]

Between the onset of World War I and the end of World War II, the economy underwent massive structural changes, and one of the many victims was the railroad industry. Guardian loved railroad bonds and, when allowed, even their preferred stock. When the railroad industry began its slow derailment in the early twentieth century, Guardian adjusted to the higher default risk by switching, beginning in earnest in 1915, to equipment trust obligations secured on rolling stock because issues of that kind invariably came through receivership or reorganization unscathed. Guardian would follow other life insurers, particularly NYLIC, gradually away from railroads and into utilities and industrials. Utilities and industrials were attractive on account of their safety and relatively high-interest yield but would not be as readily marketable as railroad bonds until after the Depression. Railroad securities continued to compose a significant portion of the company's bond portfolio for the next twenty years.[73]

When the outbreak of war in Europe in August 1914 sent European and American financial markets reeling, policyholders began to make heavy demands upon the company's funds through policy loans. Guardian responded by arranging $400,000 worth of bank loans, by calling some $600,000 of mortgages, by raising the interest rate 0.5 percent on almost $350,000 more, and by selling $300,000 worth of bonds. To aid the beleaguered industry, the New York Insurance Department allowed life insurers to value their securities, the ones that had to be marked-to-market, at their prices on 30 June 1914. That date was chosen because it was just before war-induced panic drove interest rates up and bond prices down. If Guardian needed such assistance it was for appearances only; by the end of February 1915 the company salivated at the low prices of U.S. railroad securities on the European exchanges, notably the Amsterdam, Berlin, and London exchanges, and bought. In 1920, it pounced on $100,000 Southern Pacific Railroad bonds yielding a whopping 8 percent, which the company's officers described as "an unusual opportunity, both as regards undoubted security and high yield."[74]

As Guardian's investment specialists became more alert to such transient profit opportunities in the capital markets, the Finance Committee began to loosen its reins on investment decisions. By 1921, it was clear that the committee was delegating more authority to buy and sell securities within parameters set by the committee, lest sudden bargains vanish before more ponderous decisions could be made. Rules, or to be more precise, guidelines, replaced day-to-day control, and to good effect.

To see how this worked, consider what happened in 1921 when the Finance Committee authorized investment officers to purchase general obligation municipal bonds issued by states or subdivisions where

Guardian did considerable business. The bonds had to be underwritten by a leading bond house, be highly rated by Moody's, and have maturities greater than twenty years. If issued by a state, the bonds had to yield between 5.4 and 5.9 percent per year because a lower yield was insufficiently remunerative while a higher yield signaled that the issue was too risky. Similarly, bonds issued by a city or county had to yield between 5.6 and 6.1 percent per annum. Moreover, the issuer's population had to exceed fifty thousand inhabitants. Finally, the Finance Committee further instructed, the issuer should not have a debt greater than 10 percent of its assessed valuation and should not be of mushroom growth nor dependent upon a single industry. Five years later, in contrast, the Finance Committee instructed the company's investment officers to sell municipals that did not offer significant tax benefits and to reinvest the proceeds in mortgages. Municipals became attractive again in the summer of 1933, so the Finance Committee promptly established new criteria for their purchase.[75]

There is evidence that by World War I, Guardian was taking advantage of persistent, structural inefficiencies in the capital markets. For example, the company's investment officers exploited what would later be called "the January Effect." In December 1915, as a result of a discussion among the executive officers, the Finance Committee resolved to purchase bonds shortly after the end of the year rather than later in January or February "inasmuch as at that time, by reason of the greater demand for investments owing to the re-investment of the January interest, bond prices were usually higher than toward the end of the year." Guardian did not buy the bonds low simply to resell them a month later but rather bought the bonds low so that it would not have to pay a higher price for them in late January and February.[76]

Before purchasing any issue, Guardian carefully weighed its default risk, liquidity or marketability, and after-tax return. For example, to reduce its exposure to South Carolina's premium tax in 1918, the rate of which was predicated on the level of Guardian's investment in South Carolina securities, Guardian purchased Greenville, South Carolina, 5 percent water bonds.[77]

During the late 1920s and early 1930s, bonds fell precipitously as a portion of company assets. By 1934, Guardian was playing the yield curve, buying short-term securities whose yields were much higher than long-term obligations. This state of affairs frustrated Carl Heye, who lamented the investment situation, noting "that it had become extremely difficult to make suitable [long-term] investments." He reiterated that point in 1936, when Guardian collected about $1 million per month in premiums, and could not readily invest much of it profitably in desirable instruments.[78]

Desperate for safe investment outlets, Guardian gobbled up government bonds during the Depression. At the end of 1934, the company was so top-heavy with government debt that obligations of the federal, state, and local governments accounted for about 59 percent of its bond investments, while railroads composed 33 percent of its bond portfolio and public utilities, most of the balance. Governments became such a significant part of the company's bond allocation for two reasons. Few corporations desired to take on additional debts during the business downturn, and many previously issued corporate bonds had gone into default. Guardian's investment officers were faced with spending more time, energy, and money on "bond protective committees" than the company could rightly afford. To minimize those expenses, they often simply unloaded troubled issues before they dropped too much in price. Not that they bent to every fearful scenario; when a local municipal bond house advised it in 1932 to unload $50,000 worth of North Dakota bonds because the Socialist Party of North Dakota threatened to place a five-year moratorium on all debts, the company demurred, confident that the state would honor its obligations. When default on the bonds loomed again in 1935, Guardian sublimated the urge to sell, noting that since the virtuous citizens of North Dakota owned the vast bulk of the issue, default would be unlikely.[79]

After bottoming out at 8 percent in 1932, the importance of bonds in Guardian's overall asset portfolio swelled to almost 37 percent in 1940. In the late 1930s, Guardian was busy purchasing government securities to help finance economic reconstruction, and later, with the onset of war, to aid in the military effort. Patriotism did not prove profitable, however. The Federal Reserve System pegged interest rates on Treasury bonds at extremely low levels by exchanging its notes for Treasuries in the open market whenever Treasury prices faltered. Insurance companies, including Guardian, invested heavily in low-yielding Treasuries. They did so as much out of necessity as patriotism. Restrictions against new home construction reduced demand for mortgages and numerous government contracts and advances limited corporate borrowing. Yet premiums continued to pour in. As a result, by war's end, bonds, mostly government bonds, swelled to over 60 percent of Guardian's total assets, while mortgages sagged to just over 25 percent. After the war, bond investment levels remained high, contesting with and then finally exceeding mortgages for the top asset class.[80]

Policy Loans and Other Assets

Of the remaining classes of assets held by Guardian over time, policy loans were the largest. Policy loans are good for policyholders but not usually relished by life insurers because the level of policy loans is not at their discretion. Because they are usually for small sums, policy loans are relatively expensive to make and service, and often lead to lapses and surrenders. Their volume tends to increase at unpropitious times, during business recessions when surrenders are already draining insurers' cash balances, and during inflationary or other periods when market yields exceed the contractual rate of policy loans, which is usually 5 or 6 percent per annum. As George Conklin once explained it, "increased policy loans place a handicap on investment results" because they siphon off funds that might be invested at higher rates. Policy loans, which crested in 1932–33 at slightly over 23 percent of total assets, later decreased in importance, bottoming out at around 5 percent of total assets, the level that prevailed from 1946 until 1956.[81]

Other assets included a variety of accounts receivable, like advances to agents, deferred premiums, assets denominated in foreign currencies, and equipment leases. Such assets exceeded 20 percent of the company's total in its earliest days, but have not since exceeded 10 percent.

Investment Watershed: The Postwar Environment

At the end of World War II, the economy embarked on a long, seldom interrupted boom. Guardian rode the crest of the wave along with the industry overall. Prosperity loved company. The supply of new mortgages and corporate debt instruments began to swell again, borne aloft by pent-up demand and a new wave of corporate confidence after years of deprivation. Life insurance companies took advantage of the upsurge by channeling current income flows into higher-yielding private debts, divesting themselves of government bonds, which had swelled to over 50 percent of the total assets of some companies. The resulting scramble into private investments served to keep rates low and competition keen.[82]

New government mortgage guarantees buoyed the mortgage market. Guardian sought to make arrangements for early activity under the Serviceman's Readjustment Act of 1944. "Early activity seems to be particularly advantageous not only for the purpose of making the best arrangements for the origination of such loans," it was thought, "but also because such loans made on existing housing should result in more conservative loans and at lower premiums than will be possible later." In 1946 Guardian launched its special mortgage policy, designed to fit exactly the pattern of FHA or Veterans Administration insured mortgages, and by the summer of 1947, 13 percent of Guardian's mortgage portfolio was partially guaranteed by the Veterans Administration. When Guardian finally expanded into farm mortgages, in 1950, it was on the strength of government guarantees. By 1966, over half of the company's mortgages had government guarantees.[83]

Even before the war had ended, Guardian began to feel competitive pressures in the mortgage market, particularly in Florida, where real estate values were soaring. Moreover, its mortgage investments, though much more widely spread than in the pre–World War I era, were still largely confined to New York, New Jersey, Pennsylvania, Ohio, and Illinois. Guardian responded to both of those pressures by continuing to sign up mortgage correspondents in places like Dallas, Texas; Fort Lauderdale, Florida; Memphis, Tennessee; Minneapolis, Minnesota; New Haven, Connecticut; New Orleans, Louisiana; Oakland, California; Oklahoma City, Oklahoma; and Portland, Oregon. Competition forced more decentralization in asset management. In 1946, the board of directors formed a Real Estate Committee, which then granted Guardian's mortgage department the authority to approve mortgages, up to certain amounts, that met the committee's criteria. This arrangement, much as the delegation of authority in the securities field had done after the previous war, enabled managers to approve mortgage applications much more quickly. The new system, at first a temporary measure, proved so effective that by the end of the decade it became accepted practice.[84]

Competitive pressures also led Guardian to drop the requirement of earthquake insurance on California mortgages, to issue loan commitments en masse, to overhaul its mortgage insurance requirements, and—when necessary to maintain a steady stream of business for itself and its correspondents—to cut interest rates on guaranteed mortgages.[85]

Although loan commitments were not unknown to Guardian before World War II, they took on heightened importance in the new era. The length of commitment ranged from a few weeks up to one year. About six months was the most common lag between promise and payment on mortgage commitments, while the average commitment on private placements was closer to ten months. When capital markets were relatively tight, Guardian and other lenders could extract a fee, from 0.5 to 2 percent of the principal, for the commitment. When competition between lenders was strong, many dropped the fees and were content simply to secure an outlet for their funds.[86]

Low interest rates and high influxes of premiums continued to be a problem for Guardian and other insurers in the early postwar years. Interest rates had been relatively high during the early years of the Depression, but had sagged during the New Deal and remained low through the entire war and early postwar period. The net yield for all U.S. life insurance companies in 1949 was a mere 3.04 percent, just slightly higher than the all-time low of 2.88 percent set in 1947. Guardian's net return in 1949 was 3.2 percent, higher than the industry average, partly because of a successful jaunt into preferred stocks, common stock-bond hybrid securities. The company therefore joined five other life insurers to lobby the New York State legislature for the right to invest in common stocks, an asset class that had been rendered largely inaccessible to life insurers by tradition and law. Bolstered by purchases of common stocks by other conservative institutional investors and an impressive array of academic papers calling for deregulation of life insurance equity investment, the companies argued that "if the country is to move ahead economically on an even keel the volume of equity financing must keep pace with the creation of debt." The companies also expressed the need to "realize a better rate of return on its investments" so that they could offer policyholders "insurance protection at the lowest possible cost." The companies also feared competition from abroad. Canadian life insurers could legally invest up to 15 percent of their assets in common stocks and British insurers faced no restrictions at all.[87]

The legislators were impressed. In 1951, they began to allow life insurers to invest a small percentage of their assets in the common shares of nonfinancial corporations. In 1957, the legislature would again liberalize the restrictions by allowing life companies to purchase common shares in banks and other life insurers. Guardian and most life insurance companies, however, continued to shy away from common stocks, largely because they thought them too volatile in terms of both market value and

income. The importance to the industry of common stocks would remain low until the late 1960s.[88]

It is important to remember that from the time of Guardian's founding until the mid-twentieth century, the economy of the United States
had experienced tremendous growth and massive structural transformation. Octogenarian American citizens had lived through scientific and engineering revolutions in electricity and electronics, in chemistry and
metallurgy, and in automotive and air travel. All this occurred in the context of large and profound demographic changes. Government, once
small, had become large in a highly regulated, albeit largely free economy.
Growth and change provided opportunities for life insurers, but the challenges that confronted them in their investment strategies, particularly in
the first half of the twentieth century, were due less to the economy's
structural changes than to the trials and travails of war, boom, depression, and more war.

Through it all, as noted at the outset, Guardian's investments fared relatively well. And during the period for which we have reliable compara-
tive data, Guardian's investments performed at or above the industry average. Perhaps what is most impressive about Guardian's historical performance is how it fared during the Great Depression. Like the vintner
who can make decent wines in bad years, Guardian generally outperformed its industry in the hardest of times.

Also during the course of the Depression, Guardian experienced a
larger improvement in its ratio of investment funds to total disbursements than all but two major life insurance companies. As table 12-1
demonstrates, in 1932 and 1933 Guardian's ratio was less favorable than
the average and median major life company, but by 1938, its ratio had improved considerably, far outstripping the improvements made by the average and median major company.

Precisely how Guardian managed to succeed over the long haul is
clearly reflected in the record. In response to changing circumstances, the
company's investment officers and Finance Committee members were always willing to improve their investing habits, to change their preferences, and to alter the mix of the company's assets. They took advantage
of new market opportunities and market imperfections but always with
an eye to the risks involved. The object was not to *maximize,* but to *opti-
mize* returns consistent with the safety of the policyholder's claims. The
company's senior managers seem rarely to have challenged the hands
they were dealt by government regulators, perhaps because they did not

TABLE 12-1
Ratio of Investment Funds to Total Disbursements at Selected Companies, 1932–38

Company/Year	1932	1933	1938
Metropolitan	51.4	47.0	108.6
Prudential	41.2	57.2	91.0
New York Life	37.0	48.9	120.5
Equitable	45.2	68.8	249.7
Mutual of New York	25.6	34.2	107.3
Northwestern Mutual	36.1	27.9	107.6
Travelers	39.5	44.3	96.8
John Hancock	36.2	48.1	105.2
Penn Mutual	57.5	41.1	134.7
Mutual Benefit	38.5	26.1	98.7
Massachusetts Mutual	37.9	46.0	105.7
Aetna	30.4	32.3	174.2
New England Mutual	37.5	61.1	134.3
Union Central	10.1	10.0	109.0
Provident Mutual	40.4	55.5	136.9
Connecticut Mutual	58.1	64.1	126.4
Connecticut General	48.2	54.5	155.1
Phoenix Mutual	43.2	53.9	135.8
National Life (Vt.)	65.5	170.5	111.7
State Mutual	38.6	40.9	115.2
Equitable Life (Iowa)	40.4	65.8	238.5
Western & Southern	61.1	83.3	71.6
Guardian Life	**34.0**	**33.3**	**162.8**
Average	41.5	52.8	130.3
Median	39.5	48.1	115.2

Source: Walter, *Investment Process*, 47. Permission to reproduce granted by Harvard Business School Press.

need to; likewise, they were content to capitalize on regulatory protections.

In other words, from a strategic standpoint, they were prudent and savvy investors, careful yet adaptive. There were important organizational changes, too. As the company, and hence its portfolio, grew, and as competitive pressures increased, the company's directors learned to delegate investment authority to specialists. In the latter half of the twentieth century, the investment specialty would become even more sharply defined within life insurance companies, more professional and more rigorous. Guardian would lead that transformation and continue to outperform the industry.

13

Flexibility and Quality

George Conklin's Legacy

After World War II, several individuals emerged as champions or drivers of Guardian's investment history. The three most important were the scholarly economist George Taylor Conklin, the popular "doomsday" forecaster Ashby Bladen, and Wall Street investment banker Frank Jones. Conklin's role was the longest, and seminal. His fingerprints are all over the company's investment policies and strategies from the 1940s into the early 1990s.

Conklin, with the help of board members like commercial banker Jim Jackson and financial consultant Darragh Park, professionalized the company's investment staff in the postwar era, and pushed Guardian's historically robust investment performance even further above the pack in an increasingly competitive environment. He did so by generally adhering to the time-honored Guardian policy of maintaining low cash balances. Guardian's asset allocation strategies continued to evolve, however, as Conklin innovated in private placement and loan commitment techniques. In the process, he readjusted the company's attitude toward credit and market risk.[1]

Conklin was born into an old Long Island family in 1914. He took a bachelors degree and a masters degree from Dartmouth. His first professional job was with his cousin's boutique brokerage. He did not find serving the firm's clientele, mostly widows who would call every day to check up on their stocks, to be to his tastes, so he quickly jumped ship, joining Guardian's Investment Department in 1939. He advanced to assistant to James McLain, the company's president, on 1 January 1944 but soon thereafter left for a twenty-two month stint in the service, returning to the home office in February 1946 as assistant to the president and director of research. Conklin, who earned a Ph.D. in finance from Columbia and a

Ph.D. in economics from New York University, later taught as an adjunct at New York University, where he made important contacts.

Guardian's senior managers saw much promise in this "brilliant" young investment scholar, making him second vice president on 1 January 1949, making him financial vice president on 1 October 1953, and bringing him on to the company's board as a director in 1957. He became an executive vice president in 1964, at age forty-eight, and president on 1 January 1969, and finally capped his service as board chairman, 1977–80. He stepped down from the chairmanship in 1980 but continued to serve at least two days a week as a board director and chairman of the Finance Committee from 1980 to 1984. Thereafter, he served as consulting director (1984–85), as chairman of the Auditing Committee (1987–89), and in various other capacities until the end of 1995. He also served as a director, trustee, or member of a significant number of other organizations, including Central Savings Bank, TIAA, the American Finance Association, the American Stock Exchange, and the Business Economists Council.[2]

The young Conklin was a studious, serious man, "academic" in dress, style, and temperament and yet at times prone to mischief. While such qualities of mind are more highly regarded in finance than in other business realms, Conklin's formal demeanor appeared "a bit stuffy" to some of his colleagues at NYU, and invited some teasing from his business colleagues; the hard-bitten company president Dan Lyons liked to call him "schoolboy." Conklin did not always take it well, but he was deeply respected and given a wide berth by his superiors. As he grew older, age increasingly suited his mien, and he became revered as "one of the heroes of the Guardian." Even the field force was in awe of his "very keen insight on investments and interest rates," proclaiming his 1966 speech on the subject "the finest discourse they had ever heard." During the course of his career, his widely followed investment prognostications spread the theretofore little-known name of Guardian in financial circles.[3]

One of Conklin's more important forecasts came in January 1955, when the *Wall Street Journal* summarized an address he made to the National Association of Home Builders in which he warned that credit was likely to tighten in the coming months. A surge in new housing starts increased the demand for loanable funds while the supply of loanable funds was likely to stay flat, Conklin reasoned. "The Federal Reserve will also act to tighten the market," Conklin predicted, because "the Government doesn't want an all-out boom now and then a decline in 1956 just before the elections." Conklin was right; by early February moderate credit rationing was taking place and mortgage rates were poised to increase. By the end of March, lenders obtained higher down payments, shorter re-payment periods, and higher rates on conventional mortgages. His fame—outside of the company—was made. Insiders knew that his view of the national economic picture had been correct since 1947.[4]

A career-long student of life insurance investment strategies, Conklin served on the advisory boards of scholarly studies of interest rates with the likes of Milton Friedman, Raymond Goldsmith, W. Braddock Hick-man, and Sidney Homer. He also read and made valuable comments on the manuscript version of James Walter's *Investment Process as Character-ized by Leading Life Insurance Companies*. In his own right, he authored several important pieces on the subject, including a brilliant historical analysis and a chapter in an important textbook where he explained how life insurers engage in an "unremitting search for the highest possible rate of return at an acceptable level of risk."[5]

Precisely what constituted an acceptable level of risk was, of course, a matter of some debate. A large life insurer like Guardian could purchase individual securities that were somewhat risky because it could spread its assets over a great many borrowers. As Conklin realized, even if losses clustered, the company's surplus, which was substantial, could be used to buffer them. Finally, Conklin understood that even the best investment strategy could turn into a disaster if it were not properly executed. In other words, investors had to undertake careful due diligence, conduct intelligent analyses of individual securities, and then choose the best among them. Guardian of course suffered through its share of defaults, but its overall experience was more favorable than at other companies with comparatively high yields on invested assets. Guardian learned to rely relatively less on market cues, and more on its own internal credit as-sessment capabilities, and in the process did a superb job of maximizing returns at the level of risk that it chose to assume.[6]

Forging Greatness: Guardian's Emphasis on Private Placements and Credit Analysis

Mortgages remained an important part of Guardian's portfolio during the 1950s, as higher interest rates and lower closing and servicing costs drove average net yields on urban mortgages from 3.64 percent in 1952 to 4.84 percent a decade later. Tighter conditions in the mortgage market were apparent by March 1955, when Conklin announced that Guardian already had acquired enough mortgage commitments to last nine months. "We can afford to be more selective in the kinds of loans we want," he noted. Guardian, like other life insurers, used the excess demand for mortgage loans to insist on stricter terms, including higher rates, larger down payments, and shorter terms. Thirty-year mortgages with no down payment increasingly gave way to twenty-five-year deals with 5 to 10 percent down.[7]

Guardian was much aided in its real estate and mortgage decision making by director William A. Clarke, a Delaware Valley Quaker and graduate of Swarthmore College who joined the Guardian's board in 1949. Clarke, long a mortgage correspondent of the Guardian for the Philadelphia region, was a mortgage consultant to the Federal Reserve System and was influential in shaping the philosophy of mortgage lending and of setting Federal Housing Authority policy in the 1950s. Despite his other obligations, Clarke was very attentive to the affairs of the company and a constant attendant at board meetings.[8]

In June 1958, Guardian entered into a warehousing agreement to help it manage its mortgage loan commitments. Under the arrangement, a commercial bank initially purchased mortgages from Guardian's correspondents. Guardian then had up to one year to purchase the loan from the bank. The warehousing arrangement enabled the company to close loans on schedule, regardless of its cash position, and it worked so well that in 1962 it was extended to securities, though extensive use of the securities warehousing agreement did not take place until the early 1970s.[9]

The warehousing agreements made it possible for Guardian to hew to its traditional principle of remaining as fully invested as possible. It kept its transaction balances extremely low, backing them with "secondary reserves" in the form of T-bills, corporate commercial paper, and negotiable certificates of deposit. Most postwar mortgages were amortized monthly, an innovation introduced by Acacia in 1933 but first suggested as early as 1919. Monthly amortization provided Guardian with a predictable monthly inflow of cash as opposed to the semiannual mortgage payments of the past. The percentage of assets held as cash shrank from an average of just over 1 percent immediately after the war to well under 0.5 percent by the late 1960s. Cash grew so thin that the general agents were alarmed until Conklin assuaged their fears by reminding them that he well knew what he was doing.[10]

Guardian became somewhat more disposed in the postwar era to bor-row during normal money market conditions. For example, in 1958, with a new federal tax bill pending that would greatly increase Guardian's tax exposure, Conklin suggested that Guardian borrow to fund the acquisi-tion of tax-exempt municipals. He reasoned that bond prices were low enough to justify the borrowing strategy regardless of the outcome of the tax bill. After the tax situation eventually sorted itself out, prices of "munis" rose sufficiently to induce Guardian to sell them and reinvest the proceeds in higher-yielding securities. Guardian also tried to essentially borrow from policyholders by offering to credit them 4 percent com-pound interest on premiums paid in advance.[11]

Thanks to higher net yields, a refurbished correspondent system, warehousing agreements, and government mortgage guarantees, the im-portance of mortgages in Guardian's investment portfolio again grew, from around 26 percent of total assets in 1946 to around 46 percent a decade later. From 1956 until 1965, mortgages accounted for between 40 and just under 50 percent of the company's total assets. Mortgage corre-spondents, which numbered about two score in 1960, serviced over 90 percent of the company's mortgages. In the postwar period, mortgage loans on single-family dwellings accounted for over 90 percent of all of Guardian's mortgages by number and over 80 percent by dollar value.[12]

Conversely, the importance of bonds decreased after the war from 62 percent of total assets in 1946 to just under 42 percent in 1956, a level, plus or minus 4 percent, maintained until 1965. The key change, though, was in the composition of the bond category. After the war, Guardian sold its government bonds, Treasuries as well as municipals, in favor of corporate bonds, especially industrial issues. Tax reforms underlay those changes. Increased federal income taxes drew individual investors to the tax-ex-empt municipal bond market, making those securities too expensive for institutional investors, like life companies, that did not benefit as much from the exemption. Meanwhile, new corporate tax laws made it cheaper for corporations to issue debt than equity. Industrial firms therefore greatly increased their bonded debt, which attracted insurance compa-nies like Winnie the Pooh to honey.[13]

Also in the early postwar period, Guardian began to enter into pur-chase-lease agreements. Within months of the end of the war, for in-stance, the company approved in principle investments in gasoline filling stations. One large deal involved some $1 million in filling station pur-chase-lease agreements with Sun Oil. Similarly, in early 1947, Guardian purchased the sales and service branches of Fruehauf Trailer Company, a manufacturer of tractor-trailers, then leased the properties back to Fruehauf. Equipment purchase-lease agreements became very popular with Guardian in the 1950s. In 1955, for example, it purchased and leased some $2 million of motor vehicles. Such arrangements were lucrative, long one of the highest-yielding items in Guardian's investment portfolio.[14]

Many of Guardian's postwar loans to corporations were so-called direct placements or private placements, a field unknown to it as late as 1939. Under a direct or private placement arrangement, the issuer (borrower) sold its bonds directly to the company, not to the open market or via an investment banker or other intermediary. Issuers liked private placements because such deals reduced the amount of regulatory oversight by the SEC; because they were truly "private" and hence did not force the borrower to provide the entire market, including competitors, with detailed information about the firm's operations; and because they greatly reduced transaction costs, including the length of time needed to consummate the deal. Lenders such as Guardian liked private placements because they could negotiate contract terms, including bond maturity, size of issue, and restrictive covenants, to suit their needs. Placements also allowed borrowers and lenders to forge long-term relationships, with resulting expense savings for both parties.[15]

Private placements originated sometime before 1900 but constituted only about 10 percent of corporate bond sales until passage of the Securities Act of 1933 increased federal oversight of publicly offered corporate bond issues and the travails of the Depression caused lenders to screen potential borrowers more carefully. After the revival of the nation's capital markets and the exodus of the individual investor from the corporate bond market, private placements quickly grew in importance until by the late 1940s they constituted about half of all corporate bond offerings. Guardian, which first began to investigate private placements in 1940, was well positioned to take advantage of the shift because Conklin made himself an expert on the subject. For decades, Guardian was pretty high up on the private placement leaders list.[16]

From screening loan applications to monitoring existing loans to cleaning up the few defaults that occurred, Guardian's credit analysts were top-notch. James Pirtle, who later headed up Guardian's investments, recalled that Conklin tended quickly to reject the vast bulk of applications. Those that made the first cut were then discussed in a weekly meeting, when more would be dropped. Then the in-depth screening work began. The process worked well; default rates on the company's mortgages and securities were extremely low in the postwar era. In 1964, delinquent mortgages represented less than 2.5 percent of its total mortgage portfolio, well below the industry average. Moreover, only three securities were in arrears. Although Guardian suffered through some periods with modestly elevated default rates, most of the time its president could report, as Conklin did in 1973, that "securities in arrears as to principal and interest are extremely low as a percentage of assets, as is the case likewise with the mortgage portfolio."[17]

Outside observers of that era regarded Guardian as having one of the best credit analysis procedures in the business. Although it kept one eye on what S&P and Moody analysts had to say, the company did not trust or rely upon outside sources. Instead, it delegated the credit review process to junior analysts. Moreover, the Finance Committee watched the analysts closely to ensure that information had been received and checked. Guardian analysts maintained a book of summary historical data, including times interest earned, trend, and the like, for each industry and periodically prepared summary statistics for intra-office circulation. In this way, the burden for oversight was spread efficiently, while a large number of personnel became expert at it.[18]

Up-front due diligence was particularly important in direct placements, but what happened afterward was even more important. Guardian took postinvestment monitoring especially seriously, forcing its corporate borrowers to adhere to the restrictive covenants that they had agreed to as conditions of their loans. In 1951, for example, Guardian called in its loan to the New York Merchandise Company because that firm, in anticipation of higher prices and scarcities, built up its inventories very substantially. Although the speculation proved quite profitable, it had resulted in a reduction in the year-end current ratio to about two-to-one compared with the 2.75 ratio required under the terms of the loan. The borrower did not have the cash to pay up, so it negotiated a new loan with Guardian at a rate of interest fifty basis points higher than the initial loan. About the same time, the San Antonio Drug Company also exceeded one of its restricted financial ratios, but it rectified the problem before Guardian had to take action.[19]

Selection of the right risks and close postloan monitoring were crucial components in the execution of Guardian's investment strategy. Minimizing losses when they occurred, however, was also important. In 1965, for instance, the Atlantic Acceptance Corporation blew up, forcing

Guardian executives to trek to Toronto to meet with other creditors and arrange an acquisition. In 1971, Guardian and two other creditors filed a petition of bankruptcy against Sheffield Watch Corporation, a deeply distressed manufacturer of low-priced fashion watches that owed Guardian $600,000. Guardian, which by this point probably wished that it had not allowed Sheffield to purchase a Guam watch manufacturer in 1969, and the other petitioners claimed that Sheffield, which had been in trouble since at least mid-1970, had made large payments to certain preferred creditors. Sheffield's trade creditors then requested that all creditors give the troubled concern a ninety-day moratorium to get its affairs in order. Guardian and the other bondholders agreed to a sixty-day moratorium to give Sheffield an opportunity to rehabilitate its financial affairs. Guardian continued to monitor the troubled firm for a number of years, and eventually the watchmaker made good on its obligations.[20]

Flexible Strategies and Personnel

Guardian, as always, remained alert to market inefficiencies. It took advantage of temporary market demand and consequent overpricing of certain securities by shorting them—selling them high and buying them back at a lower price later. It worked hard to find unusual situations that permitted it to invest wisely, safely, and with a good rate of return. Guardian was rather unusual in this respect. According to a study by industry analyst James E. Walter,

> The closest approximation to systematic search activity observed during the interviews [of insurance company investment officers conducted by the author] was the repeated attempt by one medium-sized company [Guardian] to uncover areas in which funds were temporarily in short supply before competition entered the picture. The chief financial officer of this company argued that small and medium-sized companies should take full advantage of their inherent flexibility.

Flexibility was key in the day-to-day markets but also in the implementation of longer-term investment strategies. Under Conklin, Guardian stood prepared not only to capitalize on short-lived market inefficiencies but also, when necessary, to change its entire investment emphasis to meet the exigencies of a rapidly evolving world.[21]

In 1958, Guardian exceeded a 4 percent pretax net rate of return, the first time that it had done so in twenty years. It accomplished that feat by sale of securities at a loss to invest at higher rates, a strategy that it continued to employ in 1959. The trend in after-tax net rate of return was flat, however, and though better than the industry average, Guardian's returns were not soaring as high above average as they had before the war. Guardian therefore reviewed its investment strategies in a November 1960 meeting. President McLain spoke first, reviewing the investment policy of the company from his own experience over the past forty years. Conklin followed with an outline of the general principles that guided company in its investment policies, followed by a review of the Guardian's investment portfolio, highlighted by slides showing the percentage of company participation in the several fields of investment open to it. The Finance Committee must have noticed that, compared to the rest of the industry, Guardian was extremely underweight in stocks, slightly underweight in bonds, slightly overweight in mortgages and real estate, and overweight in policy loans and other assets. In any event, such broad strategy meetings became common in the 1960s and 1970s as the company's investment policies, both short and long term, came increasingly under Conklin's sway. The increased strategic flexibility worked well; Guardian started to beat the industry average ever more handily.[22]

To implement flexible strategies, the company had to have personnel up to the task. Guardian's investment results remained strong as the years advanced, because its investment team was increasingly staffed with better-trained specialists. In 1960, most companies with assets of between $400 million and $1 billion employed fewer than ten nonclerical investment analysts. Guardian, which controlled about $517 million at the end of 1960, employed ten full-time professional investors. Moreover, its board, which included an unusually large number of commercial bankers, and one of its actuaries were very active in the investment area. More importantly, the people were of high caliber. By the early 1960s, Guardian truly had a distinctive orientation, a modern, scientific view of investment strategy. While juniors handled the specialized and routine tasks, Guardian's senior investment officers, three of whom, in addition to Conklin, held Ph.D.'s in economics, devoted a sizable fraction of their time to research projects designed to identify the basic risks and other strategic factors associated with specific investment categories. They researched and wrote major studies of public utilities, railroads, and revenue bonds, for example, while simultaneously diffusing major problems as they arose.[23]

Because of its strong internal research programs, Guardian could to some extent foresee and adapt to changing conditions. For example, what it considered an acceptable level of risk changed over time. By the early 1950s, Conklin clearly understood one of the main points of W. Braddock Hickman's book, *Volume of Corporate Bond Financing since 1900*, which showed that the market consistently underpriced lower-rated bonds. In other words, investors demanded risk premiums that were too high. Guardian capitalized on this knowledge by building up an outstanding staff of credit risk analysts who were able to help the company choose wisely from among second-tier offerings. In essence, Guardian was buying the equivalent of AAA debt at AA, A, or even BBB prices. Slowly, other companies caught on, bidding up the prices of lower-grade debt. By early 1967 risk premiums had become unattractively low, so Guardian, under Conklin's guidance, changed its overall investment policy from a relatively aggressive policy to a relatively conservative one. At the same time, it laid bare the fundamental attributes of its investment philosophy:

Flexibility—To keep flexibility to the maximum extent possible in directing our funds into the various alternative investment channels so that we may take advantage of the most attractive investment outlets at any given time.

Quality—To invest in mortgages and securities in the area where life insurance companies generally invest, where the speculative elements are judged not to be predominant, and where the yield advantage over the highest quality issues is judged to be adequate. To invest a moderate amount in fixed income securities where equity risks are present, provided adequate equity participation is obtained.

Market—To invest in mortgage and direct placements to the extent that the additional yield, and/or protective features, are judged to be adequate compared with the public market.

Term—To primarily invest in long term securities with maturities of 10 years or longer. To use short term securities where necessary together with the warehouse to even out our cash flow.

Commitment Policy—To commit forward to the extent necessary to keep our investment flow operational and to take advantage of unusual opportunities. Total commitments will not exceed a level which, taking into consideration the warehouse, will leave less than approximately a 25% margin for investment over the succeeding twelve month period.

Warehouse Policy—To utilize the warehouse to even out cash flow and to implement our commitment policy, reserving capacity related to near term commitments.

Reserves—To set aside the maximum permissible amount under the Mandatory Security Valuation Reserve, and to maintain a portion of surplus allocated as an investment reserve to the maximum extent consistent with our overall surplus objectives.[24]

Innovations in Common Stock Investment

Guardian's greatest claim to fame in investing circles is that it was one of a small number of companies, including TIAA-CREF, that led the modern life insurance industry's movement into common stock investments. As noted above, Guardian had pushed regulators to relax restrictions against common stock ownership as early as 1950. The company clearly understood the corporate governance implications of holding equity stakes in corporations. Since 1947, it had been the company's policy to exercise its voting rights in connection with stock holdings in every case, executing proxies to management for routine matters or courses of action not unfavorable to its interests. By 1960, the investment staff had conducted research to try to determine whether institutional investors could obtain above-average returns on common stocks and whether the expected returns were competitive with other investments. Guardian was still wary of common stocks, and was quite content to hold a small investment in common stocks after the stock market gyrations of 1962. The big step came in January 1967, when Guardian's investment officers, led by Conklin, urged the Finance Committee to approve a modest dollar averaging program of investment in common stocks of recognized standing. The committee approved investment of an aggregate of $750,000 per quarter in a number of blue chip corporations.[25]

Over the next few years, the Finance Committee modified the approved stock list by adding companies, removing companies, or changing maximum investment levels. Occasionally, the committee suspended new stock purchases or authorized sales. In July 1969, the committee approved a plan to begin investing more heavily in convertible bonds and convertible preferred shares, debt and hybrid securities that could be exchanged for common shares. The large drop in the equity indexes (including the Dow Industrial Average) that took place in 1969 due to inflation fears, rising interest rates, and a resulting business slowdown undoubtedly affected the decision. Guardian's common stock portfolio was still a small part of total assets, and its holdings were in better position than the general market, so it weathered the bear market of 1969–70—when NYSE stocks dropped 48 percent—reasonably well. (The Dow, the thirty most important NYSE stocks, did somewhat better, dropping from an intraday high of 974.92 on 14 May 1969 to an intraday low of 627.46 on 26 May 1970.) Still, the experience of "stagflation," the unusual simultaneous appearance of high inflation and business recession, did not augur well for the future.[26]

Nevertheless, stock investment strategies became a major interest of the Finance Committee and Guardian's investment officers, who were clearly bullish on the long-run prospects of common stock investments. Moreover, as a mutual company Guardian did not have to worry about its own stock price. That allowed it to take a long-term view of the stock market, and that view was a very reassuring one. In one memorable meeting, Conklin spoke on the background of general economic, business, and stock market statistics, delineating the probable range of returns on common stock investment in the future. He pointed out that while near-term results in common stocks are highly unpredictable, long-term buy and hold strategies were, if historical patterns held up, likely to be quite lucrative. Other officers followed, introducing the committee to Burton Malkiel's exposition on the Efficient Markets Hypothesis and its implications for the company's investment policy, which included avoidance of what Bladen called "high price/earnings ratio glamour stocks."[27]

By the end of 1973, Guardian had reached its statutory limit of common stocks, a limit that it almost continually bumped up against when the equities markets were strong. By 1977, it was buying $15 million of common stocks each quarter. Thanks to such a high level of purchases, the importance of stocks, common and preferred, in Guardian's investment portfolio trended strongly upward from less than 1 percent of total assets in 1966 to almost 15 percent in 1982. Stock investment levels then treaded water until 1987, when the stock market crash of that year cut deeply into the market value of Guardian's holdings, reducing stocks to less than 10 percent of total assets. Stock prices then rebounded, trending upward until March 2000. The importance of Guardian's stock holdings followed the same pattern, topping out at just over 25 percent of the company's total assets at the end of 1999.[28]

Guardian's investment in stocks came directly at the expense of mortgages, the importance of which began to wane in 1967, when Guardian initiated its common stock purchasing program. Mortgages, which accounted for almost half of total assets in 1966, dropped quickly to less than 10 percent of total assets in 1982. At first, Guardian simply slowed its acquisition of new mortgages to a trickle, noting that securities were more attractive investments. Soon, however, Guardian began an aggressive program to sell off mortgages in large blocks when their yields were close to those of highly rated bonds, thereby creating a favorable market for a switch, or when they presented attractive write-off opportunities. Mortgages almost completely disappeared from Guardian's balance sheet in the mid-1980s, and stood at only 10 percent of total assets in 1992 before again sagging in the 1990s. So, the commercial real estate crisis of the 1980s that doomed several large financial intermediaries, including Home Life, left Guardian almost completely unscathed.[29]

The reasons for the decline of mortgages are clear. First, the mortgage market became very competitive, shrinking margins. Guardian tried to innovate by experimenting with variable yield real estate investments and the handling of small house loans in larger units through debentures and participation agreements but managed no major breakthroughs. Second, Guardian discovered that it was better to hold mortgage-backed bonds than the mortgages themselves. By 1997, for instance, Mark Dunetz and John Gargana managed a $1.4 billion portfolio of mortgage-backed bonds for Guardian. Third, some of Guardian's commercial mortgages, like those on certain hotels, mimicked equities in that they contained clauses that gave Guardian a participation in income. Holding significant amounts of both mortgages and stocks, therefore, was inconsistent with the company's safety.[30]

To further hedge inflation, Guardian sought greater equity exposure in the real estate market by spinning off a wholly owned real estate subsidiary that purchased real estate equities, held foreclosed property, purchased land, and improved real estate for investment, either wholly or in joint ventures. In November 1968, Annex Realty Corporation swung into operation under the guidelines established by the superintendent of insurance on 10 September of that year. The regulations limited the subsidiary's aggregate investment to $25 million and prohibited it from entering into any investments that would be illegal for Guardian itself. The subsidiary appears to have been a tax shelter and an indirect method for Guardian to seek after-tax yields greater than those available from customary investment media utilized by the company, partly by borrowing to finance real estate development projects. Annex itself formed a subsidiary, Germania Realty, Inc., for doing business in California. As a result of the formation of those subsidiaries, real estate diminished in importance for Guardian itself, falling below 2 percent of total assets. The Annex and Germania financed a number of projects, including an apartment complex in Arizona and an industrial park in Kansas City, before merging with Guardian in 1980.[31]

Guardian continued to strive to be fully invested at nearly all times, relying on new premiums, investment income flows, and contractual payments to meet its liquidity needs. By the early 1970s, inflation and the behavior of interest rates and policy loans caused many companies to reassess the need for liquidity in life insurance investment portfolios, Conklin noted. Some companies had to sell assets, when they were at their lowest ebb no less, to meet the cash demands of policyholders. In response, many life insurers began to hold higher levels of cash and to increase policy loan rates, a tactic Guardian pursued vigorously but unsuccessfully in the late 1960s, or to make them variable rate. As early as 1946 Guardian had considered proposals to make policy loan interest rates variable.[32]

For its part, Guardian continued to keep its cash holdings razor thin, less than 1 percent of total assets, until the early 1980s. It was able to do so for three reasons. First, it kept close tabs on the level of its policy loans, which spiraled ever upward from 1956 to 1983, surrenders, and interest rates. Second, the company cut back on its use of loan commitments. This gave it greater flexibility in the use of its cash flow. Third, its banks agreed, at first informally and later formally, to honor Guardian's checks even if its accounts were temporarily overdrawn.[33]

It should be noted that Guardian was not a slave to its commitment to full investment. When conditions were right, as when it anticipated a rapid rise in interest rates in the near future, it allowed its cash balance to swell. In such an environment, holding cash from investment could be more lucrative than investing it all immediately at what would soon be relatively low rates. Similarly, when Guardian thought that interest rates had crested, they increased their forward commitments to take further advantage of the high rates. And the policy of keeping cash holdings at razor-thin margins would not prove to be a sacred cow, as the record indicates from the 1980s on.[34]

The company's higher than historic levels of cash holdings toward the end of the twentieth century stem from two sources, a change in the company's investment strategy and the development of the money market. As early as 1969, Guardian began to invest in term repurchase agreements, a collateralized short-term loan arrangement that grew to immense importance in the last three decades of the twentieth century. Extensive use of such "repos," as they are affectionately known, commercial "sweep" accounts, Eurodollar deposits, and other convenient and remunerative money market instruments made holding cash less costly. That fact became important to Guardian in the early 1980s, when its investment officers thought that another Great Depression loomed.[35]

Bracing for Impending Disaster

In 1974, Guardian's chief investment officer, Ashby Bladen, caused something of a stir in investment circles when he predicted a major economic crash similar to the Great Depression. "Any significant reduction in the availability of credit," he argued, "is likely to produce massive bankruptcies of overextended people and businesses, leading to a deflationary collapse." "The longer the crash is postponed by continuing the inflationary process of excessive credit expansion," he reasoned, "the worse [the crash] will be when it does come."[36]

Bladen had come to Guardian in 1971, after working with Wall Street legends Sidney Homer and Henry Kaufmann at Salomon Brothers before a brief stint at American Standard. He was hired, in the minds of some directors, to offset the biases of President George Conklin, who was thought to be a bit "too audacious" in the bear market environment of the times. Bladen was anything but audacious, repeatedly forecasting a second Great Depression in personal conversations, agency meetings, the national media, including a bimonthly column in *Forbes,* and finally in a short but influential book called *How to Cope with the Developing Financial Crisis* (New York: McGraw Hill, 1980). He railed against what he viewed as feckless government policy in the face of economic forces spun out of control. It was time, he argued, to hunker down.[37]

If Bladen and Conklin had been polar opposites, they could not have coexisted. They saw eye to eye on a number of important macroeconomic and monetary policy issues. Conklin agreed with Bladen that the Federal Reserve's skill in checking inflation was "sadly lacking" and that "governmental policies leave much to be desired." In August 1973, Conklin had opined in a board meeting that the Federal Reserve had placed itself "back on the horns of the same dilemma it faced in 1966 and in 1969–70, only this time the situation appears even worse." The dilemma was this: if the Federal Reserve shut off credit expansion, the economy could go into a serious depression. If it allowed the money supply to continue to rapidly increase, on the other hand, inflation would continue and worsen, leading to a further boom and bust syndrome. The government's inability to keep the economy on an even keel frustrated Guardian's senior management and directors, making them ever more prone to accept Bladen's gloomy prognostications.[38]

Moreover, Bladen was a very good bond trader who made a lot of money for Guardian and who brought on some key people, including quantitative finance gurus Charles Albers and John Neely. By the early 1980s, therefore, Bladen's foreboding strongly influenced Guardian's investment decisions. So, unlike many insurance companies, Guardian stood prepared for the trials and tribulations that plagued the industry in the mid- and late 1980s. Guardian built a large surplus designed to absorb capital losses when it replaced older, low-yield bonds with newer, high-yield issues. Bladen also pushed for the purchase of the mortgage bonds of electric utilities. Even if the companies go bankrupt, he reasoned, the underlying physical assets of the utilities would continue in operation, generating revenue to service the bonds. Thus Guardian also purchased heavily of the common stock of crucial utilities but eschewed other equities. The only equities Guardian owned, Bladen noted in 1981, were those of utilities.[39]

Bladen had begun pushing Guardian into utility securities in late 1971, soon after joining the company. Although a three-year study by Guardian's research staff had concluded that public utilities revealed little or no industry risk, the strategy was not without its critics. As early as April 1972 some members of the Finance Committee began to inquire earnestly into the reasoning behind the strategy. By July, long-time director Charles Hill Jones, a native Mississippian, a University of Virginia graduate, former vice president of Manufacturers Trust, and president and chairman of the Hershey Creamery Company, protested vigorously against additional electrical utility investments. A 20 percent increase in investment returns in the summer of 1972 quieted fears for a time. Recommendations for further purchases in October, however, brought forth negative votes from Jones and the ultracautious savings banker James Bloor. The board, which had long sought unanimity, approved the purchases anyway because most members understood that electric utility securities were underpriced. The rebuff stung Jones, who continued, in vain, to protest further acquisitions. When he threatened to resign from the Finance Committee over the issue in June 1975, the Finance Committee called him on it, because Bladen was essentially correct, if not in his macroeconomic forecasts then in his choice of investments. Jones, who had unsuccessfully attempted to block much-needed executive salary increases, declined reelection to the board in 1976.[40]

Bladen, with help from garrulous math whiz John Neely, made a killing in the market for bonds with pro rata sinking funds. Other highly sophisticated investors had miscalculated the value of those instruments, which had the unusual feature of returning part of their principal each year. They mistakenly priced the bonds as if they were typical coupon bonds that repaid their face values at maturity. Neely identified the problem and calculated the value of the bonds accurately. Bladen then took over to exploit the profit opportunity.[41]

By all accounts, Guardian's investment officers racked up impressive gains in the late 1960s and 1970s, both on the company's general account and on its separate accounts. In 1968 the company's net return on assets on a pretax basis jumped substantially, to 5.29 percent, which was among the highest returns in the industry. Unfortunately, however, the company's after-tax rate of return remained unchanged from 1967 due to a tax increase. In 1971, Guardian's net after-tax rate of return, 4.79 percent, was somewhat better than that of the industry as a whole despite the fact that the investment quality of its assets was higher than average. The following year was even better. Guardian's net after-tax returns increased thirty-three basis points, making its performance materially better than that of the industry as a whole. Though its stock portfolio took a beating in the bear market of 1974, which approached the dimensions of the 1932 depression, Guardian's portfolio behaved in much better fashion than the overall market. Thanks to deft management, good forecasting, and excellent credit analysis, strong gains continued throughout the 1970s. In 1979, President Futia could report that the "quality of our investment portfolio remains high," that "foreclosure and securities in arrears . . . are low," and that "the performance of our stock portfolio continues to be above average." In 1985, Guardian was still doing extremely well because its stock portfolio remained strong and because it had bought large sums of non-callable long-term bonds when interest rates were high.[42]

Bladen's predictions of doom and gloom never came to pass. After the steep recession of the early 1980s, the U.S. economy performed remarkably well, and its financial markets more than kept pace. The stock market crash of 1987 reduced stock prices but did not usher in recession. A recession did strike in 1990–91, but it was mild and short lived. The rest of the 1990s witnessed impressive productivity gains and unparalleled prosperity. The early years of the twenty-first century have been relatively poor ones but not nearly as bad as Bladen predicted. Bladen and Guardian decided to part ways in August 1981, when veteran bond trader James Pirtle assumed the position of chief investment officer. Pirtle, an Oberlin graduate and World War II vet, had joined the Guardian as assistant financial secretary in 1960. He was later promoted to second vice president and financial secretary, then to second vice president and treasurer, and then, in early 1973, to vice president and treasurer. When he retired in 1983, Henry Spencer succeeded him. Spencer too was a sharp one. In 1984, for instance, Guardian under his leadership decreased the duration of its money market investments in anticipation of higher short-term rates in the near future. When those rates indeed increased, Guardian had the cash to purchase large sums of higher-yielding money market instruments. Unfortunately, on Spencer's watch, the quality of the bond portfolio degenerated somewhat, a problem that would be aggressively addressed by Frank J. Jones, Guardian's chief investment officer from August 1991 until the end of 2002.[43]

Following Conklin's Footsteps

Jones, a Stanford Ph.D. in economics, had left a vice presidency at Merrill Lynch to take his new post at Guardian. Like Conklin, Jones was a well-published scholar who would eventually have some five books along with two score articles and book chapters to his credit on topics ranging from stock portfolio attribution analysis to yield curve strategies to covered call writing strategies. Among his coauthors are the investment guru Frank J. Fabozzi and Nobel laureate Franco Modigliani.[44]

Under Jones, Guardian beefed up its trading capabilities, hiring top talent from the sell side of the industry. Former sellers were "wolves," Jones liked to say, who knew the tricks of "the hunt." Converted to the buy side, they were less likely to act like "sheep" and make bad purchase decisions. To decrease the firm's reliance on outside analyst reports, Jones also hired half a dozen expert bond and equity analysts. "We have our own analysts," he said, "so the wolves can't come in and fool us."[45]

Because professional economists—who are largely proponents of efficient markets theory—have long controlled Guardian's investment portfolios, carefully calibrated asset allocation has taken precedence over market timing strategies. "Nothing" anybody on Guardian's trading floor did on Jones's watch, "ha[d] anything to do with timing." Instead, Guardian's investors continued to seek out the proportion of market-risk assets, like equities, and credit-risk assets, like junk bonds, that would, with the conservative core of every insurance company's portfolio (Treasuries and other investment grade bonds), maximize policyholder dividends. From the end of 1999 to the end of 2000, Guardian reduced its exposure to stocks and other return-oriented, market-risk assets (like below-investment-grade bonds) from 29.5 percent of invested assets to 24 percent. At the same time, it increased the share of core assets from 54.7 percent to 57.3 percent and the share of yield-oriented, credit-risk assets from 15.8 percent to 18.7 percent.[46]

Part of that shift was forced by declines in the stock market, which caused Guardian's invested equity values to fall and hence their share of total assets to drop. Part of the shift, however, was a conscious attempt to redress an imbalance in the company's asset allocation, which was now perceived as too light on credit-risk assets. The company's credit analysis continued to be top in the business, as table 13-1, which measures underperforming assets as a percentage of capital (as measured by Moody's), shows.

Buy and hold remained the basic principle, but not "buy and forget." Guardian continually monitored credit risk. The monitoring served two purposes. First, the monitoring kept default rates low, because Guardian analysts were often among the first to sniff trouble. Guardian's exposure to Enron, the giant energy concern that went bankrupt in late 2001, for instance, was next to nil. Second, close monitoring allowed the company to arbitrage risk premiums. It routinely sold bonds with risk premiums that it perceived to be too low and replaced them with bonds with risk premiums that it believed were too high.[47]

TABLE 13-1
*Underperforming Assets as a Percentage of Moody's Capital
at Selected Companies, 1996–2000*

Company	2000 (%)	1999 (%)	1998 (%)	1997 (%)	1996 (%)
Guardian	.3	.4	.4	.7	.5
Penn Mutual	.4	.7	.4	1.3	7.0
New York Life	1.1	1.4	1.7	3.9	7.8
Pacific Life	1.1	1.6	4.6	6.0	10.4
Northwestern Mutual	2.0	2.0	2.7	3.4	6.3
Phoenix Home Life	2.6	3.4	6.7	5.7	7.9
National Life (Vt.)	3.2	4.3	7.9	9.2	8.9
Prudential	3.5	4.1	4.7	6.2	12.0
Massachusetts Mutual	4.0	5.0	4.7	9.7	16.9
Provident Mutual	4.1	4.5	7.2	11.6	14.1
MONY	6.6	15.7	17.6	35.6	54.3
Principal Life	6.6	12.8	23.2	28.9	34.2
Equitable Life	9.3	11.7	14.6	30.1	44.0
Metropolitan	9.3	9.6	9.3	12.5	24.6
John Hancock	9.9	10.4	16.1	18.6	24.3

Source: "How to Choose a Life Insurance Company," Executive Presentation Client's Guide, 2001, GLIC archives.

At the turn of the twenty-first century, two aspects of Guardian's investment philosophy set it apart from most of the industry. First, it invested from the "bottom up" rather than, in typical textbook fashion, from the "top down." In other words, Guardian's analysts did not look for sectors that seemed poised to outperform the market but rather for companies that were good credit risks. They assessed the outlook for a sector only as it impinged on a particular company's credit risk, not as an end in itself or as a starting point. Second, Guardian's analysts continued to evaluate bonds on a relative value basis. They would, without compunction, sell what the company's credit analysts deemed to be overpriced bonds and use the cash to buy underpriced bonds.[48]

For example, when the spread between the bonds of a particular subsidiary corporation and its parent narrowed, it replaced the subsidiary's bonds with the bonds of the parent, which for legal reasons had considerably lower default risk. In another case, the maturity-adjusted spreads between the bonds of railroads and paper companies narrowed to the point that Guardian decided to sell the paper company bonds, which were quite a bit more volatile, and buy the relatively cheap, stable railroad bonds. Similarly, all other factors being equal, Guardian would buy the bonds of supermarkets over those of department stores because supermarkets are more stable businesses with higher entry barriers. In each of those cases, the credit risk of the issuer was scrutinized closely before the trading desk was ordered to execute.[49]

As Jones put it, "my job is to make Guardian's dividend big without undue risk." It was also to ensure that wild swings in the equities markets did not cause undue volatility of policyholder dividends. To obtain that age-old objective, Guardian averaged out capital gains over time, preserving some gains for distribution in a bear market, even holding back some of the phenomenal gains it made in 1995–99. When the equities markets entered into a long-term funk in 2000, the company began using those realized but undistributed capital gains to keep policyholder dividends high. The hope was that the stock market would regain its footing before the company's Realized Capital Gain Fund, the special surplus fund used to buffer the company from the vicissitudes of the economy, was exhausted. Dividend smoothing is simply one of the many "invisible" services that Guardian, as a financial intermediary, provides its investors.[50]

The Economic Importance of Life Insurance Investments

The efforts of the likes of Conklin, Bladen, and Jones contributed greatly to the welfare of Guardian policyholders. Without solid investment returns, a legal reserve life insurance company like Guardian would soon fold or degenerate into a wealth redistribution scheme. Life insurance investment officers, however, do more than just enrich their companies' policyholders. Investments made by life insurance companies have helped families, all levels of government, and a wide variety of firms to prosper, develop, and enrich the world economy. In 1915, insurance man William Dix stated the matter like this:

> As a developer of high class real estate through the use of the mortgage, the life insurance company stands pre-eminent. It gathers, in innumerable small amounts, the savings of the many, and sends this accumulation forth again in larger amounts to earn more money for their owners and to be one of the factors in providing the wherewithal for the building up of America. The great wheat farms of the West, the cotton industry of the South, the railroads and terminals and docks and business houses of modern America have received a generous share of the needed financial help through that greatest of economic powers for good—the life insurance company.[51]

Guardian was well aware of the influence of the industry in the capital markets, noting that its third major objective, after safety and return, was to invest "to build a better America." Moreover, life companies are among the least specialized intermediaries, standing astride all of the major dollar-denominated capital and money markets. And compared to banks, life insurance companies really stand out, because life insurers demand what banks generally cannot, the very essence of financial capital, *long-term debt.*[52]

Almost certainly, the life insurance industry increased the aggregate rate at which late-nineteenth- and early-twentieth-century Americans saved. We cannot go back in time, eliminate life insurers, and observe differences in the savings rate. Some commonsense and historical data, however, tell us that even in the depths of the Depression, when Americans were dis-saving elsewhere, more funds flowed into life companies through the receipt of premiums, investment earnings, and loan repayments than flowed out of them through the payment of death benefits, matured endowments, annuity payments, surrenders, dividends, policy loans, and operating expenses. The explanation for this is quite straightforward: Americans, especially poor and middle-class Americans, believed that they needed life insurance protection and were willing to make it a priority. They followed the advice of the industry and saved through life insurance first. As Samuel Badger of the New England Mutual explained, "with most families the payment for life insurance protection is one of the last items to be dropped from the family budget." Only in the 1950s, when the savings component of whole life policies started to become less competitive than other savings outlets, did family heads begin to reduce the rate at which they saved through life insurance.[53]

Moreover, life insurers kept the vast bulk of their assets invested in remunerative projects—constructive and destructive ones. In other words, financial intermediaries like Guardian help to steer the nation's savings to their most productive uses. Often, that has entailed the destruction of existing physical capital to make way for new, more productive facilities. Mortgage foreclosures, for instance, often indicated the obsolescence or uncompetitive nature of the real estate. Foreclosure, resale, and improvement often resulted. Consider, for instance, the melancholy story of nine houses on the 138–139 block of Edgecomb Avenue in New York. Guardian foreclosed on the properties in 1898 and carried them as real estate on its balance sheet, but the rental income that the houses generated decreased each year. By 1915, the properties had sufficiently depreciated in price that it was worthwhile for a builder to purchase the land, raze the houses, and erect new tenements. Guardian itself ordered the demolition of a good many of the properties it took during foreclosure proceedings during the Depression.[54]

In 1960, Guardian noted that its investments ran "the gamut from banana warehouses to bowling alleys, from golf bags to hospitals, from cosmetics to mobile homes." Indeed, life insurance companies finance the construction of new buildings, infrastructure, and other forms of physical capital ranging from private homes to apartments, from office buildings to factories, from farms to transportation systems, from Hawaii hotels to California condos, and from corner gas stations to transoceanic oil tankers. In 1956, for example, Public Law 1017 allowed the federal government to guarantee mortgages of ships built in this country by an American citizen for operation under the U.S. flag. Guardian and several other major life insurers took advantage of the new provision to begin making loans to shipbuilders, a group considered among the riskiest of borrowers until blessed with Uncle Sam's largesse. "Where else," asked one insurance executive, "can I get 5% government paper on a long-term loan?" Guardian agreed, investing in a considerable volume of ship loans over the next decade or so.[55]

Critics have claimed that life insurance companies have too rarely lent to new businesses. Although life companies are a far cry from venture capitalists, they did help to finance many nascent businesses and industries. For instance, insurance companies made loans to the first private atomic power plant and the first taconite pellet mills in Minnesota's Mesabi Range. They also made crucial loans to the nascent industries and small upstarts attempting to enter more mature markets. In 1946, Guardian began to investigate the merits of the aviation industry as an investment medium, purchasing twenty-year American Airline bonds in 1946. It soon jettisoned those bonds in favor of an old mainstay, railroad bonds, but it later invested in Pan Am and other airlines. Similarly, in 1949, the company began to purchase the bonds of numerous small, independent telephone companies. In 1952, it lent to companies that built electronic components for jet fighter planes like the Lockheed Starfire and to a hydroelectric turbine manufacturer. In the 1970s it purchased pollution control revenue bonds.[56]

Moreover, the rise of private placements increased medium-sized firms' access to the funds of institutional investors, especially life insurers. Regulatory restrictions, however, greatly reduced the ability of life insurance companies to lend to small businesses, those with assets of less than, say, $1 million. By New York law, for example, life insurers could not make unsecured loans to unincorporated companies, which in 1960 composed 86 percent of all business establishments in the United States and an even higher percentage of small firms. Banks, therefore, supplied small business with most of its *nonmortgage* debt. Life insurers, however, made a significant contribution to small business finance by making many mortgage loans to small firms. "The Mortgage Loan Department," noted one analyst, "often becomes in effect the small business loan department in the company in addition to performing its residential mortgage function."[57]

Nor have the investments of life companies been solely domestic. Even after Guardian extracted itself from its overseas commitments by the end of World War II, it continued to make investments overseas. In October 1964 alone, for example, the company made investments in the Philippines, Canada, the Canary Islands, and Mexico. In 1966, Guardian joined a syndicate of life insurers that lent $8 million for the construction of an apartment complex in Caracas, Venezuela. Guardian's share of the deal, which the federal government fully guaranteed, was $2.5 million. Similarly, three years later, Guardian proffered $2.5 million to another syndicate that financed seven hundred new houses in Tegucigalpa, Honduras. The guaranteed twenty-five-year loans yielded an effective interest rate of almost 11 percent.[58]

Finally, life companies have been roundly criticized for failing to lend to minority groups or to impoverished areas. To some extent, the criticism is justified, yet in a broad sense it is not so bad as critics would have it. Certainly the industry has long served as a conduit by which the wealthier, more developed areas, the North and East, have financed the economic development of poorer and newer, once undercapitalized, regions of the country in the South and West. Guardian was no exception here. It is true that insurance companies were not as keen historically about financing homes or small businesses located in urban minority neighborhoods.[59]

That said, in 1968 an industry group, including Guardian, pledged to lend over $1 billion to improve the "hard-core area of cities." Part of the reason for the pledge was simple public relations, and part stemmed from the recognition that long-term self-interest was inevitably related to more open lending policies. Guardian owned properties in and around the area afflicted by the race riots in Detroit in the summer of 1967.

Though one of its holdings, luckily "boarded up," was "in the center of the trouble," all of its properties escaped damage. The future of the race issue, however, remained uncertain and to the extent that the loans quelled discontent, life insurance executives thought them worth the risk. Investment of 1 percent of the company's assets in low-income housing and new job-producing enterprises over the next three years, Guardian's Real Estate Committee noted, was consistent with the company's continued concern for the environment in which the company operates and hence was in the interest of policyholders.[60]

And just how significant have Guardian's investment activities been to the economy? Guardian's relative importance can be roughly measured by its share of the industry's total assets. (Figure 13-1 traces the growth of both the industry's and Guardian's total assets.) By the end of the Civil War, Guardian accounted for over 1 percent of the life industry's total assets. The company's share topped out at 2.08 percent in 1888, trended downward to 0.83 percent in 1920, took a big plunge in 1921 to 0.52 (the plunge due in part to an accounting change), then trended slowly downward over the next six and a half decades, finally heading upward again in the mid-1980s after bottoming out at 0.38 percent in the early 1980s.

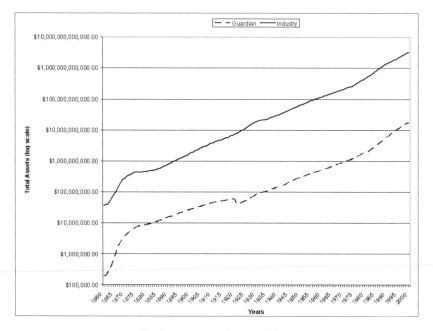

FIGURE 13-1 *Growth of Assets: Guardian and the Industry, 1860–2000*

Guardian's importance by this measure hit a plateau in the late 1990s at just over 0.5 percent of the industry's total assets. Of course, most life insurance companies have far fewer assets than Guardian does. A few huge companies have long dominated the industry, followed by a few dozen midsized companies like Guardian, and then hundreds and at times thousands of very small insurers. (See figure I-1.)

As noted above, however, the entire life industry has sharply declined in its share of overall investment in the U.S. economy since World War II, from around 43 percent to 12 percent. In that respect, the insurance industry's general account assets no longer dominate what are much larger and more diversified U.S. financial markets. Nonetheless, insurance industry assets have grown in real terms by a factor of seven, and Guardian's amount to tens of billions of dollars, hardly a trivial sum as the thousands of businesses to which Guardian lends will attest. In the final analysis, the most important consideration is the major impact that Guardian's investments have on the welfare of its seven million policyholders. Ultimately, the fate of those policyholders rests in the hands of Guardian's top managers, its mutual structure, and its ethical corporate culture, the topics to which we now turn.

Part IV

Mutuality and Performance

Guardian's history, like that of all enduring institutions, is neither quite linear nor cyclical. It is one of discontinuous progress, periods of growth and development interspersed with episodes of crisis, retrenchment, adaptation, and innovation. But in this particular history, progress prevails in a world where few companies endure for more than a few years, and fewer still grow to great size and positions of leadership in their industries. Guardian's survival and success is remarkable when we appreciate how the business of life insurance has been buffeted by constant turmoil. Since its modern beginnings in the nineteenth century, periodic outbursts of war, depression, inflation, and scandal have plagued the industry.

It is within the living memory of the authors of this history just how recent economic misfortunes adversely impacted the life insurance industry. In the inflationary 1970s, consumers shied away from whole life insurance in favor of term policies, which were less profitable to those who sold them. People also began to shift funds from life insurance companies (and other financial intermediaries) to more direct investment in financial markets, primarily though mutual and retirement funds. Life insurance companies responded to those pressures in different ways, but not all equally successfully. Then, in the course of the 1980s and early 1990s, a new series of blows, including corporate malfeasance, the implosion of the markets for commercial real estate and corporate high-yield, below-investment-grade—or junk—bonds, caused an unprecedented number of unusually large life insurers to fail. Bankruptcies, combined with a series of high-profile lawsuits that exposed fraudulent life insurance sales practices, marked an extremely troubled time for the life industry. In the course of the 1990s, a massive industry restructuring ensued, as life companies consolidated and demutualized.[1]

Guardian was one of few life insurers to come through this latest industry crisis unscathed. For most institutions, over the long haul, few things abide, while most are transient. Guardian changed in the 1990s in many ways, but its traditional core business principle, its commitment to mutuality, remained intact, as did the ethical culture on which mutuality must be based.

Guardian also stuck relatively closely to its traditional core strategy. It has always sold mostly to the upper-income and small-business market segments. "We don't try to be all things to all people," notes CEO Joseph Sargent. "We try to be all things to some people, and those some people are the upscale buyer." Hugo Wesendonck could have said much the same thing. As other insurers attempted to diversify *out* of insurance into a broader array of investment services in the 1980s and 1990s, Guardian diversified only insofar as its investment services served mainly to support the interests of its policyholders.[2]

Another abiding factor in Guardian's history, one of the utmost importance to its survival, is that it has always managed its costs reasonably well. Guardian, for much of its history, has been a low-cost company, as its well-documented struggles over the generations suggest. Since the 1950s, when the company was able to grow large enough to take advantage of scale economies, it never became so large that its management lost sight of its core enterprise and its obligations to its policyholders. On the asset side of its balance sheet, its investment returns have consistently beaten the rest of the industry. Mortality has fluctuated, but trended downward at crucial periods. Expenses were a constant struggle, but one that the company generally managed to control. All that added up to relatively low costs. As table IV-1 demonstrates, Guardian's twenty-year surrender cost index has ranked among the top ten of all insurance companies surveyed since 1985.[3]

It was a good thing that Guardian kept its costs very low in the last fifteen years of the twentieth century, too. The insurance industry would undergo many upheavals in the late 1980s and early 1990s, during which time Guardian consistently ranked at the top of *Financial World*'s most profitable life insurance companies, with return on net worth consistently near a whopping 30 percent, almost double the industry average. *Fortune* listed Guardian as one of the top ten most admired life insurance companies for three years running in the early twenty-first century, while the company also remained among *Forbes* magazine's most admired life and health companies.[4]

TABLE IV-1

The Twenty-Year Surrender Cost Index of Guardian and Other Major Insurers

Company	Surrender Cost Index ($ cost per $1,000 insurance in force)	Percent of Policies Issued upon Which Index Is Based
Northwestern	0.06	1.0
Guardian	0.59	41.8
New York Life	1.24	n/a
National Life (Vt.)	2.52	56.0
Mass Mutual	2.87	47.3
Penn Mutual	3.32	34.0
MTL Mutual	5.38	32.8

Note: This chart reflects the actual net cost of policies issued in 1982 and held for twenty years. It is based on Blease Research's Full Disclosure survey on a $250,000 policy issued to a male, age forty-five, preferred non-smoker. The Surrender Cost Index allows for direct comparison of the relative cost of similar policies. The following procedure was used to calculate the index:
   Step 1: annual premiums accumulated at 5 percent;
   Step 2: annual dividends accumulated at 5 percent;
   Step 3: difference (step 1) – (step 2);
   Step 4: cash value;
   Step 5: terminal dividend (if any);
   Step 6: difference (step 3) – (step 4) – (step 5);
   Step 7: difference (step 6) divided by factor (34.719 for twenty years).

Source: Clifford Kitchen, "The Whole Story of Whole Life," 2003, Office of the Corporate Secretary.

Independent rating agencies also attested to the basic soundness of the company's management. A. M. Best Company, the hoariest of the life insurance rating agencies, routinely gave Guardian high grades. In 1997, Standard and Poor's cut Guardian's claims-paying ability from AAA to AA+ because it felt that the company's recent performance was below expectations. Guardian's "extremely strong capitalization, . . . very strong business profile, . . . very strong operating performance, . . . conservative strategic focus [and] strong investment profile," however, continued to impress S&P's analysts. As shown in table IV-2, Moody's, the world's foremost life insurance ratings agency, ranked Guardian among the industry's most financially sound companies. In 2002, only nine other companies in the industry had a rating as high or higher.[5]

As table IV-3 documents, all the major ratings agencies placed Guardian among the industry's strongest financially. The question to which we now turn is *how* could Guardian enjoy success as a mutual company in the closing years of the twentieth century, when most other insurers could not? The answer in part is that Guardian had abundant capital with which to pursue its projects. Guardian was also effectively governed.

With respect to governance, mutuality is a mixed blessing—the fact that mutual life companies do not have to answer to stockholders is a

TABLE IV-2
Guardian's Moody Rating, 1990–2002

Year	Moody's Rating of Guardian
1990	Aaa
1991	Aaa
1992	Aaa
1993	Aaa
1994	Aaa
1995	Aaa
1996	Aa1
1997	Aa1
1998	Aa1
1999	Aa1
2000	Aa1
2001	Aa1
2002	Aa1

Source: Moody's Investor Services, various years; *Life Insurance Fact Book,* 2001.

TABLE IV-3
Major Ratings of Guardian, 1999–2001

Year	S&P (% same or higher)	Duff & Phelps-Fitch (% same or higher)	Moody's (% same or higher)	Weiss (% same or higher)
1999	AA+ (15.7)	AAA (22.6)	Aa1 (9.8)	A+ (.6)
2000	AA+ (14.4)	AAA (25.1)	Aa1 (9.9)	A– (3.9)
2001	AA+ (13.5)	AAA (18.7)	Aa1 (10.5)	A– (3.6)

Source: *The Insurance Forum,* September issue, various years.

double-edged sword. On the one hand, any profits can be shared exclusively with policyholders. On the other hand, there is no apparent concentration of power among the policyholders that can pressure management to drive toward efficiency and hence higher profitability. A common critique of mutuality, at least in theoretical terms, is that in the absence of shareholder-type governance, managers can all too easily become lazy, complacent, or, worse, self-aggrandizing.

As life insurance historian Shepard Clough noted in 1946, "important as is every branch of the life insurance business, the ultimate success of a company depends largely upon management." Of course, the key variable in any business is not the company's form but rather the quality and integrity of its management. Guardian has avoided the potential managerial pitfalls of mutuality by consistently concentrating its efforts on the needs of policyholders and by fostering and maintaining an active board that fulfills important oversight and strategic planning functions.[6] It has also built an independent, *career* agency system, which has also performed an important mediating role between the home office and the policyholders, dating back at least to the establishment of the Field Advisory Board meetings in 1948. The company's sales agents have been a powerful additional factor in what amounts, at Guardian, to a mutual system of checks and balances among the managers, the board, and the field force.

14

Swimming against the Tide

The failure of several large life insurance companies in the early 1990s shook the life insurance industry to its core. The bankruptcies caught everyone by surprise, even though in retrospect all the warning signs were there—inflation, disintermediation, deregulation, regulatory incompetence, excess capacity, and declining demand for insurance products. Those myriad problems had been stewing in a pressure cooker for almost two decades, eventually forcing many companies to take big risks, including growing too rapidly, retaining too little surplus, pricing too low, overstating the value of assets (often junk bonds and real estate), drastically changing business strategies, allowing affiliates to run amok, and a variety of other unsound practices. Big risks, combined with volatile swings in demand for health insurance and in capital and real estate markets, eventually led to big failures.[1]

It is true that life insurance company failures were commonplace in the twentieth century, and that the prime cause was failed investment strategy. But most failed companies had been young and small, weak players in an industry populated by hundreds of firms. Each year from 1975 to 1985, inclusive, except for 1983, when twenty small to medium-sized companies failed, eleven or fewer life insurers involuntarily exited the industry. Again except for 1983, when the assets of failed companies topped 0.75 percent of total industry assets, the assets of failed companies came to less than 0.25 percent of total industry assets per year. The late 1980s and early 1990s were significantly different, however. For starters, as shown in table 14-1, the number of annual failures suddenly increased, and now big companies were failing. The assets of failed life insurers in 1991 amounted to a whopping 3.18 percent of the industry's total assets that year.[2]

The Executive Life Insurance Company was an extreme, but salient, example of the problem that the industry as a whole was facing. That

TABLE 14-1
Number of Failed U.S. Insurers, 1987–92

Year	Number of Failed Insurers
1987	20
1988	19
1989	42
1990	41
1991	58
1992	32

Sources: Spector, *Law and Practice*, passim; Wallison, *Optional Federal Chartering*, 113.

company had buckled under the weight of the unhappy confluence of several events, each of which was driven by its CEO's opportunistic quest for profits in the turbulent economic environment of the 1980s. First, Executive Life had lost large sums in a risky foray into reinsurance. A bigger problem, as it would turn out, was that it had been a steady and heavy buyer of Drexel Burnham Lambert's junk bonds, which fueled much of the corporate merger wave of the mid- to late 1980s. When Drexel's own scandals and the concurrent savings and loan crisis resulted in the sudden collapse of the junk bond market in 1990, Executive Life's balance sheet was in tatters. Executive Life had $15.2 billion in assets when it failed in May 1991; its bankruptcy was the fourth largest in history.

To make matters worse, industry regulators responded in counterproductive fashion. Because the regulation of life insurance companies focused squarely on the solvency of each insurer, and not on weeding out inefficient insurers, insurance regulators strove to keep even the most marginal insurers afloat. That would not have been so bad, if the regulators had intervened *before* the market caught wind of problems. But in this case, the market was aware of Executive Life's problems before the regulators could do anything, and it reacted with punishing swiftness. Executive Life's liability holders, both its policyholders and its Guaranteed Investment Contract holders, "ran" on the company, demanding policy loans and repayments of principal. Opportunistic brokers induced policyholders to surrender their policies outright, which enabled them to earn first-year commissions when their clients purchased new policies from different companies. And because all brokers feared that Executive Life would not be able to make good on commissions, they sent new prospects elsewhere as well. Bleeding cash from every pore and unable to obtain a transfusion, Executive Life quickly expired.[3]

It would take months before an acquirer of the junk bond and insurance portfolios of Executive Life could be found, and the delay caused considerable unease in the markets for both. Industry experts and policyholders alike were left to wonder whether the same economic pressures that caused the death of Executive Life could cause the demise of even more conservative, more venerable companies. When the failing Home Life Insurance Company, which like Guardian began business in 1860, was folded into Phoenix Life in 1992, their question was answered in the affirmative. The failures that followed—Mutual Benefit, New England Life, General American, and Connecticut Mutual—were less bloody if only because government-sponsored bailouts also cushioned the blow to policyholders to some degree, and because regulators, or the faltering companies' managers themselves, found acquirers for the distressed businesses on a more timely basis.[4]

Compounding the insurance industry's problems were mounting revelations of shady dealings by brokers and agents that resulted in a flurry of multi-billion-dollar settlements. Fraudulent sales schemes were directly linked to the inflation-disintermediation-deregulation-industry maturation pressure cooker. Agents and brokers facing decreasing commissions turned to such schemes as offering policies with "vanishing premiums," essentially promises that in a few years dividends would be large enough to cover the entire annual premium payment, promises that were often unfulfilled under prevailing market conditions. Or, they induced policyholders to lapse their polices in order to replace them with new ones—a practice called "churning" or "twisting," which amounted to outright fraud.

The technology of fraud has changed remarkably little over almost two centuries of life insurance history. Agents have been known to grossly exaggerate dividend illustrations and to steal money from the insured or the insurer by forging checks, receipts, policy change forms, and so on. During times of duress such behavior, which is usually the behavior of a few rogue agents, can become rampant. The giant Prudential Life Insurance Company was implicated in both insurance-sales and investment-brokerage fraud, but it was just the highest-profile case of what was happening in too many pockets of the industry during the 1980s and early 1990s.[5]

In 1993, in the wake of the most spectacular life insurance failures and scandals in nearly a century, declining demand, financial performance, expense management, and control of the distribution system topped the

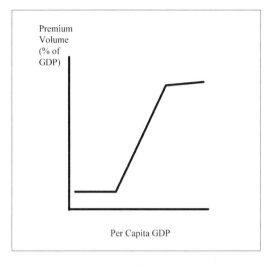

FIGURE 14-1　*S-Curve of Insurance Penetration*

concerns of U.S. life insurance CEOs. Most companies saw all four problems as largely intractable. The proliferation of sales scandals convinced many CEOs of their inability to control agent behavior. Moreover, as profit margins decreased, few industry CEOs could see how to squeeze out lower expenses, and traditionally conservative investment yields could not easily be offset by taking on higher risk, as the Executive Life debacle had shown. And all of this had come to a head when people were finding alternatives to traditional whole life insurance; it was simply harder to sell. Too much supply relative to demand. (See figure 14-1.) The long bull market, dating back to 1981, had diverted investors away from whole life insurance into the equity markets. Industry consolidation, diversification, and the corresponding disappearance of many venerable firms was all but inevitable.[6]

For its part, Guardian would weather what would be a great wave of industry consolidation because it faced only one major problem—expenses. Only high expenses could derail the company. Knowing that, Guardian's board and officers were reasonably sanguine about the company's ability to remain in business and stand alone as a mutual life insurance company. The company enjoyed a good, and relatively stable, mid-to-high-income market, and its sales and investment teams remained effective in their niche specialties. While most of the industry rushed to diversify and demutualize, Guardian was poised to capitalize on the impending industry reorganization by innovating without losing sight of its traditional mission and principles. Those principles allowed the company to maintain its strong career field force and to sustain the competitiveness of its general account at a time when other insurers with weaker distribution systems and general account investment returns had to flee to the relative safety of variable products and the separate accounts backing them.[7]

The Mutual Logic of Diversification

Diversification was a generally rational response to fundamental economic changes gripping the industry. Facing declining returns from their traditional whole life business, most life insurers in the last three decades of the twentieth century diversified their businesses substantially beyond the provision of life insurance. Some went so far as to tap the cash flows from the insurance business in order to exit from it. Because diversification required additional capital, a rare commodity for many insurers, the economically favorable way to raise it in the 1990s was to sell stock. For mutual insurers, of course, that meant changing their charters in order to become stockholder-owned companies. But there were hazards to this approach. Companies that demutualized did so by diminishing the strategic value of their insurance businesses. And taking on shareholders implied diminishing the claims their policyholders had on corporate cash flows.[8]

Guardian had begun to invest in noninsurance financial businesses in the late 1960s, after New York State regulatory changes permitted it to do so, and it continued to do so into the twenty-first century. But there was a difference. Guardian invested in such new ventures when they were seen to support, or relate in some economically justifiable way, to its traditional core business: individual whole life. Guardian, in other words, remained a life insurance company that also sold other financial products at a time when many of its peers had evolved into financial service companies that also sold life insurance.[9]

Guardian's new core-related businesses included GIAC's 1996 acquisition of First International Life Insurance Corporation (now Park Avenue Life Insurance Company, or PALIC) as a vehicle for acquiring blocks of life insurance business from third-party insurers. (PALIC, for example, purchased Family Services Life Insurance Company, a block of paid-up burial insurance, in 1998.) The July 2001 acquisition of Berkshire Life Insurance Company of America enlarged the company's position in the disability income insurance market.[10]

To enhance its position with retail investors, Guardian set up Park Avenue Securities (PAS) in 1998 as a registered retail broker-dealer that offered mutual funds from Guardian's Park Avenue portfolio as well as proprietary and nonproprietary variable life and annuity products. The following year, Guardian purchased Innovator Underwriters Inc., a commissioned-based brokerage that specialized in the placement of high-risk life insurance coverage for agents of Guardian and other insurers. It also established Guardian Trust Company, a federally chartered savings association authorized solely to exercise trust powers. Guardian Trust also operated on a fee basis and was formed to help field agents retain business formerly lost to banks.[11]

Over the last decade Guardian has become more diverse in its insurance operations as well, adding dental insurance subsidiaries, including a number of dental HMOs, such as First Commonwealth, Inc., and Managed Dental Care, to its family. The company's entrance into the dental field is instructive; Guardian built its group dental business around an entrepreneurial young actuary and a strong proprietary network of dentists. The point was not simply to buy up assets in areas of interest, but to key on acquisitions for which Guardian had the in-house human capital, if not to manage, at least to analyze.[12]

The company moved into new areas cautiously, and not always successfully. In 1990, for instance, Guardian formed Guardian Asset Management Corporation, or GAMCORP, a registered investment advisor organized to manage, for a fee, the investment accounts of other insurance companies, charities, and pension plans. The subsidiary had difficulty in developing clients, so it was shuttered within three years. Guardian did not lose its shirt on that or other failed forays, if only because it was quick to cut its losses when the handwriting was on the wall.[13]

To cope with the diversification of its operations, Guardian organized all its businesses into five broad "profit centers," essentially five divisions: individual life, disability, group insurance, group pensions, and equity products. The three major centers, the "three legs of the stool," as company managers viewed the core of their enterprise, were individual life, group, and equity products. Disability was still a relatively small but growing part of Guardian's overall business thanks to the acquisition of

Berkshire, which made it the second-largest issuer of "his occ noncan" policies (disability policies that charge a level premium, that cannot be canceled by the company, and that pay if the insured cannot return to his or her *specific* occupation). Group pensions failed to turn a profit.[14]

Overarching this structure was a guiding business principle: Guardian's mix of businesses, including its noninsurance businesses, was designed to enhance the economic value of the whole life policy. Guardian's profit centers and subsidiaries, in other words, were not economic ends in themselves. They served the policyholders' interests rather than those, say, of shareholders, which might have led to a different way of thinking about diversification. Each business was a kind of private equity investment that paid a dividend to the life insurance enterprise. "We don't have a business that just stands alone on its own just because it's nice to have that business," explains Joseph Caruso. "It has to show some benefit to the participating policyholders."[15]

This logic was evident in Guardian's Participating Business Assessment Program in 2001, a creation of Guardian's chief actuary, Armand de Palo. The program ensured that the subsidiaries subsidize the core insurance business, and not the other way around. Such internal accounting charges have long been important parts of Guardian's business strategy. In 1960, for example, Guardian charged its new group department $100,000 for "indirect expenses." Such charges ensured that departments, profit centers, and subsidiaries were economically viable on their own merits and that they fulfilled their main mission of benefiting participating policyholders. The Participating Business Assessment Program extended the principle and made the calculation of the intrabusiness transfers more actuarially precise.[16]

Underlying these accounting reforms was a virtue of controlled diversification that had become vividly apparent by the 1990s. The whole life, group, and equity businesses were at once distinct lines of business and mutually supportive. Any added complexity of managing these different businesses was more than offset by the differential ways in which they traversed market and economic cycles.

For example, in the high-interest-rate environment of the early 1980s, Joseph Sargent recalled, when short-term rates surged above long-term rates, it was a terrible time for the life insurance business. Premium proceeds were largely tied up in fixed-income investments while policyholders rushed to borrow against their policy values to invest in high-interest-bearing CDs and other relatively high-return instruments. The cash drain was offset by the robust cash flows generated mainly by the group and, to a lesser extent, the equity businesses. In the mid-1990s, when the miserable performance of medical insurance seriously impaired the overall business of the group division, the life insurance and equity businesses were strong. At the turn of the century, strong life insurance and group sales more than compensated for weak equity sales in a down securities market. In each of these periods, corporate cash flows overall remained strong enough to enable ongoing investments in technology, product development, and acquisitions.[17]

As a matter of course, many of the new businesses enabled the life insurance sales force to remain financially viable (and, hence, less prone to fraud or policy pushing) by providing additional products that they could sell. Park Avenue Securities, for example, helped the thirty-six hundred Guardian sales reps with securities licenses to more easily sell securities, mutual funds, and retirement products to Guardian policyholders. Unlike Guardian's other broker-dealer, Guardian Investor Services Corp., which sold mainly to other broker-dealers, Park Avenue Securities concentrated its efforts on the retail market. The new subsidiary performed well on the back of products like Guardian Park Avenue Small Cap Fund, a mutual fund that outperformed the Russell 2000 small-cap index in 1999 and 2000.[18]

Guardian allowed the managers of its departments, subsidiaries, and profit centers to behave like entrepreneurs, to grow their businesses in profitable directions. The company's entrepreneurial spirit and profit center structure did not come without costs. Interbusiness communication and coordination were always problems. "We had in our areas what we would call silos," Robert Ryan, a manager at the Northeast Regional Office explained. "Over the years, we had life insurance, disability insurance, and we developed a new company with variable annuities," each with its own customer service function. "We were difficult to do business with." The problem was how to focus all these activities on the common needs of customers across the business lines. The company addressed this problem by putting all its life insurance policyholder service related activities under the control of a single department. The profit center structure also inhibited information flow across centers, which demanded a continuous updating of internal information mechanisms, both laterally across divisional lines, and up and down, from the divisions to Guardian's general management.[19] It was recognition, in structural terms, of the economic interdependency of the life and group businesses.

Board Governance and Corporate Culture

In a 1939 speech to the Association of Life Insurance Counsel in Hot Springs, Virginia, Guardian's assistant secretary, Orville F. Grahame, argued that the management of a mutual life insurance company was subject to five major controls:

1. The potential voting rights of policyholders.
2. The regulatory rights of Insurance Departments.
3. The "voice of law."
4. The tradition of management, based on the interest and work of those making life insurance a career.
5. Outside directors serving as a public duty.

The same thing could be said about the governance of Guardian today without qualification, though one might note that the "public duty" of its board members does not, now as then, go uncompensated.[20]

Board directors are the mutual policyholder's direct representatives. Strictly speaking, the directors of mutual companies are not fiduciaries, but they are legally subject to the same duties and liabilities as directors of any corporation. Because policyholders own a contract that they can neither sell nor afford to lose, however, the directors' representation is arguably more important in a mutual life insurance company than in a stock company, where shareholders can realize returns in an open market. Generally speaking, Guardian's board has been a conservative one, composed of a majority of "outside" directors but also consisting of former CEOs and active managers whose expertise and experience weigh heavily in the discussions.[21] A key factor is that at no time, at least in the company's modern history, has Guardian's board been dominated by the company's chief executive.

The board, at least since the early decades of the company's existence, has played the determining role in managerial succession; it was not a matter left to the retiring CEOs. Within living memory, Guardian's board has generally tried to select from a choice of CEO candidates the person whose strengths best complement the company's weakest facet. (A limiting factor, it would seem, is that the candidates were invariably internal.) James McLain was an agency man brought in at the end of the Depression when sales were flat. John Cameron, Daniel Lyons, and John Angle were actuaries brought in to help the company strengthen its policies and move into new lines of business. George Conklin was an investment expert who did not pay much attention to the insurance side of the business, but who successfully moved Guardian's investment returns to the top of the industry. Leo Futia was a former sales agent and life insurance evangelist who acceded to the top job when that business was struggling. Arthur Ferrara was a strong leader, a people person who attracted loyal, high-quality managers when they were hard to find in the industry. Joseph Sargent was a jack-of-all-trades at a time when the industry was pressured on all sides, and Dennis Manning, a general agent for most of his career, came in at a time when the distribution system needed some shoring up.[22]

The board's most important function has been to ensure that Guardian's officers continue to be solidly committed to the company's ethical culture. One can reach back as far as 1862 to find in the records of Guardian's board a recognition that "the welfare of thousands of families depends upon the good management of the Company." Ethical considerations loom large in the pronouncements of Guardian board members to this day. John Angle explained simply, "They have been ethical people." Guardian has survived and prospered, he argued in 1977, because the company emphasized what it believes "is right, regardless of what a few in the industry may do." It was a matter of doing well by doing good, recognizing that the Golden Rule was, in business terms, a "golden opportunity." "One common thread through all the CEOs that I worked for in Guardian," Leo Futia said, "was that they were men of integrity . . . , guys that you'd go to bat for because you can trust them."[23]

Ethical culture in corporate enterprise speaks to reputation—goodwill—over the long run. Once lost, reputation is hard to restore. History is littered with the sad stories of companies whose ethical lapses proved fatal, or nearly so. In the closing years of the twentieth century, it was Prudential—once "the Rock" upon which millions of Americans trusted the financial futures of themselves, their spouses, and their children—that suffered the largest reputational damage among insurers. It took all the formidable skills of Prudential's new CEO, Arthur Ryan, to realign that company's operations with basic precepts of ethical conduct in the late 1990s, and then to make the perception of reform stick in the marketplace after years of lost opportunities.[24]

Ethics and reputation are largely dependent on the quality and commitment of a company's senior managers. Guardian's practice historically was to grow its own senior managers. All its CEOs—even those who, like John Angle, started their careers elsewhere—were carefully nurtured from within the organization's ranks and were immersed in Guardian's ethical culture, which, above all, stressed the fundamental importance of policyholder welfare. And while turning office boys into presidents has a quaint, nineteenth-century flavor to it, Guardian was still building its leadership from within in the early twenty-first century. A 1951 policy that explicitly mandated building a staff of younger officers from among its employees in order to assure continuity of management dedicated to policyholder service still applied more than fifty years later.[25]

By then, one could recount several Guardian leaders who were at some point in their careers recruited from the outside. For John Angle, Guardian's history mattered a lot; he was an ardent student of it. He "knew" Hugo Wesendonck as well as anyone could from such a distance in time. For some, history was a less visible yet implicitly powerful force. "When I got here," said Guardian CIO Frank Jones, "I didn't know what Guardian's history was, and I did what I thought was right and found it consistent. Maybe Art Ferrara knew how I was, that I would fit. . . . I had my own biases when I got here and I implemented them before I knew what the history of the place was," Jones notes, "but I've found that I'm amazingly consistent with Guardian's history. . . . Fundamentally, John [Angle] and I were the same. George Conklin and I fundamentally are the same." It mattered that one's peers shared one's beliefs, values, and sense of tradition.[26]

While homegrown, peer-driven management may not always be the answer to a company's problems, in Guardian's case, it worked to reduce the risk of ethical misfortune. It helped that Guardian was relatively small, and controllable, and that it could afford to be selective in hiring managerial talent. Long after World War II, Guardian's corporate culture remained quite distinctive, as the company's management spoke of "Guardianizing" new departments, such as group sales, and of the need to "Guardianize" new officers hired from outside the company. Once new hires were imbued with Guardian's philosophy, they were quickly accepted into the "family." As corporate culture and company loyalty went out of fashion in the U.S. economy amid the wholesale restructuring in the 1980s and 1990s, and as financial service industry personnel turnover increased to dizzyingly high levels, institutional loyalties went by the boards. Yet Guardian's managers continued to speak of Guardian's distinctive culture, and its commitment to ethics, without embarrassment.

Guardian "in many ways was and still continues to be like a large small town," said Joseph Caruso, with some of the intimacy of the traditional "corporate family." News, even bad news, could travel quickly from its source to the place where it needed to be heard. Perquisites for top management were kept within seemly bounds, even in the high-flying 1990s.[27]

Compensating Management

Compensation for top management became extremely competitive in the U.S. economy in the 1990s, and stock options, especially after legislation applied tax penalties to "excessive" executive cash compensation in 1993, took on added importance. The life insurance industry was no exception to this general trend. (It is perhaps more than coincidental in the life insurance industry that the increasing attractiveness of stock options and demutualization moved in tandem.) And because growing numbers of life insurance CEOs come not from the field or the home office but from commercial banking, investment banking, and even academia, there was added upward pressure on industry executive compensation. If anything, according to Jack Wahlquist, president and CEO of Lone Star Life Insurance Company, the insurance industry was at a disadvantage in developing and retaining adequate successor management. Generally speaking, insurers did not exploit the unique capacity life insurance has for achieving both individual development and corporate growth. In that context, Guardian had to find a way to remain competitive in its executive ranks without either becoming a stock corporation (which would have violated the company's stated raison d'être) or driving expenses significantly upward.[28]

One way was to offer a high degree of job satisfaction to executives who were not primarily focused on personal incomes. Guardian executives constantly talked about the pleasures of their working environment, the value of their colleagues, and the adequate time they had for leisure and family. As for training and preparation, time-honored methods sufficed. Guardian's senior executives had a tradition of training prospective successors by ensuring that they received exposure to key facets of the business, board committees, and the like. And the assignments were not pushovers. Irving Rosenthal's rambling description of meetings between senior and junior executives in which the hidden agenda was often personnel development gives the flavor:

There were general discussions and then they would take up department by department, and we'd bring the officers down from the various departments and, frequently, without any preparation, cold turkey, just let 'em have it, and it was tough on them, and the senior officers had a chance to see how the junior officers responded, whether they were just negative and resentful that anybody would question them or whether they understood that they had a responsibility to explain to these people whose lives are involved in this; and no matter what question is asked, you don't brush it aside.[29]

Intangibles were important to the executive compensation package, even at the end of the twentieth century. Given their strong human capital endowments, Guardian executives earned relatively little by broad financial service industry standards. Years earlier, there had been a simple explanation for that state of affairs. A 1959 survey noted that life insurance executives were *the* lowest paid and yet had the highest percentage of Phi Beta Kappas and college graduates of any industry. But they did not work that hard, either. Insurance executives worked "bankers' hours," typically fifty hours per week, compared with the fifty-four hours put in by appliance-electronics executives or the fifty-six hours put in by textile industry executives, not to mention the grueling and endless hours put in by transaction-driven investment bankers. By the late twenty-first century, insurance executives and employees were more likely than their predecessors to burn the midnight oil, but their schedules were still relatively sane by broader financial industry standards.[30]

As table 14-2 shows, at Guardian, the average total compensation of Guardian's top four executives in 1999 was low compared to that of other major life insurers.[31]

In 2001, 1,201 individuals in 235 insurance companies each received over $600,000 of total compensation. Only seven Guardianites made the list. Guardian's most highly paid executive that year, Joseph Sargent, was compensated less than the top two hundred insurance executives, even though Guardian was a Fortune 200 company. It is worth noting that top-producing general agents working for Guardian could make significantly more than the company's top officers.[32]

Historically, Guardian executives were also granted modest perquisites. In the early 1960s—the heyday of the "three-martini lunch"—Guardian officers were instructed to fly coach when possible and use first class only under unusual circumstances. Irving Rosenthal

TABLE 14-2
Compensation of Top Industry Executives, 1999

Average Compensation of Top 4 Corporate Officers, 1999 ($)	Company
900,806.50	**Guardian**
6,791,865.25	Aetna
4,727,321.00	Equitable
4,678,940.00	Hartford Financial
3,286,517.75	John Hancock
6,417,531.50	Lincoln National
1,659,023.75	Massachusetts Mutual
7,666,527.00	Metropolitan
3,218,872.75	NYLIC
2,349,456.75	Northwestern Mutual
1,866,415.75	Pacific Life Ins Co.
1,272,013.00	Penn Mutual
5,146,905.75	Prudential
3,121,277.00	Southwestern Life
4,880,546.75	TIAA

Source: *The Insurance Forum*, July 2001 and June 2002.

once read the head actuary of the group insurance division the riot act when group representatives were flown first class to a conference. Guardian eschewed such fancy extras as corporate jets and limousines during the 1970s, when such amenities were generally considered basic entitlements of high office in corporate America. Guardian's executives did not then, or later, have their own lunchroom, or even elaborately furnished offices. The executive suites, then as now, were best described as simple, comfortable, functional.[33]

So how was this relative disparity in executive compensation compensated for? The testimonies of Guardian executives reveal their belief that their quality of life on the job was high and that they believed in the social value of their work, which they expressed as service to policyholders. Their incomes in the late twentieth century were steady, not subject to massive fluctuations like those of executives of stock companies or managers of cyclical companies. And most of the time, since the company ran smoothly and was relatively immune from the shocks that upset wide swaths of the industry, their jobs were relatively less stressful than they might have been. There was little need to work on weekends; vacations were real vacations. Perhaps most important, in a business sense, Guardian could attract and keep strong executive talent by allowing officers to be entrepreneurs, to make decisions, take risks, and reap the rewards of their efforts. That many found the challenge as important as the cash conforms to what historians know to be the hallmark of entrepreneurial character.[34]

It should come as no surprise that academic studies have found that managers of mutual life companies generally earn less than managers of stock companies, and that the compensation of mutual managers is less closely tied to the performance of their companies. This finding might suggest that mutual insurers run a greater risk of mismanagement. (Lower salaries both lead to, and are a sign of, lower productivity; less correlation between salaries and performance results in inefficiency.) Joseph Sargent referred to the potential hazard, whenever he noted that "*well-managed* mutual companies"—the adjectives and noun were invariably joined in his rhetoric—were superior to stock corporations in the life insurance business. So how did Guardian ensure that it would be a well-managed mutual if its executive compensation were to remain modest by stock corporation standards, job satisfaction aside?[35]

Only part of the answer lay in the structure of compensation. Beginning in 1961, about the same time as other major U.S. corporations, Guardian began to offer deferred compensation contracts to its top executives. The agreements provided for deferred compensation of 12.5 percent, contingent on the officer's continued employment, solely for Guardian, until his retirement or death. That was not sufficient by 1974, when an ad hoc salary committee composed of nonofficer board members surveyed the salaries of senior officers at peer life insurance companies. When the committee found the salaries of Guardian executives at a low level compared with those of competitive companies, the committee voted, over the sharp opposition of one of its members, to raise executive salaries. But even with the increase, the company's officers were still far from being highly compensated by industry standards, and total compensation for executives still tracked company performance imperfectly.[36]

By the late 1980s, many life insurance companies began to reexamine the premise of industry executive compensation, which was typically composed of a fixed salary, deferred compensation, and standard benefits. Insurers worried that they could not attract or keep top talent in a world that was moving rapidly in the direction of tying executive remuneration to stock performance. This certainly made sense in ailing businesses where bureaucratic managers had lost sight of their obligations to maximize shareholder value, a problem then endemic to American capitalism. The context is important. The 1980s were a time of massive restructuring of mature industries, often through the threat of hostile takeovers, institutional investor pressure, and derivative shareholder lawsuits. "Make managers owners" (and board members, too) was the siren song, and see how shareholder value will increase. It made perfect sense, and in a general sense, it worked in one ailing industry after another.[37]

For many large life insurance companies, which were widely regarded, fairly or not, as bureaucratic dinosaurs, the problem was how to remain competitive in an industry marked by excess capacity, slow-growing demand, and declining margins. This was the major industry challenge of the 1990s. For most mutual life insurers, transforming themselves into stockholder corporations might solve the problem in one of two ways. As noted above, the ability to finance diversification through the sale of stock was attractive at a time when equity was becoming a cheaper alternative to debt as a source of financing. The other benefit was that executive performance could be more generously rewarded by, and tied to, stock ownership.

Joseph Sargent, who remained firmly committed to keeping Guardian a mutual company throughout his tenure as CEO, realized that the company could suffer a damaging drain in talent, as the allure of stock options grew ever stronger. Other insurers, of course, realized the same thing. Sargent was determined to address the threat without sacrificing the principle of mutuality. His chief actuary, Armand de Palo, was charged with creating a rewards-based compensation system within the constraints of the mutual form of organization.[38]

The upshot was a creative compensation scheme based on the idea of "phantom stock," which was reflected in a calculation of Guardian's "economic net worth," a proxy for market value. Any increases in the value of the phantom stock could then be credited to each executive's account based on title and level of responsibility. Since only a fraction of that credit, however, could be immediately drawn in cash (the remainder would wait until retirement), and since there were no shareholders demanding quarterly results, there was little incentive to overmanage the business for the short term.

Indeed, it was the deferred aspect of the compensation system that made it immune to manipulation. Executives either demonstrably increased the inflation-adjusted net worth of the company, or not. There was no incentive under this system to look for ways to "pump" the market value of the company, so that one could exercise one's options for a windfall profit. Guardian's economic net worth was based on long-term fundamental values, not the day-to-day movements of equity prices. Hence, by focusing executives on sustained long-term growth, the phantom stock plan was designed to increase executives' compensation through performance-based incentives, while still aligning their long-term interests with those of the policyholders.[39]

Performance-based, delayed compensation suffused the upper level of the firm, even the board of directors. Effective 1 January 2003, almost one-third of the compensation of the members of the board of directors became "at risk," directly linked to long-term company performance. "There's probably no other company out there," Caruso noted, "that's found a way yet to successfully make directors' pay dependent on how well they do the job for the mutual policyholders." Just how right Caruso was is evident in the flight from mutuality.[40]

Industry Demutualization

Tying the board's compensation to Guardian's long-term performance kept the economic incentives of individual board members compatible with the mutual form of organization. But the trend toward demutualization seemed almost irresistible for the rest of the industry. A committee of Guardian's board considered the matter of demutualization in 1999, but only in terms of the potential competitive effects upon the company of the conversion by many large insurers to stockholding corporations. The full board concluded only that management should make periodic reports on the subject. What followed was a series of reports and papers crafted by Joseph Sargent, Ed Kane, and Armand de Palo that made a staunch case for the status quo. It was an easy sell inside the company. "We talk commitment to mutuality on the podium and when we're outside," Chief Investment Officer Frank Jones said. "When we're here by ourselves, we close the door and we're the only ones that hear each other," he continued, "we talk the same line. That's not PR. That's reality."[41]

The case for demutualization was certainly not compelling so long as Guardian remained committed to its core business of life insurance. Efficiency was the byword among managers of insurance companies that abandoned mutualization. It took the pressure of shareholders—particularly the concentrated power of institutional shareholders—to make managers toe the line. And yet, for at least a century, many industry observers, researchers, and academic scholars have concluded that stock companies are not likely to be more efficient. And though it is hard to prove a counterfactual argument, there is ample historical evidence that many mutual insurance companies were arguably as efficient and effective as stock companies. Joseph Sargent repeatedly talked about the value of the "well-managed mutual insurance corporation," with the stress on the adjective. On his watch, Guardian's board of directors remained unshakably committed to the mutual form.[42]

Guardian's career agency force and general agency system were also wed to the mutual form of organization, and vice versa. "As you know," Irving Rosenthal said in 1972, "the chief aim of the Guardian is not to be forced back to operating on the branch-office or salaried manager system. We have been down that road and it is no good for a company of our type and size." Few life insurers invested as heavily as Guardian in a career field force.[43] And in turn, the general agents performed a key role in holding the home office managers' feet to the fire: pressing them ever onward toward better and more efficient policyholder service.

The agents, after all, had an enormous stake in the company. Their livelihoods were tied to corporate performance. They were not employees; they were the first line of customers for Guardian's products, and so the company had to work hard to ensure that the agency franchises remained valuable. If they did not, then distribution channels, the lifeblood of the whole enterprise, would languish. So whenever, over the years, the field force demanded better contracts, better technology, better policyholder support, and better products to sell, and even higher dividends, management had to listen. And, implicitly, what they, the field force, could not profitably sell were businesses that Guardian would leave to others—a check on temptations to diversify beyond the company's distributional capabilities.

As the century drew to a close, the overriding belief of Guardian's management was that the whole life business remained attractive, and was perhaps growing more so as other insurers redeployed their assets in favor of other financial services. As Robert Riegel, Moody's managing director for life and health, put it, demutualized insurers "are effectively exiting the business, or selling the line of business." Frank Jones put it differently: companies, he explained, do not like to publicly advertise defeat, so they stress that demutualization will help them to "diversify in other businesses." Basically, what demutualized companies implicitly admitted was that they could not any longer sell their traditional liabilities—life insurance policies—so they had to sell other types of liabilities, like GICs or, in the limit, equity products. "It's easier to sell mutual funds," said Joseph Caruso. "It's easier to sell a variable insurance product that has an investment in underlying mutual funds, especially in a booming stock market." Easier, perhaps, but not better business, necessarily, if one believed that life insurance still had large growth potential.[44]

So as long as one remained committed to the life insurance business, it was hard to sidestep the most apparent shortcoming of demutualization, which is that it placed shareholder (and managerial) interests ahead of those of policyholders. If demutualization did not hurt the whole life policyholder in the short run, it did not help, either, because gains in efficiency, if any, would accrue to stockholders. Demutualization, which was always accompanied by copious stock options, clearly enriched managers of the companies that made the switch. It was not lost on Guardian's directors that it had enriched a lot of board members as well.[45]

In one gambit, demutualization could be accomplished not through the creation not of a stock company, but instead of a so-called mutual stock company or mutual insurance holding company, a form of window-dressing that many felt amounted to fraud. This approach made it possible for managers to effectively demutualize without paying policyholders a cent. (Normally policyholders would either receive shares in the new stock company or cash—sometimes at their option, sometimes not.) Provident Mutual's policyholders were able to get a court order to block that company's 1999 bid to turn itself into a mutual stock company. Their victory was short lived, however, as Provident Mutual then agreed to merge with Nationwide. When the deal was consummated in August 2002, six departing Provident Mutual executives in effect appropriated some $36 million in severance payouts.[46]

Accruing gains for management that were not passed along to the company's policyholders was not a recipe for long-term success. Moody's Riegel came to the same conclusion in May 2002. "The realities of demutualization are credit negative," he explained, "because it creates an inherent conflict between shareholders and policyholders." (He might have added managers to the mix.) Moreover, Riegel added, demutualization "forces management to focus on short-term performance." On the other hand, Riegel was prepared to argue that demutualization might have some positive credit implications, such as providing greater access to the capital markets and an equity currency to fund potential acquisitions. Demutualization might enable insurers to attract and retain better managers. It might also promote greater financial reporting discipline and accountability. Such arguments would fall away in time, as evidence mounted that demutualization "actually changed very little other than the companies' organizational structure." A study of a "decade's worth of demutualization in life insurance" by Conning Research and Consulting, Inc., implied that the postreorganization performance of companies that had made the switch did not justify the costs of the demutualization process. The collective performance of former mutual life insurers that had gone public lagged behind that of those that had not.[47]

Even before such interim results were in, Guardian's managers were prepared to make the positive case for mutuality on all accounts. They thought that they had long since established that Guardian had been able to attract and retain top talent. Its financial reporting was far superior—that is, more transparent, less complicated—than that of the typical large stock corporation, and while it could not, by definition, raise equity capital, it had no problem financing the projects it had aspired to during the 1990s and thereafter. Guardian had simply paid cash out of its ample surplus for its acquisition of Fiduciary Insurance Company of America, a health insurer, and for First Commonwealth, a dental HMO. (Northwestern paid $1 billion in cash for money manager Frank Russell, which is best known for its Russell stock indexes.) And it was possible to make an acquisition *without paying a dime,* as happened when Guardian acquired the western Massachusetts–based Berkshire Life by assuming its liabilities, taking control of its assets, and entering an agreement whereby Berkshire policyholders exchanged their old policies for identical or superior Guardian policies. (As there was no outside class of equity holders to compensate, Berkshire was not so much sold as transferred.) The effective price was vouched for fairness by Goldman Sachs and the actuarial consulting firm Milliman and Robertson.[48]

Policyholders generally undervalued participating whole life contracts relative to nonparticipating ones, and the government, John Angle once complained, rarely acted as if it understood the difference between mutual and stock insurers. So why remain committed to either the product or the organization? The most compelling reason, for Guardian's managers, was almost invariably stated in ethical terms. The argument went as follows: whole life insurance is a long-term—for most people who buy it, a very long-term—financial investment. Why place the control of the companies that provide it into the hands of stockholders, particularly institutional holders, who tend to have short-term interests? It was, and is, at bottom, an ethical matter. Life insurers ought not to set themselves up for inherent, structural conflicts of interest in the management of their assets and liabilities.[49]

In that respect and others, Guardian exhibited a strong contrarian streak in an industry of conformists. To sum up, Guardian remained focused on its traditional core business in whole life insurance while other life insurers diversified out of it. It remained a mutual company while most of its peers converted to stock corporations. Guardian made a strong symbolic statement when it moved from its Union Square headquarters downtown, to Hanover Square, after a mass migration of high-profile financial service firms out of New York's traditional financial district to Midtown, and beyond, even out of town. The reason for Guardian's contrarian streak was largely pragmatic; it was thought to be smarter, even cheaper, to buck trends than to follow them.[50]

Force Majeure

In his annual report of February 2001, Guardian CEO Joseph Sargent looked soberly forward to "a very challenging year." He did not know how challenging. The U.S. economy had been teetering on the edge of recession following years of unprecedented growth and productivity gains. The nation's equity markets had been languishing ever since the long-lived bull market finally bubbled and then collapsed nearly a year earlier. Insurance sales were slack, and expenses were once again pushing upward to uncomfortable levels. There was plenty for a CEO to worry about. Knowing that his job was to make "three or four decisions a year," he was concerned to make the right ones. Two were aimed at cutting expenses and committing the organization to long-term thinking. With its recent FOCUS initiative, Guardian had set out to prune nonproductive expenses, reduce employees where possible, and streamline operations. Businesses have to do that from time to time. The Horizon program attempted to galvanize the organization around a set of ambitious, long-term goals designed to make Guardian one of the nation's most successful, and most admired, financial services companies by 2010. Just the kind of forward thinking any good company ought to do. So long as Guardian continued to focus and keep its expenses in line, its policyholders could expect that their investments were more than merely secure.[51]

What Sargent could not foresee, we now know, was much worse than he could possibly have envisioned—the enormous toll on the New York region's economy and the nation's morale that followed the terrorist at-tacks on the World Trade Center. There was no plan, no programmatic response, for that kind of event.

The total destruction of the massive Twin Towers and their surround-ing buildings took place just six blocks from Guardian's headquarters, which had only recently relocated to Hanover Square. Many of the com-pany's employees had a clear view of the fuel-laden jetliners as they struck and exploded at the beginning of the workday on 11 September. Guardian's senior managers locked down the building and walked each floor to comfort their employees, of whom many were fearful and grief-stricken. It was a good thing, too; Guardian's employees were safer in the home office than they would have been on the streets when the towers came down, filling lower Manhattan with a thick cloud of dust and de-bris. After the second tower fell, the employees were given lunch and bot-tled water and sent home. But since mass transit services in lower Man-hattan had ceased functioning, and automobile travel was out of the question, people had to trek northward to the bridges or to take refuge in public spaces or with friends who lived on Manhattan Island. Sargent himself walked the eighty blocks to Grand Central Station where the trains were at rest. It was the worst disruption of the company's business since the blackout of 9 November 1965 and the subsequent thirteen-day transit strike, when John Cameron and scores of his employees spent the night in the home office and when countless others had to hitchhike into work from their homes in the outer boroughs and beyond—inconve-nient, but nowhere nearly as traumatic nor as economically devastating as 9/11 would prove to be.[52]

Guardian's recovery from this sudden blow was rapid. Its home office was shut down for several days, as the lower part of Manhattan was sealed off for rescue efforts and environmental cleanup. But since most of its op-erations were spread across the nation in regional offices, the ordinary business of the company continued without much interruption. The company's executives communicated via conference calls. When the home office reopened for business, much of the western side of New York's financial district looked like what it was, a war zone, but Guardian's access points in Hanover Square seemed eerily calm. From street level, no one would have noticed the difference, save for the cloud of dust and smoke that lingered overhead. Under the cloud, business resumed.[53]

Guardian had to turn quickly to the problem of how to handle at-tack-related death claims arising from the scores of lives lost in the four hijacked airplanes and the thousands lost in the Trade Center and Pentagon. Immediately following the disaster, rumors circulated that life insurance companies would try to deny such death claims by seeking refuge in a stipulation presumed by many to be built into life contracts that absolved insurers from paying benefits on deaths from an "act of war." Whether the attack would be classified as an "act of war" was, of course, a question that only the courts could decide, but with the president of the United States treating the attacks as an act of war and his own declaration of "war on terror," there was little doubt what decision the courts would be likely to make. Guardian settled the matter for its own affected policyholders quickly. When asked if his company planned to dispute the claims, Joseph Sargent responded without hesitation that Guardian would pay, even before the full extent of its exposure to the event became clear.[54]

That was no minor decision. On the evening of 11 September, the total day's terror-related casualty expectations ranged as high as ten thousand. (The actual number turned out to be less than four thousand, still shockingly high and significant in actuarial terms.) Guardian had twenty-five hundred group life contracts with firms that were tenants in the World Trade Center, while the number of individual policyholders who worked in the Towers could not be ascertained. Given the company's market penetration in New York and in the upper-middle-income category, the numbers were likely to be significant. The next day, Guardian informed its field force that it would pay all attack-related death claims. Once Guardian spoke, other insurers could not suffer the negative publicity that would have arisen had they attempted to deny claims on their policies. Whether out of patriotism or competitive necessity (or both), insurers would fall in line and pay. Guardian's decision not only to pay the claims but also to *expedite* them exerted even more pressure on other insurers to do likewise. Guardian sped WTC claims along by setting up a special claims station near "Ground Zero" and by establishing a special 24/7 hotline.

Guardian's posture won it some friends. One insurance broker, formerly with an office in the WTC, decided to send all his business to Guardian. (Of the dozen different insurers with which he had large dealings, only Guardian called to see if he was safe and asked what it could do to help.) Unspoken, of course, is that there would be no protest, no opportunity for political attacks or regulatory criticism. No one who knew Sargent could believe that his response had been anything but reflexive, uncalculating. But, once again, as had often been the case, the ethical choice to defend the policyholder's interest was simply good business.

The lingering impact of 11 September 2001 on Guardian was but part and parcel of its impact on the overall economy. As the company recovered during 2002, it still had to cope with an unexpectedly anxious economy. World trade slowed. War loomed. The recession dragged on. Guardian was especially hard hit among life insurers, if only because of its relatively strong equity holdings. Its normally robust investment returns fell below the industry average for the second straight year.

Uncertainty and Conviction

Of course, nobody knows what lies over the horizon, as the terrorist attacks of 11 September all too tragically demonstrated. But people and businesses still need life insurance and probably always will.[55] In 2003, Guardian's planners were projecting growth for the company's niche market in insurance for the foreseeable future, even as large portions of the life insurance industry were scaling back their expectations.

Ironically, the biggest immediate issue that Guardian had to face at the end of 2000 was an unfamiliar problem with its investments. While the company did extremely well relative to its peers during the stock market boom of the late 1990s, its investment performance, as table 14-3 documents, plunged dramatically when the equity markets stalled in March 2000.

Increased financial market volatility threatened Guardian's risk-based capital ratio, a regulatory test of the risk-adjusted adequacy of insurers' capital base that was "computed by dividing actual capital by a formula-derived *required* capital." (The higher the ratio, the greater the insurer's presumed financial strength.) If the ratio were to fall below desirable limits, it would most certainly trigger reviews by independent rating agencies, if not by regulators themselves. If those reviews were less positive than they had been during the 1990s, the fear was that sales could be negatively impacted. (See table 14-4.)

A promising sign was that Guardian's persistency rate, which by 2002 had exceeded 92.5 percent since at least 1996, was one of the best, and most stable, in the business. High persistency was both a sign of a good business and a cause of more good business. A consistently high and stable persistency rate meant that policyholders were satisfied with their

TABLE 14-3

Total Investment Return (%) of Guardian and Other Leading Companies, 1996–2001

Company	1996	1997	1998	1999	2000	2001
Guardian	9.36	10.39	7.38	8.11	2.77	3.65
Equitable	7.35	8.66	9.03	7.82	9.64	6.30
John Hancock	8.29	7.94	7.63	7.24	8.35	6.81
Massachusetts Mutual	8.75	7.70	7.53	6.92	7.10	6.92
Metropolitan	7.55	8.22	7.48	6.99	6.76	8.33
MONY	7.16	7.40	6.26	7.10	7.42	3.81
National Life, VT	7.65	7.85	7.78	7.69	6.88	6.20
New York Life	7.50	8.32	8.74	8.01	6.18	5.52
Northwestern Mutual	9.03	9.15	7.85	8.65	7.46	6.24
Pacific Life	8.46	8.45	8.12	7.44	10.34	7.11
Penn Mutual	7.81	8.14	8.29	8.39	9.70	6.66
Phoenix Home Life	7.46	7.91	7.03	9.04	11.23	3.46
Principal Life	7.43	7.80	6.84	7.63	8.32	7.44
Provident Mutual	8.31	8.91	8.19	7.46	7.50	6.45
Prudential	8.09	8.09	7.39	7.60	6.20	5.78
Average	**8.01**	**8.33**	**7.70**	**7.74**	**7.72**	**6.05**
Median	**7.73**	**8.12**	**7.71**	**7.62**	**7.48**	**6.30**
Guardian's Edge **(Guardian – Average)**	1.35	2.06	−0.32	0.37	−4.95	−2.40

Source: "How to Choose a Life Insurance Company," Executive Presentation Client's Guide, 2001, 2002, GLIC archives.

TABLE 14-4

Guardian's Risk-Based Capital Ratio, 1997–2001

Year	Risk-Based Capital Ratio
1997	227
1998	220
1999	189
2000	205
2001	301
2002	353

Source: *The Insurance Forum*, August 2002; Office of the Corporate Secretary.

products. In addition, good persistency kept premiums flowing in for investment on a more or less predictable basis, which greatly facilitated the company's liquidity management and investment strategies.[56]

As for its operating performance, the FOCUS program aimed to cut expenses some $50 to $75 million. It was a problem that all life insurers struggled with, to be sure, but Guardian was determined to make the cuts with as little pain as possible, through attrition and well-compensated early retirements wherever possible. The mass layoffs or across-the-board salary reductions preferred by some other companies (and by Wall Street analysts!) were avoided. The business concern, explained Joseph Sargent's successor, Dennis Manning, was to trim the fat without cutting the muscle or nicking an artery.[57]

It was all aimed, of course, at keeping the company's expense ratio low, but the real key to that goal was, as always, to maintain a strong, productive field force that could write large amounts of quality business. Guardian held out the promise that motivated and productive representatives could make "a lot of money," while making their own hours, running their own businesses. Guardian would provide the training. It was a winning offer. While the total number of agents in the life insurance industry shrank in the latter half of the 1990s, Guardian's field force continued to grow, by a whopping 10 percent in 2000 alone.[58]

Following its acquisition of Berkshire, Guardian remained actively on the lookout for small but well-run insurers—specialized or niche firms that were too small to cover the large fixed costs of operating in the information age. What Guardian had to offer were scale economies and an ample surplus that might be tapped to purchase better computer systems or better access to large distribution networks. Though many such companies resisted absorption by larger concerns, Guardian had an attractive story to tell. Insofar as Berkshire was a precedent, managers of potential merger partners could rest easy if they wanted to stay in their jobs. Berkshire was reorganized as a wholly owned stock subsidiary of Guardian— Berkshire Life Insurance Company of America (BLICOA)—and was capitalized with its own assets. Berkshire's top management stayed on. After Guardian turned Berkshire's Pittsfield, Massachusetts, headquarters into a Guardian regional office, the merger actually resulted in an immediate increase of employment in western Massachusetts.[59]

Technological factors promised to change the landscape for insurance dramatically, in ways that were only partly foreseeable. The communications revolution, particularly the rise of the Internet, was transforming the way insurance was sold and underwritten. It was now easier and faster than ever to obtain life insurance protection. One company, the Hartford, created a program that allowed bankers and securities brokers to sign up their clients for life insurance in just eight days, without medical examination or complicated forms. The information age was perforce transforming customer service expectations. Guardian's managers knew that the Internet was going to transform their business, but they did not know how much or how quickly. After waiting while others innovated, the company developed its own website and plunged in.[60]

It had to. Policyholders were demanding prompter, more courteous service. When it took Joseph Sargent six months to get his new address listed on his twelve Guardian policies in 1995, he knew that the company had to catch up. As Guardian anticipated the deregulation of the insurance industry, its managers prepared for it by investing more heavily than it ever had in service and technology, $35 million. As Guardian's policyholder service improved, its competitors' did likewise.[61]

One area of high uncertainty but great importance was the potential, and perhaps inevitable, use of genetic testing in underwriting. Insurers, on the one hand, were reluctant to require genetic testing because of the storm of controversy such a requirement would probably entail. On the other hand, if insurers did not require genetic testing, they might increasingly face adverse selection, an age-old problem in insurance, in a newer and politically sensitive form. For example, if newly insured individuals who learned that they have high predispositions to deadly diseases purchased term life insurance while those who learned that they have healthy genes purchased life annuities, insurers and their existing policyholders would suffer. As genetic tests became cheaper and more accurate, the problem was bound to increase. Insurers would ultimately be forced to take action (just as they had been forced to begin testing for AIDS in the 1980s). At the very least, they were going to have to ensure that individuals who underwent genetic testing shared the results with potential insurers.[62]

A more immediate threat to life insurers was posed by variable life insurance policies that carried a "secondary guarantee." Broadly speaking, variable life policies burdened the policyholder with investment risk. A variable policy, for instance, might be worth $100,000 one year, but only $50,000 the next, depending on the performance of the assets underlying the policy. In an effort to increase sales of variable policies, a number of companies began guaranteeing minimum policy values, which made some risk-averse policyholders feel safer and posed little threat to insurers, at least during the time of the great bull market of the 1990s. After 2000, the markets were not so kind to holders of variable policies. If companies were to reach the point where they could not make good on their guarantees, the result would be a crisis for the entire life industry.[63]

Another uncertain, if not ominous, sign for the industry is the specter of federal regulation. In the past, coalitions of life insurers and state regulators joined successfully to rebuff attempts to regulate the life insurance industry at the national level. In the wake of financial deregulation that opened the path to the merger of banks and insurance companies, however, a number of large life insurers, including Guardian, have quietly begun to consider backing at least an optional federal insurance system. If the federal government became a unitary regulator instead of the fifty-first regulator, a federal insurance regulatory system would probably prove to be cheaper and more efficient than the hodgepodge of state regulations currently in place. But that is an unlikely scenario.[64]

Health insurance was another great area of uncertainty. As Armand de Palo pointed out, the current system was "madness." It was certainly in crisis. The insured essentially subsidized the uninsured, medical and pharmaceutical costs were spiraling, and nothing stood in the way. Employers struggled to lay off the rising premium costs. Worse yet, the political system appeared incapable of tackling the problem. Politicians feared the wrath of voters if they did anything that would require higher taxes or lower subsidies, of trial lawyers if they tried to cap medical malpractice suits, and of doctors and other health professionals if they attempted anything that might decrease their incomes. Of all the interest groups that might be affected by change, only the insurers, who could always be accused of price gouging, were politically vulnerable to attack. No end to the crisis was in sight. Fortunately, health insurance, though hardly a trivial component, was not the mainstay of Guardian's business.[65]

Finally, Guardian always had to make the calculation as to whether its core business was the right business. Throughout the broad financial services industry, consolidation, diversification, and expansion into foreign territories were the dominant trends. Most large insurers had followed suit. Guardian had once been an international company, but once it had retreated to the confines of the United States after World War I, it had never looked back. In 1973, Guardian's general agents worried that banks were encroaching upon the insurance business, and George Conklin considered the prospects of entering banking. But the regulatory barriers could not have been overcome in that period, even if Conklin had concluded (and he did not) that the merger of banking and insurance would be efficient. When Joseph Sargent talked the talk of diversification in 2001—"Guardian is building a diversified financial services company"— he was quick to add, "on the chassis of a great mutual life insurance company."[66]

Strategies must always be reconsidered. Institutions must change. No large insurance company is likely to survive on insurance alone. But looking ahead, Guardian has concluded that its life insurance business is indeed its best business, its policyholder its bedrock stakeholder, its general agents and career field representatives its first customers, and its mutual form of governance its best assurance that the company will remain robustly competitive as far as one can reasonably see into the twenty-first century.

Appendix

The authors' contention that technological changes were at least as important as broad socioeconomic factors to the growth of life insurance in the United States in the nineteenth century is formally presented in figure A-1. The upward sloping lines represent the supply of life insurance at various prices at different points in time. Supply increased modestly (the supply curve shifted to the right) after the financial revolution of the 1790s. It increased more (shifted further right) after the growth of mutual insurers and stock companies offering participating insurance in the 1840s. Supply increased still more after the proliferation of Elizur

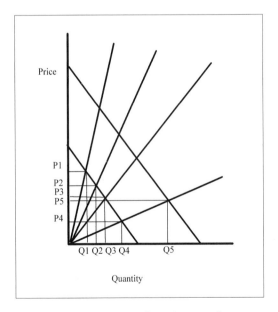

FIGURE A-1 *Supply and Demand for Life Insurance over Time*

Wright's level premium concept and the entry of new companies, including Guardian, in the middle decades of the century.

The two downward sloping lines represent the demand for life insurance at various prices at two points in time. Demand remained largely unchanged until the advent of the sales agency system, which increased demand (shifted the demand curve to the right). Agents made certain that prospects repeatedly confronted their need for protection until they signed up.

The intersection of the supply and demand curves indicates the point of market equilibrium, where the quantity of policies supplied was equal to the quantity demanded. The point of equilibrium provides us with two important pieces of information: the price of policies (net cost to the insured), indicated by a horizontal line running from the equilibrium to a point on the vertical axis; and the quantity of insurance contracted, indicated by a vertical line running from the equilibrium to a point on the horizontal axis. Note that the increased supply of life insurance led to lower net costs (P_1, P_2, P_3, P_4) and slightly higher quantities of insurance sold (Q_1, Q_2, Q_3, Q_4). The increased demand that accompanied the widespread implementation of the agency system increased net costs (P_5) but greatly increased the quantity of insurance sold (Q_5).

Notes

Notes placed at ends of paragraphs contain all citations for the paragraph, in the following order:

1. textual explanations, definitions, explications, etc.;
2. secondary sources;
3. periodicals not published by Guardian;
4. periodicals published by Guardian;
5. the authors' interviews with Guardian officers;
6. non-Guardian archival materials;
7. materials in Guardian's corporate archives;
8. materials in Guardian's office of the corporate secretary.

NOTES TO THE PREFACE

1. Carl Heye Speech, 1930, Office of the Secretary, Scott, Box 64; James A McLain to Lavinia Dudley, 8 September 1947, Public Relations Department Records, Box 84, GLIC archives.

2. *Guardian Scene*, September 1964. Interview with Dennis Manning, 1 December 2001; interview with Art Ferarra, 2 May 2002.

3. MacLean, *Life Insurance*, 25.

4. *Proceedings of the Twelfth Annual Meeting of Life Insurance Association of America*, 1918, 33; Fiske, "Life Insurance Investments"; Gephart, "Loans," 334; Hurrell, "America First in Life Insurance"; Krooss and Blyn, *History of Financial Intermediaries*, 109. Speech by Irving Rosenthal, Group Conference, 14 April 1969, Office of the Executive Vice President, Rosenthal, Box 183, GLIC archives.

5. Buley, *American Life Convention*, xx.

6. Lane, *A Maine Heritage*, 7.

7. Kalmbach, "Chairman's Address."

NOTES TO THE INTRODUCTION

1. The insurer would not have paid a double indemnity or accident benefit if it could prove that Loman's demise was suicide and not an automobile accident. But it could not have denied payment of the policy's face value. In one case a man went into one of the large New York mutuals threatening to kill himself if his policy was not paid. The company of course declined to make payment. The man proceeded to the lobby, where he blew his own brains out. The company paid the claim.

Loman had no other reason to fear that the insurer would not make good on the policy. After 1907 all New York life insurance policies were incontestable for any reason, including misrepresentation on the application, two years and a day after their issuance. Before 1907, most companies voluntarily offered an incontestability clause, though such clauses naturally varied somewhat from company to company. McCall, *A Review*, 52; Villaronga, *Incontestable Clause*. Interview with Ed Kane, 22 February 2002.

2. Annual Report, 1952, Box 3; Memorandum, 21 June 1934, Claim Department Records, Box 77, GLIC archives.

3. Bosch-Domench and Silvestre, "Risk Aversion?"; Campbell, Ritchie, "Demand for Life Insurance"; Fischer, "Life Cycle Model"; Kreinin et al., "Life Insurance Premiums"; Manes, "Economic History of Insurance"; Pissarides, "Wealth-Age Relation"; Roover, "Marine Insurance"; Ruwell, *American Marine Insurance*; Yaari, "Uncertain Lifetime."

4. Bernheim, "Bequest Motives?"; Kreinin et al., "Life Insurance Premiums"; Winterhalder, "Social Foraging"; Winterhalder and Smith, "Human Behavioral Ecology"; Winterhalder et al., "Risk-Sensitive Adaptive Tactics."

5. Black and Skipper, *Life Insurance*; Genovese, "Insurance Costs of Slaveholding," 146–47; Lewis, "Demand for Life Insurance"; Savitt, "Slave Life Insurance," 587. Field Advisory Board Meeting Proceedings, 21 April 1966, Box 75, GLIC archives. Minutes of the Board of Directors, 25 July 2001, Office of the Corporate Secretary.

6. Axelson, "Opportunities in Life Insurance"; Babbel, "Price Elasticity of Demand."

7. Fama, "Agency Problems"; Ross, "Economic Theory of Agency"; Zimmerman, "Research in Agency Management."

8. *Proceedings of the Fourteenth Annual Meeting of Life Insurance Association of America*, 1920, 11; Hughes, "Life Insurance Enterprise"; Hull, "What's Happening?"; Johnson, "Regulation of Life Insurance Companies," 158; Mathewson, "Information," 131–33; Zartman, "Control of Life Insurance Companies."

9. Krooss and Blyn, *History of Financial Intermediaries.*

10. Axelson, "Opportunities in Life Insurance"; Diamond, "Economic Impact"; Hurrell, "America First in Life Insurance"; Life Insurance Association of America, *Life Insurance Companies*; Stevens, "Greatest Service"; Sylla, "Financial Systems."

11. Hacker, *Hamilton in the American Tradition.*

12. Buley, *American Life Convention*; Wright, Robert E., "Banking and Politics in New York."

13. Buley, *American Life Convention*; Knapp, *Science of Life Insurance*; North, "Entrepreneurial Policy"; North, "Life Insurance and Investment Banking"; Ransom and Sutch, "Tontine Insurance"; Zartman, "Control of Life Insurance Companies."

14. Legend had it that a pelican mother would pierce her own breast to feed her fledglings during time of famine. Presumably this symbolizes the parents' forgone consumption to provide life insurance. Axelson, "Opportunities in Life Insurance"; Stone, *Since 1845*, 4, 16. Name Cases, Legal Department Records, Box 219, GLIC archives.

15. *Profile of Life Insurance Ownership*; Geren, "Contribution of Life Insurance," 48; *Life Insurance Fact Book.*

16. Mishkin, *Money, Banking, and Financial Markets.*

17. Leung, "Why Do Some Households Save So Little?"

18. Charles Rudd to Carl Heye, 26 October 1918, Carl Heye to Charles Rudd, 28 October 1918, Office of the President, Heye, Box 51, GLIC archives. Minutes of the Board of Directors, 28 February, 25 April 2001, Office of the Corporate Secretary.

19. Chen et al., "Risk-Taking Behaviour."

20. For a good overview of these issues, see Baker and Smith, *New Financial Capitalists.* John C. Angle, "Golden Opportunities," 21 January 1984, Office of the President, Angle, Box 195, GLIC archives.

21. Carr and Mathewson, "Unlimited Liability."

22. Haeger, "Eastern Financiers"; Mackie, *Facile Princeps*; Wallace, "Friendly Societies"; Zartman, "Control of Life Insurance Companies." Other important sources for the history of life insurance in the nineteenth-century United States include Abbott, *Story of NYLIC*; Buley, *American Life Convention*; Clough, *Mutual Life Insurance Company of New York*; Collier, *A Capital Ship*; Fowler, *History of Insurance in Philadelphia*; Knight, "History of Life Insurance"; O'Donnell, *History of Life Insurance*; Pritchett, *Financing Growth*; Stalson, *Marketing Life Insurance*; White, *Massachusetts Hospital Life Insurance Company*; Williamson and Smalley, *Northwestern Mutual Life.*

23. Mayers and Smith, "Contractual Provisions"; Orren, *Corporate Power*; Verbrugge, "Stock versus Mutual Performance"; Zartman, "Control of Life Insurance Companies."

24. Clough, *Mutual Life Insurance Company of New York,* 210; Kellner and Mathewson, "Economies in the Life Insurance Industry"; MacLean, *Life Insurance,* 25; Smith, B., and Stutzer, "Mutual Formation and Moral Hazard." Interview with Joseph Caruso, 30 November 2001. Minutes of the Board of Directors, 28 February, 25 April 2001, Office of the Corporate Secretary.

25. The subject of this study, formerly called the Germania Life Insurance Company, should not be confused with Guardian Mutual Life Insurance Company of New York, which operated from 1859 to 1873, nor with Guardian Life of Seattle (reinsured in 1909), Guardian Life of Madison, Wisconsin (National Guardian after 1919), Guardian Mutual Life Insurance Company of Dallas (later Guardian International Life), Guardian Life Insurance Company of Texas (later Guardian American Life), Guardian Life and Hospital Aid Company of Greenville, South Carolina (later Guardian Life Insurance Company of South Carolina), Guardian National Life Insurance Company of Lincoln, Nebraska (reinsured in 1944), United Guardian Life Association of New Jersey (principals imprisoned in 1940), or any other number of life insurers, most minuscule, that used the Guardian name. Drucker, *Essential Drucker,* 40; Pritchett, *Capital Mobilization.* James Scott to J. C. Barnsley, 5 August 1949, M. Hewitt, n.d., Office of the Secretary, Scott, Box 64; Executive Officers Committee Minutes, 5 July 1939, 16 January 1940, Box 178; Executive Officers Committee Minutes, 4, 18, 25 April, 9, 23 May, 10 October 1944, 29 January, 19 February, 12 March 1946, 2 March 1948, Box 179; James Gardiner to John Angle, 15 December 1983, History Files, John C. Angle, Box 199; Price Topping to Philip Dalsimer, 9 May 1957, Guardian Symbols Registration, Name Cases, Legal Department Records, Box 219; Before the Commissioners of Insurance, State of Iowa, 1 November 1962, Guardian vs. American Guardian Life Insurance Company, Utah, 1962, Legal Department Records, Box 220, GLIC archives.

26. Annual Report, 1945, Box 2; Annual Statement, 1869, Box 106; "Special Committee" Minutes, 9 July 1862, Box 125, GLIC archives.

27. de Palo, *Dividend Study Note*; Norberg, "Theory of Bonus in Life Insurance."

28. Ourusoff and Meschi, "Staying Power." Interview with Joseph Caruso, 30 November 2001.

29. See Houston and Simon, "Economies of Scale," which concludes that "average cost functions for the life insurance industry . . . show increasing and then constant returns . . . beyond $100 million [in 1970 dollars] of premiums." Clough, *Mutual Life Insurance Company of New York,* 201; Drucker, *Essential Drucker,* 10; Geehan, "Returns to Scale"; Kellner and Mathewson, "Economies in the Life Insurance Industry"; North, "Capital Accumulation," 252; Palyi, "Life Insurance," 66. Interview with Joseph Caruso, 30 November 2001; interview with John Angle, 21 March 2002. Annual Report, 1946, Box 2, GLIC archives.

30. Abbott, *Story of NYLIC,* preface.

NOTES TO PART I

1. The company frequently used the term "Guardianite" to refer to Guardian employees. Sullivan, "Life Insurance," 346. *The Guardian Family News,* January 1921; *Service,* 2 April 1923; *The Bond,* January 1944; *Home Office Newsletter,* 14 April 1950; *Newsletter,* 25 September 1979. Annual Report, 1963, Box 4; John C. Angle, "Guardian Life: 1981 General Agents Conference, Closing Address," 23 January 1981, Office of the President, Angle, Box 195, GLIC archives.

2. "After Two Years," 1903, Office of the President, Doremus, Box 45, GLIC archives.

3. Douglass, *American Business,* 153, 156; Drucker, *Essential Drucker,* 20; Johnson, William C., "Regulation of Life Insurance Companies," 155–56; Murphy, Sharon, "Life Insurance"; North, "Capital Accumulation," 238–39; Norton, "A Brief History," 1089; Zelizer, *Morals and Markets.* Annual Report, 1954, Box 3, GLIC archives.

4. Buley, *American Life Convention,* xii, 25; Fowler, *History of Insurance in Philadelphia,* 607; John, "Insurance Investment."

5. Douglass, *American Business*, 152–53; Fowler, *History of Insurance in Philadelphia*, 608, 614–20; Mackie, *Facile Princeps*; Mackie, *"That Is to Say"*; Manes, "Economic History of Insurance," 30, 33; Poitras, *History of Financial Economics*, 187; Smith, Robert Sydney, "Barcelona"; Stone, *A Short History*.

6. Clough, *Mutual Life Insurance Company of New York*, 7; Manes, "Economic History of Insurance," 31; Norton, "A Brief History," 1090. Walter Grosser, "Writing a Riddle Maker," *The Guardian Life Service*, 26 September 1921.

7. Manes, "Economic History of Insurance," 32–33. *The Guardian*, 30 October 1961. Annual Report, 1964, Box 4, GLIC archives.

8. John, "Insurance Investment." For a fuller description of the financial revolutions, especially that of the United States, see Wright, *Wealth of Nations Rediscovered* and Wright, *Hamilton Unbound*.

9. *Proposals of the Pennsylvania Company*; Abbott, *Story of NYLIC*, 14; Buley, *American Life Convention*, 49; Douglass, *American Business*, 152, 154; Fowler, *History of Insurance in Philadelphia*, 610–11, 623–42; Haeger, "Eastern Financiers"; Stone, *A Short History*, 28; White, *Massachusetts Hospital Life Insurance Company*.

10. *Proposals of the Pennsylvania Company*; Buley, *American Life Convention*, 17; Pearson, "Moral Hazard," 7; Zelizer, *Morals and Markets*, 42.

11. Horack et al., "Regulation of Insurance," 197.

12. To this day, Guardian and other life insurers use *consulting* actuaries, i.e., business consultants skilled in the actuarial sciences, who help them with complex issues, a fundamentally different function than the one performed by Homans and other nineteenth-century itinerants. See, for example, Milliman and Robertson to Peter Tompa, 19 April 1963, Office of the Executive Vice President, Rosenthal, Box 183, GLIC archives.

13. According to Buley, "mankind in the mass [is] . . . constitutionally incapacitated, in applying the generally known rules of simple arithmetic to financial matters beyond the limited experience of the individual." *American Life Convention*, 124; Clough, *Mutual Life Insurance Company of New York*, 57; Moorhead, *History of the Actuarial Profession*. "Actuaries Who Practiced in North America Up to 1869," *The Actuary* (April 1983): 4–5. "The New Policy Reviewed," *New York Daily Courier*, 7 December 1872, Public Relations Department Records, Box 85; Dr. A. Zillmer, "Contributions to Life Insurance Companies' Theory of the Premium Reserve," 1863, "William Bard," n.d., History Files, John C. Angle, Box 199, GLIC archives.

14. Buck, *Quill Pens*; Buley, *American Life Convention*, 81; Murphy, Ray, "Sale of Annuities by Governments"; Murphy, Ray, "Significant Annuity Developments"; Pearson, "Moral Hazard," 9; Poitras, *History of Financial Economics*, 155, 201–7; Scoles, "Development of Life Annuities." A. C. Webster, "Report on Underwriting," May 1971, Office of the Executive Vice President, Rosenthal, Box 184; Dr. A. Zillmer, "Contributions to Life Insurance Companies' Theory of the Premium Reserve," 1863, History Files, John C. Angle, Box 199, GLIC archives.

15. Campbell, "Mortality Tables," 425–27; Clough, *Mutual Life Insurance Company of New York*, 59–61.

16. Clough, *Mutual Life Insurance Company of New York*, 26; Douglass, *American Business*, 153, 308–9; Poitras, *History of Financial Economics*, 208. John C. Angle, "The Actuary As a Professional," Office of the President, Angle, Box 195, GLIC archives.

17. Fowler, *History of Insurance in Philadelphia*, 610; Manes, "Economic History of Insurance," 31; Pearson, "Moral Hazard," 11–15, 19–27; Pressnell, "Rate of Interest in the Eighteenth Century"; Tuckett, *Practical Remarks*, 27. "Life Insurance Assets and 'Profits' as Tests of Prosperity," *New York Times*, 7 January 1870, Public Relations Department Records, Box 85, GLIC archives.

18. Buley, *American Life Convention*, 35–36; Collier, *A Capital Ship*; Douglass, *American Business*, 156–58; Fortune, "A Theory of Optimal Life Insurance," 591; Fowler, *History of Insurance in Philadelphia*, 646–73; Hutcheson, "Some Facts"; Murphy, Sharon, "Life Insurance"; North, "Capital Accumulation," 244; Packard, *Hidden Persuaders*, 68–78; Roover, "Marine In-

surance"; Tuckett, *Practical Remarks,* 31; Wainwright, *A Philadelphia Story.* Annual Report, 1946, Box 2; Minutes of the Department Head Meeting, 20 February 1930, Home Office Records, Box 74, GLIC archives.

19. Douglass, *American Business,* 158; North, "Capital Accumulation," 238, 240.

20. Hudnut, *Semi-Centennial History,* v.

NOTES TO CHAPTER 1

1. Except where otherwise noted, this section draws on Kesslinger, *Guardian,* and Rapone, *Guardian.* Germania Life Insurance Company Charter, 1860, Box 1, GLIC archives.

2. *Days of Knights;* Beito, *Mutual Aid;* Kacy, *Unique and Different,* 10–11; Palyi, "Life Insurance," 61–63; Soyer, *Jewish Immigrant Associations;* Wallace, "Friendly Societies." Carl Heye Speech, 1930, Office of the Secretary, Scott, Box 64; "Germania Lebens Versicherungs Gessellschaft," 3 December 1867, Circulars, Box 94, GLIC archives.

3. Buley, *American Life Convention,* 47, 64; Hudnut, *Semi-Centennial History,* 48; Pritchett, *Capital Mobilization,* 408. Cornelius Doremus, "Address of the President to the Company's Managers," 30 May 1901, Home Office Records, Box 74, GLIC archives.

4. Record of the Certificates Issued and Cancelled, n.d., Germania Life Insurance Company, Box 137, GLIC archives.

5. When Kling died in 1872, his wife received $3,636.36, the face of the policy plus dividends, and all for premium payments of just $1,157.52. President's Report, 11 July, 30 September, 31 December 1860, Box 42; Advertisement: "This Was Wall Street," *Saturday Evening Post,* 27 June 1959, Public Relations Department Records, Box 84; "Special Committee" Minutes, 9 March 1861, 9 April 1862, Box 125, GLIC archives.

6. Buley, *American Life Convention,* 73–74; Clough, *Mutual Life Insurance Company of New York,* 46; MacLean, *Life Insurance,* 527. President's Reports, 30 June 1861, Box 42, GLIC archives.

7. James, *Metropolitan,* 59; Lane, *A Maine Heritage,* 10; Stone, *Since 1845,* 74.

8. President's Reports, 31 December 1861, 30 September 1862, 31 March 1863, Box 42; "Special Committee" Minutes, 9 April 1862, Box 125, GLIC archives.

9. The statement "cash only" refers to the company itself, not its agents, who were allowed well into the twentieth century to accept promissory notes, "AT THEIR OWN RISK AND PERIL." and on what regulators called a "strictly limited" basis. The matter was a personal one between the agents and the policyholder as the company immediately charged the agent's account for the amount of the premium, the policy went into effect, and the agent earned all interest on the note. The distinction blurred somewhat during the Depression, however, when Guardian advanced large sums to many of its agents. *Testimony Taken before the Joint Committee,* 5,519–20; Douglass, *American Business,* 158; Tuckett, *Practical Remarks;* Williamson and Smalley, *Northwestern Mutual Life,* 29. Reports on the Examination of the Guardian, 1933, Box 70; Reports on the Examination of the Guardian, 1952, Box 71; Hooning v. McMurphey and Guardian, 1923, Legal Department Records, Box 79; "Business Instructions for Agents," 1903, Manuals, Box 96; Executive Officers Committee Minutes, 20 September 1921, 10 September 1940, Box 178, GLIC archives.

10. Abbott, *Story of NYLIC,* 93; Hudnut, *Semi-Centennial History,* 43; Rapone, *Guardian,* 39–43. "Special Committee" Minutes, 9 April 1862, Box 125, GLIC archives.

11. President's Reports, 30 June 1862, Box 42; Carl Heye Speech, 1930, Office of the Secretary, Scott, Box 64, GLIC archives.

12. Buley, *American Life Convention,* 76.

13. President's Reports, 30 June 1861, Box 42; "Interesting Statistics of Life Insurance," *New York Daily Tribune,* 23 June 1869, Public Relations Department Records, Box 85; "Special Committee" Minutes, 8 April 1863, Box 125, GLIC archives.

14. President's Reports, 30 June 1861, Box 42, GLIC archives.

15. "Expenses of Twenty-Seven of the Oldest and Largest Life Insurance Companies," *New*

York Tribune, 20 November 1869, Public Relations Department Records, Box 85; "Special Committee" Minutes, 9 May 1865, 9 April 1870, Box 125, GLIC archives.

16. Buley, *American Life Convention,* 91; Wallison, *Federal Chartering,* 35. John E. Albert, "Historical Facts and Data Regarding the Germania Life Insurance Co. of America," 1950, Office of the Secretary, Scott, Box 64; Executive Officers Committee Minutes, 6 February 1940, Box 178, GLIC archives.

17. Buley, *American Life Convention,* 92; McCall, *A Review,* 22–24. Carl Heye Speech, 1930, Office of the Secretary, Scott, Box 64, GLIC archives.

18. "The Germania Life-Insurance Company," *King's Handbook,* 1892: 673–74, Public Relations Department Records, Box 85; "To the Company's Medical Examiners," 1 November 1877, "To the Company's Agents!" 1 December 1878, Circulars, Box 94; Minutes of the Board of Directors, 25 January 1893, Box 121, GLIC archives.

19. Advisory Committee Minutes, 27 February 1895, Office of the Secretary, Scott, Box 64; Minutes of the Board of Directors, 25, 30 January 1893, Box 121, GLIC archives.

20. Interview with Armand de Palo, 27 January 2003. Germania Life Insurance Company Charter, 1860, Box 1; Solomon Hanford to Germania, 17 May 1924, Office of the Secretary, Heye and Neuendorffer, Box 54; Carl Heye to Joseph Kirby, 5 December 1924, Office of the President, Heye, Box 51; Carl Heye Speech, 1930, Office of the Secretary, Scott, Box 64; Minutes of the Board of Directors, 12 December 1896, Box 121, GLIC archives.

21. *Testimony Taken before the Joint Committee,* 5,507. Except where otherwise noted, Germania's stock prices are compliments of Ben Chabot of the University of Wisconsin.

22. Palyi, "Life Insurance . . . Continued," 175–76; Rapone, *Guardian,* 109–11. "Germania Life Stock Subscription," 8 May 1919, Office of the President, Heye, Box 48; Carl Heye to Former Stockholders of the Germania, 17 December 1925, Office of the President, Heye, Box 51; "Misc. Stock Correspondence" folders, n.d., Office of the Secretary, Heye and Neuendorffer, Boxes 54–55; Cornelius Doremus, "Address of the President to the Company's Managers," 30 May 1901, Home Office Records, Box 74; Stockholders Records, n.d., Boxes 86–90; Stock Transfer Book, n.d., Box 139; John C. Angle to David Mayers, 29 June 1982, History Files, John C. Angle, Box 198, GLIC archives.

23. Mishkin, *Money, Banking, and Financial Markets;* Westerfield, *Branch Banking.*

24. Fowler, *History of Insurance in Philadelphia,* 627–28. Robert Stewart Buchanan Papers, New York Historical Society.

25. Buley, *American Life Convention,* 106. Scrapbook, 1869–77, Public Relations Department Records, Box 85; Minutes of the Board of Directors, 12 October 1887, Box 121; "Board of Directors Minutes, Extracts—Agencies, 1860–1946," Office of the Secretary, 1942–75, Box 180, GLIC archives.

26. "The Guardian Life Insurance Company of America," 6 September 1918, Office of the President, Heye, Box 47; Minutes of the Board of Directors, 26 October 1910, Box 122, GLIC archives.

27. Buley, *American Life Convention,* 107; Douglass, *American Business,* 306–7.

28. Abbott, *Story of NYLIC,* 126–27, 145; Buley, *American Life Convention,* 107–11; Clough, *Mutual Life Insurance Company of New York,* 163; Hudnut, *Semi-Centennial History,* 150; North, "Capital Accumulation," 247; Whatley, "Agency System." "European Business," 1 September 1904, Circulars, Box 94; Kenneth Black, "International Life Insurance: Opportunities and Problems," 14 July 1981, History Files, John C. Angle, Box 198, GLIC archives.

29. Douglass, *American Business,* 302.

30. Grant, *Insurance Reform,* 25. "Deeply Absurd," *Collier's,* 6 February 1909, 10. "Expenses of Twenty-Seven of the Oldest and Largest Life Insurance Companies," *New York Tribune,* 20 November 1869, Public Relations Department Records, Box 85, GLIC archives.

31. Buley, *American Life Convention,* 92; Keller, *Life Insurance Enterprise,* 136; North, "Capital Accumulation," 248. Scrapbook, 1869–77, Public Relations Department Records, Box 85, GLIC archives.

32. Buley, *American Life Convention,* 217; North, "Life Insurance and Investment Banking."

33. The story of Perkins's dual role has been told by various Morgan biographies, the best of which is Strouse, *Morgan,* 409ff.

34. Abbott, *Story of NYLIC,* 167; Buley, *American Life Convention,* 47, 133, 151; McElreath, *History of the Industrial Life,* 65; North, "Capital Accumulation," 252; Walker, *Guaranteed Investment Contracts,* 33; Williamson and Smalley, *Northwestern Mutual Life,* 254.

35. Grant, *Insurance Reform,* 28–29.

36. Except where otherwise noted, this section is based on the following sources: Carosso, *Investment Banking in America;* Douglass, *American Business,* 307; Grant, *Insurance Reform,* 40–44; Johnson, "Regulation of Life Insurance Companies," 168–70; Keller, *Life Insurance Enterprise;* North, "Capital Accumulation," 251–52; Pusey, *Charles Evans Hughes.*

37. Buley, *American Life Convention,* 214; North, "Capital Accumulation," 250–51; North, "Life Insurance and Investment Banking."

38. Douglass, *American Business,* 309–10. Carl Heye, "50th Anniversary," September 1939, Office of the President, Heye, Box 202, GLIC archives.

39. Keller, *Life Insurance Enterprise,* 195–96, 257.

40. Douglass, *American Business,* 309; Grant, *Insurance Reform,* 53–60.

41. *Testimony Taken before the Joint Committee,* 5,501–62 and 5,567–70, which pages are in volume 6 of this consecutively paginated source. For Germania's "exhibits," see volume 9, exhibits 808–20, 825–26. "Germania Life," *Insurance Monitor,* 1906, 52–53. Reports on the Examination of the Germania, 1901, Box 70; "Materials Intended for the Public," Public Relations Department Records, Box 95, GLIC archives.

42. Cornelius Doremus to H. P. Reager, 28 December 1901, Office of the Secretary, Scott, Box 64; "Elected to Succeed Cornelius Doremus," *The Surveyor: A Weekly Insurance Journal,* 1 January 1915, Public Relations Department Records, Box 85; Minutes of the Board of Directors, 28 January 1903, 25 January 1905, 24 April 1907, Box 122, GLIC archives.

43. Buck, *Quill Pens,* 42; Buley, *American Life Convention,* 224; Clough, *Mutual Life Insurance Company of New York,* 221; Collier, *A Capital Ship;* Grant, *Insurance Reform,* 42; Stone, *Since 1845,* 114.

44. Burkholder, "Ives"; Feder, *Ives;* Perlis, *Ives;* Rossiter, *Ives.* James J. Nugent, 1920, Field Offices, Box 202, GLIC archives.

45. Buley, *American Life Convention,* xiii, 591 n.40. Executive Officers Committee Minutes, 17 January 1922, 6 December 1938, 21 February 1939, Box 178; Carl Heye, "50th Anniversary," September 1939, Office of the President, Heye, Box 202, GLIC archives.

46. *Proceedings of the Fiftieth Annual Meeting of the Life Insurance Association of America,* 1956, 157; Buley, *The American Life Convention,* 247ff.; Clough, *Mutual Life Insurance Company of New York,* 239–44; Hughes, "Life Insurance Enterprise."

47. Johnston, "Savings Deposits and Life Insurance."

48. *Testimony Taken before the Joint Committee,* 5,551. Minutes of the Board of Directors, 12 December 1914, Box 5, GLIC archives.

49. President's Report, 22 October 1958, 27 April 1960, Box 43; Reports on the Examination of the Guardian, 1955, 1961, Box 72, GLIC archives.

50. Minutes of the Board of Directors, 22 April 1914, Box 5; Carl Heye Speech, 1930, Office of the Secretary, Scott, Box 64; Reports on the Examination of the Guardian, 1914, Box 70, GLIC archives.

NOTES TO CHAPTER 2

1. Abbott, *Story of NYLIC,* 122–27; Clough, *Mutual Life Insurance Company of New York,* 158–63. Minutes of the Board of Directors, 23 July 1919, Box 5; Minutes of the Board of Directors, 13 September, 26 October 1910, Box 122, GLIC archives.

2. Finance Committee Minutes, 8 March 1916, Box 15; "Historical Facts and Data Regarding the Germania Life Insurance Co. of America," John E. Albert, 1950, Office of the Secretary, Scott, Box 64; Minutes of the Board of Directors, 22 October 1902, Box 122; "Board of Direc-

tors Minutes, Extracts—Agencies, 1860–1946," Office of the Secretary, 1942–75, Box 180, GLIC archives.

3. Minutes of the Board of Directors, 1 January 1915, 15 December 1917, Box 5; Audrey Nichols to John Angle, 6 December 1983, History Files, John C. Angle, Box 199, GLIC archives.

4. Minutes of the Board of Directors, 28 October 1914, 28 July, 27 October 1915, 26 January, 26 April, 26 July 1916, October 1917, Box 5; "Correspondence with Department of State," Office of the President, Heye, Box 48, GLIC archives.

5. Most other insurers had also removed war clauses from their contracts in the prewar period. Recommendations within the industry called for extra premiums ranging from 5 to 20 percent. Hutcheson, "Life Insurance and the War." Minutes of the Board of Directors, 16 December 1916, Box 5; "Supplementary Statements to Be Made by Every Applicant," 1914, "Memorandum Re Treatment of New Applicants," 29 April 1914, "Notes," 1 May 1914, Carl Heye to Robert Lynn Cox, 2 May 1914, Hubert Cillis to the Company's Representatives, 8 May 1914, Hubert Cillis to the Company's Representatives, copy, 8 May 1914, "Memorandum," 11 May 1914, Office of the President, Heye, Box 47; Hubert Cillis to the Company's Representatives, 8 May 1914, Circulars, Box 94, GLIC archives.

6. Rittenhouse, "National Physical Preparedness." *Guardian Service,* March 1916. "War Risk on European Business," 12 August 1918, "The Germania Life Insurance Company of America," 6 September 1918, "Memorandum in re National Economic Mobilization of Life Insurance Policyholders," n.d., Office of the President, Heye, Box 47; "World War I Problems re European Business," n.d., John E. Albert, "Historical Facts and Data Regarding the Germania Life Insurance Co. of America," 1950, Office of the Secretary, Scott, Box 64; "How to Lengthen Your Life," 1916, Advertisement, *Red Cross Magazine,* June 1918, Public Relations Department Records, Box 84; "War Doesn't Bother U.S. Insurance Companies," *New York Evening Sun,* 25 September 1914, "To Visit Germania Agents," *The Eastern Underwriter,* 7 May 1915, Public Relations Department Records, Box 85; Carl Heye to the Company's Representatives, 29 September 1914, Hubert Cillis to the Company's Representatives, 6 April, 15 June, 29 September 1917, 10 May, 19 July 1918, Circulars, Box 94, GLIC archives.

7. Finance Committee Minutes, 25 April, 16 May 1917, Box 15; Hubert Cillis to Jesse Phillips, 25 April 1918, "Memorandum in re National Economic Mobilization of Life Insurance Policyholders," n.d., Office of the President, Heye, Box 47; Carl Heye to the Company's Managers, 17 May 1917, Hubert Cillis to the Company's Managers and Cashiers, 8, 31 October 1917, T. Louis Hansen to the Company's Managers, 2 November 1917, Hubert Cillis to the Company's Fieldmen, 23 January 1918, Circulars, Box 94, GLIC archives.

8. Minutes of the Board of Directors, 22 July 1914, 24 October 1917, Box 5; "Memorandum in re All-American Brokers, Inc.," 25 July 1921, Office of the President, Heye, Box 48; Carl Heye Speech, 1930, Office of the Secretary, Scott, Box 64, GLIC archives.

9. Finance Committee Minutes, 3 October 1917, Box 15; John E. Albert, "Historical Facts and Data Regarding the Germania Life Insurance Co. of America," 1950, Office of the Secretary, Scott, Box 64; Executive Officers Committee Minutes, 22 May 1923, Box 178; Memorandum, 5 November 1917, Expressions of the Company's Managers Who Attended the New Orleans, Louisiana Convention, 12 November 1917, "German American of Baltimore Changes Name," *Insurance Journal,* 27 April 1918, Office of the Secretary, Box 189; Ed Miller to Bill Smith, 7 July 1982, History Files, John C. Angle, Box 199, GLIC archives.

10. "Confidential," n.d., "Confidential," 17 October 1917, T. Louis Hansen speech, 24 October 1917, Expressions of the Company's Managers Who Attended the New Orleans, Louisiana Convention, 12 November 1917, Office of the Secretary, Box 189, GLIC archives.

11. Stalker Advertising Co. to Carl Heye, 12, 20 October, 21 December 1917, Hubert Cillis to Jesse Phillips, 22 November 1917, Dulon and Roe to Francis Hugo, 22 November 1917, Carl Heye to H. H. Stalker, 24 December 1917, Office of the Secretary, Box 189, GLIC archives.

12. Minutes of the Board of Directors, 5 December 1917, Box 5; Carl Heye Speech, 1930, Office of the Secretary, Scott, Box 64; Carl Heye to H. H. Stalker, 24 December 1917, Statement, n.d., Office of the Secretary, Box 189; *ARGHOE,* May 1981, History Files, John C. Angle, Box

198; John Angle to Audrey Nichols, 1 December 1983, History Files, John C. Angle, Box 199, GLIC archives.

13. "To Drop Name 'Germania,'" *New York Times,* 6 December 1917. Minutes of the Board of Directors, 5, 15 December 1917, Box 5, GLIC archives.

14. Minutes of the Board of Directors, 5 December 1917, Box 5, GLIC archives.

15. For the attacks on Guardian, see, for instance, *Insurance Index,* various dates 1921–24, Office of the Secretary, Box 189, GLIC archives. Buley, *American Life Convention,* 188. Memorandum, 24 April 1918, Office of the President, Heye, Box 47; J. Frazer Kempson to Jesse Phillips, 5, 15 April 1918, Jesse Phillips to J. Frazer Kempson, 13, 19 April 1918, Office of the President, Heye, Box 48, GLIC archives.

16. J. Frazer Kempson to Hubert "Cillas," 27 April 1918, Office of the President, Heye, Box 48, GLIC archives.

17. Hubert Cillis to J. Frazer Kempson, 30 April 1918, Hubert Cillis to Alien Property Custodian, 30 April 1918, Hubert Cillis to Jesse Phillips, 30 April 1918, Office of the President, Heye, Box 48, GLIC archives.

18. "Approximately correct statement based on stenographic notes taken in the adjoining room of a meeting between Carl Heye and F. J. Andrews," 30 April 1918, "Approximately correct statement based on stenographic notes taken in the adjoining room of a meeting between Carl Heye and F. J. Andrews," 2 May 1918, Office of the President, Heye, Box 48, GLIC archives.

19. For more on the epidemic, see Moir, "Epidemic Waste of Human Life." Finance Committee Minutes, 23 October, 27 November 1918, Box 15, GLIC archives.

20. "To Drop Name 'Germania,'" *New York Times,* 6 December 1917. Minutes of the Board of Directors, 24 April 1918, Box 5; Hubert Cillis to Dulon and Roe, 24 April 1918, Dulon and Roe to Hubert Cillis, 27 April 1918, "Memorandum," 12 August 1918, Office of the President, Heye, Box 47; S. C. Morgan to Germania Life, 1 March 1918, Germania to Dulon and Roe, 21 April 1919, Dulon and Roe to Germania, 22 April 1919, Office of the Secretary, Heye and Neuendorffer, Box 54, GLIC archives.

21. Minutes of the Board of Directors, 10 May, 22 August 1918, 23 July 1919, Box 5; Hubert Cillis to Jesse R. Phillips, 22 August 1918, Memorandum, 22 April 1919, Secretary of the Nominating Committee to George C. Austin, 26 June, 9 July 1919, Secretary of the Nominating Committee to John Grier, William Cruikshank, Charles MacDonald, and William Woodward, 26 June, 9 July 1919, Office of the President, Heye, Box 47; "Germania Life Stock Subscription," 8 May 1919, Carl Heye to W. W. Berliner, 17 September 1928, Office of the President, Heye, Box 48; Dulon and Roe to Germania, 9 May 1918, Hartwell Cabell to Carl Heye, 9 May 1918, Carl Heye to Frederick Fleitmann, 9 May 1918, Office of the Secretary, Heye and Neuendorffer, Box 54; "Correspondence with Managers re Co. Stock," 1919, 1921, A. W. Fetter to T. Louis Hansen, 17 June 1919, T. Louis Hansen to Arthur Niemeyer, 27 June 1919, T. Louis Hansen to A. W. Fetter, 14 July 1919, Office of the Vice President and Agency Managers, Hansen, Box 66; Interview with Irving Rosenthal, 6 July 1984, Box 250, GLIC archives.

22. "Small Dividends Should Cause No Dissatisfaction," *Chicago Evening Post,* 30 December 1918. Minutes of the Board of Directors, 14, 26 December 1918, Box 5; Hubert Cillis to the company's policyholders, 1 February 1919, Public Relations Department Records, Box 84, GLIC archives.

23. Bixby, *Kansas City Life*; Buley, *American Life Convention,* 538. Minutes of the Board of Directors, 19 January 1919, Box 5; Finance Committee Minutes, 8, 22 January 1919, Box 15; Max A. Wesendonck to Germania Fieldmen, 25 January 1919, Memorandum, Office of the President, Heye, Box 47; Albert Conway to Germania, 27 June 1930, Office of the President, Heye, Box 52; Carl Heye, "Mr. Cillis," 21 February 1923, Office of the President, Heye, Box 202, GLIC archives.

24. Finance Committee Minutes, 19 February 1919, Box 15, GLIC archives.

25. Cornelius Doremus to Hubert Cillis, 18 August 1913, Office of the President, Heye, Box 47; "Memorandum in Re Financial Situation of Company's European Branch," 8 October 1917, Office of the President, Heye, Box 48; Executive Officers Committee Minutes, 1 Novem-

ber 1921, Box 178; John C. Angle to John L. Cameron, 2 December 1981, Office of the President, Angle, Box 197, GLIC archives.

26. Finance Committee Minutes, 6 August 1919, 9 November 1921, Box 15, GLIC archives.

27. Finance Committee Minutes, 3 March 1920, Box 15; "Insurance on Shipments of U.S. Currency Abroad," Office of the President, Heye, Box 48, GLIC archives.

28. Finance Committee Minutes, 19 January 1921, Box 15, GLIC archives.

29. Finance Committee Minutes, 9 November 1921, Box 15, GLIC archives.

30. "Gist of Letter received from the Basler Lebens-Versicherungs Gesellschaft in Basel dated November 21st, 1921," Carl Heye to La Baloise Compagnie d'Assurances, 19 December 1921, Carl Heye, Memorandum, 19 January 1922, Office of the President, Heye, Box 46; Memorandum, 26 April, 23 October 1922, Office of the President, Heye, Box 48, GLIC archives.

31. Finance Committee Minutes, 30 August, 8 November 1922, Box 15; Carl Heye, Memorandum, 3 October 1922, Memorandum, 5 December 1928, Office of the President, Heye, Box 48, GLIC archives.

32. Minutes of the Board of Directors, 24 October 1923, Box 5; Memorandum, 26 September 1924, Office of the President, Heye, Box 48, GLIC archives.

33. Memorandum, 4 June 1923, Report of T. Louis Hansen, 15 October 1923, Office of the President, Heye, Box 48, GLIC archives.

34. Report of T. Louis Hansen, 15 October 1923, Office of the President, Heye, Box 48, GLIC archives.

35. Report of T. Louis Hansen, 15 October 1923, Office of the President, Heye, Box 48; Minutes of the Imperial Department for Private Insurance, 15 December 1930, Office of the President, Heye, Box 52, GLIC archives.

36. Report of T. Louis Hansen, 15 October 1923, Carl Heye to John Foster Dulles, draft, n.d., Memorandum, 4 June 1926, "Memorandum in re John Foster Dulles' opinion of June 1st in Dr. Waldeck's Case," 7 June 1926, John Foster Dulles to the Phoenix Life Insurance Company of Vienna, 10 June 1926, "Memorandum re: Accumulative Dividends of European Policyholders," n.d., Office of the President, Heye, Box 48, GLIC archives.

37. Minutes of the Board of Directors, 23 January, 22 October 1924, Box 5; Memorandum, 6 June 1923, Office of the President, Heye, Box 48, GLIC archives.

38. F. R. Stoddard to Carl Heye, 6, 18 October, 1 November 1923, Report of T. Louis Hansen, 15 October 1923, Carl Heye to Nelson Hadley, 19 November 1923, Memorandum, 26 September 1924, Carl Heye to James A. Beha, 18, 23, 26, 31 March, 7 April 1925, Office of the President, Heye, Box 48; Memorandum, 9 April 1936, Folders 7, 9, Office of the President, Heye, Box 53, GLIC archives.

39. Dr. Berliner to the Germania, 14 September 1923, Dr. Berliner to T. Louis Hansen, 15 December 1923, Memorandum, 26 January 1924, Office of the President, Heye, Box 48; Executive Officers Committee Minutes, 4 April 1922, Box 178, GLIC archives.

40. Minutes of the Board of Directors, 26 October 1927, Box 5; Report of T. Louis Hansen, 15 October 1923, Office of the President, Heye, Box 48; Carl Heye to Francisco Kubusch, 27 December 1927, "Credits Available in Excess of Sale of Remaining European Business to Phoenix as Contemplated under Contract Dated 19 August 1927," n.d., Office of the President, Heye, Box 49, GLIC archives.

41. Carl Heye to W. W. Berliner, 17 September 1928, 7, 31 December 1928, 1, 20 March 1929, 31 December 1930, Memorandum, Translation, n.d., Office of the President, Heye, Box 48; various documents, Box 52, GLIC archives. "Synopsis of Legal Opinion," n.d., "Legal Opinion," ? June 1927, Office of the President, Heye, Box 53, GLIC archives.

42. New York regulators thought $230,000, including court costs, the proper settlement value. Guardian's attorneys thought it safe under the circumstances for Guardian to exceed the regulators' recommendation because they had not accounted for Guardian's German real estate holdings. The attorneys were right; the superintendent approved the settlement on 19 March 1931. Guardian made the final payment on 30 April 1932. Albert Conway to Guardian, 27 June 1930, Sullivan and Cromwell to Guardian, 5 March 1931, Office of the President, Heye,

Box 52; George Van Schaick to Carl Heye, n.d., Office of the President, Heye, Box 53, GLIC archives.

43. As early 1923 attorneys Dulon and Roe advised Guardian "that should any action be brought upon policies of your Company written in Germany . . . payable in German currency . . . your company will be compelled to pay, under our law, only the value of the money designated in the contract, as of the date when the indebtedness became due." Minutes of the Board of Directors, 22 October 1930, Box 5; Dulon and Roe to Guardian, 9, 11 May 1923, Office of the President, Heye, Box 48; Memorandum, 7 August 1930, Minutes of the Imperial Department for Private Insurance, 15 December 1930, Rudolf Goose to Carl Heye, 15 December 1930, Sullivan and Cromwell to Guardian, 5 March 1931, Office of the President, Heye, Box 52; Memorandum, 9 April 1936, Office of the President, Heye, Box 53, GLIC archives.

44. Minutes of the Board of Directors, 26 October 1932, Box 5; Finance Committee Minutes, 27 July, 26 October 1932, Box 16, GLIC archives.

45. Carl Heye to W. W. Berliner, 31 December 1930, 21 March, 1 April, 20 May, 29 June, 17 September, 27 November 1931, 30 June, 12 August 1932, Office of the President, Heye, Box 48; Agreement, 12 January 1938, Carl Heye to Louis H. Pink, 28 February 1938, Memo, n.d., I. Schapp to Guardian, 18 April 1939, Carl Heye to I. Schaap, 28 April 1939, Office of the President, Heye, Box 53; Carl Heye Speech, 1930, Office of the Secretary, Scott, Box 64; Reports on the Examination of the Guardian, 1946, Box 71; "Austrian Leaders Got Phoenix Funds," *New York Times*, 29 April 1936, Public Relations Department Records, Box 85; Interview with Irving Rosenthal, 6 July 1984, Box 250, GLIC archives.

46. Memorandum in re: Mexican Gold Policies, 14 October 1931, Organ Box 19; Minutes of the Board of Directors, 23 April, 23 July 1947, 27 October 1948, 26 October 1949, 24 October 1951, Box 6; Finance Committee Minutes, 25 August 1948, 26 October 1949, Box 18; Real Estate Committee Minutes, 23 August 1967, Box 37; "Liquidation of Business," various dates, various folders, Office of the Vice President and Actuary, Barnsley, Boxes 67, 68, 69; Reports on the Examination of the Guardian, 1949, Box 71; Executive Officers Committee Minutes, 9 April, 3 September 1940, Box 178; Executive Officers Committee Minutes, 9, 23 March, 13 April 1948, Box 179, GLIC archives.

47. "Insurers Urged to Boycott Reds," *New York Times*, 6 October 1954. Real Estate Committee Minutes, 22 December 1971, Box 38; Minutes of the Board of Directors, 23 February 1972, Box 206, GLIC archives.

48. Group Advisory Committee Minutes, 22 March 1961, Office of the Executive Vice President, Rosenthal, Box 183; Minutes of the Board of Directors, 25 November 1970, Box 206, GLIC archives.

NOTES TO CHAPTER 3

1. Finance Committee Minutes, 9 November 1921, Box 15, GLIC archives.

2. Charles Rudd to Carl Heye, 26 October 1918, Carl Heye to Charles Rudd, 28 October 1918, Office of the President, Heye, Box 51; Henry Moir to Carl Heye, 14 April 1916, Carl Heye to Henry Moir, 17 April 1916, Office of the Secretary, Heye and Neuendorffer, Box 54, GLIC archives.

3. Charles Rudd to Carl Heye, 26 October 1918, Carl Heye to Charles Rudd, 28 October 1918, Office of the President, Heye, Box 51, GLIC archives.

4. Albert Conway to Guardian, 27 June 1930, Office of the President, Heye, Box 52, GLIC archives.

5. Minutes of the Board of Directors, 13 December 1919, 28 January 1920, Box 5; Annual Report, 1921, Office of the President, Heye, Box 46; Fieldmen Memorandum, 1920, Office of the Secretary, Scott, Box 64, GLIC archives.

6. Fieldmen Memorandum, 1920, Office of the Secretary, Scott, Box 64, GLIC archives.

7. Minutes of the Board of Directors, 27 October 1920, Box 5; Fieldmen Memorandum,

1920, James McLain to T. Louis Hansen, 13 January 1923, Office of the Secretary, Scott, Box 64, GLIC archives.

8. "Retirement of Equitable's Capital," *The Eastern Underwriter,* 15 February 1918; "Provident Life and Trust Company to Be Purely Mutual Company," *The Eastern Underwriter,* 2 December 1921. Finance Committee Minutes, 9 November 1921, Box 15; Charles Rudd to Carl Heye, 26 October 1918, "Plan for the acquisition of the shares of the capital stock of Home Life Insurance Company," 3 April 1916, George Ide to the Policyholders, 2 May 1916, "Special Report of the Executive Committee to the Board of Directors," 25 November 1924, T. Louis Hanson to Carl Heye, 29 June 1921, Carl Heye to Jesse Phillips, 22 June 1921, Office of the President, Heye, Box 51; T. Louis Hansen to R. Bardwell, 19 January 1921, to Charles Brust, 24 January 1921, Office of the Vice President and Agency Managers, Hansen, Box 66, GLIC archives.

9. "Special Report of the Executive Committee to the Board of Directors," 25 November 1924, Carl Heye to Albrecht Pagenstecher, 8 July 1921, Office of the President, Heye, Box 51, GLIC archives.

10. Corporate bond yields peaked at 5.27 percent in 1920. Homer and Sylla, *Interest Rates,* 337.

11. MacLean, *Life Insurance,* 36. T. Louis Hanson to Carl Heye, 29 June 1921, Carl Heye to Albrecht Pagenstecher, 8 July 1921, Office of the President, Heye, Box 51; John C. Angle, "Closing Address, Leaders Club Conference," 19 June 1980, Office of the President, Angle, Box 195, GLIC archives.

12. "In view of the proposed mutualization," 2 August 1921, Office of the President, Heye, Box 51; Carl Heye Speech, 1930, Office of the Secretary, Scott, Box 64; T. Louis Hansen to R. Bardwell, 19, 31 January 1921, Office of the Vice President and Agency Managers, Hansen, Box 66, GLIC archives.

13. "Beha Explains His Stand on Directors," *The Eastern Underwriter,* 20 March 1925. Carl Heye to James Beha, 7 November 1924, Office of the President, Heye, Box 51, GLIC archives.

14. Minutes of the Board of Directors, 25 November 1924, 28 January 1925, Box 5; Finance Committee Minutes, 14 January 1925, Box 15; James Beha to Carl Heye, 8, 18 November 1924, "Minutes of the Special Meeting of Stockholders of the Guardian Life," 15 December 1924, Carl Heye to the Stockholders of the Guardian, 16 December 1924, 28 January 1925, Carl Heye to Middlebrook and Borland, 20 January 1925, Office of the President, Heye, Box 51; List of Stockholders of the Guardian Life Insurance Company of America, 15 December 1924, History Files, John C. Angle, Box 199, GLIC archives.

15. Mutualization, Organ Boxes 2, 3; "Heye Correspondence Mutualization," n.d., Carl Heye to the Company's Policyholders, 28 January 1925, Carl Heye to the Company's Managers, 28 January 1925, to the Guardian Field Force, 16 December 1924, to Mrs. Paul B. Phillips, 29 June 1925, Office of the President, Heye, Box 51; Carl Heye Speech, 1930, Office of the Secretary, Scott, Box 64, GLIC archives.

16. "Guardian Life Mutualized," *New York Times,* 4 January 1946. Finance Committee Minutes, 22 July 1925, Box 15; Dulon and Roe to Carl Heye, 13 November 1924, J. Schaefer to Guardian Life, 30 April 1926, Harry Rosenthal to Guardian, 12 August 1925, George W. Cook to Carl Heye, 17 April 1925, W. B. Barney to Guardian, 28 April 1925, Mrs. Paul B. Phillips to Carl Heye, 13 June 1925, Office of the President, Heye, Box 51; "Investment Questionnaire," TNEC Records, Box 59; John Cameron to James Scott, 27 February 1945, Office of the Secretary, Scott, Box 64; James A McLain to Guardian personnel, 2 January 1946, Office of the Cashier, Hahn, Box 69; Reports on the Examination of the Guardian, 1946, Box 71; John C. Angle to David Mayers, 29 June 1982, History Files, John C. Angle, Box 198, GLIC archives.

17. Finance Committee Minutes, 1 March 1922, Box 15; Carl Heye, Memorandum, 19 January 1922, Carl Heye, Memorandum, n.d., Office of the President, Heye, Box 46; Carl Heye Speech, 1930, Office of the Secretary, Scott, Box 64; Interview with Irving Rosenthal, 6 July 1984, Box 250, GLIC archives.

18. T. Louis Hansen to Carl Heye, 15 February 1922; Carl Heye to T. Louis Hansen, 18, 27 February 1922, T. Louis Hansen to Carl Heye, 1 March 1922, Office of the President, Heye, Box

46; Executive Officers Committee Minutes, 31 January 1922, Box 178; Regulatory report, 7 December 1925, History Files, John C. Angle, Box 198; Interview with Irving Rosenthal, 6 July 1984, Box 250, GLIC archives.

19. Life insurers did not have to mark investment grade bonds to market. For more on the history of valuation of life insurance assets, see Fraine, *Valuation of Securities Holdings*; Fraine, "Valuation of Security Holdings"; O'Leary, "Valuation of Life Insurance Company Holdings."

20. Rosenthal, *Short and Confidential History*. Minutes of the Board of Directors, 24 October 1923, 22 October 1924, Box 5; Finance Committee Minutes, 8 November 1922, 24 October 1923, 28 October 1925, Box 15; Memorandum, 3 November 1924, Office of the President, Heye, Box 51; Executive Officers Committee Minutes, 21 October 1924, Box 178, GLIC archives.

21. *Guardian Service*, 21 December 1925.

22. Rosenthal, *Short and Confidential History*. "Record by Guardian Life," *New York Times*, 6 February 1928. Minutes of the Board of Directors, 24 October 1928, Box 5; Carl Heye Speech, 1930, Office of the Secretary, Scott, Box 64; McNamara v. Guardian, 1943, Legal Department Records, Box 80; Executive Officers Committee Minutes, 15 November 1921, 30 June, 29 September 1925, Box 178; Interview with Irving Rosenthal, 6 July 1984, Box 250, GLIC archives.

23. Minutes of the Board of Directors, 7 September 1927, Box 5, GLIC archives.

24. We have seen frequent contemporary references to the stock market crash and subsequent recession as a debacle. For example, see Ecker, "Stabilizing Life." John E. Albert, "Historical Facts and Data Regarding The Guardian Life Insurance Co. of America," 1950, Office of the Secretary, Scott, Box 64; Interview with Irving Rosenthal, 6 July 1984, Box 250, GLIC archives.

25. Buley, *American Life Convention*, 682; Ecker, "Stabilizing Life." "Guardian Life Near Peak," *New York Times*, 3 February 1931. Annual Report, 1930, Box 2; Minutes of the Board of Directors, 23 April 1930, Box 5; Interview with Irving Rosenthal, 6 July 1984, Box 250, GLIC archives.

26. Buley, *American Life Convention*, 699. "Gains for Guardian Life," *New York Times*, 11 February 1932. Annual Report, 1931, Box 2; Minutes of the Department Head Meeting, 29 January 1931, Home Office Records, Box 74, GLIC archives.

27. Minutes of the Board of Directors, 26 October 1932, Box 5; Finance Committee Minutes, 28 October 1931, 27 January 1932, Box 16, GLIC archives.

28. Minutes of the Board of Directors, 26 October 1932, Box 5; Finance Committee Minutes, 27 April, 27 July, 26 October 1932, 26 April, 26 July 1933, 25 July 1934, 15 January 1936, Box 16; Reports on the Examination of the Guardian, 1933, Box 70, GLIC archives.

29. "Cut Policy-Holders' Dividends," *New York Times*, 4 November 1932; "Guardian Life's Assets," *New York Times*, 4 February 1933. Annual Report, 1932, Box 2, GLIC archives.

30. Minutes of the Board of Directors, 27 January 1932, 24 October 1934, Box 5, GLIC archives.

31. "Guardian Life Insurance Company of America," *New York Times*, 3 February 1934. *Guardian Service*, 26 January 1925. Minutes of the Board of Directors, 26 October 1932, Box 5; Carl Heye Speech, 1930, Office of the Secretary, Scott, Box 64; McNamara v. Guardian, Vol. 1, 1943, Legal Department Records, Box 80; Interview with Irving Rosenthal, 6 July 1984, Box 250, GLIC archives.

32. Rosenthal, *Short and Confidential History*; Sullivan, "Life Insurance"; Wright, H. P., "Financial Problems." Interview with Irving Rosenthal, 6 July 1984, Box 250, GLIC archives.

33. "Insurance Leader Hopeful on Trade," *New York Times*, 18 July 1935.

34. The effect of this liberal policy was marginal for Guardian. The difference in value in Guardian's securities holdings between the regular assessment and the more lenient convention values allowed by the regulators during the Depression was about $832,569. Buley, *American Life Convention*, 749. Interview with John Angle, 21 March 2002. Minutes of the Board of Directors, 27 January 1932, Box 5, GLIC archives.

35. Annual Report, 1933, Box 2; Minutes of the Board of Directors, 25 October 1933, Box 5; Finance Committee Minutes, 25 October 1933, Box 16, GLIC archives.

36. Life insurers had known the risks posed by the coming of the automobile age since at least 1917. Frankel, "The Increasing Automobile Hazard." "Gain for Guardian Life," *New York Times,* 9 February 1934; "Guardian Life Insurance Company," *New York Times,* 22 July 1934; "Guardian Life has 34 Rise," *New York Times,* 7 February 1935. Annual Report, 1934, Box 2; Finance Committee Minutes, 23 January 1935, Box 16, GLIC archives.

37. *Proceedings of the Fifty-Fourth Annual Meeting of Life Insurance Association of America,* 1960, 236; Rosenthal, *Short and Confidential History*; Smith, Thomas, "Banking and Life Insurance." "Insurance Leader Hopeful on Trade," *New York Times,* 18 July 1935. Annual Report, 1934, 1935, Box 2; Minutes of the Board of Directors, 24 October 1934, 23 January 1935, Box 5; Finance Committee Minutes, 24 October 1934, 23 October 1935, Box 16; Finance Committee Minutes, 26 October 1938, 25 January 1939, Box 17, GLIC archives.

38. Finance Committee Minutes, 23 May 1934, Box 16, GLIC archives.

39. "Gain for Guardian Life," *New York Times,* 1 February 1937. Annual Report, 1936, Box 2; Minutes of the Board of Directors, 18 December 1935, 22 January 1936, 28 July 1937, 26 January 1938, Box 5; Executive Officers Committee Minutes, 28 September 1937, Box 178, GLIC archives.

40. Rydgren, "Impact of Lower Interest Earnings." Reports on the Examination of the Guardian, 1940, Box 70; Interview with Irving Rosenthal, 6 July 1984, Box 250, GLIC archives.

41. Despite some early claims to the contrary, it now appears that life insurance prospects are sensitive to net cost. Babbel, "Price Elasticity of Demand," 235; Winter, "On the Rate Structure," 81. "Income Sets Mark for Guardian Life," *New York Times,* 31 January 1939; "Guardian Life Insurance Company of America," *New York Times,* 22 August 1939; "Guardian Life Reports," *New York Times,* 30 January 1940; "Gain for Guardian Life in 1940," *New York Times,* 27 January 1941. Annual Report, 1938, 1939, 1940, 1945, Box 2; Executive Officers Committee Minutes, 6, 12 July, 6 September 1938, Box 178, GLIC archives.

42. "Financial Notes," *New York Times,* 21 December 1940. Rosenthal, *Short and Confidential History.* Interview with Ed Kane, 30 November 2001. Minutes of the Board of Directors, 20 December 1939, Box 5; Carl Heye to Wilhelm Remppis, 3 January 1940, Office of the President, Heye, Box 53; Interview with Irving Rosenthal, 6 July 1984, Box 250, GLIC archives.

43. Buley, *American Life Convention,* 932. "Changes in Corporations," *New York Times,* 28 October 1930; "J. A. M'Lain Heads Guardian Life," *New York Times,* 21 December 1939; "Cameron Will Succeed McLain as Guardian Life Chairman, Chief Officer," *Wall Street Journal,* 6 August 1963. Interview with Ed Kane, 30 November 2001; interview with John Angle, 21 March 2002. Annual Report, 1963, Box 4; Minutes of the Board of Directors, 17 December 1924, 22 October 1930, Box 5; "The Story of 25 Years," 1945, Office of the Secretary, Scott, Box 64; John C. Angle interview with Daniel J. Lyons, 7 March 1982, Office of the President, Angle, Box 197; Minutes of the Board of Directors, 18 May 1977, Box 207, GLIC archives.

44. John C. Angle, "A Report on Guardian History," 18 November 1981, Office of the President, Angle, Box 195; John C. Angle interview with Daniel J. Lyons, 7 March 1982, Office of the President, Angle, Box 197; Minutes of the Board of Directors, 18 May 1977, Box 207; Interview with Irving Rosenthal, 6 July 1984, Box 250, GLIC archives.

45. *Proceedings of the Twenty-Ninth Annual Convention of the Association of Life Insurance Presidents,* 1935, 126–27; Buley, *American Life Convention,* 874, 916, 931–32, 938, 952, 954, 963, 996–97, 1004; McLain, "Stewardship." Interview with Ed Kane, 30 November 2001. Minutes of the Board of Directors, 26 July 1944, 15 December 1948, Box 6; Interview with Irving Rosenthal, 6 July 1984, Box 250, GLIC archives.

46. "Guardian Life Lists $8,128,934 Asset Gain," *New York Times,* 29 January 1942. Annual Report, 1940, Box 2; President's Reports, Summary, 1941, Box 42, GLIC archives.

47. Annual Report, 1939, 1940, Box 2; President's Reports, Summary, 1941, Box 42, GLIC archives.

48. Annual Financial Statement, 1940; Annual Report, 1940, 1941, Box 2; Minutes of the

Board of Directors, 28 October 1942, Box 5; Finance Committee Minutes, 26 January 1944, Box 17; Executive Officers Committee Minutes, 30 June, 14 October 1942, Box 178, GLIC archives.

49. *The Bond,* December 1942; *Home Office Newsletter,* 15 December 1950. Executive Officers Committee Minutes, 9, 16 December 1941, 24 February, 3 March, 4 August 1942, Box 178; "Register of Records Microfilmed," Office of the Secretary, 1942–75, Box 180; "Recordak," Subsidiaries, Box 227, GLIC archives.

50. *The Bond,* September 1942; *Guardian Life,* July 1959. The Guardian War Cabinet, Memoranda, 1942–46, Minutes of the Guardian War Cabinet, 1942–46, Office of the Secretary, Scott, Box 179, GLIC archives.

51. Annual Report, 1941, 1945, Box 2; Executive Officers Committee Minutes, 18 December 1941, Box 178, GLIC archives.

52. Rusk, "America's Number One Medical Problem." "Insurance Policies Eased," *New York Times,* 28 August 1945. Annual Report, 1942, Box 1; Annual Report, 1941, 1945, Box 2, GLIC archives.

53. "Insurance Concerns Report Increases," *New York Times,* 5 February 1942; "Guardian Coverage Sets Mark," *New York Times,* 31 January 1944; "Guardian Life Reports," *New York Times,* 4 February 1943. *The Bond,* September 1942. Annual Report, 1941, Box 2; Minutes of the Board of Directors, 23 October 1940, 22 April 1942, Box 5; Minutes of the Board of Directors, 27 October 1943, Box 6; Reports on the Examination of the Guardian, 1943, Box 71; Executive Officers Committee Minutes, 31 December 1940, Box 178; Executive Officers Committee Minutes, 3 April 1945, Box 179; Interview with Irving Rosenthal, 6 July 1984, Box 250, GLIC archives.

54. Annual Report, 1941, Box 2, GLIC archives.

55. Rosenthal, *Short and Confidential History.* "Advertising News," *New York Times,* 5 February 1944; "Guardian Life Business Up," *New York Times,* 26 May 1944. Annual Report, 1945, Box 2; Reports on the Examination of the Guardian, 1943, Box 71; James A McLain to Supervisory Staff, 15 June 1943, 20 June 1944, Home Office Records, Box 74; Executive Officers Committee Minutes, 10 April 1945, Box 179, GLIC archives.

56. Rosenthal, *Short and Confidential History.*

57. Annual Report, 1946, Box 2; Reports on the Examination of the Guardian, 1946, 1949, Box 71, GLIC archives.

58. "Insurance Office Added to His Baseball Interests," *New York Times,* 17 December 1945; "Insurance Notes," *New York Times,* 20 December 1945. Minutes of the Board of Directors, 24 October, 19 December 1945, Box 6; "The Story of 25 Years," 1945, Office of the Secretary, Scott, Box 64, GLIC archives.

59. Rosenthal, *Short and Confidential History.* Minutes of the Board of Directors, 27 October 1948, Box 6, GLIC archives.

60. Rosenthal, *Short and Confidential History.* Minutes of the Board of Directors, 22 January 1947, Box 6; Reports on the Examination of the Guardian, 1940, Box 70; Executive Officers Committee Minutes, 19 November, 3 December 1940, 11 February 1941, 19 May 1942, Box 178; Interview with Irving Rosenthal, 6 July 1984, Box 250, GLIC archives.

61. In early 1928 Guardian voluntarily changed its home office working hours to 8:45 A.M. to 4:15 P.M. to help the city "to relieve subway congestion." Saturday hours ceased in 1933 at the behest of the N.R.A. "Help in Stagger Plan," *New York Times,* 31 January 1928. John E. Albert, "Historical Facts and Data Regarding The Guardian Life Insurance Co. of America," 1950, Office of the Secretary, Scott, Box 64; Minutes of the Department Head Meeting, 27 January 1928, Home Office Records, Box 74, GLIC archives.

62. Guardian modified those hours during crises. During World War I, for instance, it kept the office closed on Mondays in deference to the government's coal conservation policy. It opened the office an hour earlier for the rest of the week, however, to make up some of the time. John E. Albert, "Historical Facts and Data Regarding The Guardian Life Insurance Co. of America," 1950, Office of the Secretary, Scott, Box 64, GLIC archives.

63. Annual Report, 1946, Box 2; "Rules of Conduct," n.d., Office of the President, Doremus, Box 45; Supervisors' Manual, 1 June 1926, Temporary Advisory Board to Home Office Staff, 23 May 1946, Home Office Records, Box 74; Employment Manual, 1925, 1928 Personnel Department Records, Box 83, GLIC archives.

64. Lunchroom, n.d., Home Office Records, Box 74; Tom Quinn interview with Helen Sulyma, 2-9 Group Underwriting Department Manager, n.d., Office of the President, Angle, Box 197; Carl Heye, "50th Anniversary," September 1939, Office of the President, Heye, Box 202, GLIC archives.

65. Rosenthal, *Short and Confidential History. Home Office Newsletter,* 14 April 1950, 15 May 1956. Annual Report, 1946, 1948, Box 2; Minutes of the Board of Directors, 24 July 1946, 17 December 1947, Box 6; Temporary Advisory Board to Home Office Staff, 23 May 1946, Home Office Records, Box 74; Executive Officers Committee Minutes, 13 June 1944, Box 179, GLIC archives.

66. Minutes of the Board of Directors, 23 October 1946, 25 October 1950, Box 6, GLIC archives.

67. Rosenthal, *Short and Confidential History.* Minutes of the Board of Directors, 27 October 1948, Box 6, GLIC archives.

68. Rosenthal, *Short and Confidential History.* Interview with Ed Kane, 30 November 2001.

NOTES TO CHAPTER 4

1. Annual Report, 1949, Box 3, GLIC archives.

2. Annual Report, 1948, Box 2; Minutes of the Board of Directors, 27 April 1949, Box 6; Field Advisory Board Meeting Proceedings, 7 January 1948, 30 June 1949, Box 75, GLIC archives.

3. Executive Officers Committee Minutes, 7, 14 January, 25 February 1947, Box 179, GLIC archives. Daniel Reidy to George A. Bisson, 23 June 1953, Office of the Secretary, Box 189, GLIC archives.

4. Minutes of the Board of Directors, 27 July, 26 October 1949, 26 April 1950, 26 January 1955, Box 6, GLIC archives.

5. Guardian was not writing business in Alaska, Arizona, Delaware, Hawaii, Idaho, Maine, Mississippi, Montana, Nevada, New Hampshire, New Mexico, Rhode Island, Texas, Utah, Vermont, or Wyoming. Some of those states, like Montana and Rhode Island, Guardian had exited because agency costs had exceeded the profits from new business. It abandoned Texas because of regulatory conflicts. "To Drop Name 'Germania,'" *New York Times,* 6 December 1917. Executive Officers Committee Minutes, 10 May 1921, Box 178; "Board of Directors Minutes, Extracts—Agencies, 1860–1946," Office of the Secretary, 1942–75, Box 180, GLIC archives.

6. "Guardian Life's Sales Up," *Wall Street Journal,* 31 January 1955. Annual Report, 1954, 1955, Box 3, GLIC archives.

7. This industrial insurance company, which formed in 1944, was at first called Guardian Life and Hospital Aid Company. Minutes of the Board of Directors, 26 April 1950, Box 6; Reports on the Examination of the Guardian, 1949, 1952, Box 71; "Memos re: Guardian Life Insurance Co. of S. Carolina," 1948, Public Relations Department Records, Box 84; Executive Officers Committee Minutes, 10 October 1944, 24 February, 4, 11 May 1948, Box 179; Memorandum to John C. Slattery, 27 December 1951, Office of the Secretary, Box 189, GLIC archives.

8. Brimmer, *Life Insurance Companies in the Capital Market,* 18. Minutes of the Board of Directors, 27 January 1954, Box 6, GLIC archives.

9. Minutes of the Board of Directors, 21 December 1955, Box 6, GLIC archives.

10. Annual Report, 1960, Box 3; President's Reports, 25 January 1961, Box 43; "Centennial Celebration Ideas," 1959–60, Office of the Secretary, Burrell, Box 65; Reports on the Examination of the Guardian, 1961, Box 72; Field Advisory Board Meeting Proceedings, 9 January 1959, Box 75; John Cameron, "Opening Address for 1960 Leaders' Club Meeting," 1960, Office of the President, Cameron, Box 202, GLIC archives.

11. According to the U.S. Census, the total population was 178,554,916 in 1960. *Proceedings of*

the Fifty-Sixth Annual Meeting of Life Insurance Association of America, 1962, 10–11; Davis, Frank, "Economic Freedom"; Hurrell, "America First in Life Insurance"; Life Insurance Marketing and Research Association, *Profile of Life Insurance Ownership*; Oates, *Business and Social Change,* 11; Rosenthal, *Short and Confidential History*; Sick, "Let's Get Excited." Annual Report, 1961, Box 3, GLIC archives.

12. Shale Goodman to Irving Rosenthal, 13 April 1966, Office of the Executive Vice President, Rosenthal, Box 184, GLIC archives.

13. There were warning signs of this trend as early as 1954. Rosenthal, *Short and Confidential History*. Annual Report, 1961, Box 3; Minutes of the Board of Directors, 27 January 1960, 24 April 1963, Box 6; President's Reports, 27 January 1960, Box 43; Field Advisory Board Meeting Proceedings, 21 January 1954, Box 75; Lawrence Lubin to Company Officers, 19 May 1965, Office of the Assistant Actuary, Lubin, Box 202, GLIC archives.

14. Remarks by Ashby Bladen, Field Advisory Board Meeting Proceedings, 20 September 1974, Box 75, GLIC archives.

15. President's Reports, 27 July, 26 October 1960, 25 January 1961, Box 43, GLIC archives.

16. Rosenthal, *Short and Confidential History*. Annual Report, 1963, Box 4, GLIC archives.

17. Annual Report, 1963, Box 4; President's Reports, 24 January 1962, Box 43; Field Advisory Board Meeting Proceedings, 1 April 1963, Box 75; Coordinating Committee Minutes, 13 August, 18 December 1963, Office of the Secretary, Reilly, Box 179; Irving Rosenthal, "Comments on New Mortality Study (1948–1969)," Office of the Executive Vice President, Rosenthal, Box 184, GLIC archives.

18. *Guardian Scene,* October 1965. Annual Report, 1965, Box 4; Field Advisory Board Meeting Proceedings, 12 April, 4 November 1965, 21 April 1966, 27 April 1967, Box 75; Irving Rosenthal to Daniel J. Lyons, 21 October 1966, John E. Gray to Irving Rosenthal et al., 1 December 1965, Office of the Executive Vice President, Rosenthal, Box 183, GLIC archives.

19. Higgins, "Small-Business Market," 42; Holtz-Eakin et al., "Estate Taxes." Annual Report, 1965, Box 4, GLIC archives.

20. Annual Report, 1966, 1967, Box 4, GLIC archives.

21. Field Advisory Board Meeting Proceedings, 17 November 1966, 27 April 1967, Box 75; Minutes of the Board of Directors, 27 July 1966, Box 206, GLIC archives.

22. Annual Report, 1967, Box 4; Field Advisory Board Meeting Proceedings, 17 November 1966, 28 September 1967, 12 September 1968, Box 75, GLIC archives.

23. Field Advisory Board Meeting Proceedings, 15 January, 1 May 1969, Box 75; Tom Quinn interview with Arthur Ferrara, Executive Vice President, n.d., Office of the President, Angle, Box 197, GLIC archives.

24. Field Advisory Board Meeting Proceedings, 1 May 1969, 9 September 1971, 21 September 1972, Box 75, GLIC archives.

25. Field Advisory Board Meeting Proceedings, 18 September 1969, 10 September 1970, 28 January, 5 April 1971, Box 75, GLIC archives.

26. Field Advisory Board Meeting Proceedings, 10 September 1970, 5 April 1971, Box 75, GLIC archives.

27. Interview with Ed Kane, 22 February 2002; interview with Leo Futia, 12 April 2002. Tom Quinn interview with Arthur Ferrara, Executive Vice President, n.d., Office of the President, Angle, Box 197, GLIC archives.

28. John C. Angle, "Guardian Life: 1981 General Agents Conference, Closing Address," 23 January 1981, John C. Angle, "Summation of the Evidence," 21 January 1983, Office of the President, Angle, Box 195; Interview with Irving Rosenthal, 6 July 1984, Box 250, GLIC archives.

29. Interview with John Angle, 21 March 2002. "The Record of The Guardian Life," Reports on the Examination of the Guardian, 1974, Box 187; Minutes of the Board of Directors, 28 November 1973, Box 206, GLIC archives.

30. Interview with Ed Kane, 22 February 2002; interview with John Angle, 21 March 2002. Irving Rosenthal to George Conklin, 23 May 1972, Office of the Executive Vice President, Rosenthal, Box 185, GLIC archives.

31. Annual Report, 1973, Box 4, GLIC archives.

32. Day, "Significance"; Hurrell, "America First in Life Insurance"; Shanks, "Life Insurance on the Inflation Treadmill."

33. Annual Report, 1946, Box 2; Field Advisory Board Meeting Proceedings, 6 January 1948, Box 75, GLIC archives.

34. *Proceedings of the Forty-Eighth Annual Meeting of the Life Insurance Association of America*, 1954, 118; Call, "The Policyholder's Stake in Sound Economics"; Fortune, "A Theory of Optimal Life Insurance," 600; Holland, "Cross Currents." Field Advisory Board Meeting Proceedings, 25 January 1952, Box 75, GLIC archives.

35. President's Report, 25 February 1976, Box 44; Irving Rosenthal to Fiscal Advisory Committee, 19 May 1961, Guardian Major Medical Policy, 1 October 1954, Office of the Executive Vice President, Rosenthal, Box 183, GLIC archives.

36. *Proceedings of the Fiftieth Annual Meeting of the Life Insurance Association of America*, 1956, 161. James McLain to Members of the Home Office Staff, 14 January 1949, Home Office Records, Box 74; Field Advisory Board Meeting Proceedings, 24 July 1975, Box 75, GLIC archives.

37. Nollen, "Recent Fluctuations"; Schott, "Disintermediation through Policy Loans"; Walker, Kenneth, *Guaranteed Investment Contracts*, 2. Interview with John Angle, 21 March 2002. Finance Committee Minutes, 23 May 1973, Box 20; President's Reports, Summary, 1941, Box 42; President's Report, 28 August 1974, Box 44; John C. Angle, "The Legacy of Queen Anne: Price-Fixed Interest Rates and the Cost of Life Insurance," Office of the President, Angle, Box 195, GLIC archives.

38. Rosenthal, *Short and Confidential History*. President's Report, 28 August 1974, Box 44, GLIC archives.

39. The German hyperinflation of the early 1920s, for example, forced the company to write off its German mortgages as it had been found impossible "to compel mortgagors to pay their mortgages upon maturity in gold instead of the depreciated Mark currency." At the same time, the company had to fend off policyholders who wanted claims paid in gold even though they made premium payments in worthless paper money. Clough, *Mutual Life Insurance Company of New York*, 224; Keller, *Life Insurance Enterprise*, 137; Reilly, "Guardian." Minutes of the Board of Directors, 23 January 1924, Box 5; "Historical Facts and Data Regarding The Guardian Life Insurance Co. of America," John E. Albert, 1950, Office of the Secretary, Scott, Box 64, GLIC archives.

40. "Adoption of the Statement on the Monetary Problem"; Buley, *American Life Convention*, 794; Call, "The Policyholder's Stake in Sound Economics." Annual Report, 1940, 1945, Box 2; Executive Officers Committee Minutes, 2 September 1941, Box 178; Executive Officers Committee Minutes, 20 April 1943, 3 September 1946, Box 179, GLIC archives.

41. O'Leary, "Investment Trends"; Riefler, "Inflation." Annual Report, 1945, 1948, 1950, Box 3, GLIC archives.

42. Annual Report, 1951, 1952, Box 3, GLIC archives.

43. "McLain of Guardian Predicts Switch from Term to Reserve Life," 1952?, Public Relations Department Records, Box 84, GLIC archives.

44. *Proceedings of the Fifty-Second Annual Meeting of the Life Insurance Association of America*, 1958, 164–68; *Proceedings of the Fifty-Sixth Annual Meeting of Life Insurance Association of America*, 1962, 203; *Proceedings of the Fifty-Seventh Annual Meeting of Life Insurance Association of America*, 1963, 181–86. *Home Office Newsletter*, 15 March 1951; *Guardian Life*, April 1960. Annual Report, 1958, Box 3; Minutes of the Board of Directors, 23 October 1957, Box 6; President's Report, 28 January 1959, Box 43, GLIC archives.

45. Call, "The Policyholder's Stake in Sound Economics." John C. Angle, "Guardian Life: 1981 General Agents Conference, Closing Address," 23 January 1981, Office of the President, Angle, Box 195, GLIC archives.

46. Camp, *Liberty National Life*, 104; Jacobsson, "International Balance of Payments"; Kacy,

Unique and Different, 23. Finance Committee Minutes, 26 May, 8 September 1971, 14 February 1973, Box 20; President's Reports, 22 August 1973, Box 43, GLIC archives.

47. Sylla, "Breakdown of Bretton Woods."

48. President's Report, 27 November 1974, Box 44; Irving Rosenthal to Daniel J. Lyons, 6 July 1970, Office of the Executive Vice President, Rosenthal, Box 185, GLIC archives.

49. President's Report, 26 February 1975, 23 February, 16 November 1977, 24 May, 23 August, 29 November 1978, 23 May 1979, Box 44; Remarks by Ashby Bladen, Field Advisory Board Meeting Proceedings, 20 September 1974, Box 75; Coordinating Committee Minutes, 11 July, 13 August 1963, 13 June 1967, Office of the Secretary, Reilly, Box 179, GLIC archives.

50. Interview with John Angle, 21 March 2002. President's Report, 27 November 1974, Box 44, GLIC archives.

51. Bixby, *Kansas City Life,* 22. Rosenthal, *Short and Confidential History.* Irving Rosenthal to Daniel J. Lyons, 6 July 1970, Office of the Executive Vice President, Rosenthal, Box 185, GLIC archives.

52. Rosenthal, *Short and Confidential History.* Field Advisory Board Meeting Proceedings, 4 May 1978, Box 75; John Angle to Irving Rosenthal, 24 August 1977, Office of the Executive Vice President, Rosenthal, Box 183; Reports on the Examination of the Guardian, 1974, 1979, Box 187, GLIC archives.

53. Annual Report, 1977, 1978, Box 4; President's Report, 22 February 1978, 28 February 1979, Box 44; Field Advisory Board Meeting Proceedings, 9 September 1976, 21 September 1978, Box 75; "Share in the Difference" Agency Department, Product/Sales Promotion, Box 194, GLIC archives.

54. Hamwi, *Surrender Benefits*; MacLean, *Life Insurance,* 47.

55. *Proceedings of the Fifty-Third Annual Meeting of the Life Insurance Association of America,* 1959, 174–94; Hull, "What's Happening?"; Sick, "Let's Get Excited." President's Reports, 27 April 1960, Box 43; Field Advisory Board Meeting Proceedings, 29 January 1970, Box 75, GLIC archives.

56. Babbel and Staking, "Life Insurance Costs." Field Advisory Board Meeting Proceedings, 24 September 1962, Box 75, GLIC archives.

57. New York regulators began allowing life insurers to form subsidiaries in 1962. *Proceedings of the Fifty-Sixth Annual Meeting of Life Insurance Association of America,* 1962, 77; Reilly, "Guardian." Interview with Ed Kane, 22 February 2002. Annual Report, 1968, 1981, Box 4; President's Report, 28 May, 27 August 1969, Box 43; Reports on the Examination of the Guardian, 1969, Box 72; John E. Gray to Irving Rosenthal, 5 August 1969, Office of the Executive Vice President, Rosenthal, Box 183; William C. Brown to All Guardian Agencies, June 1971, Irving Rosenthal to Leo Futia, 10 April 1972, Office of the Executive Vice President, Rosenthal, Box 185; Interview with Irving Rosenthal, 6 July 1984, Box 250, GLIC archives.

58. Plan of Agreement and Merger of Guardian Advisors into GLICOA Associates, 1973, Subsidiaries, Box 227, GLIC archives.

59. "Broker Units of 4 Insurers Challenge SEC on Exchange Membership for Institutions," *Wall Street Journal,* 28 November 1972. Annual Report, 1970, 1972, Box 4; Finance Committee Minutes, 24 January 1973, Box 20; William C. Brown to George Conklin, 16 June 1972, Office of the Executive Vice President, Rosenthal, Box 183; Reports on the Examination of the Guardian, 1974, Box 187; Minutes of the Board of Directors, 24 November 1971, 28 February, 22 August 1973, 22 May, 27 November 1974, Box 206, GLIC archives. Records of Subsidiaries, Office of the Corporate Secretary.

60. Field Advisory Board Meeting Proceedings, 15 September 1977, Box 75; Reports on the Examination of the Guardian, 1984, Box 187; "Guardian Plusses," 1982, Agency Department, Product/Sales Promotion, Box 194; Minutes of the Board of Directors, 27 August 1975, 23 February 1977, 22 February 1978, Box 206, Minutes of the Board of Directors, 28 February 1979, 27 February 1980, 25 February 1981, Box 207, GLIC archives. Records of Subsidiaries, Office of the Corporate Secretary.

61. Annual Report, 1977, Box 4; Field Advisory Board Meeting Proceedings, 15 September 1977, Box 75; Reports on the Examination of the Guardian, 1984, Box 187; Minutes of the Board of Directors, 28 February 1979, 27 February 1980, 25 February, 26 August 1981, Box 207, GLIC archives. Records of Subsidiaries, Office of the Corporate Secretary.

62. Annual Report, 1969, Box 4; Executive Officers Committee Minutes, 13 November 1945, Box 179; Minutes of the Board of Directors, 22 May 1974, Box 206; Subsidiaries, Box 227, GLIC archives.

63. Drucker's work had a profound influence on numerous Guardianites, including John C. Angle, who cited him repeatedly in speeches. Guardian's Office of the Corporate Secretary sports at least one of Drucker's tomes. See Drucker, *Essential Drucker,* 10, 40, 42–44, 65, 101–2, 125, 128–29, 142. Jack Welch, who is very much a Druckerite, therefore also indirectly influenced the company. Welch and Byrne, *Jack,* 108, 397. Interview with Joseph Sargent, 30 May 2002. John Angle to Leo Futia, 24 November 1981, Office of the President, Angle, Box 197; Leo Futia, President's Report, 28 November 1979, Office of the President, Angle, Box 195, GLIC archives.

64. GICs are fixed income instruments for which there is no active secondary market; hence they do not fall under SEC regulation. They are carried at book value and therefore do not fluctuate with interest rates. While many insurers found them useful for financing projects, Guardian eschewed them on the grounds that it should owe no money to anyone but its policyholders. Interview with Art Ferrara, 2 May 2002. Annual Report, 1983, 1984, Box 4; Minutes of the Board of Directors, 23 January 1957, Box 6, GLIC archives.

65. Walker, Kenneth, *Guaranteed Investment Contracts,* 47.

66. Kalmbach, "Chairman's Address"; Wallison, *Federal Chartering,* 31–33. Joseph Belth, "The Financial Strength of Life-Health Insurance Companies," *The Insurance Forum* 27 (September 2000): 85. Interview with Joseph Sargent, 30 May 2002.

67. Interview with Irving Rosenthal, 6 July 1984, Box 250, GLIC archives.

68. In the wake of the Armstrong reforms, many insurance executives would have agreed with William C. Johnson, who asked why the state should be empowered to determine how much safety cushion a company needed. Only companies in conjunction with their policyholders, it was argued, should make determinations about how much surplus should be committed to ensuring policyholder safety. But that argument was a losing one. See Johnson, William C., "Regulation of Life Insurance Companies," 174.

69. President's Report, 27 November 1974, Box 44; John C. Angle, "Reserves, Contingency Reserves and Surplus," 21 October 1975, John C. Angle, "A Proposal to Establish a Reinsurance Department," 28 May 1980, Office of the President, Angle, Box 195, GLIC archives.

70. Lencsis, *Insurance Regulation,* 85. Minutes of the Board of Directors, 28 February, 25 April 2001, Office of the Corporate Secretary.

NOTES TO PART II

1. http://sandiego.fbi.gov/surebuck/surebuck.htm. Interview with Robert Evraets, 22 March 2002.

2. As one nineteenth-century critic put it, if any company has a reputation for litigation, prospects should "avoid the office as he would a pestilence." Tuckett, *Practical Remarks,* 29; Tully, "Policy Claims." *Guardian Life,* August 1960. McKeithen v. Guardian, 1923, Legal Department Records, Box 79, GLIC archives.

3. Statements like the following permeate Guardian's archives: "We are somewhat behind the eight-ball in the development of our three new products—association life, long term disability and baby group. I think it would be very unwise to develop any further new programs until we have these sufficiently under control." T. Robert Wilcox to John E. Gray, 29 January 1964, Office of the Executive Vice President, Rosenthal, Box 183; Interview with Irving Rosenthal, 6 July 1984, Box 250, GLIC archives.

NOTES TO CHAPTER 5

1. S. Bulow to James Scott, 18 August 1949, Office of the Secretary, Scott, Box 64, GLIC archives.

2. Annual Report, 1952, Box 3, GLIC archives.

3. Oates, *Business and Social Change*, 4.

4. Annual Report, 1940, Box 2, GLIC archives.

5. Reports on the Examination of the Guardian, 1952, Box 71, GLIC archives.

6. Douglass, *American Business*, 155. Reports on the Examination of the Guardian, 1911, Box 70; Harwood E. Ryan, "Report on Dividend System—Germania Life Insurance Company," 3 January 1911, History Files, John C. Angle, Box 198, GLIC archives.

7. Wilde, "Effective Expense Control." Irving Rosenthal, "How to Compete against the 'New' Joint Life Policies," 24 August 1966, Office of the Executive Vice President, Rosenthal, Box 184; John C. Angle, "The Actuary As a Professional," Office of the President, Angle, Box 195, GLIC archives.

8. "Financial Notes," *New York Times*, 24 January 1941; "Insurance Notes," *New York Times*, 5 February 1943; "A New Chief Executive," *New York Times*, 24 December 1966. Interview with Ed Kane, 30 November 2001. Annual Report, 1963, Box 4; Minutes of the Board of Directors, 23 April 1930, Box 5; Minutes of the Board of Directors, 24 January 1968, Box 206, GLIC archives.

9. "Changes in Guardian Life," *New York Times*, 1 January 1943; "Cameron Will Succeed McLain as Guardian Life Chairman, Chief Officer," *Wall Street Journal*, 6 August 1963. Interview with Frank Jones, 30 November 2001; interview with John Angle, 21 March 2002; interview with Leo Futia, 12 April 2002; interview with Art Ferarra, 2 May 2002. Annual Report, 1963, Box 4; Minutes of the Board of Directors, 16 December 1942, 28 July 1948, Box 6; John Angle interview with Irving Rosenthal, 26 February 1982, John C. Angle interview with Daniel J. Lyons, 7 March 1982, Office of the President, Angle, Box 197, GLIC archives.

10. Rosenthal, *Short and Confidential History*. "A New Chief Executive," *New York Times*, 24 December 1966; "Guardian Life Elects Two Top Executives," *New York Times*, 26 December 1966. Interview with Art Ferrara, 2 May 2002. Tom Quinn interview with George T. Conklin, 5 March 1982, Office of the President, Angle, Box 197; Minutes of the Board of Directors, 16 December 1953, 16 December 1970, Box 206; Interview with Irving Rosenthal, 6 July 1984, Box 250, GLIC archives.

11. Interview with John Angle, 21 March 2002; interview with Art Ferarra, 2 May 2002. Minutes of the Board of Directors, 17 December 1941, Box 5; Field Advisory Board Meeting Proceedings, 18 January 1950, Box 75; Irving Rosenthal to Art Ferarra, 28 January 1969, Speech by Irving Rosenthal, Group Conference, 14 April 1969, Office of the Executive Vice President, Rosenthal, Box 183; Irving Rosenthal to Shale Goodman, 15 April 1966, Office of the Executive Vice President, Rosenthal, Box 184; "Rosenthal, Irving," Office of the President, Angle, Box 197; Interview with Irving Rosenthal, 6 July 1984, Box 250, GLIC archives.

12. Interview with Ed Kane, 22 February 2002. Tom Quinn interview with Anthony Peloso, Director of Group Administration, n.d., Office of the President, Angle, Box 197, GLIC archives.

13. Rosenthal, *Short and Confidential History*. "Financial Notes," *New York Times*, 24 January 1941; "Guardian," *New York Times*, 19 December 1963. Minutes of the Board of Directors, 28 November, 19 December 1973, Box 206, GLIC archives.

14. Interview with Joseph Caruso, 30 November 2001; interview with John Angle, 21 March 2002. Minutes of the Board of Directors, 23 May, 22 August 1973, Box 206, GLIC archives.

15. John C. Angle, "Closing Remarks, Group Regional Meeting," 1974, Office of the President, Angle, Box 195; Minutes of the Board of Directors, 23 May 1973, Box 206, GLIC archives.

16. "Guardian Life Insurance Co. of America," *Wall Street Journal*, 8 May 1980; "Guardian Life Insurance Names New Chairman," *New York Times*, 27 May 1980; "Who's News," *Wall*

Street Journal, 20 December 1984; "Who's News," *Wall Street Journal,* 30 December 1988. John C. Angle, "Health Care Delivery in the 1970's," 16 April 1970, Office of the President, Angle, Box 195, GLIC archives.

17. Angle and McCuistion, "Substandard Risks," 333–35. John C. Angle, "A Report on Guardian History," 18 November 1981, Office of the President, Angle, Box 195, GLIC archives.

18. de Palo, *Dividend Study Note,* 1997. Interview with Armand de Palo, 27 January 2003. Minutes of the Board of Directors, 25 February 1981, Box 207, GLIC archives.

19. Interview with Armand de Palo, 27 January 2003.

20. President's Report, 22 February 1978, Box 44, GLIC archives.

21. Interview with Irving Rosenthal, 6 July 1984, Box 250, GLIC archives.

22. Annual Report, 1877, Box 1, GLIC archives.

23. Joseph M. Belth, "The Age 100 Problem in Life Insurance," *The Insurance Forum* 28 (January 2001): 163.

24. Annual Report, 1877, Box 1, GLIC archives.

25. Minutes of the Board of Directors, 13 October 1886, Box 121, GLIC archives.

26. Nathan R. Smith to Frank Weidenborner, 20 October 1954, Office of the Secretary, Scott, Box 64, GLIC archives.

27. Clough, *Mutual Life Insurance Company of New York,* 151–52; McCall, *A Review,* 46.

28. Grant, *Insurance Reform,* 25; Tuckett, *Practical Remarks,* 28; Villaronga, *Incontestable Clause.*

29. Taylor, John M., *'Incontestable' Insurance.*

30. Buley, *American Life Convention,* 721; Cragin, "Medical Preparedness"; Geren, "Contribution of Life Insurance," 44; Stone, *Since 1845,* 153, 168. "Historical Facts and Data Regarding The Guardian Life Insurance Co. of America," John E. Albert, 1950, Office of the Secretary, Scott, Box 64; "Guardian Guardianship," 1935?, Home Office Records, Box 74; Facts of Interest in the History of the Germania Life Insurance Company, 1910, Public Relations Department Records, Box 84; Minutes of the Board of Directors, 11 July 1888, 26 October 1892, Box 121; Executive Officers Committee Minutes, 15 March 1921, Box 178, GLIC archives.

31. Hamwi, *Surrender Benefits*; Sullivan, "Life Insurance."

32. Charles B. Rudd to Carl Heye, 10 July 1919, on verso of letterhead, Office of the Vice President and Agency Managers, Hansen, Box 66, GLIC archives.

33. Annual Report, 1877, Box 1, GLIC archives.

34. Gephart, "Loans"; Hudnut, *Semi-Centennial History,* 200. "Historical Facts and Data Regarding The Guardian Life Insurance Co. of America," John E. Albert, 1950, Office of the Secretary, Scott, Box 64, GLIC archives.

35. Annual Report, 1965, Box 4, GLIC archives.

36. President's Report, 25 February 1981, Leo Futia to Guardian Associates, 23 January 1981, Box 44; Reports on the Examination of the Guardian, 1984, Box 187, GLIC archives.

37. Babbel and Staking, "Life Insurance Costs." Interview with Leo Futia, 12 April 2002; interview with Art Ferrara, 2 May 2002. Annual Report, 1985, 1986, Box 1; "Share in the Difference," Agency Department, Product/Sales Promotion, Box 194; John C. Angle, "The Legacy of Queen Anne: Price-Fixed Interest Rates and the Cost of Life Insurance," Office of the President, Angle, Box 195, GLIC archives.

38. Charles B. Rudd to Carl Heye, 10 July 1919, on verso of letterhead, Office of the Vice President and Agency Managers, Hansen, Box 66, GLIC archives.

39. Hunter, "The Problem."

40. Minutes of the Board of Directors, 24 April 1946, 27 July 1955, Box 6; Reports on the Examination of the Guardian, 1946, Box 71; Frank F. Weidenborner to All Company Managers, 19 April 1946, J. C. Barnsley to All Guardian Managers, 3 February 1947, Irving Rosenthal to All Managers and Cashiers, 25 October 1954, Circulars, Box 94; Executive Officers Committee Minutes, 13 August 1940, 7 August 1945, Box 179, GLIC archives.

41. Davis, Malvin E., *Industrial Insurance,* 52–59; Douglass, *American Business,* 305; McElreath, *History of the Industrial Life,* 87; North, "Capital Accumulation," 243–44.

42. Davis, Malvin E., *Industrial Insurance.*

43. Buley, *American Life Convention,* 122–30; Clough, *Mutual Life Insurance Company of New York,* 151; Douglass, *American Business,* 304–5; Woodson, Carter G., "Insurance Business among Negroes," 207. "Investment Questionnaire," TNEC Records, Box 59; "Historical Facts and Data Regarding The Guardian Life Insurance Co. of America," John E. Albert, 1950, Office of the Secretary, Scott, Box 64; Reports on the Examination of the Guardian, 1937, Box 70; Executive Officers Committee Minutes, 9 June 1925, Box 178, GLIC archives.

44. McElreath, *History of the Industrial Life,* 86–87. Annual Report, 1947, Box 2, GLIC archives.

45. *Testimony Taken before the Joint Committee,* 5,523–24. Minutes of the Board of Directors, 24 July 1940, Box 5; Minutes of the Board of Directors, 27 April 1910, Box 122; Executive Officers Committee Minutes, 15 February, 17, 24 May, 7 June, 18 October 1921, 9 June 1925, Box 178; Interview with Irving Rosenthal, 6 July 1984, Box 250, GLIC archives.

46. Geren, "Contribution of Life Insurance," 47; Myers, "Social Security"; Oates, *Business and Social Change,* 18.

47. Annual Report, 1877, Box 1; "The Accommodation Plan," 1875, Circulars, Box 94; Annual Statement, 1873, Box 106; Minutes of the Board of Directors, 10 April 1889, Box 121, GLIC archives.

48. Abbott, *Story of NYLIC,* 9; Horack et al., "Regulation of Insurance," 190–91.

49. Clough, *Mutual Life Insurance Company of New York,* 127; Douglass, *American Business,* 152, 304; North, "Capital Accumulation," 240–41; Washington Tontine, "As Many of the Stockholders Have Expressed a Wish to Obtain a Complete List," 1805.

50. "Sheppard Homans," *The National Cyclopaedia of American Biography,* 6:539; Buley, *American Life Convention,* 94–95, 101; Douglass, *American Business,* 309; North, "Capital Accumulation," 245; Stone, *Since 1845,* 107.

51. Boney, "Public Service"; Hudnut, *Semi-Centennial History,* 226; Johnson, William C., "Regulation of Life Insurance Companies," 170–71; North, "Capital Accumulation," 242.

52. North, "Capital Accumulation"; Ransom and Sutch, "Tontine Insurance."

53. Buley, *American Life Convention,* 112; Hunter, "Insurance of Impaired Lives." "Business Instructions for Agents," 1903, Manuals, Box 96, GLIC archives.

54. J. C. Barnsley to Charles Dubuar, 29 April 1947, Reinsurance, Organ Box 14; Annual Report, 1940, Box 2; Minutes of the Board of Directors, 23 April 1952, 28 July 1954, Box 6; Reports on the Examination of the Guardian, 1937, Box 70; Reports on the Examination of the Guardian, 1943, Box 71; "Guardian's Centennial Year," 1960, Public Relations Department Records, Box 84, GLIC archives.

55. Oates, *Business and Social Change,* 16–17. Field Advisory Board Meeting Proceedings, 21 April 1966, Box 75, GLIC archives.

56. Rosenthal, *Short and Confidential History.* Annual Report, 1948, Box 2; Annual Report, 1950, Box 3; Minutes of the Board of Directors, 27 October 1948, Box 6; "Guardian's Centennial Year," 1960, Public Relations Department Records, Box 84; Executive Officers Committee Minutes, 27 June 1939, Box 178; Executive Officers Committee Minutes, 20 November 1945, 7 August, 10, 31 December 1946, 8 October 1948, Box 179, GLIC archives.

57. Annual Report, 1954, Box 3; Reports on the Examination of the Guardian, 1952, Box 71; Field Advisory Board Meeting Proceedings, 6 January 1948, Box 75; Advertisement: "Guardian of Your Most Valuable Business Asset," *Business Week,* 22 June 1957, Public Relations Department Records, Box 84; "Notes on the New Guardian Preferred Risk Policies," 1948, Underwriting Secretary and Assistant Secretary, Box 185, GLIC archives.

58. "Wife insurance" should not be confused with the so-called wives' insurance, i.e., policies taken out for the benefit of wives, protected from creditors under the laws of New York and many other states. Hudnut, *Semi-Centennial History,* 11. *The Guardian,* 12 November 1962, 28 January 1963, 27 April 1964. Rosenbaum v. Guardian, Guardian v. Rosenbaum and Rosenbaum, 1921, Legal Department Records, Box 79; Germania Life Insurance Company Prospec-

tus, 1861, Box 84; Executive Officers Committee Minutes, 11 June 1940, Box 178; Interview with Irving Rosenthal, 6 July 1984, Box 250, GLIC archives.

59. Phyllis Lee Levin, "Wives Cause Re-Appraisal of Insurance," *New York Times,* 26 June 1957. Annual Report, 1966, Box 4, GLIC archives.

60. "The Germania's Child's Endowment," *The Insurance Monitor* 52 (1904): 202. "Actuary B. R. Neuske Dead," *Eastern Underwriter,* 22 January 1954, Office of the Secretary, Scott, Box 64, GLIC archives.

61. Executive Officers Committee Minutes, 15 May 1923, Box 178, GLIC archives.

62. "Insurance Notes," *New York Times,* 3 March 1945. Minutes of the Board of Directors, 24 April 1946, 27 July 1955, Box 6, GLIC archives.

63. Annual Report, 1940, Box 2; Minutes of the Board of Directors, 26 July 1950, 22 January 1958, Box 6; Advertisement: "Let's Make It Simple," *Fortune,* August 1938, Public Relations Department Records, Box 84; Executive Officers Committee Minutes, 14 February, 12 March, 2, 16 April, 7 May 1940, Box 178; Interview with Irving Rosenthal, 6 July 1984, Box 250, GLIC archives.

64. Clough, *Mutual Life Insurance Company of New York,* 269–70. Minutes of the Board of Directors, 25 October 1916, 27 December 1916, 27 July 1955, Box 6; Carl Heye to T. Louis Hansen, 15 December 1916, Office of the President, Heye, Box 46; "Historical Facts and Data Regarding The Guardian Life Insurance Co. of America," John E. Albert, 1950, Office of the Secretary, Scott, Box 64, GLIC archives.

65. Geren, "Contribution of Life Insurance," 50; Goldberg, "Some Aspects of Competition"; Murphy, Robert E., "Are We in Focus?"; Woodson, Benjamin, "What Can Be Done?"

66. Annual Report, 1877, Box 1; "The Accommodation Plan," 1875, Circulars, Box 94, GLIC archives.

67. Murphy, Ray, "Significant Annuity Developments"; Oates, *Business and Social Change,* 13.

68. Murphy, Ray, "Significant Annuity Developments"; Scoles, "Development of Life Annuities." Reports on the Examination of the Guardian, 1937, Box 70; Field Advisory Board Meeting Proceedings, 20 November 1964, Box 75; John Gray to Irving Rosenthal, 5 August 1969, Leo Futia to All Agencies, 3 December 1969, Office of the President, Angle, Box 197; John C. Angle to Robert D. Shapiro, 19 May 1986, Office of the President, Angle, Box 201, GLIC archives.

69. Life insurance companies, including Guardian, were slow to catch on to the possibilities of various types of "supplemental insurance," probably because they considered a standard health policy backed by a whole life policy with a high savings component to be equal to the task of insuring against catastrophic or long-term illness. AFLAC, however, proved that many American families thought otherwise. Shubin, *Man from Enterprise.* For a good introduction to disability benefits, see Hunter, "The Problem"; Maclean, "Development of Disability Benefits."

70. Stone, *A Short History,* 76–77. "Historical Facts and Data Regarding The Guardian Life Insurance Co. of America," John E. Albert, 1950, Office of the Secretary, Scott, Box 64; Minutes of the Board of Directors, 25 January 1911, Box 122, GLIC archives.

71. Jesse Phillips to John Fuhrer, 13 December 1915, John Fuhrer to Jesse Phillips, 9 December 1915, Jesse Phillips to John Fuhrer, 27 December 1916, Amended Charter of the Germania Life Insurance Company of New York, 31 December 1915, Office of the Secretary, Heye and Neuendorffer, Box 54; "Historical Facts and Data Regarding The Guardian Life Insurance Co. of America," John E. Albert, 1950, Office of the Secretary, Scott, Box 64; Reports on the Examination of the Guardian, 1937, Box 70, GLIC archives.

72. Clough, *Mutual Life Insurance Company of New York,* 267–68; Keesling, "Moral Hazard." Reports on the Examination of the Guardian, 1933, Box 70, GLIC archives.

73. For more details about the Barry case, see Box 8, folders 1–8; Box 13, folder 17, Winfield K. Denton Papers, Indiana Historical Society, Indianapolis, Indiana. Executive Officers Committee Minutes, 24 October 1922, 18 August, 8 October 1925, Box 178; Interview with Irving Rosenthal, 6 July 1984, Box 250, GLIC archives.

74. Buley, *American Life Convention,* 721; Maclean, "Development of Disability Benefits." Annual Report, 1954, Box 3; Finance Committee Minutes, 27 October 1937, Box 16; Reports on the Examination of the Guardian, 1937, Box 70; Various memos, correspondence, calculations, competition analyses, and industry commentary, Claim Department Records, Box 77; Interview with Irving Rosenthal, 6 July 1984, Box 250, GLIC archives.

75. Reports on the Examination of the Guardian, 1940, Box 70, Reports on the Examination of the Guardian, 1943, Box 71; Disability Claim Survey folder, various dates, Claim Department Records, Box 77; Executive Officers Committee Minutes, 29 March 1938, Box 178; "Compromise Settlements of Disability Claims," 1942, Office of the Executive Vice President, Rosenthal, Box 185, GLIC archives.

76. "Agents' Manual: The Guardian Life Insurance Company of America," 1938, Manuals, Box 96, GLIC archives.

77. Maclean, "Development of Disability Benefits." Annual Report, 1940, 1941, Box 2; Reports on the Examination of the Guardian, 1943, Box 71, GLIC archives.

78. Rosenthal, *Short and Confidential History.* Annual Report, 1949, 1950, Box 3, GLIC archives.

79. Minutes of the Board of Directors, 22 January 1958, Box 6, GLIC archives.

80. Annual Report, 1977, Box 4; Field Advisory Board Meeting Proceedings, 12 April 1965, 5 April 1971, 15 September 1977, 4 May 1978, Box 75; John C. Angle, "Moderator's Opening Remarks," Office of the President, Angle, Box 195; Gerald S. Parker to All Agencies, 7 July 1976, Circular Letters, Agency Communication and Sales Promotion, Box 212, GLIC archives.

81. 70 N.Y.2d 888; 519 N.E.2d 288; 524 N.Y.S.2d 377; 1987 N.Y. LEXIS 19936.

82. Smith, J. Henry, "The Nation's Needs in Medical Economics." Interview with John Angle, 21 March 2002.

83. Annual Report, 1952, Box 3; Minutes of the Board of Directors, 26 October 1949, Box 6; John Cameron to Home Office Staff, 1 November 1944, Home Office Records, Box 74; Executive Officers Committee Minutes, 5 November 1941, Box 178; Office of the Executive Vice President, Rosenthal, Box 183, GLIC archives.

84. Annual Report, 1951, 1952, Box 3, GLIC archives.

85. Annual Report, 1953, 1955, Box 3, GLIC archives.

86. *Home Office Newsletter,* 15 October 1952. Field Advisory Board Meeting Proceedings, 6 July 1951, Box 75; Interview with Irving Rosenthal, 6 July 1984, Box 250, GLIC archives.

87. Yandell Smith, "'Disaster' Insurance Spreads Rapidly but Some Problems Appear," *Wall Street Journal,* 20 December 1955; "Guardian Life Insurance Net Rose to $8,278,000 in 1955," *Wall Street Journal,* 28 February 1956. Finance Committee Minutes, 14 May 1952, Box 18; Interview with Irving Rosenthal, 6 July 1984, Box 250, GLIC archives.

88. Guardian Major Medical Policy, 1 October 1954, Office of the Executive Vice President, Rosenthal, Box 183; William Mauke to Guardian Group, 14 January 1982, Office of the President, Angle, Box 197, GLIC archives.

89. Angle and McCuistion, "Substandard Risks," 335. Interview with Irving Rosenthal, 6 July 1984, Box 250, GLIC archives.

90. Interview with Armand de Palo, 27 January 2003. John C. Angle, "Health Care from the Viewpoint of Insurance Companies and Business Executives," 14 October 1981, Office of the President, Angle, Box 195, GLIC archives.

91. Annual Report, 1956, Box 3; Minutes of the Board of Directors, 25 July 1956, 22 October 1958, Box 6; President's Report, 23 October 1957, Box 43; Reports on the Examination of the Guardian, 1955, 1961, Box 72, GLIC archives.

92. *Proceedings of the Forty-Fifth Annual Meeting of the Life Insurance Association of America,* 1951, 108. *The Guardian,* 12 March 1962. Annual Report, 1962, Box 4; President's Report, 28 July 1965, Box 43; Field Advisory Board Meeting Proceedings, 24 September 1962, 20 November 1964, Box 75; "Theory of Major Medical Premiums," 1960, "Some Notes on Net Supplementary Major Medical Premiums," 1962–63, Irving Rosenthal to Peter Tompa, 14 January

1963, Irving Rosenthal to Fiscal Advisory Committee, 19 May 1961, Office of the Executive Vice President, Rosenthal, Box 183, GLIC archives.

93. Annual Report, 1958, Box 3; President's Reports, 27 April 1960, 24 October 1962, Box 43; Irving Rosenthal to George Conklin, 23 May 1972, Office of the Executive Vice President, Rosenthal, Box 185, GLIC archives.

94. President's Report, 24 April 1963, 22 April, 28 October 1964, 28 July 1965, Box 43; Coordinating Committee Minutes, 10 March 1964, Office of the Secretary, Reilly, Box 179, GLIC archives.

95. President's Report, 27 October 1965, 26 January 1966, Box 43; Coordinating Committee Minutes, 7 July 1966, Office of the Secretary, Reilly, Box 179; Gerald S. Parker to All Agencies, 24 March, 11 August 1976, Robert Damon to All Agencies, 13 February 1980, Circular Letters, Agency Communication and Sales Promotion, Box 212, GLIC archives.

96. Interview with Joseph Sargent, 30 May 2002. President's Report, 27 July 1966, Box 43; Minutes of the Board of Directors, 25 February 1981, Box 207; Gerald S. Parker to All Agencies, 11 September 1975, Circular Letters, Agency Communication and Sales Promotion, Box 212, GLIC archives.

97. Interview with Armand de Palo, 27 January 2003.

98. A recently completed database of early securities prices allows us to extend this generalization back to 1790. Sylla et al., "Database of Securities Prices"; Walker, *Guaranteed Investment Contracts,* 21. *New York Times,* 19 November 1962. John E. Gray to Irving Rosenthal, 5 August 1969, Irving Rosenthal to George Conklin, 14 August 1972, Office of the Executive Vice President, Rosenthal, Box 183; Tom Quinn interview with Anthony Peloso, Director of Group Administration, n.d., Office of the President, Angle, Box 197, GLIC archives.

99. MacLean, *Life Insurance,* 47. Sal Nuccio, "Mutual Funds: A New Role as Life Insurer?" *New York Times,* 19 November 1962.

100. *Proceedings of the Forty-Ninth Annual Meeting of the Life Insurance Association of America,* 1955, 108–9; Woodson, Benjamin, "What Can Be Done?"; Sal Nuccio, "Mutual Funds: A New Role as Life Insurer?" *New York Times,* 19 November 1962.

101. Sal Nuccio, "Mutual Funds: A New Role as Life Insurer?" *New York Times,* 19 November 1962; H. J. Maidenberg, "Four Insurers Join in a Fund Venture," *New York Times,* 29 April 1969. *The Guardian,* 12 February 1962. Interview with Joseph Caruso, 30 November 2001. Field Advisory Board Meeting Proceedings, 20 April 1972, Box 75, GLIC archives.

102. Blue Sky laws were state level securities regulations. Macey and Miller, "Blue Sky Laws"; Mahoney, "Blue Sky Laws." Finance Committee Minutes, 14 August 1968, Box 19; Finance Committee Minutes, 23 July 1969, Box 20; President's Report, 26 February, 27 August, 26 November 1969, Box 43, GLIC archives.

103. Interview with Joseph Caruso, 30 November 2001; interview with Don Sullivan, 22 March 2002. Annual Report, 1986, Box 1; Annual Report, 1981, 1982, 1983, 1984, Box 4; President's Report, 28 May, 27 August 1969, Box 43; Leo Futia to Guardian Associates, 4 August 1981, Box 44; Field Advisory Board Meeting Proceedings, 31 January 1968, 18 September 1969, 5 April 1971, 20 April 1972, 24 July 1975, 21 September 1978, Box 75, GLIC archives. Minutes of the Board of Directors, 18 November 1992, Office of the Corporate Secretary.

104. John C. Angle to Robert D. Shapiro, 19 May 1986, Office of the President, Angle, Box 201, GLIC archives.

105. Irving Rosenthal to George Conklin, 23 September 1971, Office of the Executive Vice President, Rosenthal, Box 184; Irving Rosenthal, "Life Insurance in the U.S. Needs an Equity Investment Element," *Probe,* 1968, Irving Rosenthal to Leo Futia, 10 April 1972, Office of the Executive Vice President, Rosenthal, Box 185; Interview with Irving Rosenthal, 6 July 1984, Box 250, GLIC archives.

106. Interview with Joseph Caruso, 30 November 2001, 21 August 2002. Annual Report, 1972, Box 4; Field Advisory Board Meeting Proceedings, 20 April 1972, 13 September 1973, 24 July 1975, Box 75; William C. Brown to Irving Rosenthal, 15 June 1972, Office of the Executive Vice President, Rosenthal, Box 183, GLIC archives.

107. Annual Report, 1968, Box 4; Field Advisory Board Meeting Proceedings, 17 November 1966, Box 75, GLIC archives.

108. Field Advisory Board Meeting Proceedings, 30 April 1968, President's Report, 26 February, 26 November 1969, 9 September 1971, Box 75, GLIC archives.

109. Interview with Bruce Long, 30 November 2001.

110. It is clear, however, that over the decades a number of people had developed similar ideas upon which Dinney drew. Black and Skipper, *Life Insurance,* 83–96.

NOTES TO CHAPTER 6

1. A good overview is Beers, "Group Coverages." Interview with Gary Lenderink, 7 December 2001.

2. Reports on the Examination of the Guardian, 1961, Box 72, GLIC archives.

3. Davis, Malvin E., *Industrial Insurance,* 234–38; Davis, Malvin E., "Industrial Life." Peter Tompa to T. Robert Wilcox, 20 April 1960, Group Advisory Committee Minutes, 21 December 1961, Office of the Executive Vice President, Rosenthal, Box 183, GLIC archives.

4. Buley, *American Life Convention,* 377; Day, "Significance"; Grant, *Insurance Reform,* 60; Outerbridge, "Promoting Stability in Labor Groups."

5. Buley, *American Life Convention,* 417. Minutes of the Board of Directors, 12 March 1890, Box 121, GLIC archives.

6. Buley, *American Life Convention,* 420.

7. Kavanaugh, "Advancing Social Welfare"; Outerbridge, "Promoting Stability in Labor Groups."

8. Guardian also wrote a group policy on the Seng Company, soon afterward, that terminated in early 1921. Finance Committee Minutes, 13 December 1916, Finance Committee Minutes, 20 December 1933, Box 16; Reports on the Examination of the Guardian, 1937, Box 70; Reports on the Examination of the Guardian, 1952, Box 71; Executive Officers Committee Minutes, 5 April, 22 November 1921, 6, 13 July, 9 November, 7 December 1937, 6, 12 July, 22 November 1938, 31 January, 7 March, 21, 28 March, 4 April, 2 May, 27 June, 5, 11 July, 22 August, 19, 26 September, 28 November, 12 December 1939, 2 January, 3 December 1940, 25 November 1941, Box 178; Executive Officers Committee Minutes, 5 December 1944, 19 February, 8, 15, 22 October, 26 November, 10 December 1946, Box 179; Interview with William W. Mauke, Senior Vice President for Group Insurance, 25 March 1982, Office of the President, Angle, Box 197, GLIC archives.

9. Executive Officers Committee Minutes, 13 January, 12 April 1922, 17 April 1923, 6 February, 11 November, 9 December 1924, Box 178, GLIC archives.

10. Minutes of the Board of Directors, 22 April 1925, Box 5; "Agents' Manual: The Guardian Life Insurance Company of America," 1938, Manuals, Box 96; Executive Officers Committee Minutes, 13 January, 17, 31 March, 9, 14 April, 5 May, 15 December 1925, 1 October 1940, Box 178, GLIC archives.

11. Minutes of the Board of Directors, 16 December 1936, 24 July 1940, Box 5; "Operating Results and Investments of the Twenty-Six Largest Legal Reserve Life Insurance Companies in the U.S., 1929–1938," TNEC Records, Box 59, GLIC archives.

12. *Proceedings of the Forty-Eighth Annual Meeting of the Life Insurance Association of America,* 1954, 107. Field Advisory Board Meeting Proceedings, 6 January 1948, 19 January 1949, 31 August 1955, 24 September 1962, Box 75; Executive Officers Committee Minutes, 27 May 1947, Box 179; Group Advisory Committee Minutes, 1 March, 6 November 1961, John E. Gray to Irving Rosenthal, 28 January 1964, Office of the Executive Vice President, Rosenthal, Box 183; Special Report of the Executive Committee to the Board of Directors, 19 December 1956, Tom Quinn interview with George T. Conklin, 5 March 1982, Office of the President, Angle, Box 197; Interview with Irving Rosenthal, 6 July 1984, Box 250, GLIC archives.

13. *Proceedings of the Forty-Ninth Annual Meeting of the Life Insurance Association of America,* 1955, 154. *Business Week,* 26 September 1953, 120. Robert C. McQueen to E. A. Dougherty, 6

April 1954, Irving Rosenthal to Robert C. McQueen, 11 June 1956, Office of the Executive Vice President, Rosenthal, Box 183; Wendell Milliman, "A Supplemental Report on Group Insurance for Guardian Life Insurance Company," March 1956, Special Report of the Executive Committee to the Board of Directors, 19 December 1956, Office of the President, Angle, Box 197, GLIC archives.

14. "Pension Trust," n.d., Public Relations Department Records, Box 84, GLIC archives.

15. Minutes of the Board of Directors, 22 October, 17 December 1941, Box 5; Executive Officers Committee Minutes, 1, 9, 15, 22 November 1938, Box 178, GLIC archives.

16. Annual Report, 1985, Box 1; Executive Officers Committee Minutes, 18 June 1940, 4 August, 17, 24 November, 8 December 1942, 19, 26 January, 2 March, 11 May 1943, Box 179, GLIC archives.

17. Annual Report, 1945, 1947, Box 2; Annual Report, 1954, Box 3; Reports on the Examination of the Guardian, 1943, Box 71; Executive Officers Committee Minutes, 17, 22, 29 June, 3, 10 August 1943, Box 179, GLIC archives.

18. Hull, "What's Happening?"; Sommers, "Life Insurance Companies and Corporate Pensions"; Walker, Kenneth, *Guaranteed Investment Contracts,* 9. Sal Nuccio to Henry Stral, 27 May 1975, Organ Box 17A-#1; Annual Report, 1985, Box 1; Minutes of the Board of Directors, 22 May 1974, 27 August 1975, Box 206, GLIC archives.

19. Saul Nuccio, "Mutual Funds: Role of Institutional Buying," *New York Times,* 26 November 1962. Field Advisory Board Meeting Proceedings, 15 September 1977, Box 75; Irving Rosenthal to George Conklin, 14 August 1972, Office of the Executive Vice President, Rosenthal, Box 183, GLIC archives.

20. Richard E. Ullman, "Should We Make a Major Investment in Group Pensions? The Facts," 17 February 1967, Office of the President, Angle, Box 197; Interview with Irving Rosenthal, 6 July 1984, Box 250, GLIC archives. Minutes of the Board of Directors, 24 April 2002, Office of the Corporate Secretary.

21. Annual Report, 1987, Box 1; Annual Report, 1956, Box 3; Minutes of the Board of Directors, 27 July 1955, 19 December 1956, Box 6; Reports on the Examination of the Guardian, 1958, Box 72, GLIC archives.

22. Reports on the Examination of the Guardian, 1961, Box 72; Group Advisory Committee Minutes, 19 February 1960, Office of the Executive Vice President, Rosenthal, Box 183, GLIC archives.

23. *The Guardian,* 12 March 1962. Interview with Gary Lenderink, 7 December 2001; interview with Art Ferrara, 2 May 2002. President's Report, 23 October 1957, 22 January, 23 April 1958, Box 43; Harley Kight to John Angle, 25 March 1982, Office of the President, Angle, Box 197, GLIC archives.

24. Field Advisory Board Meeting Proceedings, 6 February 1957, 20 November 1964, 12 April 1965, 17 November 1966, 27 April 1967, 13 September 1973, Box 75; T. Robert Wilcox to Irving Rosenthal, 17 June 1964, Office of the Executive Vice President, Rosenthal, Box 183, GLIC archives.

25. *The Guardian,* 11 December 1961, 26 March 1962. Reports on the Examination of the Guardian, 1961, Box 72; Tom Quinn interview with Howard Abel, Chartered Life Underwriter, n.d., Office of the President, Angle, Box 197, GLIC archives.

26. Field Advisory Board Meeting Proceedings, 24 September 1962, 27 April 1967, Box 75; Coordinating Committee Minutes, 21 January 1964, Office of the Secretary, Reilly, Box 179; T. Robert Wilcox to Edward Mallon, 25 May 1964, William Mauke to John Gray, 25 May 1964, T. Robert Wilcox to Irving Rosenthal, 24 June 1964, Office of the Executive Vice President, Rosenthal, Box 183, GLIC archives.

27. Interview with Ed Kane, 30 November 2001.

28. Reports on the Examination of the Guardian, 1969, Box 72; Legal Memorandum: The Guardian Multiple Employer Trust Program, September 1972, Office of the Executive Vice President, Rosenthal, Box 183; Reports on the Examination of the Guardian, 1974, Box 187, GLIC archives.

29. *Guardian Service,* May–June 1969; *Newsletter,* 15 February 1979.

30. In 1965 Provident paid out $834,000 of dividends when its losses were $673,000 on $10 million of premiums. Guardian paid only $391,000 of dividends on $14 million worth of premiums when it was earning modest profits. Irving Rosenthal to Daniel J. Lyons, 21 October 1966, Office of the Executive Vice President, Rosenthal, Box 183, GLIC archives.

31. *The Guardian,* 1 July, 12 August 1963. Interview with Armand de Palo, 27 January 2003. Group Advisory Committee Minutes, 15 September 1960, Office of the Executive Vice President, Rosenthal, Box 183; Interview with Irving Rosenthal, 6 July 1984, Box 250, GLIC archives.

32. *Guardian Life,* December 1960. Field Advisory Board Meeting Proceedings, 15 September 1977, 28 September 1979, Box 75, GLIC archives.

33. Group Advisory Committee Minutes, 22 March 1961, Office of the Executive Vice President, Rosenthal, Box 183, GLIC archives.

34. Field Advisory Board Meeting Proceedings, 12 September 1968, 18 September 1969, 5 April, 9 September 1971, Box 75, GLIC archives.

35. President's Report, 27 August 1969, Box 43, GLIC archives.

36. Field Advisory Board Meeting Proceedings, 10 September 1970, Box 75; John C. Angle, "Presentation of Professionalism Award," 8 June 1977, John C. Angle, "1975 Guardian Group Conference," Office of the President, Angle, Box 195, GLIC archives.

37. Interview with Gary Lenderink, 7 December 2001.

38. Interview with Gary Lenderink, 7 December 2001. Field Advisory Board Meeting Proceedings, 25 September 1980, 19 May 1981, Box 75; Reports on the Examination of the Guardian, 1984, Box 187, GLIC archives. Minutes of the Board of Directors, 23 September, 2 December 1992, Office of the Corporate Secretary.

39. Greg Steinmetz, "Eight Insurers End Individual Policies in New York State," *Wall Street Journal,* 5 February 1993. Interview with Armand de Palo, 27 January 2003. Minutes of the Board of Directors, 24 February, 22 September, 1 December 1993, 30 November 1994, 28 February, 22 May 1996, 3 December 1997, Office of the Corporate Secretary.

40. Interview with Gary Lenderink, 7 December 2001.

41. Annual Report, 1957, Box 3; Group Advisory Committee Minutes, 1 March 1961, Gerald S. Parker, memorandum, 3 May 1973, Office of the Executive Vice President, Rosenthal, Box 183, GLIC archives.

42. *Guardian Scene,* October 1963. Reinsurance, Organ Box 14; Speech by Irving Rosenthal, Group Conference, 14 April 1969, Office of the Executive Vice President, Rosenthal, Box 183; Tom Quinn interview with Howard Abel, n.d., Tom Quinn interview with Arthur Ferrara, n.d., "John E. Gray," n.d., Office of the President, Angle, Box 197, GLIC archives.

43. Lencsis, *Insurance Regulation,* 100–103; Menge, "Reinsurance of Life Risks."

44. Rapone, *Guardian,* 75. "Supplemental Investment Questionnaire," TNEC Records, Box 59, GLIC archives.

45. Executive Officers Committee Minutes, 26 June 1922, 22 May, 19 June 1923, 29 April 1924, 17 March 1925, Box 178, GLIC archives.

46. Reports on the Examination of the Guardian, 1933, Box 70; Executive Officers Committee Minutes, 16, 21 March, 14 November 1922, 30 January, 20 March, 8, 22 May, 19 June 1923, Box 178, GLIC archives.

47. Irving Rosenthal, "Comments on New Mortality Study (1948–1969)," Executive Vice President, Rosenthal, Box 184, GLIC archives.

48. Reports on the Examination of the Guardian, 1958, Box 72; Irving Rosenthal, "Comments on New Mortality Study (1948–1969)," Executive Vice President, Rosenthal, Box 184; John C. Angle interview with Daniel J. Lyons, 7 March 1982, Office of the President, Angle, Box 197; Minutes of the Board of Directors, 19 December 1979, Box 207; Interview with Irving Rosenthal, 6 July 1984, Box 250, GLIC archives.

49. In 1972 Guardian had joined Met, Equitable, Home Life, Prudential, and other companies in an extended reinsurance pool on aviation risks. War Risks—Pooling Agreements, Organ Box 21; Annual Report, 1985, Box 1; Minutes of the Board of Directors, 23 January 1952,

Box 6; Coordinating Committee Minutes, 19 February 1963, Office of the Secretary, Reilly, Box 179, GLIC archives.

50. Reinsurance agreements and life catastrophe insurance, Organ Box 14A, 14A-#1, 14B; Minutes of the Board of Directors, 23 April, 23 July 1952, 25 April 1956, 26 October 1960, Box 6; Reports on the Examination of the Guardian, 1961, Box 72; Field Advisory Board Meeting Proceedings, 9 September 1971, Box 75; Group Advisory Committee Minutes, 28 April 1961, Office of the Executive Vice President, Rosenthal, Box 183; "Life Catastrophe Reinsurance," Executive Vice President, Rosenthal, Box 184, GLIC archives.

51. Field Advisory Board Meeting Proceedings, 20 November 1964, 15 September 1977, 5 April 1979, Box 75; Minutes of the Board of Directors, 17 December 1980, Box 207, GLIC archives.

52. Richard A. Hess, Memo, 1972, Irving Rosenthal to Edward Zeiger, 6 December 1972, Office of the Executive Vice President, Rosenthal, Box 185; Reports on the Examination of the Guardian, 1974, Box 187; John C. Angle, "A Proposal to Establish a Reinsurance Department," 28 May 1980, John C. Angle, "Reinsurance Assumed," 11 March 1981, Office of the President, Angle, Box 195, GLIC archives.

53. John C. Angle, "Why Guardian Wishes to Become a Life Reinsurer," 26 July 1979, Office of the President, Angle, Box 201, GLIC archives.

54. John C. Angle to George Conklin, Leo Futia, and Art Ferrara, 8 October 1979, Office of the President, Angle, Box 201, GLIC archives.

55. Annual Report, 1985, Box 1; Reports on the Examination of the Guardian, 1984, Box 187; Thomas Kabele to John C. Angle, 24 June 1980, Tillinghast, Nelson and Warren, "Reinsurance Potential for the Guardian Life," 26 November 1979, John C. Angle, "Risk and Reward in Reinsurance," 12 March 1986, Office of the President, Angle, Box 201, GLIC archives.

NOTES TO CHAPTER 7

1. Sage, "Prevention." Interview with Robert Ryan, 22 March 2002.

2. North, "Capital Accumulation," 248.

3. Williamson and Smalley, *Northwestern Mutual Life*, 18, 21. *The Guardian Family News*, September 1921. Letterhead of Guardian Agent Charles Rudd, various boxes, GLIC archives.

4. North, "Capital Accumulation," 248. John Cameron, "Opening Address for 1960 Leaders' Club Meeting," 1960, Office of the President, Cameron, Box 202, GLIC archives.

5. Julian, "Is Supervision at the Crossroads?" Minutes of the Board of Directors, 25 January 1950, 27 January 1960, Box 6, GLIC archives.

6. Germania Life Insurance Company Prospectus, 1861, Public Relations Department Records, Box 84, GLIC archives.

7. Germania Life Insurance Company Charter and By-Laws, 1860, Box 1; Germania Life Insurance Company Charter and By-Laws, 1867, Box 2, GLIC archives.

8. "The Germania Life Insurance Co. of New York," 1905, "The Germania Life Insurance Company of New York," 1909, "Germania," *Daily Rocky Mountain News*, 8 September 1870, Public Relations Department Records, Box 84; Scrapbook, 1869–77, Public Relations Department Records, Box 85; "European Business," 1 September 1904, Circulars, Box 94; John C. Angle, "Histories: My own; Guardian Life's; and that of J. F. Entz," 17 September 1983, Office of the President, Angle, Box 195, GLIC archives.

9. Rapone, *Guardian*, 80, photograph 15. "The Germania Life Insurance Company," 1902, Lewis Hargreaves to George Conklin, 13 September 1957, Public Relations Department Records, Box 84, GLIC archives.

10. Reports on the Examination of the Guardian, 1878, Box 70, GLIC archives.

11. Johnson, William C., "Regulation of Life Insurance Companies," 167. Annual Report, 1871, 1877, Box 1, GLIC archives.

12. "The Germania in Germany," *Insurance Monitor*, 1904, 385.

13. "The Germania Life Insurance Company," *Insurance Monitor*, 1907, 90.

14. Grant, *Insurance Reform,* 59.

15. "Memorandum: The Germania Life Insurance Company," 1886, "Postcards, 1910–1918," Public Relations Department Records, Box 84; "Materials Intended for the Public," Public Relations Department Records, Box 95, GLIC archives.

16. Premium and Loan Interest Receipts, 1912, 1931–32, "Charles Kruse folder," Office of the President, Heye, Box 53; "Premium Receipts," Office of the Secretary, Scott, Box 64, GLIC archives.

17. Supervisors' Manual, 1 June 1926, Home Office Records, Box 74; "Looking for Lost Policyholders," n.d., Public Relations Department Records, Box 84, GLIC archives.

18. "A Few Reasons Why to Apply for Insurance to the Germania Life Insurance Company," 1913, Public Relations Department Records, Box 84; Margaret Boehme, letter in the *Pottsville Standard,* 26 June 1869, Public Relations Department Records, Box 85, GLIC archives.

19. Marchand, *Advertising.* Carl Heye to Policyholders, 1 June 1927, Public Relations Department Records, Box 84, GLIC archives.

20. Day, "Significance." Annual Report, 1919, Box 1, GLIC archives.

21. Annual Report, 1923, 1927, 1929, Box 1; Executive Officers Committee Minutes, 12 July 1921, Box 178, GLIC archives.

22. Annual Report 1942, Box 1; Annual Report, 1940, Box 2, GLIC archives.

23. "The Case of Jack Horner," 1930?, Public Relations Department Records, Box 84, GLIC archives.

24. Annual Report, 1934, Box 2; Minutes of the Board of Directors, 19 December 1934, 18 December 1935, Box 5; "National Advertisements," 1935–38, "Guardian of American Families advertisements," 1935–38, Public Relations Department Records, Box 84, GLIC archives.

25. Minutes of the Board of Directors, 18 December 1935, 16 December 1936, 15 December 1937, 21 December 1938, Box 5; Field Advisory Board Meeting Proceedings, 8 July 1948, Box 75; "Guardian of American Families advertisements," 1935–38, Public Relations Department Records, Box 84, GLIC archives.

26. Annual Report, 1941, Box 2, GLIC archives.

27. Alternatively, on major anniversaries, the slogan was "Guardian of American Families for XXX Years." Annual Report, 1943, 1944, Box 1; Annual Report, 1934, Box 2; Memorandum to John C. Slattery, 27 December 1951, Office of the Secretary, Box 189; Price Topping to Philip Dalsimer, 9 May 1957, Price Topping to John Buckley, 27 March 1967, "Guardian Symbols Registration," Legal Department Records, Box 219; Price Topping to Philip T. Dalsimer, 9 May 1957, Legal Department Records, Box 220, GLIC archives.

28. "Insurance Campaign in Papers," *New York Times,* 13 May 1946. Reports on the Examination of the Guardian, 1949, Box 71, GLIC archives.

29. James A McLain to Home Office Staff, 15 March 1948, Circulars, Box 94, GLIC archives.

30. Annual Report, 1949, Box 3, GLIC archives.

31. Annual Report, 1950, 1957, Box 3; Annual Report, 1958–64, Box 4, GLIC archives.

32. Annual Report, 1985, 1986, 1987, Box 1, GLIC archives.

33. *The Guardian,* 30 October 1961. Field Advisory Board Meeting Proceedings, 30 June 1949, Box 75; Daniel J. Reidy, "The Lawyer and His Taxes," *New York State Bar Bulletin,* February 1952, 39–46, Herbert Seibert to Charles Robinson, 28 December 1946, Public Relations Department Records, Box 84; "Model Agent Film," *Eastern Underwriter,* 10 June 1949, Public Relations Department Records, Box 85; Executive Officers Committee Minutes, 8 October 1948, Box 179, GLIC archives.

34. Reports on the Examination of the Guardian, 1952, Box 71; Executive Officers Committee Minutes, 18 June 1940, Box 178; Coordinating Committee Minutes, 10 September, 8 October, 10 December 1963, Office of the Secretary, Reilly, Box 179, GLIC archives.

35. The face value of Roosevelt's policy, which was taken out in 1931 by the Georgia Warm Springs Foundation, founded by FDR to study the prevention and treatment of polio, was $50,000. After some debate, Guardian accepted the then governor of New York at standard rates, but reinsured $20,000 of the risk with Lincoln National. The policy was but one of half

a million dollars' worth of policies that FDR took out at that time. Guardian did not require submission of the usual proof of death forms in this case. "F.D. Roosevelt" folder, Claim Department Records, Box 78, GLIC archives.

36. "Memos re: policyholders of note, 1944–1954," Office of the Secretary, Scott, Box 64, GLIC archives.

37. *Home Office Newsletter,* 15 September 1955. Annual Report, 1955, Box 3; Minutes of the Board of Directors, 26 October 1955, Box 6; Reports on the Examination of the Guardian, 1955, Box 72, GLIC archives.

38. Hedges and Henslee, *Compensation of Life Insurance Agents,* 28. Advertisements, 1956–58, Public Relations Department Records, Box 84; Agency Department, Product/Sales Promotion, Box 194, GLIC archives.

39. *Guardian Life,* July 1960. Annual Report, 1959, 1960, Box 3; "Centennial Committee," 1958–61, "Centennial Celebration Ideas," 1959–60, Office of the Secretary, Burrell, Box 65; "Our Centennial Year," 1959, Public Relations Department Records, Box 84; "Guardian Honors US Guardians," *United States Review,* 2 July 1960, Public Relations Department Records, Box 85, GLIC archives.

40. Lane, *A Maine Heritage,* 8. *The Guardian,* 29 January 1962; *Guardian Scene,* January 1964. Annual Report, 1961, Box 3; Field Advisory Board Meeting Proceedings, 24 September 1962, Box 75; "Guardian—Because You Care" advertisements, 1960–63, Public Relations Department Records, Box 84, GLIC archives.

41. *The Guardian,* 25 February 1963; *Guardian Scene,* August 1964. Field Advisory Board Meeting Proceedings, 17 November 1966, Box 75; "Joe Scott" advertisements, 1963, Public Relations Department Records, Box 84; Coordinating Committee Minutes, 21 January 1964, 14 January 1965, Office of the Secretary, Reilly, Box 179, GLIC archives.

42. Annual Report, 1966, Box 4; "How My Guardian Agent" advertisements, 1966, Public Relations Department Records, Box 84; Coordinating Committee Minutes, 14 June 1966, Office of the Secretary, Reilly, Box 179; Lawrence Lubin to Company Officers, 19 May 1965, Office of the Assistant Actuary, Lubin, Box 202, GLIC archives.

43. Interview with Leo Futia, 12 April 2002. Field Advisory Board Meeting Proceedings, 18 September 1969, 7 May 1970, Box 75, GLIC archives.

44. Field Advisory Board Meeting Proceedings, 20 April 1972, 9 September 1976, 15 September 1977, 5 April 1979, Box 75, GLIC archives.

45. Annual Report, 1982, Box 4; "Guardian Life Proudly Announces" advertisements, 1976–78, Public Relations Department Records, Box 84; Jeanne Berres to Arthur Ferrara, 12 September 1983, Public Relations, Box 209, GLIC archives.

46. Palyi, "Life Insurance," 67. Annual Report, 1985, Box 1; Sales Campaigns, Agency Communication and Sales Promotion, Box 212; President's Report, 1991, unboxed, GLIC archives.

47. Interview with Dennis Manning, 1 December 2001. Field Advisory Board Meeting Proceedings, 20 April 1972, Box 75; Agency Department, Product/Sales Promotion, Box 194; Before the Commissioners of Insurance, State of Iowa, 1 November 1962, Guardian vs. American Guardian Life Insurance Company, Utah, 1962, Legal Department Records, Box 220, GLIC archives.

48. Slattery, "Manning." Interview with Joseph Sargent, 30 May 2002. Executive Officers Committee Minutes, 4 May 1948, Box 179; Manuals: Agents and Managers, Field Training, 1988, Field Offices, Box 202, GLIC archives. "How to Choose a Life Insurance Company," Executive Presentation Client's Guide, 2001, Office of the Corporate Secretary.

NOTES TO CHAPTER 8

1. This story is based on our interview with Leo Futia, 12 April 2002, and one of the authors' experiences living in Buffalo from 1987 to 1995.

2. This accords with the industry rule of thumb: "call 10, see 3, and sell 1." *The Insurance Forum,* August 2001.

3. Interview with Leo Futia, 12 April 2002.

4. Davis, Malvin E., *Industrial Insurance,* 50; Sage, "Prevention"; Solberg, "Consumer Valuation," 636.

5. Solberg, "Consumer Valuation," 635.

6. Interview with Joseph Caruso, 30 November 2001.

7. Regulatory report, 7 December 1925, History Files, John C. Angle, Box 198, GLIC archives.

8. Field Advisory Board Meeting Proceedings, 17 November 1966, Box 75; "Special Committee" Minutes, 8 April 1863, Box 125, GLIC archives.

9. *The Guardian,* 29 January 1962. Minutes of the Board of Directors, 26 October 1949, Box 6; Advisory Committee Minutes, 14 April 1897, copy, "History of Guardian Life on West Coast: Contribution to Expansion," 1956, Office of the Secretary, Scott, Box 64, GLIC archives.

10. "Business Instructions for Agents," 1889, Manuals, Box 96, GLIC archives.

11. "Insurance Notes," *New York Times,* 25 February 1946. Finance Committee Minutes, 19 May 1926, Box 15; Executive Officers Committee Minutes, 14 June 1938, Box 178, Executive Officers Committee Minutes, 24 July, 4 September 1945, Box 179, GLIC archives.

12. Abbott, *Story of NYLIC,* 144–53. Regulatory report, 7 December 1925, History Files, John C. Angle, Box 198, GLIC archives.

13. "Sales Questionnaire," TNEC Records, Box 59; Reports on the Examination of the Guardian, 1937, 1940, Box 70, GLIC archives.

14. "Sales Questionnaire," TNEC Records, Box 59; Field Advisory Board Meeting Proceedings, 1 July 1949, Box 75, GLIC archives.

15. Technically, a lapse occurs only when a policyholder stops making premium payments before two full annual premiums are paid. It is usually indicative of a poor or pressured sales effort and should not be confused with legitimate terminations due to death, disability, maturity, expiry, decrease, or surrender. Hedges and Henslee, *Compensation of Life Insurance Agents,* 8–11.

16. Issues, Lapses, and Net Increase in Business, 1910–15, Organ Box 9; Reports on the Examination of the Guardian, 1946, Box 71; Executive Officers Committee Minutes, 9 January 1940, 18 March, 22 July 1941, Box 178, GLIC archives.

17. The company would add Alaska, Hawaii, and the Territory of Puerto Rico in due course. *Home Office Newsletter,* 15 June 1950. Annual Report, 1950, 1958, Box 3; Annual Report, 1968, Box 4; Minutes of the Board of Directors, 24 April 1963, Box 6; Finance Committee Minutes, 27 January 1954, Box 18; President's Report, 22 October 1958, 25 January 1961, Box 43; Reports on the Examination of the Guardian, 1969, Box 72; Coordinating Committee Minutes, 10 March 1964, Office of the Secretary, Reilly, Box 179, Executive Officers Committee Minutes, 8 August 1944, Box 179; Minutes of the Board of Directors, 28 November 1979, 27 February 1980, Box 207, GLIC archives.

18. Rosenthal, *Short and Confidential History.* Interview with Ed Kane, 30 November 2001. Reports on the Examination of the Guardian, 1949, Box 71; Irving Rosenthal to Murray Krowitz (Chief of the Life Bureau), 28 September 1972, Office of the Executive Vice President, Rosenthal, Box 183; John C. Angle, "Chairman's Address and Report on Progress during 1984," 27 February 1985, Office of the President, Angle, Box 201, GLIC archives.

19. Interview with John Angle, 21 March 2002.

20. Interview with Dennis Manning, 1 December 2001.

21. Rosenthal, *Short and Confidential History.* Field Advisory Board Meeting Proceedings, 9 September 1976, Box 75, GLIC archives.

22. Annual Report, 1948, Box 2; Field Advisory Board Meeting Proceedings, 6 January 1948, Box 75; Interview with Irving Rosenthal, 6 July 1984, Box 250, GLIC archives.

23. *Guardian Service,* August 1989. Field Advisory Board Meeting Proceedings, 9 September 1976, 5 May 1977, 15 September 1977, 5 April 1979, Box 75, GLIC archives.

24. Davis, Frank, "Economic Freedom"; Davis, Malvin E., *Industrial Insurance,* 51. Interview with Joseph Caruso, 30 November 2001.

25. Hedges and Henslee, *Compensation of Life Insurance Agents,* 3.

26. Hedges and Henslee, *Compensation of Life Insurance Agents,* 20; Westfall, "Agency Manager's Function."

27. Buley, *American Life Convention,* 49; Williamson and Smalley, *Northwestern Mutual Life,* 37.

28. Frank Weidenborner to All Guardian Managers and Cashiers, 14 March 1949, Circulars, Box 94, GLIC archives.

29. "Sales Questionnaire," TNEC Records, Box 59, GLIC archives.

30. "Business Instructions for Agents," 1889, 1903, Manuals, Box 96, GLIC archives.

31. Davis, Frank, "Economic Freedom"; Hedges and Henslee, *Compensation of Life Insurance Agents,* 3, 7–8; Huebner, "A New Vision"; Jaeger, "Agency Resourcefulness"; McLain, "Stewardship"; Parkinson, "Selling Self-Reliance"; Westfall, "Agency Manager's Function"; Westfall, J. V. E., "Relation of the Agent"; Whatley, "Agency System"; Woods, "Relation of the Agent"; Zimmerman, "Research in Agency Management." *The Guardian,* 27 November 1961.

32. *Proceedings of the Forty-Sixth Annual Meeting of the Life Insurance Association of America,* 1952, 157–58; Abbott, *Story of NYLIC,* 152–65. Fieldmen Memorandum, 1920, Office of the Secretary, Scott, Box 64, GLIC archives.

33. First Annual Convention, Germania Life Fieldmen, 24–25 September 1917, "Guardian Guardianship," 1935?, Home Office Records, Box 74; "Service to Agents: Service to Public," *Insurance Times,* March 1916, 60, Public Relations Department Records, Box 85, GLIC archives.

34. Minutes of the Board of Directors, 28 October 1936, Box 5; Reports on the Examination of the Guardian, 1937, Box 70, GLIC archives.

35. Hedges and Henslee, *Compensation of Life Insurance Agents,* 73. Interview with Dennis Manning, 1 December 2001. Minutes of the Board of Directors, 22 July, 28 October 1942, Box 5; Field Advisory Board Meeting Proceedings, 18 January 1950, Box 75; Executive Officers Committee Minutes, 6 November 1940, Box 178, GLIC archives.

36. *Proceedings of the Thirty-Fifth Annual Convention of the Association of Life Insurance Presidents,* 1941, 61–62. Annual Report, 1938, 1940, Box 2; Minutes of the Board of Directors, 19 December 1956, Box 6, GLIC archives.

37. McLain, "Stewardship." Annual Report, 1941, 1946, Box 2, GLIC archives.

38. Zimmerman, "Research in Agency Management." President's Reports, Summary, 1941, Box 42, GLIC archives.

39. Hedges and Henslee, *Compensation of Life Insurance Agents,* 21, 29. Executive Officers Committee Minutes, 29 February 1944, Box 179, GLIC archives.

40. Finance Committee Minutes, 9 June 1943, Box 17; Reports on the Examination of the Guardian, 1940, Box 70; Reports on the Examination of the Guardian, 1946, Box 71; Executive Officers Committee Minutes, 23 May 1944, 30 January 1945, Box 179, GLIC archives.

41. *Newsletter,* February 1979. Annual Report, 1946, Box 2; Reports on the Examination of the Guardian, 1946, Box 71; Frank Weidenborner to All Managers and Field Representatives, 18 August 1948, Circulars, Box 94; John C. Angle interview with Daniel J. Lyons, 7 March 1982, Office of the President, Angle, Box 197, GLIC archives.

42. Interview with John Angle, 22 March 2002. Annual Report, 1947, Box 2, GLIC archives.

43. Reports on the Examination of the Guardian, 1949, Box 71; Field Advisory Board Meeting Proceedings, 9 July 1948, Box 75; Advertisement, *Fortune,* 1949, Public Relations Department Records, Box 84; Executive Officers Committee Minutes, 11 December 1945, Box 179, GLIC archives.

44. Mathewson, "Information," 132–33. Reports on the Examination of the Guardian, 1949, Box 71; Executive Officers Committee Minutes, 23 September 1946, Box 179; Agency Department, Product/Sales Promotion, Box 194, GLIC archives.

45. Reports on the Examination of the Guardian, 1961, Box 72; Field Advisory Board Meeting Proceedings, 4 May 1978, Box 75, GLIC archives.

46. Interview with Ed Kane, 30 November 2001; interview with Leo Futia, 12 April 2002.

"Field Representatives Plan Revision," 1974, Office of the Executive Vice President, Rosenthal, Box 183, GLIC archives.

47. Field Advisory Board Meeting Proceedings, 1 April 1963, 21 April 1966, 31 January 1968, 20 April 1972, Box 75, GLIC archives.

48. Murphy, Robert E., "Are We in Focus?" Field Advisory Board Meeting Proceedings, 2 May 1974, Box 75; "Field Representatives Plan Revision," 1974, Office of the Executive Vice President, Rosenthal, Box 183, GLIC archives.

49. In 1946, for instance, Guardian's Julius M. Eisendrath agency lured A. Aaron Press from his fifteen-year stint at Prudential. "Backing Up the Agent," *The Eastern Underwriter,* 2 December 1921; "Annual Statement," *The Eastern Underwriter,* 20 March 1925; "Insurance Notes," *New York Times,* 18 January 1946. Interview with Leo Futia, 12 April 2002. Field Advisory Board Meeting Proceedings, 12 September 1968, Box 75, GLIC archives.

50. Finance Committee Minutes, 31 December 1924, 14 January 1925, Box 15; Carl Heye Speech, 1930, Office of the Secretary, Scott, Box 64; McNamara v. Guardian, Vol. 1, 1943, Legal Department Records, Box 80, GLIC archives.

51. Rosenthal, *Short and Confidential History.* Minutes of the Board of Directors, 26 October 1932, Box 5; John C. McNamara to Carl Heye, 30 December 1932, Office of the President, Heye, Box 49, GLIC archives.

52. Minutes of the Board of Directors, 28 July 1943, 26 April 1944, 25 July 1945, Box 6; McNamara v. Guardian, 1943, Legal Department Records, Boxes 80–82; "Supreme Court Trial Term," *New York Law Journal,* 16 February 1944, Public Relations Department Records, Box 85; Executive Officers Committee Minutes, 8, 13 July 1937, 16 February, 12 July, 4 October 1938, 21 February 1939, 7 May 1940, 4 February, 11 March 1941, Box 178; Executive Officers Committee Minutes, 23 February 1944, Box 179; Interview with Irving Rosenthal, 6 July 1984, Box 250, GLIC archives.

53. Annual Report, 1940, Box 2, GLIC archives.

54. *Guardian Service,* May 1916, March 1918, 19 January 1925, 21 July 1930, 13 July 1931, Winter 1971. Guardian VIPs, 1971–88, Agency Communication and Sales Promotion, Boxes 212, 213, GLIC archives.

55. Annual Report, 1950, Box 3, GLIC archives.

56. Finance Committee Minutes, 8 April 1925, 10 March 1926, Box 15; Finance Committee Minutes, 23 May 1951, Box 18, GLIC archives.

57. Interview with Leo Futia, 12 April 2002. Minutes of the Board of Directors, 22 April 1925, 28 April 1926, 27 April 1927, 25 April 1928, Box 5; Reports on the Examination of the Guardian, 1964, 1969, Box 72; Field Advisory Board Meeting Proceedings, 20 January 1949, Box 75, GLIC archives.

58. Annual Report, 1932, 1933, 1934, 1935, Box 2; Finance Committee Minutes, 6 January 1932, 27 September 1933, 2 January 1935, 21 April 1937, Box 16, GLIC archives.

59. "Insurance Leader Hopeful on Trade," *New York Times,* 18 July 1935; "Guardian Life's Jubilee," *New York Times,* 19 July 1935; "Dinner for J. A. McLain," *New York Times,* 19 January 1940. Finance Committee Minutes, 3 July 1935, Box 16; President's Reports, 22 July 1959, Box 43, GLIC archives. To track the history of the elite sales clubs, see Reports on the Examination of the Guardian, various years, Boxes 71–74; Coordinating Committee Minutes, Office of the Secretary, Reilly, Box 179; Agency Records, Box 208, GLIC archives.

60. Weidenborner, "Strengthening Agency Assets"; Zimmerman, "Research in Agency Management." Annual Report, 1945, 1946, Box 2; Reports on the Examination of the Guardian, 1946, 1949, Box 71; Field Advisory Board Meeting Proceedings, 21 September 1978, Box 75, GLIC archives.

61. Guardian completely avoided the churning scandals because it did not grant commissions when agents replaced one Guardian policy with another. So agents had no incentive to "churn." Like most companies, Guardian did use "vanishing premium" language in some of its advertising and sales pitches. It avoided the *scandals* related to vanishing premiums because, unlike some companies, it always made clear that dividends would soon offset all pre-

miums only if expectations of high interest rates held true and that they were *not* selling policies that would in all events be "paid up" after seven or ten premium payments. President's
Report, 23 April 1958, Box 43; Field Advisory Board Meeting Proceedings, 27 April 1967, 5 April
1971, 20 April 1972, Box 75, GLIC archives.

62. Annual Report, 1985, 1986, Box 1, GLIC archives. President's Report, 1996, 1999, 2000;
Minutes of the Board of Directors, 1 December 1993, 28 February 1996, 3 December 1997,
Office of the Corporate Secretary.

63. Hull, "What's Happening?"; Murphy, Robert E., "Are We in Focus?" Minutes of the
Board of Directors, 23 April 1958, Box 6; "After Two Years," 1903, Office of the President, Doremus, Box 45; Field Advisory Board Meeting Proceedings, 20 April 1972, 15 September 1977, Box
75; Minutes of the Board of Directors, 16 December 1970, Box 206, GLIC archives.

64. Interview with Ed Kane, 22 February 2002; interview with Don Sullivan, 22 March 2002.

65. *The Insurance Forum,* August 2001, October 2002; Johnson and Randle, "New Life Insurance Products."

66. Interview with Joseph Caruso, 30 November 2001. Field Advisory Board Meeting Proceedings, 21 April 1966, Box 75, GLIC archives.

67. "Management—Personnel Notes," *Wall Street Journal,* 31 December 1956. Tom Quinn
interview with Arthur Ferrara, Executive Vice President, n.d., Office of the President, Angle,
Box 197, GLIC archives.

68. "Who's News," *Wall Street Journal,* 20 December 1984; "Who's News," *Wall Street Journal,* 30 December 1988; "Who's News," *Wall Street Journal,* 14 December 1995. Interview with
Art Ferrara, 2 May 2002. Minutes of the Board of Directors, 27 January 1960, Box 6; Minutes
of the Board of Directors, 23 February 1972, Box 206; Minutes of the Board of Directors, 19
November 1980, Box 207, GLIC archives.

69. Annual Report, 1970, Box 4; Minutes of the Board of Directors, 28 January 1959, Box 6;
Reports on the Examination of the Guardian, 1961, Box 72; Field Advisory Board Meeting
Proceedings, 2 May 1974, Box 75; Group Advisory Committee Minutes, 3 March 1960, Office of
the Executive Vice President, Rosenthal, Box 183; Interview with William W. Mauke, Senior
Vice President for Group Insurance, 25 March 1982, Special Report of the Executive Commit-
tee to the Board of Directors, 19 December 1956, Tom Quinn interview with Howard Abel,
Chartered Life Underwriter, n.d., John Angle interview with Irving Rosenthal, 26 February
1982, R.G.O., n.d., Office of the President, Angle, Box 197, GLIC archives.

70. Interview with Art Ferrara, 2 May 2002. Group Conference, 1971, Office of the Executive
Vice President, Rosenthal, Box 183, GLIC archives.

71. Field Advisory Board Meeting Proceedings, 21 April 1966, 28 January, 5 April 1971, 9 Sep-
tember 1971, 9 September 1976, Box 75; Irving Rosenthal to George Conklin, 12 March 1971,
Group Advisory Committee Minutes, 13 October 1960, Group Conference, 1971, Office of the
Executive Vice President, Rosenthal, Box 183, GLIC archives.

72. Irving Rosenthal to John E. Gray, 17 March 1971, Office of the Executive Vice President,
Rosenthal, Box 183; "John E. Gray," n.d., John Angle interview with Irving Rosenthal, 26 February 1982, Office of the President, Angle, Box 197; Interview with Irving Rosenthal, 6 July
1984, Box 250, GLIC archives.

73. Various Annual Statements, GLIC archives.

74. Interview with John Angle, 22 March 2002. John Angle interview with Irving Rosenthal,
26 February 1982, Office of the President, Angle, Box 197, GLIC archives.

75. Interview with Don Sullivan, 22 March 2002. President's Reports, 25 January 1961, Box
43; Reports on the Examination of the Guardian, 1952, 1955, Box 71; Reports on the Examination of the Guardian, 1958, Box 72; Field Advisory Board Meeting Proceedings, 19 January
1949, Box 75, GLIC archives.

76. Interview with Armand de Palo, 27 January 2003. Annual Report, 1947, Box 2, GLIC
archives.

77. McLain, "Stewardship."

78. Guardian regularly donated nontrivial sums to the Life Insurance Medical Research

Fund. It later made contributions to other medical research foundations as well. Annis, "Recent Advances in Medicine"; Campbell, "Mortality Tables," 437–38; Cox, Robert Lynn, "National Health"; Cragin, "Medical Preparedness"; Hughes, "Life Insurance Enterprise"; Hunter, "Insurance of Impaired Lives"; Quayle, "Reclamation of Men Rejected by the Draft." *Guardian Service,* February 1919. Annual Report, 1947, Box 2; Minutes of the Board of Directors, 23 April 1952, 24 October 1962, Box 6; Minutes of the Board of Directors, 25 November 1970, Box 206, GLIC archives.

79. Westfall, "Relation of the Agent." Annual Report, 1940, Box 2; Irving Rosenthal, "Comments on New Mortality Study (1948–1969)," Executive Vice President, Rosenthal, Box 184; "Notes on the New Guardian Preferred Risk Policies," 1948, Underwriting Secretary and Assistant Secretary, Box 185, GLIC archives.

80. Frank Weidneborner to All Guardian Managers and Cashiers, 14 March 1949, Circulars, Box 94; "Business Instructions for Agents," 1889, Manuals, Box 96, GLIC archives.

81. Lane, *A Maine Heritage,* 8. "Mortality of Persons Engaged in Liquor Business," 31 March 1877, Circulars, Box 94; "Business Instructions for Agents," 1889, Manuals, Box 96; "Guardian Gives Underwriting Credit for Non-Smokers," Press Release, 1 April 1970, Public Relations, Box 209, GLIC archives.

82. "Business Instructions for Agents," 1903, Manuals, Box 96, GLIC archives.

83. Grant, *Insurance Reform,* 8; Hudnut, *Semi-Centennial History,* 250; North, "Capital Accumulation," 247. "Business Instructions for Agents," 1903, Manuals, Box 96, GLIC archives.

84. "Business Instructions for Agents," 1909, Manuals, Box 96, GLIC archives.

85. Advisory Committee Minutes, 29 May 1895, 6 January 1897, copies, Office of the Secretary, Scott, Box 64; "Business Instructions for Agents," 1889, 1920, Manuals, Box 96, GLIC archives.

86. Race was an issue for many companies. MetLife, Prudential, and three other insurers made multi-million-dollar settlements in 2002 to African-American policyholders charged higher rates based solely on their race. See, for example, the report in Reuters, 23 December 2002.

87. Henderson, *Atlanta Life*; Puth, "Supreme Life"; Shepherd, "Principals and Problems"; Stuart, *Economic Detour*; Weare, *Black Business*; Woodson, Carter G., "Insurance Business among Negroes." Field Advisory Board Meeting Proceedings, 6 July 1951, Box 75, GLIC archives. Minutes of the Board of Directors, 25 July 2001, Office of the Corporate Secretary.

88. "Selection and Rating of Risks," 1922, Manuals, Box 96, GLIC archives.

89. "Agents' Manual: The Guardian Life Insurance Company of America," 1938, Manuals, Box 96; Executive Officers Committee Minutes, 12 April 1938, Box 178, GLIC archives.

90. Shepherd, "Principals and Problems." *Home Office Newsletter,* 16 January 1950. Reports on the Examination of the Guardian, 1943, Box 71; "Agents' Manual: The Guardian Life Insurance Company of America," 1938, Manuals, Box 96; Executive Officers Committee Minutes, 29 July, 2, 6 December 1924, Box 178, GLIC archives.

91. Field Advisory Board Meeting Proceedings, 5 April 1971, 9 September 1971, 26 January, 20 April 1972, 2 May 1974, 28 September 1979, Box 75; Frank Weidenborner to All Guardian Managers and Cashiers, 14 March 1949, Circulars, Box 94, GLIC archives.

92. Shepherd, "Principals and Problems." Annual Report, 1940, Box 2; Leo Futia to All Agencies, 9 July 1975, Circular Letters, Agency Communication and Sales Promotion, Box 212, GLIC archives.

93. Shepherd, "Principals and Problems." Field Advisory Board Meeting Proceedings, 28 September 1967, Box 75, GLIC archives.

94. For Guardian's underwriting rules, see "Classification of Risks," 1938–47, Underwriting Secretary and Assistant Secretary, Box 185, GLIC archives.

95. Interview with Armand de Palo, 27 January 2003. Field Advisory Board Meeting Proceedings, 9 September 1971, Box 75; A. C. Webster, "Report on Underwriting," May 1971, Charles H. Edwards to Irving Rosenthal, 12 October 1972, John L. Cameron to Irving Rosen-

thal, 28 October 1972, Office of the Executive Vice President, Rosenthal, Box 184, GLIC archives.

96. President's Report, 25 October 1967, 26 February 1969, Box 43, GLIC archives.

97. "Finance," *Wall Street Journal,* 20 May 1977; "Guardian Life Insurance Co. of America," *Wall Street Journal,* 8 May 1980; "Guardian Life Insurance Names New Chairman," *New York Times,* 27 May 1980; "Who's News," *Wall Street Journal,* 20 December 1984. Interview with Leo Futia 12 April 2002. Tom Quinn interview with Leo Futia, 4 April 1982, Office of the President, Angle, Box 197; Minutes of the Board of Directors, 26 July 1967, 16 December 1970, Box 206, GLIC archives.

98. Field Advisory Board Meeting Proceedings, 5 April 1971, Box 75; Mortality Studies, 1969–72, Irving Rosenthal, "Comments on New Mortality Study (1948–1969)," John L. Cameron to Irving Rosenthal, 28 October 1972, Office of the Executive Vice President, Rosenthal, Box 184, GLIC archives.

99. Interview with Leo Futia, 12 April 2002. Irving Rosenthal, "Comments on New Mortality Study (1948–1969)," John L. Cameron to Irving Rosenthal, 28 October 1972, Office of the Executive Vice President, Rosenthal, Box 184, GLIC archives.

100. Leo Futia to Charles H. Edwards, 27 March 1972, Office of the Executive Vice President, Rosenthal, Box 184, GLIC archives.

101. Interview with Leo Futia, 12 April 2002.

NOTES TO CHAPTER 9

1. Rosenthal, *Short and Confidential History.* Annual Report, 1877, Box 1; Annual Report, 1940, Box 2; Elie Charlier to Germania, 12 May 1894, Cornelius Doremus to Elie Charlier, 2 June 1894, Decker, Howell, and Co. to Germania, 24 April 1894, Office of the Secretary, Heye and Neuendorffer, Box 54; Reports on the Examination of the Guardian, 1914, 1937, Box 70, GLIC archives.

2. The same writer addressed another missive to the "Fourth Vice-President in Charge of Condoning the Defrauding of Widows" and joked that he hoped that the stenographers "will get a laugh out of retyping this pleasant epistle." Paul G. Lutzeier to Guardian, 5 January, 24 July 1937, Office of the Secretary, Scott, Box 64; Supervisors' Manual, 1 June 1926, Minutes of the Department Head Meeting, 14 October 1927, "Guardian Guardianship," 1935?, Home Office Records, Box 74, GLIC archives.

3. Field Advisory Board Meeting Proceedings, 6 January 1948, 19 January 1950, Box 75, GLIC archives.

4. For more on Hopf and his rocky relationship with Guardian, see Rapone, *Guardian,* 130–40. Burgh Johnson, a native of Rock Hill, South Carolina, who joined the company in 1930, took over where Neuendorffer left off. Rosenthal, *Short and Confidential History.* Minutes of the Board of Directors, 23 July 1947, Box 6; Memorandum, 16, 31 October, 1, 11 November 1913, 25 February 1914, Office of the President, Heye, Box 46, GLIC archives.

5. Supervisors' Manual, 1 June 1926, Home Office Records, Box 74, GLIC archives.

6. Supervisors' Manual, 1 June 1926, Home Office Records, Box 74, GLIC archives.

7. Drucker, *Essential Drucker,* 125. *Home Office Newsletter,* 15 July 1954. Supervisors' Manual, 1 June 1926, Home Office Records, Box 74; Executive Officers Committee Minutes, 19 March 1940, Box 178; Edward Mallon to Officers and Supervisory Staff, Coordinating Committee Minutes, 15 April 1963, Office of the Secretary, Reilly, Box 179, GLIC archives.

8. Interview with Ed Kane, 30 November 2001. Annual Report, 1940, 1946, Box 2, GLIC archives.

9. Annual Report, 1946, Box 2; "Analysis of Employee Jobs," 1893, Office of the Assistant Secretary, Meidt, Box 66, GLIC archives.

10. According to John Byrne, "Inside McKinsey," *Business Week,* 8 July 2002, Marvin Bower of McKinsey and Company invented "modern management consulting" circa 1933. There was nothing apparently "premodern" about the consultants that Guardian hired before that date,

however. Leffingwell, *Office Management.* Annual Report, 1953, 1955, Box 3; Minutes of the Board of Directors, 22 July 1942, Box 5; Executive Officers Committee Minutes, 14 April, 5 May 1942, Box 178; Executive Officers Committee Minutes, 5 July 1944, Box 179, GLIC archives.

11. Minutes of the Board of Directors, 22 April 1953, Box 6, GLIC archives.

12. Helpful Communication Tips, 1 April 1957, Home Office Records, Box 74; Executive Officers Committee Minutes, 3 July 1945, Box 179, GLIC archives.

13. President's Reports, 27 April 1960, Box 43; Coordinating Committee Minutes, 11 April 1961, Office of the Secretary, Reilly, Box 179, GLIC archives.

14. *Guardian Scene,* May 1964. "Policyholder Service and Relations," Coordinating Committee Minutes, 12 September 1962, Office of the Secretary, Reilly, Box 179, GLIC archives.

15. President's Report, 26 February, 27 August 1969, 27 May 1970, Box 43; Field Advisory Board Meeting Proceedings, 5 April 1971, Box 75; Minutes of the Board of Directors, 27 November 1968, Box 206, GLIC archives.

16. Interview with Ed Kane, 22 February 2002.

17. Executive Officers Committee Minutes, 21 May, 11 June 1940, Box 178, GLIC archives.

18. Clough, *Mutual Life Insurance Company of New York,* 332.

19. Clough, *Mutual Life Insurance Company of New York,* 111. Minutes of the Board of Directors, 26 April 1916, 28 July 1926, 21 December 1932, Box 5; 16 December 1959, Box 6, GLIC archives.

20. Supervisors' Manual, 1 June 1926, Home Office Records, Box 74, GLIC archives.

21. Minutes of the Board of Directors, 27 December 1916, 17 December 1941, Box 5; "Lohmeyer Recollections," 1943, Office of the Secretary, Scott, Box 64; James A McLain to All Officers, 6 July 1943, Home Office Records, Box 74, GLIC archives.

22. James A McLain to Home Office Staff, 26 October 1950, Home Office Records, Box 74, GLIC archives.

23. Supervisors' Manual, 1 June 1926, Home Office Records, Box 74; Executive Officers Committee Minutes, 17 April 1923, Box 178, GLIC archives.

24. James A McLain to Supervisory Staff, 15 June 1943, James A McLain to All Officers, 6 July 1943, Home Office Records, Box 74; Executive Officers Committee Minutes, Memoranda: 1937, Box 178, GLIC archives.

25. *Proceedings of the Fiftieth Annual Meeting of the Life Insurance Association of America,* 1956, 153. *Guardian Scene,* February–March, June 1967. Interview with Don Sullivan, 22 March 2002. "The How and Why of Guardian's Salary Scales," 1949, Personnel Department Records, Box 83, GLIC archives.

26. Compounding matters, Guardian did not always understand the best ways to attract certain professional categories. In general, for instance, it did not do a good job of hiring entry-level actuaries, at least until John Angle arrived on the scene. "They thought what you did was to call an employment agency and then have them send over some students," Angle recalls. Harkavy, *Leadership for Life Insurance.* Interview with John Angle, 21 March 2002.

27. *Home Office Newsletter,* 15 May 1956. Minutes of the Department Head Meeting, 24 June 1926, 30 January 1930, John Cameron to All Officers and Department Heads, 26 January 1948, 14 January 1949 Salary Policy, 1955, Form X-41A-55, "Performance Rating," 1955, Home Office Records, Box 74, GLIC archives.

28. Merit Rating Program, ? November 1953, Home Office Records, Box 74, GLIC archives.

29. Harkavy, *Leadership for Life Insurance,* 204–9.

30. John Geortner to Supervising Officers and Department Managers, Coordinating Committee Minutes, 18 December 1963, Office of the Secretary, Reilly, Box 179, GLIC archives.

31. James A McLain to Home Office Clerical Staff, 12 December 1955, Home Office Records, Box 74, GLIC archives.

32. President's Report, 27 January 1965, Box 43; Coordinating Committee Minutes, 8 September 1964, 21 September 1965, Office of the Secretary, Reilly, Box 179, GLIC archives.

33. Minutes of the Board of Directors, 15 December 1943, Box 5; Minutes of the Board of Directors, 29 April 1908, Box 122, GLIC archives.

34. Minutes of the Board of Directors, 17 December 1941, Box 5; Minutes of the Board of Directors, 24 April 1946, 28 July 1948, 25 January 1950, 25 July 1951, 22 July 1953, 15 December 1954, 27 July 1955, 22 July 1959, Box 6, GLIC archives.

35. *Home Office Newsletter,* 15 February 1950; *Guardian Scene,* September 1967. Reports on the Examination of the Guardian, 1952, Box 71; "The Blue Cross Hospital Plan and the Surgical Plan for Our Employees," 1948, Personnel Department Records, Box 83, GLIC archives.

36. Clough, *Mutual Life Insurance Company of New York,* 110; *Proceedings of the Fifty-Eighth Annual Meeting of Life Insurance Association of America,* 1964, 61. *Guardian Scene,* January 1967, April 1967. President's Report, 27 July 1966, Box 43; Memorandum, 15 November 1917, Office of the President, Heye, Box 46; Reports on the Examination of the Guardian, 1969, Box 72; Executive Officers Committee Minutes, 1 November 1938, Box 178, GLIC archives.

37. Minutes of the Board of Directors, 16 December 1936, 20 December 1939, Box 5, 25 April 1956, Box 6; Group Advisory Committee Minutes, 28 April 1961, Office of the Executive Vice President, Rosenthal, Box 183, GLIC archives.

38. Annual Report, 1950, Box 3; Minutes of the Board of Directors, 20 December 1950, Box 6, GLIC archives.

39. Interview with Ruth Klain, 3 April 2003; interview with Doug Kramer, 3 April 2003.

40. Interview with Ruth Klain, 3 April 2003; interview with Doug Kramer, 3 April 2003.

41. Annual Report, 1940, Box 2, GLIC archives.

42. The agent Frederic S. Doremus was duly feted and presented with a silver tray and a scroll to honor him on the sixtieth anniversary of his service to the company. "Doremus Is Honored," *New York Times,* 28 October 1942. *The Guardian Family News,* May 1922; *Home Office Newsletter,* 15 September 1950; *Guardian Life,* August, October 1959; *Guardian Scene,* April 1967. Annual Report, 1940, 1946, Box 2; Executive Officers Committee Minutes, 27 May 1941, Box 178; Tom Quinn interview with Helen Sulyma, 2-9 Group Underwriting Department Manager, n.d., Office of the President, Angle, Box 197, GLIC archives.

43. Finance Committee Minutes, 13 June 1917, Box 15; Memorandum, n.d., Carl Heye to George Leyser, 20 December 1916, Office of the President, Heye, Box 46, GLIC archives.

44. *Home Office Newsletter,* 15 January 1952. Reports on the Examination of the Guardian, 1969, Box 72; Minutes of the Department Head Meeting, 1 June 1928, Home Office Operations on Outing Day, 1 March 1955, Home Office Records, Box 74; Field Advisory Board Meeting Proceedings, 31 January 1955, Box 75; Executive Officers Committee Minutes, 29 May 1923, Box 178; Coordinating Committee Minutes, 15 June 1961, 13 July 1965, Office of the Secretary, Reilly, Box 179; Minutes of the Board of Directors, 22 August 1979, Box 207; Agency Records, Box 208, GLIC archives.

45. *Home Office Newsletter,* 15 December 1953, 14 October 1955, 15 March 1956; *Guardian Life,* March, June, August 1960.

46. Interview with Ed Kane, 22 February 2002. Annual Report, 1950, Box 3; Tom Quinn interview with Anthony Peloso, Director of Group Administration, n.d., Office of the President, Angle, Box 197, GLIC archives.

47. Interview with Don Sullivan, 22 March 2002; interview with Ruth Klain, 3 April 2003; interview with Doug Kramer, 3 April 2003. Coordinating Committee Minutes, 11 May 1965, Office of the Secretary, Reilly, Box 179, GLIC archives.

48. *Guardian Scene,* April 1963, February–March 1967. Field Advisory Board Meeting Proceedings, 21 April 1966, 12 September 1968, Box 75; Coordinating Committee Minutes, 21 January 1964, Office of the Secretary, Reilly, Box 179, GLIC archives.

49. Employee Benefit Programs, Organ Boxes 8A-8E; President's Report, 26 February 1969, 23 February 1972, Box 43; Field Advisory Board Meeting Proceedings, 7 May 1970, Box 75; "Retirement Plan," 1969–77, Box 227, GLIC archives.

50. Interview with Joseph Caruso, 30 November 2001. "The Record of the Guardian Life," Reports on the Examination of the Guardian, 1974, Box 187, GLIC archives.

51. Interview with Ruth Klain, 3 April 2003; interview with Doug Kramer, 3 April 2003. Field Advisory Board Meeting Proceedings, 9 September 1971, 2 May 1974, Box 75, GLIC archives.

52. Field Advisory Board Meeting Proceedings, 7 May 1970, Box 75, Minutes of the Board of Directors, 16 December 1970, Box 206; 22 August 1979, Box 207, GLIC archives.

53. Interview with Ruth Klain, 3 April 2003; interview with Doug Kramer, 3 April 2003.

54. *Guardian Service,* November 1916. Interview with Robert Ryan, 22 March 2002; interview with Ruth Klain, 3 April 2003; interview with Doug Kramer, 3 April 2003.

55. *The Guardian Family News,* March 1921, May 1922. Minutes of the Department Head Meeting, 10 December 1925, 29 April 1926, 1 December 1927, Supervisors' Manual, 1 June 1926, Home Office Records, Box 74; "'Service' to Agents: Service to Public," *Insurance Times,* March 1916, 60, Public Relations Department Records, Box 85, GLIC archives.

56. Collins, "Employee Education." Minutes of the Department Head Meeting, 30 January 1930, Home Office Records, Box 74; Executive Officers Committee Minutes, 17 January, 17 October 1922, 9 June 1925, Box 178, GLIC archives.

57. Indoctrination Program, 1 November 1951, 1 March 1955, Home Office Records, Box 74; Executive Officers Committee Minutes, 20 November, 4 December 1945, Box 179, GLIC archives.

58. Get Acquainted Course, 1 November 1951, Home Office Records, Box 74, GLIC archives.

59. Employee Education Program, 15 June 1952, Home Office Records, Box 74; Coordinating Committee Minutes, 10 September 1963, 9 February, 13 July 1965, 11 October 1966, Office of the Secretary, Reilly, Box 179, GLIC archives.

60. *Guardian Scene,* October 1963, May 1966, May 1967. Interview with Ruth Klain, 3 April 2003; interview with Doug Kramer, 3 April 2003. Hower Letter Improvement Service, 1 March 1951, Home Office Records, Box 74; Coordinating Committee Minutes, 22 January 1946, 8 October 1948, 8 January, 14 May 1963, Office of the Secretary, Reilly, Box 179, GLIC archives.

61. Group Advisory Committee Minutes, 21 September 1960, Office of the Executive Vice President, Rosenthal, Box 183, GLIC archives.

62. Interview with Ruth Klain, 3 April 2003; interview with Doug Kramer, 3 April 2003.

63. *Guardian Service,* November 1916; *The Guardian Family News,* March, August 1921; *Home Office Newsletter,* 15 February, 15 September 1950, 16 June, 15 July 1952; *Guardian Scene,* September 1964, August–September 1966. Interview with Ruth Klain, 3 April 2003; interview with Doug Kramer, 3 April 2003. Tom Quinn interview with Howard Abel, n.d., Tom Quinn interview with Anthony Peloso, Director of Group Administration, n.d., Office of the President, Angle, Box 197, GLIC archives. Minutes of the Board of Directors, 1 December 1993, Office of the Corporate Secretary.

64. Interview with Ed Kane, 22 February 2002.

65. Interview with Armand de Palo, 27 January 2003. Reports on the Examination of the Guardian, 1964, Box 72; Coordinating Committee Minutes, 6, 12 September 1962, Office of the Secretary, Reilly, Box 179; Tom Quinn interview with George T. Conklin, 5 March 1982, Office of the President, Angle, Box 197; Interview with Irving Rosenthal, 6 July 1984, Box 250, GLIC archives.

66. Guardian also employed George Mills, a "colored messenger and porter," from 1908 until 1923, when he resigned to go into business, and again from 1924 until 1937, when he retired at the age of eighty-two. *Guardian Life,* August 1959. Minutes of the Board of Directors, 27 October 1937, Box 5; Minutes of the Department Head Meeting, 1 December 1927, Home Office Records, Box 74, GLIC archives.

67. "Lohmeyer Recollections," 1943, Office of the Secretary, Scott, Box 64, GLIC archives.

68. Lipartito, "When Women Were Switches"; McIntosh, "Life Insurance and the Modern Woman." *Home Office Newsletter,* 16 March 1953, 15 February, 15 July, 14 October 1955; *Guardian Life,* August 1959, February, December 1960. Biographical Data, Directors and Officers, Organ Box 23-B; Tom Quinn interview with Anthony Peloso, Director of Group Administration, n.d., Office of the President, Angle, Box 197; Interview with Irving Rosenthal, 6 July 1984, Box 250, GLIC archives.

69. *Home Office Newsletter,* 15 January 1952, 15 July 1954, 16 August 1954; *Guardian Life,* August 1959, May 1960. Tom Quinn interview with Howard Abel, Chartered Life Underwriter,

n.d., Tom Quinn interview with Anthony Peloso, Director of Group Administration, n.d., Office of the President, Angle, Box 197, GLIC archives.

70. *Guardian Service,* May 1967. Interview with Armand de Palo, 27 January 2003. Pearl Goldman to Irving Rosenthal, 4 May 1973, Office of the Executive Vice President, Rosenthal, Box 184; Tom Quinn interview with Helen Sulyma, 2-9 Group Underwriting Department Manager, n.d., Tom Quinn interview with Anthony Peloso, Director of Group Administration, n.d., Office of the President, Angle, Box 197, GLIC archives.

71. Orren, *Corporate Power,* 148.

72. "Rights Accord Set on Insurance Jobs," *New York Times,* 11 December 1971. Interview with Armand de Palo, 27 January 2003; interview with Ruth Klain, 3 April 2003; interview with Doug Kramer, 3 April 2003. Minutes of the Board of Directors, 27 May 1970, Box 206, GLIC archives. Minutes of the Board of Directors, 1 December 1993, Office of the Corporate Secretary.

NOTES TO CHAPTER 10

1. Annual Report, 1950, Box 3, GLIC archives.

2. Annual Report, 1948, Box 2, GLIC archives.

3. "Guardian Life Insurance Co. in Empire State Building," *New York Times,* 17 January 1933. Minutes of the Department Head Meeting, ? October 1926, 28 February 1929, 29 October 1930, Home Office Records, Box 74; Executive Officers Committee Minutes, 15 March 1921, 16 March 1922, 15 October 1924, Box 178, GLIC archives.

4. Supervisors' Manual, 1 June 1926, Home Office Records, Box 74; Executive Officers Committee Minutes, 8 April, 17 June 1941, 2 February, 7 July 1943, Box 179, GLIC archives.

5. *Home Office Newsletter,* 16 March 1953. Minutes of the Board of Directors, 25 October 1950, Box 6; Finance Committee Minutes, 10 January 1951, Box 18; George L. Zevnik to Home Office Staff, 28 October 1953, Office of the Vice President and Actuary, Barnsley, Box 69; Reports on the Examination of the Guardian, 1969, Box 72, GLIC archives.

6. *Home Office Newsletter,* 15 September, 16 October 1950, 15 February 1955. Interview with Leo Futia, 12 April 2002. Minutes of the Board of Directors, 23 July, 17 December 1952, 22 July 1953, 26 October 1955, 25 April 1956, Box 6, GLIC archives.

7. "Guardian Life Plans to Enlarge Offices," *New York Times,* 7 February 1953; "New Wing Slated by Guardian Life," *New York Times,* 25 January 1957. New Rochelle and White Plains Home Office Building Documents, Organ Box 20; Annual Report, 1986, Box 1; Minutes of the Board of Directors, 25 April, 24 October 1956, 24 April, 24 July 1957, Box 6; Reports on the Examination of the Guardian, 1961, Box 72; George Keim to John Angle, 10 March 1982, Office of the President, Angle, Box 197, GLIC archives.

8. "Cabaret Zoning Faces Court Test," *New York Times,* 22 January 1967. *Guardian Scene,* July–August 1967. Minutes of the Board of Directors, 25 October 1961, Box 6; Union Square Improvement Project, 1977–80, Office of the President, Angle, Box 201; Minutes of the Board of Directors, 17 November 1976, 17 December 1980, 27 May 1981, Box 207, GLIC archives.

9. Hawfield, *Ninety Years.* Annual Report, 1986, Box 1; Minutes of the Board of Directors, 25 November 1970, Box 206, GLIC archives.

10. Interview with Joseph Caruso, 30 November 2001; interview with John Angle, 21 March 2002. Annual Report, 1986, Box 1; Minutes of the Board of Directors, 25 October 1950, 23 July 1952, Box 6; Reports on the Examination of the Guardian, 1952, Box 71; Field Advisory Board Meeting Proceedings, 21 September 1972, Box 75, GLIC archives.

11. Interview with Ruth Klain, 3 April 2003; interview with Doug Kramer, 3 April 2003; interview with Robert Ryan, 22 March 2002; interview with Don Sullivan, 22 March 2002. Annual Report, 1986, Box 1, GLIC archives.

12. Interview with Joseph Caruso, 30 November 2001; interview with Robert Ryan, 22 March 2002.

13. Annual Report, 1986, Box 1; William Mauke to John Gray, 21 July 1964, Office of the Executive Vice President, Rosenthal, Box 183, GLIC archives.

14. Interview with John Angle, 21 March 2002. Coordinating Committee Minutes, 5 January 1967, Office of the Secretary, Reilly, Box 179, GLIC archives.

15. New York City Press Office Release, 13 January 1998; Christina Binkley, "Marriott, Starwood Outlooks Send Stocks Higher," *Wall Street Journal*, 4 February 1999. Interview with Joseph Caruso, 30 November 2001; interview with Joseph Sargent, 30 May 2002. Minutes of the Board of Directors, 22 August 1979, Box 207, GLIC archives. Minutes of the Board of Directors, 28 January 1998, Office of the Corporate Secretary.

16. "Guardian Life Insurance Company of America: Case Study," Washington State University Cooperative Extension Energy Program and Commuter Challenge, April 1999, online.

17. Interview with Joseph Caruso, 30 November 2001.

18. Interview with John Angle, 21 March 2002. "Misc Stock Corr. w/ Sup. of Insurance" folder, Office of the Secretary, Heye and Neuendorffer, Box 54; "Historical Facts and Data Regarding The Guardian Life Insurance Co. of America," John E. Albert, 1950, Office of the Secretary, Scott, Box 64; Reports on the Examination of the Guardian, 1901, 1911, Box 70; Minutes of the Department Head Meeting, 12 December 1929, Home Office Records, Box 74; Press Release, 31 January 1946, Public Relations Department Records, Box 84, GLIC archives.

19. Yates, "Co-evolution." Reports on the Examination of the Guardian, 1911, Box 70, GLIC archives.

20. *The Guardian Family News,* April 1922. "Historical Facts and Data Regarding The Guardian Life Insurance Co. of America," John E. Albert, 1950, Office of the Secretary, Scott, Box 64; Minutes of the Department Head Meeting, 12 December 1929, Burgh S. Johnson to All Officers and Supervisors, 18 June 1953, Folder 3 Home Office Records, Box 74; Executive Officers Committee Minutes, 14 June 1938, 13 January, 17 February 1942, Box 178; Executive Officers Committee Minutes, 23 April, 7 May 1946, Coordinating Committee Minutes, 10 September 1963, Office of the Secretary, Reilly, Box 179, GLIC archives.

21. Minutes of the Board of Directors, 27 December 1916, 24 April 1929, 20 December 1939, Box 5; Carl Heye to T. Louis Hansen, 15 December 1916, Office of the President, Heye, Box 46; "Forged Checks," 1949, Office of the Secretary, Scott, Box 64; Reports on the Examination of the Guardian, 1949, Box 71; Minutes of the Department Head Meeting, 14 May 1930, Home Office Records, Box 74; Executive Officers Committee Minutes, 9 May 1939, 22 October 1940, Box 178, GLIC archives.

22. Dividend cards, 1925, 1928, "Charles Kruse folder," Office of the President, Heye, Box 53; Executive Officers Committee Minutes, 10, 24 October, 20 December 1922, Box 178, GLIC archives.

23. *Guardian Service,* June 1916. Supervisors' Manual, 1 June 1926, Home Office Records, Box 74; Coordinating Committee Minutes, 10 March 1964, Office of the Secretary, Reilly, Box 179, GLIC archives.

24. *The Guardian,* 30 October 1961. Minutes of the Board of Directors, 22 October 1924, Box 5; Minutes of the Department Head Meeting, 14 May, 25 September 1930, Supervisors' Manual, 1 June 1926, Home Office Records, Box 74; Field Advisory Board Meeting Proceedings, 1 May 1969, 5 April 1971, Box 75; Executive Officers Committee Minutes, 24 July 1924, 24 February, 3 March 1925, Box 178; Coordinating Committee Minutes, 8 December 1964, Office of the Secretary, Reilly, Box 179; Minutes of the Board of Directors, 16 November 1977, 23 August 1978, Box 207, GLIC archives.

25. Yates, "Co-evolution." *The Guardian Family News,* March 1922. Annual Report, 1946, Box 2; Minutes of the Board of Directors, 22 April 1931, Box 5; James A McLain to Supervisory Staff, 20 June 1944, Home Office Records, Box 74; Executive Officers Committee Minutes, 13 August 1940, Box 178; Executive Officers Committee Minutes, 29 February 1944, 6 February 1945, Box 179, GLIC archives.

26. Annual Report, 1947, Box 2; Annual Report, 1949, Box 3; James A McLain to Supervisory Staff, 20 June 1944, Home Office Records, Box 74, GLIC archives.

27. Field Advisory Board Meeting Proceedings, 30 June 1949, 21 April, 17 November 1966, 26 January 1972, 13 September 1973, 28 September 1979, Box 75; Executive Officers Committee

Minutes, 3 July 1945, Box 179; Tom Quinn interview with Howard Abel, Chartered Life Underwriter, n.d., Office of the President, Angle, Box 197, GLIC archives.

28. Annual Report, 1946, Box 2; Minutes of the Department Head Meeting, 15 May 1929, 20 March 1930, Home Office Records, Box 74; Executive Officers Committee Minutes, 3 August 1943, 20 April 1948, Box 179, GLIC archives.

29. Yates, "Co-evolution." *The Guardian Family News,* May 1922. Reports on the Examination of the Guardian, 1937, Box 70; Reports on the Examination of the Guardian, 1946, Box 71; Executive Officers Committee Minutes, 10 May 1921, 4 April 1922, 22 December 1925, 16 August 1938, 26 March, 19, 26 November, 3 December 1940, 18 March 1941, 29 September 1942, Box 178; Executive Officers Committee Minutes, 15 October 1946, Box 179, GLIC archives.

30. Annual Report, 1946, Box 2; Executive Officers Committee Minutes, 17 September 1946, 24 June, 8 July, 30 September, 2 December 1947, 2 March 1948, Box 179, GLIC archives.

31. Memorandum, 12 April 1944, Office of the Secretary, Scott, Box 64; Executive Officers Committee Minutes, 19 March 1946, Box 179, GLIC archives.

32. Rosenthal, *Short and Confidential History. Home Office Newsletter,* 16 January 1950; *Guardian Life,* August 1959. Interview with Ed Kane, 30 November 2001. Coordinating Committee Minutes, 11 April 1961, Office of the Secretary, Reilly, Box 179, GLIC archives. Miervaldis Dobelis, "IBM-Based Computer System Implementation at GLIC," 29 August 2002, Office of the Corporate Secretary.

33. *Proceedings of the Forty-Sixth Annual Meeting of the Life Insurance Association of America,* 1952, 141.

34. "Management—Personnel Notes," *Wall Street Journal,* 31 December 1956. *Guardian Scene,* January 1967. Annual Report, 1955, Box 3; Minutes of the Board of Directors, 26 April 1961, Box 6; President's Reports, 24 January 1962, Box 43; Group Advisory Committee Minutes, 5 February 1960, Office of the Executive Vice President, Rosenthal, Box 183, GLIC archives.

35. Fisher et al., *IBM,* 56–57; Olegario "IBM." *Guardian Scene,* May 1966. Biographical Data, Directors and Officers, Organ Box 23-B; Annual Report, 1956, Box 3; Minutes of the Board of Directors, 26 April 1961, Box 6; President's Reports, 27 April 1960, 22 July 1964, Box 43; Coordinating Committee Minutes, 11 August 1964, Office of the Secretary, Reilly, Box 179, GLIC archives.

36. *Home Office Newsletter,* 16 November 1953; *Guardian Life,* February 1960. Miervaldis Dobelis, "IBM-Based Computer System Implementation at GLIC," 29 August 2002, Office of the Corporate Secretary.

37. President's Reports, 25 January, 26 April, 25 October 1961, Box 43, GLIC archives.

38. Rosenthal, *Short and Confidential History.* Field Advisory Board Meeting Proceedings, 14 September 1961, 24 September 1962, Box 75; Irving Rosenthal to Shale Goodman, 15 April 1966, Office of the Executive Vice President, Rosenthal, Box 184; Interview with Irving Rosenthal, 6 July 1984, Box 250, GLIC archives.

39. *Guardian Scene,* May 1966. President's Reports, 24 July 1963, 22 July, 28 October 1964, Box 43; Coordinating Committee Minutes, 12 March, 9 April, 10 December 1963, 11 August 1964, Office of the Secretary, Reilly, Box 179; Minutes of the Board of Directors, 27 April 1966, Box 206, GLIC archives. Miervaldis Dobelis, "IBM-Based Computer System Implementation at GLIC," 29 August 2002, Office of the Corporate Secretary.

40. Olegario, "IBM," 367; Flamm, *Creating the Computer.* Coordinating Committee Minutes, 12 April 1966, Office of the Secretary, Reilly, Box 179, GLIC archives. Miervaldis Dobelis, "IBM-Based Computer System Implementation at GLIC," 29 August 2002, Office of the Corporate Secretary.

41. President's Report, 27 November 1968, 28 May, 27 August, 26 November 1969, Box 43; Reports on the Examination of the Guardian, 1969, Box 72; Field Advisory Board Meeting Proceedings, 17 November 1966, Box 75, GLIC archives. Miervaldis Dobelis, "IBM-Based Computer System Implementation at GLIC," 29 August 2002, Office of the Corporate Secretary.

42. Tom Quinn interview with Anthony Peloso, Director of Group Administration, n.d., Office of the President, Angle, Box 197, GLIC archives. Miervaldis Dobelis, "IBM-Based Computer System Implementation at GLIC," 29 August 2002, Office of the Corporate Secretary.

43. Bold figures and the 5 percent discount rate are the authors' estimations. Present value estimations assume all costs and benefits accrue at once, at the beginning of each year. President's Report, 25 February, 27 May 1970, Box 43, GLIC archives.

44. *Home Office Newsletter,* 15 May 1952. *The Guardian,* 30 July 1962. Coordinating Committee Minutes, 22 May 1962, 19 February 1963, Office of the Secretary, Reilly, Box 179; Minutes of the Board of Directors, 26 February 1969, 23 February 1972, Box 206; Interview with Irving Rosenthal, 6 July 1984, Box 250, GLIC archives.

45. President's Report, 26 May, 25 August 1971, Box 43; Field Advisory Board Meeting Proceedings, 7 May 1970, Box 75; Minutes of the Board of Directors, 23 February 1972, 22 August 1973, Box 206, GLIC archives. Miervaldis Dobelis, "IBM-Based Computer System Implementation at GLIC," 29 August 2002, Office of the Corporate Secretary.

46. Pearl Goldman to Irving Rosenthal, 4 May 1973, Office of the Executive Vice President, Rosenthal, Box 184, GLIC archives. Miervaldis Dobelis, "IBM-Based Computer System Implementation at GLIC," 29 August 2002, Office of the Corporate Secretary.

47. President's Report, 25 August 1976, Box 44; Minutes of the Board of Directors, 27 August 1975, Box 206; Minutes of the Board of Directors, 24 May, 29 November 1978, 23 May 1979, 25 February, 27 May 1981, Box 207, GLIC archives.

48. Annual Report, 1986, Box 1; Field Advisory Board Meeting Proceedings, 5 April 1979, Box 75; "The Record of The Guardian Life," Reports on the Examination of the Guardian, 1974, Box 187; John C. Angle, "Summation of the Evidence," 21 January 1983, Office of the President, Angle, Box 195, GLIC archives.

49. Projections, like that summarized for the IBM 360, above, were estimations based on assumptions that may not have, in reality, panned out. Such was the case with the 360/40. The company's rapid growth, combined with continued rapid development of new computer technology, required modification of the original plan, namely, the expansion of the IBM 360 to allow multiprogramming and a memory upgrade. Interview with Joseph Caruso, 30 November 2001. Annual Report, 1967, Box 4; Field Advisory Board Meeting Proceedings, 13 September 1973, Box 75; John C. Angle, "Summation of the Evidence," 21 January 1983, John C. Angle, "Guardian Life: 1981 General Agents Conference, Closing Address," 23 January 1981, Office of the President, Angle, Box 195; Minutes of the Board of Directors, 26 July 1967, Box 206, GLIC archives. Miervaldis Dobelis, "IBM-Based Computer System Implementation at GLIC," 29 August 2002, Office of the Corporate Secretary.

50. Minutes of the Board of Directors, 22 February, 20 December 1978, Box 207, GLIC archives. Thomas Baker and John Pallota to the Audit Committee, 16 May 1994, Office of the Corporate Secretary.

51. Interview with James Pirtle, 6 June 2002.

52. Interview with Art Ferrara, 2 May 2002. Annual Report, 1985, Box 1; Field Advisory Board Meeting Proceedings, 20 April 1972, 28 September 1979, 25 September 1980, 19 May 1981, Box 75; John C. Angle, "Chairman's Address and Report on Progress during 1984," 27 February 1985, Office of the President, Angle, Box 201, GLIC archives.

53. Reports on the Examination of the Guardian, 1974, Box 187, GLIC archives.

54. Interview with Joseph Caruso, 30 November 2001.

55. Minutes of the Board of Directors, 23 February 2000, 25 April 2001, Office of the Corporate Secretary.

NOTES TO CHAPTER 11

1. Rare but not spotless. One detailed account, for example, concerns a December 1936 incident in which the home office received a frantic letter from Paul Lutzeier of Detroit, the son of an old widow apparently defrauded by sales agent Allen McKee. When Mrs. Lutzeier's en-

dowment policy fell due in October 1933, McKee had convinced Mrs. Lutzeier to keep it on deposit with Guardian. Instead of making the deposit, however, McKee invested the money in a new policy. Mrs. Lutzeier did not discover the fraud until 1936, when she needed to withdraw the funds. After thorough investigation of the situation, which included a trip to Detroit by a home office employee, Guardian settled the matter to the satisfaction of Mrs. Lutzeier, and McKee's agency was terminated. *Guardian Service,* Summer 1985. "Policyholder Complaint Letters," 1936–37, Office of the Secretary, Scott, Box 64; Reports on the Examination of the Guardian, 1961, Box 72; "Business Instructions for Agents," 1920, Manuals, Box 96; Executive Officers Committee Minutes, 8 August 1922, Box 178, GLIC archives.

2. Interview with Leo Futia, 12 April 2002. President's Report, 26 August 1981, Box 44, GLIC archives.

3. *The Guardian,* 10 September 1962. Field Advisory Board Meeting Proceedings, 24 July 1975, 9 September 1976, Box 75; Arthur Ferrara to All Agencies, 22 June 1977, Circular Letters, Agency Communication and Sales Promotion, Box 212, GLIC archives.

4. Field Advisory Board Meeting Proceedings, 18 September 1969, Box 75, GLIC archives.

5. Robert Gettlin, "Insurers Scrambling to Salvage Image," *Best's Review—Life-Health Edition,* October 1996, 44.

6. Cox, "Activities of All-Industry Committee"; Lencsis, *Insurance Regulation*; Wallison, *Federal Chartering,* 21–27.

7. Orren, *Corporate Power,* 18–24.

8. Halaas, "Legal Control."

9. Johnson, "Regulation of Life Insurance Companies," 164; MacLean, *Life Insurance,* 467; Orren, *Corporate Power,* 65; Monk, "Cooperation"; North, "Capital Accumulation," 249; Parkinson, "Legislative Contribution to Progress"; Patterson, *Insurance Commissioner,* 5–6. Interview with Joseph Caruso, 30 November 2001.

10. Patterson, *Insurance Commissioner,* 8–9.

11. Ellsworth, "Progress of Life Insurance"; Kalmbach, "Chairman's Address"; Monk, "Cooperation"; Palyi, "Life Insurance," 70; Sick, "Let's Get Excited"; Wysong, "Reserves." "Few Would Use State Regulators to Resolve Disputes, ACLI Survey Finds," Internet Wire, 17 June 2002.

12. On employee pensions, see chapter 9 above. *Testimony Taken Before the Joint Committee,* 5,568. Minutes of the Board of Directors, 22 April 1908, Box 122; John C. Angle, "Histories: My own; Guardian Life's; and that of J. F. Entz," 17 September 1983, Office of the President, Angle, Box 195, GLIC archives.

13. Minutes of the Board of Directors, 28 April 1926, 23 April 1930, Box 5; William C. Brown to Irving Rosenthal, 15 June 1972, Office of the Executive Vice President, Rosenthal, Box 183; Reports on the Examination of the Guardian, 1974, Box 187, GLIC archives.

14. Otto Kelsey to Cornelius Doremus, 9 October 1908, Cornelius Doremus to Heinrich Rose, 20 October 1908, State of New York Insurance Department Circular, 19 May, 16 June 1908, Office of the President, Doremus, Box 45; Minutes of the Board of Directors, 25 October 1905, 28 April 1909, Box 122, GLIC archives.

15. Finance Committee Minutes, 4, 18 May 1927, Box 15, GLIC archives.

16. Reports on the Examination of the Guardian, 1921, 1933, Box 70, GLIC archives.

17. Johnson, "Regulation of Life Insurance Companies," 165; Lencsis, *Insurance Regulation,* 43–51. *Home Office Newsletter,* 15 March 1950. Interview with Joseph Caruso, 21 August 2002. Minutes of the Board of Directors, 23 February 1994, Office of the Corporate Secretary.

18. The issue at hand was the regulation of wholesale life policies. Kesslinger, *Guardian,* 53. William J. Burrell to T. Robert Wilcox, 22 May 1964, Office of the Executive Vice President, Rosenthal, Box 183, GLIC archives.

19. Kesslinger, *Guardian,* 54. Annual Report, 1947, Box 2, GLIC archives.

20. Reports on the Examination of the Guardian, 1933, Box 70; Arthur Ferrara to All Agencies, 14 December 1979, Circular Letters, Agency Communication and Sales Promotion, Box 212, GLIC archives.

21. Minutes of the Board of Directors, 28 July 1909, Box 122, GLIC archives.

22. President's Report, 27 November 1974, Box 44; Reports on the Examination of the Guardian, 1979, Box 187; Interview with Irving Rosenthal, 6 July 1984, Box 250, GLIC archives. Minutes of the Board of Directors, 17 November, 1 December 1993, Office of the Corporate Secretary.

23. Interview with Art Ferrara, 2 May 2002.

24. Buley, *American Life Convention,* 463. "New York Life Firms Ask State Law Change to Permit Expansion," *Wall Street Journal,* 15 January 1960.

25. Camp, *Liberty National Life,* 106–7. Field Advisory Board Meeting Proceedings, 21 September 1972, Box 75; Daniel J. Lyons to Irving Rosenthal, 10 July 1972, Irving Rosenthal to George Conklin, 23 May 1972, Office of the Executive Vice President, Rosenthal, Box 185, Interview with Irving Rosenthal, 6 July 1984, Box 250, GLIC archives.

26. Real Estate Committee Minutes, 28 June 1978, Box 38; Minutes of the Board of Directors, 24 April 1907, Box 122; Minutes of the Board of Directors, 23 August 1978, Box 207, GLIC archives.

27. President's Report, 24 May 1978, 22 August 1979, Box 44, GLIC archives.

28. Interview with John Angle, 21 March 2002. Minutes of the Board of Directors, 16 December 1970, Box 206, GLIC archives.

29. Orren, *Corporate Power,* 36–38. Interview with Ashby Bladen, 6 June 2002.

30. *Proceedings of the Fifty-Seventh Annual Meeting of Life Insurance Association of America,* 1963, 89; Buley, *American Life Convention,* 301–8; Cox, Robert Lynn, "Robertson Law." Annual Report, 1947, Box 2; Minutes of the Board of Directors, 26 April 1916, 28 July 1920, Box 5; Minutes of the Board of Directors, 23 April 1947, Box 6; Finance Committee Minutes, 27 August 1925, Box 15; Minutes of the Board of Directors, 19 June 1907, Box 122, GLIC archives.

31. Gerald S. Parker to All Agencies, 9 December 1976, Circular Letters, Agency Communication and Sales Promotion, Box 212, GLIC archives. Minutes of the Board of Directors, 24 February 1993, 26 May 1993, Office of the Corporate Secretary.

32. Finance Committee Minutes, 21 October 1925, Box 15; Finance Committee Minutes, 5 July 1933, Box 16, GLIC archives.

33. Carl Heye to Charles Hughes, 16 January 1919, Office of the President, Heye, Box 48, GLIC archives.

34. For the differences between GAAP and STAT or statutory accounting, see Lencsis, *Insurance Regulation,* 33–34; Raymond, "Financial Statements." Interview with John Angle, 21 March 2002. John C. Angle, "The State of the Life Insurance Industry," 27 September 1988, Office of the President, Angle, Box 201, GLIC archives. Minutes of the Board of Directors, 23 February 1994, 25 September 1996, Office of the Corporate Secretary.

35. The same could be said of the circa 1940 TNEC investigation, the questionnaire of which asked questions so arcane that Rosenthal found himself making up answers on a wing and a prayer. Reports on the Examination of the Guardian, "Correspondence and Response," 1952, Box 71; Interview with Irving Rosenthal, 6 July 1984, Box 250, GLIC archives.

36. Even a seemingly harmless, rational move like moving the equity markets to decimal pricing could severely hurt secondary market liquidity. Latto, "Federal Regulation." Interview with Eric Larson, 6 June 2002.

37. Annual Report, 1976, Box 4, GLIC archives.

38. Johnson, "Regulation of Life Insurance Companies," 161–62. John C. Angle, "Discussion at Concurrent Session B, Society of Actuaries Annual Meeting," 24 October 1977, Office of the President, Angle, Box 195, GLIC archives.

39. Buley, *American Life Convention,* 142; Davis, Malvin E., *Industrial Insurance,* 326–29; Johnson, "Regulation of Life Insurance Companies," 184–85; Lencsis, *Insurance Regulation,* 111–13. Executive Officers Committee Minutes, 19 March 1940, Box 178, GLIC archives.

40. Harman, "Life Insurance Company Taxation—Part I"; Valenti, "Federal Taxation."

41. Clough, *Mutual Life Insurance Company of New York,* 335–36; Fiske, "Life Insurance In-

vestments"; Johnson, "Regulation of Life Insurance Companies," 181–84; MacLean, *Life Insurance,* 477. Annual Report, 1935, Box 2, GLIC archives.

42. Blackburn, "State Taxation"; Davis, "Menace of Taxation"; Gephart, "Loans"; Keller, *Life Insurance Enterprise,* 198; McCall, *A Review,* 10; Rhodes, "Federal Taxation"; Young, "Economic Aspects."

43. "Legal Opinions of Counsel," 1860–1920, Legal Department Records, Box 79; "Special Committee" Minutes, 12 July 1864, Box 125, GLIC archives.

44. Adams, "Increase of Public Expenditures and Taxes." Annual Report, 1949, Box 3, GLIC archives.

45. Guardian deposited bonds with the Manhattan Bank for the benefit of the collector instead. Finance Committee Minutes, 25 January 1922, 26 January 1927, Box 15; Wing and Russell to Guardian Life Insurance Company, 29 January 1920, Legal Department Records, Box 79, GLIC archives.

46. Finance Committee Minutes, 24 May, 14 September 1933, 23 May 1934, Box 16, GLIC archives.

47. Finance Committee Minutes, 10 April 1935, 21 October 1936, Box 16; Executive Officers Committee Minutes, 12 March 1940, Box 178, GLIC archives.

48. "Tax on Insurance by State Upheld," *New York Times,* 13 May 1943. Reports on the Examination of the Guardian, 1946, Box 71; Executive Officers Committee Minutes, 18 June 1940, Box 178; Executive Officers Committee Minutes, 18 May 1943, Box 179, GLIC archives.

49. "Edge Charges Inefficiency and Neglect of Duty in the State Division of Tax Appeals," *New York Times,* 19 July 1945; "Hague on Witness Stand," *New York Times,* 16 November 1946; "Annuity Receipts Ruled Not Taxable by N.Y. City," *New York Times,* 21 May 1948. Finance Committee Minutes, 24 June 1942, 19 July 1944, Box 17; Real Estate Committee Minutes, 22 January 1947, Box 33; 28 September, 9 November 1949, Box 34, GLIC archives.

50. Young, "Economic Aspects." Annual Report, 1940, Box 2, GLIC archives.

51. *Home Office Newsletter,* 15 February 1952. Finance Committee Minutes, 22 May 1946, Box 18, GLIC archives.

52. Harman, "Life Insurance Company Taxation—Part I"; Sick, "Let's Get Excited." Interview with Armand de Palo, 27 January 2003. President's Report, 28 January 1959, Box 43; Tax memo, n.d., Irving Rosenthal to Ashby Bladen, 16 March 1973, Office of the Executive Vice President, Rosenthal, Box 185, GLIC archives

53. Minutes of the Board of Directors, 28 October 1959, Box 6; Minutes of the Board of Directors, 16 December 1970, Box 206, GLIC archives.

54. Interview with Armand de Palo, 27 January 2003. President's Reports, 28 October 1959, Box 43, GLIC archives.

55. President's Report, 22 July, 28 October 1964, 28 July, 27 October 1965, 26 January 1966, 27 November 1968, 26 February 1969, Box 43; President's Report, 26 February 1975, 25 February 1976, Box 44; "Status of Federal Tax Audits," 15 April 1971, Office of the Executive Vice President, Rosenthal, Box 185; Minutes of the Board of Directors, 23 February, 23 August 1972, Box 206, GLIC archives.

56. Interview with John Angle, 21 March 2002. Irving Rosenthal to Daniel J. Lyons, 6 July 1970, John E. Gray to Irving Rosenthal, 23 November 1971, Irving Rosenthal to Edward Zeiger, 8 May 1972, Office of the Executive Vice President, Rosenthal, Box 185; John C. Angle, "The State of the Life Insurance Industry," 27 September 1988, Office of the President, Angle, Box 201, GLIC archives.

57. Interview with John Angle, 21 March 2002. President's Reports, 22 August 1973, 27 February 1974, Box 43; Remarks by Ashby Bladen, Field Advisory Board Meeting Proceedings, 20 September 1974, Box 75; Subsidiary Analysis, 20 November 1972, Office of the Executive Vice President, Rosenthal, Box 185, GLIC archives.

58. Annual Report, 1985, Box 1; President's Report, 25 February 1981, Box 44; President's Report, 1991, unboxed, GLIC archives.

59. *Taxing Life Insurance Companies;* Graetz, *Life Insurance Company Taxation;* Harman,

"Life Insurance Company Taxation—Part I"; Harman, "Life Insurance Company Taxation—Part II."

NOTES TO PART III

1. Interview with Eric Larson, 6 June 2002.

2. "Naturally, Guardian cannot control interest rates; they are determined by the Government's fiscal policy and by supply and demand." Sproul, "Central Banking and the Private Economy." Annual Report, 1946, Box 2, GLIC archives.

3. Cornelius Doremus, "Address of the President to the Company's Managers," 30 May 1901, Home Office Records, Box 74, GLIC archives.

4. "Schwendler was the financial genius of the organization." Carl Heye Speech, 1930, Office of the Secretary, Scott, Box 64, GLIC archives.

NOTES TO CHAPTER 12

1. Conklin, "Company Investments," 1023; Conklin, "Portfolio Management."

2. Clough, *Mutual Life Insurance Company of New York,* 299; New York State Insurance Department, "Income of State-Licensed Life Insurance Companies by Source, New York State—1987, 1992 and 1997." Interview with Joseph Sargent, 30 May 2002.

3. Unless, of course, their mortality or cost experiences were sufficiently better than expected to make up for the deficit in investment returns.

4. Davis, E. Philip, "Portfolio Regulation"; Gentry and Pike, "Risk-Return Hypothesis"; Law, "Investment Trends"; Smith and Sparks, "Life Insurance Company Mortgage Investment."

5. *Testimony Taken before the Joint Committee,* 5,513; Cox, "Life Insurance Investments."

6. Speech, 1915, Office of the Secretary, Scott, Box 64, GLIC archives.

7. California did not suspend gold payments during the Civil War, so Guardian had to keep a reserve of gold on deposit in San Francisco to make its payments there. Jones, Charles P., *Investments,* 518. "Early Guardian History in California," 1948, "History of Guardian Life on West Coast: Contribution to Expansion," 1956, Office of the Secretary, Scott, Box 64; "Special Committee" Minutes, 12 July 1864, Box 125, GLIC archives.

8. Rapone, *Guardian,* 92.

9. "Cash" is a generic term that refers to highly liquid assets ranging from physical currency (notes and coins) to demand deposits in banks to bank time deposits to short-term financial instruments.

10. Badger, "Unusual Features of Life Insurance Investing," 78–79. Cornelius Doremus to Hubert Cillis, 18 August 1913, Office of the President, Heye, Box 47, GLIC archives.

11. One exception was the Liberty National Life. See Camp, *Liberty National Life,* 58–59; Walter, *Investment Process,* 22. Cornelius Doremus to Hubert Cillis, 18 August 1913, Office of the President, Heye, Box 47, GLIC archives.

12. The bombing sketch is based on Daniel Gross, "Previous Terror on Wall Street: A Look at the 1920 Bombing," *TheStreet.com,* 20 September 2001. Finance Committee Minutes, 5 September 1917, 29 October 1919, 29 September 1920, 28 November 1928, Box 15; Finance Committee Minutes, 12 April 1933, Box 16; "Lohmeyer Recollections," 1943, Office of the Secretary, Scott, Box 64, GLIC archives.

13. Before the machine could be operated, two locks, each with a different key, had to be disengaged. Checks written in amounts greater than $500, or for other than salary, disability, examination, or dividends were void. The company also extended its fraud insurance to cover misuse of the machine.

14. Annual Report, 1940, Box 2; Finance Committee Minutes, 24 April 1929, 16 April 1930, Box 15; Finance Committee Minutes, 27 January 1932, 16 January 1935, Box 16; Reports on the Examination of the Guardian, 1952, Box 71, GLIC archives.

15. Keller, *Life Insurance Enterprise,* 135. Finance Committee Minutes, 27 January, 10 February 1915, Box 15, GLIC archives.

16. Hartzel, "Bank and Life Insurance Company Resources"; Johnston, "Savings Deposits and Life Insurance." Finance Committee Minutes, 14 July, 29 December 1915, Box 15, GLIC archives.

17. Finance Committee Minutes, 28 July, 22 September 1915, 22 March, 5 April, 17 May, 13 December 1916, 10 January, 5 September 1917, 24 July 1918, 2 April 1919, 5 January 1921, 19 May 1926, Box 15; "Independence Trust Company," Office of the President, Heye, Box 45, GLIC archives.

18. Finance Committee Minutes, 2 July, 13 August 1913, 17 June, 22 July 1914, 8 January 1919, Box 15, GLIC archives.

19. Brimmer, *Life Insurance Companies in the Capital Market,* 100–101. Cornelius Doremus to Hubert Cillis, 12 March 1912, Finance Committee Minutes, 11 March 1914, 10 July 1918, Box 15, GLIC archives.

20. Finance Committee Minutes, 14 September 1921, Box 15, GLIC archives.

21. Guardian "very rarely made few call loans in the nineteenth century" because, according to Doremus, "they are not attractive in any way as an investment. In the first place it is only a temporary thing." *Testimony Taken before the Joint Committee,* 5,524.

22. Brimmer, *Life Insurance Companies in the Capital Market,* 69; Halaas, "Legal Control," 329, 332; Law, "Investment Trends." Finance Committee Minutes, 21 January, 18 February, 31 March 1920, 2 July 1923, 23 January 1929, Box 15; Memorandum in Re Collateral Loans, 3 August 1948, Office of the Secretary, Scott, Box 64, GLIC archives.

23. Finance Committee Minutes, 18 September 1929, Box 15, GLIC archives.

24. Finance Committee Minutes, 27 November 1929, Box 15; Finance Committee Minutes, 7 January 1931, Box 16, GLIC archives.

25. Pesando, "Life Insurance Company Cash Flow Forecasts"; Walter, *Investment Process,* 20–21. Finance Committee Minutes, 16, 30 September 1931, 6 January, 30 March, 31 August, 14 September, 21 December 1932, 18 January 1933, 17 January 1934, 16 January 1935, Box 16, GLIC archives.

26. Finance Committee Minutes, 1, 15 March 1933, Box 16, GLIC archives.

27. Badger, "Unusual Features of Life Insurance Investing," 79; Buley, *American Life Convention,* 753–4; Krooss and Blyn, *History of Financial Intermediaries,* 202–3; Walter, *Investment Process,* 8. Minutes of the Board of Directors, 25 April 1934, 24 April 1935, Box 5; Finance Committee Minutes, 18 January 1928, Box 15; Finance Committee Minutes, 12 April, 7 June 1933, Box 16; Executive Officers Committee Minutes, 15 June 1947, Box 179, GLIC archives.

28. Finance Committee Minutes, 11 November 1931, 26 July 1933, Box 16, GLIC archives.

29. Nerlove, "Common Stocks—I," 44; Rosenthal, *Short and Confidential History.* Finance Committee Minutes, 3 January, 14 March, 11 April, 9 May 1934, Box 16; Reports on the Examination of the Guardian, 1935, Box 70, GLIC archives.

30. Finance Committee Minutes, 16 December 1914, Box 15; Carl Heye Speech, 1930, Office of the Secretary, Scott, Box 64, GLIC archives.

31. Finance Committee Minutes, 24 January 1917, Box 15; Finance Committee Minutes, 20 September 1939, Box 17; John P. Leo to Carl Heye, 12, 14 June 1917, Office of the President, Heye, Box 46, GLIC archives.

32. Finance Committee Minutes, 4 April 1917, Box 15; Reports on the Examination of the Guardian, 1933, Box 70, GLIC archives.

33. "Operating Results and Investments of the Twenty-Six Largest Legal Reserve Life Insurance Companies in the U.S., 1929–1938," TNEC Records, Box 59, GLIC archives.

34. Camp, *Liberty National Life,* 12; Saulnier, *Urban Mortgage Lending,* 80. Interview with James Pirtle, 6 June 2002. Annual Report, 1955, Box 3; President's Reports, Summary, 1939, 1941, Box 42; Reports on the Examination of the Guardian, 1952, Box 71, GLIC archives.

35. *Testimony Taken before the Joint Committee,* 5,514–15. "Germania Life," *Insurance Moni-*

tor, 1906, 52–53. Carl Heye Speech, 1930, Speech, 1915, Office of the Secretary, Scott, Box 64; Reports on the Examination of the Guardian, 1933, Box 70, GLIC archives.

36. Reports on the Examination of the Guardian, 1921, Box 70; Minutes of the Board of Directors, 23 September 1913, Box 122, GLIC archives.

37. *Testimony Taken before the Joint Committee,* 5,516, 5,546. Alfred Roelker to the Finance Committee, 20 April 1891, and related documents, Cornelius Doremus to Hubert Cillis, 12 March 1912, Finance Committee Minutes, 8 October 1913, Box 15; "After Two Years," 1903, Office of the President, Doremus, Box 45; Reports on the Examination of the Guardian, 1901, 1911, 1933, Box 70, GLIC archives.

38. Reports on the Examination of the Guardian, 1933, Box 70, GLIC archives.

39. Finance Committee Minutes, 13 August 1913, Box 15, GLIC archives.

40. William Renecker to Cornelius Doremus, 24 October 1890, Box 15; T. Louis Hansen to Carl Heye, 18 February 1922, Office of the President, Heye, Box 46, GLIC archives.

41. Halaas, "Legal Control," 325; Spring, *Laws Controlling the Investment of Insurance Funds,* 8–9.

42. Finance Committee Minutes, 29 November 1916, 21 August 1918, Box 15, GLIC archives.

43. Finance Committee Minutes, 9 July 1919, Box 15, GLIC archives.

44. Among the earliest calls for heavy investment in farm mortgages by life insurers is Clark, "Rural Credit Problems" and Taylor, Charles, "Getting Closer to the Farmer." For an overview of farm mortgages, see Breiling, "Policyholders' Contribution"; Kingsley, "Farm Mortgage"; Woodruff, *Farm Mortgage Loans.* Minutes of the Board of Directors, 24 January 1917, Box 5; Memorandum, ? January 1917, "Farm Mortgages," "Investment in Farm Mortgages," n.d., Office of the President, Heye, Box 46, GLIC archives.

45. From the study, "it appeared that the experience of such Companies with [farm mortgage] investments during the abnormal conditions which prevailed during the past twelve months, had continued generally favorable; that 20 of the Companies were investing the same amount or more in such mortgages than heretofore and but three less owing to an increased demand for policy loans." Woodruff, *Farm Mortgage Loans,* 25–26, 60–68, 73–74. "Investment Questionnaire," TNEC Records, Box 59; Finance Committee Minutes, 10 January 1917, 31 March, 7 July 1920, 28 September 1921, Box 15, GLIC archives.

46. Snowden, "Mortgage Securitization"; Woodruff, *Farm Mortgage Loans,* 14. Finance Committee Minutes, 28 September 1921, Box 15, GLIC archives.

47. *The Bond,* August 1945. Finance Committee Minutes, 13, 26 October 1921, Box 15, GLIC archives.

48. Finance Committee Minutes, 9 November 1921, 15 March, 26 April 1922, Box 15, GLIC archives.

49. Finance Committee Minutes, 17 November 1915, 22 January 1919, 5 January 1921, Box 15, GLIC archives.

50. Finance Committee Minutes, 30 January 1924, 23 February 1925, Box 15; Field Advisory Board Meeting Proceedings, 13 September 1973, Box 75; Executive Officers Committee Minutes, 15 September 1925, Box 178, GLIC archives.

51. Brimmer, *Life Insurance Companies in the Capital Market,* 86–87; Hartzel, "Bank and Life Insurance Company Resources," 683; Saulnier, *Urban Mortgage Lending,* 31. Finance Committee Minutes, 24 May, 30 August 1922, 2 July 1923, 2 June 1926, Box 15, GLIC archives.

52. "Insurance Company to Erect House Opposite Tammany Hall," *New York Times,* 5 March 1931. Minutes of the Board of Directors, 22 July 1931, Box 5, GLIC archives.

53. Finance Committee Minutes, 10 December 1930, 10 June, 8 July 1931, Box 16, GLIC archives.

54. Saulnier, *Urban Mortgage Lending,* 31. Finance Committee Minutes, 22 June 1932, 1, 15, 29 March, 5 July, 30 August, 8 November 1933, 17 January, 14 February 1934, Box 16, GLIC archives.

55. Camp, *Liberty National Life,* 9. Minutes of the Board of Directors, 24 January 1945, Box 6; Finance Committee Minutes, 25 July 1934, Box 16; Finance Committee Minutes, 7 Septem-

ber 1938, 4 February 1942, Box 17; Reports on the Examination of the Guardian, 1933, Box 70, GLIC archives.

56. Finance Committee Minutes, 30 March 1932, Box 16, GLIC archives.

57. Finance Committee Minutes, 16 January, 13 February, 13 March, 9 October 1935, 15 January 1936, Box 16; Reports on the Examination of the Guardian, 1933, Box 70, GLIC archives.

58. Brimmer, *Life Insurance Companies in the Capital Market,* 218. *Guardian Life,* April 1960. Finance Committee Minutes, 4 November, 2 December 1936, Box 16, GLIC archives.

59. Saulnier, *Urban Mortgage Lending,* 86. Finance Committee Minutes, 5 July, 26 July 1933, Box 16; Reports on the Examination of the Guardian, 1933, Box 70; Reports on the Examination of the Guardian, 1940, Box 71; Interview with Irving Rosenthal, 6 July 1984, Box 250, GLIC archives.

60. Finance Committee Minutes, 24 March, 29 December 1937, Box 16; Finance Committee Minutes, 9 March, 28 December 1938, 22 March, 14 June, 13 December 1939, 7 August 1940, 5 February, 5 March 1941, 8 November 1944, 28 March 1945, Box 17; Reports on the Examination of the Guardian, 1940, Box 70, GLIC archives.

61. Nerlove, "Common Stocks—I," 41; Saulnier, *Urban Mortgage Lending,* 32–33. Annual Report, 1945, 1947, Box 2; Finance Committee Minutes, 27 November 1940, Box 17, GLIC archives.

62. "Guardian Life Lists $8,128,934 Asset Gain," *New York Times,* 29 January 1942. Finance Committee Minutes, 27 December 1939, 23 April, 29 October, 13 November 1941, Box 17; Executive Officers Committee Minutes, 20 February 1940, Box 178, GLIC archives.

63. Finance Committee Minutes, 13 December 1939, Box 17; Real Estate Committee Minutes, 22 January 1947, Box 33; Real Estate Committee Minutes, 8 September 1948, Box 34, GLIC archives.

64. Finance Committee Minutes, 1 May 1940, 25 June 1941, Box 17, GLIC archives.

65. "Will Cut Dividend Rate," *New York Times,* 5 December 1942. Finance Committee Minutes, 17 February, 3 March 1943, Box 17; Executive Officers Committee Minutes, 23 June 1942, Box 178, GLIC archives.

66. Montana Central Railway Company circular, George K. Sistare circular, 13 May 1870, Box 15, GLIC archives.

67. William Meredith to Hugo Wesendonck, 20 October 1888, Box 15, GLIC archives.

68. Finance Committee Minutes, 10 January 1917, Matthews and Whitaker to Vermilye and Co., 29 October 1888, Spencer Trask and Company to Guardian, n.d., Box 15; Speech, 1915, Office of the Secretary, Scott, Box 64, GLIC archives.

69. The company did make a low volume of call loans early on. *Testimony Taken before the Joint Committee,* 5,516; Spring, "New York," in *Laws Controlling the Investment of Insurance Funds,* 18–19; North, "Life Insurance and Investment Banking," 213. "Germania Life," *Insurance Monitor,* 1906, 52–53. New York Statutes, Chapter 361, 10 May 1883, Box 15; "Special Committee" Minutes, 10 July 1867, Box 125, GLIC archives.

70. Finance Committee Minutes, 16 July 1913, 3 June 1914, Box 15, GLIC archives.

71. Finance Committee Minutes, 3 June, 2 December 1914, Box 15; Hubert Cillis to Banco Mexicano De Comercio E Industria, 14 January 1918, Hubert Cillis to Mexico City Banking Company, S.A., 4 April 1918, Office of the President, Heye, Box 46; "War Risk on European Business," 12 August 1918, Office of the President, Heye, Box 47, GLIC archives.

72. Minutes of the Board of Directors, 23 September 1913, Box 12; Finance Committee Minutes, 17 December 1913, 11 February, 22 July 1914, 17 March 1920, Box 15; Cornelius Doremus to Hubert Cillis, 18 August 1913, Cornelius Doremus to Heinrich Rose, 15 August 1913, Office of the President, Heye, Box 47, GLIC archives.

73. *Proceedings of the Eleventh Annual Meeting of Life Insurance Association of America,* 1917, 120–25. Finance Committee Minutes, 27 January 1915, 16 October 1916, Box 15; Finance Committee Minutes, 23 August 1939, Box 17, GLIC archives.

74. Finance Committee Minutes, 26 August, 9 September, 2 December 1914, 24 February 1915, 22 December 1920, Box 15, GLIC archives.

75. Finance Committee Minutes, 20 June 1921, 30 June 1926, Box 15; Finance Committee Minutes, 2, 30 August 1933, Box 16, GLIC archives.

76. Finance Committee Minutes, 29 December 1915, Box 15, GLIC archives.

77. Finance Committee Minutes, 7 August 1918, Box 15, GLIC archives.

78. Finance Committee Minutes, 29 August 1934, 13 February 1935, 15 January, 25 March 1936, Box 16, GLIC archives.

79. Nerlove, "Common Stocks—I," 48–49. Finance Committee Minutes, 27 May 1931, 8, 22 June 1932, 13, 27 February 1935, Box 16, GLIC archives.

80. Nerlove, "Common Stocks—I," 41; O'Leary, "Effects of Recent Credit and Debt Management Policies," 309. "Guardian Life Reports," *New York Times,* 4 February 1943.

81. Gephart, "Loans"; Nollen, "Recent Fluctuations"; Pesando, "Life Insurance Company Cash Flow Forecasts," 1108; Sage, "Prevention"; Schott, "Disintermediation through Policy Loans"; Sullivan, "Life Insurance," 348. "Guardian Life Lists $8,128,934 Asset Gain," *New York Times,* 29 January 1942. President's Reports, 26 February, 27 August 1969, Box 43, GLIC archives.

82. Camp, *Liberty National Life,* 39; O'Leary, "Effects of Recent Credit and Debt Management Policies," 309; O'Leary, "Investment Trends."

83. Annual Report, 1945, Box 2; Finance Committee Minutes, 10 January 1951, Box 18; Real Estate Committee Minutes, 9 January 1946, 11 June 1947, Box 33; Real Estate Committee Minutes, 11 July 1950, Box 34; Coordinating Committee Minutes, 5 January 1967, Office of the Secretary, Reilly, Box 179, GLIC archives.

84. Finance Committee Minutes, 28 February 1945, Box 17; Real Estate Committee Minutes, 22 May, 27 November, 26 December 1946, 9 April, 14 May, 25 June 1947, 10 March, 9 June 1948, Box 33; Real Estate Committee Minutes, 12 January 1949, Box 34; Reports on the Examination of the Guardian, 1946, Box 71, GLIC archives.

85. Real Estate Committee Minutes, 22 May, 28 August 1946, 27 August 1947, Box 33; Real Estate Committee Minutes, 9 March, 28 December 1949, Box 34, GLIC archives.

86. Brimmer, *Life Insurance Companies in the Capital Market,* 104, 108; Smith and Sparks, "Life Insurance Company Mortgage Investment," 20. Reports on the Examination of the Guardian, 1958, Box 72, GLIC archives.

87. Drummond, "Canadian Life Insurance"; Geren, "Contribution of Life Insurance," 50–51; Halaas, "Legal Control," 332–34; Hobbs, "Problems of Supervision"; Hood and Main, "Canadian Life Insurance Companies"; Huebner et al., "Investments in Life Insurance Companies"; Jones, Homer, "Investment in Equities"; Ketchum, "Life Insurance Companies"; Nerlove, "Common Stocks—I"; Nerlove, "Common Stocks—II"; O'Leary, "Investment Trends"; Rydgren, "Impact of Lower Interest Earnings." Thomas P. Swift, "Insurance Giants Eye Equity Stocks," *New York Times,* 25 June 1950. Office of the President, Heye, Box 45; Reports on the Examination of the Guardian, 1949, Box 71; Executive Officers Committee Minutes, 20 April 1948, Box 179, GLIC archives.

88. Brimmer, *Life Insurance Companies in the Capital Market,* 69, 353; Jones, Homer, "Investment in Equities," 190; Ketchum, "Life Insurance Companies," 31; Nerlove, "Common Stocks—II," 60. Reports on the Examination of the Guardian, 1946, Box 71, GLIC archives.

NOTES TO CHAPTER 13

1. Minutes of the Board of Directors, 24 January 1962, Box 6; James A McLain to My Associates in the Field and Home Office, 16 December 1948, Circulars, Box 94; Reports on the Examination of the Guardian, 1974, Box 187, GLIC archives.

2. "Guardian Life Advances Conklin," *New York Times,* 21 December 1943; "Insurance Notes," *New York Times,* 14 March 1946; "Cameron Will Succeed McLain as Guardian Life Chairman, Chief Officer," *Wall Street Journal,* 6 August 1963; "Guardian Life Elects Two Top Executives," *New York Times,* 26 December 1966; "Finance," *Wall Street Journal,* 20 May 1977; "Guardian Life Insurance Co. of America," *Wall Street Journal,* 8 May 1980. *The Bond,* January

1944; *Home Office Newsletter,* 16 March 1955. Interview with John Angle, 21 March 2002; interview with Arthur Ferrara, 2 May 2002. Benjamin Rushmore Papers, 1815–17; Isaac Van Scoy Papers, 1831–32, New York Historical Society. Biographical Data, Directors and Officers, Organ Box 23-B; Annual Report, 1963, Box 4; Minutes of the Board of Directors, 15 December 1943, 20 December 1944, 24 April 1946, 28 October 1953, Box 6; James A McLain to My Associates in the Field and Home Office, 16 December 1948, Circulars, Box 94; John C. Angle, "1975 Guardian Group Conference," Office of the President, Angle, Box 195; Tom Quinn interview with George T. Conklin, 5 March 1982, Office of the President, Angle, Box 197; John C. Angle to Robert D. Shapiro, 19 May 1986, Office of the President, Angle, Box 201; Minutes of the Board of Directors, 19 December 1979, 13 December 1995, Box 207, GLIC archives.

3. *Proceedings of the Forty-Seventh Annual Meeting of the Life Insurance Association of America,* 1953, 84; *Proceedings of the Fifty-Second Annual Meeting of the Life Insurance Association of America,* 1958, 164–68; *Proceedings of the Fifty-Fourth Annual Meeting of Life Insurance Association of America,* 1960, 234–35; *Proceedings of the Fifty-Fifth Annual Meeting of Life Insurance Association of America,* 1961, 175; *Proceedings of the Fifty-Seventh Annual Meeting of Life Insurance Association of America,* 1963, 181–86; *Proceedings of the Fifty-Eighth Annual Meeting of Life Insurance Association of America,* 1964, 90, 93, 170. Conversation with Robert Kavesh, economist at New York University's Stern School of Business; interview with Frank Jones, 30 November 2001. Annual Report, 1947, Box 2; Field Advisory Board Meeting Proceedings, 21 April 1966, Box 75, GLIC archives.

4. "Home Builders Warned of a Tight Market If Starts Soar," *Wall Street Journal,* 19 January 1955; "Many Builders Plan Spring Dwelling Starts above High 1954 Rate," *Wall Street Journal,* 7 February 1955; George E. Cruikshank, "Some Lenders Tighten Terms a Bit; May Slow Pace of New Home Sales," *Wall Street Journal,* 22 March 1955. Field Advisory Board Meeting Proceedings, 20 January 1950, Box 75, GLIC archives.

5. Friedman was a Nobel laureate and coauthor of *A Monetary History of the United States,* among other works. Goldsmith was a Yale professor and author of the three-volume classic, *Saving in the United States.* Hickman, who worked for the Federal Reserve, was author of *Corporate Bond Financing.* Homer was the author of *A History of Interest Rates,* which, with the help of Richard Sylla, has gone through three editions and several revisions. Homer worked at Salomon Brothers. Conard, *Behavior of Interest Rates;* Conklin, "Portfolio Management"; Conklin, "Company Investments," 1024; Walter, *Investment Process,* vii.

6. Walter, *Investment Process,* 7, 11, 14, 18. Finance Committee Minutes, 11 August 1971, Box 20, GLIC archives.

7. *Proceedings of the Fifty-Seventh Annual Meeting of Life Insurance Association of America,* 1963, 119. George E. Cruikshank, "Some Lenders Tighten Terms a Bit; May Slow Pace of New Home Sales," *Wall Street Journal,* 22 March 1955.

8. Minutes of the Board of Directors, 28 April 1965, Box 6, GLIC archives.

9. Minutes of the Board of Directors, 23 July 1958, Box 6; Finance Committee Minutes, 11 June, 23 July, 22 October 1958, 10 January 1962, Box 19; Finance Committee Minutes, 8 December 1971, Box 20; President's Report, 22 October 1958, Box 43; Reports on the Examination of the Guardian, 1958, Box 72; John C. Angle to Robert D. Shapiro, 19 May 1986, Office of the President, Angle, Box 201, GLIC archives.

10. Mortgages amortized monthly began to gain favor during the Depression. Camp, *Liberty National Life,* 24; Ecker, "Problem of Housing"; Kacy, *Unique and Different,* 20. Finance Committee Minutes, 25 April 1962, Box 19; Field Advisory Board Meeting Proceedings, 9 September 1971, Box 75, GLIC archives.

11. Annual Report, 1961, Box 3; Finance Committee Minutes, 27 August 1958, Box 19; President's Reports, 24 July 1963, Box 43, GLIC archives.

12. *Guardian Life,* April 1960. Reports on the Examination of the Guardian, 1955, 1958, Box 72, GLIC archives.

13. Conklin, "Direct Placements." Reports on the Examination of the Guardian, 1955, Box 72, GLIC archives.

14. *Home Office Newsletter,* 15 April 1953. Annual Report, 1955, Box 3; Finance Committee Minutes, 19 December 1945, Box 17; Finance Committee Minutes, 22 January 1947, 9 January 1952, Box 18; Finance Committee Minutes, 26 January 1955, Box 19; Reports on the Examination of the Guardian, 1955, Box 72; Coordinating Committee Minutes, 9 June 1964, Office of the Secretary, Reilly, Box 179, GLIC archives.

15. Brimmer, *Life Insurance Companies in the Capital Market,* 84, 177; Walter, *Investment Process,* 28. "Investment Questionnaire," "Operating Results and Investments of the Twenty-Six Largest Legal Reserve Life Insurance Companies in the U.S., 1929–1938," TNEC Records, Box 59, GLIC archives.

16. Brimmer, *Life Insurance Companies in the Capital Market,* 199; Conklin, "Direct Placements"; O'Leary, "Investment Trends." Field Advisory Board Meeting Proceedings, 20 January 1950, Box 75; Executive Officers Committee Minutes, 30 April 1940, Box 178; Coordinating Committee Minutes, 14 June 1966, Office of the Secretary, Reilly, Box 179, GLIC archives.

17. Interview with James Pirtle, 6 June 2002. President's Reports, 22 July 1964, 28 November 1973, Box 43, GLIC archives.

18. Walter, *Investment Process,* 33–34, 147–48. Interview with Joseph Sargent, 30 May 2002.

19. Finance Committee Minutes, 25 April, 23 May 1951, Box 18, GLIC archives.

20. "A Petition Is Filed against Sheffield," *New York Times,* 3 June 1971; "Three Creditors File Bankruptcy Petition for Sheffield Watch," *Wall Street Journal,* 3 June 1971; "Creditors Propose Help for Sheffield," *New York Times,* 19 June 1971; "Sheffield Moratorium Set," *New York Times,* 24 June 1971. Finance Committee Minutes, 8, 15, 22 September, 24 November 1965, Box 19; Finance Committee Minutes, 23 April 1969, 24 June 1970, Box 20; Reports on the Examination of the Guardian, 1964, Box 72; Coordinating Committee Minutes, 21 September 1965, Office of the Secretary, Reilly, Box 179, GLIC archives.

21. Walter, *Investment Process,* 27. Finance Committee Minutes, 14 February 1962, Box 19; Coordinating Committee Minutes, 14 June 1966, Office of the Secretary, Reilly, Box 179, GLIC archives.

22. Conklin, "Fundamental Considerations"; McKinley, "Lending to Small Business," 291; Walter, *Investment Process,* 7, 206. Annual Report, 1963, Box 4; Finance Committee Minutes, 10 November 1960, 12 May, 10 November 1965, Box 19; 22 July, 12 August 1970, 8 September 1971, Box 20; President's Reports, 28 January 1959, 27 January 1960, Box 43; Coordinating Committee Minutes, 9 April 1963, 13 September 1966, Office of the Secretary, Reilly, Box 179, GLIC archives.

23. One of those Ph.D.'s was Paul Grundgeiger. *Guardian Life,* August 1959. Another of the Ph.D.'s was an actuary who devoted half of his time to investment issues. Walter, *Investment Process,* 147–48, 200. On the constitution of life insurance boards, see Arthur Young and Company, *Profile.*

24. Reilly, "Guardian." Interview with Joseph Sargent, 30 May 2002; interview with James Pirtle, 6 June 2002. Finance Committee Minutes, 16 January 1967, Box 19; Finance Committee Minutes, 11 August 1971, Box 20; Remarks by Ashby Bladen, Field Advisory Board Meeting Proceedings, 20 September 1974, Box 75, GLIC archives.

25. The list included Allied Chemical, Aluminum Company of America, American Telephone and Telegraph, Baltimore Gas and Electric, Bank of America, National Trust and Savings Association, Central and South West Corp., Citizens and Southern National Bank, Deere and Co., Dow Chemical, Du Pont, General Electric, General Foods, General Motors, Goodyear, International Paper, Otis Elevator, Owens-Illinois, Procter and Gamble, Safeway Stores, Sears, Roebuck, Southern California Edison, Standard Oil of California, Standard Oil of New Jersey, Union Carbide, Upjohn, Virginia Electric and Power, Warner-Lambert Pharmaceutical, Westinghouse Electric. Walter, *Investment Process,* 147–48. *Guardian Life,* March 1960. Finance Committee Minutes, 23 July 1947, Box 18; Finance Committee Minutes, 16, 25 January, 8 February 1967, Box 19; President's Reports, 25 July 1962, Box 43, GLIC archives.

26. Farrell, *Dow Jones Averages.* Finance Committee Minutes, 23 February 1967, Box 19; Finance Committee Minutes, 8 January, 26 March, 23 April, 9, 23 July, 13 August 1969, 24 March,

13 October 1971, 24 May, 27 September 1972, 28 February, 14, 28 March, 11 April, 28 November 1973, Box 20; President's Report, 25 February, 27 May 1970, Box 43, GLIC archives.

27. Malkiel, *Random Walk.* Interview with Joseph Sargent, 30 May 2002. Finance Committee Minutes, 25 June 1969, 14 June 1972, Box 20; President's Reports, 27 February 1974, Box 43, GLIC archives. Guardian Park Avenue Funds, Records of Subsidiaries, Office of the Corporate Secretary.

28. Finance Committee Minutes, 28 November 1973, 5 October 1977, Box 20; President's Report, 25 August 1976, Box 44, GLIC archives.

29. Interview with John Angle, 21 March 2002; interview with Howard Most, 6 June 2002; interview with Thomas Sorell, 6 June 2002. President's Reports, 23 August 1972, 28 February 1973, 22 August 1973, Box 43; President's Reports, 22 May, 28 August 1974, 28 February 1978, Box 44, GLIC archives.

30. Brimmer, *Life Insurance Companies in the Capital Market,* 48. Marc Hochstein, "Asset-Backed Securities Now Have New Wrinkle," *Wall Street Journal,* 8 September 1997. Real Estate Committee Minutes, 24 April, 12 June 1968, 8 January 1969, Box 37; President's Report, 26 February 1969, Box 43, GLIC archives.

31. Germania Realty Inc., Corporate Records, Organ Box 17A-#2; Annual Report, 1971, Box 4; Real Estate Committee Minutes, 14 August, 13 November 1968, Box 37; Real Estate Committee Minutes, 11 August 1971, 10 May, 8 November 1972, 9 May 1973, Box 38; President's Report, 28 May 1980, Box 44; Reports on the Examination of the Guardian, 1974, Box 187; Minutes of the Board of Directors, 27 February 1980, Box 207; Subsidiaries, Box 227, GLIC archives.

32. Conklin, "Company Investments," 1027–28. President's Report, 26 October 1966, 26 April 1967, 26 February 1969, Box 43; President's Report, 27 February 1980, Box 44; Executive Officers Committee Minutes, 7 August 1946, Box 179, GLIC archives.

33. Finance Committee Minutes, 11 March, 22 April, 22 July, 12 August, 23 September, 28 October 1970, 10 February, 9, 23 June, 28 July, 8 September 1971, Box 20; President's Report, 22 May 1974, Box 44; Reports on the Examination of the Guardian, 1974, Box 187, GLIC archives.

34. President's Report, 26 October 1966, 22 August 1973, 28 August, 27 November 1974, 29 November 1978, Box 44; Remarks by Ashby Bladen, Field Advisory Board Meeting Proceedings, 20 September 1974, Box 75; Coordinating Committee Minutes, 10 March 1964, Office of the Secretary, Reilly, Box 179; John C. Angle to Robert D. Shapiro, 19 May 1986, Office of the President, Angle, Box 201, GLIC archives.

35. Finance Committee Minutes, 9 April 1969, Box 20; Minutes of the Board of Directors, 25 February 1981, Box 207, GLIC archives.

36. Leonard Silk, "Inflation: The Mood Turns Foul," *New York Times,* 22 May 1974.

37. Reilly, "Guardian." Interview with John Angle, 21 March 2002. John C. Angle, "Guardian Life: 1981 General Agents Conference, Closing Address," 23 January 1981, Office of the President, Angle, Box 195, GLIC archives.

38. President's Report, 22 August 1973, 27 February 1974, 22 August 1979, Box 44, GLIC archives.

39. Albers joined the company 25 January 1971. He was appointed assistant financial secretary in early 1973. "Author of Financial Gloom Book Runs Guardian Life Portfolio," *Wall Street Journal,* 27 January 1981. Interview with Ashby Bladen, 6 June 2002. Minutes of the Board of Directors, 26 May 1971, 20 December 1972, Box 206, GLIC archives.

40. "Actions based on decisions arrived at in Board and Committee meetings, while not requiring a unanimous vote, are rarely, if ever, taken without such a vote, and this applies particularly to the actions of the Finance Committee regarding investment of the Company's funds." Walter, *Investment Process,* 147–48. *Service,* January 1954. Annual Report, 1940, Box 2; Minutes of the Board of Directors, 28 October 1953, Box 6; Finance Committee Minutes, 13 October, 24 November 1971, 26 April, 14 June, 26 July, 25 October 1972, 12 December 1973, 11 June 1975, Box 20; Minutes of the Board of Directors, 27 November 1974, Box 206; Minutes of the Board of Directors, 25 February 1976, Box 207, GLIC archives.

41. Interview with Ashby Bladen, 6 June 2002.

42. Annual Report, 1985, 1986, Box 1; Finance Committee Minutes, 28 April 1976, 12 January 1977, Box 20; President's Report, 26 February 1969, 23 February 1972, 28 February 1973, Box 43; President's Report, 27 November 1974, 18 May 1977, 29 November 1978, 28 February, 22 August 1979, Box 44; "The Record of the Guardian Life," Reports on the Examination of the Guardian, 1974, Box 187, GLIC archives.

43. *Pensions and Investment Age,* 14 May 1984. Interview with Leo Futia, 12 April 2002; interview with Ashby Bladen, 6 June 2002; interview with James Pirtle, 6 June 2002. Minutes of the Board of Directors, 16 December 1959, Box 6; Minutes of the Board of Directors, 28 May 1969, 23 February, 20 December 1972, Box 206; Minutes of the Board of Directors, 26 August 1981, Box 207, GLIC archives.

44. "Who's News," *Wall Street Journal,* 23 August 1991. *Guardian Scene,* Fall 2002.

45. Interview with Frank Jones, 30 November 2001, 6 June 2002.

46. "How to Choose a Life Insurance Company," Executive Presentation Client's Guide, 2001, GLIC archives.

47. Interview with Howard Most, 6 June 2002; interview with Thomas Sorell, 6 June 2002. Annual Report, 1980, Box 4; John C. Angle to Robert D. Shapiro, 19 May 1986, Office of the President, Angle, Box 201, GLIC archives.

48. Jones, Charles P., *Investments,* 390.

49. Interview with Howard Most, 6 June 2002; interview with Thomas Sorell, 6 June 2002.

50. Davis, E. Philip, "Portfolio Regulation." Interview with Frank Jones, 30 November 2001. Annual Report, 1987, 2001, Box 1; Reports on the Examination of the Guardian, 1911, Box 70, GLIC archives.

51. *Economic and Social Contributions of Life Insurance,* 25–30; Dix, "Life Insurance Investments," 16; Drummond, "Canadian Life Insurance"; Hood and Main, "Canadian Life Insurance Companies"; Life Insurance Association of America, *Life Insurance*; Oates, *Business and Social Change,* 50–51; Pritchett, *Capital Mobilization,* 1–2.

52. Brimmer, *Life Insurance Companies in the Capital Market,* 40; Clough, *Mutual Life Insurance Company of New York,* 338. *Guardian Life,* March 1960. Annual Report, 1952, Box 3, GLIC archives.

53. Badger, "Unusual Features of Life Insurance Investing," 79; Brimmer, *Life Insurance Companies in the Capital Market,* 32; Fulcher, "Life Insurance Saving"; Geren, "Contribution of Life Insurance," 34, 42, 48–50; Krooss and Blyn, *History of Financial Intermediaries,* 236–37; Leung, "Why Do Some Households Save So Little?"; Loewry, "The Flow of Net Cash Savings"; Sullivan, "Life Insurance," 360; Wright, Kenneth, "Gross Flows of Funds."

54. Diamond, "Economic Impact." Finance Committee Minutes, 21 April 1915, Box 15; Finance Committee Minutes, 13 March 1935, 19 May 1937, Box 16, GLIC archives.

55. McKinley, "Lending to Small Business," 291; Ricks, "Imputed Equity Returns," 921. Mitchell Gordon, "Insurance Companies, Banks, Pension Funds Provide Money for Vessels," *Wall Street Journal,* 22 January 1957. *Guardian Life,* March 1960; *Guardian Scene,* March 1963. Annual Report, 1956, Box 3; Finance Committee Minutes, 9 June 1965, Box 19; Real Estate Committee Minutes, 25 October, 13 December 1972, Box 38; Coordinating Committee Minutes, 9 June, 11 August 1964, Office of the Secretary, Reilly, Box 179, GLIC archives.

56. Krooss and Blyn, *History of Financial Intermediaries,* 144. Annual Report, 1950, 1952, Box 3; Finance Committee Minutes, 22 May, 11, 26 December 1946, 11 February 1947, 28 September 1949, Box 18; Finance Committee Minutes, 26 January 1955, Box 19; Minutes of the Board of Directors, 23 February 1977, Box 207, GLIC archives.

57. Brimmer, *Life Insurance Companies in the Capital Market,* 325–28; Conklin, "Direct Placements"; McKinley, "Lending to Small Business."

58. "Four Insurers to Lend $8 Million to Finance Venezuelan Apartments," *Wall Street Journal,* 20 July 1966; "Insurers Join A.I.D. on Honduras Loan," *New York Times,* 17 June 1969. Coordinating Committee Minutes, 10 November 1964, Office of the Secretary, Reilly, Box 179, GLIC archives.

59. Brimmer, *Life Insurance Companies in the Capital Market,* 15, 218; Haeger, "Eastern Fi-

nanciers"; McKinley, "Lending to Small Business," 291–92; Orren, *Corporate Power,* 149. Annual Report, 1952, Box 3, GLIC archives.

60. Camp, *Liberty National Life,* 93. Real Estate Committee Minutes, 9 August, 13 September 1967, Box 37, GLIC archives.

NOTES TO PART IV

1. Failure here means *involuntary* liquidation, receivership, conservatorship, cease-and-desist order, suspension, license revocation, administrative order, or regulatory supervision.

2. Interview with Joseph Sargent, 30 May 2002.

3. Babbel, "Price Elasticity of Demand," 235; McDowell, *Deregulation and Competition*; Walker, *Guaranteed Investment Contracts,* 58; Winter, "On the Rate Structure," 88–89. Interview with Joseph Sargent, 30 May 2002; interview with Joseph Caruso, 21 August 2002. Executive Officers Committee Minutes, 18 February 1941, Box 178, GLIC archives.

4. Ourusoff and Meschi, "Staying Power," 52–53. Interview with Robert Ryan, 22 March 2002; interview with Joseph Sargent, 30 May 2002.

5. For a good summary of insurance rating companies, see Walker, *Guaranteed Investment Contracts.* Rodney Clark and Mark Puccia, "Summary: Guardian Life Insurance Co. of America," Standard and Poor's Ratings Services, 29 May 2002. "How to Choose a Life Insurance Company," Executive Presentation Client's Guide, 2001; Minutes of the Board of Directors, 25 September 1996, Office of the Corporate Secretary.

6. Clough, *Mutual Life Insurance Company of New York,* 319.

NOTES TO CHAPTER 14

1. Spector, *Law and Practice.*

2. American Bar Association, *Reference Handbook on Insurance Company Insolvency,* 52–81; Spector, *Law and Practice.*

3. Kohn, *Money, Banking*; McDowell, *Deregulation and Competition*; Modugno, *Broken Promises*; Spector, *Law and Practice.*

4. *Home Life Insurance Company.* Minutes of the Board of Directors, 23 September 1992, 17 November 1993, Office of the Corporate Secretary.

5. Grant, *Insurance Reform,* 8; Lencsis, *Insurance Regulation,* 108; North, "Capital Accumulation," 247.

6. Demand for life insurance, many believe, follows an S-shaped curve when GDP per capita is plotted against premium volume as a percentage of GDP. In other words, as depicted in figure 14-1, demand for insurance in poor economies is quite low. As economies grow richer, demand for insurance increases more rapidly than income, forcing premiums as a percentage of GDP to rise. But at some point, apparently reached by the United States in the 1980s, demand for life insurance slackens. In this final phase, the top part of the S-curve, people demand more insurance in absolute terms as they grow richer, but insurance does not increase as a percentage of people's income. In the terms of economists, insurance in very poor and very rich economies has an income elasticity of about one. In middle-income economies, by contrast, consumption of insurance grows at a faster rate than income. Pearson, "Growth, Crisis."

7. Berry and Tuohy, *1993 Life Insurance Industry CEO Survey.* Minutes of the Board of Directors, 30 November 1994, Office of the Corporate Secretary.

8. John C. Angle, "Chairman's Address and Report on Progress during 1984," 27 February 1985, Office of the President, Angle, Box 201, GLIC archives.

9. John C. Angle, "The State of the Life Insurance Industry," 27 September 1988, Office of the President, Angle, Box 201, GLIC archives. Minutes of the Board of Directors, 25 April 2001, Office of the Corporate Secretary.

10. Minutes of the Board of Directors, 22 May 1996; PALIC, Records of Subsidiaries; Family Services Life Insurance Corporation, Records of Subsidiaries, Office of the Corporate Secretary.

11. Slattery, "Manning." PAS, Records of Subsidiaries, Office of the Corporate Secretary.

12. Interview with John Angle, 21 March 2002; interview with Art Ferrara, 2 May 2002. John C. Angle, "The State of the Life Insurance Industry," 27 September 1988, Office of the President, Angle, Box 201; interview with Irving Rosenthal, 6 July 1984, Box 250, GLIC archives. Minutes of the Board of Directors, 22 May 1996; Records of Subsidiaries, Office of the Corporate Secretary.

13. Minutes of the Board of Directors, 2 December 1992, 26 May 1993; GAMCORP, Records of Subsidiaries, Office of the Corporate Secretary.

14. Interview with Bruce Long, 30 November 2001. Minutes of the Board of Directors, 30 November 1994, 24 April 2002, Office of the Corporate Secretary.

15. Minutes of the Board of Directors, 28 February, 25 April 2001, Office of the Corporate Secretary.

16. Interview with Armand de Palo, 27 January 2003. Group Advisory Committee Minutes, 5 February 1960, Office of the Executive Vice President, Rosenthal, Box 183, GLIC archives.

17. Interview with Joseph Sargent, 25 March, 11 April 2003.

18. "Guardian Life Insurance Co. of America: Broker-Dealer United Planned for Life-Insurance Clients," *Wall Street Journal,* 3 May 1999; Bridget O'Brian, "Fund Track: Investors Hold Bank on Stock Funds in June," *Wall Street Journal,* 31 July 2001.

19. Interview with Dennis Manning, 1 December 2001; interview with Robert Ryan, 22 March 2002. John C. Angle, "Opening at Skytop," 1985, Office of the President, Angle, Box 201, GLIC archives. Minutes of the Board of Directors, 3 December 1997, Office of the Corporate Secretary.

20. "Grahame Talks on Mutuality Phases," *New York Journal of Commerce,* 5 June 1939. Orville F. Grahame, "Introduction to Mutuality," 1939, Office of the Cashier, Hahn, Box 69, GLIC archives.

21. Arthur Young and Company, *Profile of the Chief Executive Officer.* Minutes of the Board of Directors, 28 February 1996, 28 February, 25 April 2001, Office of the Corporate Secretary.

22. Arthur Young and Company, *Profile of the Chief Executive Officer.* Interview with Ed Kane, 30 November 2001; interview with Dennis Manning, 1 December 2001; interview with Art Ferrara, 2 May 2002. Minutes of the Board of Directors, 27 May 1992, Office of the Corporate Secretary.

23. Interview with John Angle, 21 March 2002; interview with Leo Futia, 12 April 2002. "Special Committee" Minutes, 9 July 1862, Box 125; John C. Angle, "Have We Gone Full Circle?" 12 May 1977, John C. Angle, "Golden Opportunities," 21 January 1984, Office of the President, Angle, Box 195, GLIC archives.

24. Walker et al., "Business Risks and Controls at Prudential."

25. Annual Report, 1951, Box 3, GLIC archives.

26. Interview with Frank Jones, 30 November 2001.

27. *Home Office Newsletter,* 15 January 1954. Interview with Joseph Caruso, 30 November 2001; interview with Art Ferrara, 2 May 2002. Field Advisory Board Meeting Proceedings, 9 February 1961, 17 November 1966, 27 April 1967, Box 75; Tom Quinn interview with Anthony Peloso, Director of Group Administration, n.d., Tom Quinn interview with Helen Sulyma, 2-9 Group Underwriting Department Manager, n.d., Tom Quinn interview with Howard Abel, n.d., Tom Quinn interview with Anthony Peloso, Director of Group Administration, n.d., Office of the President, Angle, Box 197, GLIC archives.

28. *Proceedings of the Fifty-Fourth Annual Meeting of Life Insurance Association of America,* 1960, 184; Wallison, *Federal Chartering,* 66.

29. Interview with Irving Rosenthal, 6 July 1984, Box 250, GLIC archives.

30. "1,700 Top Executives," *Fortune* (November 1959): 138–43.

31. We used two sources of data. First, we used compensation exhibits in documents filed by public companies with the Securities and Exchange Commission ("SEC"). The exhibits show six dollar items: salary, bonus, "other annual compensation," "restricted stock awards," "long-term incentive plan payouts," and "all other compensation." We used the sum of those items. We did not include the value of "securities underlying stock options" or the value of "option grants in 2001." Second, we used compensation exhibits filed with the Nebraska insurance department by companies doing business in the state. The exhibits show salary, bonus, "all other compensation," and the sum of those items. We used the sum. *The Insurance Forum*, July 2002.

32. *The Insurance Forum*, July 2002. See also Sclafane, "Top Dogs Get Top Dollars"; "CEO's Pay Jumps in 2000," *Business Insurance*, 3 September 2001. Interview with Dennis Manning, 1 December 2001.

33. Interview with Don Sullivan, 22 March 2002. Coordinating Committee Minutes, 11 April 1961, Office of the Secretary, Reilly, Box 179; "The Record of The Guardian Life," Reports on the Examination of the Guardian, 1974, Box 187; John Angle interview with Irving Rosenthal, 26 February 1982, Tom Quinn interview with Leo Futia, 4 April 1982, Office of the President, Angle, Box 197, GLIC archives.

34. *Proceedings of the Fifty-Fourth Annual Meeting of Life Insurance Association of America*, 1960, 190–94. Interview with Bruce Long, 30 November 2001; interview with Robert Ryan, 22 March 2002.

35. Mayers and Smith, "Executive Compensation." But see also Wilson and Higgins, "CEO Pay/Firm Performance."

36. Hansman and Larrabee, *Deferred Compensation*. Deferred Compensation Agreements, Organ Box 17A-#1; Reports on the Examination of the Guardian, 1964, Box 72; Minutes of the Board of Directors, 17 December 1969, 27 November 1974, Box 206, GLIC archives.

37. Galarza-Vega, "Executive Compensation"; Tauber, *Executive Compensation 1984*.

38. Bell, "Executive Compensation." Interview with Joseph Sargent, 30 May 2002; interview with Armand de Palo, 27 January 2003.

39. Interview with Joseph Sargent, 30 May 2002. "The Guardian Life Insurance Company of America Long-Term Incentive Compensation Plan for Senior Officers," 1 April 1999, 1 January 2002, Office of the Corporate Secretary.

40. Interview with Joseph Caruso, 30 November 2001. Minutes of the Board of Directors, 14 November 2001, Office of the Corporate Secretary.

41. Interview with Frank Jones, 30 November 2001; interview with Armand de Palo, 27 January 2003. Minutes of the Board of Directors, 22 September 1999, 13 December 2000, 28 February, 25 April 2001, Office of the Corporate Secretary.

42. Pearson, "Mutuality Tested"; Zartman, "Control of Life Insurance Companies," 531. John C. Angle, "Chairman's Address and Report on Progress during 1984," 27 February 1985, Office of the President, Angle, Box 201, GLIC archives.

43. Berry and Tuohy, "1993 Life Insurance Industry CEO Survey." Interview with Armand de Palo, 27 January 2003. Irving Rosenthal to Murray Krowitz, 28 September 1972, Office of the Executive Vice President, Rosenthal, Box 183, John C. Angle, "At the Top," 21 January 1987, Office of the President, Angle, Box 201, GLIC archives.

44. Insurance-portal.com, 16 May 2002; *The Insurance Forum*, August 2002. Interview with Joseph Caruso, 30 November 2001; interview with Frank Jones, 30 November 2001; interview with Ed Kane, 22 February 2002; interview with Armand de Palo, 27 January 2003. John C. Angle to Robert D. Shapiro, 19 May 1986, Office of the President, Angle, Box 201, GLIC archives.

45. Clough, *Mutual Life Insurance Company of New York*, 96; Lencsis, *Insurance Regulation*, 85. Interview with Joseph Caruso, 30 November 2001; interview with Ed Kane, 30 November 2001; interview with John Angle, 21 March 2002; interview with Robert Ryan, 22 March 2002; interview with Armand de Palo, 27 January 2003.

46. Thompson, "When Is Ownership?" Peter Keating, "Whose Company Is It, Anyway?" *Money Magazine,* 1 October 1998; "A Big Payday for Six Departing Executives of Provident Mutual," *The Insurance Forum,* August 2002. Interview with Armand de Palo, 27 January 2003.

47. Insurance-portal.com, 16 May 2002. Conning Research, *Demutualization,* 2003.

48. Cornett and De, "Medium of Payment"; Martin, "Method of Payment"; Servaes and Zenner, "Role of Investment Banks"; Walker, *Guaranteed Investment Contracts,* 9. Interview with Gary Lenderink, 7 December 2001; interview with Joseph Sargent, 30 May 2002; interview with Armand de Palo, 27 January 2003. John C. Angle, "Golden Opportunities," 21 January 1984, Office of the President, Angle, Box 195, GLIC archives. Fiduciary Insurance Company of America, Records of Subsidiaries, Minutes of the Board of Directors, 26 July, 29 August 2000, 25 April 2001, Office of the Corporate Secretary.

49. Mathewson, "Information," 145–47. Interview with Armand de Palo, 27 January 2003. John C. Angle, "Golden Opportunities," 21 January 1984, John C. Angle, "Chairman's Address and Report on Progress during 1984," 27 February 1985, Office of the President, Angle, Box 201, GLIC archives. Minutes of the Board of Directors, 30 November 1994, 13 December 2000, 25 July, 14 November 2001, Office of the Corporate Secretary.

50. Interview with Frank Jones, 30 November 2001. Minutes of the Board of Directors, 28 January 1998, Office of the Corporate Secretary.

51. Slattery, "Manning." Interview with Joseph Sargent, 30 May 2002. Minutes of the Board of Directors, 27 September, 13 December 2000, Joseph Sargent, President's Report, 28 February 2001, Office of the Corporate Secretary.

52. *Guardian Scene,* December 1965, January–February 1966, Fall 2002. Interview with Joseph Sargent, 30 May 2002. Annual Report, 2001, Office of the Corporate Secretary.

53. Minutes of the Board of Directors, 19 September, 24 October 2001, Office of the Corporate Secretary.

54. Minutes of the Board of Directors, 19 September 2001, Office of the Corporate Secretary.

55. Minutes of the Board of Directors, 13 December 2000, Office of the Corporate Secretary.

56. "How to Choose a Life Insurance Company," Executive President Client's Guide, 2001, GLIC archives.

57. Interview with Bruce Long, 30 November 2001; interview with Dennis Manning, 1 December 2001. Minutes of the Board of Directors, 24 October 2001, 24 April 2002, Office of the Corporate Secretary.

58. Slattery, "Manning." Minutes of the Board of Directors, 3 December 1997, Office of the Corporate Secretary.

59. Interview with John Angle, 22 March 2002; interview with Joseph Sargent, 30 May 2002. BLICOA, Records of Subsidiaries, Office of the Corporate Secretary.

60. "Making It Simpler to Ring Up More Life Insurance Sales," *Insurance Letter,* 23 July 2002. Interview with Joseph Sargent, 30 May 2002.

61. Pearson, "Growth, Crisis." Interview with Joseph Sargent, 30 May 2002. Minutes of the Board of Directors, 15 December 1999, Office of the Corporate Secretary.

62. The extent of the problem currently is thought to be low but is not known with precision. Harper, "Genetic Testing"; Ridley, *Genome,* 267–68; Shepherd, "Principals and Problems." Interview with Joseph Caruso, 21 August 2002; interview with Armand de Palo, 27 January 2003. "AIDS: An Actuarial Perspective," August 1987, Group Actuarial Division, Box 202, GLIC archives.

63. Interview with Joseph Caruso, 21 August 2002; interview with Armand de Palo, 27 January 2003.

64. Interview with Joseph Caruso, 21 August 2002; interview with Armand de Palo, 27 January 2003. Wallison, *Federal Chartering*; Lencsis, *Insurance Regulation.*

65. Interview with Armand de Palo, 27 January 2003.

66. Some studies have suggested that risks can be reduced (or returns increased without

increasing risk) by combining banks, brokerages, and insurers. The real-world experience of CitiGroup, however, may suggest otherwise. Similarly, some international mergers of financial giants seem to have been profitable, but studies suggest that scale diseconomies lurk in the shadows, ready to pounce. For a recent overview of these issues, see Berger et al., "Globalization of Financial Institutions." Pearson, "Growth, Crisis." Interview with Joseph Caruso, 21 August 2002. Field Advisory Board Meeting Proceedings, 13 September 1973, Box 75, GLIC archives.

Bibliography

Primary Sources

Archival Materials

Guardian Life Insurance Company of America, Archives, 7 Hanover Square, New York, New York
Annual Reports (for policyholders)
Annual Statements ("Convention Blanks," for regulators)
Circulars
Claim Department Records
Executive Officers Committee Minutes
Executive Presentation Client's Guide
Field Advisory Board Meeting Proceedings
Finance Committee Minutes
History Files, John C. Angle
Home Office Records
Legal Department Records
Manuals
Minutes of the Board of Directors
Office of the Assistant Actuary, Lubin
Office of the Assistant Secretary, Meidt
Office of the Cashier, Hahn
Office of the Executive Vice President, Rosenthal
Office of the President, Angle
Office of the President, Cameron
Office of the President, Doremus
Office of the President, Heye
Office of the Secretary, Burrell
Office of the Secretary, Heye and Neuendorffer
Office of the Secretary, Reilly
Office of the Secretary, Scott
Office of the Vice President and Actuary, Barnsley
Office of the Vice President and Agency Managers, Hansen
Personnel Department Records
President's Reports (to the Board of Directors)
Public Relations Department Records
Real Estate Committee Minutes
Reports on the Examination of the Guardian
"Special Committee" Minutes
Stockholders Records
Subsidiaries

TNEC Records

Guardian Life Insurance Company of America, Office of the Corporate Secretary, 7 Hanover
  Square, New York, New York
    Minutes of the Board of Directors
    Records of Subsidiaries

New York Historical Society Library, 2 West Seventy-Seventh Street, New York, New York
    Benjamin Rushmore Papers, 1815–17
    Bergen Turnpike Company Papers, 1804–35
    Isaac Van Scoy Papers, 1831–32
    Robert Stewart Buchanan Papers
    Walter E. Stephens Papers, 1831–36

W. H. Smith Memorial Library, Indiana Historical Society, 450 West Ohio Street, Indianapolis, Indiana
    Winfield K. Denton Papers

Oral Interviews

Angle, John, 21 March 2002
Bladen, Ashby, 6 June 2002
Caruso, Joseph, 30 November 2001; 21 August 2002
de Palo, Armand, 27 January 2003
Evraets, Robert, 22 March 2002
Ferrara, Arthur, 2 May 2002
Futia, Leo, 12 April 2002
Jones, Frank, 30 November 2001; 6 June 2002
Kane, Ed, 30 November 2001; 22 February 2002
Klain, Ruth, 3 April 2003
Kramer, Doug, 3 April 2003
Larson, Eric, 6 June 2002
Lenderink, Gary, 7 December 2001
Long, Bruce, 30 November 2001
Manning, Dennis, 1 December 2001
Most, Howard, 6 June 2002
Pirtle, James, 6 June 2002
Ryan, Robert, 22 March 2002
Sargent, Joseph, 30 May 2002; 25 March 2003; 11 April 2003
Sorell, Thomas, 6 June 2002
Sullivan, Don, 22 March 2002

Published Sources
Periodicals

Actuary
ARGHOE (Association of Retired Guardian Home Office Employees) (Guardian)
Best's Insurance News
Bond (Guardian)
Business Week
Chicago Evening Post
Collier's
Flitcraft's Compend
Guardian (Guardian)
Guardian Family News (Guardian)

Guardian Life (Guardian)
Guardian Life Service (Guardian)
Guardian Scene (Guardian)
Guardian Service (Guardian)
Home Office Newsletter (Guardian)
Insurance Forum
Insurance Monitor
Life Insurance Fact Book
Newsletter (Guardian)
New York Times
Proceedings of the Life Insurance Association of America
Service (Guardian)
TheStreet.com
Wall Street Journal

Books and Articles

Abbott, Lawrence. *The Story of NYLIC: A History of the Origin and Development of the New York Life Insurance Company from 1845 to 1929.* New York: New York Life Insurance Company, 1930.

Adams, Thomas. "Increase of Public Expenditures and Taxes." *Proceedings of the Tenth Annual Meeting of Life Insurance Association of America.* New York: 1916.

"Adoption of the Statement on the Monetary Problem." *Proceedings of the Twenty-Seventh Annual Convention of the Association of Life Insurance Presidents.* New York: 1933.

American Bar Association. *Reference Handbook on Insurance Company Insolvency.* Chicago: 1986.

Angle, John C., and John J. McCuistion. "Risk Selection and Substandard Risks," in *Life and Health Insurance Handbook,* 3rd ed., Davis Gregg and Vane Lucas, eds. Homewood, Ill.: Richard D. Irwin, 1973: 333–47.

Annis, Edward R. "Recent Advances in Medicine." *Proceedings of the Fifty-Eighth Annual Meeting of Life Insurance Association of America.* New York: 1964.

Arthur Young and Company. *Profile of the Chief Executive Officer and Boards of Directors of Life Insurance Companies.* Life Office Management Association, 1983.

Axelson, C. F. "Opportunities in Life Insurance Salemanship for a College Graduate." *University Journal of Business* 5 (1927): 88–105.

Babbel, David. "The Price Elasticity of Demand for Whole Life Insurance." *Journal of Finance* 40 (1985): 225–39.

Babbel, David, and Kim Staking. "A Capital Budgeting Analysis of Life Insurance Costs in the United States: 1950–1979." *Journal of Finance* 38 (1983): 149–70.

Badger, Sherwin. "Unusual Features of Life Insurance Investing." *Journal of Finance* 6 (1951): 77–84.

Baker, George, and George David Smith. *The New Financial Capitalists: Kohlberg Kravis Roberts and the Creation of Corporate Value.* New York: Cambridge University Press, 1998.

Beers, Henry. "The Growing Field of Group Coverages," in *Life Insurance Trends at Mid-Century,* David McCahan, ed. Philadelphia: University of Pennsylvania Press, 1950: 133–55.

Beito, David T. *From Mutual Aid to the Welfare State: Fraternal Societies and Social Services, 1890–1967.* Chapel Hill: University of North Carolina Press, 2000.

Bell, Jill. "Executive Compensation: The New Philosophy Revisited." *Resource* (April 1991): 32–34.

Berger, Allen, Robert DeYoung, Hesna Genay, and Gregory Udell. "Globalization of Financial Institutions: Evidence from Cross-Border Banking Performance." *Brookings-Wharton Papers on Financial Services* (2000): 23–158.

Bernheim, B. Douglas. "How Strong Are Bequest Motives? Evidence Based on Estimates of the Demand for Life Insurance and Annuities." *Journal of Political Economy* 99 (1991): 899–927.

Berry, Richard, and Michale Tuohy. *1993 Life Insurance Industry CEO Survey.* New York: Towers Perrin, 1993.

Bixby, W. E. *Kansas City Life Insurance Company: Since 1895 . . . One Hundred Years of Quality Service.* New York: Newcomen Society of the United States, 1996.

Black, Kenneth, and Harold Skipper. *Life Insurance.* Englewood Cliffs, N.J.: Prentice Hall, 1988.

Blackburn, Thomas. "State Taxation of Life Insurance." *Proceedings of the Fourteenth Annual Meeting of Life Insurance Association of America.* New York: 1920.

Boney, Dan C. "The Public Service of Insurance Supervision." *Proceedings of the Twenty-Eighth Annual Convention of the Association of Life Insurance Presidents.* New York: 1934.

Bosch-Domench, Antoni, and Joaquim Silvestre. "Does Risk Aversion or Attraction Depend on Income?" *Economics Letters* 65 (1999): 265–73.

Breiling, Louis. "Policyholders' Contribution to Agricultural Readjustment." *Proceedings of the Thirteenth Annual Meeting of Life Insurance Association of America.* New York: 1919.

Brimmer, Andrew. *Life Insurance Companies in the Capital Market.* East Lansing: Michigan State University Press, 1962.

Buck, Wendell. *From Quill Pens to Computers: An Account of the First One Hundred and Twenty-Five Years of the Manhattan Life Insurance Company of New York, N.Y.* New York: Manhattan Life Insurance Company, 1975.

Buley, R. Carlyle. *The American Life Convention, 1906–1952: A Study in the History of Life Insurance.* New York: Appleton-Century-Crofts, 1953.

Burkholder, J. Peter. "Ives, Charles." *The New Grove Dictionary of Music.* Online ed. (Accessed 10 December 2002), http://www.grovemusic.com.

Call, Asa. "The Policyholder's Stake in Sound Economics." *Proceedings of the Forty-Third Annual Meeting of the Life Insurance Association of America.* New York: 1949.

Camp, Ehney. *A History of the Investment Division of Liberty National Life Insurance Company.* Tuscaloosa: University of Alabama Press, 1978.

Campbell, J. A. "Mortality Tables in Life Insurance Management." *Canadian Journal of Economics and Political Science* 6 (1940): 424–39.

Campbell, Ritchie. "The Demand for Life Insurance: An Application of the Economics of Uncertainty." *Journal of Finance* 35 (1980): 1155–72.

Carosso, Vincent. *Investment Banking in America.* Cambridge: Harvard University Press, 1970.

Carr, Jack L., and G. F. Mathewson. "Unlimited Liability as a Barrier to Entry." *Journal of Political Economy* 96 (1988): 766–84.

Chen, Carl, Thomas Steiner, and Ann White. "Risk-Taking Behaviour and Managerial Ownership in the United States Life Insurance Industry." *Applied Financial Economics* 11 (2001): 165–71.

Clark, Jesse. "Rural Credit Problems." *Proceedings of the Ninth Annual Meeting of Life Insurance Association of America.* New York: 1915.

Clark, Rodney, and Mark Puccia. "Summary: Guardian Life Insurance Co. of America," Standard and Poor's Ratings Services, 29 May 2002.

Clough, Shepard. *A Century of American Life Insurance: A History of the Mutual Life Insurance Company of New York, 1843–1943.* Westport, Conn.: Greenwood Press, 1970.

Collier, Abram. *A Capital Ship: New England Life, a History of America's First Chartered Mutual Life Insurance Company, 1835–1985.* Boston: New England Mutual Life Insurance Company, 1985.

Collins, R. G. Rowland. "The Responsibility of Top Management for Employee Education." *Proceedings of the Forty-Second Annual Meeting of the Life Insurance Association of America.* New York: 1948.

Conard, Joseph W. *The Behavior of Interest Rates: A Progress Report.* New York: Columbia University Press, 1966.

Conklin, George T., Jr. "Direct Placements." *Journal of Finance* 6 (1951): 85–118.

——. "A Century of Life Insurance Portfolio Management," in *Investment of Life Insurance Funds,* David McCahan, ed. Philadelphia: University of Pennsylvania Press, 1953: 246–88.

——. "Some Fundamental Considerations of Investment Policy." *American Life Convention, 1954* (1954): 312–19.

——. "Company Investments," in *Life and Health Insurance Handbook,* 3rd ed., Davis Gregg and Vane Lucas, eds. Homewood, Ill.: Richard D. Irwin, 1973: 1022–35.

Conning Research and Consulting. *Life Insurance Demutualization: An Interim Report Card.* 2003.

Cornett, Marcia, and Sankar De. "Medium of Payment in Corporate Acquisitions: Evidence from Interstate Bank Mergers." *Journal of Money, Credit, and Banking* 23 (1991): 767–76.

Cox, Berkeley. "Activities of All-Industry Committee." *Proceedings of the Thirty-Eighth, Thirty-Ninth, and Fortieth Annual Meetings (including 1946 Spring Meeting) of the Life Insurance Association of America.* New York: 1946.

Cox, Guy. "Life Insurance Investments: A Material Resource of American Foresight." *Proceedings of the Thirtieth Annual Convention of the Association of Life Insurance Presidents.* New York: 1936.

Cox, Robert Lynn. "National Health in the Life Insurance Mirror." *Proceedings of the Fifteenth Annual Meeting of Life Insurance Association of America.* New York: 1921.

——. "Statutory Direction of Life Insurance Investments, with Special Reference to the Robertson Law of Texas." *Proceedings of the Eighteenth Annual Meeting of Life Insurance Association of America.* New York: 1924.

Cragin, Donald. "Medical Preparedness." *Proceedings of the Thirty-Fourth Annual Convention of the Association of Life Insurance Presidents.* New York: 1940.

Davis, E. Philip. "Portfolio Regulation of Life Insurance Companies and Pension Funds." *Financial Market Trends* 80 (2001): 133–89.

Davis, Frank. "Broadcasting Economic Freedom." *Proceedings of the Twenty-First Annual Meeting of Life Insurance Association of America.* New York: 1927.

Davis, Malvin E. *Industrial Insurance in the United States.* New York: McGraw-Hill, 1944.

——. "Modern Industrial Life Insurance," in *Life Insurance Trends at Mid-Century,* David McCahan, ed. Philadelphia: University of Pennsylvania Press, 1950: 115–32.

Davis, William. "The Menace of Taxation to Life Insurance." *Proceedings of the Nineteenth Annual Meeting of Life Insurance Association of America.* New York: 1925.

Day, W. A. "The Significance of the Increasing Volume of Life Insurance." *Proceedings of the Thirteenth Annual Meeting of Life Insurance Association of America.* New York: 1919.

de Palo, Armand. *Advanced Policyowner Dividend Study Note.* Schaumburg, Ill.: Society of Actuaries, 1997.

Diamond, Daniel. "The Economic Impact of Life Insurance Investments on the American Economy." Ph.D. diss., New York University, 1958.

Dix, William F. "The Relation of Life Insurance Investments to City Development." *Proceedings of the Ninth Annual Meeting of Life Insurance Association of America.* New York: 1915.

Douglass, Elisha P. *The Coming of Age of American Business.* Chapel Hill: University of North Carolina Press, 1971.

Drucker, Peter. *The Essential Drucker: Selections from the Management Works of Peter F. Drucker.* New York: HarperCollins, 2001.

Drummond, Ian. "Canadian Life Insurance Companies and the Capital Market, 1890–1914." *Canadian Journal of Economics and Political Science* 28 (1962): 204–24.

Ecker, Frederick. "The Problem of Housing the American People." *Proceedings of the Thirteenth Annual Meeting of Life Insurance Association of America.* New York: 1919.

——. "Stabilizing Life through Life Insurance." *Proceedings of the Twenty-Third Annual Meeting of Life Insurance Association of America.* New York: 1929.

Economic and Social Contributions of Life Insurance to the Nation, The. New York, N.Y.: Institute of Life Insurance, 1959.

Ellsworth, Frank. "The Progress of Life Insurance through Constructive Regulation." *Proceedings of the Fourteenth Annual Meeting of Life Insurance Association of America.* New York: 1920.

Fama, Eugene. "Agency Problems and the Theory of the Firm." *Journal of Political Economy* 88 (1980): 288–307.

Farrell, Maurice, ed. *The Dow Jones Averages, 1885–1970.* New York: Dow Jones, 1972.

Feder, Stuart. *Charles Ives, "My Father's Song": A Psychoanalytic Biography.* New Haven, Conn.: Yale University Press, 1992.

Fischer, Stanley. "A Life Cycle Model of Life Insurance Policies." *International Economic Review* 14 (1973): 132–52.

Fisher, Franklin M., James W. McKie, and Richard B. Mancke. *IBM and the U.S. Data Processing Industry: An Economic History.* New York: Praeger, 1983.

Fiske, Haley. "Life Insurance Investments: What, Where, and Why?" *Proceedings of the Fourteenth Annual Meeting of Life Insurance Association of America.* New York: 1920.

Flamm, Kenneth. *Creating the Computer: Government, Industry, and High Technology.* Washington, D.C.: Brookings Institute, 1988.

Fortune, Peter. "A Theory of Optimal Life Insurance: Development and Test." *Journal of Finance* 28 (1973): 587–600.

Fowler, J. A. *History of Insurance in Philadelphia for Two Centuries (1683–1882).* Philadelphia: Review Publishing and Printing Company, 1888.

Fraine, Harold G. "The Valuation of Security Holdings of Life Insurance Companies." *Journal of Finance* 6 (1951): 124–38.

———. *Valuation of Securities Holdings of Life Insurance Companies.* Homewood, Ill.: Richard D. Irwin, 1962.

Frankel, Lee. "The Increasing Automobile Hazard." *Proceedings of the Eleventh Annual Meeting of Life Insurance Association of America.* New York: 1917.

Friedman, Milton, and Anna Schwartz. *A Monetary History of the United States, 1867–1960.* Princeton, N.J.: Princeton University Press, 1963.

From the Days of Knights: A History of the American United Life Insurance Company of Indianapolis, Indiana, 1877–1977. Indianapolis: American United Life, 1977.

Fulcher, Gordon S. "Life Insurance Saving of American Families." *Review of Economic Statistics* 26 (1944): 93–94.

Galarza-Vega, Zoila. "Executive Compensation: A New Philosophy." *Resource* (November/December 1985): 43–45, 75.

Geehan, Randall. "Returns to Scale in the Life Insurance Industry." *Bell Journal of Economics* 8 (1977): 497–514.

Genovese, Eugene. "The Medical and Insurance Costs of Slaveholding in the Cotton Belt." *Journal of Negro History* 45 (1960): 141–55.

Gentry, James, and John Pike. "An Empirical Study of the Risk-Return Hypothesis Using Common Stock Portfolios of Life Insurance Companies." *Journal of Financial and Quantitative Analysis* 5 (1970): 179–85.

Gephart, W. F. "Loans on Life Insurance Policies." *American Economic Review* 4 (1914): 332–39.

Geren, Paul. "The Contribution of Life Insurance to the Savings Stream." *Journal of Political Economy* 51 (1943): 33–51.

Goldberg, Milton J. "Some Aspects of Competition." *Proceedings of the Fiftieth Annual Meeting of the Life Insurance Association of America.* New York: 1956.

Goldsmith, Raymond. *A Study of Saving in the United States.* 3 vols. Princeton, N.J.: Princeton University Press, 1955–56.

Graetz, Michael. *Life Insurance Company Taxation: The Mutual vs. Stock Differential.* Larchmont, N.Y.: Rosenfeld, Emanuel, 1986.

Grant, H. Roger. *Insurance Reform: Consumer Action in the Progressive Era.* Ames: Iowa State University Press, 1979.

Hacker, Louis. *Alexander Hamilton in the American Tradition.* New York: McGraw-Hill, 1957.

Haeger, John. "Eastern Financiers and Institutional Change: The Origins of the New York Life and Trust Company and the Ohio Life Insurance and Trust Company." *Journal of Economic History* 39 (1979): 259–73.

Halaas, E. T. "Legal Control of Life Insurance Company Investments." *Journal of Business of the University of Chicago* 5 (1932): 321–34.

Hamwi, Iskander. *Growth of Life Insurance Surrender Benefits in the United States, 1945 to 1970.* Hattiesburg, Miss.: Bureau of Business Research, 1973.

Hansman, Robert, and John Larrabee. *Deferred Compensation.* Lexington, Mass.: D.C. Heath, 1983.

Harkavy, Oscar. *Leadership for Life Insurance: The College Graduate in the Life Insurance Company Home Office.* Chapel Hill: University of North Carolina Press, 1955.

Harman, William B., Jr. "The Structure of Life Insurance Company Taxation: The New Pattern under the 1984 Act—Part I." *Journal of the American Society of CLU* 39 (1985): 56–66.

———. "The Structure of Life Insurance Company Taxation: The New Pattern under the 1984 Act—Part II." *Journal of the American Society of CLU* 39 (1985): 76–88.

Harper, P. S. "Genetic Testing, Life Insurance, and Adverse Selection." *Philosophical Transactions of the Royal Society of London* (1997): 1063–66.

Hartzel, Elmer. "A Balance Sheet of the Banking System and a Consolidated Statement of Bank and Life Insurance Company Resources." *Journal of Political Economy* 41 (1933): 673–85.

Hawfield, Michael. *Ninety Years and Growing: The Story of Lincoln National.* Indianapolis: Guild Press of Indiana, 1995.

Hedges, Joseph, and Lem Henslee. *Compensation of Life Insurance Agents.* Bloomington: Indiana School of Business, 1942.

Henderson, Alexa. *Atlanta Life Insurance Company: Guardian of Black Economic Dignity.* Tuscaloosa: University of Alabama Press, 1990.

Hickman, W. Braddock. *The Volume of Corporate Bond Financing since 1900.* Princeton, N.J.: Princeton University Press, 1953.

Higgins, Barry. "Small-Business Market for Retirement Plans Is Wide Open," *National Underwriter,* 20 August 2001: 42.

Hobbs, Charles. "Problems of Supervision in the National Emergency." *Proceedings of the Thirty-Fifth Annual Convention of the Association of Life Insurance Presidents.* New York: 1941.

Holland, Benjamin L. "Cross Currents." *Proceedings of the Fifty-First Annual Meeting of the Life Insurance Association of America.* New York: 1957.

Holtz-Eakin, Douglas, John Phillips, and Harvey Rosen. "Estate Taxes, Life Insurance, and Small Business." *Review of Economics and Statistics* 83 (2001): 52–63.

Home Life Insurance Company: A Record of Fifty Years, 1860–1910. Cambridge, Mass.: Riverside Press, 1910.

Homer, Sidney. *A History of Interest Rates.* New Brunswick, N.J.: Rutgers University Press, 1963.

Homer, Sidney, and Richard E. Sylla. *A History of Interest Rates.* 3rd ed., revised. New Brunswick, N.J.: Rutgers University Press, 1996.

Hood, William C., and O. W. Main. "The Role of Canadian Life Insurance Companies in the Post-War Capital Market." *Canadian Journal of Economics and Political Science* 22 (1956): 467–80.

Horack, Frank, W. G. Langworthy Taylor, Frederick Cleveland, Frederick Hoffman, Lewis Anderson, and William Johnson. "The Regulation of Insurance—Discussion." *Publications of the American Economic Association* 9 (1906): 189–203.

Houston, David B., and Richard M. Simon. "Economies of Scale in Financial Institutions: A Study in Life Insurance." *Econometrica* 38 (1970): 856–64.

Hudnut, James. *Semi-Centennial History of the New York Life Insurance Company, 1845–1895.* New York: New York Life Insurance Company, 1895.

Huebner, Solomon. "A New Vision in Salesmanship." *Proceedings of the Twenty-Third Annual Meeting of Life Insurance Association of America.* New York: 1929.

Huebner, Solomon, Robert Riegel, S. H. Nerlove, M. C. Rorty, H. D. Corey, J. Lloyd Mahony, and Dwight C. Rose. "Investments in Life Insurance Companies." *American Economic Review* 22 (1932): 128–36.

Hughes, Charles Evans. "The Life Insurance Enterprise from the Standpoint of the Public." *Proceedings of the Twentieth Annual Meeting of Life Insurance Association of America.* New York: 1926.

Hull, Roger. "What's Happening—What's Ahead—in the Life Insurance Business?" *Proceedings of the Fifty-Seventh Annual Meeting of Life Insurance Association of America.* New York: 1963.

Hunter, Arthur. "The Problem of the Disabled Policyholder." *Proceedings of the Nineteenth Annual Meeting of Life Insurance Association of America.* New York: 1925.

———. "Insurance of Impaired Lives and Its Economic Aspects." *Proceedings of the Twenty-Fourth Annual Convention of the Association of Life Insurance Presidents.* New York: 1930.

Hurrell, Alfred. "America First in Life Insurance." *Proceedings of the Tenth Annual Meeting of Life Insurance Association of America.* New York: 1916.

Hutcheson, William. "Life Insurance and the War." *Proceedings of the Eleventh Annual Meeting of Life Insurance Association of America.* New York: 1917.

———. "Some Facts in the Development of Life Insurance in the United States." *Proceedings of the Fourteenth Annual Meeting of Life Insurance Association of America.* New York: 1920.

Jacobsson, Per. "The International Balance of Payments Position." *Proceedings of the Fifty-Sixth Annual Meeting of Life Insurance Association of America.* New York: 1962.

Jaeger, William. "Agency Resourcefulness—A Company Resource." *Proceedings of the Twenty-Seventh Annual Convention of the Association of Life Insurance Presidents.* New York: 1933.

James, Marquis. *The Metropolitan Life: A Study in Business Growth.* New York: Viking, 1947.

John, A. H. "Insurance Investment and the London Money Market of the Eighteenth Century." *Economica* 20 (1953): 137–58.

Johnson, I. Richard, and Paul Randle. "Old Wine in New Wineskins? Evaluating New Life Insurance Products." *CPA Journal* 65 (1995): 30–36.

Johnson, William C. "The Principles Which Should Govern the Regulation of Life Insurance Companies." *Publications of the American Economic Association* (1907): 155–88.

Johnston, V. D. "The Combination of Savings Deposits and Life Insurance." *University Journal of Business* 1 (1922): 23–33.

Jones, Charles P. *Investments: Analysis and Management.* New York: John Wiley and Sons, 2002.

Jones, Homer. "Investment in Equities by Life Insurance Companies." *Journal of Finance* 5 (1950): 179–91.

Julian, Frank. "Is Supervision at the Crossroads?" *Proceedings of the Thirty-Second Annual Convention of the Association of Life Insurance Presidents.* New York: 1938.

Kacy, Howard. *A Unique and Different Company.* Princeton, N.J.: Newcomen Society, 1964.

Kalmbach, Leland J. "Chairman's Address." *Proceedings of the Fifty-Eighth Annual Meeting of Life Insurance Association of America.* New York: 1964.

Kavanaugh, James. "Advancing Social Welfare through Group Insurance." *Proceedings of the Twenty-Second Annual Meeting of Life Insurance Association of America.* New York: 1928.

Keesling, Francis. "Moral Hazard in Relation to Democracy." *Proceedings of the Thirty-Fifth Annual Convention of the Association of Life Insurance Presidents.* New York: 1941.

Keller, Morton. *The Life Insurance Enterprise, 1885–1910: A Study in the Limits of Corporate Power.* Cambridge: Harvard University Press, 1963.

Kellner, S., and G. Frank Mathewson. "Entry, Size Distribution, Scale, and Scope Economies in the Life Insurance Industry." *Journal of Business* 56 (1983): 25–44.

Kesslinger, J. M. *Guardian of a Century, 1860–1960.* New York: Guardian Life Insurance Company of America, 1960.

Ketchum, Marshall. "Can Life Insurance Companies Use Formula Plans?" *Journal of Business of the University of Chicago* 22 (1949): 30–49.

Kingsley, William. "The Farm Mortgage: The Pulse of Agricultural Health." *Proceedings of the Sixteenth Annual Meeting of Life Insurance Association of America.* New York: 1922.

Knapp, Moses. *Lectures on the Science of Life Insurance, Addressed to Families, Societies, Trades, Professions—Considerate Persons of All Classes.* Philadelphia: E. S. Jones, 1853.

Knight, Charles. "The History of Life Insurance in the United States to 1870, with an Introduction to Its Development Abroad." Ph.D. diss., University of Pennsylvania, 1920.

Kohn, Meir. *Money, Banking, and Financial Markets.* 2nd ed. New York: Dryden Press, 1993.

Kreinin, Mordechai, John Lansing, and James Morgan. "Analysis of Life Insurance Premiums." *Review of Economics and Statistics* 39 (1957): 46–54.

Krooss, Herman E., and Martin R. Blyn. *A History of Financial Intermediaries.* New York: Random House, 1971.

Lane, Carleton. *A Maine Heritage: A Brief History of Union Mutual Life Insurance Company, 1848–1968.* New York: Newcomen Society in North America, 1968.

Latto, Larry. "Federal Regulation of the Contracts Issued by Life Insurance Companies," in *The Financial Services Revolution: Understanding the Changing Role of Banks, Mutual Funds, and Insurance Companies,* Clifford Kirsch, ed. Chicago: Irwin Professional Publishing, 1997: 29–62.

Law, William. "Investment Trends and Traditions." *Proceedings of the Twenty-Fifth Annual Convention of the Association of Life Insurance Presidents.* New York: 1931.

Leffingwell, William Henry. *Office Management: Principles and Practice.* New York: McGraw Hill, 1925.

Lencsis, Peter. *Insurance Regulation in the United States: An Overview for Business and Government.* Westport, Conn.: Quorum Books, 1997.

Leung, Siu Fang. "Why Do Some Households Save So Little? A Rational Explanation." *Review of Economic Dynamics* 3 (2000): 771–800.

Lewis, Frank D. "Dependents and the Demand for Life Insurance." *American Economic Review* 79 (1989): 452–67.

Life Insurance Association of America. *Life Insurance Companies as Financial Institutions.* Englewood Cliffs, N.J.: Prentice-Hall, 1962.

Life Insurance Marketing and Research Association. *A Profile of Life Insurance Ownership in the United States.* Harford, Conn.: Life Insurance Marketing and Research Association, 1978.

Lipartito, Kenneth. "When Women Were Switches: Technology, Work, and Gender in the Telephone Industry, 1890–1920." *American Historical Review* 99 (1994): 1074–1111.

Loewry, Harris. "The Flow of Net Cash Savings through Life Insurance Companies." Ph.D. diss., University of Wisconsin, 1954.

Macey, Jonathan, and Geoffrey Miller. "Origin of the Blue Sky Laws." *Texas Law Review* 70 (1991): 347–97.

Mackie, Alexander. *Facile Princeps: The Story of the Beginning of Life Insurance in America.* Lancaster, Penn.: Presbyterian Ministers' Fund, 1956.

———. *"That Is to Say"; or, A Preacher Talks about Life Assurance.* New York: Newcomen Society, 1959.

MacLean, Joseph. *Life Insurance.* 5th ed. New York: McGraw-Hill, 1939.

———. "Development of Disability Benefits in Life Insurance Contracts" in *Life Insurance Trends at Mid-Century,* David McCahan, ed. Philadelphia: University of Pennsylvania Press, 1950: 100–114.

Mahoney, Paul. "The Origins of the Blue Sky Laws: A Test of Competing Hypotheses." *Journal of Law and Economics* 46 (2003): forthcoming.

Malkiel, Burton. *A Random Walk down Wall Street.* New York: Norton, 1973.

Manes, Alfred. "Outlines of a General Economic History of Insurance." *Journal of Business* 15 (1942): 30–48.

Marchand, Roland. *Advertising the American Dream: Making Way for Modernity, 1920–1940.* Los Angeles: University of California Press.

Martin, Kenneth. "The Method of Payment in Corporate Acquisitions, Investment Opportunities, and Management Ownership." *Journal of Finance* 51 (1996): 1227–46.

Mathewson, G. F. "Information, Search, and Price Variability of Individual Life Insurance Contracts." *Journal of Industrial Economics* 32 (1983): 131–48.

Mayers, David, and Clifford W. Smith. "Contractual Provisions, Organizational Structure, and Conflict Control in Insurance Markets." *Journal of Business* 54 (1981): 407–37.

———. "Executive Compensation in the Life Insurance Industry." *Journal of Business* 65 (1992): 51–74.

McCall, John. *A Review of Life Insurance from the Date of the First National Convention of Insurance Officials.* Milwaukee, Wis.: n.p., 1898.

McDowell, Banks. *Deregulation and Competition in the Insurance Industry.* New York: Quorum Books, 1989.

McElreath, Walter. *History of the Industrial Life and Health Insurance Company.* Atlanta, Ga.: Industrial Life and Health Insurance Company, 1935.

McIntosh, Millicent C. "Life Insurance and the Modern Woman." *Proceedings of the Forty-Sixth Annual Meeting of the Life Insurance Association of America.* New York: 1952.

McKinley, Gordon W. "Life Insurance Company Lending to Small Business." *Journal of Finance* 16 (1961): 291–303.

McLain, James. "Stewardship—and the American Agency System." *Proceedings of the Twenty-Ninth Annual Convention of the Association of Life Insurance Presidents.* New York: 1935.

Menge, Walter. "Reinsurance of Life Risks," in *Life Insurance Trends at Mid-Century,* David McCahan, ed. Philadelphia: University of Pennsylvania Press, 1950: 68–83.

Miller, Arthur. *Death of a Salesman.* New York: Penguin Books, 1949.

Mishkin, Frederic. *The Economics of Money, Banking, and Financial Markets.* New York: Addison Wesley, 2001.

Modugno, Vic. *Broken Promises: The Inside Story of the Failure of Executive Life.* Torrance, Calif.: Pacific Insurance Press, 1992.

Moir, Henry. "Epidemic Waste of Human Life." *Proceedings of the Twelfth Annual Meeting of Life Insurance Association of America.* New York: 1918.

Monk, Wesley. "Cooperation in State Insurance Supervision." *Proceedings of the Twentieth Annual Meeting of Life Insurance Association of America.* New York: 1926.

Moorhead, E. J. *Our Yesterdays: The History of the Actuarial Profession in North America, 1809–1979.* Schaumburg, Ill.: Society of Actuaries, 1989.

Murphy, Ray. "Sale of Annuities by Governments." *Proceedings of the Thirty-Third Annual Convention of the Association of Life Insurance Presidents.* New York: 1939.

———. "Significant Annuity Developments," in *Life Insurance Trends at Mid-Century,* David McCahan, ed. Philadelphia: University of Pennsylvania Press, 1950: 84–99.

Murphy, Robert E. "Are We in Focus?" *Proceedings of the Fifty-Sixth Annual Meeting of Life Insurance Association of America.* New York: 1962.

Murphy, Sharon. "Life Insurance in the United States through World War I." *Eh.Net Encyclopedia.* http://www.eh.net/encyclopedia/murphy.life.insurance.us.php (accessed 15 December 2002).

Myers, R. J. "The Effect of Social Security on the Life Insurance Needs of Labor." *Journal of Political Economy* 45 (1937): 681–86.

Nerlove, S. H. "Common Stocks as Investments for American Life Insurance Companies: A Non-Academic View—I." *Journal of Finance* 3 (1948): 39–51.

———. "Common Stocks as Investments for American Life Insurance Companies: A Non-Academic View—II." *Journal of Finance* 4 (1949): 60–77.

Nollen, Henry. "Recent Fluctuations in Policy Loans." *Proceedings of the Fifteenth Annual Meeting of Life Insurance Association of America.* New York: 1921.

Norberg, Ragnar. "A Theory of Bonus in Life Insurance." *Finance and Stochastics* 3 (1999): 373–90.

North, Douglass. "Entrepreneurial Policy and Internal Organization in the Largest Life Insurance Companies at the Time of the Armstrong Investigation of Life Insurance." *Explorations in Entrepreneurial History* 5 (1953): 139–61.

———. "Life Insurance and Investment Banking at the Time of the Armstrong Investigation of 1905–1906." *Journal of Economic History* 14 (1954): 209–28.

———. "Capital Accumulation in Life Insurance between the Civil War and the Investigation of 1905," in *Men in Business: Essays on the Historical Role of the Entrepreneur,* William Miller, ed. New York: Harper and Row, 1962: 238–53.

Norton, Paul A. "A Brief History," in *Life and Health Insurance Handbook,* 3rd ed., Davis Gregg and Vane Lucas, eds. Homewood, Ill.: R. D. Irwin, 1973, 1089–1102.

Oates, James. *Business and Social Change: Life Insurance Looks to the Future.* New York: McGraw-Hill, 1968.

O'Donnell, Terence, ed. *History of Life Insurance in Its Formative Years.* American Conservation Company, 1936.

Olds, Glenn A. "Our Achilles Heel." *Proceedings of the Fifty-Eighth Annual Meeting of Life Insurance Association of America.* New York: 1964.

O'Leary, James J. "Investment Trends and Problems," in *Life Insurance Trends at Mid-Century,* David McCahan, ed. Philadelphia: University of Pennsylvania Press, 1950: 33–46.

———. "The Effects of Recent Credit and Debt Management Policies upon Life Insurance Company Investments." *Journal of Finance* 7 (1952): 307–20.

———. "Valuation of Life Insurance Company Holdings of Corporate Bonds and Stocks—Some Recent Developments." *Journal of Finance* 9 (1954): 160–77.

Olegario, Rowena. "IBM and the Two Thomas J. Watsons," in *Creating Modern Capitalism: How Entrepreneurs, Companies, and Countries Triumphed in Three Industrial Revolutions,* Thomas K. McCraw, ed. Cambridge: Harvard University Press, 1997: 349–95.

Orren, Karen. *Corporate Power and Social Change: The Politics of the Life Insurance Industry.* Baltimore, Md.: Johns Hopkins University Press, 1974.

Ourusoff, Alexandra, and Robert Meschi. "Staying Power: Profitability Is Up for Insurers Despite Tougher Capital Requirements." *Financial World* (1994): 50–56.

Outerbridge, Eugenius. "Group Insurance as an Influence in Promoting Stability in Labor Groups." *Proceedings of the Twelfth Annual Meeting of Life Insurance Association of America.* New York: 1918.

Packard, Vance. *The Hidden Persuaders.* New York: Washington Square Press, 1957.

Palyi, Melchoir. "Life Insurance and the Financial Frontier." *Journal of Business of the University of Chicago* 12 (1939): 51–79.

———. "Life Insurance and the Financial Frontier, Continued." *Journal of Business of the University of Chicago* 12 (1939): 175–208.

Parkinson, Thomas. "Legislative Contribution to Progress." *Proceedings of the Nineteenth Annual Meeting of Life Insurance Association of America.* New York: 1925.

———. "Selling Self-Reliance." *Proceedings of the Twenty-Fifth Annual Convention of the Association of Life Insurance Presidents.* New York: 1931.

Patterson, Edwin. *The Insurance Commissioner in the United States: A Study in Administrative Law and Practice.* Cambridge: Harvard University Press, 1927.

Pearson, Robin. "Growth, Crisis, and Change in the Insurance Industry: A Retrospect." *Accounting, Business, and Financial History* 12 (2002): 487–504.

———. "Moral Hazard and the Assessment of Insurance Risk in Eighteenth- and Early Nineteenth-Century Britain." *Business History Review* 76 (2002): 1–36.

———. "Mutuality Tested: The Rise and Fall of Mutual Fire Insurance Offices in Eighteenth-Century London." *Business History* 44 (2002): 1–28.

Perlis, Vivian. *Charles Ives Remembered: An Oral History.* New Haven, Conn.: Yale University Press, 1974.

Pesando, James E. "On the Accuracy and Formation of Life Insurance Company Cash Flow Forecasts." *Journal of Business* 48 (1975): 20–26.

Pissarides, C. A. "The Wealth-Age Relation with Life Insurance." *Economica* 47 (1980): 451–57.

Poitras, Geoffrey. *The Early History of Financial Economics, 1478–1776: From Commercial Arithmetic to Life Annuities and Joint Stocks.* Northampton, Mass.: Edward Elgar, 2000.

Pressnell, L. S. "The Rate of Interest in the Eighteenth Century," in *Studies in the Industrial Revolution,* L. S. Pressnell, ed. London: Athlone Press, 1960: 178–214.

Pritchett, Bruce. *A Study of Capital Mobilization: The Life Insurance Industry of the Nineteenth Century.* New York: Arno Press, 1977.

———. *Financing Growth: A Financial History of American Life Insurance through 1900.* Philadelphia: Huebner Foundation for Insurance Education, 1985.

Profile of Life Insurance Ownership in the United States, A. Hartford, Conn.: Life Insurance Marketing and Research Association, 1978.

Proposals of the Pennsylvania Company for Insurance on Lives and Granting Annuities. Philadelphia: James Kay, Jr., & Brother, 1837.

Pusey, Merlo. *Charles Evans Hughes.* New York: Macmillan, 1951.

Puth, Robert. "Supreme Life: The History of a Negro Life Insurance Company." Ph.D. diss., Northwestern University, 1968.

Quayle, John H. "Reclamation of Men Rejected by the Draft and Its Relation to Life Insurance." *Proceedings of the Eleventh Annual Meeting of Life Insurance Association of America.* New York: 1917.

Ransom, Roger, and Richard Sutch. "Tontine Insurance and the Armstrong Investigation: A Case of Stifled Innovation, 1868–1905." *Journal of Economic History* 47 (1987): 379–90.

Rapone, Anita. *Guardian Life Insurance Company, 1860–1920: A History of a German-American Enterprise.* New York: New York University Press, 1987.

Raymond, Robert. "Financial Statements of Life Insurance Companies." Ph.D. diss., Michigan State University, 1964.

Reilly, Jim. "Guardian Life Finds Its Ways through the Volatility Maze," *Market Chronicle,* 16 April 1981: 2, 16.

Rhodes, E. E. "Federal Taxation of Life Insurance." *Proceedings of the Fourteenth Annual Meeting of Life Insurance Association of America.* New York: 1920.

Ricks, R. Bruce. "Imputed Equity Returns on Real Estate Financed with Life Insurance Company Loans." *Journal of Finance* 24 (1969): 921–37.

Ridley, Matt. *Genome: The Autobiography of a Species in Twenty-Three Chapters.* New York: HarperCollins, 1999.

Riefler, Winfield W. "Inflation and the Life Insurance Industry." *Proceedings of the Forty-Fourth Annual Meeting of the Life Insurance Association of America.* New York: 1950.

Rittenhouse, E. E. "The Relationship of Life Insurance to National Physical Preparedness." *Proceedings of the Tenth Annual Meeting of Life Insurance Association of America.* New York: 1916.

Roover, Florence. "Early Examples of Marine Insurance." *Journal of Economic History* 5 (1945): 172–200.

Rosenthal, Irving. *A Short and Confidential History of a Half-Century of Guardian's Net Cost Development (1926–1976).* GLIC archives (1977).

Ross, S. "The Economic Theory of Agency: The Principal's Problem." *American Economic Review* 63 (1973): 134–39.

Rossiter, Frank. *Charles Ives and His America.* New York: Liveright, 1975.

Rusk, Howard A. "America's Number One Medical Problem." *Proceedings of the Forty-Second Annual Meeting of the Life Insurance Association of America.* New York: 1948.

Ruwell, Mary. *Eighteenth-Century Capitalism: The Formation of American Marine Insurance.* New York: Garland, 1993.

Rydgren, A. "The Impact of Lower Interest Earnings," in *Life Insurance Trends at Mid-Century,* David McCahan, ed. Philadelphia: University of Pennsylvania Press, 1950: 1–18.

Sage, John D. "Prevention of Life Insurance Lapses by Educating the Insured." *Proceedings of the Sixteenth Annual Meeting of Life Insurance Association of America.* New York: 1922.

Saulnier, R. J. *Urban Mortgage Lending by Life Insurance Companies.* New York: National Bureau of Economic Research, 1950.

Savitt, Todd. "Slave Life Insurance in Virginia and North Carolina." *Journal of Southern History* 43 (1977): 583–600.

Schott, Francis H. "Disintermediation through Policy Loans at Life Insurance Companies." *Journal of Finance* 26 (1971): 719–29.

Sclafane, Susanne. "Top Dogs Get Top Dollars As Salaries Soar," *National Underwriter,* 13 October 1997: 35ff.

Scoles, Donald. "The Development and Scope of Life Insurance Annuities in the United States." Ph.D. diss., University of Pennsylvania, 1954.

Servaes, Henri, and Marc Zenner. "The Role of Investment Banks in Acquisitions." *Review of Financial Studies* 9 (1996): 787–815.

Shanks, Carroll. "Life Insurance on the Inflation Treadmill." *Proceedings of the Forty-Fourth Annual Meeting of the Life Insurance Association of America.* New York: 1950.

Shepherd, Pearce. "Principals and Problems of Selection and Underwriting," in *Life Insurance Trends at Mid-Century,* David McCahan, ed. Philadelphia: University of Pennsylvania Press, 1950: 47–67.

Shubin, Seymour. *The Man from Enterprise: The Story of John B. Amos, Founder of AFLAC.* Macon, Ga.: Mercer University Press, 1998.

Sick, T. A. "Let's Get Excited." *Proceedings of the Fifty-Seventh Annual Meeting of Life Insurance Association of America.* New York: 1963.

Slattery, Thomas J. "Manning, 'On Message.'" *National Underwriter: Life and Health Edition,* 23 April 2001: 27.

Smith, Bruce, and Michael Stutzer. "A Theory of Mutual Formation and Moral Hazard with Evidence from the History of the Insurance Industry." *Review of Financial Studies* 8 (1995): 545–77.

Smith, J. Henry. "The Nation's Needs in Medical Economics." *Proceedings of the Fifty-Second Annual Meeting of the Life Insurance Association of America.* New York: 1958.

Smith, Lawrence, and Gordon Sparks. "Specification and Estimation of Financial Stock Adjustment Models, with Special Reference to Life Insurance Company Mortgage Investment." *International Economic Review* 12 (1971): 14–26.

Smith, Robert Sydney. "Life Insurance in Fifteenth-Century Barcelona." *Journal of Economic History* 1 (1941): 57–59.

Smith, Thomas. "Banking and Life Insurance Face the Future Together." *Proceedings of the Thirtieth Annual Convention of the Association of Life Insurance Presidents.* New York: 1936.

Snowden, Kenneth. "Mortgage Securitization in the United States: Twentieth-Century Developments in Historical Perspective," in *Anglo-American Financial Systems: Institutions and Markets in the Twentieth Century,* Michael Bordo and Richard Sylla, eds. New York: Irwin Professional Publishing, 1995: 261–98.

Solberg, Harry. "A Method for Consumer Valuation of Life Insurance Policies by Type." *Journal of Finance* 17 (1962): 634–45.

Sommers, Davidson. "Life Insurance Companies and Corporate Pensions." *Proceedings of the Fifty-Sixth Annual Meeting of Life Insurance Association of America.* New York: 1962.

Soyer, Daniel. *Jewish Immigrant Associations and American Identity in New York, 1880–1939.* Cambridge: Harvard University Press, 1997.

Spector, David, ed. *Law and Practice of Life Insurance Company Insolvency.* Chicago: American Bar Association, 1993.

Spring, Samuel. *Laws Controlling the Investment of Insurance Funds.* Boston: Financial Publishing Company, 1921.

Sproul, Allan. "Central Banking and the Private Economy." *Proceedings of the Forty-Fifth Annual Meeting of the Life Insurance Association of America.* New York: 1951.

Stalson, J. Owen. *Marketing Life Insurance, Its History in America.* Cambridge: Harvard University Press, 1942.

Stevens, Raymond. "The Greatest Service of Life Insurance." *Proceedings of the Eighteenth Annual Meeting of Life Insurance Association of America.* New York: 1924.

Stone, Mildred. *A Short History of Life Insurance.* Indianapolis, Ind.: Insurance Research and Review Service, 1942.

———. *Since 1845: A History of the Mutual Benefit Life Insurance Company.* New Brunswick, N.J.: Rutgers University Press, 1957.

Strouse, Jean. *Morgan: American Financier.* New York: Random House, 1999.

Stuart, Merah. *An Economic Detour: A History of Insurance in the Lives of American Negroes.* College Park, Md.: McGrath Publishing, 1940.

Sullivan, James P. "The Life Insurance Company as a Banking Concern." *Journal of Business of the University of Chicago* 5 (1932): 346–61.

Sylla, Richard E. "The Breakdown of Bretton Woods and the Revival of Global Finance." *Jahrbuch fur Wirtschafts Geschichte* (2002–2001): 81–88.

———. "Financial Systems and Economic Modernization." *Journal of Economic History* 62 (2002): 277–92.

Sylla, Richard E., Jack Wilson, and Robert E. Wright. *Database of Early U.S. Securities Prices.* Inter-university Consortium for Political and Social Research, 2004.

Tauber, Yale D. *Executive Compensation, 1984.* New York: Practising Law Institute, 1984.

Taxing Life Insurance Companies. Danvers, Mass.: Organization for Economic Co-operation and Development, 2001.

Taylor, Charles. "Getting Closer to the Farmer." *Proceedings of the Ninth Annual Meeting of Life Insurance Association of America.* New York: 1915.

Taylor, John M. *A Look at So-Called Incontestable Insurance.* 1882.

Testimony Taken before the Joint Committee of the Senate and Assembly of the State of New York to Investigate and Examine into the Business and Affairs of Life Insurance Companies Doing Business in the State of New York. Albany, N.Y.: Brandow Printing, 1905.

Thompson, Claud. "When Is Ownership Not Ownership?" Working Paper, University of Wisconsin, 17 April 2000.

Tuckett, Harvey. *Practical Remarks on the Present State of Life Insurance in the United States, Showing the Evils Which Exist, and Rules for Improvement.* Philadelphia: Smith and Peters, 1850.

Tully, William. "Policy Claims: A Moral Test of Life Insurance." *Proceedings of the Fourteenth Annual Meeting of Life Insurance Association of America.* New York: 1920.

Valenti, Raymond. "Federal Taxation of Life Insurance Companies: The Savings Institution Approach." Ph.D. diss., Syracuse University, 1959.

Verbrugge, James. "A Multivariate Analysis of Stock versus Mutual Performance in the Savings and Loan Industry." *Journal of Financial and Quantitative Analysis* 11 (1976): 573.

Villaronga, Luis M. *The Incontestable Clause: An Historical Analysis.* Philadelphia: Huebner Foundation, 1976.

Wainwright, Nicholas. *A Philadelphia Story: The Philadelphia Contributionship, 1752–1952.* Philadelphia: Philadelphia Contributionship for the Insurance of Houses from Loss by Fire, 1952.

Walker, Kenneth. *Guaranteed Investment Contracts: Risk Analysis and Portfolio Strategies.* Homewood, Ill.: Dow Jones–Irwin, 1989.

Walker, Paul L., William G. Shenkir, and C. Stephen Hunn, "Developing Risk Skills: An Investigation of Business Risks and Controls at Prudential Insurance Company of America." *Issues in Accounting Education* (2001): 291–313.

Wallace, Elizabeth. "The Needs of Strangers: Friendly Societies and Insurance Societies in Late Eighteenth-Century England." *Eighteenth-Century Life* 24 (2000): 53–72.

Wallison, Peter, ed. *Optional Federal Chartering and Regulation of Insurance Companies.* Washington, D.C.: AEI Press, 2000.

Walter, James E. *The Investment Process as Characterized by Leading Life Insurance Companies.* Cambridge: Harvard Business School Press, 1962.

Weare, Walter B. *Black Business in the New South: A Social History of the North Carolina Mutual Life Insurance Company.* Chicago: University of Illinois Press, 1973.

Weidenborner, Frank. "Strengthening Agency Assets." *Proceedings of the Thirty-Fifth Annual Convention of the Association of Life Insurance Presidents.* New York: 1941.

Welch, Jack, and John Byrne. *Jack, Straight from the Gut.* New York: Warner Books, 2001.

Westerfield, Ray. *Historical Survey of Branch Banking in the United States.* New York: American Economists Council, 1939.

Westfall, J. V. E. "Relation of the Agent to Some Executive Problems." *Proceedings of the Fourteenth Annual Meeting of Life Insurance Association of America.* New York: 1920.

———. "The Agency Manager's Function in Progressive Field Organization and Development." *Proceedings of the Seventeenth Annual Meeting of Life Insurance Association of America.* New York: 1923.

Whatley, Seaborn. "Our Agency System: An Example of American Foresight." *Proceedings of the Thirtieth Annual Convention of the Association of Life Insurance Presidents.* New York: 1936.

White, Gerald. *A History of the Massachusetts Hospital Life Insurance Company.* Cambridge: Harvard University Press, 1955.

Wilde, Frazar. "Effective Expense Control in the Field." *Proceedings of the Forty-Third Annual Meeting of the Life Insurance Association of America.* New York: 1949.

Williamson, Harold, and Orange Smalley. *Northwestern Mutual Life: A Century of Trusteeship.* Evanston, Ill.: Northwestern University Press, 1957.

Wilson, Alex, and Eric Higgins. "CEO Pay/Firm Performance Sensitivity in the Insurance Industry." *Journal of Insurance Issues* (Spring 2001): 1–16.

Winter, Ralph. "On the Rate Structure of the American Life Insurance Market." *Journal of Finance* 36 (1981): 81–96.

Winterhalder, Bruce. "Social Foraging and the Behavioral Ecology of Intragroup Resource Transfers." *Evolutionary Anthropology* 5 (1996): 46–57.

Winterhalder, Bruce, and Erice Alden Smith. "Analyzing Adaptive Strategies: Human Behavioral Ecology at Twenty-Five." *Evolutionary Anthropology* 9 (2000): 51–72.

Winterhalder, Bruce, Flora Lu, and Bram Tucker. "Risk-Sensitive Adaptive Tactics: Models and Evidence from Subsistence Studies in Biology and Anthropology." *Journal of Archaeological Research* 7 (1999): 301–48.

Woodruff, Archibald. *Farm Mortgage Loans of Life Insurance Companies.* New Haven, Conn.: Yale University Press, 1937.

Woods, Edward. "Relation of the Agent to Life Insurance Investments." *Proceedings of the Ninth Annual Meeting of Life Insurance Association of America.* New York: 1915.

Woodson, Benjamin. "What Can Be Done in the Marketing Area to Increase the Flow of Life Insurance Savings?" *Proceedings of the Fifty-Sixth Annual Meeting of Life Insurance Association of America.* New York: 1962.

Woodson, Carter G. "Insurance Business among Negroes." *Journal of Negro History* 14 (1929): 202–26.

Wright, H. P. "Financial Problems of Life Insurance," *National Underwriter,* 3 October 1930.

Wright, Kenneth. "Gross Flows of Funds through Life Insurance Companies." *Journal of Finance* 15 (1960): 140–56.

Wright, Robert E. "Banking and Politics in New York, 1784–1829." Ph.D. diss., State University of New York at Buffalo, 1997.

———. *Hamilton Unbound: Finance and the Creation of the American Republic.* Westport, Conn.: Greenwood, 2002.

———. *The Wealth of Nations Rediscovered: Integration and Expansion in American Financial Markets, 1780–1850.* New York: Cambridge University Press, 2002.

Wysong, Clarence. "Reserves Built through Supervision." *Proceedings of the Twenty-Fourth*

Annual Convention of the Association of America of Life Insurance Presidents. New York: 1930.

Yaari, Menahem. "Uncertain Lifetime, Life Insurance, and the Theory of the Consumer." *Review of Economic Studies* 32 (1965): 137–50.

Yates, JoAnne. "Co-evolution of Information-Processing Technology and Use: Interaction between the Life Insurance and Tabulating Industries." *Business History Review* 67 (1993): 1–52.

Young, George B. "Some Economic Aspects of State Taxation of Life Insurance." *Proceedings of the Seventeenth Annual Meeting of Life Insurance Association of America.* New York: 1923.

Zartman, Lester. "Control of Life Insurance Companies." *Journal of Political Economy* 15 (1907): 531–41.

Zelizer, Viviana. *Morals and Markets: The Development of Life Insurance in the United States.* New Brunswick, N.J.: Transaction, 1983.

Zimmerman, Charles. "Research in Agency Management," in *Investment of Life Insurance Funds,* David McCahan, ed. Philadelphia: University of Pennsylvania Press, 1953: 156–70.

Index

About the Authors

Robert E. Wright received a Ph.D. in history from the State University of New York at Buffalo in 1997. He has published numerous scholarly treatments of the history of money, banking, corporate finance and governance, diet, government regulation, politics, primary and secondary securities markets, and trade. He is also the author or coauthor of four other books, the most recent of which, *Financial Founding Fathers,* is forthcoming. At present, he teaches business and financial history at New York University's Stern School of Business and resides in Pennsylvania with his wife and four children.

George David Smith holds a Ph.D. in history from Harvard University. He has taught at Harvard and at New York University's Stern School of Business where he is presently Clinical Professor of Economics and Academic Director of Executive MBA Programs. Author and coauthor of numerous books and articles on business and financial history, Professor Smith is currently at work with a colleague on a history of Wall Street. He has consulted widely to numerous corporations and sits on the board of the Winthrop Group, Inc., a consulting firm he cofounded in 1982. He lives cheerfully in Hastings on Hudson, New York, with his wife, son, dog, and cat.